THE CLAY SANSKRIT LIBRARY
FOUNDED BY JOHN & JENNIFER CLAY

GENERAL EDITOR

SHELDON POLLOCK

EDITED BY

ISABELLE ONIANS

WWW.CLAYSANSKRITLIBRARY.ORG
WWW.NYUPRESS.ORG

Artwork by Robert Beer.
Typeset in Adobe Garamond at 10.25 : 12.3+pt.
Editorial input from Muktak Aklujkar, Ridi Faruque,
Chris Gibbons, Tomoyuki Kono & Eszter Somogyi.
Printed and Bound in Great Britain by
TJ International, Cornwall on acid free paper

THE OCEAN OF THE RIVERS OF STORY

VOLUME TWO

TRANSLATED BY

Sir James Mallinson

NEW YORK UNIVERSITY PRESS

JJC FOUNDATION

2009

First Edition 2009

The Clay Sanskrit Library is co-published by
New York University Press
and the JJC Foundation.

Further information about this volume
and the rest of the Clay Sanskrit Library
is available at the end of this book and
on the following websites:
www.claysanskritlibrary.org
www.nyupress.org

ISBN 978-0-8147-9558-3

Library of Congress Cataloging-in-Publication Data
[Kathāsaritsāgara. English & Sanskrit]
The ocean of the rivers of story / by Somadeva ;
translated by James Mallinson.
p. cm. – (The Clay Sanskrit library)
In English and Sanskrit (romanized) on facing pages;
Includes translation from Sanskrit.
Includes bibliographical references and index.
ISBN 978-0-8147-9558-3
1 Tales–India–Early works to 1800. I.Title.
PK3741.S7E5 2006
891.21–dc22
2006032846

CONTENTS

CSL CONVENTIONS

Sanskrit Alphabetical Order

Vowels:	*a ā i ī u ū ṛ ṝ ḷ ḹ e ai o au ṃ ḥ*
Gutturals:	*k kh g gh ṅ*
Palatals:	*c ch j jh ñ*
Retroflex:	*ṭ ṭh ḍ ḍh ṇ*
Dentals:	*t th d dh n*
Labials:	*p ph b bh m*
Semivowels:	*y r l v*
Spirants:	*ś ṣ s h*

Guide to Sanskrit Pronunciation

a	b*u*t
ā, â	f*a*ther
i	s*i*t
ī, î	f*ee*
u	p*u*t
ū, û	b*oo*
ṛ	vocalic *r*, American p*ur*dy or English p*re*tty
ṝ	lengthened *ṛ*
ḷ	vocalic *l*, ab*le*
e, ê, ē	m*a*de, esp. in Welsh pronunciation
ai	b*i*te
o, ô, ō	r*o*pe, esp. Welsh pronunciation; Italian s*o*lo
au	s*ou*nd
ṃ	*anusvāra* nasalizes the preceding vowel
ḥ	*visarga*, a voiceless aspiration (resembling the English *h*), or like Scottish lo*ch*, or an aspiration with a faint echoing of the last element of the preceding vowel so that *taiḥ* is pronounced *taih*[i]
k	luc*k*
kh	bloc*kh*ead
g	*g*o
gh	bi*gh*ead
ṅ	a*n*ger
c	*ch*ill
ch	mat*chh*ead
j	*j*og
jh	aspirated *j*, he*dgeh*og
ñ	ca*ny*on
ṭ	retroflex *t*, *t*ry (with the tip of tongue turned up to touch the hard palate)
ṭh	same as the preceding but aspirated
ḍ	retroflex *d* (with the tip

	of tongue turned up to touch the hard palate)
ḍh	same as the preceding but aspirated
ṇ	retroflex *n* (with the tip of tongue turned up to touch the hard palate)
t	French *t*out
th	ten*t h*ook
d	*d*inner
dh	guil*dh*all
n	*n*ow
p	*p*ill
ph	u*ph*eaval
b	*b*efore
bh	a*bh*orrent
m	*m*ind
y	*y*es
r	trilled, resembling the Italian pronunciation of *r*
l	*l*inger
v	*w*ord
ś	*sh*ore
ṣ	retroflex *sh* (with the tip of the tongue turned up to touch the hard palate)
s	hi*ss*
h	*h*ood

CSL Punctuation of English

The acute accent on Sanskrit words when they occur outside of the Sanskrit text itself, marks stress, e.g., Ramáyana. It is not part of traditional Sanskrit orthography, transliteration, or transcription, but we supply it here to guide readers in the pronunciation of these unfamiliar words. Since no Sanskrit word is accented on the last syllable it is not necessary to accent disyllables, e.g., Rama.

The second CSL innovation designed to assist the reader in the pronunciation of lengthy unfamiliar words is to insert an unobtrusive middle dot between semantic word breaks in compound names (provided the word break does not fall on a vowel resulting from the fusion of two vowels), e.g., Maha·bhárata, but Ramáyana (not Rama·áyana). Our dot echoes the punctuating middle dot (·) found in the oldest surviving samples of written Indic, the Ashokan inscriptions of the third century BCE.

The deep layering of Sanskrit narrative has also dictated that we use quotation marks only to announce the beginning and end of every direct speech, and not at the beginning of every paragraph.

CSL Punctuation of Sanskrit

The Sanskrit text is also punctuated, in accordance with the punctuation of the English translation. In mid-verse, the punctuation will not alter the sandhi or the scansion. Proper names are capitalized. Most Sanskrit meters have four "feet" (*pāda*); where possible we print the common *śloka* meter on two lines. In the Sanskrit text, we use French *Guillemets* (e.g., *«kva saṃcicīrṣuḥ?»*) instead of English quotation marks (e.g., "Where are you off to?") to avoid confusion with the apostrophes used for vowel elision in sandhi.

SANDHI

Sanskrit presents the learner with a challenge: *sandhi* (euphonic combination). Sandhi means that when two words are joined in connected speech or writing (which in Sanskrit reflects speech), the last letter (or even letters) of the first word often changes; compare the way we pronounce "the" in "the beginning" and "the end."

In Sanskrit the first letter of the second word may also change; and if both the last letter of the first word and the first letter of the second are vowels, they may fuse. This has a parallel in English: a nasal consonant is inserted between two vowels that would otherwise coalesce: "a pear" and "an apple." Sanskrit vowel fusion may produce ambiguity.

The charts on the following pages give the full sandhi system.

Fortunately it is not necessary to know these changes in order to start reading Sanskrit. All that is important to know is the form of the second word without sandhi (pre-sandhi), so that it can be recognized or looked up in a dictionary. Therefore we are printing Sanskrit with a system of punctuation that will indicate, unambiguously, the original form of the second word, i.e., the form without sandhi. Such sandhi mostly concerns the fusion of two vowels.

In Sanskrit, vowels may be short or long and are written differently accordingly. We follow the general convention that a vowel with no mark above it is short. Other books mark a long vowel either with a bar called a macron (*ā*) or with a circumflex (*â*). Our system uses the

VOWEL SANDHI

Final vowels: a	ā	i	ī	u	ū	ṛ	e	ai	o	au	Initial vowels:
' â	" â	y a	y a	v a	v a	r a	e '	ā a	o '	āv a	a
' ā	" ā	y ā	y ā	v ā	v ā	r ā	a ā	ā ā	a ā	āv ā	ā
' ê	" ê	' î	" î	v i	v i	r i	a i	ā i	a i	āv i	i
' ē	" ē	' ī	" ī	v ī	v ī	r ī	a ī	ā ī	a ī	āv ī	ī
' ô	" ô	y u	y u	' û	" û	r u	a u	ā u	a u	āv u	u
' ō	" ō	y ū	y ū	' ū	" ū	r ū	a ū	ā ū	a ū	āv ū	ū
a' r	a" r	y ṛ	y ṛ	v ṛ	v ṛ	' ṛ̂	a ṛ	ā ṛ	a ṛ	āv ṛ	ṛ
' âi	" âi	y e	y e	v e	v e	r e	a e	ā e	a e	āv e	e
' āi	" āi	y ai	y ai	v ai	v ai	r ai	a ai	ā ai	a ai	āv ai	ai
' âu	" âu	y o	y o	v o	v o	r o	a o	ā o	a o	āv o	o
' āu	" āu	y au	y au	v au	v au	r au	a au	ā au	a au	āv au	au

CONSONANT SANDHI

Permitted finals:							(Except āḥ/aḥ)			Initial letters:
k	ṭ	t	p	ṅ	n	m	ḥ/r	āḥ	aḥ	
k	ṭ	t	p	ṅ	n	ṃ	ḥ	āḥ	aḥ	k/kh
g	ḍ	d	b	ṅ	n	ṃ	r	ā	o	g/gh
k	ṭ	c	p	ṅ	ṃś	ṃ	ś	āś	aś	c/ch
g	ḍ	j	b	ṅ	ñ	ṃ	r	ā	o	j/jh
k	ṭ	ṭ	p	ṅ	ṃṣ	ṃ	ṣ	āṣ	aṣ	ṭ/ṭh
g	ḍ	ḍ	b	ṅ	ṇ	ṃ	r	ā	o	ḍ/ḍh
k	ṭ	t	p	ṅ	ṃs	ṃ	s	ās	as	t/th
g	ḍ	d	b	ṅ	n	ṃ	r	ā	o	d/dh
k	ṭ	t	p	ṅ	n	ṃ	ḥ	āḥ	aḥ	p/ph
g	ḍ	d	b	ṅ	n	ṃ	r	ā	o	b/bh
ṅ	ṇ	n	m	ṅ	n	ṃ	r	ā	o	*nasals* (n/m)
g	ḍ	d	b	ṅ	n	ṃ	r	ā	o	y/v
g	ḍ	d	b	ṅ	n	ṃ	*zero*[1]	ā	o	r
g	ḍ	l	b	ṅ	l̃[2]	ṃ	r	ā	o	l
k	ṭ	c ch	p	ṅ	ñ ś/ch	ṃ	ḥ	āḥ	aḥ	ś
k	ṭ	t	p	ṅ	n	ṃ	ḥ	āḥ	aḥ	ṣ/s
gg h	ḍḍ h	dd h	bb h	ṅ	n	ṃ	r	ā	o	h
g	ḍ	d	b	ṅ/ṅṅ[3]	n/nn[3]	m	r	ā	a[4]	*vowels*
k	ṭ	t	p	ṅ	n	m	ḥ	āḥ	aḥ	*zero*

[1]ḥ or r disappears, and if a/i/u precedes, this lengthens to ā/ī/ū. [2]e.g. tān+lokān=tāl̃ lokān.
[3]The doubling occurs if the preceding vowel is short. [4]Except: aḥ+a=o '.

macron, except that for initial vowels in sandhi we use a circumflex to indicate that originally the vowel was short, or the shorter of two possibilities (*e* rather than *ai*, *o* rather than *au*).

When we print initial *â*, before sandhi that vowel was *a*

î or *ê*,	*i*
û or *ô*,	*u*
âi,	*e*
âu,	*o*
ā,	*ā*
ī,	*ī*
ū,	*ū*
ē,	*ī*
ō,	*ū*
ai,	*ai*
āu,	*au*

', before sandhi there was a vowel *a*

When a final short vowel (*a*, *i*, or *u*) has merged into a following vowel, we print ' at the end of the word, and when a final long vowel (*ā*, *ī*, or *ū*) has merged into a following vowel we print " at the end of the word. The vast majority of these cases will concern a final *a* or *ā*. See, for instance, the following examples:

What before sandhi was *atra asti* is represented as *atr' âsti*

atra āste	*atr' āste*
kanyā asti	*kany" âsti*
kanyā āste	*kany" āste*
atra iti	*atr' êti*
kanyā iti	*kany" êti*
kanyā īpsitā	*kany" ēpsitā*

Finally, three other points concerning the initial letter of the second word:

(1) A word that before sandhi begins with *ṛ* (vowel), after sandhi begins with *r* followed by a consonant: *yatha" rtu* represents pre-sandhi *yathā ṛtu*.

(2) When before sandhi the previous word ends in *t* and the following word begins with *ś*, after sandhi the last letter of the previous word is *c*

and the following word begins with *ch*: *syāc chāstravit* represents pre-sandhi *syāt śāstravit*.

(3) Where a word begins with *h* and the previous word ends with a double consonant, this is our simplified spelling to show the pre-sandhi form: *tad hasati* is commonly written as *tad dhasati*, but we write *tadd hasati* so that the original initial letter is obvious.

COMPOUNDS

We also punctuate the division of compounds (*samāsa*), simply by inserting a thin vertical line between words. There are words where the decision whether to regard them as compounds is arbitrary. Our principle has been to try to guide readers to the correct dictionary entries.

Exemplar of CSL Style

Where the Devanagari script reads:

कुम्भस्थली रक्षतु वो विकीर्णसिन्धूररेणुर्द्विरदाननस्य ।
प्रशान्तये विघ्नतमश्छटानां निष्ठ्यूतबालातपपल्लवेव ॥

Others would print:

kumbhasthalī rakṣatu vo vikīrṇasindūrareṇur dviradānanasya /
praśāntaye vighnatamaśchaṭānāṃ niṣṭhyūtabālātapapallaveva //

We print:

kumbha|sthalī rakṣatu vo vikīrṇa|sindūra|reṇur dvirad'|ānanasya
praśāntaye vighna|tamaś|chaṭānāṃ niṣṭhyūta|bāl'|ātapa|pallav" êva.

And in English:

May Ganésha's domed forehead protect you! Streaked with vermilion dust, it seems to be emitting the spreading rays of the rising sun to pacify the teeming darkness of obstructions.

("Nava·sáhasanka and the Serpent Princess" I.3)

Wordplay

Classical Sanskrit literature can abound in puns (*śleṣa*). Such paronomasia, or wordplay, is raised to a high art; rarely is it a *cliché*. Multiple meanings merge (*ślisyanti*) into a single word or phrase. Most common are pairs of meanings, but as many as ten separate meanings are attested. To mark the parallel senses in the English, as well as the punning original in the Sanskrit, we use a *slanted* font (different from *italic*) and a triple colon (⁝) to separate the alternatives. E.g.

yuktaṃ Kādambarīṃ śrutvā kavayo maunam āśritāḥ
Bāṇa|dhvanāv an|adhyāyo bhavat' îti smṛtir yataḥ.

It is right that poets should fall silent upon hearing the Kadámbari, for the sacred law rules that recitation must be suspended when *the sound of an arrow* ⁝ *the poetry of Bana* is heard.

(Soméshvara·deva's "Moonlight of Glory" I.15)

INTRODUCTION

THIS SECOND CSL volume of the "Ocean of the Rivers of Story" (*Kathāsaritsāgara*) finds the main narrative in full flow after the scene-setting of volume one. The ministers of Údayana, the king of Vatsa, dismayed at how he has lost almost his entire kingdom because he whiles away his time with his beloved queen Vásava·datta, have used various stories to convince him to conquer the world. In the first two waves of volume two, which are the last waves of 'Lavá-naka,' the third part or Attainment of the "Ocean of the Rivers of Story," he does so and then returns to Kaushámbi, where Vásava·datta gives birth to a son. The boy, Nara·váhana·datta, is the protagonist of the main narrative of the "Ocean of the Rivers of Story." Before his birth Shiva tells his parents in a dream that he will be a partial incarnation of Kama, the god of love, and become the emperor of all the sorcerers. The remainder of this volume (which covers three Attainments: 'The birth of Nara·váhana·datta,' 'Four Girls' and 'Mádana·mánchuka') sees him given the conventional education of a mortal royal (but not yet acquire the magical sciences necessary to make him a sorcerer), grow to manhood and be made crown prince by Údayana. It finishes with his falling in love with and marrying Mádana·mánchuka. An incarnation of Rati, the wife of Kama, she is the first of his twenty-six wives and his greatest love.

Throughout the "Ocean of the Rivers of Story" the main narrative is swamped in a flood of tributary tales. These draw on a wide range of sources, which in this volume include well-established myths of the gods, such as the birth of Karttikéya (3.6.58–100), and famous legends, such as that of Chitra·lekha and Anirúddha (6.5.11–33), as well as more obscure (and often comical) stories, such as that in which a stupid brahmin's cunning daughter tricks a *piśāca* (a goblin-like creature) with a ruse beyond the pale of the text's early translators (6.2.156–184), and the barber's story of how he made King Dridha·varman think that his wife, with whom the king was having an affair, was a witch (6.6.146–170). Many of the tributary tales can be found in other works and, sometimes, elsewhere within the "Ocean of the Rivers of Story" itself. Thus the tale of King Víkrama·sinha and the two brahmins (6.1.135ab–210) is not only the same as that of Madirávati found in Attainment 14 but also forms the plot of the eighth-century dramatist Bhava·bhuti's "Málati and Mádhava" (*Mālatīmādhava*), as well as appearing in the "Treasury of Tales" (*Kathākośa*) and the Persian "Parrot's Tales" (*Ṭūṭīnāmeh*).

In volume one of the "Ocean of the Rivers of Story," we were told how the text is a reworking of the "Long Story" (*Bṛhatkathā*), a compendium of tales which was lost long ago, if indeed it ever existed. There are four other works which are said to be based upon the "Long Story": the *Bṛhatkathāślokasaṃgraha* of Budha·svamin (the extant part of which has been translated in two CSL volumes as the "Emperor of the Sorcerers"); the "Flowering of the Long Story" (*Bṛhatkathāmañjarī*) of Ksheméndra; "Vasu·deva's Travels" (*Vasudevahiṇḍi*), a work of Jaina tradition written in Old Jaina Maharashtri of which there are two versions, one by Sangha·dasa·gani and one (also known as the "Medium-length Saga," *Majjhimakhaṇḍa*) composed by Dharma·dasa·gani; and the "Long Story" (*Peruṅkatai*) of Konguvelir, another Jaina work, written in Tamil. Although these works are all very different, attempts can and have been made to determine the elements shared by all five and thus posit the contents of an ur-text, which may or may not have been the "Long Story." To do this one must begin by removing the different frames found around the main narrative in each of the works.

In the first Attainment of the "Ocean of the Rivers of Story," which is called 'Story's Throne,' it was said that the god Shiva told the "Long Story" to his wife Párvati. He was overheard by his servant Pushpa·danta, who told it to the *piśāca* Kana·bhuti, who told it to Gunádhya, the mortal incarnation of Pushpa·danta's friend Mályavan. Gunádhya translated it into Paisháchi, the language of the *piśāca*s, before destroying all but one hundred thousand of its seven hundred thousand verses, which he then gave to King Shata·váhana. It appears that Soma·deva, the author of the "Ocean of the Rivers of Story," felt that the complexity of this multiple boxing of speakers, which is perhaps an allegory of the complex transmission of the "Long Story," needed to be swept aside in order for the main narrative to continue afresh.

Thus in this second volume, at the beginning of the sixth Attainment when Nara·váhana·datta is eight years old, the anonymous omniscient narrator, who started to tell the main narrative at the beginning of the second Attainment and who—the logic of the first Attainment's frames dictates—must be Soma·deva, announces that the rest of the story is henceforth to be told by Nara·váhana·datta, as a flashback: "Now hear all the amazing adventures of Nara·váhana·datta, which he himself told from the beginning, in the third person, after he had become the ruler of the sorcerers and was questioned about them at some time or other by the great sages and their wives." The logical conundrum of introducing the protagonist of the main story as also its teller in the middle of telling his tale is found in three of the four other works said to be based on the "Long Story" (it is not in the *Peruṅkatai*) and is likely to have been a feature of their ur-text. However, only the Kashmiri versions—the "Ocean of the Rivers of Story" and the *Bṛhatkathāmañjarī*—have Nara·váhana·datta talk about himself in the third rather than first person. This would seem to be a way of paying homage to the ur-text while still allowing the reader to forget about the complex scaffolding of intertwined frames and to plunge into the story unencumbered.

This twist in the frame is reflected in twists found in many of the individual tales, in which various types of reincarnation create a fluidity of identity. Divine beings fall to earth, cursed to become mortals, while mortals remember and relive their past lives. Thus the sorcerer Jimúta·váhana, while describing his past life as Vasu·datta, reports how when he was about to meet his sweetheart, "her arrival had been indicated by this right eye of mine throbbing as if with the desire to see her" (4.2.106). In a similar fashion, countless characters tell their life-stories in the third person before announcing to their audiences at the end that they are in fact the protagonists of their stories.

Once he has swept aside the complexities of the frames of the "Long Story," Soma·deva creates a masterpiece of coherent storytelling, sustained over nearly twenty thousand verses. His languid detachment and stylistic simplicity (the latter having made the "Ocean of the Rivers of Story" a favorite text for students of Sanskrit) belie a perspicacity and descriptive talent that set him apart from other Sanskrit poets.

It is not just Soma·deva's attitude that detaches him from his story. Unusually for the author of a Sanskrit epic tale, he plays no part in the narrative. This suggests that he is indeed retelling Gunádhya's tale and might account for his indifference towards the fortunes of the actors in the tales he retells. However, this indifference is accompanied by a marked reluctance to let his own opinions float to the surface anywhere in the flow of the main narrative. Very rarely do we hear moral judgments when he is recounting the deeds of the protagonists, nor does Soma·deva himself announce the pithy aphorisms found throughout the text. These are only to be found within the subsidiary tales or voiced by the protagonists themselves. Indeed, the "Ocean of the Rivers of Story" does not teach any overarching moral philosophy. When a moral standpoint is argued, almost always by way of illustration in a story, it is often controverted in another story. Despite being populated by all kinds of characters, many of them otherworldly, their aims are decidedly worldly. Life in classical India traditionally had four possible goals: material profit (*artha*), pleasure (*kāma*), righteousness (*dharma*) and liberation (*mokṣa*). Few of the characters in the "Ocean of the Rivers of Story" seek anything other than *artha*. *Kāma*, through the winning of lovers, does sometimes stir both men and women to action, and *dharma* is occasionally invoked as a means of getting what one wants, but it is wealth and power that are the ultimate aims.

At the very end of the "Ocean of the Rivers of Story," we hear that Soma·deva has created it in order to divert ("for just a moment"!) Queen Súryavati of Kashmir, who has adorned her country with excellent monasteries and built beautiful temples, who supports the population with gifts of countless jewels and gold pieces, thousands of cows, mountains of riches and so forth, who is always striving to worship Shiva, perform sacrifices and practice charity, and who wears herself out by constantly listening to sacred teachings. Soma·deva has no desire or need, nor is it his place, to educate the queen in the ways of righteousness or to help her to liberation. We know from the "Taste of the Flow of Kings" (*Rājataraṅginī*) of Kálhana that Kashmir during the reign of King Anánta·deva, Súryavati's husband, was in a state of upheaval and that Kálasha·deva, their son, was seeking, with ultimate success, to dethrone his father. Soma·deva wants to distract a troubled and pious queen and let her have some fun.

Even though Soma·deva contrives to do away with the complexity of the multiple frames of the "Ocean of the Rivers of Story" at the beginning of the sixth Attainment and the main narrative is allowed to flow unchecked from then on, it still gets swamped in the flood of tales and tales within tales, so in order to help readers keep their heads above water a synopsis of the contents of this volume follows.

Attainment III: Lavánaka

FIFTH WAVE

1–15: Údayana decides to conquer the world and wins Shiva's favor through austerities. 16–55: Yaugándharáyana tells the story of Deva·dasa and the treasure. 56–73: Údayana's army sets forth for Varanasi. 74–88: Yaugándharáyana's spies in Varanasi help him foil Brahma·datta's schemes and Brahma·datta submits to Údayana. 89–97: Údayana conquers the east and south, then travels to Ujjain. 98–118: Údayana conquers the west and north, then returns to Lavánaka.

SIXTH WAVE

1–3: Údayana voices concern that Brahma·datta might still move against him. 4–219: Yaugándharáyana disagrees and replies by telling him the story of Soma·datta. (54–190:) Queen Kuvalayávali tells Soma·datta the story of how she got her magical powers from the witch Kala·ratri. (58–100:) To illustrate the powers of Ganésha, Kuvalayávali's friends tell the story of Karttikéya's being born in order to kill Táraka. (115–185:) The tale of Súndaraka, a pupil of Kala·ratri's brahmin husband. 220–230: Údayana returns to Kaushámbi.

Attainment IV: The Birth of Nara·váhana·datta

FIRST WAVE

1–16: Údayana enjoys himself by sporting with his queens and hunting. 17–37: Nárada comes and tells him the story of Pandu dying as a result of a curse incurred by killing a sage in the form of a deer while hunting. 38–53: Píngalika seeks refuge with the king. He sends her to Vásava·datta who treats her hospitably and asks her to tell a story. 54–101: Píngalika tells the tale of the impoverished prince Deva·datta and his wife, the rich merchant's daughter. 102–123: Píngalika tells Vásava·datta her story. 124–148: Vásava·datta longs for children. She and Údayana worship Shiva, who appears in a dream and tells them that they will have a son who will be a partial incarnation of Kama and the lord of the sorcerers.

SECOND WAVE

1–15: Vásava·datta falls pregnant and craves anything to do with sorcerers. 16–257: Yaugándharáyana tells the story of the sorcerer Jimúta·váhana. (56–170:) Jimúta·váhana tells Mittra·vasu the story of his previous life as Vasu·datta, when they became friends. (136–144:) Chitrángada tells the story of him and his daughter, Manóvati, Vasu·datta's wife. (181–257:) The story of the snake-man Shankha·chuda.

THIRD WAVE

1–29: Vásava·datta reports a dream in which Shiva makes a prophesy about the arrival of a wicked woman. The prophesy comes true. 31–51: Vasántaka tells the story of Sinha·parákrama. 52–94: The birth and childhood of Nara·váhana·datta.

Attainment V: Four Girls

FIRST WAVE

19–5.3.284: Shakti·vega, who used to be a man called Shakti·deva and is now a sorcerer king, tells Údayana and

Vásava·datta his story, which starts with that of princess Kánaka·rekha, who says she will only marry the man who has seen Kánaka·puri. (82–201:) Kánaka·rekha tells the story of the rogues Shiva and Mádhava. (204–227:) Her father Paropakárin tells the story of Hara·svamin.

SECOND WAVE

74–297: The brahmin Vishnu·datta in Útsthala tells Shakti·deva the story of Ashóka·datta and Víjaya·datta.

THIRD WAVE

Shakti·deva reaches Kánaka·puri. 53–72: Chandra·prabha tells him her story. 195–255: Bindu·rekha tells the story of Deva·datta.

Attainment VI: Mádana·mánchuka

FIRST WAVE

From here onwards (6.1.3–4) the main narrator is said to be Nara·váhana·datta, talking about himself in the third person.

10–54: A merchant boy from Taksha·shila is taught righteousness by King Kalínga·datta. 59–74: The story of the *apsaras* Súrabhi·datta being cursed and entering the womb of Tara·datta, the wife of Kalínga·datta. 79–106: Tara·datta tells the story of Dharma·datta and his wife Naga·shri. 109–118: Kalínga·datta tells the story of the seven brahmins. 119–132: Kalínga·datta tells the story of two ascetics, one a brahmin the other an outcaste. 135–210: Kalínga·datta tells the story of King Víkrama·sinha and the two brahmins.

SECOND WAVE

9–43: Kalínga·datta repeats the tale about seven princesses which he overheard from a monk. (18–40:) The prince who became a monk and tore out his eye. (26–38:) The prince/monk tells the story of the ascetic who forgives the king who attacks him. 51–95: An old brahmin in the palace tells Kalínga·datta the story of Sulóchana to illustrate the goodness of daughters. 113–153: Soma·prabha tells Kalínga·sena the story of the prince and the merchant's son. 156–184: Kalínga·sena tells Soma·prabha the story of the brahmin, his daughter and the *piśāca*.

THIRD WAVE

Soma·prabha brings Kalínga·sena various magical wooden toys and takes her to her home on a flying machine. 69–197: Kalínga·sena tells Soma·prabha the story of Kirti·sena, who was mistreated by her mother-in-law.

FOURTH WAVE

72–142: Soma·prabha tells Kalínga·sena the story of Tejásvati. (90–139:) A minister tells the king the story of the brahmin Hari·sharman.

FIFTH WAVE

11–33: Kalínga·sena tells Soma·prabha the story of Chitra·lekha and Anirúddha. Soma·prabha takes Kalínga·sena to meet the king of Vatsa. They want to marry but Yaugándharáyana contrives to have the astrologers set the date a long way off.

SIXTH WAVE

42–89: Soma·prabha tells Kalínga·sena the story of Vishnu·datta and his seven foolish companions. 98–190: Soma·prabha tells Kalínga·sena the story of Kádali·garbha. (146–170:) The old barber tells Dridha·varman's senior queen the story of his wife and Dridha·varman's father.

SEVENTH WAVE

25–80: Yaugándharáyana tells the king of Vatsa the story of Shruta·sena in the context of Vásava·datta and Padmávati's apparent acquiescence to the king of Vatsa's love for Kalínga·sena. 7.28–67: The brahmin Agni·sharman tells Shruta·sena about two miracles he has witnessed. 7.35–51: A farmhand tells an ascetic the story of the three brahmin brothers. 7.52–67: The second miracle—the sight of Vidyud·dyota. 7.62–66: Agni·sharman tells the story of Deva·sena and Unmádini. 106–130: Yaugándharáyana tells Yogéshvara the story of the mongoose, the owl, the cat and the mouse. 133–156: Yaugándharáyana tells Yogéshvara the story of King Prasénajit and the brahmin who lost his buried treasure.

EIGHTH WAVE

10–20: Kalínga·sena tells the king of Vatsa the story of King Indra·datta. 67–89: Yaugándharáyana tells the king of Vatsa the story of the *yakṣa* Virupáksha. 90–173: Nara·váhana·datta is made crown prince and engaged to Mádana·mánchuka. 182–187: To illustrate the snake-like nature of women, Go·mukha tells the story of Shatrúghna. 189–213: Go·mukha and the others, on being asked by him, tell Nara·váhana·datta the essence of statecraft. 206–212: By way of illustration they tell the stories of Shura·sena and Hari·sinha. Nara·váhana·datta and Mádana·mánchuka get married.

A Note on the Edition and Translation

This new translation is based on the Nirnaya Sagar Press's 1915 edition of the Sanskrit text, which is very accurate and has needed correction and emendation in only a few places. I have sought to translate literally without sacrificing readability. To ensure the latter, I have on occasion found it necessary not to translate some conjunctive particles, in particular *atha*, *ca* and *tataḥ*, because the repetition of "and" or "then" can become jarring in English.

I would like to acknowledge and thank MUKTAK AKLUJKAR for the help he has given me with my work on the *Kathāsaritsāgara*. His encyclopedic knowledge of the *Bṛhatkathā* cycle and keen eye for mistakes and infelicities in both Sanskrit and English have resulted in numerous improvements to both the text and translation and additions to the explanatory notes.

Bibliography

The Kathāsaritsāgara of Somadevabhaṭṭa, edited by PANDIT DURGAPRASAD and KASINATH PANDURANG PARAB. 3rd ed., revised by WASUDEV LAXMAN SHASTRI PANSIKAR. Bombay: Nirnaya Sagar Press, 1915. [Ed]

The Katha Sarit Sagara or Ocean of the Streams of Story, translated from the original Sanskrit by C.H. TAWNEY, M.A. Calcutta: The Asiatic Society, 1880. [T]

Koṅkuvēḷir iyaṟṟiya Peruṅkatai, edited by U.V. CĀMINĀTAIYAR. 2nd ed. Ceṉṉai: Kēcari Accukkūṭam, 1935.

The Bṛhatkathāmañjarī of Kshemendra, edited by MAHAMAHOPADHYAYA PANDIT SIVADATTA & KASHINATHA PANDURANG PARAB. Bombay: Nirnaya Sagara Press, Kāvyamālā 69, 1901.

The Emperor of the Sorcerers or *Bṛhatkathāślokasaṃgraha* of Budhasvāmin, edited and translated by SIR JAMES MALLINSON. 2 vols. New York University Press/JJC Foundation. 2005.

Vasudevahiṇḍiprathamakhaṇḍam, *Ātmānanda-Jaina-Granthamālā*, nos. 80 & 81 (2 vols.), edited by CATURVIJAYAMUNI & PUNYAVIJAYAMUNI. Bhāvnagar: Bhāvnagar Śrījaina-Ātmānanda-Sabhā, 1930–31.

NELSON, DONALD. "Bṛhatkathā Studies: The Problem of an Ur-Text." *Journal of Asian Studies*, vol. 37, no. 4 (Aug., 1978), 663–76.

Bibliography

[illegible]aritsāgara of Somadevabhaṭṭa, edited by Paṇḍit Durgāprasād and Kāśīnāth Pāṇḍurang Parab, 3rd ed. revised by W[illegible] Laxman Shāstrī Paṇsīkar. Bombay: Nirṇaya-Sāgar Press, [illegible]

[illegible] Sarit Sāgara [illegible], translated from the original Sanskrit by C. H. Tawney, M.A. [illegible]

[illegible]

[illegible] edited by [illegible]

[illegible]

[illegible] edited and translated by [illegible] 2 vols. [illegible] University Press [illegible]

[illegible] edited by [illegible]

[illegible]

[illegible]

THE OCEAN OF THE RIVERS OF STORY

VOLUME TWO

ATTAINMENT III
LAVÁNAKA

5

3.5.1 Tato Vats'|ēśvaraṃ prāha tatra Yaugandharāyaṇaḥ
«rājan, daiv'|ānukūlyaṃ ca vidyate pauruṣaṃ ca te.
nīti|mārge ca vayam apy atra kiṃ|cit|kṛta|śramāḥ
tad yathā|cintitaṃ śīghraṃ kuruṣva vijayaṃ diśām.»

ity ukte mantri|mukhyena rājā Vats'|ēśvaro 'bravīt
«astv etad bahu|vighnās tu sadā kalyāṇa|siddhayaḥ.
atas tad|arthaṃ tapasā Śaṃbhum ārādhayāmy aham
vinā hi tat|prasādena kuto vāñchita|siddhayaḥ.»

3.5.5 tac chrutvā ca tapas tasya mantriṇo 'py anumenire
setu|bandh'|ôdyatasy' âbdhau Rāmasy' eva kap'|īśvarāḥ.
tatas taṃ saha devībhyāṃ sacivaiś ca tapaḥ|sthitam
tri|rātr'|ôpoṣitaṃ bhūpaṃ Śivaḥ svapnaṃ samādiśat.
«tuṣṭo 'smi te tad uttiṣṭha nirvighnaṃ jayam āpsyasi
sarva|vidyā|dhar'|âdhīśaṃ putraṃ c' âiv' â|cirād iti.»

tataḥ sa bubudhe rājā tat|prasāda|hṛta|klamaḥ
ark'|âṃśu|racit'|āpyāyaḥ pratipac|candramā iva.
ānandayac ca sacivān prātaḥ svapnena tena saḥ
vrat'|ôpavāsa|klānte ca devyau dve puṣpa|komale.

3.5.10 tat|svapna|varṇanen' âiva śrotra|peyena tṛptayoḥ
tayoś ca vibhavāy' âiva jātaḥ svādv|auṣadha|kramaḥ.
lebhe sa rājā tapasā prabhāvaṃ pūrvajaiḥ samam
puṇyāṃ pati|vratānāṃ ca tat|patnyau kīrtim āpatuḥ.

5

THEN YAUGÁNDHARÁYANA said to the king of Vatsa there, 3.5.1
"Sire, fate is favorable to you and you are brave, and we, for our part, have taken a certain amount of trouble over how to proceed correctly in this matter, so you should quickly conquer the directions as planned."

When the chief minister said this, the king of Vatsa replied, "Would that I could, but there are always a lot of obstacles to the attainment of good fortune, so to that end I shall propitiate Shiva with austerities, for without his grace desires are not fulfilled."

When they heard this the ministers consented to his per- 3.5.5
forming austerities, just as the monkey chiefs approved of Rama's austerities when he was trying to build a causeway across the ocean. Then, while he was performing austerities with his two queens and his ministers and had fasted for three nights, in a dream Shiva instructed the king thus: "I am pleased with you so arise! You shall achieve victory unhindered and before long you shall have a son who is the emperor of all the sorcerers."

After this the king woke up, his fatigue removed by Shiva's grace as if he were the new moon having been made to grow by the rays of the sun. By recounting the dream that morning he brought joy to the ministers and the two queens, who, tender as flowers, were exhausted from their
observances and fasting. The telling of his dream was a tonic 3.5.10
to the ears of those two delighted ladies and produced in them a succession of sweet elixirs which directly brought about their recovery. By means of his austerities the king obtained a power equal to that of his ancestors and his wives

utsava|vyagra|paure ca vihite vrata|pāraṇe
Yaugandharāyaṇo 'nyedyur iti rājānam abravīt.
«dhanyas tvaṃ yasya c' âiv' êtthaṃ prasanno bhagavān Haraḥ
tad idānīṃ ripūñ jitvā bhaja lakṣmīṃ bhuj'|ârjitām.
sā hi sva|dharma|saṃbhūtā bhūbhṛtām anvaye sthirā
nija|dharm'|ârjitānāṃ hi vināśo n' âsti saṃpadām.
3.5.15 tathā ca cira|bhūmi|ṣṭho nidhiḥ pūrva|ja|saṃbhṛtaḥ
praṇaṣṭo bhavatā prāptaḥ kiṃ c' âtr' âitāṃ kathāṃ śṛṇu.

babhūva Devadās'|ākhyaḥ pure Pāṭaliputrake
purā ko 'pi vaṇik|putro mahā|dhana|kul'|ôdgataḥ.
abhavat tasya bhāryā ca nagarāt Pauṇḍravardhanāt
pariṇītā samṛddhasya kasy' âpi vaṇijaḥ sutā.
gate pitari pañcatvaṃ krameṇa vyasan'|ânvitaḥ
sa Devadāso dyūtena sarvaṃ dhanam ahārayat.
tataś ca tasya sā bhāryā duḥkha|dāridrya|duḥkhitā
etya nītā nijaṃ gehaṃ sva|pitrā Pauṇḍravardhanam.
3.5.20 śanaiḥ so 'pi vipat|khinnaḥ sthātum icchan sva|karmaṇi
mūly'|ârthī Devadāsas taṃ śvaśuraṃ yācituṃ yayau.
prāptaś ca saṃdhyā|samaye tat puraṃ Pauṇḍravardhanam
rajo|rūkṣaṃ vivastraṃ ca vīkṣy' ātmānam acintayat.
‹īdṛśaḥ praviśām' îha kathaṃ śvaśura|veśmani?
varaṃ hi mānino mṛtyur na dainyaṃ sva|jan'|âgrataḥ.›

won the righteous renown of women who are devoted to their husbands.

On the next day, when the fast had been broken and the city was busy celebrating, Yaugándharáyana said to the king, "You are fortunate that lord Shiva has graced you thus, so now you must defeat your enemies and enjoy the prosperity won by your arm. When prosperity arises through kings carrying out their natural duty it remains with their descendants, because riches won by carrying out one's duty
are never lost. Thus the long since buried treasure which 3.5.15
was amassed by your ancestors and had been lost was found by you. By the same token listen to this story on the matter:

Long ago in the city of Pátali·putra there lived a certain young merchant called Deva·dasa who had been born to a very rich family. He married a girl from the city of Paundra·várdhana, the daughter of some prosperous merchant. When his father died he gradually became addicted to vice and lost all his wealth at gambling. At this the father of that wife of his, who was distressed by her sorrows and poverty, came and took her home to Paundra·várdhana.

Deva·dasa slowly became depressed by his misfortune. 3.5.20
He wanted to get established in his business and needed capital, so he went to entreat his father-in-law. When he reached the city of Paundra·várdhana at dusk and realized that he was caked in dust and unsuitably dressed, he said to himself, 'How can I enter my father-in-law's house here like this? For a proud man death is preferable to destitution in front of one's family.'

ity ālocy' āpaṇe gatvā sa kv' âpi vipaṇer bahiḥ
naktaṃ saṃkucitas tasthau tat|kālaṃ kamal'|ôpamaḥ.
kṣaṇāc ca tasyāṃ vipaṇau praviśantaṃ vyalokayat
yuvānaṃ vaṇijaṃ kaṃ|cid udghāṭita|kavāṭakam.
3.5.25 kṣaṇ'|ântare ca tatr' âiva niḥśabda|padam āgatām
drutam antaḥ praviṣṭāṃ ca striyam ekāṃ dadarśa saḥ.
jvalat|pradīpe yāvac ca dadau dṛṣṭiṃ tad|antare
pratyabhijñātavāṃs tāvat tāṃ nijām eva gehinīm.
tataḥ so 'rgalita|dvārāṃ bhāryāṃ tām anya|gāminīm
dṛṣṭvā duḥkh'|âśani|hato Devadāso vyacintayat.
‹dhana|hīnena deho 'pi hāryate strīṣu kā kathā
nisarga|niyataṃ v" āsāṃ vidyutām iva cāpalam.
tad iyaṃ sā vipat puṃsāṃ vyasan'|ârṇava|pātinām
gatiḥ s" êyaṃ sva|tantrāyāḥ striyāḥ pitṛ|gṛha|sthiteḥ.›
3.5.30 iti saṃcintayaṃs tasyā bhāryāyāḥ sa bahiḥ sthitaḥ
rat'|ânta|visrambha|juṣaḥ kath"|ālāpam iv' âśṛṇot.
upetya ca dadau dvāri sa karṇaṃ s" âpi tat|kṣaṇam
ity abravīd upapatiṃ pāpā taṃ vaṇijaṃ rahaḥ.
‹śṛṇv idaṃ kathayāmy adya rahasyaṃ te 'nurāgiṇi
mad|bhartur Vīravarm'|ākhyaḥ pur" âbhūt prapitāmahaḥ.
sva|gṛhasy' âṅgaṇe tena catvāraḥ svarṇa|pūritāḥ
kumbhāś caturṣu koṇeṣu nigūḍhāḥ sthāpitā bhuvi.
tad ekasyāḥ sva|bhāryāyāḥ sa cakre viditaṃ tadā
tad|bhāryā c' ânta|kāle sā snuṣāyai tad avocata.
3.5.35 s" âpi snuṣāyai mac|chvaśrve mac|chvaśrūr abravīc ca me
ity ayaṃ mat|pati|kule śvaśrū|krama|mukh'|āgamaḥ.
sva|bhartus tac ca na mayā daridrasy' âpi varṇitam

After thinking this, he went to some market and spent
the night outside a shop, huddled up like a lotus at that
same hour. A moment later he noticed a certain young merchant open the door and go into the shop and immediately 3.5.25
after that he saw a woman steal up to that very place and
hurry inside. As he looked within, where a lamp was burning, he recognized the woman as his own wife. Then, seeing his wife behind a bolted door with another man, Deva·
dasa was struck by the thunderbolt of grief and said to himself, 'The man without wealth loses even his body, to say
nothing of his wife—women are fickle by nature, like lightning. So what we have here is the sorry state that befalls
men who plunge into the sea of vice and the behavior that
results from a woman living freely in her father's house.'

As he was thinking this while standing outside, he heard 3.5.30
what sounded like the chatter of his wife delighting in post-
coital intimacy. He went up and put his ear to the door, and
at that moment the wicked woman was saying in private to
her lover, the merchant, 'Listen, since I am in love with you,
I'm now going to tell you a secret. Long ago there lived my
husband's paternal great-grandfather, who was called Vira·
varma. In the four corners of the courtyard of his house
he hid in the ground four pots filled with gold. He told
only his wife about it and then on her deathbed she told
her daughter-in-law. She too told her daughter-in-law, who 3.5.35
was my mother-in-law and my mother-in-law told me. This
has thus been passed on in my husband's family by word
of mouth from daughter-in-law to daughter-in-law. I have
not told my husband even though he is poor, because he is
addicted to gambling and contemptible. You, however, are

sa hi dyūta|rato dveṣyas tvaṃ tu me paramaḥ priyaḥ.
tat tatra gatvā mad|bhartuḥ sakāśāt tad|gṛhaṃ dhanaiḥ
krītvā tat prāpya ca svarṇam ih' âitya bhaja māṃ sukham.›
evam uktaḥ kuṭilayā sa tay" ôpapatir vaṇik
tutoṣa tasyai manvāno nidhiṃ labdham a|yatnataḥ.

Devadāso 'pi ku|vadhū|vāk|śalyais tair bahir gataḥ
kīlitām iva tat|kālaṃ dhan'|āśāṃ hṛdaye dadhau.
3.5.40 jagāma ca tataḥ sadyaḥ puraṃ Pāṭaliputrakam
prāpya ca sva|gṛhaṃ labdhvā nidhānaṃ svī|cakāra tat.
ath' ājagāma sa vaṇik tad|bhāryā|cchanna|kāmukaḥ
tam eva deśaṃ vāṇijya|vyājena nidhi|lolupaḥ.
Devadāsa|sakāśāc ca krīṇāti sma sa tad|gṛham
Devadāso 'pi mūlyena bhūyasā tasya tad dadau.
tato gṛha|sthitiṃ kṛtvā yuktyā śvaśura|veśmanaḥ
sa Devadāsaḥ śīghraṃ tām ānināya sva|gehinīm.
evaṃ kṛte ca tad|bhāryā|kāmukaḥ sa vaṇik|śaṭhaḥ
a|labdha|nidhir abhyetya Devadāsam uvāca tam.
3.5.45 ‹etad bhavad|gṛhaṃ jīrṇaṃ mahyaṃ na khalu rocate
tad dehi me nijaṃ mūlyaṃ sva|gṛhaṃ svī|kuruṣva ca.›

iti jalpaṃś ca sa vaṇig Devadāsaś ca vibruvan
ubhau vivāda|saktau tau rāj'|âgram upajagmatuḥ.
tatra sva|bhāryā|vṛttāntaṃ vakṣaḥ|stha|viṣa|duḥsaham
Devadāso nar'|êndr'|âgre kṛtsnam udgirati sma tam.
tataś c' ānāyya tad|bhāryāṃ tattvaṃ c' ânviṣya bhū|patiḥ
adaṇḍayat taṃ sarvasvaṃ vaṇijaṃ pāra|dārikam.
Devadāso 'pi ku|vadhūṃ kṛtvā tāṃ chinna|nāsikām
anyāṃ ca pariṇīy' âtra tasthau labdha|nidhiḥ sukham.

supremely dear to me. So go there, buy my husband's house from him, get the gold, come back here and enjoy me in luxury.' When her lover the merchant heard this from that crooked woman, he was pleased with her, thinking that he had come by a treasure without trying.

Deva·dasa, meanwhile, went outside holding in his heart
the hope of wealth as if it had been impaled there at that
very moment by those barbed words from his wicked wife.
He immediately went from there to the city of Pátali·putra 3.5.40
and on reaching his house he found the treasure and took it
for himself. Then the merchant, his wife's secret lover, being
greedy for the treasure arrived at that very same place on
the pretext of doing business and bought Deva·dasa's house
from him. Deva·dasa gave it to him for a large sum. Then
Deva·dasa set up house and before long contrived to fetch
that wife of his from his father-in-law's house. And when
he had done this, his wife's lover, that rogue of a merchant,
after failing to find the treasure, went up to Deva·dasa and
said, 'I really don't like this ramshackle house of yours, so 3.5.45
give me my money and take your house.'

With the merchant saying this and Deva·dasa disagreeing, the two of them were at loggerheads and they went before the king. Once there Deva·dasa spewed forth before the king everything that his wife had done, which was as unbearable as poison in his chest. Then the king had his wife brought in and, on inquiring after the truth, he fined the adulterous merchant all his property. Deva·dasa cut off his wicked wife's nose, married another woman and now that he had obtained the treasure, lived there in luxury.

3.5.50 ittham dharm'|ârjitā lakṣmīr ā|saṃtaty an|apāyinī
itarā tu jalā|pāta|tuṣāra|kaṇa|naśvarī.
ato yateta dharmeṇa dhanam arjayitum pumān
rājā tu sutarāṃ yena mūlaṃ rājya|taror dhanam.
tasmād yathāvat saṃmānya siddhaye mantri|maṇḍalam
kuru dig|vijayaṃ, deva, labdhuṃ dharm'|ôttarāṃ śriyam.
śvaśura|dvaya|bandhūnāṃ prasakt'|ânuprasaktitaḥ
vikurvate na bahavo rājānas te milanti ca.
yas tv eṣa Brahmadatt'|ākhyo Vārāṇasyāṃ mahī|patiḥ
nityaṃ vairī sa te tasmād vijayasva tam agrataḥ.
3.5.55 tasmiñ jite jaya prācī|prakrameṇ' âkhilā diśaḥ
uccaiḥ kuruṣva vai Pāṇḍor yaśaś ca kumud'|ôjjvalam.»
ity ukto mantr|imukhyena tath" êti vijay'|ôdyataḥ
Vatsa|rājaḥ prakṛtiṣu prayāṇ'|ārambham ādiśat.
dadau Vaideha|deśe ca rājyaṃ Gopālakāya saḥ
sat|kāra|hetor nṛ|patiḥ śvaśuryāy' ânugacchate.
kiṃ ca Padmāvatī|bhrātre prāyacchat Siṃhavarmaṇe
saṃmānya Cedi|viṣayaṃ sainyaiḥ samam upeyuṣe.
ānāyayac ca sa vibhur bhilla|rājaṃ Pulindakam
mittraṃ balair vyāpta|diśaṃ prāvṛṭ|kālam iv' âmbudaiḥ.
3.5.60 abhūc ca yātrā|saṃrambho rāṣṭre tasya mahā|prabhoḥ
ākulatvaṃ tu śatrūṇāṃ hṛdi citram ajāyata.
Yaugandharāyaṇaś c' âgre cārān Vārāṇasīṃ prati
prāhiṇod Brahmadattasya rājño jñātuṃ viceṣṭitam.

Thus riches attained through righteousness remain as 3.5.50
long as one's descendants, but those attained otherwise are
as fleeting as a cool drop of spray from a waterfall. So a
man should strive to attain wealth by means of righteousness, but a king should try even harder because wealth is
the root of the tree of kingship. Therefore, your majesty,
to be successful you should duly honor all your ministers
before conquering the directions in order to add riches to
righteousness.

Because of the close ties between the relatives of your two
fathers-in-law, not many kings are moving against you; they
are falling in with you. But there is a king in Varánasi called
Brahma·datta who has always been your enemy so defeat
him first. With him defeated, starting in the east conquer 3.5.55
all the directions and truly exalt the glory of Pandu which
is as dazzling as a white lotus."

The king of Vatsa was keen for conquest and after being
told this by the chief minister he agreed and instructed his
subjects to prepare to march forth. With the intention of
honoring him, the king gave his obedient brother-in-law
Go·pálaka sovereignty over the land of Vaidéha. In addi-
tion, he honored Padmávati's brother Sinha·varman, who
had come to him with his troops, by giving him the region of Chedi. The king summoned Pulíndaka, ruler of
the Bhillas, his friend whose forces filled the directions like
clouds in the rainy season. A flurry of preparation for the 3.5.60
march arose in the great lord's realm, but, strange to say,
panic was produced in the hearts of his enemies. Yaugándharáyana sent spies ahead to Varánasi to find out what
King Brahma·datta was doing.

tataḥ śubhe 'hani prīto nimittair jaya|śaṃsibhiḥ
Brahmadattaṃ prati prācyāṃ pūrvaṃ Vats'|ēśvaro yayau.
ārūḍhaḥ procchrita|cchattraṃ prottuṅgaṃ jaya|kuñjaram
giriṃ praphull'|âika|taruṃ mṛg'|êndra iva durmadaḥ.
prāptayā siddhi|dūty" êva śaradā datta|saṃmadaḥ
darśayanty" âti|sugamaṃ mārgaṃ svalp'|âmbu|nimnagam.
3.5.65 pūrayan bahu|nādābhir vāhinībhir bhuvas talam
kurvann a|kāṇḍa|nirmegha|varṣā|samaya|saṃbhramam.
tadā ca sainya|nirghoṣa|pratiśabd'|ākulī|kṛtāḥ
parasparam iv' ācakhyus tad|āgama|bhayaṃ diśaḥ.

celuś ca hema|saṃnāha|saṃbhṛt'|ârka|prabhā hayāḥ
tasya nīrājana|prīta|pāvak'|ânugatā iva.
virejur vāraṇāś c' âsya sita|śravaṇa|cāmarāḥ
vigalad|gaṇḍa|sindūra|śoṇa|dāna|jalāḥ pathi.
śarat|pāṇḍu|payod'|âṅkāḥ sa|dhātu|rasa|nirjharāḥ
yātr"|ânupreṣitā bhītair ātmajā iva bhū|dharaiḥ.
3.5.70 n' âiv' âiṣa rājā sahate pareṣāṃ prasṛtaṃ mahaḥ
it' îva tac|camū|reṇur arka|tejas tirodadhe.

padāt padaṃ ca dve devyau mārge tam anujagmatuḥ
nṛpaṃ naya|*guṇ*'|ākṛṣṭe iva kīrti|jaya|śriyau.
«namat" âtha palāyadhvam! ity» ūce vidviṣām iva
pavan'|ākṣipta|vikṣiptais tasya senā|dhvaj'|âṃśukaiḥ.
evaṃ yayau sa dig|bhāgān paśyan phulla|sit'|âmbujān
mahī|marda|bhay'|ôdbhrānta|Śeṣ'|ôtkṣipta|phaṇān iva.

Then on an auspicious day, gladdened by omens proclaiming victory, the king of Vatsa first traveled eastwards towards Brahma·datta. He mounted a towering elephant of victory with a parasol raised above it as if he were a raging lion climbing a mountain on which a single tree is blooming. Fall arrived like a messenger of success, exhilarating him as she pointed out a very easy route, along which the
rivers had little water. By covering the surface of the earth 3.5.65
with his noisy troops, he created the untimely illusion that it was the rainy season, without the clouds. Then the directions, resounding with the echoes of the shouts of the army, seemed to tell one another of their fear of its arrival.

The brightness of the sun was concentrated by the golden armor of his horses, as if fire, delighted by the weapons' ceremonial lustration, were following them. On the way his elephants, their white ears like chowries, the rut fluid dripping from their temples as red as vermilion, made it look as if the terrified mountains had sent forth on the march offspring marked with the white clouds of fall, their streams
red with the juice of mineral ores. As if thinking that the 3.5.70
king would not put up with glory spreading forth from anyone else, the dust from his army concealed the splendor of the sun.

The two queens followed the king from place to place along the way as if they were the goddesses of renown and victory drawn by the *virtue : rope* of political wisdom. "Bow down or run away!" his army's silken banners seemed to say to his enemies as they flapped about in the wind. He journeyed on like this looking in all directions, where the

atr' ântare ca te cārā dhṛta|Kāpālika|vratāḥ
Yaugandharāyaṇ'|ādiṣṭāḥ prāpur Vārāṇasīṃ purīm.
3.5.75 teṣāṃ ca kuhak'|âbhijño jñānitvam upadarśayan
śiśriye gurutām ekaḥ śeṣās tac|chiṣyatāṃ yayuḥ.
«ācāryo 'yaṃ tri|kāla|jña iti» vyāja|guruṃ ca tam
śiṣyās te khyāpayām āsur bhikṣ"|âśinam itas tataḥ.
yad uvāc' âgni|dāh'|ādi sa jñānī bhāvi pṛcchatām
tac|chiṣyās tat tathā guptaṃ cakrus tena sa paprathe.
rañjitaṃ kṣudra|siddhyā ca tatratyaṃ nṛpa|vallabham
svī|cakre sa kam apy ekaṃ rāja|putram upāsakam.
tan|mukhen' âiva rājñaś ca Brahmadattasya pṛcchataḥ
so 'bhūt tatra rahasya|jñaḥ prāpte Vats'|ēśa|vigrahe.
3.5.80 ath' âsya Brahmadattasya mantrī Yogakaraṇḍakaḥ
cakāra Vatsa|rājasya vyājān āgacchataḥ pathi.
adūṣayat pratipathaṃ viṣ'|ādi|dravya|yuktibhiḥ
vṛkṣān kusuma|vallīś ca toyāni ca tṛṇāni ca.
vidadhe viṣa|kanyāś ca sainye paṇya|vilāsinīḥ
prāhiṇot puruṣāṃś c' âiva niśāsu cchadma|ghātinaḥ.
tac ca vijñāya sa jñāni|liṅgī cāro nyavedayat
Yaugandharāyaṇāy' āśu sva|sahāya|mukhais tadā.
Yaugandharāyaṇo 'py etad buddhvā pratipadaṃ pathi
dūṣitaṃ tṛṇa|toy'|ādi pratiyogair aśodhayat.
3.5.85 a|pūrva|strī|samāyogaṃ kaṭake niṣiṣedha ca
avadhīd vadhakāṃs tāṃś ca labdhvā saha Rumaṇvatā.

blossoming white lotuses made it seem that Shesha,* panicked by the fear that the world would be destroyed, had raised his hoods.

Meanwhile, at the order of Yaugándharáyana the spies in that region adopted the guise of *kapálika*s* and arrived
at the city of Varánasi. One of them was a skilled fraudster 3.5.75
and, pretending to be a soothsayer, he assumed the role of a guru while the rest became his pupils. The pupils made it known all around that their fake guru, who lived off alms, was a teacher who knew the past, present and future. Whatever the soothsayer said would happen, such as fires and so forth, to those who asked him was secretly brought about by his pupils as he had predicted and thus his reputation spread. Using his contemptible powers he charmed a certain Rajput there, a favorite of the king, and gained him as a devotee. When the war with the king of Vatsa had begun and King Brahma·datta was questioning the guru via that same Rajput, the spy found out the secrets of the place.

Then Brahma·datta's minister Yoga·karándaka* laid traps 3.5.80
in the path of the advancing king of Vatsa. Craftily using poisons and other substances, he polluted the trees, flowering creepers, water and grasses along his route. He deployed poison-maidens as prostitutes among the army and he sent out men to kill by stealth at night. When the spy disguised as a sage discovered all this, he quickly had his followers inform Yaugándharáyana. When Yaugándharáyana found out about it, he used antidotes to purify the polluted
grass, water and so forth all along their route, he forbade 3.5.85
intercourse with unknown women in the camp, and with Rumánvat's help he found and killed the assassins.

tad buddhvā dhvasta|māyaḥ
san sainya|pūrita|diṅ|mukham
Vats'|ēśvaraṃ Brahmadatto
mene durjayam eva tam.
saṃmantrya dattvā dūtaṃ ca śiro|viracit'|âñjaliḥ
tataḥ sa nikaṭī|bhūtaṃ Vats'|ēśaṃ svayam abhyagāt.
Vatsa|rājo 'pi taṃ prāptaṃ pradatt'|ôpāyanaṃ nṛpam
prītyā saṃmānayām āsa śūrā hi praṇati|priyāḥ.

itthaṃ tasmiñ jite prācīṃ śamayan namayan mṛdūn
unmūlayaṃś ca kaṭhinān nṛpān vāyur iva drumān.
3.5.90 prāpa ca prabalaḥ prācyaṃ calad|vīci|vighūrṇitam
Vaṅg'|âvajaya|vitrāsa|vepamānam iv' âmbudhim.
tasya velā|taṭ'|ânte ca jaya|stambhaṃ cakāra saḥ
pātāl'|â|bhaya|yācñ"|ârthaṃ nāga|rājam iv' ôdgatam.

avanamya kare datte Kaliṅgair agragais tataḥ
āruroha Mahendr'|âdriṃ yaśas tasya yaśasvinaḥ.
Mahendr'|âbhibhavād bhītair Vindhya|kūṭair iv' āgataiḥ
gajair jitv" âṭavīṃ rājñāṃ sa yayau dakṣiṇāṃ diśam.
tatra cakre sa niḥsāra|pāṇḍurān apagarjitān
parvat'|āśrayiṇaḥ śatrūñ śarat|kāla iv' âmbudān.
3.5.95 ullaṅghyamānā Kāverī tena saṃmarda|kāriṇā
Colak'|ēśvara|kīrtiś ca kāluṣyaṃ yayatuḥ samam.
na paraṃ Muralānāṃ sa sehe mūrdhasu n' ônnatim
karair āhanyamāneṣu yāvat kāntā|kuceṣv api.
yat tasya sapta|dhā bhinnaṃ papur Godāvarī|payaḥ
mātaṅgās tan|mada|vyājāt saptadh" âiv' āmucann iva.

When Brahma·datta found out about this, now that his tricks had been overcome he considered the king of Vatsa, whose army filled the directions, to be utterly invincible. After holding a council and sending an envoy, he then went in person to the king of Vatsa, who was nearby, with his palms pressed together at his head. And when that king reached him proffering a gift, the king of Vatsa honored him affectionately, for heroes like deference.

After Brahma·datta had been conquered thus, the mighty king of Vatsa, quelling the east by making pliant kings bow down and uprooting stubborn ones as if he were the wind
and they were trees, arrived at the eastern ocean, made 3.5.90
rough by rolling waves as if trembling with fear at the conquest of the country of Vanga.* At the furthest point on its shores he built a victory column which looked like the king of the serpents arisen to request safety for the underworld.

When the chiefs of Kalínga submitted and paid tribute, the renown of that renowned king attained the heights of mount Mahéndra. As if they were the peaks of the Vindhya mountains come in terror at the defeat of Mahéndra, he used his elephants to conquer a forest of kings and then journeyed southwards. There he made his enemies run for the mountains like clouds in fall—spent and pale, their
thunder gone. On being crossed by that devastating king, 3.5.95
the river Kavéri and the glory of the king of the Cholas were simultaneously besmirched. No longer did he put up with the Múralas holding their heads high, so much so that they were beaten down by *hands : tributes* into their beloveds' breasts. His elephants seemed to discharge in the form of

ath' ôttirya sa Vats'|ēśo Revām Ujjayinīm agāt
praviveśa ca tāṃ Caṇḍamahāsena|puraskṛtaḥ.
sa mālya|ślatha|dhammilla|śobhā|dvaiguṇya|śālinām
Mālava|strī|kaṭākṣāṇāṃ yayau c' âtr' âiva lakṣyatām.
3.5.100 tasthau ca nirvṛtas tatra tathā śvaśura|satkṛtaḥ
visasmāra yath" âbhīṣṭān api bhogān sva|deśa|jān.
āsīd Vāsavadattā ca pituḥ pārśva|vivartinī
smarantī bāla|bhāvasya saukhye 'pi vimanā iva.
rājā Caṇḍamahāsenas tayā tanayayā yathā
tath" âiva Padmāvaty" âpi nandati sma samāgataḥ.

viśramya ca niśāḥ kāś|cit prīto Vats'|ēśvaras tataḥ
anvitaḥ śvāśuraiḥ sainyaiḥ prayayau paścimāṃ diśam.
tasya khaḍga|latā nūnaṃ pratāp'|ânala|dhūmikā
yac|cakre Lāṭa|nārīṇām udaśru|kaluṣā dṛśaḥ.
3.5.105 «asau mathitum ambhodhiṃ mā mām unmūlayiṣyati»
it' îva tad|gaj'|ādhūta|vano 'vepata Mandaraḥ.
satyaṃ sa ko 'pi tejasvī bhāsvad|ādi|vilakṣaṇaḥ
pratīcyām *udayaṃ prāpa prakṛṣṭam* api yaj jayī.

a seven-fold fluid of rut the seven separate streams of the Godávari which they had drunk.*

Then the king of Vatsa crossed the Nármada and went to Ujjain. He entered the city after being honored by Chanda·maha·sena. As soon as he was there he became the target of the women of Málava's side glances, whose allure was doubled by their plaits slipping from their garlands. Treated 3.5.100
hospitably by his father-in-law, he stayed there in such comfort that he forgot the delights of his own land even though he had been longing for them. Vásava·datta remained at her father's side, thinking about her childhood, seeming downcast even in this happy situation. King Chanda·maha·sena took just as much pleasure in meeting Padmávati as he did in being united with his daughter Vásava·datta.

After resting for a few nights, the happy king of Vatsa then journeyed westward joined by his father-in-law's troops. His creeper of a sword must have been a tendril of smoke from his blazing valor, for it made the eyes of the women of Lata turbid with tears. As if thinking that he was 3.5.105
going to uproot it to churn the ocean after his elephants had laid waste to its forests, mount Mándara trembled.* Truly he was some luminary other than the sun and the stars, for, by being victorious in the west, he *achieved great success : rose high* there.

tataḥ Kubera|tilakām Alakā|saṅga|śaṃsinīm
Kailāsa|hāsa|subhagām āśām abhisasāra saḥ.
Sindhu|rājaṃ vaśī|kṛtya *hari|sainyair* anudrutaḥ
kṣapayām āsa ca mlecchān Rāghavo rākṣasān iva.
Turuṣka|turaga|vrātāḥ kṣubdhasy' âbdher iv' ūrmayaḥ
tad|gaj'|êndra|ghaṭā velā|vaneṣu dalaśo yayuḥ.
3.5.110 *gṛhīt'|âri|karaḥ śrīmān* pāpasya *puruṣ'|ôttamaḥ*
Rāhor iva sa ciccheda Pārasīka|pateḥ śiraḥ.
Hūṇa|hāni|kṛtas tasya mukharī|kṛta|diṅ|mukhā
kīrtir dvitīyā Gaṅg" êva vicacāra Himācale.
nadantīṣv asya senāsu bhaya|stimita|vidviṣaḥ
pratīpaḥ śuśruve nādaḥ śaila|randhreṣu kevalam.
apacchattreṇa śirasā Kāmarūp'|êśvaro 'pi tam
naman *vicchāyatāṃ* bheje yat tadā na tad adbhutam.
tad|dattair anvito nāgaiḥ samrāḍ vivávṛte 'tha saḥ
adribhir jaṅgamaiḥ śailaiḥ karī|kṛty' ârpitair iva.
3.5.115 evaṃ vijitya Vats'|ēśo vasudhāṃ sa|paricchadaḥ
Padmāvatī|pituḥ prāpa puraṃ Magadha|bhū|bhṛtaḥ.
Magadh'|êśaś ca devībhyāṃ sahite 'sminn upasthite
s'|ôtsavo 'bhūn niśā|jyotsnāvati candra iva Smaraḥ.
a|vijñāta|sthitām ādau punaś ca vyaktim āgatām
mene Vāsavadattāṃ ca so 'dhika|praśray'|āspadam.
tato Magadha|bhū|bhṛtā sa|nagareṇa ten' ârcitaḥ

Then he advanced towards the region adorned by Kubéra which proclaims the delights of Álaka and is made lovely by Kailása's laugh.* He subdued the king of Sindh and *accompanied by his cavalry : an army of monkeys* he then crushed the barbarians just as Rama crushed the *rákshasa*s. Like the waves of a stormy sea breaking on forests on the shore, the Turkish cavalry was scattered by his host of elephants. As if 3.5.110
he were *Vishnu, discus in hand and accompanied by Lakshmi*, cutting off the head of Rahu, that *glorious finest of men accepted the tribute of his enemies* and cut off the head of the wicked king of the Persians. When he crushed the Huns, his fame resounded in every quarter and flowed through the Himálaya like a second Ganga. His foes were transfixed with fear and an opposing voice to his thundering armies was heard only in mountain caves. It was not remarkable then that when even the king of Kama·rupa was bowing before him, his head uncovered by a parasol,* he was *without shade : pale.* The emperor then returned accompanied by elephants given to him by that king, as if the mountains had given to him in tribute hills that could move.

Having thus conquered the earth, the king of Vatsa and 3.5.115
his entourage arrived at the city of the king of Mágadha, Padmávati's father. The king of Mágadha was overjoyed by him being there in the company of his two queens, like the god of love when the moon is accompanied by night and moonlight. And he considered Vásava·datta, with whom he had previously been unacquainted and who had now been revealed to him, to be an abode of abundant modesty. Then, after being honored by the king of Mágadha and his city,

samagra|jana|mānasair anugato 'nurāg'|āgataiḥ
nigīrṇa|vasudhā|talo bala|bhareṇa Lāvāṇakaṃ
jagāma viṣayaṃ nijaṃ sa kila Vatsa|rājo jayī.

iti mahā|kavi|śrī|Somadeva|bhaṭṭa|viracite Kathāsaritsāgare
Lāvāṇaka|lambake pañcamas taraṅgaḥ.

6

3.6.1 TATAḤ SA SENĀ|VIŚRĀNTYAI tatra Lāvāṇake sthitaḥ
rahasy uvāca Vats'|ēśo rājā Yaugandharāyaṇam.
«tvad|buddhyā nirjitāḥ sarve pṛthivyāṃ bhū|bhṛto mayā
upāya|svī|kṛtās te ca n' âiva vyabhicaranti me.
Vārāṇasī|patis tv eṣa Brahmadatto durāśayaḥ
jāne vyabhicaraty eko viśvāsaḥ kuṭileṣu kaḥ.»
iti Vats'|ēśvareṇ' ôkta āha Yaugandharāyaṇaḥ
«na, rājan, Brahmadattas te bhūyo vyabhicariṣyati.
3.6.5 ākrānt'|ôpanatas tv eṣa bhṛśam sammānitas tvayā
śubh'|ācārasya kaḥ kuryād a|śubhaṃ hi sa|cetanaḥ?
kurvīta vā yas tasy' âiva tad|ātmany a|śubhaṃ bhavet
tathā ca śrūyatām atra kathāṃ te varṇayāmy aham.
babhūva Padma|viṣaye purā ko 'pi dvij'|ôttamaḥ
khyātimān Agnidatt'|ākhyo bhū|bhṛd|datt'|âgrahāra|bhuk.
tasy' âikaḥ Somadatt'|ākhyaḥ putro jyāyān ajāyata
dvitīyaś c' âbhavad Vaiśvānaradatt'|ākhyayā sutaḥ.
ādyas tayor abhūn mūrkhaḥ svākṛtir durvinītakaḥ
aparaś c' âbhavad vidvān vinīto 'dhyayana|priyaḥ.

and followed by the minds of all the people, which had come to him out of love, it is said that the victorious king of Vatsa, who had devoured the surface of the earth with his great army, entered Lavánaka, his own territory.

Thus ends the fifth wave in the Lavánaka Attainment
in the "Ocean of the Rivers of Story" composed by
the glorious and learned great poet Soma·deva.

6

THEN THE KING of Vatsa, staying there in Lavánaka to 3.6.1
rest his army, said in private to Yaugándharáyana, "By means of your intelligence, I have conquered all the kings on the earth. They have been won over by statecraft and will not turn against me. But that king of Varánasi, Brahma·datta, is ill-intentioned. I think that he alone will cause trouble. One cannot trust the crooked."

When the king of Vatsa said this, Yaugándharáyana replied, "Sire, Brahma·datta will not move against you
again. You treated him with great respect when he surren- 3.6.5
dered after being defeated. What sensible man would do bad to one who behaves well? Should someone behave thus, he himself will suffer for it. Just listen—I shall tell you a story on this subject.

Long ago in the country of Padma there lived the finest of brahmins. Agni·datta by name, he was well known and lived off a donation of land from the king. The first son born to him was called Soma·datta, the second Vaishvánara·datta. The eldest was foolish, handsome and unruly. The
second was clever, polite and fond of study. Then, when 3.6.10

3.6.10 kṛta|dārāv ubhau tau ca pitary astaṃ gate tataḥ
tadīyasy' âgra|hār'|āder ardham ardhaṃ vibhejatuḥ.
tan|madhyāt sa kanīyāṃś ca rājñā saṃmānito 'bhavat
jyeṣṭhas tu Somadatto 'bhūc capalaḥ kṣatra|karma|kṛt.
ekadā baddha|goṣṭhīkaṃ śūdraiḥ saha vilokya tam
Somadattaṃ pitṛ|suhṛd|dvijaḥ ko 'py evam abravīt.
‹Agnidatta|suto bhūtvā śūdravan, mūrkha, ceṣṭase!
nijam ev' ânujaṃ dṛṣṭvā rāja|pūjyaṃ na lajjase!›
tac chrutvā kupitaḥ so 'tha Somadattaḥ pradhāvya tam
vipraṃ pāda|prahāreṇa jaghān' ôjjhita|gauravaḥ.
3.6.15 tatra vipraḥ sa kṛtv" ânyān sākṣiṇas tat|kṣaṇaṃ dvijān
gatvā pād'|āhati|kruddho rājānaṃ taṃ vyajijñapat.
rāj" âpi Somadattasya bandhāya prāhiṇod bhaṭān
te ca nirgatya tan|mittrair jaghnire śastra|pāṇibhiḥ.
tato bhūyo balaṃ preṣy' âvaṣṭabdhasy' âsya bhū|patiḥ
krodh'|ândhaḥ Somadattasya śūl'|āropaṇam ādiśat.
āropyamāṇaḥ śūlāyām ath' â|kasmāt sa ca dvijaḥ
prakṣipta iva ken' âpi nipapāta tataḥ kṣitau.
rakṣanti bhāvi kalyāṇaṃ bhāgyāny eva yato 'sya te
andhī|babhūvur vadhakāḥ punar āropaṇ'|ôdyatāḥ.
3.6.20 tat|kṣaṇaṃ śruta|vṛttāntas tuṣṭo rājā kanīyasā
bhrātr" âsya kṛta|vijñaptir vadhād enam amocayat.
tato maraṇa|nistīrṇaḥ Somadatto gṛhaiḥ saha
gantuṃ rāj'|âvamānena deś'|ântaram iyeṣa saḥ.
yadā ca n' āicchan gamanaṃ sametās tasya bāndhavāḥ
tyakta|rāj'|âgrahār'|ârdhāṃ pratipede tadā sthitim.

they had both married and their father had died, they divided his estate equally between them. Of the two, the younger was honored by the king, but Soma·datta, the capricious elder brother, led the life of a warrior.

One day a certain brahmin friend of his father's saw Soma·datta having a conversation with some shudras and said the following, 'You are the son of Agni·datta and you carry on like a shudra, you idiot! You see your very own younger brother being honored by the king and are not ashamed!'

When he heard this the enraged Soma·datta ran at the brahmin and, abandoning his deference, gave him a kick.
The brahmin immediately made the other brahmins there 3.6.15
his witnesses and, furious at having been kicked, went to the king and informed him. The king in turn sent some soldiers to arrest Soma·datta but on going out they were killed by friends of his wielding arms. At this the king again sent out some troops and when Soma·datta had been arrested, in a blind rage he ordered him to be impaled. Then, as he was being lifted onto the stake, that brahmin suddenly fell from it onto the ground as if someone had hurled him down. When the executioners tried to lift him up again they were blinded, for the fates protect a man destined for happiness.

The king immediately found out what had happened and 3.6.20
was delighted. On being requested by the man's younger brother he stayed his execution. Then, having been saved from death, Soma·datta wanted to go with his family to a different country because he had been slighted by the king. When his assembled relatives did not assent to his depar-

tato vṛtty|antar'|âbhāvāt kartuṃ sa cakame kṛṣim
tad|yogyāṃ ca bhuvaṃ draṣṭuṃ śubhe 'hany aṭavīṃ yayau.
tatra lebhe śubhāṃ bhūmiṃ saṃbhāvya phala|saṃpadam
tan|madhye ca mahā|bhogam aśvattha|tarum aikṣata.
3.6.25 taṃ *kalyāṇa/ghana/cchāyāc* channa|sūry'|âṃśu|śītalam
prāvṛṭ|kālam iv' ālokya kṛṣy|arthī toṣam āpa saḥ.
‹yo 'dhiṣṭhāt" âtra tasy' âiva bhakto 'sm' îty› abhidhāya ca
kṛta|pradakṣiṇo 'śvattha|vṛkṣaṃ taṃ praṇanāma saḥ.
saṃyojy' âtha balīvarda|yugaṃ racita|maṅgalaḥ
kṛtvā baliṃ tasya taror ārebhe kṛṣim atra saḥ.
tasthau tasy' âiva c' âdhastād drumasya sa divā|niśam
bhojanaṃ tasya c' āninye tatr' âiva gṛhiṇī sadā.
kāle tatra ca pakveṣu tasya sasyeṣv a|śaṅkitam
sā bhūmiḥ para|rāṣṭreṇa daivād etya vyaluṇṭhyata.
3.6.30 tataḥ para|bale yāte naṣṭe sasye sa sattvavān
āśvāsya rudatīṃ bhāryāṃ kiṃ|cic cheṣaṃ tad" ādadau.
prāgvat kṛta|balis tasthau tatr' âiv' âtha taror adhaḥ
nisargaḥ sa hi dhīrāṇāṃ yad āpady adhikaṃ dṛḍhāḥ.
atha cintā|vinidrasya sthitasy' âikākino niśi
tasy' âśvattha|taros tasmād uccacāra sarasvatī.
‹bhoḥ Somadatta, tuṣṭo 'smi tava tad gaccha bhū|pateḥ
Ādityaprabha|saṃjñasya rāṣṭraṃ Śrīkaṇṭha|deśa|gam.

ture, he agreed to remain but gave up his half of the king's grant of land.

Next, because he had no other way of making a living, he wanted to work the land, and on an auspicious day went to the forest to find a suitable lot. He found there some good land, reckoning that it would produce an abundant harvest, and in its middle he saw an *ashváttha* tree of great girth.
Seeing that because of *its lovely thick shade : the shade of a* 3.6.25
lovely cloud it was cool and hid the rays of the sun as if it were the rainy season, he was satisfied in his desire for land to cultivate. Announcing, 'I devote myself to none other than he who presides here,' he performed a clockwise circumambulation and bowed before the *ashváttha* tree. Then he yoked a pair of oxen, recited an auspicious verse, made a sacrificial offering to the tree and started to plow there. Day and night he remained beneath that same tree and his wife kept bringing his food to that very spot. In time, when his corn there had ripened, by a stroke of fate an army from an enemy kingdom suddenly arrived in that land and plundered it. Then, when the enemy army had left, and his corn 3.6.30
had been lost, that brave man comforted his weeping wife and gave her the little that was left. Next he made a sacrificial offering as he had before and remained right there underneath the tree, for it is the nature of brave men that they become more resolute in time of disaster.

Then one night when he was sleepless with worry and alone, a divine voice came forth from the *ashváttha* tree: 'Oh Soma·datta, I am pleased with you, so go to the country of the king called Adítya·prabha in the land of Shri·kantha. Once there, you should recite the mantras of the evening

tatra tasy' ânavaratam dvāra|deśe mahī|pateḥ
vadeḥ paṭhitvā saṃdhy"|âgni|hotra|mantrān idaṃ vacaḥ.
3.6.35 «Phalabhūtir ahaṃ nāmnā
vipraḥ śṛṇuta vacmi yat
bhadra|kṛt prāpnuyād bhadram
a|bhadraṃ c' âpy a|bhadra|kṛt.»
evaṃ vadaṃś ca tatra tvaṃ mahatīm ṛddhim āpsyasi
saṃdhy"|âgni|hotra|mantrāṃś ca matta eva paṭh' âdhunā.
ahaṃ ca yakṣa ity› uktvā sva|prabhāveṇa tat|kṣaṇam
tam adhyāpya ca tān mantrān vaṭe vāṇī tirodadhe.
prātaḥ sa Somadattaś ca pratasthe bhāryayā saha
Phalabhūtir iti prāpya nāma yakṣa|kṛtaṃ kṛtī.
atikramy' âṭavīs tās tā viṣamāḥ parivartinīḥ
durdaśā iva saṃprāpa Śrīkaṇṭha|viṣayaṃ ca saḥ.
3.6.40 tatra saṃdhy"|âgni|kāry'|ādi paṭhitvā dvāri bhū|pateḥ
yathāvan nāma saṃśrāvya Phalabhūtir iti svakam
so 'vādīd ‹bhadra|kṛd bhadram
a|bhadraṃ c' âpy a|bhadra|kṛt
prāpnuyād iti› lokasya
kautuk'|ôtpādakaṃ vacaḥ.
muhuś ca tad|vadantaṃ taṃ tatr' Ādityaprabho nṛpaḥ
buddhvā praveśayām āsa Phalabhūtiṃ kutūhalī.
so 'pi praviśya tasy' āgre tad eva muhur abravīt
jahāsa tena sa nṛpas tadā pārśva|sthitaiḥ saha.
sa|sāmantaś ca vastrāṇi dattvā c' ābharaṇāni saḥ
grāmān rājā dadau tasmai na toṣo mahatāṃ mṛṣā.
3.6.45 evaṃ ca tat|kṣaṇaṃ prāpa guhyak'|ânugraheṇa saḥ
Phalabhūtiḥ kṛśo bhūtvā vibhūtiṃ bhū|bhṛd|arpitām.
sadā tad eva ca vadan pūrv'|ôktaṃ prāpa bhūpateḥ
vāllabhyam īśvarāṇāṃ hi vinoda|rasikaṃ manaḥ.

fire sacrifice at the king's door and then repeat over and
over again these words: "I am a brahmin called Phala·bhuti. 3.6.35
Listen to what I have to say. He who does good shall obtain
good and he who does evil shall obtain evil." By saying this
there you shall obtain a great fortune. Now recite after me
the mantras of the evening fire sacrifice. By the way, I am a
yaksha.'

Immediately after saying this the voice in the tree used
its powers to teach Soma·datta the mantras and then it fell
quiet. In the morning the gratified Soma·datta adopted the
name Phala·bhuti given by the *yaksha* and set out with his
wife. After passing through various dangerous and different
forests as if they were his misfortunes, he arrived at the land
of Shri·kantha. Once there he recited the mantras and so 3.6.40
forth for the evening fire sacrifice at the king's door, duly
announced that his name was Phala·bhuti and said 'He who
does good shall obtain good and he who does evil shall obtain evil,' arousing the interest of the people.

When King Adítya·prabha found out about him repeatedly saying this there, he was curious and had Phala·bhuti
brought in. He went in and said that same thing over and
over again in front of the king, at which the king laughed,
along with those at his side. The king and his vassals gave
him clothes and ornaments and bestowed villages on him.
The happiness of the great is never barren. And thus at 3.6.45
that moment, through the grace of the *yaksha*, Phala·bhuti,
who had been poor, received a fortune granted to him by
the king. By constantly repeating the same words that he
had spoken before he became a favorite of the king, for

kramād rāja|gṛhe c' âsmin rāṣṭreṣv antaḥ|pureṣu ca
rāja|priya iti prītiṃ bahumānām avāpa saḥ.
kadā|cid atha so 'ṭavyāḥ kṛtv" ākheṭakam āgataḥ
Ādityaprabha|bhū|pālaḥ sahas" ântaḥ|puraṃ yayau.
dvāḥ|stha|saṃbhrama|s'|āśaṅkaḥ praviśy' âiva dadarśa saḥ
devīṃ dev'|ârcana|vyagrāṃ nāmnā Kuvalayāvalīm.
3.6.50 digambarām ūrdhva|keśīṃ nimīlita|vilocanām
sthūla|sindūra|tilakāṃ japa|prasphurit'|ādharām.
vicitra|varṇaka|nyasta|mahā|maṇḍala|madhya|gām
asṛk|surā|mahā|māṃsa|kalpit'|ôgra|bali|kriyām.
s" âpi praviṣṭe nṛpatau saṃbhram'|ākalit'|âṃśukā
tena pṛṣṭā kṣaṇād evam avocad yācit'|â|bhayā.
‹tav' âiv' ôdaya|lābh'|ârthaṃ kṛtavaty asmi pūjanam
atra c' āgama|vṛttāntaṃ siddhiṃ ca śṛṇu me, prabho.
pur" âhaṃ pitṛ|veśma|sthā kanyā madhu|mah"|ôtsave
evam uktā vayasyābhiḥ samety' ôdyāna|vartinī.
3.6.55 «ast' îha pramad'|ôdyāne taru|maṇḍala|madhya|gaḥ
dṛṣṭa|prabhāvo vara|do deva|devo Vināyakaḥ.
tam upāgatya bhaktyā tvaṃ pūjaya prārthita|pradam
yena nirvighnam ev' āśu sv'|ôcitaṃ patim āpsyasi.»

the minds of rulers delight in diversion. And gradually, because the king was fond of him, he gained affection and respect among the royal household, the people and the female apartments.

Then one day King Adítya·prabha returned from the forest having been hunting and went into the female apartments unexpectedly. The panic of the doormen made him
suspicious and as soon as he went in he saw a queen called
Kuvalayávali busy worshipping the gods. She was naked, 3.6.50
her hair was standing on end, her eyes were shut, she had
a forehead mark of thick vermilion, her lips quivered as
she chanted mantras, she was in the middle of a big circle marked with various colored paints and she was offering a fearsome oblation made from blood, alcohol and human flesh. When the king entered she hurriedly put on
her clothes and, on being questioned by him, immediately
asked him to spare her and said the following. 'I was carrying out the worship just then in order to procure prosperity.
In this context, hear about my powers and how I obtained
them, my lord. Long ago when I was a young girl living in
my father's house, I was in the park at the time of the great
spring festival when some friends whom I met there told me
the following. "Here in the ladies' pleasure garden, in the 3.6.55
middle of a circle of trees, there dwells Ganésha, the god of
gods, the giver of boons whose power has been proven. You
should devoutly go up and worship that granter of wishes
so that without any hindrance you quickly get a husband
appropriate to you."

tac chrutvā paryapṛcchyanta sakhyas tā maugdhyato mayā
«kanyā labhante bhartāraṃ kiṃ Vināyaka|pūjayā?»
atha tāḥ pratyavocan māṃ «kim etāvat tvay" ôcyate?
tasminn a|pūjite n' âsti siddhiḥ k" âp' îha kasya cit.
tathā c' âitat|prabhāvaṃ te varṇayāmo vayaṃ śṛṇu»
ity uktvā ca vayasyā me kathām akathayann imām.
3.6.60 «purā Pur'|âres tanayaṃ senānyaṃ prāptum icchati
Tārak'|ôpadrute Śakre dagdhe ca Kusum'|āyudhe.
ūrdhva|retasam aty|ugraṃ su|dīrgha|tapasi sthitam
Gaurī kṛta|tapāḥ prārthya prāpya ca Try|ambakaṃ patim.
ācakāṅkṣa suta|prāptiṃ Madanasya ca jīvitam
na ca sasmāra siddhy|arthaṃ sā vighn'|êśvara|pūjanam.
abhīṣṭ'|âbhyarthinīṃ tāṃ ca kāntām ity avadac Chivaḥ
‹priye, Prajāpateḥ pūrvaṃ mānasād ajani Smaraḥ.
«*kaṃ darpayām' îti?*» madāj jāta|mātro jagāda ca
tena Kaṃdarpa|nāmānaṃ taṃ cakāra Catur|mukhaḥ.
3.6.65 «ati|dṛpto 'si cet, putra, tat Tri|netrasya laṅghanam
ekasya rakṣer mā nāma mṛtyuṃ tasmād avāpsyasi.»
itthaṃ ca vedhas" ôkto 'pi saṃkṣobhāy' āgataḥ śaṭhaḥ
mayā dagdho na tasy' âsti sa|dehasy' ôdbhavaḥ punaḥ.
bhavatyās tu sva|śakty" âiva putram utpādayāmy aham
na hi me Madan'|ôtsāha|hetukā lokavat prajā.›

On hearing this, out of naivete I asked those friends of mine, "What? Do girls get husbands through worshiping Ganésha?"

They then answered me by saying, "Why do you mention only that? Without worshipping him, no one gets any kind of success in this life. On this note we shall tell you about his power. Listen."

After saying this my friends told me the following story.
"Long ago, when Indra had been attacked by Táraka and 3.6.60
wanted to get Shiva's son to lead his army, and the god of love had been consumed by fire, Párvati performed austerities and after wooing him, won as her husband the three-eyed god, who was celibate, extremely fearsome and engaged in very lengthy austerities. She wanted to have a son and for the god of love to be revived, but she did not remember to worship Ganésha in order to be successful. When she was asking for what she wanted, Shiva said to his sweetheart, 'My dear, long ago the god of love was born from the mind of Brahma, and as soon as he was born he arrogantly announced, "*Whom shall I drive mad?** : I shall drive Brahma mad!*" As a result of this, four-faced Brahma
gave him the name Kandárpa, saying, "If you are to be so 3.6.65
very arrogant, my son, then, in particular, you should avoid offending three-eyed Shiva, or you shall receive death from him." Even though he had been told this by the creator, the rogue came to disturb me. I burned him up and he shall never again be born in a body. But I shall use my power to create a son in you, for unlike everyone else, my offspring are not caused by the efforts of the god of love.'

evaṃ vadata ev' âsya Pārvatīṃ Vṛṣa|lakṣmaṇaḥ
āvir|babhūva purato Brahmā Śata|makh'|ânvitaḥ.
tena stutvā sa vijñaptas Tārak'|âsura|śāntaye
aṅgī|cakre Śivaḥ sraṣṭuṃ devyām ātmajam aurasam.

3.6.70 anumene ca Kāmasya janma cetasi dehinām
sarga|viccheda|rakṣ"|ârtham a|mūrtasy' âiva tad|girā.
dadau ca nija|citte 'pi so 'vakāśaṃ Manobhuvaḥ
tena tuṣṭo yayau dhātā mudaṃ prāpa ca Pārvatī.

tato yāteṣu divaseṣv ekadā rahasi sthitaḥ
siṣeve surata|krīḍām Umayā saha Śaṃkaraḥ.
yadā n' âbhūd rat'|ânto 'sya gateṣv abda|śateṣv api
tadā tad|upamardena cakampe bhuvana|trayam.
tato jagan|nāśa|bhayād rata|vighnāya śūlinaḥ
vahniṃ smaranti sma surāḥ Pitāmaha|nideśataḥ.

3.6.75 so 'py Agniḥ smṛta|mātraḥ sann
a|dhṛṣyaṃ Madan'|ântakam
matvā palāyya devebhyaḥ
praviveśa jal'|ântaram.
tat|tejo|dahyamānāś ca tatra bhekā divaukasām
vicinvatāṃ śaśaṃsus tam Agnim antar|jala|sthitam.
tatas tān an|abhivyakta|vācaḥ śāpena tat|kṣaṇam
bhekān kṛtvā tiro|bhūya bhūyo 'gnir Mandaraṃ yayau.
tatra taṃ koṭar'|ânta|sthaṃ devāḥ śambūka|rūpiṇam
prāpur gaja|śuk'|ākhyātaṃ sa c' âiṣāṃ darśanaṃ dadau.
kṛtvā jihvā|viparyāsaṃ śāpena śuka|dantinām
pratipede ca devānāṃ sa kāryaṃ taiḥ kṛta|stutiḥ.

Just as he whose insignia is the bull was saying this to Párvati, Brahma appeared before him accompanied by Indra.
After Brahma had hymned him and asked him to pacify the
demon Táraka, Shiva agreed to bring forth in the goddess
his own self-born son. And at their bidding, he consented 3.6.70
that the god of love be born in the minds of embodied beings, albeit without taking a body himself, in order to pre-
vent the stoppage of procreation. And he gave the god of
love the opportunity to enter his own mind. Pleased by this,
the creator went on his way and Párvati was delighted.

Then the days passed until one day, sitting in private,
Shiva started to enjoy himself by making love with Párvati.
Hundreds of years passed without their lovemaking coming
to an end and then the three worlds began to shake with its
violence. Frightened that the world would be destroyed, at
the instruction of Brahma the gods called to mind the god
of fire in order to interrupt Shiva's lovemaking. The god 3.6.75
of fire, for his part, thinking the killer of the god of love
to be invincible, ran away from the gods as soon as he was
thought of and went into the water. There the frogs, being
burned up by his heat, told the gods, who were searching
for him, that the god of fire was in the water. Then the god
of fire immediately cursed the frogs to be inarticulate, disappeared once more and went to mount Mándara. There he
was betrayed by the elephants and parrots. The gods found
him at the top of a tree in the form of a snail and he revealed
himself to them. He cursed the parrots and elephants to ex-
change tongues and after being hymned by them agreed to
do what the gods needed done.

3.6.80 gatvā ca sv'|ôṣmaṇā so 'gnir nivārya suratāc chivam
śāpa|bhītyā praṇamy' âsmai deva|kāryaṃ nyavedayat.
Śarvo 'py ārūḍha|vego 'gnau tasmin vīryaṃ svam ādadhe
tadd hi dhārayituṃ śakto na Vahnir n' Âmbik" âpi vā.

‹na mayā tanayas tvattaḥ saṃprāpta iti› vādinīm
kheda|kop'|ākulāṃ devīm ity uvāca tato Haraḥ.
‹vighno 'tra tava jāto 'yaṃ vinā vighn'|ēśa|pūjanam
tad arcay' âinaṃ yen' āśu vahnau no janitā sutaḥ.›

ity uktā Śaṃbhunā devī cakre vighn'|êśvar'|ârcanam
analo 'pi sa|garbho 'bhūt tena vīryeṇa dhūr|jaṭeḥ.
3.6.85 tat tejaḥ śāṃbhavaṃ bibhrat sa tadā divaseṣv api
antaḥ|praviṣṭa|tigm'|âṃśur iva sapt'|ârcir ābabhau.
udvavāma ca Gaṅgāyāṃ tat tejaḥ so 'tha durdharam
Gaṅg" âinam atyajan Merau vahni|kuṇḍe Har'|ājñayā.
tatra saṃrakṣyamāṇaḥ san sa garbhaḥ śāmbhavair gaṇaiḥ
niḥsṛty' âbda|sahasreṇa kumāro 'bhūt ṣaḍ|ānanaḥ.
tato Gaurī|niyuktānāṃ kṛttikānāṃ payo|dharān
ṣaṇṇāṃ ṣaḍbhir mukhaiḥ pītvā svalpaiḥ sa vavṛdhe dinaiḥ.

atr' ântare deva|rājas Tārak'|âsura|nirjitaḥ
śiśriye Meru|śṛṅgāṇi durgāṇy ujjhita|saṃgaraḥ.
3.6.90 devāś ca sākam ṛṣibhiḥ ṣaṇ|mukhaṃ śaraṇaṃ yayuḥ
ṣaṇ|mukho 'pi surān rakṣann āsīt taiḥ parivāritaḥ.

So the god of fire went and with his heat interrupted 3.6.80
Shiva's lovemaking, and, fearful of a curse, bowed before him and told him what the gods needed done. Shiva ejaculated and deposited his semen in the god of fire. The god of fire was not able to hold on to it, and nor too was Párvati.

At this Shiva said to the goddess, who was beside herself with regret and rage and saying, 'I have not received a son from you,' 'This obstacle has arisen for you in this matter because you have not worshipped Ganésha, the lord of obstacles, so worship him in order for a son to be born to us soon in the god of fire.'

After Shiva said this to her, the goddess worshipped the lord of obstacles and the god of fire became pregnant by
the semen of he of the heavy matted locks. Then, carry- 3.6.85
ing that brilliant semen of Shiva, the fire shone as if it had been entered by the sun even by day. And he then vomited that insufferable semen into the Ganga. At the order of Shiva, Ganga cast it into a sacrificial fire pit on mount Meru. While being looked after there by Shiva's *ganas*,* after a thousand years it came forth and became a six-faced boy. Then, after drinking with his six mouths at the breasts of the six *kríttikas* employed by the goddess, he came of age in a few days.

In the meantime, the king of the gods, defeated by the *ásura* Táraka, gave up the fight and took refuge on the inaccessible peaks of mount Meru. The gods, together with the 3.6.90
sages, went to the six-faced one for safety and the six-faced one, while protecting the gods, was surrounded by them.

tad buddhvā hāritaṃ matvā rājyam Indro 'tha cakṣubhe
yodhayām āsa gatvā ca kumāraṃ sa sa|matsaraḥ.
tad|vajr'|âbhihatasy' âṅgāt ṣaṇ|mukhasy' ôdbabhūvatuḥ
putrau Śākha|Viśākh'|ākhyāv ubhāv a|tula|tejasau.
sa|putraṃ ca tam ākrānta|śata|kratu|parākramam
upetya tanayaṃ Śarvaḥ svayaṃ yuddhād avārayat.
‹jāto 'si Tārakaṃ hantuṃ rājyaṃ c' Êndrasya rakṣitum
tat kuruṣva nijaṃ kāryam iti› c' âinaṃ śaśāsa saḥ.

3.6.95 tataḥ praṇamya prītena tat|kṣaṇaṃ Vṛtra|vairiṇā
sain'|âpaty'|âbhiṣeko 'sya kumārasy' ôpacakrame.
svayam utkṣipta|kalaśa|stabdha|bāhur abhūd yadā
tataḥ Śakraḥ śucam agād ath' âinam avadac Chivaḥ.
‹na pūjito gaja|mukhaḥ senānyam vāñchatā tvayā
ten' âiṣa vighno jātas te tat kuruṣva tad|arcanam.›

tac chrutvā tat tathā kṛtvā mukta|bāhuḥ Śacī|patiḥ
abhiṣek'|ôtsavaṃ samyak senānye niravartayat.
tato jaghāna na cirāt senānīs Tārak'|âsuram
nananduḥ siddha|kāryāś ca devā Gaurī ca putriṇī.
3.6.100 tad evaṃ, devi, devānām api santi na siddhayaḥ
Herambe 'n|arcite tasmāt pūjay' âinaṃ var'|ârthinī.»

ity ukt" âhaṃ vayasyābhir udyān'|âik'|ânta|vartinam
ārya|putra, purā gatvā vighna|rājam apūjayam.
pūj"|âvasāne c' âpaśyam a|kasmād gagan'|âṅgaṇe
utpatya viharantīs tāḥ sva|sakhīr nija|siddhitaḥ.
tad dṛṣṭvā kautukād vyomnaḥ samāhūy' âvatārya ca

When he found out about this, Indra then considered his kingdom to have been taken away from him and was troubled. In his jealousy he went and fought the boy. From the body of the six-faced one, which had been struck by Indra's thunderbolt, there were born two boys of unrivaled splendor called Shakha and Vishákha. And Shiva went up to his son, whose valor surpassed that of Indra, and personally forbade him and his boys to fight. He ordered him, 'You were born to kill Táraka and to protect the kingdom of Indra, so do the duty that is yours.'

At this the delighted Indra immediately bowed before 3.6.95
him and performed Karttikéya's consecration as general of the army. Then, when his arm became stiff from holding up the water pot on his own, Indra became upset and Shiva said to him, 'The elephant-faced one was not venerated by you when you wanted a general for the army, which is why this obstacle has arisen for you, so carry out his worship.'

On hearing this Indra did just that and his arm was freed and he duly completed the rite of consecration on his general. Soon after that the general killed the *ásura* Táraka and the gods rejoiced that they had succeeded in what they had
to do and Párvati rejoiced at having a son. So in this way, O 3.6.100
lady, even for the gods nothing succeeds without Ganésha being venerated, so worship him when you want a boon."

After being told this by my friends, O noble husband, a long time ago I went and worshipped at a temple to Ganésha in an isolated spot in a park. And when the worship had come to an end, I saw that those friends of mine, using their magical powers, had suddenly flown up into the

mayā siddhi|sva|rūpaṃ tāḥ pṛṣṭāḥ sadyo 'bruvann idam.
«imā nṛ|māṃs'|âśana|jā ḍākinī|mantra|siddhayaḥ
Kāla|rātrir iti khyātā brāhmaṇī gurur atra naḥ.»
3.6.105 evaṃ sakhībhir ukt" âhaṃ khecarī|siddhi|lolubhā
nṛ|māṃs'|âśana|bhītā ca kṣaṇam āsaṃ sa|saṃśayā.
atha tat|siddhi|lubdhatvād avocaṃ tāḥ sakhīr aham
«upadeśo mam' âpy eṣa yuṣmābhir dāpyatām iti.»
tato mad|abhyarthanayā gatvā tat|kṣaṇam eva tāḥ
āninyuḥ Kāla|rātriṃ tāṃ tatr' âiva vikaṭ'|ākṛtim.
milad|bhruvaṃ kātar'|âkṣīṃ nyañcac|cipiṭa|nāsikām
sthūla|gaṇḍīṃ karāl'|âuṣṭhīṃ danturāṃ dīrgha|kaṃdharām.
lamba|stanīm udariṇīṃ vidīrṇ'|ôtphulla|pādukām
dhātrā vairūpya|nirmāṇa|vaidagdhīṃ darśitām iva.
3.6.110 sā māṃ pād'|ānatāṃ snātāṃ kṛta|vighn'|êśvar'|ârcanām
vivastrāṃ maṇḍale bhīmāṃ bhairav'|ârcām akārayat.
abhiṣicya ca sā mahyaṃ tāṃs tān mantrān nijān dadau
bhakṣaṇāya nṛ|māṃsaṃ ca dev'|ârcana|balī|kṛtam.
ātta|mantra|gaṇā bhukta|mahā|māṃsā ca tat|kṣaṇam
nirambar" âiv' ôtpatitā sa|sakhīk" âham ambaram.
kṛta|krīḍ" âvatīry' âtha gaganād gurv|anujñayā
gat" âbhūvam ahaṃ, deva, kanyak"|ântaḥ|puraṃ nijam.

sky, where they were having fun. When I saw this I was curious and called them, making them come down from the sky, and on being asked by me about the nature of their magical power, they immediately said the following: "These powers are witches' spells and are produced by eating human flesh. Our teacher in this is a brahmin lady called Kala·ratri."

After being told this by my friends, I wanted to have 3.6.105
the magical power of flight. Frightened of eating human flesh, I was hesitant for a moment. Then out of greed for that magical power, I said to my friends, "You must have this teaching given to me too!" Then at my request they immediately went and brought to that very spot that lady Kala·ratri, who looked hideous. Her eyebrows met, her eyes were shifty, her nose was pendulous and flat, her cheeks were rough, her lips were wide open, her teeth stuck out, her neck was long, her breasts were droopy, her belly was large and her feet were cracked and broad: it was as if in her the creator had shown off his skill for producing ugliness.
She had me bow down and touch her feet, bathe, worship 3.6.110
Ganésha, remove my clothes and, inside a circle, perform a terrifying worship of Bháirava. After anointing me she gave me various of her spells and some human flesh to eat which had been presented as a sacrificial offering in the worship of the gods. After taking all the spells and eating the human flesh I immediately flew up into the sky, completely naked, in the company of my friends. After playing about I then came down from the sky at the order of my teacher and I went, my lord, to my own ladies' apartments.

evaṃ bālye 'pi jāt" âhaṃ ḍākinī|cakra|vartinī
bhakṣitās tatra c' âsmābhiḥ sametya bahavo narāḥ.
3.6.115 asmin kath"|ântare c' âitāṃ, mahā|rāja, kathāṃ śṛṇu
Viṣṇusvām" îty abhūt tasyāḥ Kālarātryāḥ patir dvijaḥ.
sa ca tasminn upādhyāyo deśe nānā|dig|āgatān
śiṣyān adhyāpayām āsa veda|vidyā|viśāradaḥ.
śiṣya|madhye ca tasy' âiko nāmnā Sundarako yuvā
babhūva śiṣyaḥ śīlena virājita|vapur|guṇaḥ.
tam upādhyāya|patnī sā Kālarātriḥ kadā|cana
vavre rahasi kām'|ârtā patyau kv' âpi bahir gate.
nūnaṃ virūpair adhikaṃ hāsanaiḥ krīḍati Smaraḥ
yat s" ân|avekṣya svaṃ rūpaṃ cakre Sundaraka|spṛhām.
3.6.120 sa tu sarv'|ātmanā n' āicchad arthyamāno 'pi viplavam
striyo yathā viceṣṭantāṃ niṣkampaṃ tu satāṃ manaḥ.
tataḥ s" âpasṛte tasmin Kālarātriḥ krudhā tadā
svam aṅgaṃ pāṭayām āsa svayaṃ danta|nakha|kṣataiḥ.
vikīrṇa|vastra|keś'|ântā rudatī tāvad āsta ca
gṛhaṃ yāvad upādhyāyo Viṣṇusvāmī viveśa saḥ.
praviṣṭaṃ tam avādīc ca «paśya Sundarakeṇa me
avasthā vihitā, svāmin, balāt|kār'|âbhilāṣiṇā.»
tac chrutvā sa upādhyāyaḥ krudhā jajvāla tat|kṣaṇam
pratyayaḥ strīṣu muṣṇāti vimarśaṃ viduṣām api.
3.6.125 sāyaṃ ca taṃ Sundarakaṃ gṛha|prāptaṃ pradhāvya saḥ
sa|śiṣyo muṣṭibhiḥ pādair laguḍaiś c' âpy atāḍayat.
kiṃ ca prahāra|niśceṣṭaṃ śiṣyān ādiśya taṃ bahiḥ
tyājayām āsa rathyāyāṃ nirapekṣatayā niśi.

Thus even as a girl I came to take part in the witches' circle, and there we met and consumed many men. In the con- 3.6.115
text of this story, listen, great king, to this tale. There was a brahmin called Vishnu·svamin who was the husband of that lady Kala·ratri. Adept in the Vedas and the sciences, he was a teacher in that land and taught pupils who came from various lands. Among his pupils there was one young man called Súndaraka. His looks and talents were embellished by his character. One day Kala·ratri, his teacher's wife, stricken by desire, propositioned him in private when her husband had gone out somewhere. The god of love must play with ugly people as objects of ridicule, in that she, disregarding her own appearance, desired Súndaraka. But despite be- 3.6.120
ing requested, in no way did he want to incur sin: however women may behave, the minds of good men are still immovable. Then when he had gone away, Kala·ratri angrily bit and scratched her own body and she stayed crying, her clothes and hair disheveled, until the teacher Vishnu·svamin entered the house. When he came in she said to him, "Look, my lord, at what Súndaraka has done to me in his desire to have me by force." When he heard this the teacher was immediately consumed with rage, for trust in women steals the reasoning of even clever men. And when 3.6.125
Súndaraka came to the house in the evening, he ran at him with his other pupils and punched, kicked and beat him with sticks. Moreover, when he was unconscious from the blows, he gave his pupils an order and had them throw him out into the street that night regardless.

tataḥ śanaiḥ Sundarakaḥ sa niś”|ânila|vījitaḥ
tath” âbhibhūtam ātmānaṃ paśyann evam acintayat.
«aho strī|preraṇā nāma *rajasā laṅghit’|ātmanām*
puṃsāṃ vāty” êva sarasām āśaya|kṣobha|kāriṇī.
yen’ âvicārya vṛddho ’pi vidvān api ca tat tathā
atikrodhād upādhyāyo viruddham akaron mayi.
3.6.130 athavā daiva|saṃsiddhāv ā sṛṣṭer viduṣām api
kāma|krodhau hi viprāṇāṃ mokṣa|dvār’|ârgalāv ubhau.
tathā hi kiṃ na munayaḥ sva|dāra|bhraṃśa|śaṅkinaḥ
deva|dāru|vane pūrvam api Śarvāya cakrudhuḥ?
na c’ âinaṃ vividur devaṃ kṛta|kṣapaṇ’|ākṛtim
Umāyai darśayiṣyantam ṛṣīṇām apy a|śāntatām.
datta|śāpāś ca te sadyas tri|jagat|kṣobha|kāraṇam
buddhvā taṃ devam Īśānaṃ tam eva śaraṇaṃ yayuḥ.
tad evaṃ kāma|kop’|ādi|ripu|ṣaḍ|varga|vañcitāḥ
munayo ’pi vimuhyanti śrotriyeṣu kath” âiva kā?»
3.6.135 iti Sundarakas tatra dhyāyan dasyu|bhayān niśi
āruhya śūnya|govāṭa|harmye tasthau samīpage.
tatr’ âika|deśe yāvac ca kṣaṇaṃ tiṣṭhaty a|lakṣitaḥ
tāvat tatr’ âiva harmye sā Kālarātrir upāyayau.
ākṛṣṭa|vīra|cchurikā mukta|phūt|kāra|bhīṣaṇā
nayan’|ānana|vānt’|ôlkā ḍākinī|cakra|saṃgatā.
tāṃ dṛṣṭvā tādṛśīṃ tatra Kālarātrim upāgatām
sasmāra mantrān rakṣo|ghnān bhītaḥ Sundarako ’tha saḥ.
tan|mantra|mohitā c’ âtha taṃ dadarśa na sā tadā

At this Súndaraka, fanned by the evening breeze and slowly realizing how injured he was, thought the following: "Oh, the urges of women trouble the hearts of men *sullied by passion*, just as a strong wind disturbs the depths of lakes *sullied by dust*. That is why the teacher didn't think even though he is old and wise and, in his extreme anger, behaved so badly towards me. Have not passion and anger 3.6.130
both been bolts on the door of liberation for brahmins, even wise ones, ever since their creation? For did not the sages, fearful that their own wives would go astray, long ago get angry with Shiva in the deodar forest? They did not know that he was a god for he had assumed the guise of a Jain mendicant and was wanting to show Párvati that even sages are not peaceful. Having bestowed their curse, they suddenly discovered that he was the mighty god Shiva, who shakes the three worlds, and they went straight to him for refuge. So thus even sages, when tricked by the group of six enemies,* passion, anger and so forth, can be deluded, to say nothing of learned brahmins."

Thinking this there that night, Súndaraka, fearful of rob- 3.6.135
bers, climbed into a nearby deserted cowshed and stayed there. And when he had been waiting there, unseen, for a moment in that same place, Kala·ratri came into that very shed. She had drawn her magical knife, she was shrieking terrifyingly, flames were pouring forth from her eyes and mouth and she was in the midst of a circle of witches. When the terrified Súndaraka saw her arrive there like that, he brought to mind spells that kill *rákshasa*s, and bewildered by his spells, she then did not see him hiding in the corner, his limbs drawn in with fear. Then Kala·ratri and her 3.6.140

bhaya|saṃpiṇḍitair aṅgair ekānte nibhṛta|sthitam.
3.6.140 ath' ôtpatana|mantraṃ sā paṭhitvā sa|sakhī|janā
Kālarātriḥ sa|govāṭa|harmy" âiv' ôdapatan nabhaḥ.
tam ca mantraṃ sa jagrāha śrutvā Sundarakas tadā
sa|harmyā s" âpi nabhasā kṣipram Ujjayinīṃ yayau.
tatr' âvatārya harmyaṃ sā mantrataḥ śāka|vāṭake
gatvā śmaśāne cikrīḍa ḍākinī|cakra|madhya|gā.
tat|kṣaṇaṃ ca kṣudh"|ākrāntaḥ śāka|vāṭe 'vatīrya saḥ
tatra Sundarakaś cakre vṛttim utkhāta|mūlakaiḥ.
kṛta|kṣut|pratighāte 'smin prāgvad govāṭam āśrite
pratyāyayau Kālarātrī rātri|madhye niketanāt.
3.6.145 tato 'dhirūḍha|govāṭā pūrvavan mantra|siddhitaḥ
ākāśena sa|śiṣyā sā niśi sva|gṛham āyayau.
sthāpayitvā yathā|sthānaṃ tac ca govāṭa|vāhanam
visṛjy' ânucarīs tāś ca śayyā|veśma viveśa sā.
so 'pi Sundarako nītvā tāṃ niśāṃ vighna|vismitaḥ
prabhāte tyakta|govāṭo nikaṭaṃ suhṛdāṃ yayau.
tatr' ākhyāta|sva|vṛttānto videśa|gaman'|ônmukhaḥ
taiḥ samāśvāsito mittrais tan|madhye sthitim agrahīt.
upādhyāya|gṛhaṃ tyaktvā bhuñjānaḥ sattra|sadmani
uvāsa tatra viharan sva|cchandaḥ sakhibhiḥ saha.
3.6.150 ekadā nirgatā kretuṃ gṛh'|ôpakaraṇāni sā
dadarśa taṃ Sundarakaṃ Kālarātriḥ kil' āpaṇe.
upetya ca jagād' âinaṃ punar eva smar'|āturā
«bhaja, Sundarak,' âdy' âpi māṃ tvad|āyatta|jīvitām.»

friends chanted a spell for flying, and, complete with the cowshed, flew into the sky.

Súndaraka listened to the spell and learned it. Meanwhile Kala·ratri quickly flew to Ujjain in the cowshed. There she used a spell to have the cowshed land in a vegetable garden. Then she went to the cremation ground and enjoyed herself in the midst of the circle of witches. Súndaraka, overcome with hunger, immediately got down into the vegetable garden there and made do with some roots that he dug up. Having kept his hunger at bay, he took shelter in the cowshed as before and, in the middle of the night, Kala·ratri returned from the temple. Then, after climbing into the cow- 3.6.145
shed, like before she used spells to fly with her pupils to her house that night. She put her chariot, the cowshed, back in its place and, after dismissing her attendants, went into her bedroom.

As for Súndaraka, well, after getting through that night amazed at his misfortune, in the morning he left the cowshed and went to his friends. There he related what had happened to him and, keen to go to another land, was reassured by those friends of his and took up residence with them. He left the teacher's house and, eating at an almshouse for brahmins, he lived there independently, enjoying himself with his friends.

One day it seems Kala·ratri went out to buy some house- 3.6.150
hold goods and saw Súndaraka in the market. Stricken by love once more, she went up to him and said, "Súndaraka, this time make love to me! My life depends on you!"

evam uktas tayā so 'tha sādhuḥ Sundarako 'bravīt
«m" âivaṃ vadīr na dharmo 'yaṃ mātā me guru|patny asi.»
tato 'bravīt Kālarātrir «dharmaṃ ced vetsi dehi tat
prāṇān me prāṇa|dānād dhi dharmaḥ ko 'bhyadhiko bhavet.»
atha Sundarako 'vādīn «mātar, m" âivaṃ kṛthā hṛdi
guru|talp'|âbhigamanaṃ kutra dharmo bhaviṣyati?»

3.6.155 evaṃ nirākṛtā tena tarjayantī ca taṃ ruṣā
pāṭayitvā sva|hastena sv'|ôttarīyam agād gṛham.
«paśya Sundarakeṇ' êdaṃ dhāvitvā pāṭitaṃ mama!»
ity uvāca patiṃ tatra darśayitv" ôttarīyakam.
sa ca tasyāḥ patiḥ krodhād gatvā vadhyam udīrya ca
sattre Sundarakasy' āśu vārayām āsa bhojanam.
tataḥ Sundarakaḥ khedāt taṃ deśaṃ tyaktuṃ udyataḥ
jānann utpatane vyomni mantraṃ govāṭa|śikṣitam.
tato 'varohe 'py aparaṃ śikṣitaṃ śruta|vismṛtam†
tad eva śūnya|govāṭa|harmyaṃ niśi punar yayau.

3.6.160 tatra tasmin sthite prāgvat Kālarātrir upetya sā
tath" âiv' ôtpatya harmya|sthā vyomn" âiv' Ôjjayinīṃ yayau.
tatr' âvatārya mantreṇa govāṭaṃ śāka|vāṭake
jagāma rātri|caryāyai punaḥ sā pitṛ|kānanam.
taṃ ca Sundarako mantraṃ bhūyaḥ śrutv" âpi n' âgrahīt
vinā hi gurv|ādeśena saṃpūrṇāḥ siddhayaḥ kutaḥ?
tato 'tra bhuktvā kati|cin mūlakāny aparāṇi ca
netuṃ prakṣipya govāṭe tatra tasthau sa pūrvavat.
ath' âity' ārūḍha|govāṭā sā gatvā nabhasā niśi
viveśa Kālarātriḥ svaṃ sadma sthāpita|vāhanā.

Addressed thus by her, the goodly Súndaraka then replied, "Don't speak to me like that. It's not right. As the wife of my guru, you are my mother."

At this Kala·ratri said, "If you know what's right, then let me live, for what could be more right than giving life?"

Then Súndaraka said "Mother, don't entertain this desire—what would be right in sleeping with one's guru's
wife?" Thus spurned by him, while angrily scolding him she 3.6.155
tore her upper garment with her hand before going home. There she showed her husband the upper garment and said to him, "Look how Súndaraka ran at me and ripped this!" Her husband angrily rushed off and, saying that he should be put to death, immediately had Súndaraka's food in the almshouse stopped. At this Súndaraka was so upset that he wanted to leave that place and, knowing the spell for flying up into the sky which he had learned in the cowshed but having forgotten what he had heard when he learned how to get down from there, he went again that night to the very
same cowshed. When he was there Kala·ratri arrived like 3.6.160
before and in the same way flew in the cowshed to Ujjain. There she used a spell to land the cowshed in the vegetable garden and went once more to carry out nocturnal rituals in the grove of the ancestors. Even though he had heard the spell once more, he still did not remember it, for without the instructions of a teacher magical powers are never mastered. Next he ate a few roots there, put some more in the cowshed to take with him and stayed there as before. Then Kala·ratri arrived, climbed into the cowshed, flew into the night and, after parking her vehicle, went into her house.

3.6.165 so 'pi Sundarakaḥ prātar govāṭān nirgatas tataḥ
yayau bhojana|mūly'|ârthī vipaṇīm ātta|mūlakaḥ.
vikrīṇānasya tasy' âtra mūlakaṃ rāja|sevakāḥ
Mālavīyā vinā mūlyaṃ jahrur dṛṣṭvā sva|deśa|jam.
tataḥ sa kalahaṃ kurvan baddhvā suhṛd|anudrutaḥ
pāṣāṇa|ghāta|dāy" îti rāj'|âgraṃ tair anīyata.
«‹Mālavāt katham ānīya Kānyakubje 'tra mūlakam
vikrīṇiṣe sad" êty› eṣa pṛṣṭo 'smābhir na jalpati.
hanti pratyuta pāṣāṇair» ity uktas taiḥ śaṭhair nṛpaḥ
taṃ tad adbhutam aprākṣīt tatas tat|suhṛdo 'bruvan.
3.6.170 «asmābhiḥ saha yady eṣa prāsādam adhiropyate
tad" âitat kautukaṃ, deva, kṛtsnaṃ jalpati n' ânyathā.
«tath" êty» āropito rājñā sa|prāsādo 'sya paśyataḥ
utpapāta sa mantreṇa sadyaḥ Sundarako nabhaḥ.
sa|mitras tena gatvā ca Prayāgaṃ prāpya ca kramāt
śrāntaḥ kam api rājānaṃ snāntaṃ tatra dadarśa saḥ.
saṃstabhya c' âtra prāsādaṃ Gaṅgāyāṃ khān nipatya ca
vismay'|ôdvīkṣitaḥ sarvais taṃ sa rājānam abhyagāt.
«kas tvaṃ kiṃ c' âvatīrṇo 'si gaganād? iti śaṃsa naḥ»
rājñā prahveṇa pṛṣṭaḥ sann evaṃ Sundarako 'bravīt.
3.6.175 «ahaṃ Murajako nāma gaṇo devasya dhūr|jaṭeḥ
prāpto mānuṣa|bhog'|ârthī tvat|sakāśaṃ tad|ājñayā.»

As for Súndaraka, well, in the morning he went out of the 3.6.165
cowshed, and, taking the roots, went to the market in hope
of getting some money for food. When he was selling them
there, some servants of the king, who were from Málava,
took a root away without paying for it after seeing that it
was from their native land. Then while he was arguing he
was bound by them and, followed by his friends, was taken
before the king, where it was said that he had been throwing
stones.

"'How can you keep on bringing this root here to Kanya·
kubja from Málava and selling it?' When we ask him this
he says nothing, on the contrary, he hits us with stones."

When those rogues said this to the king, he questioned
him about this miracle, to which his friends replied, "If he 3.6.170
is put on the palace with us, your highness, he shall explain the whole curious matter, but not otherwise." The
king gave his consent and had him put on it. As the king
looked on, Súndaraka used the spell to fly up suddenly into
the sky along with the palace. He traveled along in it with
his friends until eventually he reached Prayága,* exhausted.
There he saw some king or other who was taking a bath.
After stopping the palace there, he fell from the sky into
the Ganga and, watched in astonishment by all, went up
to the king. When the bowing king asked him to tell them
who he was and why he had come down from the sky, Súndaraka said the following: "I am a *gana* of the god with the 3.6.175
heavy matted locks and I go by the name of Murájaka. At
his command, I have come to you in search of the pleasures
of men."

tac chrutvā satyam āśaṅkya sasy'|āḍhyaṃ ratna|pūritam
sa|strīkaṃ s'|ôpakaraṇaṃ dadau tasmai puraṃ nṛpaḥ.
praviśy' âtha pure tasminn utpatya divi s'|ânugaḥ
ciraṃ Sundarakaḥ svecchaṃ nirdainyaṃ vicacāra saḥ.
śayāno hema|paryaṅke vījyamānaś ca cāmaraiḥ
sevyamāno vara|strībhir aindraṃ sukham avāpa saḥ.
ath' âikadā dadau tasmai mantraṃ vyom'|âvarohaṇe
siddhaḥ ko 'pi kil' ākāśa|cārī saṃjāta|saṃstavaḥ.
3.6.180 prāpt'|âvatāra|mantraḥ sa gatvā Sundarakas tataḥ
Kānyakubje nije deśe vyoma|mārgād avātarat.
sa|puraṃ pūrṇa|lakṣmīkam avatīrṇaṃ nabhas|talāt
buddhvā tatra svayaṃ rājā kautukāt tam upāyayau.
parijñātaś ca pṛṣṭaś ca rāj'|âgre so 'tha kālavit
Kālarātri|kṛtaṃ sarvaṃ sva|vṛttāntaṃ nyavedayat.
tataś c' ānāyya papraccha Kālarātriṃ mahī|patiḥ
nirbhayā s" âpy a|vinayaṃ svaṃ sarvaṃ pratyapadyata.
kupite ca nṛpe tasyāḥ karṇau ca cchettum udyate
sā gṛhīt" âpi paśyatsu sarveṣv eva tirodadhe.
3.6.185 tataḥ sva|rāṣṭre vāso 'syās tatra rājñā nyaṣidhyata
tat|pūjitaḥ Sundarakaḥ śiśriye ca nabhaḥ punaḥ.›
ity uktvā tatra bhartāram Ādityaprabha|bhū|patim
ābhāṣata punaś c' âinaṃ rājñī Kuvalayāvalī.
‹bhavanty evaṃ|vidhā, deva, ḍākinī|mantra|siddhayaḥ
etac ca mat|pitur deśe vṛttaṃ sarvatra viśrutam.

When the king heard this he thought it to be true and gave to him a city which was rich in corn and filled with jewels, together with its women and its ornaments. Then, after going into the city, Súndaraka flew up into the sky with his followers, and roamed about at will for a long time, free from sadness. Lying on a golden bed, being fanned with yaks' tails and waited on by beautiful women, he was as happy as Indra.

Then one day it seems that some sky-roving *siddha* whose acquaintance he had made gave him a spell for descending
from the air. Having obtained the mantra for descending, 3.6.180
Súndaraka went from there to Kanya·kubja, his own land, and came down from the sky. When the king there found out that he had come down from the sky with a city and possessed a fortune, he was so curious he came in person to meet him. On being recognized and questioned before the king, Súndaraka, seeing his moment, related everything that had happened to him at the hands of Kala·ratri. Then the king had Kala·ratri fetched and he questioned her. She fearlessly confirmed all the bad deeds she had done, and when the angry king wanted her ears to be cut off and she
was seized, she vanished while everyone looked on. Then 3.6.185
she was forbidden by the king from living there in his kingdom and after being worshipped by him, Súndaraka flew once more into the sky.'

Having said this there to her husband King Áditya·prabha, Queen Kuvalayávali continued by saying to him, 'My lord, powers such as these from the spells of witches do exist. This happened in my father's land and is celebrated everywhere. I am a pupil of Kala·ratri, as I told you first of

Kālarātreś ca śiṣy" âham ity ādau varṇitaṃ mayā
pati|vratātvāt siddhis tu tato 'py abhyadhikā mama.
bhavatā c' âdya dṛṣṭ" âhaṃ śreyo|'rthaṃ te kṛt'|ârcanā
upahārāya puruṣaṃ mantreṇ' ākraṣṭum udyatā.
3.6.190 tad asmadīye 'tra naye tvam api praviś' âdhunā
siddhi|yoga|jitānāṃ ca rājñāṃ mūrdhni padaṃ kuru.›

tac chrutvā ‹kva mahā|māṃsa|bhojanaṃ ḍākinī|naye
kva ca rājatvam› ity uktvā sa rājā niṣiṣedha tat.
prāṇa|tyāg'|ôdyatāyāṃ tu rājñyāṃ tat pratyapadyata
viṣay'|ākṛṣyamāṇā hi tiṣṭhanti su|pathe katham?
tataḥ sā taṃ praveśy' âiva maṇḍale pūrva|pūjite
gṛhīta|samayaṃ santaṃ rājānam idam abravīt.
‹ya eṣa Phalabhūty|ākhyaḥ sthito vipras tav' ântike
sa may" âtr' ôpahār'|ârtham ākraṣṭum upakalpitaḥ.
3.6.195 ākarṣaṇaṃ ca s'|āyāsaṃ tat kaś|cit sūpa|kṛd varam
naye 'tra sthāpyatāṃ yas taṃ svayaṃ hanti pacaty api.
na kāryā ca ghṛṇā yasmāt tan|māṃsa|bali|bhakṣaṇāt
samāpite 'rcane pūrṇā siddhiḥ syād uttamo hi saḥ.›

ity uktaḥ priyayā rājā pāpa|bhīto 'pi tat punaḥ
aṅgī|cakāra dhig aho kaṣṭāṃ strīṣv anurodhitām!.
ānāyya sūpa|kāraṃ ca tataḥ sāhasik'|âbhidham
viśvāsya dīkṣitaṃ kṛtvā daṃpatī tau sah' ôcatuḥ.
‹rājā devī|dvitīyo 'dya bhokṣyate tat tvarāṃ kuru
āhārasy' êti› yo 'bhyetya tvāṃ brūyāt taṃ nipātayeḥ.

all, but because I am a devoted wife, my powers are greater even than hers. And today you saw me after I had performed a rite for the good of you and I was trying to attract a man with a spell so that I could offer him as a sacrifice. So you 3.6.190
too must now get involved in this cult of ours and humble the kings by defeating them using magical powers.'

When he heard this, the king forbade it, saying that the eating of human flesh according to the cult of witchcraft was incompatible with kinghood. However, when the queen became intent on killing herself, he agreed to it, for how can those who are being drawn by the objects of the senses remain on the path of righteousness? Then she had the king enter a circle which had been previously consecrated and said to him when he had taken a vow, 'I have been preparing the brahmin called Phala·bhuti who is close to you to be brought here to be sacrificed. Enticing him here will be 3.6.195
difficult so it would be better if some cook or other were to be initiated into this cult who will then kill and cook him himself. Do not be disgusted, because by eating the sacrificial offering of his flesh, the magical power will be complete at the end of the ritual because he is of the highest birth.'

When the king was told this by his sweetheart, even though he was scared of committing a sin, he still agreed to it. Oh how wrong it is to indulge the wishes of women! Then the couple had a cook called Sáhasika brought in. After reassuring him, they initiated him and then both said together, 'You are to kill the man who comes to you and

3.6.200 ‹tan|māṃsaiś ca rahaḥ kuryāḥ prātar nau svādu bhojanam›
iti sūpa|kṛd† ādiṣṭas ‹tath" êty› uktvā gṛhaṃ yayau.
prātaś ca Phalabhūtiṃ taṃ prāptaṃ rājā jagāda saḥ
‹gaccha Sāhasikaṃ brūhi sūpa|kāraṃ mahā|nase.
«rājā devī|dvitīyo 'dya bhokṣyate svādu bhojanam
atas tvaritam āhāram uttamaṃ sādhayer» iti.›
‹tath" êti› nirgataṃ taṃ ca Phalabhūtiṃ bahis tadā
etya Candraprabho nāma rājñaḥ putro 'bravīd idam.
‹anena śīghraṃ hemnā me kāray' âdy' âiva kuṇḍale
yādṛśe bhavatā pūrvam, ārya|tātasya kārite.›
3.6.205 ity ukto rāja|putreṇa Phalabhūtis tad" âiva saḥ
kṛt'|ânurodhaḥ prahito yayau kuṇḍalayoḥ kṛte.
rāja|putro 'py agāt svairaṃ kathitaṃ Phalabhūtinā
rāj'|ādeśaṃ gṛhītvā tam ekāky eva mahā|nasam.
tatr' ôkta|rāj'|ādeśaṃ taṃ sthita|saṃvit sa sūpa|kṛt
rāja|putraṃ churikayā sadyaḥ Sāhasiko 'vadhīt.
tan|māṃsaiḥ sādhitaṃ tena bhojanaṃ ca kṛt'|ârcanau.
abhuñjātām a|jānantau tattvaṃ rājñī nṛpas tathā.

says, "The king shall eat with the queen today so quickly prepare some food" and in the morning you are secretly 3.6.200
to make for us a delicious meal out of his flesh.' After being instructed thus, the cook agreed and went home. And in the morning when Phala·bhuti arrived, the king said to him, 'Go and say to the cook Sáhasika in the kitchen, "The king shall eat a delicious meal with the queen today, so quickly prepare some food of the highest quality."'

After Phala·bhuti had agreed and gone outside, a son of the king called Chandra·prabha then came to him and said the following, 'Use this gold to have quickly made for me this very day a pair of earrings like the one you had made before for my noble father.'

After being told this by the prince, Phala·bhuti, oblig- 3.6.205
ing him, immediately went off on his errand to have the earrings made. The prince, meanwhile, happily went on his own to the kitchen with the message from the king that he had been told by Phala·bhuti. There the cook Sáhasika, keeping his word, when the prince passed on the king's message, suddenly killed him with a knife. He prepared a meal with his flesh, and, after they had performed a ritual, the king and queen ate it without knowing the truth.

nītvā ca s'|ânutāpas tāṃ rātriṃ rājā dadarśa saḥ
prātaḥ kuṇḍala|hastaṃ taṃ Phalabhūtim upāgatam.
3.6.210 bibhrāntaḥ kuṇḍal'|ôddeśāt taṃ ca papraccha tat|kṣaṇam
ten' ākhyāta|sva|vṛttāntaḥ papāta ca bhuvas tale.
‹hā putr' êti› ca cakranda nindan bhāryāṃ sah' ātmanā
pṛṣṭaś ca sacivaiḥ sarvaṃ yathā|tattvam avarṇayat.
uvāca c' âitad uktaṃ tat
pratyahaṃ Phalabhūtinā
‹«bhadra|kṛt prāpnuyād bhadram
a|bhadraṃ c' âpy a|bhadra|kṛt.»
kanduko bhitti|niḥkṣipta iva pratiphalan muhuḥ
āpataty ātmani prāyo doṣo 'nyasya cikīrṣitaḥ.
pāp'|ācārair yad asmābhir brahma|hatyāṃ cikīrṣubhiḥ
sva|putra|ghātanaṃ kṛtvā prāptaṃ tan|māṃsa|bhakṣaṇam.›
3.6.215 ity uktvā bodhayitvā ca mantriṇaḥ svān adho|mukhān
tam eva Phalabhūtiṃ ca nije rājye 'bhiṣicya saḥ.
rājā pradatta|dānaḥ sann a|putraḥ pāpa|śuddhaye
sa|bhāryaḥ pravives' âgniṃ dagdho 'py anuśay'|âgninā.
Phalabhūtiś ca tad rājyaṃ prāpya pṛthvīṃ śaśāsa saḥ
evaṃ bhadram a|bhadraṃ vā kṛtam ātmani kalpyate.»
iti Vats'|ēśvarasy' âgre kathayitvā kathām imām
Yaugandharāyaṇo bhūyo bhū|patiṃ tam abhāṣata.
«tasmāt tava sa, rāj|êndra, jitv" âpy ācarataḥ śubham
Brahmadatto vikurvīta yadi hanyās tvam eva tam.»

And after he had passed that night in regret, in the morning the king saw Phala·bhuti arrive with the earrings in his hand. Confused, he immediately asked him about the ear- 3.6.210
rings and when Phala·bhuti told him his story, the king fell to the ground and wailed, 'Oh my son!,' blaming his wife and himself. On being questioned by his ministers, he related everything as it had happened and he said what Phala·bhuti had said every day: '"He who does good shall obtain good while he who does bad shall obtain bad." Like a ball thrown against a wall bouncing back over and over again, harm intended to be done to others usually falls on oneself: in wishing to murder a brahmin, we sinners have killed our own son and eaten his flesh.'

After saying this and informing his ministers, their faces 3.6.215
looking down, he had that same Phala·bhuti anointed and installed on his throne. After giving donations, the king, who had no son, in order to purify himself of his sin went with his wife into the flames, even though he had already been consumed by the fire of regret.

And Phala·bhuti, on obtaining the throne, ruled the earth. In this way the good or bad that one does befalls oneself."

After telling this tale before the king of Vatsa, Yaugándharáyana continued speaking to the king. "Therefore, O king of kings, if Brahma·datta were to move against you even after you behaved well having defeated him, you yourself should kill him."

3.6.220 ity ukto mantri|mukhyena tad|vākyam abhinandya saḥ
utthāya dina|kartavyaṃ Vats'|ēśo niravartayat.
anyedyuś ca sa saṃpanna|sarva|dig|vijayaḥ kṛtī
Lāvāṇakād udacalat Kauśāmbīṃ sva|purīṃ prati.
krameṇa nagarīṃ prāpa kṣit'|īśaḥ sa|paricchadaḥ
utpatākā|bhuja|latāṃ nṛtyantīm utsavād iva.
viveśa c' âināṃ paura|strī|nayan'|ôtpala|kānane
vitanvānaḥ pratipadaṃ pravāt'|ārambha|vibhramam.
cāraṇ'|ôdgīyamānaś ca stūyamānaś ca bandibhiḥ
nṛpaiḥ praṇamyamānaś ca rājā mandiram āyayau.
3.6.225 tato vinamreṣv adhiropya śāsanaṃ
sa Vatsa|rājo 'khila|deśa|rājasu
pūrvaṃ nidhān'|âdhigataṃ kul'|ôcitaṃ
prasahya siṃh'|āsanam āruroha tat.
tat|kāla|maṅgala|samāhata|tāra|dhīra|
tūryā|rava|pratiravaiś ca nabhaḥ pupūre
tan|mantri|mukhya|paritoṣita|loka|pāla|
dattair iva pratidiśaṃ sama|sādhu|vādaiḥ.
vividham atha vitīrya vīta|lobho
vasu vasudhā|vijay'|ârjitaṃ dvijebhyaḥ
akṛta kṛta|mah"|ôtsavaḥ kṛt'|ârthaṃ
kṣiti|pati|maṇḍalam ātma|mantriṇaś ca.
kṣetreṣu varṣati tad" ânuguṇaṃ *nar'/êndre*
tasmin *dhvanad/ghana/mṛdaṅga/*nināditāyām
saṃbhāvya bhāvi bahudhānya|phalaṃ* jano 'pi
tasyāṃ puri prati|gṛhaṃ *vihit'/ôtsavo* 'bhūt.

On being told this by the chief minister, the king of Vatsa welcomed what he had said, stood up and completed the days duties. And on the next day, satisfied at having completed his conquest of all the directions, he set forth from Lavánaka for Kaushámbi, his city. 3.6.220

In time the king and his entourage reached the city which, with its banners resembling creeper-like arms, looked like it was dancing for joy. And he went in, spreading with every step the flutter brought on by the start of a breeze in the garden of the lotus eyes of the women of the city. Celebrated by singers, hymned by bards and bowed down before by kings, the king arrived at the palace. Then the king 3.6.225
of Vatsa, after laying commands on bowing kings from every land, without further ado ascended the throne which he had earlier acquired as a treasure and which befitted his family. And the skies were filled with the high and low notes and echoes of the drums being struck in the auspicious ceremonies at that time, and it was as though it were being filled everywhere with simultaneous shouts of bravo from the guardians of the directions, delighted with the king's chief minister. Then the king, who was free from greed, gave away to the brahmins various riches that had been acquired in his conquest of the world, and then, after holding great celebrations, he satisfied all the kings and his own ministers. Then in that city, which was resounding to *booming drums : the noisy drumming of clouds*, while *the king : Indra* rained down suitably on *worthy recipients : the fields*, the people too, expecting *lots of other rewards : a great harvest, held a celebration : celebrated the festival of Indra* in every house.

evaṃ vijitya jagatīṃ sa kṛtī Rumaṇvad|
Yaugandharāyaṇa|niveśita|rājya|bhāraḥ
tasthau yath"|êccham atha Vāsavadattay" âtra
Padmāvatī|sahitayā saha Vatsa|rājaḥ.

3.6.230 kīrti|śriyor iva tayor ubhayoś ca devyor
madhya|sthitaḥ sa vara|cāraṇa|gīyamānaḥ
candr'|ôdayaṃ nija|yaśo|dhavalaṃ siṣeve
śatru|pratāpam iva sīdhu papau ca śaśvat.

iti mahā|kavi|śrī|Somadeva|bhaṭṭa|viracite Kathāsaritsāgare
Lāvāṇaka|lambake ṣaṣṭhas taraṅgaḥsamāptaś c' âyaṃ
Lāvāṇaka|lambakas tṛtīyaḥ.

After thus conquering the world, the satisfied king of Vatsa invested Rumánvat and Yaugándharáyana with the burdens of state and then stayed there at his pleasure, in the company of Vásava·datta and Padmávati. In the middle of 3.6.230
those two queens, who were like Fame and Fortune, and hymned by the finest singers, he enjoyed the rising of the moon, which was as dazzling as his own renown, and continually drank spirits just as he had consumed the strength of his enemies.

Thus ends the sixth wave in the Lavánaka Attainment
in the Ocean of the Rivers of Story composed by
the glorious and learned great poet Soma·deva
and this third Attainment, Lavánaka, is complete.

After thus conquering the world, the exalted King of Vatsa dwelt in Kaumbhī [illegible] and Yaugandharāyaṇa [illegible] burden of state and then stayed there at his pleasure, in the company of Vāsavadattā and Padmāvatī. In the middle of those two queens, who were like Rati and Prīti, and hymned by the bards [illegible] he enjoyed the flattery of the moon, which was dwelling at his own eclipse, and continually [illegible] as he had assumed the [illegible] of [illegible].

[illegible]

ATTAINMENT IV

THE BIRTH OF NARA·VÁHANA·DATTA

MAHĀ|KAVI|ŚRĪ|SOMADEVA|bhaṭṭa|viracitaḥ Kathāsaritsāgaraḥ. Naravāhanadatta|jananaṃ nāma caturtho lambakaḥ.

idaṃ guru|gir'|îndra|jā|praṇaya|Mandar'|ândolanāt
purā kila kath"|âmṛtaṃ Hara|mukh'|âmbudher udgatam
prasahya sarayanti ye vigata|vighna|labdh'|arddhayo
dhuraṃ dadhati vaibudhīṃ bhuvi Bhava|prasādena te.

The "Ocean of the Rivers of Story," composed by the glorious and learned great poet Soma·deva. The fourth Attainment, called the birth of Nara·váhana·datta.

This nectar of story is said to have arisen long ago from the ocean of Hara's mouth as a result of its being churned by mount Mándara in the form of the insistent entreaties of the daughter of the lord of the mountains. Those who make it flow freely lose their troubles and gain riches, and through Bhava's grace it puts them on a divine pedestal on earth.

I

4.1.1 Karṇa|tāla|bal'|āghāta|sīmantita|kul'|âcalaḥ
panthānam iva siddhīnāṃ diśañ jayati vighna|jit.

tato Vats'|ēśvaro rājā sa Kauśāmbyām avasthitaḥ
ek'|ātapatrāṃ bubhuje jitām Udayano mahīm.
vidhāya sa|Rumaṇvatke bhāraṃ Yaugandharāyaṇe
vihār'|âika|rasaś c' âbhūd Vasantaka|sakhaḥ sukhī.
svayaṃ sa vādayan vīṇāṃ devyā Vāsavadattayā
Padmāvatyā ca sahitaḥ saṃgītakam asevata.
4.1.5 devī|kākali|gītasya tad|vīṇā|ninadasya ca
abhede vādan'|âṅguṣṭha|kampo 'bhūd bheda|sūcakaḥ.
harmy'|âgre nija|kīrty" êva jyotsnayā dhavale ca saḥ
dhārā|vigalitaṃ sīdhu papau madam iva dviṣām.
ājahruḥ svarṇa|kalaśais tasya vār'|âṅganā rahaḥ
Smara|rājy'|âbhiṣek'|âmbha iva *rāg'|ôjjvalaṃ* madhu.
ārakta|surasa|svaccham antaḥ|sphurita|tan|mukham
upaninye dvayor madhye sa sva|cittam iv' āsavam.
īrṣyā|ruṣām abhāve 'pi bhaṅgura|bhruṇi rāgiṇi
na mukhe tat tayo rājñyos tad|dṛṣṭis tṛptim āyayau.
4.1.10 sa|madhu|sphaṭik'|ân|eka|caṣakā tasya pāna|bhūḥ
babhau bāl'|ātap'|ārakta|sita|padm" êva padminī.

I

May the conqueror of obstacles, who, with mighty 4.1.1
blows from his flapping ears, makes a parting in the chief mountain ranges as if he were marking the way to success, be victorious!

Then Údayana, king of Vatsa, stayed in Kaushámbi and enjoyed the conquered earth, which was now under a single parasol. He placed the burdens of state on Yaugándharáyana and Rumánvat, and with Vasántaka as his companion he happily devoted himself to nothing but fun. Playing the lute himself, he enjoyed making music with Vásava·datta
and Padmávati. In the absence of any difference between 4.1.5
the sweet song of the queens and the sound of his lute, it was left to the flickering of his playing thumb to show that they were separate. And on the terrace of his palace, which the moonlight, as if it were his glory, made dazzling white, he drank wine flowing in torrents as if he were drinking the pride of his enemies. In private his courtesans brought *brilliantly red* wine *ablaze with passion* in golden pots as if it were water for consecrating him as the ruler of the kingdom of the god of love. As if it were his heart—*impassioned, amorous and pure, their faces appearing within*—he placed the drink—*red, delicious and clear, their faces appearing within*—between the two queens. Even though they were neither jealous nor angry, those queens' faces were red with passion and had knitted brows: the king could not get
enough of looking at them. There were many crystal glasses 4.1.10
full of wine in the place where he drank and it glowed as if it were a bed of lotuses, its white flowers reddened by the morning sun.

antarā ca milad|vyādhaḥ palāśa|śyāma|kañcukaḥ
sa sa|bāṇāsano bheje sv'|ôpamaṃ mṛga|kānanam.
jaghāna paṅka|kaluṣān varāha|nivahāñ śaraiḥ
timir'|âughān a|viralaiḥ karair iva marīcimān.
vitrasta|prasṛtās tasmin kṛṣṇa|sārāḥ pradhāvite
babhuḥ pūrv'|âbhibhūtānāṃ kaṭākṣāḥ kakubhām iva.

reje rakt'|âruṇā c' âsya mahī mahiṣa|ghātinaḥ
sev'|āgat" êva tac|chṛṅga|pāta|muktā van'|ābjinī.
4.1.15 vyātta|vaktra|patat|prāsa|proteṣv api mṛg'|âriṣu
s'|ântar|garjita|niṣkrānta|jīviteṣu tutoṣa saḥ.
śvānaḥ śvabhre vane tasmiṃs tasya vartmasu vāgurāḥ
sā sv'|āyudh'|âika|siddhe 'bhūt prakriyā mṛgayā|rase.

evaṃ sukh'|ôpabhogeṣu vartamānaṃ tam ekadā
rājānam āsthāna|gataṃ Nārado munir abhyagāt.
nija|deha|prabhā|baddha|maṇḍalo maṇḍanaṃ divaḥ
kṛt'|âvatāras tejasvi|jāti|prīty" âṃśumān iva.

sa tena racit'|ātithyo muhuḥ prahveṇa bhū|bhṛtā
prītaḥ kṣaṇam iva sthitvā rājānaṃ tam abhāṣata.
4.1.20 «śṛṇu saṃkṣiptam etat te, Vats'|ēśvara, vadāmy aham
babhūva Pāṇḍur iti te rājā pūrva|pitāmahaḥ.
tav' êva tasya dve eva bhavye bhārye babhūvatuḥ
ekā Kuntī dvitīyā ca Mādrī nāma mah"|âujasaḥ.

Now and then he would get together with some hunters, take his bow and, wearing a jacket as dark green as a *palásha* tree, enjoy himself in the game park, which he resembled. With his arrows he killed hordes of mud-besmirched boars, like the sun destroying with its dense rays the ranks of darkness. When he chased them, the spotted antelopes fled, terrified, looking like side-glances from the directions which had earlier been conquered.

And when he killed buffalo, the ground would shine red with blood, as if a bed of lotuses from the jungle, liberated from the goring of the buffaloes' horns, had come
to worship him. When the lions too were speared by his 4.1.15
javelins falling in their gaping jaws, their life-breaths departing with a stifled roar, he was delighted. In his fondness for the chase, which he carried out using only his own weapons, his method was to have dogs down the holes in that forest and traps on the paths.

While the king was living thus, enjoying these pleasures, one day the sage Nárada came to him when he was in his hall of audience. He wore a halo formed by the glow from his body and it was as if the sun, the adornment of the sky, had come down to earth out of affection for a fellow luminary.

Showing him hospitality and bowing repeatedly, the king pleased Nárada, and after standing there for a moment or
two, he said to the king, "Listen to this short tale that I am 4.1.20
about to tell you, O king of Vatsa. You had an ancestor, a king called Pandu. Like you, that powerful king had just two lovely wives. One was called Kunti, the other Madri. Pandu conquered this earth with its girdle of oceans and

sa Pāṇḍuḥ pṛthivīm etāṃ jitvā jaladhi|mekhalām
sukhī kadā|cit prayayau mṛgayā|vyasanī vanam.
tatra Kindama|nāmānaṃ sa muniṃ mukta|sāyakaḥ
jaghāna mṛga|rūpeṇa sa|bhāryaṃ surata|sthitam.
sa munir mṛga|rūpaṃ tat tyaktvā kaṇṭha|vivartibhiḥ
prāṇaiḥ śaśāpa taṃ Pāṇḍuṃ viṣaṇṇaṃ mukta|kārmukam.
4.1.25 ‹svaira|stho nirvimarśena hato 'haṃ yat tvayā tataḥ
bhāryā|saṃbhoga|kāle te madvan mṛtyur bhaviṣyati.›
ity āpta|śāpas tad|bhītyā tyakta|bhoga|spṛho 'tha saḥ
patnībhyām anvitaḥ Pāṇḍus tasthau śānte tapo|vane.
tatra|stho 'pi sa śāpena preritas tena c' âikadā
a|kasmāc cakame Mādrīṃ priyāṃ prāpa ca pañcatām.
tad evaṃ mṛgayā nāma pramādo, nṛpa, bhū|bhṛtām
kṣapitā hy anay" ânye 'pi nṛpās te te mṛgā iva.
ghora|nād" āmiṣ'|âik'|âgrā rūkṣā dhūmr'|ôrdhva|mūrdha|jā
kunta|dantā kathaṃ kuryād rākṣas" îva hi sā śivam?
4.1.30 tasmād viphalam āyāsaṃ jahīhi mṛgayā|rasam
vanya|vāhana|hantṝṇāṃ samānaḥ prāṇa|saṃśayaḥ.
tvaṃ ca tvat|pūrva|ja|prītyā priyaḥ kalyāṇa|pātra me
putraś ca tava Kām'|âṃśo yathā bhāvī tathā śṛṇu.
pur" ân|aṅg'|âṅga|saṃbhūtyai Ratyā stutibhir arcitaḥ
tuṣṭo rahasi saṃkṣepam idaṃ tasyāḥ Śivo 'bhyadhāt.
‹avatīrya nij'|âṃśena bhūmāv ārādhya māṃ svayam
Gaurī putr'|ârthinī Kāmaṃ janayiṣyaty asāv iti.›
ataś Caṇḍamahāsena|sutā devī, nar'|êndra, sā

one day the happy king, who was addicted to hunting, went to the forest. There he let fly an arrow and killed a sage called Kíndama who was making love with his wife in the form of a deer. The sage abandoned his form as a deer and as his life-breaths struggled in his throat he cursed Pandu,
who was despondent and had cast aside his bow. 'Because 4.1.25
you willfully killed me without thinking while I was making love with my wife, your death shall be like mine.'

After receiving this curse, he was terrified by it and lost the desire for pleasure. Accompanied by his two wives, Pandu took up residence in a peaceful penance grove. But while he was there, one day, driven on by the curse, he suddenly made love to his beloved Madri and died. Thus, O king, that which is called the chase is a folly of kings, for other kings too have been destroyed by it, just like all those deer. The chase is like a demoness—she has a terrific roar, thinks only of flesh, is cruel, her hair stands on end like smoke and her teeth are spears. How could she bring
good? So give up your love of hunting—it is a vain exer- 4.1.30
tion. The danger to the lives of those who kill wild animals is universal.

And because of my affection for your ancestors, you, who are a worthy recipient of good fortune, are dear to me. Hear how your future son is to be a partial incarnation of the god of love. Long ago, when he had been worshipped with hymns of praise by Rati in order to restore the body of the bodiless god of love and was pleased, in private Shiva announced to her the following brief declaration: "Having partially incarnated herself, Párvati, desirous of a son, shall personally worship me on earth and she shall give birth to

jātā Vāsavadatt" êyaṃ saṃpannā mahiṣī ca te.
4.1.35 tad eṣā Śaṃbhum ārādhya Kām'|âṃśaṃ soṣyate sutam
sarva|vidyā|dharāṇāṃ yaś cakra|vartī bhaviṣyati.»

ity ukten' ādṛta|vacā rājñā pṛthvīṃ tad|arpitām
pratyarpya tasmai sa yayau Nārada'|rṣir a|darśanam.
tasmin gate Vatsa|rājaḥ sa tad Vāsavadattayā
jāta|putr'|êcchayā sākaṃ ninye tac|cintayā dinam.

anyedyus taṃ sa Vats'|ēśam upety' āsthāna|vartinam
Nityodit'|ākhyaḥ pravaraḥ pratīhāro vyajijñapat.
«śiśuka|dvaya|saṃyuktā brāhmaṇī k" âpi durgatā
dvāri sthitā, mahā|rāja, deva|darśana|kāṅkṣiṇī.»
4.1.40 tac chrutv" âiv' âbhyanujñāte tat|praveśe mahī|bhṛtā
brāhmaṇī sā viveś' âtra kṛśa|pāṇḍura|dhūsarā.
mānen' êva viśīrṇena vāsasā vidhurī|kṛtā
duḥkha|dainya|nibhāv aṅke vibhratī bālakāv ubhau.
kṛt'|ôcita|praṇāmā ca sā rājānaṃ vyajijñapat
«brāhmaṇī kula|jā c' âham īdṛśīṃ durgatiṃ gatā.
daivād yugapad etau ca jātau dvau tanayau mama
tad, deva, n' âsti me stanyam etayor bhojanaṃ vinā.
ten' êha kṛpaṇā, nātha, śaraṇ'|āgata|vatsalam
prāpt" âsmi devaṃ śaraṇaṃ pramāṇaṃ adhunā prabhuḥ.»

the god of love." And so, O king, the goddess has been born as Chanda·maha·sena's daughter, Vásava·datta here, and has become your chief queen. So she, after worshipping Shiva, 4.1.35
shall give birth to a son who is a partial incarnation of the god of love and will be the emperor of all the sorcerers." When the king, whose words were respected, was told this, he offered Nárada the earth; the sage gave it back to him and vanished. After he had gone, the king of Vatsa and Vásava·datta, in whom the desire for a son had arisen, spent the day worrying about it.

The next day, when the king of Vatsa was in his hall of audience, the head chamberlain, Nityódita by name, went up and announced to him, "Sire, some poor brahmin lady is at the gate with two children and wants to have an audience with your highness."

As soon as he heard this, the king gave his permission for 4.1.40
her to enter and the brahmin lady came in. She was thin, pale and dusty. Made miserable by wearing clothes as tattered as her pride, she was carrying on her hips two children as if they were sorrow and poverty. After bowing appropriately before the king, she said to him, "I am a brahmin lady from a good family and this wretched state has befallen me. It happened that these two boys were born to me simultaneously, so, your highness, not having any food, I have no milk for them. Thus, my lord, in my state of wretchedness, I have come here to your highness, who is kind to those who come to him for protection, for help. Now it is up to your majesty."

4.1.45 tac chrutvā sa|dayo rājā sa pratīhāram ādiśat
«iyaṃ Vāsavadattāyai devyai nītv" ârpyatām iti.»
tataś ca karmaṇā svena śubhen' êv' âgra|yāyinā
nīt" âbhūn nikaṭaṃ devyāḥ pratīhāreṇa tena sā.
rājñā visṛṣṭāṃ buddhvā tāṃ pratīhārād upāgatām
devī Vāsavadattā sā brāhmaṇīṃ śraddadhe|tarām.
yugm'|âpatyāṃ ca paśyantī dīnām etāṃ vyacintayat
«aho vām'|âika|vṛttitvaṃ kim|apy etat Prajāpateḥ!
aho vastuni mātsaryam aho bhaktir a|vastuni!
n' âdy' âpy eko 'pi me jāto jātau tv asyāṃ yamāv imau!»
4.1.50 evaṃ saṃcintayantī ca sā devī snāna|kāṅkṣiṇī
brāhmaṇyāś ceṭikās tasyāḥ snapan'|ādau samādiśat.
snapitā datta|vastrā ca tābhiḥ svādu ca bhojitā
brāhmaṇī s" âmbu|sikt" êva taptā bhūḥ samudaśvasat.
samāśvastā ca sā yuktyā kath"|ālāpaiḥ parīkṣitum
kṣaṇ'|ântare nijagade devyā Vāsavadattayā,
«bho brāhmaṇi kathā kā|cit tvayā naḥ kathyatām iti»
tac chrutvā sā «tath" êty» uktvā kathāṃ vaktuṃ pracakrame.
«pur" âbhūj Jayadatt'|ākhyaḥ sāmānyaḥ ko 'pi bhū|patiḥ
Devadatt'|âbhidhānaś ca putras tasy' ôdapadyata.
4.1.55 yauvana|sthasya tasy' âtha vivāhaṃ tanayasya saḥ
vidhātum icchan nṛpatir matimān ity acintayat,
‹veśy" êva balavad|bhogyā rāja|śrīr ati|cañcalā
vaṇijāṃ tu kula|str" îva sthirā lakṣmīr an|anya|gā.
tasmād vivāhaṃ putrasya karomi vaṇijāṃ gṛhāt
rājye 'sya bahu|dāyāde yena n' āpad bhaviṣyati.›

When he heard this, the king took pity and instructed 4.1.45
his chamberlain to take the woman to Vásava·datta and entrust her to her. At this, leading her on as if he were her own good karma, the chamberlain took her to the queen. When Queen Vásava·datta found out from the chamberlain that the brahmin woman who had arrived had been sent by the king, she had greater trust in her. Seeing that the poor woman had two children, she thought, "Oh! This is a piece of the creator's unswerving perversity! How niggardly he is towards one who is worthy and how kind to one who is not! I still have not had even one son, but this woman has
had twin boys!" While thinking this, the queen, who was 4.1.50
wanting to take a bath, instructed her servant girls to attend to the brahmin woman's toilet. After being bathed, clothed and fed delicious food by them, the brahmin lady was as refreshed as scorched earth on being sprinkled with water. And soon after she had been refreshed, Queen Vásava·datta contrived to find out about her in conversation and said to her, "O brahmin lady, please tell us some story." On hearing this, she said yes and started to tell a tale.

"Long ago there lived some run-of-the-mill king called Jaya·datta and a son called Deva·datta was born to him.
Then, when the boy had grown up and the king was want- 4.1.55
ing to arrange his marriage, being a wise man he thought to himself, 'Like a courtesan, the prosperity of a king is extremely fickle and is to be enjoyed by he who has power, but the prosperity of merchants, like a woman from a respectable family, is assured and does not go elsewhere. Therefore I shall find my son a wife from a merchant household

iti niścitya putrasya kṛte vavre sa bhūpatiḥ
vaṇijo Vasudattasya kanyāṃ Pāṭaliputrakāt.
Vasudatto 'pi sa dadau ślāghya|saṃbandha|vāñchayā
dūra|deś'|ântare 'py asmai rāja|putrāya tāṃ sutām.
4.1.60 pūrayām āsa ca tathā ratnair jāmātaraṃ sa tam
agalad bahumāno 'sya yathā sva|pitṛ|vaibhave.
avāpt'|āḍhya|vaṇik|putrī|sahiten' âtha tena saḥ
tanayena samaṃ tasthau Jayadatta|nṛpaḥ sukham.

ekadā tatra c' āgatya s'|ôtkaḥ saṃbandhi|sadmani
sa vaṇig Vasudattas tāṃ nināya sva|gṛhaṃ sutām.
tato 'kasmāt sa nṛ|patir Jayadatto divaṃ yayau
udbhūya gotra|jais tasya tac ca rājyam adhiṣṭhitam.
tad|bhītyā tasya tanayo jananyā nijayā niśi
Devadattas tu nīto 'bhūd anya|deśam a|lakṣitaḥ.
4.1.65 tatr' āha rāja|putraṃ taṃ mātā duḥkhita|mānasā
‹devo 'sti cakra|vartī naḥ prabhuḥ pūrva|dig|īśvaraḥ
tat|pārśvaṃ vraja. rājyaṃ te sādhayiṣyati, vatsa, saḥ›

ity uktaḥ sa tadā mātrā rāja|putro jagāda tām,
‹tatra māṃ niṣparikaraṃ gataṃ ko bahu maṃsyate?›

tac chrutvā punar apy evaṃ sā mātā tam abhāṣata,
‹śvaśurasya gṛhaṃ gatvā tvaṃ hi prāpya tato dhanam
kṛtvā parikaraṃ gaccha nikaṭaṃ cakra|vartinaḥ.›

so that no disaster will befall his kingdom, to which there are many claimants.'

After deciding this, the king chose for his son the daughter of a merchant called Vasu·datta from Pátali·putra. And Vasu·datta, in his desire for a commendable alliance, betrothed his daughter to the prince, even though he was in
a far-off land. He loaded his son-in-law with so many jew- 4.1.60
els that the boy's respect for his father's greatness dripped away. Then King Jaya·datta lived happily in the company of his son and the rich merchant's daughter whom he had obtained.

One day the merchant Vasu·datta came expectantly to the house of his daughter's in-laws and took her to his home. Then suddenly King Jaya·datta died and the kingdom was taken over by relatives of his who had risen up. In fear of them the king's son Deva·datta was taken away by
his mother at night, unseen, to another country. There his 4.1.65
mother, her mind troubled, said to the prince, 'Our lord is his highness, the emperor, the ruler of the east. Go to him. He will get the kingdom for you.'

When his mother said this to him, the prince replied, 'If I go there without a retinue, no one will show me respect.'

When she heard this, his mother insisted, saying, 'Go to your father-in-law's house, take some money from him, get a retinue and go to the emperor.'

iti sa prerito mātrā sa|lajjo 'pi nṛp'|ātmajaḥ
kramāt pratasthe sāyaṃ ca prāpa tac|chvāśuraṃ gṛham.
4.1.70 pitṛ|hīno vinaṣṭa|śrīr bāṣpa|pāt'|âbhiśaṅkayā
a|kāle n' âśakac c' âtra praveṣṭuṃ lajjayā niśi.
nikaṭe sattra|bāhye 'tha sthitaḥ śvaśura|mandirāt
naktaṃ rajjv" âvarohantīm a|kasmāt striyam aikṣata.
kṣaṇāc ca bhāryāṃ svām eva tāṃ ratna|dyuti|bhāsvarām
ulkām iv' âbhra|patitāṃ parijñāy' âbhyatapyata.
sā tu taṃ dhūsara|kṣāmaṃ dṛṣṭv" âpy a|parijānatī
‹ko 's' îty› apṛcchat tac chrutvā ‹pāntho 'ham iti› so 'bravīt.
tataḥ sā sattra|śāl"|ântaḥ praviveśa vaṇik|sutā
anvagād rāja|putro 'pi sa tāṃ guptam avekṣitum.
4.1.75 sā c' âtra puruṣaṃ kaṃ|cid upāgāt puruṣo 'pi tām
‹tvaṃ cireṇ' āgat" âs' îti› pāda|ghātair atāḍayat.
tataḥ sā dvi|guṇī|bhūta|rāgā pāpā prasādya tam
puruṣaṃ tena sahitā tatra tasthau yadṛcchayā.
tad dṛṣṭvā tu sa su|prajño rāja|putro vyacintayat
‹kopasy' âyaṃ na kālo me sādhyam anyadd hi vartate.
kathaṃ ca prasaratv etac chastraṃ kṛpaṇayor dvayoḥ
śatru|yogyaṃ striyām asyām asmin vā nṛpaśau mama?
kim etayā ku|vadhvā vā kṛtyam etadd hi durvidheḥ
mad|dhairy'|ālokana|krīḍā|naipuṇye duḥkha|varṣiṇaḥ.
4.1.80 a|tulya|kula|saṃbandhaḥ s" âiṣā kiṃ v" âparādhyati
muktvā bali|bhujaṃ kākī kokile ramate katham?›

Urged on thus by his mother, the prince, even though he
was ashamed, set forth and eventually reached his father-
in-law's house in the evening. He had lost his father and 4.1.70
his fortune, and shame and the fear of shedding tears made
him unable to enter there at that untimely moment that
night, so he stayed on the verandah of a nearby almshouse.
During the night he suddenly noticed a woman climbing
down a rope from his father-in-law's house. A moment later
he became very distressed when he recognized the woman
as none other than his wife. Resplendent with the glitter of
jewels, she resembled a shooting star fallen from a cloud.
Even though she saw him, he was dusty and thin, and she
did not recognize him. She asked him who he was and he
replied that he was a traveler. Then the merchant's daughter
went into the hall of the almshouse and the prince followed,
in order to watch her in secret. Once inside she went up 4.1.75
to some man and the man, after telling her that she was
late, kicked her repeatedly. Then the wicked girl, her passion
redoubled, gratified him and willingly stayed there with the
man. But on seeing this, the prince, who was very wise,
said to himself, 'Now is not the time for me to be angry for
there is something else that I must see through. And how
might this sword of mine, which is for worthy enemies,
range against two wretches, this woman and this brute of a
man? Anyway, there is no need to bother with my wicked
wife, for this is the work of cruel fate, which, cleverly having
fun by testing my fortitude, is raining down sorrows. It is 4.1.80
the union of unequal families rather than this lady herself
which is at fault. How is a lady crow to leave her husband,
an eater of temple offerings, and sport with a koyal?'

ity ālocya sa tāṃ bhāryām upaikṣata sa|kāmukām
satāṃ guru|jigīṣe hi cetasi strī|tṛṇaṃ kiyat?
tat|kālaṃ ca rat'|āvega|vaśāt tasyāḥ kil' âpatat
vaṇik|sutāyāḥ śravaṇāt san|mukt'|āḍhyaṃ vibhūṣaṇam.

tac ca sā na dadarś' âiva surat'|ânte ca satvarā
yayau yath"|āgataṃ geham āpṛcchy' ôpapatiṃ tataḥ.
tasminn api gate kv' âpi drutaṃ pracchanna|kāmuke
sa rāja|putro dṛṣṭvā tad|ratn'|ābharaṇam agrahīt.

4.1.85 sphurad|ratna|śikhā|jālaṃ dhātrā moha|tamo|'paham
hasta|dīpam iva prattaṃ praṇaṣṭa|śrī|gaveṣaṇe.
mah"|ârghaṃ ca tad ālokya rāja|putraḥ sa tat|kṣaṇam
nirgatya siddha|kāryaḥ san Kānyakubjaṃ tato yayau.
tatra bandhāya dattvā tat svarṇa|lakṣeṇa bhūṣaṇam
krītvā hasty|aśvam agamat sa pārśvaṃ cakra|vartinaḥ.
tad|dattaiś ca balaiḥ sākam etya hatvā ripūn raṇe
prāpa tat paitṛkaṃ rājyaṃ kṛtī mātr" âbhinanditaḥ.
tac ca bandhād vinirmocya bhūṣaṇaṃ śvaśur'|ântikam
prāhiṇot prakaṭī|kartuṃ rahasyaṃ tad a|śaṅkitam.

4.1.90 so 'pi tac|chvaśuro dṛṣṭvā sva|sutā|karṇa|bhūṣaṇam
tat tath" ôpāgataṃ tasyai saṃbhrāntaḥ samadarśayat.
s" âpi pūrva|paribhraṣṭaṃ cāritram iva vīkṣya tat
buddhvā ca bhartrā prahitaṃ vyākul" âiva samasmarat.
‹idaṃ me patitaṃ tasyāṃ rātrau sattra|gṛh'|ântare
yasyāṃ tatra sthito dṛṣṭaḥ sa ko 'pi pathiko mayā.

After thinking this through, he watched his wife and her lover with indifference, for when good men's minds are desirous of obtaining something important, women mean as much to them as straw. And it seems that at that moment in the haste of their embrace a piece of jewelry rich in fine pearls fell from the merchant's daughter's ear. She did not see it and when their lovemaking was over she said goodbye to her lover and hurried off to her house the way she had come. And after her secret lover had also rushed off somewhere, the prince found that jeweled ornament and took it.

With the many rays from its sparkling gems it dispelled 4.1.85
the darkness of despair and it was as if the creator had placed in his hand a torch with which to search for his lost fortune. On realizing that it was very valuable, the prince immediately went outside and, his task accomplished, journeyed from there to Kanya·kubja. There he pawned the piece of jewelry for one hundred thousand gold coins, bought some elephants and horses, and went to the emperor. Together with some troops given by him, that clever prince went and killed his enemies in battle, and, applauded by his mother, won back his father's kingdom. Then he got back the jewelry from the pawnbroker and sent it to his father-in-law in order to make public that surprising secret.

His father-in-law, on seeing his daughter's ear ornament 4.1.90
arrive like that, was confused and showed it to her. It had fallen long before, like her virtue, and when she saw it and discovered that it had been sent by her husband, she recalled it with a start. 'It's mine and it fell off that night in the almshouse when I saw the traveler there. So he must have been my husband, come to test my conduct, but I didn't

tan nūnaṃ so 'tra bhartā me śīla|jijñāsay" āyayau
mayā tu sa na vijñātas ten' êdaṃ prāpi bhūṣaṇam.›
ity evaṃ cintayantyāś ca durnaya|vyakti|viklavam
vaṇik|sutāyā hṛdayaṃ tasyāḥ kātaram asphuṭat.
4.1.95 tatas tasyā rahasya|jñāṃ pṛṣṭvā ceṭīṃ sva|yuktitaḥ
tat|pitā sa vaṇig buddhvā tattvaṃ tatyāja tac|chucam.
rāja|putro 'tha saṃprāpta|rājyo labdhvā guṇ'|ârjitām
sa cakra|varti|tanayāṃ bhāryāṃ bheje 'parāṃ śriyam.

tad itthaṃ sāhase strīṇāṃ hṛdayaṃ vajra|karkaśam
tad eva sādhvas'|āvega|saṃpāte puṣpa|pelavam.
tās tu kāś|cana sad|vaṃśa|jātā muktā iv' âṅganāḥ
yāḥ *suvṛtt'*|âccha|hṛdayā yānti bhūṣaṇatāṃ bhuvi.
hariṇ" îva ca rāja|śrīr evaṃ viplavinī sadā
dhairya|pāśena banddhuṃ ca tām eke jānate budhāḥ.
4.1.100 tasmād āpady api tyājyaṃ na sattvaṃ sampad|eṣibhiḥ
ayam ev' âtra vṛttānto mam' âtra ca nidarśanam,
yan mayā vidhure 'py asmiṃś cāritraṃ, devi, rakṣitam
yuṣmad|darśana|kalyāṇa|prāptyā tat phalitaṃ hi me.»

iti tasyā mukhāc chrutvā brāhmaṇyās tat|kṣaṇaṃ kathām
devī Vāsavadattā sā sādarā samacintayat,
«brāhmaṇī kulavaty eṣā dhruvam asyā hy udāratām
bhaṅgiḥ sva|śīl'|ôpakṣepe vacaḥ|prauḍhiś ca śaṃsati.
rāja|saṃsat|praveśe 'syāḥ prāvīṇyam ata eva ca
iti saṃcintya devī tāṃ brāhmaṇīṃ punar abravīt:

recognize him and he got hold of this piece of jewelry.' As the merchant's daughter was thinking this, her timid heart
burst, alarmed at the revelation of her misconduct. At this, 4.1.95
using his own cunning, her father the merchant questioned a servant of hers who was privy to the secret, found out the truth and cast off his sorrow for her. Then the prince, having won the kingdom, obtained the emperor's daughter as his wife, having acquired her through his virtues, and enjoyed unrivaled prosperity.

Thus, when it comes to being bold, women's hearts are as hard as diamond, but, when sudden consternation befalls them, they are as soft as a flower. However there are some women, born into good families, who are like pearls: their hearts are *virtuous : well-rounded* and clear, and they become ornaments to the world. Thus a king's prosperity is always like a flighty doe and it is only the wise who know
how to bind it with the tether of fortitude. So, even in times 4.1.100
of disaster, courage is not to be abandoned by those seeking prosperity: what has happened to me here is an example of this, since even in these hard times I have safeguarded my virtue, O queen, and that has born fruit for me in my obtaining the good fortune of meeting you."

As soon as she heard these words from the brahmin lady's mouth, Queen Vásava·datta was impressed and said to herself, "This brahmin lady must be from a good family, for the way in which she indirectly alluded to her own virtue and the assurance of her speech proclaim her nobility. And that must be how she was so skillful in getting into the king's assembly." After thinking this, the queen addressed the brahmin lady once more: "Whose wife are you and what is your 4.1.105

4.1.105 «bhāryā tvaṃ kasya ko vā te vṛttāntaḥ? kathyatāṃ tvayā»
tac chrutvā brāhmaṇī bhūyaḥ s" âtha vaktuṃ pracakrame.
«Mālave, devi, ko 'py āsīd Agnidatta iti dvijaḥ
nilayaḥ Śrī|Sarasvatyoḥ svayam ātta|dhano 'rthibhiḥ.
tasya ca sv'|ânurūpau dvāv utpannau tanayau kramāt
jyeṣṭhaḥ Śaṃkaradatt'|ākhyo nāmnā Śāntikaro 'paraḥ.
tayoḥ Śāntikaro 'kasmād vidy'|ârthī sva|pitur gṛhāt
sa bāla eva nirgatya gataḥ kv' âpi, yaśasvini.
dvitīyaś ca sa tad|bhrātā jyeṣṭho māṃ pariṇītavān
tanayāṃ Yajñadattasya yajñ'|ârtha|bhṛta|saṃpadaḥ.
4.1.110 kālena tasya mad|bhartuḥ so 'gnidatt'|âbhidhaḥ pitā
vṛddho lok'|ântaraṃ yāto bhāryay" ânugataḥ svayā.
tīrth'|ôddeśāc ca mad|bhartā dhṛta|garbhāṃ vimucya mām
gatvā Sarasvatī|pūre śoken' ândho jahau tanum.
vṛttānte kathite c' âsminn etya tat|sahayāyibhiḥ
sva|janebhyo mayā labdhaṃ n' ânugantuṃ sa|garbhayā.
tato mayy ārdra|śokāyām a|kasmād etya dasyubhiḥ
asman|nivāsaḥ sakalo 'py agrahāro viluṇṭhitaḥ.
tat|kṣaṇaṃ tisṛbhiḥ sārdhaṃ brāhmaṇībhir ahaṃ tataḥ
śīla|bhraṃśa|bhayād ātta|svalpa|vastrā palāyitā.
4.1.115 deśa|bhaṅgād vidūraṃ ca gatvā deśaṃ tad|anvitā
māsa|mātraṃ sthit" âbhūvaṃ kṛcchra|karm'|ôpajīvinī.
śrutvā c' â|nātha|śaraṇaṃ lokād Vats'|ēśvaraṃ tataḥ

story? Pray tell." On hearing this, the brahmin lady then started to speak once again.

"Your highness, there was a certain brahmin called Agni·datta in the region of Málava. He was home to the goddesses of fortune and learning and he happily let his wealth be taken by those who asked for it. In time two sons were born to him in his own image. The eldest was called Shánkara·datta, the other Shanti·kara. Of these two, O illustrious lady, Shanti·kara, though just a boy, desired knowledge and suddenly left his father's house and went off somewhere. The other son, his elder brother, married me, the daughter of Yajña·datta, who acquired wealth to perform sacrifices.
In time my husband's father, who was called Agni·datta, 4.1.110
grew old and went to the next world, followed by his wife. I was pregnant but my husband abandoned me on the pretext of going on pilgrimage and, blind with grief, went and cast off his body in the torrent of the river Sarásvati. When his companions came and told me the news, my relatives stopped me from doing the same because I was pregnant. Then, while my grief was still fresh, bandits suddenly came and plundered our house together with the entire brahmin village. In fear of my virtue being violated, I immediately fled from there in the company of three brahmin ladies,
taking just a few clothes. At the overthrow of the country, 4.1.115
I went with them to a far off land and had stayed there for just a month, providing for myself by doing menial jobs, when I heard from people that the king of Vatsa gave shelter to the needy, and from there I came here with the brahmin ladies, my virtue my only provision for the journey. As soon as I arrived I gave birth to twin boys. And even though

sa|brāhmaṇikā śīl'|âika|pāthey" âham ih' âgatā.
āgaty' âiva prasūt" âsmi yugapat tanayāv ubhau
sthitāsu c' āsu tisṛṣu brāhmaṇīṣu sakhīṣv api
śoko videśo dāridryaṃ dvi|guṇaḥ prasavo 'py ayam
aho apāvṛtaṃ dvāram āpadāṃ mama vedhasā!
tad etayor gatir n' âsti bālayor vardhanāya me
ity ālocya parityajya lajjāṃ yoṣid|vibhūṣaṇam.
4.1.120 mayā praviśya Vats'|ēśo rājā sadasi yācitaḥ
kaḥ śaktaḥ soḍhum āpanna|bāl'|âpaty'|ârti|darśanam?
tad|ādeśena ca prāptaṃ mayā tvac|caraṇ'|ântikam
vipadaś ca nivṛttā me dvārāt pratihatā iva.
ity eṣa mama vṛttānto nāmnā Piṅgalik" âpy aham
ābāly'|âgni|kriyā|dhūmair yan me piṅgalite dṛśau.
sa tu Śāntikaro, devi, devaro me videśa|gaḥ
kutra tiṣṭhati deśe 'sāv iti n' âdy' âpi budhyate»

evam ukta|sva|vṛttāntāṃ kulīn" êty avadhārya tām
prīty" ênāṃ brāhmaṇīṃ devī sā vitarky' âivam abravīt
4.1.125 «iha Śāntikaro nāma sthito 'smākaṃ purohitaḥ
vaideśikaḥ sa jāne 'haṃ devaras te bhaviṣyati.»

ity uktvā brāhmaṇīm utkāṃ nītvā rātriṃ tad" âiva tām
devī Śāntikaraṃ prātar ānāyy' âpṛcchad anvayam.
ukt'|ânvayāya tasmai ca sā saṃjāta|su|niścayā
«iyaṃ te bhrātṛ|jāy" êti» brāhmaṇīṃ tām adarśayat.
jātāyāṃ ca parijñaptau jñāta|bandhu|kṣayo 'tha saḥ
brāhmaṇīṃ bhrātṛ|jāyāṃ tāṃ ninye Śāntikaro gṛham.
tatr' ânuśocya pitarau bhrātaraṃ ca yath"|ôcitam
āśvāsayām āsa sa tāṃ bālaka|dvitay'|ânvitām.

I have these three brahmin ladies on hand as my companions, I have bereavement, exile and poverty too, and now these two offspring. Oh! The creator has opened for me the door to disasters! So, realizing that there was no way for me to bring up these two boys, I put aside my shame—a woman's ornament—and went into the king of Vatsa's as- 4.1.120
sembly where I petitioned him. Who can bear the sight of the suffering of unfortunate young offspring? At his bidding, I have arrived at your feet, and my disasters have gone away, as if turned back at the door. That is my story and my name is Píngalika, because since childhood my eyes have been reddened by the smoke from fire sacrifices. It is still not known in which country that brother-in-law of mine, Shanti·kara, who went abroad, is living."

When the brahmin lady had thus told her story, the queen determined that she was from a respectable family and after some thought said the following to her with affection. "There lives here a foreigner called Shanti·kara. He 4.1.125
is our priest. I think he will turn out to be your brother-in-law."

After saying this to the expectant brahmin lady, the queen then passed that night and in the morning summoned Shanti·kara and asked him about his family. When he had described his lineage, she became convinced and showed him the brahmin lady, saying, "Here is your brother's wife." When they recognized each other and Shanti·kara found out about the demise of his relatives, he took the brahmin lady, his brother's wife, to his house. Once there, he grieved for his parents and brother in an appropriate fashion and then comforted the woman and her two boys.

4.1.130 devī Vāsavadatt" âpi tasyās tau bālakau sutau
purohitau sva|putrasya bhāvinaḥ paryakalpayat.
jyeṣṭhas tayoḥ Śāntisomo nāmnā Vaiśvānaro 'paraḥ
kṛtas tay' âiva devyā ca vitīrṇa|bahu|saṃpadā.
andhasy' êv' âsya lokasya phala|bhūmiṃ sva|karmabhiḥ
purogair nīyamānasya hetu|mātraṃ sva|pauruṣam.
yad etya labdha|vibhavās tatra sarve 'pi saṃgatāḥ
bālakau tau tayoḥ sā ca mātā Śāntikaraś ca saḥ.
tato gacchatsu divaseṣv ekadā pañcabhiḥ sutaiḥ
sah' āgatām upādāya śarāvān kumbha|kārikām.
4.1.135 dṛṣṭvā sva|mandire kāṃ|cid devyā Vāsavadattayā
sā brāhmaṇī Piṅgalikā jagade pārśva|vartinī.
«pañc' âitasyāḥ suto 'dy' âpi n' âiko me, sakhi, dṛśyatām!
puṇyānām īdṛśaṃ pātram īdṛśy api na mādṛśī!»
tataḥ Piṅgalik" âvādīd «devi, duḥkhāya jāyate
praj" êyaṃ pāpa|bhūyiṣṭhā daridreṣv eva bhūyasī.
yuṣmādṛśeṣu jāyeta yaḥ sa ko 'py uttamo bhavet
tad alaṃ tvarayā prāpsyasy a|cirāt sv'|ôcitaṃ sutam.»
iti Piṅgalik"|ôkt" âpi s'|ôtsukā suta|janmani
abhūd Vāsavadattā sā tac|cint"|ākrānta|mānasā.
4.1.140 «girīś'|ārādhana|prāpyaṃ putraṃ te Nārado 'bhyadhāt
tad, devi, varado 'vaśyam ārādhyaḥ sa Śivo 'tra naḥ.»
ity uktā Vatsa|rājena tat|kālaṃ c' āgatena sā
devī labdh'|āśayen' āśu cakāra vrata|niścayam.
tasyām ātta|vratāyāṃ tu sa rāj" âpi sa|mantrikaḥ
sa|rāṣṭraś c' âpi vidadhe Śaṃkar'|ārādhana|vratam.

Queen Vásava·datta, meanwhile, decided that the two young boys would be her future son's priests and she gave the eldest of the two the name Shanti·soma and the other Vaishvánara, and presented them with large fortunes. People are like blind men, led to the place of their rewards by their actions, their own courage being nothing but a catalyst. 4.1.130

After going there and obtaining riches, those two boys, their mother and Shanti·kara, all lived there together. The 4.1.135
days then went by until on one of them, Queen Vásava·datta saw that a certain potter woman with five sons had arrived in her palace, bringing plates, and she said to the brahmin woman Píngalika, who was at her side, "Look, my friend. This woman has five sons and I still don't have one! A person like her is rich in merit, while a woman like me is nothing of the sort!

Píngalika replied, "O queen, offspring are for the most part sinners, born to poor people in great numbers in order to suffer. A boy born to a woman like you will be someone of the highest rank, so stop being impatient: before long you shall have a son befitting you."

Even after being told this by Píngalika, Vásava·datta longed for the birth of a son and her mind was overrun with
anxiety about it. At that moment the king of Vatsa arrived 4.1.140
and, realizing what she was feeling, said to her, "Nárada announced that you would get a son through worshipping Shiva, so, queen, we must worship that giver of boons here," at which the queen quickly decided to undertake an oath. When she had made her pledge, the king and his ministers, together with the people, took a vow to worship Shiva. And when the couple had fasted for three nights, the Lord

tri|rātr'|ôpoṣitau tau ca daṃpatī sa vibhus tataḥ
prasāda|prakaṭī|bhūtaḥ svayaṃ svapne samādiśat.
«uttiṣṭhatāṃ! sa yuvayoḥ Kām'|âṃśo janitā sutaḥ
nātho vidyā|dharāṇāṃ yo bhavitā mat|prasādataḥ.»

4.1.145 iti vacanam udīrya candra|maulau
sapadi tiro|hitatāṃ gate prabudhya
adhigata|varam āśu daṃpatī tau
pramadam a|kṛtrimam āpatuḥ kṛt'|ârthau.
utthāya c' ôṣasi tataḥ prakṛtīr vidhāya
tat|svapna|kīrtana|sudhā|rasa|tarpitās tāḥ
devī ca sā nara|patiś ca sa|bandhu|bhṛtyau
baddh'|ôtsavau vidadhatur vrata|pāraṇāni.
katipaya|divas'|âpagame tasyāḥ
svapne jaṭā|dharaḥ puruṣaḥ
ko 'py atha devyā Vāsavadattāyāḥ phalam upetya dadau.
tataḥ sa vinivedita|sphuṭa|tathā|vidha|svapnayā
saha pramuditas tayā samabhinandito mantribhiḥ
vicintya śaśi|maulinā phala|nibhena dattaṃ sutaṃ
manoratham a|dūra|gaṃ gaṇayati sma Vats'|ēśvaraḥ.

iti mahā|kavi|śrī|Somadeva|bhaṭṭa|viracite Kathāsaritsāgare
Naravāhanadatta|janana|lambake prathamas taraṅgaḥ.

2

4.2.1 ATHA VĀSAVADATTĀYĀ Vats'|ēśa|hṛday'|ôtsavaḥ
saṃbabhūv' â|cirād garbhaḥ Kām'|âṃś'|âvatar'|ôjjvalaḥ.
sā babhau lola|netreṇa mukhen' ā|pāṇḍu|kāntinā
śaś'|âṅken' êva garbha|stha|Kāma|prem'|ôpagāminā.
āsīnāyāḥ pati|snehād Rati|Prītī iv' āgate

was pleased and himself appeared in a dream and ordered, "Arise! The son who will be born to you shall, through my grace, be a partial incarnation of the god of love and the lord of the sorcerers." After the god with the moon as his 4.1.145
diadem had said this, he suddenly disappeared and the couple woke up. They had quickly received both a boon and real joy: their wish had been fulfilled. Then in the morning they got up and sprinkled the people with the nectar that was the telling of their dream, and the king and queen, with their relatives and dependents, celebrated and broke their fast.

Then, after a few days had passed, in a dream a man with matted locks came to Queen Vásava·datta and gave her a fruit. When the queen made the contents of her dream known, the royal couple were delighted and the king was congratulated by his ministers. Thinking that in the form of a fruit he had been given a son by Shiva, the god with the moon in his diadem, he considered that the fulfillment of his desire was not far away.

Thus ends the first wave in the Attainment called Nara·váhana·datta's birth in the "Ocean of the Rivers of Story" composed by the glorious and learned great poet Soma·deva.

2

Not long afterwards Vásava·datta became pregnant 4.2.1
with a glorious partial incarnation of the god of love, and the king of Vatsa's heart rejoiced. With her complexion a little lightened and her eyes rolling, her face made it seem as if the moon had arrived out of affection for the god of love in her womb, and she looked radiant. When she sat down

rejatuḥ pratime tasyā maṇi|paryaṅka|pārśvayoḥ.
bhāvi|vidyā|dhar'|âdhīśa|garbha|sev"|ârtham iṣṭa|dāḥ
mūrtā vidyā iv' āyātāḥ sakhyas tāṃ paryupāsata.
4.2.5 vinīla|pallava|śyāma|mukhau s" âtha payo|dharau
sūnor garbh'|âbhiṣekāya babhāra kalaśāv iva.
svaccha|sphurita|sa|cchāya|maṇi|kuṭṭima|śobhinaḥ
sukha|śayyā|gatā madhye mandirasya rarāja sā.
bhāvi|tat|tanay'|ākrānti|śaṅkā|kampita|vāribhiḥ
upetya sevyamān" êva samantād ratna|rāśibhiḥ.
tasyā vitāna†|madhya|stha|ratn'|ôtthā pratimā babhau
vidyā|dhara|śrīr nabhasā praṇām'|ârtham iv' āgatā.

mantra|sādhana|saṃnaddha|sādhak'|êndra|kathāsu ca
babhūva sā dohadinī prasaṅg'|ôpanatāsu ca.
4.2.10 sa|ras'|ārabdha|saṃgītā vidyā|dhara|var'|āṅganāḥ
svapne tām ambar'|ôtsaṅgam ārūḍhām upatasthire.
prabuddhā sevituṃ sākṣāt tad ev' âbhilalāṣa sā
nabhaḥ|krīḍā|vilasitaṃ lakṣya|bhū|tala|kautukam.
taṃ ca dohadam etasyā devyā Yaugandharāyaṇaḥ
yantra|mantr'|Êndra|jāl'|ādi|prayogaiḥ samapūrayat.
vijahāra ca sā tais taiḥ prayogair gagana|sthitā
paura|nārī|jan'|ôtpakṣma|locan'|āścarya|dāyibhiḥ.
ekadā vāsaka|sthāyās tasyāś ca samajāyata
hṛdi vidyā|dhar'|ôdāra|kathā|śravaṇa|kautukam.
4.2.15 tatas tay" ârthito devyā tatra Yaugandharāyaṇaḥ
tasyāḥ sarveṣu śṛṇvatsu nijagāda kathām imām.

and two images of her reflected in the sides of her jeweled bed, it was as if Rati and Priti had come out of love for their husband.* Her companions sat around her like incarnations of the wish-fulfilling sciences, come to worship the future emperor of the sorcerers in her womb. She bore breasts like 4.2.5
pots for anointing the son in her womb, and their nipples grew as dusky as dark blue buds. She looked resplendent when she lay down to relax in the palace, which shone with its inlaid floor of clear, sparkling, beautiful jewels: it was as if she were being worshipped by that store of gems, the ocean, troubled by the fear of being overcome by her future son. An image of her was reflected in the jewels in the middle of her canopy, as if the goddess of the sorcerers' prosperity had come through the sky to make obeisance.

She developed a pregnancy craving for stories, segued into her conversations, of great magicians armed with powers conjured up by spells. When in a dream she rose up 4.2.10
into the firmament, lovely sorcerer ladies served her and started to sing beautiful songs. On waking she would want to have that same pleasure of sporting in the sky, with the fun of looking at the surface of the earth. Yaugándharáyana fulfilled the queen's pregnancy craving by using machines, spells, trickery and so forth. Through those various techniques, which brought astonishment to the eyes, their lashes upturned, of the womenfolk of the city, she roamed about in the sky. One day, when she was in her bedroom, a desire arose in her heart to hear the illustrious tales of the sorcerers. So, Yaugándharáyana, on being asked by the 4.2.15
queen there, told her the following story while everyone listened on.

«asty Ambikā|janayitā nag'|êndro Himavān iti
na kevalaṃ girīṇāṃ yo gurur Gaurī|pater api.
vidyā|dhara|nivāse ca tasmin vidyā|dhar'|âdhipaḥ
uvāsa rājā Jīmūtaketur nāma mah"|âcale.
tasy' âbhūt kalpa|vṛkṣaś ca gṛhe pitṛ|kram'|āgataḥ
nāmn" ânvarthena vikhyāto yo manoratha|dāyakaḥ.

kadā|cic ca sa Jīmūtaketū rāj" âbhyupetya tam
udyāne devat"|ātmānaṃ kalpa|drumam ayācata.
4.2.20 ‹sarvadā prāpyate 'smābhis tvattaḥ sarvam abhīpsitam
tad a|putrāya me dehi, deva, putraṃ guṇ'|ânvitam.›
tataḥ kalpa|drumo 'vādīd ‹rājann, utpatsyate tava
jāti|smaro dāna|vīraḥ sarva|bhūta|hitaḥ sutaḥ.›

tac chrutvā sa prahṛṣṭaḥ san kalpa|vṛkṣaṃ praṇamya tam
gatvā nivedya tad rājā nijāṃ devīm anandayat.
atha tasy' âcirād eva rājñaḥ sūnur ajāyata
Jīmūtavāhanaṃ taṃ ca nāmnā sa vidadhe pitā.
tataḥ sahajayā sākaṃ sarva|bhūt'|ânukampayā
jagāma sa mahā|sattvo vṛddhim Jīmūtavāhanaḥ.
4.2.25 kramāc ca yauva|rājya|sthaḥ paricaryā|prasāditam
lok'|ânukampī pitaraṃ vijane sa vyajijñapat.
‹jānāmi, tāta, yad bhāvā bhave 'smin kṣaṇa|bhaṅgurāḥ
sthiraṃ tu mahatām ekam ākalpam amalaṃ yaśaḥ.
par'|ôpakṛti|saṃbhūtaṃ tad eva yadi hanta tat
kim anyat syād udārāṇāṃ dhanaṃ prāṇ'|âdhika|priyam.
saṃpac ca vidyud iva sā loka|locana|kheda|kṛt

"There is a great mountain called Himávat, the father of Párvati, who is respected by not only the mountains, but by Shiva too. On that mountain, which is the abode of sorcerers, there lived the emperor of the sorcerers, a king called Jimúta·ketu. In his house there was a wish-fulfilling tree which he had inherited from his forefathers and was appropriately called the granter of desires.

One day that King Jimúta·ketu went up to the divine wish fulfilling tree in the garden and made a request of it:
'We always get everything we want from you, so, O di- 4.2.20
vine one, since I am childless, give me a son endowed with virtues.' The wish-fulfilling tree replied, 'O king, you shall have a son who remembers his past lives, is heroically generous and good to all beings.'

When he heard this, the king was overjoyed. He bowed before the wish-fulfilling tree before going and delighting his queen by telling her what had happened. And very soon afterwards a son was born to the king, to whom his father gave the name Jimúta·váhana. Then, in company with his natural compassion for all beings, the magnanimous Jimúta·váhana grew up. In time, when he had be- 4.2.25
come crown prince, in his compassion for the world he said in private to his father, who was pleased with his devotion, 'Father, I know that the things that exist in this world disappear in an instant and only the spotless renown of the great is permanent and lasts as long as an eon. If it arises from helping others, then for the noble there can be no other wealth; it is dearer to them than life. And a fortune which is not used to help others is like lightning: it brings pain to people's eyes and, being fickle, disappears somewhere else.

lolā kv' âpi layaṃ yāti yā par'|ân|upakāriṇī.
tad eṣa kalpa|viṭapī kāma|do yo 'sti naḥ sa cet
par'|ârthaṃ viniyujyeta tad" āptaṃ tat phalaṃ bhavet.
4.2.30 tat tath" âhaṃ karom' îha yath" âitasya samṛddhibhiḥ
a|daridrā bhavaty eṣa sarv'|ârthi|jana|saṃhatiḥ.›

iti vijñāpya pitaraṃ tad|anujñām avāpya saḥ
Jīmūtavāhano gatvā taṃ kalpa|drumam abravīt.
‹deva, tvaṃ śaśvad asmākam abhīṣṭam phala|dāyakaḥ
tad ekam idam adya tvaṃ mama pūraya vāñchitam.
a|daridrāṃ kuruṣv' âitāṃ pṛthivīm akhilāṃ, sakhe.
svasty astu te pradatto 'si lokāya draviṇ'|ârthine!›

ity uktas tena dhīreṇa kalpa|vṛkṣo vavarṣa saḥ
kanakaṃ bhūtale bhūri nananduś c' âkhilāḥ prajāḥ.
4.2.35 dayālur bodhisattv'|âṃśaḥ ko 'nyo Jīmūtavāhanāt
śaknuyād arthisāt kartum api kalpa|drumaṃ kṛtī?
iti jāt'|ânurāgāsu tato dikṣu vidikṣv api
Jīmūtavāhanasy' ôccaiḥ paprathe viśadaṃ yaśaḥ.
tataḥ putra|prath"|ābaddha|mūlaṃ rājyaṃ sa|matsarāḥ
dṛṣṭvā Jīmūtaketos tad|gotra|jā vikṛtiṃ yayuḥ.
dān'|ôpayukta|sat|kalpa|vṛkṣa|yukt'|āspadaṃ† ca tat
menire niṣprabhāvatvāj jetuṃ su|karam eva te.
tataḥ sambhūya yuddhāya kṛta|buddhiṣu teṣu ca
pitaraṃ tam uvāc' âivaṃ dhīro Jīmūtavāhanaḥ.
4.2.40 ‹yathā śarīram ev' êdaṃ jala|budbuda|saṃnibham
pravāta|dīpa|capalās tathā kasya kṛte śriyaḥ?
tā apy any'|ôpamardena manasvī ko 'bhivāñchati?
tasmāt, tata, mayā n' âiva yoddhavyaṃ gotra|jaiḥ saha.
rājyaṃ tyaktvā tu gantavyam itaḥ kv' âpi vanaṃ mayā

So if this wish-fulfilling tree of ours, which grants desires, were to be used for the benefit of others, we might obtain that reward. Therefore I shall use its riches to stop all these 4.2.30
needy people here from being poor.'

After telling his father this and getting his consent, Jimúta·váhana went and spoke to the wish-fulfilling tree. 'O divine one, you always give us the rewards we desire, so now you must fulfill this one wish of mine. Make this entire world free from poverty, my friend. May you be successful, you who have been given to all those who want wealth!'

After being addressed thus by that resolute man, the wish-fulfilling tree poured forth copious amounts of gold on the earth and the entire populace was delighted. What 4.2.35
compassionate partial incarnation of a bodhisattva other than Jimúta·váhana would be capable enough to bestow a wish-fulfilling tree upon the needy? Thus the whole world grew to love him and Jimúta·váhana's brilliant renown spread all around. Then Jimúta·ketu's jealous relatives, seeing that his kingdom was well established thanks to the fame of his son, started to move against him. And they thought that it had to be easy to conquer the place where the goodly wish-fulfilling tree was employed in charity, because it was lacking in might. Then when they had assembled and made up their minds to fight, the resolute Jimúta·váhana said the following to his father. 'In the same way that this 4.2.40
body is like a bubble in water, so riches are as unsteady as a candle in the wind—what is the point of them? And what wise man desires to obtain them through the destruction

āsatāṃ kṛpaṇā ete mā bhūt sva|kula|saṃkṣayaḥ.›

ity uktavantaṃ Jīmūtavāhanaṃ sa pitā tataḥ
Jīmūtaketur apy evaṃ jagāda kṛta|niścayaḥ.
‹may" âpi, putra, gantavyaṃ kā hi vṛddhasya me spṛhā
rājye tṛṇa iva tyakte yūn" âpi kṛpayā tvayā?›
4.2.45 evam uktavatā sākaṃ sa|bhāryeṇa ‹tath" êti› saḥ
pitrā jagāma Jīmūtavāhano Malay'|âcalam.
tatr' âdhivāse siddhānāṃ candana|cchanna|nirjhare
sa tasthāv āśrama|pade paricaryā|paraḥ pituḥ.
atha siddh'|âdhirājasya vaśī Viśvāvasoḥ sutaḥ
mittraṃ Mittrāvasur nāma tasy' âtra samapadyata.
tat|svasāraṃ ca so 'paśyad ek'|ânte jātu kanyakām
janm'|ântara|priyatamāṃ jñānī Jīmūtavāhanaḥ.
tat|kālaṃ ca tayos tulyaṃ yūnor anyonya|darśanam
abhūn mano|mṛg'|â|manda|vāgurā|bandha|saṃnibham.
4.2.50 tato 'kasmāt samabhyetya tri|jagat|pūjyam ekadā
Jīmūtavāhanaṃ prītaḥ sa Mittrāvasur abhyadhāt.
‹kanyā Malayavaty|ākhyā svasā me 'sti kanīyasī.
tām ahaṃ te prayacchāmi mam' êcchāṃ m" ânyathā kṛthāḥ.›

of others? Therefore, father, I must not fight with my kinsmen. I should leave the kingdom and go from here to somewhere in the forest. Let these wretches live here—our family must not be destroyed.'

After Jimúta·váhana had said this, his father Jimúta·ketu, having made up his mind, said the following to him. 'I too, my son, must go, for what desire can I, an old man, have for the kingdom when out of pity you, even though you are young, have given it up as if it were a piece of straw?'

On his speaking thus, Jimúta·váhana said, 'So be it,' and 4.2.45
went to mount Málaya with his father, who was accompanied by his wife. He lived there in an ashram in a settlement of *siddhas*, where the streams were hidden by sandalwood trees, and devoted himself to looking after his father. Then the self-disciplined son of Vishva·vasu, the ruler of the *siddhas*, who was called Mittra·vasu, became his friend. And one day in a secluded spot, Jimúta·váhana, who had second sight, came across a girl, Mittra·vasu's sister, who had
been his sweetheart in a former life. As soon as those two 4.2.50
youngsters looked at one another in the same way, it was as if the deer of the heart had suddenly been captured in a net. Mittra·vasu was delighted and one day he unexpectedly came up to Jimúta·váhana, who was to be worshipped by the three worlds, and said, 'I have a younger sister, a maiden called Málayavati. I am offering her to you. Do not disappoint me.'

tac chrutv" âiva sa Jīmūtavāhano 'pi jagāda tam
‹yuva|rāja, mam' âbhūt sā bhāryā pūrve 'pi janmani
tvaṃ ca tatr' âiva me jāto dvitīyaṃ hṛdayaṃ suhṛt
jāti|smaro 'smy ahaṃ sarvaṃ pūrva|janma smarāmi tat.›
ity uktavantaṃ tat|kālaṃ Mittrāvasur uvāca tam
‹janm'|ântara|kathāṃ tāvac chaṃs' âitāṃ kautukaṃ hi me.›
4.2.55 etan Mittrāvasoḥ śrutvā tasmai Jīmūtavāhanaḥ
sukṛtī kathayām āsa pūrva|janma|kathām imām.
‹asti pūrvam ahaṃ vyoma|cārī vidyā|dharo 'bhavam
himavac|chṛṅga|mārgeṇa gato 'bhūvaṃ kadā|cana.
tataś c' âdhaḥ sthitas tatra krīḍan Gauryā samaṃ Haraḥ
śaśāp' ôllaṅghana|kruddho «martya|yonau pat' êti» mām.
«prāpya vidyā|dharīṃ bhāryāṃ niyojya sva|pade sutam
punar vaidyādharīṃ yoniṃ smṛta|jātiḥ prapatsyase.»
evaṃ niśamya śāp'|ântam uktvā Śarve tirohite
a|cireṇ' âiva jāto 'haṃ bhūtale vaṇijāṃ kule.
4.2.60 nagaryāṃ Valabhī|nāmnyāṃ Mahādhana|vaṇik|sutaḥ
Vasudatt'|âbhidhānaḥ san vṛddhiṃ ca gatavān aham.
kālena yauvana|sthaś ca pitrā kṛta|paricchadaḥ
dvīp'|ântaraṃ gato 'bhūvaṃ vaṇijyāyai tad|ājñayā.
āgacchantaṃ tato 'ṭavyāṃ taskarā vinipatya mām
hṛta|svam anayan baddhvā sva|pallīṃ Caṇḍikā|gṛham.
vilola|dīrghayā ghoraṃ rakt'|âṃśuka|patākayā
jighatsataḥ paśu|prāṇān kṛt'|ântasy' êva jihvayā.
tatr' âham upahār'|ârtham upanīto nijasya taiḥ
prabhoḥ Pulindak'|ākhyasya devīṃ pūjayato 'ntikam.

As for Jimúta·váhana, well, the moment he heard this he said to him, 'Prince, she was my wife in a former life too and in that same life you became my friend, a second heart to me. I can recall my past lives and I remember all of that previous birth.'

When he said this, Mittra·vasu immediately replied, 'Please tell the story of your previous birth, for I am curious.' On hearing this from Mittra·vasu, the virtuous Jimúta· 4.2.55
váhana told him the following story about his former birth.

'Once upon a time I was a sky-roving sorcerer. One day I was flying through the peaks of the Himálaya and then there below me was Shiva, having fun with Párvati. Enraged at being overflown he cursed me, saying, "Go down and be born in a mortal's womb. When you have found a sorceress wife and have put your son in your place, you will once again be born as a sorcerer and will remember your past lives." Shiva said this and disappeared, and, having thus heard how the curse would end, I was very soon afterwards
born on earth into a family of merchants. I grew up in a 4.2.60
city called Válabhi as the son of the merchant Maha·dhana and I was called Vasu·datta. In time, when I was a young man and had been given a retinue by my father, at his bidding I went overseas to trade. On my way back, bandits fell upon me in the wilderness, seized my goods, captured me and took me to the temple of Chándika in their village. With its long, fluttering, red, silken banner looking like the tongue of death wanting to eat up the life-breaths of sacrificial victims, it was terrifying. There they took me before their chief, who was called Pulíndaka and was worshipping
the goddess, in order to be sacrificed. Even though he was a 4.2.65

4.2.65 sa dṛṣtv" âiv' ârdra|hṛdayaḥ śabaro 'py abhavan mayi.
vakti janm'|ântara|prītiṃ manaḥ snihyad a|kāraṇam.
tato māṃ mocayitv" âiva vadhāt sa śabar'|âdhipaḥ
aicchad ātm'|ôpahāreṇa kartuṃ pūjā|samāpanam.
«m" âivaṃ kṛthāḥ prasann" âsmi tava yācasva māṃ varam»
ity ukto divyayā vācā prahṛṣṭaś ca jagāda saḥ.
«tvaṃ prasannā varaḥ ko 'nyas tath" âpy etāvad arthaye
janm'|ântare 'pi me sakhyam anena vaṇij" âstv iti.»
«evam astv iti» śāntāyāṃ vāci māṃ śabaro 'tha saḥ
pradatta|sa|viśeṣ'|ârthaṃ prajighāya nijaṃ gṛham.
4.2.70 mṛtyor mukhāt pravāsāc ca tataḥ pratyāgate mayi
akaroj jñāta|vṛttāntaḥ pitā mama mah"|ôtsavam.
kālena tatra c' âpaśyam ahaṃ sārth'|âvaluṇṭhanāt
vaṣṭabhy' ānāyitaṃ rājñā tam eva śabar'|âdhipam.
tat|kṣaṇaṃ pitur āvedya vijñapya ca mahī|patim
mocitaḥ svarṇa|lakṣeṇa sa mayā vadha|nigrahāt.
prāṇa|dān'|ôpakārasya kṛtv" âivaṃ pratyupakriyām
ānīya ca gṛhaṃ prītyā pūrṇaṃ saṃmānitaś ciram.
sat|kṛtya preṣitaś c' âtha hṛdayam prema|peśalam
nidhāya mayi pallīṃ svāṃ prāyāt sa śabar'|âdhipaḥ.
4.2.75 tatra pratyupakār'|ârthaṃ cintayan prābhṛtaṃ mama
svalpaṃ sa mene svādhīnaṃ muktā|kastūrik'|ādy api.
tataḥ s'|âtiśayaṃ prāptuṃ muktā|sāraṃ sa mat|kṛte
dhanur|dvitīyaḥ prayayau gajān hantuṃ him'|âcalam.

tribal, the moment he saw me his heart melted with pity. A mind that feels affection for no reason tells of friendship in a previous life. No sooner had the chief of the tribals saved me from being killed than he wanted to finish his worship by sacrificing himself. A divine voice said to him, "Don't do it! I am pleased with you so ask me for a boon." Delighted, he replied, "You are pleased—what more could I want? Even so, let me ask for this much: may I be friends with this merchant in another life."

Then, when the voice had said, "So be it," and fallen quiet, the tribal, after giving me extraordinary riches, sent me home.

And then, when I had returned—both from the jaws of 4.2.70
death and from being away—and my father heard my story, he held a great celebration. After some time, I saw there that very same tribal chieftain. He had been arrested and brought in by the king after the robbing of a caravan. I immediately informed my father and made a request to the king, and for one hundred thousand gold coins I saved him from being executed. Having thus returned the favor of one who had saved my life, I brought him to my house and looked after him affectionately and with the greatest respect for a long time. And after treating him hospitably, I sent the tribal chieftain on his way, and he, having given me his heart, tender with love, went to his village.

There, while thinking about a present for me in return for 4.2.75
my help, he decided that even the pearls, musk and so forth that he had at his disposal were inadequate. So, in order to obtain for me the very finest pearls, he took his bow and went to the Himálaya to kill elephants.* While wandering

bhramaṃś ca tatra tīra|stha|dev'|āgāraṃ mahat saraḥ
prāpa tulyaiḥ kṛta|prītis tad|abjair *mittra*|rāgibhiḥ.
tatr' āśaṅky' âmbu|pān'|ârtham āgamaṃ vanya|hastinām
channaḥ sa tasthāv ekānte sa|cāpas taj|jighāṃsayā.

tāvat tatra saras|tīra|gataṃ pūjayituṃ Haram
āgatām adbhut'|ākārāṃ kumārīṃ siṃha|vāhanām.
4.2.80 sa dadarśa tuṣār'|âdri|rāja|putrīm iv' âparām
paricaryā|parāṃ Śaṃbhoḥ kanyakā|bhāva|vartinīm.
dṛṣṭvā ca vismay'|ākrāntaḥ śabaraḥ sa vyacintayat
«k" êyaṃ syād? yadi martya|strī tat kathaṃ siṃha|vāhanā?
atha divyā kathaṃ dṛśyā mādṛśais? tad iyaṃ dhruvam
cakṣuṣoḥ pūrva|puṇyānāṃ mūrtā pariṇatir mama.
anayā yadi mittraṃ taṃ yojayeyam ahaṃ tataḥ
k" âpy any" âiva mayā tasya kṛtā syāt pratyupakriyā.
tad etām upasarpāmi tāvaj jijñāsituṃ varam»
ity ālocya sa mittraṃ me śabaras tām upāyayau.
4.2.85 tāvac ca s" âvatīry' âiva siṃhāc chāyā|niṣādinaḥ
kany" āgatya saraḥ padmāny avacetuṃ pracakrame.

taṃ ca dṛṣṭv" ântika|prāptaṃ śabaraṃ sā kṛt'|ānatim
a|pūrvam atithi|prītyā svāgaten' ânvarañjayat.
«kas tvaṃ? kiṃ c' āgato 'sy etāṃ
bhūmim atyanta|durgamām?»
iti pṛṣṭavatīṃ tāṃ ca
śabaraḥ pratyuvāca saḥ.
«ahaṃ Bhavānī|pād'|âika|śaraṇaḥ śabar'|âdhipaḥ

about there he came across a huge lake with a temple on its shore and its lotuses, by loving *the sun : their friend* like him, delighted him. Thinking that wild elephants would come there to drink water, he waited there with his bow, hidden in a secret spot, wanting to kill them.

Meanwhile he saw arrive there to worship at the Shiva 4.2.80
temple on the shore of the lake a young lady of amazing appearance riding a lion, looking like a second Párvati, daughter of the Himálaya, intent on serving Shiva while in her maidenhood. And on seeing her, that tribal was overcome with astonishment and said to himself, "Who might this girl be? If she is a mortal woman, then how is she riding on a lion? But if she is divine, how could she be visible to people like me? So she must be the embodied result of my eyes' past merits. If I were to marry my friend to her, then I need not do anything else for him to repay his help, so I'd better just go up to her and inquire." After reflecting thus,
that friend of mine the tribal went up to her. And the girl, 4.2.85
meanwhile, got down from the lion, who was resting in the shade, and immediately went to the lake and started to pick lotuses.

When she saw the strange tribal approach her and bow, out of her liking for guests she delighted him with a welcome. She asked him who he was and why he had come to that extremely inaccessible land, to which the tribal replied, "My only refuge is the feet of Bhaváni and I am a tribal chieftain. I have come to this wilderness to get pearls from elephants. And when I saw you just now, O goddess, I thought of my close friend, who saved my life, the illustrious merchant's son Vasu·datta. For like you, O beautiful 4.2.90

āgato 'smi ca mātaṅga|muktā|hetor idaṃ vanam.
tvāṃ ca dṛṣṭv" âdhun" ātmīyo, devi, prāṇa|pradaḥ suhṛt
sārthavāha|sutaḥ śrīmān Vasudatto mayā smṛtaḥ.
4.2.90 sa hi tvam iva rūpeṇa yauvanena ca, sundari
a|dvitīyo 'sya viśvasya nayan'|âmṛta|nirjharaḥ.
sā dhanyā kanyakā loke yasyās ten' êha gṛhyate
maittrī|dāna|dayā|dhairya|nidhinā kaṅkaṇī karaḥ.
tat tvad|ākṛtir eṣā cet tādṛśena na yujyate
vyarthaṃ vahati tat Kāmaḥ kodaṇḍam iti me vyathā.
iti vyādh'|Êndra|vacanaiḥ sadyo 'pahṛta|mānasā
s" âbhūt kumārī kaṃdarpa|moha|mantr'|âkṣarair iva.
uvāca taṃ ca śabaraṃ preryamāṇā manobhuvā
«kva sa te suhṛd? ānīya tāvan me darśyatām iti.»
4.2.95 tac chrutvā ca «tath" êty» uktvā tām āmantrya tad" âiva saḥ
kṛt'|ârtha|mānī muditaḥ pratasthe śabaras tataḥ.
prāpya sva|pallīm ādāya muktā|mṛga|mad'|ādikam
bhūri bhāra|śatair hāryam asmad|gṛham ath' āyayau.
sarvaiḥ puraskṛtas tatra praviśya prābhṛtaṃ ca tat
mat|pitre sa bahu|svarṇa|lakṣa|mūlyaṃ nyavedayat.
utsavena ca yāte 'smin dine rātrau sa me rahaḥ
kanyā|darśana|vṛttāntaṃ tam āmūlād avarṇayat.
«ehi tatr' âiva gacchāva! ity» uktvā ca samutsukam
māṃ ādāya niśi svairaṃ sa prāyāc chabar'|âdhipaḥ.
4.2.100 prātaś ca māṃ gataṃ kv' âpi buddhvā sa|śabar'|âdhipam
tat|prīti|pratyayāt tasthau dhṛtim ālambya mat|pitā.
ahaṃ ca prāpito 'bhūvaṃ kramāt tena tarasvinā
śabareṇa tuṣār'|âdriṃ kṛt'|âdhva|parikarmaṇā.
tac ca prāpya saraḥ sāyaṃ snātvā svādu|phal'|âśanau

one, he is peerless in looks and youthful vigor, a cascade of the nectar of immortality into the eyes of this world. Blessed is the girl on this earth whose hand with its bracelets is taken by that man, who is a store of friendship, generosity, compassion and resolve. So if this beauty of yours is not to be joined with one like him, then I am afraid that the god of love carries his bow for no reason."

The girl's mind was immediately captivated by these words from that finest of hunters, as if by the syllables of the spell of enchantment of the god of love. Urged on by the god of love, she said to the tribal, "Where is this friend of yours?
Fetch him and show him to me." When he heard this he 4.2.95
said he would and immediately took his leave of her. Then the delighted tribal, thinking that he had achieved his aim, went on his way. After arriving at his village, he took large amounts of pearls, musk and so forth, to be carried in hundreds of loads, and then came to my house. Having been honored by everyone there, he went inside and offered my father the gifts, which were worth several hundred thousand gold coins. And when that day had passed in celebration, in the night he took me aside and told me from the very beginning the story of his meeting the girl. I was very eager, and after saying, "Come, let's go straight there!," that night the tribal chief quietly set off, taking me with him.

When in the morning my father discovered that I had 4.2.100
gone away with the tribal chief, he remained composed because he was convinced of the tribal's affection. Eventually that energetic tribal, attending to my needs along the way, brought me to the Himálaya. In the evening we reached the lake. After bathing he and I spent one night there in

ahaṃ ca sa ca tām ekāṃ vane tatr' ôṣitau niśām.
latābhiḥ kīrṇa|kusumaṃ bhṛṅgī|saṃgīta|sundaram
śubha|gandha|vahaṃ hāri jvalit'|âuṣadhi|dīpikam.
Rates tad vāsa|veśm' êva viśrāntyai giri|kānanam
āvayor abhavan naktaṃ pibatos tat|saro|jalam
4.2.105 tato 'nyedyuḥ pratipadaṃ tat|tad|utkalikā|bhṛtā
pratyudgat" êva manasā mama tan|mārga|dhāvinā.
cakṣuṣā dakṣiṇen' âpi sūcit'|āgaman" âmunā
didṛkṣay" êva sphuratā sā kany" âtr' āgat" âbhavat.
sa|ṭāla|siṃha|pṛṣṭha|sthā subhrūr dṛṣṭā mayā ca sā
śarad|ambho|dhar'|ôtsaṅga|saṅgin" îv' êndavī kalā.
vilasad|vismay'|āutsukya|sādhvasaṃ paśyataś ca tām
mam' āvartata tat|kālaṃ na jāne hṛdayaṃ katham.
ath' âvatīrya siṃhāt sā puṣpāṇy uccitya kanyakā
snātvā sarasi tat|tīra|gataṃ Haram apūjayat.
4.2.110 pūj"|âvasāne c' ôpetya sa sakhā śabaro mama
praṇamy' ātmānam āvedya tām avocat kṛt'|ādarām.
«ānītaḥ sa mayā, devi, suhṛd yogyo varas tava
manyase yadi tat tubhyaṃ darśayāmy adhun' âiva tam.»

tac chrutvā «darśay' êty» ukte tayā sa śabaras tataḥ
āgatya nikaṭaṃ nītvā māṃ tasyāḥ samadarśayat.
s" âpi māṃ tiryag ālokya cakṣuṣā praṇaya|srutā
madan'|āveśa|vaśagā śabar'|ēśaṃ tam abhyadhāt.
«sakhā te mānuṣo n' âyaṃ kāmaṃ ko 'py ayam āgataḥ
mad|vañcanāya devo 'dya martyasy' âiṣ" ākṛtiḥ kutaḥ.»

the forest eating delicious fruits. For us two to rest in for the night, drinking the water of the lake, that grove on the mountain. strewn with flowers from the creepers, beautiful with the buzzing of bees, giving off lovely scents, enchanting and lit by luminous herbs, was like the bedchamber of
Rati. Then on the next day the girl arrived there and my 4.2.105
mind, rushing along her path, seemed to go ahead to meet her, entertaining different desires at each step, and her arrival had been indicated by this right eye of mine throbbing as if with the desire to see her. I saw that girl with lovely eyebrows on the back of a lion with a mane and she was like a digit of the moon sitting in the lap of an fall cloud. And I do not know how my heart kept going at that moment while I was looking at her, as it manifested astonishment, desire and fear. Then the girl got down from the lion, picked some flowers, bathed in the lake and worshipped
Shiva in the temple on its shore. And when the worship was 4.2.110
over, my friend the tribal went up, bowed and introduced himself. She greeted him respectfully and he said to her, "O goddess, I have bought my friend, who is a suitable groom for you. If you deem it fit then I shall show him to you right away."

On hearing this she told the tribal to show me to her and he took me up and presented me to her. She gave me a sideways glance with an eye streaming with love and, overcome by possession by the god of love, said to the tribal chief, "This friend of yours is not a mortal—surely he is some god come to deceive me today, for mortals do not look like this."

4.2.115 tad ākarṇy' ôktavān asmi tāṃ pratyāyayituṃ svayam
«satyaṃ, sundari, martyo 'haṃ kiṃ vyājen' ârjave jane?
ahaṃ hi sārthavāhasya Valabhī|vāsinaḥ sutaḥ
Mahādhan'|âbhidhānasya Maheśvara|var'|ârjitaḥ.
tapasyan sa hi putr'|ârtham uddiśya śaśi|śekharam
samādiśyata ten' âivaṃ svapne devena tuṣyatā.
‹uttiṣṭh' ôtpatsyate ko 'pi mah"|ātmā tanayas tava
rahasyaṃ paramaṃ c' âitad alam uktv" âtra vistaram.›
etac chrutvā prabuddhasya tasya kālena c' ātmajaḥ
aham eṣa samutpanno Vasudatta iti śrutaḥ.
4.2.120 ayaṃ ca śabar'|âdhīśaḥ svayaṃvara|suhṛn mayā
deś'|ântara|gatena prāk|prāptaḥ kṛcchr'|âika|bāndhavaḥ.
eṣa me tattva|saṃkṣepa ity» uktvā virate mayi.
ābhāṣat' âtha kanyā sa lajjay" âvanat'|ānanā.
«asty etan māṃ ca jāne 'dya svapne 'rcitavatīṃ Haraḥ
‹prātaḥ prāpsyasi bhartāram iti› tuṣṭaḥ kil' ādiśat.
tasmāt tvam eva me bhartā bhrāt" âyaṃ ca bhavat|suhṛt»
iti vāk|sudhayā sā mām ānandya virat" âbhavat.
saṃmantry' âtha tayā sākaṃ vivāhāya yathā|vidhi
akārṣaṃ niścayaṃ gantuṃ sa|mittro 'haṃ nijaṃ gṛham.
4.2.125 tataḥ sā siṃham āhūya vāhanaṃ taṃ sva|saṃjñayā
«atr' āroh,' ārya|putr,' êti» māṃ abhāṣata sundarī.
ath' âhaṃ tena suhṛd" ânuyātaḥ śabareṇa tam
siṃham āruhya dayitām utsaṅge tāṃ gṛhītavān.
tataḥ prasthitavān asmi kṛta|kṛtyo nijaṃ gṛham
kāntayā saha siṃha|stho mitre tasmin puraḥ|sare.

When I heard this, in order to convince her, I myself said, "It is true, O beautiful lady: I am a mortal. What is the point of deceiving honest people? I am the son of a caravan leader called Maha·dhana who lives in Válabhi and I was obtained as a boon from Shiva. For when, in order to get a son, my father was carrying out austerities directed towards he whose diadem is the moon, the pleased Lord instructed him thus in a dream: 'Arise. An illustrious son shall be born to you. This is a great secret. I shall not discuss it at length.' After hearing this he woke up and in time I was born to him as his son and was called Vasu·datta. Some time ago when I had gone to another country I chose as my friend this tribal chieftain here, he who was my one ally in difficult times. This, in brief, is the truth about me." After saying this I fell quiet. 4.2.115 4.2.120

Then the girl, looking down in embarrassment, said, "It is so. I know—today I dreamed that I had performed my worship and Shiva, pleased, said to me, 'This morning you shall obtain a husband.' Therefore it is you who are my husband and this friend of yours is my brother!" After delighting me with the nectar that was these words, she fell silent. Then, after discussing it with her, I decided to go with my friend to my house in order to carry out the wedding appropriately. At this the beautiful girl called the lion using a gesture of hers and said to me, "Mount him, my noble lord." Next, accompanied by my tribal friend, I mounted the lion and took my sweetheart in my lap. Then, having done what I had to do, I set out for my home, accompanied by my beloved, mounted on a lion and with my friend leading the way. 4.2.125

tadīya|śara|nirbhinna|hariṇ'|āmiṣa|vṛttayaḥ
krameṇa te vayaṃ sarve saṃprāptā Valabhīṃ purīm.
tatra mām āgataṃ dṛṣṭvā siṃh'|ārūḍhaṃ sa|vallabham
s'|āścaryas tad drutaṃ gatvā mama pitre 'bravīj janaḥ.
4.2.130 so 'pi pratyudgato harṣād avatīrṇaṃ mṛg'|êndrataḥ
pād'|âvanamraṃ dṛṣṭvā mām abhyanandat sa|vismayaḥ.
an|anya|sadṛśīṃ tāṃ ca kṛta|pād'|âbhivandanām
paśyan mam' ôcitāṃ bhāryāṃ na māti sma mudā kva|cit.
praveśya mandiraṃ c' âsmān vṛttāntaṃ paripṛcchya ca
praśaṃsañ śabar'|âdhīśa|sauhārdaṃ c' ôtsavaṃ vyadhāt.
tato mauhūrtik'|ādeśād anyedyur vara|kanyakā
sā mayā pariṇīt" âbhūn milit'|âkhila|bandhunā.

tad ālokya ca so 'kasmān mad|vadhū|vāhanas tadā
siṃhaḥ sarveṣu paśyatsu saṃpannaḥ puruṣ'|ākṛtiḥ.
4.2.135 «kim etad iti?» vibhrānte jane tatra sthite 'khile
sa divya|vastr'|ābharaṇo naman mām evam abravīt.
«ahaṃ Citrāṅgado nāma vidyā|dhara iyaṃ ca me
sutā Manovatī nāma kanyā prāṇ'|âdhika|priyā.
etām aṅke sadā kṛtvā vipinena bhramann aham
prāptavān ekadā Gaṅgāṃ bhūri|tīra|tapo|vanām.
tapasvi|laṅghana|trāsāt tasyā madhyena gacchataḥ
apatan mama daivāc ca puṣpa|mālā tad|ambhasi.
tato 'kasmāt samutthāya Nārado 'ntar|jala|sthitaḥ
pṛṣṭhe tayā patitayā kruddho mām aśapan muniḥ.
4.2.140 ‹auddhatyen' âmunā, pāpa, gaccha siṃho bhaviṣyasi

Living off the flesh of deer pierced by the tribal chief's arrows, we all eventually reached the city of Válabhi. There, when the people saw me arrive mounted on a lion in the company of my sweetheart, they were astonished and rushed to tell my father. He was so happy that he came out to 4.2.130
meet me, and when he saw me get down from the lion and prostrate myself at his feet, he welcomed me in amazement. When that girl of peerless beauty respectfully touched his feet, he saw that she was a suitable wife for me and was completely beside himself with joy. He led us into the house and after asking us our story, while praising the tribal chief's friendship, he arranged a celebration. Then on the next day, at the instruction of an astrologer, with all my family and friends there, I married that beautiful girl.

Then after seeing the wedding, as everyone looked on, my wife's vehicle, the lion, suddenly assumed the form of a man. With all the people there confused as to what this 4.2.135
meant, the man, wearing divine clothes and ornaments, and bowing, said the following to me. "I am a sorcerer called Chitrángada and this girl is my daughter. Her name is Manóvati and she is dearer to me than life. When wandering through the forest, I used always to carry her in my arms. One day I arrived at the Ganga, on whose banks there are many penance groves. While journeying along the middle of the river out of fear of offending the ascetics, it so happened that my flower garland fell in her waters. Then suddenly the sage Nárada, who had been in the water, rose up and, enraged by the garland having fallen on his back, cursed me. 'Because of this insolence, you sinner, you must 4.2.140
leave! You shall become a lion and go to the Himálaya,

him'|âcale gataś c' âitāṃ sutāṃ pṛṣṭhena vakṣyasi.
yadā ca mānuṣeṇ' âiṣā sutā te pariṇeṣyate
tadā tad|darśanād eva śāpād asmād vimokṣyase.›

ity ahaṃ muninā śaptaḥ siṃhī|bhūya him'|âcale
atiṣṭhaṃ tanayām etāṃ Hara|pūjā|parāṃ vahan.
an|antaraṃ yathā yatnāc chabar'|âdhipater idam
saṃpannaṃ sarva|kalyāṇaṃ tathā viditam eva te.
tat sādhayāmi bhadraṃ vas tīrṇaḥ śāpo may" âiṣa saḥ»
ity uktvā so 'bhyudapatat sadyo vidyā|dharo nabhaḥ.

4.2.145 tatas tad|vismay'|ākrānto nandat|sva|jana|bāndhavaḥ
ślāghya|saṃbandha|hṛṣṭo me pit" ākārṣīn mah"|ôtsavam.
«ko hi nirvyāja|mittrāṇāṃ caritaṃ cintayiṣyati
suhṛtsu n' âiva tṛpyanti prāṇair apy upakṛtya ye.»
iti c' âtra na ko nāma sa|camatkāram abhyadhāt
dhyāyan dhyāyan udāraṃ tac chabar'|âdhipa|ceṣṭitam.
rāj" âpi tat tathā buddhvā tatratyas tasya san|mateḥ
atuṣyad asmat|snehena śabar'|âdhipateḥ param.
tuṣṭaś ca tasmai mat|pitrā dāpitaḥ sahas" âiva ca
aśeṣam aṭavī|rājyaṃ ratn'|ôpāyana|dāyinā.

4.2.150 tatas tayā Manovatyā patnyā mittreṇa tena ca
kṛt'|ârthaḥ śabar'|êndreṇa tatr' âtiṣṭham ahaṃ sukhī.
sa ca ślathī|kṛt'|ātmīya|deśa|vāsa|rasas tataḥ
bhūyas" âsmad|gṛheṣv eva nyavasac chabar'|âdhipaḥ.
paraspar'|ôpakāreṣu sarva|kālam a|tṛptayoḥ
sa dvayor agamat kālo mama tasya ca mittrayoḥ.

where you shall carry this daughter of yours on your back. And when this daughter of yours marries a mortal, then as soon as you see it happen you shall be freed from this curse.'

After being thus cursed by the sage, I became a lion and lived in the Himálaya, carrying this daughter of mine, who was intent on worshipping Shiva. Of course you know how in the meantime, through the efforts of the tribal chief, it turned out most auspiciously. So I shall endeavor to do good for you. I have now reached the end of my curse." As soon as he had said this, the sorcerer flew up into the sky.

Then, overcome with astonishment at this and delighted 4.2.145
by the exalted union, my father, his friends and relatives rejoicing, held a great celebration. "Who can believe the behavior of true friends, who are not satisfied even when they have helped save their friends' lives?" To a man, everyone said this in astonishment about the matter when reflecting over and over again on the noble behavior of the tribal chieftain. As for the king of the place, well, when he found out about it he was extremely pleased with that high-minded tribal chief because of his affection for my family. And being pleased, the king, when my father presented the tribal chief with a gift of jewels, was immediately inspired to give him a huge kingdom in the forest. Then, my 4.2.150
aims achieved by having Manóvati as my wife and the tribal chieftain as my friend, I lived there happily. And then the tribal chieftain, his taste for living in his own country diminished, spent most of his time in our house. Time passed for us two friends, him and me, with us never being satisfied by the constant favors we afforded one another.

a|cirāc ca Manovatyāṃ tasyām ajani me sutaḥ
bahiṣ|kṛtaḥ kulasy' êva kṛtsnasya hṛday'|ôtsavaḥ.
Hiraṇyadatta|nāmā ca sa śanair vṛddhim āyayau
kṛta|vidyo yathā|vac ca pariṇīto 'bhavat tataḥ.
4.2.155 tad dṛṣṭvā jīvita|phalaṃ pūrṇaṃ matvā ca mat|pitā
vṛddho Bhāgīrathīṃ prāyāt sa|dāro deham ujjhitum.
tato 'haṃ pitṛ|śok'|ârtaḥ kathaṃ|cid bāndhavair dhṛtim
grāhito gṛha|bhāraṃ svam udvoḍhuṃ pratipannavān.

tadā Manovatī|mugdha|mukha|darśanam ekataḥ
anyataḥ śabar'|êndreṇa saṃgamo māṃ vyanodayat.
tataḥ sat|putra|s'|ānandāḥ su|kalatra|manoramāḥ
suhṛt|samāgama|sukhā gatās te divasā mama.

kālen' âtha pravṛddhaṃ mām agrahīc cibuke jarā
«kiṃ gṛhe 'dy' âpi, putr,' êti?» prīty" êva bruvatī hitam.
4.2.160 ten' âhaṃ sahas" ôtpanna|vairāgyas tanayaṃ nijam
kuṭumba|bhār'|ôdvahane vanaṃ vāñchann ayojayam.
sa|dāraś ca gato 'bhūvaṃ giriṃ Kālañjaraṃ tataḥ
mat|sneha|tyakta|rājyena samaṃ śabara|bhū|bhṛtā.
tatra prāptena c' ātmīyā jātir vaidyādharī mayā
śāpaś ca prāpta|paryantaḥ sa śārvaḥ sahasā smṛtaḥ.
tac ca patnyai Manovatyai tad" âiv' ākhyātavān aham
sakhye ca śabar'|êndrāya mumukṣur mānuṣīṃ tanum.
«bhāryā|mittre ime eva bhūyāstāṃ smarato mama
anya|janmany ap' îty» uktvā hṛdi kṛtvā ca Śaṃkaram.

Before long Manóvati bore me a son and it was as if the joy in the hearts of the whole family had assumed external form. He was called Hiránya·datta and gradually grew up. After being duly educated he got married. On seeing this, 4.2.155
my father, an old man, considered that he had achieved everything he wanted from life and went with his wife to the river Bhagírathi to cast off his body.* At this I was stricken with grief for my parents. My friends and relatives somehow had me keep my composure and I agreed to attend to my duties as a householder.

At that time, the sight of Manóvati's lovely face, on the one hand, and, the company of the tribal chief, on the other, kept me amused. Then the days that passed for me were made blissful by my having a virtuous son, beautiful by my having a good wife and happy by my associating with my friend.

In time I became advanced in years and old age grabbed me by the chin,* as if out of affection it were rightly saying, "Why are you still at home, my son?" So I suddenly devel- 4.2.160
oped a distaste for the world and, yearning for the forest, I entrusted my son with the burden of running the household. In the company of my wife I then went to mount Kalánjara, accompanied by the tribal king, who in his affection for me had abandoned his kingdom. And when I arrived there, I suddenly remembered my birth as a sorcerer and realized that the curse from Shiva had reached its end. I immediately told this to my wife Manóvati and my friend the tribal chieftain, and wanted to cast off my human body. Saying, "May these two be my wife and friend in another life too, and may I remember them," and visualizing Shiva

4.2.165 mayā giri|taṭāt tasmān nipatya prasabhaṃ tataḥ
tābhyāṃ sva|patnī|mittrābhyāṃ saha muktaṃ śarīrakam.
so 'haṃ tataḥ samutpanno nāmnā Jīmūtavāhanaḥ
vidyā|dhara|kule 'muṣminn eṣa jāti|smaro 'dhunā.
sa c' âpi śabar'|êndras tvaṃ jāto Mittrāvasuḥ punaḥ
try|akṣa|prasādāt siddhānāṃ rājño Viśvāvasoḥ sutaḥ.
s" âpi vidyā|dharī, mittra, mama bhāryā Manovatī
tava svasā samutpannā nāmnā Malayavaty asau.
evaṃ me pūrva|patny eṣā bhaginī te bhavān api
pūrva|mittram ato yuktā pariṇetum asau mama.
4.2.170 kiṃ tu pūrvam ito gatvā mama pitror nivedaya
tayoḥ pramāṇī|kṛtayoḥ siddhyaty etat tav' êpsitam.»
itthaṃ niśamya Jīmūtavāhanāt prīta|mānasaḥ
gatvā Mittrāvasuḥ sarvaṃ tat|pitṛbhyāṃ śaśaṃsa tat.
abhinandita|vākyaś ca tābhyāṃ hṛṣṭas tad" âiva saḥ
upagamya tam ev' ârthaṃ sva|pitṛbhyāṃ nyavedayat.
tayor īpsita|saṃpatti|tuṣṭayoḥ satvaraṃ ca saḥ
yuva|rājo vivāhāya saṃbhāram akarot svasuḥ.
tato jagrāha vidhivat tasyā Jīmūtavāhanaḥ
pāṇiṃ Malayavatyāḥ sa siddha|rāja|puraskṛtaḥ.
4.2.175 babhūva c' ôtsavas tatra cañcad|dyu|cara|cāraṇaḥ
saṃmilat|siddha|saṃghāto valgad|vidyā|dhar'|ôddhuraḥ.
kṛt'|ôdvāhas tatas tasthau tasmiñ Jīmūtavāhanaḥ
Malay'|âdrau mah"|ârheṇa vibhavena vadhū|sakhaḥ.

in my heart, I then hurled myself off that cliff and aban- 4.2.165
doned my body, as well as my wife and my friend.

Then I took the birth that I have here now, under the name Jimúta·váhana and into a sorcerer family, with the ability to remember my past lives. And you, the tribal chieftain, by the grace of Shiva were born again as Mittra·vasu, the son of Vishva·vasu, king of the *siddha*s. And, friend, that sorceress, my wife Manóvati, was born as your sister, with the name Málayavati. Thus your sister was previously my wife and you were previously my friend, so it is right
that I should marry her. But first you must go from here 4.2.170
and inform my parents. Once they are given the final say on the matter, your desires will be fulfilled."

On hearing this from Jimúta·váhana, Mittra·vasu was pleased and went and told Jimúta·váhana's parents everything. They welcomed what he said, so, delighted, he immediately went and told his parents the same news. They were happy that their wishes had been fulfilled and the prince quickly made the necessary arrangements for his sister's wedding. Then with due ceremony Jimúta·váhana took Málayavati's hand in marriage and was honored by the king
of the *siddha*s. Celebrations were held there, with celestial 4.2.175
singers flitting about, all the *siddha*s getting together and cavorting sorcerers adding to the fun. After he was married, Jimúta·váhana stayed on mount Málaya with his wife and a great fortune.

ekadā ca śvaśuryeṇa sa Mittrāvasunā saha
velā|vanāni jaladher avalokayituṃ yayau.
tatr' âpaśyac ca puruṣaṃ yuvānaṃ vignam āgatam
nivartayantaṃ jananīṃ ‹hā putr' êti› virāviṇīm.
apareṇa parityaktaṃ bhaṭen' êv' ânuyāyinā
puruṣeṇa pṛth'|ûttuṅgaṃ prāpayy' âikaṃ śilā|talam.
4.2.180 ‹kas tvaṃ? kim īhase? kiṃ ca mātā tvāṃ śocat' îti?› tam
sa papraccha tataḥ so 'pi tasmai vṛttāntam abravīt.
‹purā Kaśyapa|bhārye dve Kadrūś ca Vinatā tathā
mithaḥ kathā|prasaṅgena vivādaṃ kila cakratuḥ.
ādyā śyāmān raver aśvān avādīd aparā sitān
anyonya|dāsa|bhāvaṃ ca paṇam atra babandhatuḥ.
tato jay'|ârthinī Kadrūḥ svairaṃ nāgair nij'|âtma|jaiḥ
viṣa|phūt|kāra|malinān arkasy' âśvān akārayat.
tādṛśāṃś c' ôpadarśy' âitān Vinatāṃ chadmanā jitām
dāsī|cakāra kaṣṭā hi strīṇām any"|â|sahiṣṇutā.
4.2.185 tad buddhv" āgatya Vinatā|tanayo Garuḍas tadā
sāntvena mātur dāsatva|muktiṃ Kadrūm ayācata.
tataḥ Kadrū|sutā nāgā vicinty' âivaṃ tam abruvan
«bho Vainateya! kṣīr'|âbdhiḥ prārabdho mathituṃ suraiḥ.
tataḥ sudhāṃ samāhṛtya prativastu prayaccha naḥ
mātaraṃ svī|kuruṣv' âtha bhavān hi balināṃ varaḥ.»

One day he went to look at the forests on the shore of the ocean with Mittra·vasu, his brother-in-law. There they saw a young man arrive in a panic, turning away his mother, who was wailing, "Oh! My son!" Another man, who looked like a soldier, was accompanying him. He led him to the broad and high flat surface of a rock and left him there. Jimúta· 4.2.180
váhana asked him, "Who are you? What do you want? And why is your mother grieving for you?," to which he told him his story.

'It is said that long ago the two wives of Káshyapa, Kadru and Vínata, in the course of a conversation had an argument with one another. The former said that the sun's horses were black, the other, white. They made a bet on it, the stake being that the loser would become the winner's slave. Then Kadru, in her desire to win, secretly used some snake-men, her own sons, to make the sun's horses dark by spitting venom on them. After showing them to Vínata like that and thus beating her with a trick, she made her her slave. Oh women's intolerance of one another is terrible! When Ví- 4.2.185
nata's son Gáruda found out about this, he came and used kind words to ask Kadru to free his mother from slavery. Then Kadru's sons, the snake-men, thought about it and said to him, "O Gáruda! The gods have started to churn the ocean of milk. Bring the nectar of immortality from there and then in return for giving it to us take your mother, for you, sir, are the mightiest of the mighty."

etan nāga|vacaḥ śrutvā gatvā ca kṣīra|vāri|dhim
sudh"|ârthaṃ darśayām āsa Garuḍo guru pauruṣam.
tataḥ parākrama|prīto devas tatra svayaṃ Hariḥ
«tuṣṭo 'smi te varaṃ kaṃ|cid vṛṇīṣv' êty» ādideśa tam.
4.2.190 «nāgā bhavantu me bhakṣyā iti» so 'pi Hares tataḥ
Vainateyo varaṃ vavre mātur dāsyena kopitaḥ.
«tath" êti» Hariṇ" ādiṣṭo nija|vīry'|ârjit'|âmṛtaḥ
sa c' âivam atha Śakreṇa gadito jñāta|vastunā.
«tathā, pakṣ'|îndra, kāryaṃ te yathā mūḍhair na bhujyate
nāgaiḥ sudhā yathā c' âināṃ tebhyaḥ pratyāharāmy aham.»
etac chrutvā «tath" êty» uktvā sa vaiṣṇava|var'|ôddhuraḥ
sudhā|kalaśam ādāya Tārkṣyo nāgān upāyayau.
vara|prabhāva|bhītāṃś ca mugdhān ārāj jagāda tān
«idam ānītam amṛtaṃ muktv" âmbāṃ mama gṛhyatām.
4.2.195 bhayaṃ cet sthāpayāmy etad
aham vo darbha|saṃstare
unmocy' âmbāṃ ca gacchāmi
svī|kurudhvam itaḥ sudhām.»
«tath" êty» ukte ca tair nāgaiḥ sa pavitre kuś'|āstare
sudhā|kalaśam ādhatta te c' âsya jananīṃ jahuḥ.
dāsya|muktāṃ ca kṛtv" âivaṃ mātaraṃ Garuḍe gate
yāvad ādadate nāgā niḥśaṅkās tat kil' âmṛtam.
tāvan nipatya sahasā tān vimohya sva|śaktitaḥ
taṃ sudhā|kalaśaṃ Śakro jahāra kuśa|saṃstarāt.

After hearing these words from the snake-men, Gáruda went to the ocean of milk and showed off his great strength in order to get the nectar of immortality. Then, pleased by his valor, the god there, Vishnu himself, instructed him, "I am pleased with you. Choose some boon."

At this, Gáruda, angered by his mother's servitude, chose 4.2.190
as his boon from Vishnu for the snake-men to become suitable food for him.

Vishnu said to him, "So be it," and after Gáruda had obtained the nectar of immortality by means of his own heroism, Indra, who knew what had happened, told him the following. "King of the birds, you must ensure that the foolish snake-men do not eat the nectar and I can take it back from them."

When he heard this he gave his assent and, lightened of his burden by Vishnu's boon, he took the pot of nectar and approached the snake-men. From a distance he said to those idiots, who were terrified because of the boon, "Look—I
have brought the nectar. Release my mother and take it. If 4.2.195
you are afraid, then I shall place it on a bed of *darbha* grass for you. When I have had my mother set free, I shall go. Take the nectar from here."

When the snake-men agreed to this, he put the pot of nectar on a sanctified bed of *kusha* grass and they released his mother. Having thus freed his mother from slavery, Gáruda left. It seems that while the unsuspecting snake-men were taking the nectar of immortality, Indra, having used his power to stupefy them, suddenly flew down and grabbed the pot of nectar from the bed of *kusha* grass. Then the despondent snake-men licked the bed of *darbha*

viṣaṇṇās te 'tha nāgās taṃ lilihur darbha|saṃstaram
kadā|cid amṛta|ścyota|lepo 'py asmin bhaved iti.
4.2.200 tena pāṭita|jihvās te vṛthā prāpur dvi|jihvatām
hāsyād ṛte kim anyat syād atilaulyavatāṃ phalam?
ath' â|labdh'|âmṛta|rasān nāgān vairī Harer varāt
Tārkṣyaḥ pravavṛte bhoktuṃ tān nipatya punaḥ punaḥ.
tad|āpāte ca Pātālaṃ trāsa|nirjīva|rājilam
prabhraṣṭa|garbhiṇī|garbham abhūt kṣapita|pannagam.
taṃ dṛṣṭvā c' ânvahaṃ tatra Vāsukir bhujag'|êśvaraḥ
kṛtsnam eka|pade naṣṭaṃ nāga|lokam amanyata.
tato durvāra|vīryasya sadyas tasya vicintya saḥ
samayaṃ prārthanā|pūrvaṃ cakār' âivaṃ Garutmataḥ.
4.2.205 «ekam ekaṃ pratidinaṃ nāgaṃ te preṣayāmy aham
āhāra|hetoḥ, pakṣ'|îndra, payo|dhi|pulin'|âcale.
Pātāle tu praveṣṭavyaṃ na tvayā marda|kāriṇā
nāga|loka|kṣayāt sv'|ârthas tav' âiva hi vinaśyati.»
iti Vāsukinā proktas «tath" êti» Garuḍo 'nvaham
tat|preṣitam ih' âikaikaṃ nāgaṃ bhoktuṃ pracakrame.
tena krameṇa c' â|saṃkhyāḥ phaṇino 'tra kṣayaṃ gatāḥ
ahaṃ ca Śaṅkhacūḍ'|ākhyo nāgo vāro mam' âdya ca.
ato 'haṃ Garuḍ'|āhāra|hetor vadhya|śilām imām
mātuś ca śocyatāṃ prāpto nāga|rāja|nideśataḥ.›

grass, thinking that perhaps a drop of nectar might have dripped onto it. As a result their tongues were torn and, 4.2.200
to no end, they attained the state of having two tongues.* Other than ridicule, what reward can there be for those who are overly greedy? They failed to get a taste of the nectar of immortality and then, as a result of Vishnu's boon, their enemy Gáruda started to eat them, flying down to them again and again. At his onslaught, the snake-men in Patála, their underworld home, died of fright and their pregnant women miscarried—the snake people were no more. Having watched him there day after day, Vásuki, the king of the snake people, realized that all the snake-men in Patála had been destroyed in one go. Then, on reflection, he quickly petitioned that bird of irrepressible valor and made the following arrangement with him. "Every day, O king of the 4.2.205
birds, I shall send you a snake-man to eat on the mountain by the ocean's shore. But you must not go into Patála to do violence, for the destruction of the race of the snake people will only harm your own interests."

Gáruda agreed to these words from Vásuki and started to eat the single snake-man which he sent to him here each day. In this way, countless snake-men have met their end here. I am a snake-man called Shankha·chuda and it is my turn today, so, at the command of the king of the snake people, I have come to this rock of execution to be food for Gáruda, and I have become a reason for my mother to grieve.'

4.2.210 iti tasya vacaḥ śrutvā Śaṅkhacūḍasya duḥkhitaḥ
s'|ântaḥ|khedaḥ sa Jīmūtavāhanas tam abhāṣata.
‹aho kim api niḥsattvaṃ rājatvaṃ bata Vāsukeḥ
yat sva|hastena nīyante ripor āmiṣatāṃ prajāḥ?
kiṃ na prathamam ātm" âiva tena datto Garutmate?
klīben' âbhyarthitā k" êyaṃ sva|kula|kṣaya|sākṣitā?
utpadya Kaśyapāt pāpaṃ Tārkṣyo 'pi kurute kiyat?
deha|mātra|kṛte mohaḥ kīdṛśo mahatām api?
tad ahaṃ tāvad ady' âikaṃ rakṣāmi tvāṃ Garutmataḥ
sva|śarīra|pradānena mā viṣādaṃ kṛthāḥ, sakhe.›
4.2.215 tac chrutvā Śaṅkhacūḍo 'pi dhairyād etad uvāca tam
‹śāntam etan, mahā|sattva! mā sm' âivaṃ bhāṣathāḥ punaḥ!
na kācasya kṛte jātu yuktā muktā|maṇeḥ kṣatiḥ
na c' âpy ahaṃ gamiṣyāmi kathāṃ kula|kalaṅkitām.›
ity uktvā taṃ niṣidhy? âiva sādhur Jīmūtavāhanam
matvā Garuḍa|velāṃ ca sa kṣaṇ'|ântara|gāminīm.
Śaṅkhacūḍo yayau tatra vāri|dhes tīra|vartinam
anta|kāle namaskartuṃ Gokarṇ'|ākhyam Umā|patim.
gate tasmin sa kāruṇya|nidhir Jīmūtavāhanaḥ
tat|trāṇāy' ātma|dānena bubudhe labdham antaram.
4.2.220 tatas tad|vismṛtam iva kṣipraṃ kṛtvā sva|yuktitaḥ
kāry'|âpadeśād vyasṛjan nijaṃ Mittrāvasuṃ gṛham.
tat|kṣaṇaṃ ca samāsanna|Tārkṣya|pakṣ'|ânil'|āhatā
tat|sattva|darśan'|āścaryād iva sā bhūr aghūrṇata.
ten' âhi|ripum āyāntaṃ matvā Jīmūtavāhanaḥ
par'|ânukampī tāṃ vadhya|śilām adhyāruroha saḥ.

When Jimúta·váhana heard this speech from Shankha· 4.2.210
chuda he was troubled and inwardly sad. He said to him, 'Oh, how cowardly is Vásuki's rule, that with his own hand he makes his subjects become prey for their enemy! Why didn't he first offer himself to Gáruda? Did the coward want to witness this destruction of his race? And what sin is being committed by Gáruda too, the son of Káshyapa! For the sake of their bodies alone, even the great can be completely deluded! So let me today make an offering of my own body to save you, and you alone, from the bird. Don't be sad, my friend!'

But Shankha·chuda, on hearing these words, resolutely 4.2.215
said this to him, 'Heaven forbid this, great hero! Don't speak such words again! The destruction of a pearl for the sake of glass is completely wrong, and I won't become the subject of stories about how my race has been disgraced.'

After saying this and stopping Jimúta·váhana, the goodly Shankha·chuda, thinking that Gáruda would be arriving very shortly, went to worship at the hour of his death Shiva who resides on the ocean shore with the name of Go·karna. When he had gone, Jimúta·váhana, that store of compassion, realized that now was his chance to save him by offering up his life. Then, quickly pretending to have for- 4.2.220
gotten something, he contrived to send Mittra·vasu to his house on the pretext of an errand. At that moment the earth, struck by the wind from the wings of the approaching Gáruda, shook as if in astonishment at the sight of his valor. Jimúta·váhana, realizing that the enemy of the snake-men was coming and feeling pity, climbed the rock of execution. A moment later Gáruda, blocking out the sky with

kṣaṇāc c' âtra nipaty' âiva mahā|sattvaṃ jahāra tam
āhatya cañcvā Garuḍaḥ sva|cchāy"|ācchādit'|âmbaraḥ.
parisravad|asṛg|dhāraṃ cyut'|ôtkhāta|śikhā|maṇim
nītvā bhakṣayituṃ c' âinam ārebhe śikhare gireḥ.
4.2.225 tat|kālaṃ puṣpa|vṛṣṭiś ca nipapāta nabhas|talāt
tad|darśanāc ca ‹kiṃ nv etad? iti› Tārkṣyo visismiye.

tāvat sa Śaṅkhacūḍo 'tra natvā Gokarṇam āgataḥ
dadarśa rudhirā|sāra|siktaṃ vadhya|śilā|talam.
‹hā dhiṅ mad|arthaṃ ten' ātmā datto nūnaṃ mah"|ātmanā!
tat kutra nītas Tārkṣyeṇa kṣaṇe 'smin sa bhaviṣyati.
anviṣyāmi drutaṃ tāvat kadā|cit tam avāpnuyām.›
iti sādhuḥ sa tad|rakta|dhārām anusaran yayau.
atr' ântare ca hṛṣṭaṃ taṃ dṛṣṭvā Jīmūtavāhanam
Garuḍo bhakṣaṇaṃ muktvā sa|vismayam acintayat.
4.2.230 ‹kaś|cit kim anya ev' âyaṃ bhakṣyamāṇo 'pi yo mayā
vipadyate na tu paraṃ dhīraḥ pratyuta hṛṣyati.›
ity antar vimṛśantaṃ ca Tārkṣyaṃ tādṛg|vidho 'pi saḥ
nijagāda nij'|âbhīṣṭa|siddhyai Jīmūtavāhanaḥ.
‹pakṣi|rāja, mam' âsty eva śarīre māṃsa|śoṇitam
tad a|kasmād a|tṛpto 'pi kiṃ nivṛtto 'si bhakṣaṇāt.›

tac chrutv" āścarya|vaśa|gas taṃ sa papraccha pakṣi|rāṭ
‹nāgaḥ, sādho, na tāvat tvaṃ brūhi tat ko bhavān iti.›

his silhouette, flew down there and immediately struck that great hero with his beak before carrying him off. He took him, streams of blood pouring forth, his crest jewel pulled out and thrown down, and started to eat him on the top of the mountain. At that moment a rain of flowers fell from 4.2.225
the sky. When he saw it, Gáruda was amazed, wondering what it could mean.

Meanwhile, Shankha·chuda returned there having paid his respects to Shiva Go·karna and saw that the surface of the rock of execution was sprinkled with blood. 'Oh! Alas! That noble fellow must have offered himself for my sake! So where will Gáruda have taken him in this short interval? I shall quickly look for him and perhaps I'll find him.' With this, that virtuous snake-man followed the trail of blood from there. In the meantime Gáruda, seeing that Jimúta·váhana was happy, stopped eating and said to himself in astonishment, 'But this must be someone else altogether, 4.2.230
for even though I am eating him the resolute fellow is not despondent; rather he is rejoicing!' And while doing just that, Jimúta·váhana, in order to achieve what he wanted, even said to Gáruda as he was thinking this through, 'King of the birds, flesh and blood remain in my body, so why, even though you are not full, have you suddenly stopped eating?'

When he heard this, the king of the birds, overcome with astonishment, asked him, 'O virtuous one, you are not a snake-man, so please, sir, just tell me who you are.'

‹nāga ev' âsmi. bhuṅkṣva tvaṃ
yath" ārabdhaṃ samāpaya
ārabdhā hy asamāpt" âiva
kiṃ dhīrais tyajyate kriyā?›
4.2.235 iti yāvac ca Jīmūtavāhanaḥ prativakti tam
tāvat sa Śaṅkhacūḍo 'tra prāpto dūrād abhāṣata.
‹mā! mā, Garutman! n' âiv' âiṣa nāgo nāgo hy ahaṃ tava
tad enaṃ muñca! ko 'yaṃ te jāto 'kāṇḍe, bata, bhramaḥ?›
tac chrutv" âtīva vibhrānto babhūva sa khag'|êśvaraḥ
vāñchit'|â|siddhi|khedaṃ ca bheje Jīmūtavāhanaḥ.
tato 'nyonya|samālāpa|krandad|vidyā|dhar'|âdhipam
buddhvā taṃ bhakṣitaṃ mohād Garutmān abhyatapyata.
‹aho bata! nṛśaṃsasya pāpam āpatitaṃ mama!
kiṃ vā su|labha|pāpā hi bhavanty *unmārga/vṛttayaḥ*.
4.2.240 ślāghyas tv eṣa mah"|ātm" âikaḥ par'|ârtha|prāṇa|dāyinā
«mam' êti» moh'|âika|vaśaṃ yena viśvam adhaḥ|kṛtam.›
iti taṃ cintayantaṃ ca Garuḍaṃ pāpa|śuddhaye
vahniṃ vivikṣuṃ Jīmūtavāhano 'tha jagāda saḥ.
‹pakṣ'|îndra, kiṃ viṣaṇṇo 'si? satyaṃ pāpād bibheṣi cet
tad idānīṃ na bhūyas te bhakṣyā h' îme bhujaṃgamāḥ.
kāryaś c' ânuśayas teṣu pūrva|bhukteṣu bhogiṣu
eṣo 'tra hi pratīkāro vṛth" ânyac cintitaṃ tava.›
ity uktas tena sa prītas Tārkṣyo bhūt'|ânukampinā
‹tath" êti› pratipede tad|vākyaṃ tasya guror iva.
4.2.245 yayau c' âmṛtam ānetuṃ nākāj jīvayituṃ javāt
kṣat'|âṅgaṃ tatra taṃ c' ânyān asthi|śeṣān ahīn api.

'I am a snake-man. You must eat and finish what you have started, for once they have started them, the bold do not abandon things unfinished.' While Jimúta·váhana was 4.2.235
replying thus Shankha·chuda arrived there and said from a distance, 'Don't! Don't, Gáruda! He is not a snake-man, for I am your snake-man, so let him go! Oh, alas! What is this mistake that you have suddenly made?'

When he heard this, the king of the birds was extremely disturbed and Jimúta·váhana was depressed because he had not achieved what he wanted. Then when, in the course of his conversation with the sorrowful sorcerer king, he found out that he had eaten him in ignorance, Gáruda was very distressed. 'Oh, alas! I am cruel and have committed a sin! But those who go *by the higher paths : the wrong way* incur sin easily. Moreover, this noble and singular fellow is 4.2.240
to be praised: by giving up his life to help someone else, he has put to shame the entire world, which is in the sway of nothing but the delusion that things are "mine".'

Then, while Gáruda was thinking this and wanting to enter the fire to purify himself of his sin, Jimúta·váhana said to him, 'King of the birds, why are you upset? If you are really afraid of sin, then you just have to stop eating these snake-men. And you must repent for the snake-men you have already eaten. That is how you can remedy this matter. There is no point in your worrying about anything else.'

When Gáruda was told this by Jimúta·váhana, who was compassionate towards living beings, he agreed to what he
had said as if it were the words of his guru. He quickly went 4.2.245
to fetch from the sky the nectar of immortality to heal his

tataś ca sākṣād āgatya devyā sikto 'mṛtena saḥ
Jīmūtavāhano Gauryā tad|bhāryā|bhakti|tuṣṭayā.
ten' âdhikatar'|ôdbhūta|kāntīny aṅgāni jajñire
tasya s'|ānanda|gīr|vāṇa|dundubhi|dhvanibhiḥ saha.
svasth'|ôtthite tatas tasminn ānīya Garuḍo 'pi tat
kṛtsne velā|taṭe 'py atra vavarṣ' âmṛtam ambarāt.
tena sarve samuttasthur jīvantas tatra pannagāḥ
babhau tac ca tadā bhūri|bhujaṃga|kula|saṃkulam.
4.2.250 velā|vanaṃ vinirmukta|Vainateya|bhayaṃ tataḥ
Pātālam iva Jīmūtavāhan'|ālokan'|āgatam.

tato '|kṣayeṇa dehena yaśasā ca virājitam
buddhv" âbhyanandat taṃ bandhu|jano Jīmūtavāhanam.
nananda tasya bhāryā ca sa|jñātiḥ pitarau tathā
ko na prahṛṣyed duḥkhena sukhatva|parivartinā.
visṛṣṭas tena ca yayau Śaṅkhacūḍo rasātalam
svacchandam a|visṛṣṭaṃ ca lokāṃs trīn api tad|yaśaḥ.
tataḥ prīti|prahv'|âmara|nikaram āgatya Garuḍaṃ praṇemus
taṃ vidyā|dhara|tilakam abhyetya sa|bhayāḥ
sva|dāyādāḥ sarve hima|giri|sut"|ânugraha|vaśān Mataṅg'|
ākhy'|ādyā ye suciram abhajann asya vikṛtim.

injured body there and to restore to life the other snake-men, whose only remains were their bones. Then the goddess Párvati, having been pleased by Jimúta·váhana's wife's devotion, appeared there in person and sprinkled the nectar of immortality on him. As a result, to the accompaniment of drumbeats from the blissful gods, his body reappeared and was even more beautiful than before. Then when he had stood up, healed, Gáruda fetched the nectar of immortality from heaven and rained it down along the entire shore of
the ocean there, with the result that all the snake-men there 4.2.250
stood up, alive, and then the forest on the shore, crowded with the many families of snake people and freed from the fear of Gáruda, made it seem as if Patála had come to look at Jimúta·váhana.

Then, having discovered that it was Jimúta·váhana shining forth with his indestructible body and fame, his kinsmen welcomed him. And his wife, together with her relatives, and his parents too, rejoiced. Who would not rejoice at sorrow turning into happiness? And, sent forth by him, Shankha·chuda went to the underworld, while his fame, which had not been sent forth, spread of its own accord throughout the three worlds. Then, because of the grace of the daughter of the snowy mountains, all his relations, Matánga and so forth, who for so long had moved against him, came to Gáruda, to whom the ranks of the gods were affectionately bowing, before going up to the crowning glory of the sorcerers and fearfully making obeisance.

4.2.255 tair eva c' ârthyamānaḥ su|kṛtī Jīmūtavāhanaḥ sa tataḥ
Malay'|âcalād agacchan nija|nilayaṃ tuhina|śaila|taṭam.
tatra pitṛbhyāṃ sahito Mittrāvasunā ca Malayavatyā ca
dhīraś cirāya bubhuje vidyā|dhara|cakra|varti|padam.
evaṃ sakala|jagat|traya|hṛdaya|camatkāra|kāri|caritānām
svayam anudhāvanti sadā kalyāṇa|paramparāḥ padavīm.»

ity ākarṇya kathāṃ kila devī Yaugandharāyaṇasya mukhāt
mumude Vāsavadattā garbha|bhar'|ôdāra|dohadinī.
tad|anu tad|anuṣaṅga|prāptayā prīti|bhājām
an|avarata|nideśa|pratyayād devatānām
nija|pati|nikaṭa|sthā bhāvi|vidyā|dhar'|êndra|
sva|tanaya|kathayā taṃ vāsaraṃ sā nināya.

iti mahā|kavi|śrī|Somadeva|bhaṭṭa|viracite Kathāsaritsāgare
Naravāhanadatta|janana|lambake dvitīyas taraṅgaḥ.

3

4.3.1 TATO VĀSAVADATTĀ sā Vatsa|rājaṃ samīpa|gam
vijane sacivair yuktam anyedyur idam abravīt.
«yataḥ prabhṛti garbho 'yam, ārya|putra, dhṛto mayā
tataḥ prabhṛti tad|rakṣā tīvrā māṃ hṛdi bādhate.
adya tac|cintayā c' âhaṃ suptā niśi kathaṃ|cana
jāne dṛṣṭavatī kaṃ|cit svapne puruṣam āgatam.
bhasm'|āṅga|rāga|sitayā śekharī|kṛta|candrayā
piśaṅga|jaṭayā mūrtyā śobhitaṃ śūla|hastayā.

And on being asked by them, the kindly Jimúta·váhana 4.2.255
then went from mount Málaya to his own home, a slope in the Himálaya. There, together with his parents and Mittra·vasu and Málayavati, the steadfast fellow enjoyed for a long time the position of emperor of the sorcerers. In this way a succession of fortunate events always follows of its own accord the footsteps of those whose deeds earn the admiration of the hearts of the entire three worlds."

Apparently when Queen Vásava·datta, whom the burden of pregnancy was making experience severe cravings, heard this story from the mouth of Yaugándharáyana, she was delighted. After that, because of her unceasing confidence in the instructions of the friendly gods, she spent that day at her husband's side listening to stories, inspired by him, of her son, the future king of the sorcerers.

Thus ends the second wave in the Attainment called Nara·váhana·datta's birth in the Ocean of the Rivers of Story composed by the glorious and learned great poet Soma·deva.

3

THEN ON THE next day Vásava·datta went to the king of 4.3.1
Vatsa, who was nearby in a quiet spot with his ministers, and said the following. "My noble husband, ever since I have been pregnant with this child, the difficulties of looking after it have been afflicting my heart. And in my worry about it, just now, having with difficulty got to sleep last night, I'm sure I saw some man come in a dream. With his body white from the ash smeared thereon, the moon as his crest-jewel, his tawny matted locks, and a spear in his hand,
his appearance made him resplendent. And he came up to 4.3.5

4.3.5 sa ca mām abhyupety' âiva s'|ânukampa iv' âvadat
‹putri, garbha|kṛte cintā na kāryā kā|cana tvayā.
ahaṃ tav' âinaṃ rakṣāmi datto hy eṣa may" âiva te
kiṃ|c' ânyac chṛṇu vacmy eva tava pratyaya|kāraṇam.
śvaḥ k" âpi nārī vijñapti|hetor yuṣmān upaiṣyati
avaṣṭabhy' âiva s'|ākṣepam ākarṣantī nijaṃ patim
pañcabhis tanayair yuktā bahu|bandhu|jan'|āvṛtā*
sā ca duścāriṇī yoṣit sva|bāndhava|balāt patim
taṃ ghātayitum icchantī sarvaṃ mithyā bravīti tat.
tvaṃ c' âtra, putri, Vats'|ēśaṃ pūrvaṃ vijñāpayes tathā
tasyāḥ sakāśāt sa yathā sādhur mucyeta ku|striyaḥ.›
4.3.10 ity ādiśya gate tasminn antar|dhānaṃ mah"|ātmani
prabuddhā sahas" âiv' âhaṃ vibhātā ca vibhāvarī.»
evam ukte tayā devyā Śarv'|ânugraha|vādinaḥ
tatr' āsan vismitāḥ sarve saṃvād'|âpekṣi|mānasāḥ.
tasminn eva kṣaṇe c' âtra praviśy' ārt'|ânukampinam
Vatsa|rājaṃ pratīhāra|mukhyo 'kasmād vyajijñapat.
«āgatā, deva, vijñaptyai k" âpi strī bāndhavair vṛtā
pañca|putrān gṛhītvā svam ākṣipya vivaśaṃ patim.»
tac chrutvā nṛpatir devī|svapna|saṃvāda|vismitaḥ
«praveśyatām ih' âiv' êti» pratīhāraṃ tam ādiśat.
4.3.15 svapna|satyatva|saṃjāta|sat|putra|prāpti|niścayaḥ
devī Vāsavadatt" âpi sā saṃprāpa parāṃ mudam.
atha dvār'|ônmukhaiḥ sarvair vīkṣyamāṇā sa|kautukam
pratīhār'|ājñayā yoṣid bhartṛ|yuktā viveśa sā.

me and straightaway said, as if he were feeling compassion, 'My girl, you must not in any way worry about your unborn child. I shall look after him for you, because it was I who gave him to you. Furthermore, listen to something else I shall tell you to make you believe me. Tomorrow a certain lady will come to make a request to you, dragging her captive husband and abusing him, in the company of her five sons and surrounded by several friends and relatives. That wicked woman, with the help of her relatives, will be wanting to have her husband killed and everything she says will be lies. My girl, you should first tell the king of Vatsa about this, so that the evil woman's virtuous husband might be freed from her presence.'

After that noble soul had given these instructions and 4.3.10
disappeared, I suddenly woke up and morning had dawned."

When the queen said this, everyone there was astonished and spoke of Shiva's grace, their minds anticipating what she had said would happen. At that very moment the head gatekeeper suddenly came in there and said to the king of Vatsa, who was sympathetic to those in trouble, "Your highness, a certain woman, surrounded by relatives, has come to make a request. She has five sons with her and is abusing her helpless husband."

When he heard this, the king, astonished that the queen's dream had come true, told the gatekeeper to have her
brought straight in. The truthfulness of her dream had con- 4.3.15
vinced him that they would get a virtuous son. Queen Vásava·datta, meanwhile, was supremely happy. Then, with everyone straining their necks towards the door, looking at her with curiosity, the woman entered at the gatekeeper's

praviśy' āśrita|dainyā ca yathā|krama|kṛt'|ānatiḥ
atha saṃsadi rājānaṃ sa|devīkaṃ vyajijñapat.
«ayaṃ niraparādhāyā mama bhartā bhavann api
na prayacchaty a|nāthāyā bhojan'|ācchādan'|ādikam.»

ity uktavatyāṃ tasyāṃ ca sa tad|bhartā vyajijñapat
«deva, mithyā vadaty eṣā sa|bandhur mad|vadh'|âiṣiṇī.
4.3.20 ā vatsar'|ântaṃ sarvaṃ hi dattam asyā may" âgrataḥ
etad|bandhava ev' ânye taṭa|sthā me 'tra sākṣiṇaḥ.»

evaṃ vijñāpitas tena rājā svayam abhāṣata
«devī|svapne kṛtaṃ sākṣyaṃ deven' âiv' âtra śūlinā.
tat kiṃ sākṣibhir eṣ" âiva nigrāhyā strī sa|bandhavā»

iti rājñ" ôdite 'vādīd dhīmān Yaugandharāyaṇaḥ.
«tath" âpi sākṣi|vacanāt kāryaṃ, deva, yath"|ôcitam
loko hy etad a|jānāno na pratīyāt kathaṃ|cana.»

tac chrutvā sākṣiṇo rājñā «tath" êty» ānāyya tat|kṣaṇam
pṛṣṭāḥ śaśaṃsus te c' âtra tāṃ mithyā|vādinīṃ striyam.
4.3.25 tataḥ prakhyāta|sad|bhartṛ|drohām etāṃ sa|bāndhavām
sa|putrāṃ ca sa Vats'|ēśaḥ sva|deśān niravāsayat.
visasarja ca taṃ sādhuṃ tad|bhartāraṃ day"|ârdra|dhīḥ
vivāh'|ântara|paryāptaṃ vitīrya vipulaṃ vasu.
«pumāṃsam ākulaṃ krūrā patitaṃ durdaś"|âvaṭe
jīvantam eva kuṣṇāti kāk" îva ku|kuṭumbinī.

command, accompanied by her husband. Next, after coming in and behaving as if upset, she paid her respects in the correct order and then told the king and queen in the assembly, "I have done nothing wrong, yet this man, even though he is my husband, doesn't provide me, helpless as I am, with food, clothes and so forth."

When she had said this, her husband made a plea: "Your highness, she is lying. She and her relatives want me to be executed. I have given her everything to last the year ahead. 4.3.20
She has other relatives who are fair and will bear witness on this matter for me."

After being told this, the king himself said, "The queen has had a dream in which none other than Shiva has born witness on this matter. So there is no need of witnesses—this woman and her relatives are to be punished."

When the king said this, the wise Yaugándharáyana replied, "That may be so, your highness, but it should be done correctly, according to the evidence of witnesses, for the people do not know about the dream and will never have confidence in the decision."

When he heard this, the king agreed and immediately had the witnesses brought in. On being questioned, they said that the woman was telling lies about the matter at hand. Then, her treachery towards her virtuous husband 4.3.25
having been made public, the king of Vatsa banished the woman, her relatives and her sons from his country. And, his mind made tender by pity, he dismissed that virtuous husband of hers, having given him a large fortune which was enough for him to get married again. "An evil wife is as cruel as a she-crow and tears apart her dismayed husband

snigdhā kulīnā mahatī gṛhiṇī tāpa|hāriṇī
taru|cchāy" êva mārga|sthā puṇyaiḥ kasy' âpi jāyate.»

iti c' âitat|prasaṅgena vadantaṃ taṃ mahī|patim
Vasantakaḥ sthitaḥ pārśve kathā|paṭur avocata.

4.3.30 «kiṃ ca, deva, virodho vā sneho v" âp' îha dehinām
prāg|janma|vāsan"|âbhyāsa|vaśāt prāyeṇa jāyate.
tathā ca śrūyatām atra kath" êyaṃ varṇyate mayā

āsīd Vikramacaṇḍ'|ākhyo Vārāṇasyāṃ mahīpatiḥ.
tasy' âbhūd vallabho bhṛtyo nāmnā Siṃhaparākramaḥ
yo raṇeṣv iva sarveṣu dyūteṣv apy a|samo jayī.
tasy' âbhavac ca vikṛtā vapuṣ' îv' āśaye 'py alam
khyātā Kalahakār" îti nāmn" ânvarthena gehinī.
sa tasyāḥ satataṃ bhūri rājato dyūtatas tathā
prāpya prāpya dhanaṃ dhīraḥ sarvam eva samarpayat.
4.3.35 sā tu tasya samutpanna|putra|traya|yutā śaṭhā
tath" âpi kṣaṇam apy ekaṃ na tasthau kalahaṃ vinā.
‹bahiḥ pibasi bhuṅkṣe ca n' âiva kiṃ|cid dadāsi naḥ›
ity āraṭantī sa|sutā sā taṃ nityam atāpayat.
prasādyamān" âpy āhāra|pāna|vastrair ahar|niśam
durantā bhoga|tṛṣṇ" êva bhṛśaṃ jajvāla tasya sā.

alive when he falls into the pit of disaster. Through meritorious actions, any man can have an affectionate, noble wife from a respectable family who removes the heat of affliction like the shade of a roadside tree."

As the king was saying these words in the context of the matter in hand, the skilled storyteller Vasántaka, who was at his side, said, "What's more, your highness, hostility, and 4.3.30
affection too, usually arise in living beings in this world as a result of the repeated effect of impressions from their past lives. Just listen to this story on the subject which I shall now tell.

There was a king in Varánasi called Víkrama·chanda. He had a dear servant called Sinha·parákrama who was as incomparably victorious in all his gambling bouts as he was in battles. He had a wife who was as utterly unpleasant in her appearance as she was in her disposition. She was known by the fitting name of Kálaha·kari, "quarrel-maker." Over and over again that brave man would win large amounts of money from the king through gambling and give it all to her. That wicked wife of his, together with the three sons 4.3.35
she had produced, would still not go a single moment without arguing with him. 'You drink and eat outside and you don't give us anything.' Shouting this, she and her sons continually harassed him. Even though she was appeased by him day and night with food, drink and clothes, that woman was as violently ablaze as if she were the unquenchable thirst for pleasure.

tataḥ krameṇa tan|manyu|
khinnas tyaktv" âiva tad|gṛham
sa Vindhyavāsinīṃ draṣṭum
agāt Siṃhaparākramaḥ.
sā taṃ svapne nirāhāra|sthitaṃ devī samādiśat
‹uttiṣṭha, putra, tām eva gaccha Vārāṇasīṃ purīm.
4.3.40 tatra sarva|mahān eko yo 'sti nyagrodha|pādapaḥ
tan|mūlāt khanyamānāt tvaṃ svairaṃ nidhim avāpsyasi.
tan|madhyāl lapsyase c' âikaṃ nabhaḥ|khaṇḍam iva cyutam
pātraṃ Garuḍa|māṇikya|mayaṃ nistriṃśa|nirmalam.
tatr' ârpit'|êkṣaṇo drakṣyasy antaḥ pratimitām iva
sarvasya jantoḥ prāg|jātiṃ yā syāj jijñāsitā tava.
ten' âiva buddhvā bhāryāyāḥ pūrva|jātiṃ tath" ātmanaḥ
avāpt'|ârthaḥ sukhī tatra gata|khedo nivatsyasi.›
evam uktaś ca devyā† sa prabuddhaḥ kṛta|pāraṇaḥ
Vārāṇasīṃ prati prāyāt prātaḥ Siṃhaparākramaḥ.
4.3.45 gatvā ca tāṃ purīṃ prāpya tasmān nyagrodha|mūlataḥ
lebhe nidhānaṃ tan|madhyāt pātraṃ maṇi|mayaṃ mahat.
apaśyac c' âtra jijñāsuḥ
pātre pūrvatra janmani
ghorām ṛkṣīṃ† sva|bhāryāṃ tām
ātmānaṃ ca mṛg'|âdhipam.
pūrva|jāti|mahā|vaira|
vāsanā|niścalaṃ tataḥ
buddhvā bhāry"|ātmanor dveṣaṃ
śoka|mohau mumoca saḥ.
atha bahvīḥ parijñātās tatra pātra|prabhāvataḥ

In time, Sinha·parákrama, exhausted by her hatred, left the house and went directly to have darshan of Vindhya·vásini. While he was fasting, that goddess gave him an order in a dream. 'Arise, my son. Go directly to the city of Varánasi. There is a banyan tree there, the biggest of all, by 4.3.40
digging at the foot of which you shall have no difficulty in obtaining a treasure. And in that treasure you shall find, like a fallen fragment of heaven, an emerald vessel as shiny as a sword. If you look inside it you shall see, seemingly reflected within, the past lives of every person whose past life you want to know. As soon as you have used it to find out about the previous incarnations of you and your wife, you shall get what you want and live there happily, free from sorrow.'

After being told this by the goddess, Sinha·parákrama woke up, broke his fast and set forth for Varánasi that morning.

He went to the city, obtained the treasure from the foot 4.3.45
of the banyan tree, and found in it a huge vessel made of jewels. Wanting to discover the truth, he looked inside and saw that in a past life his wife had been a terrifying she-bear and he a lion. Having discovered from it that the hatred between his wife and him was inevitable due to the impression of their great enmity in a previous life, he abandoned his sorrow and delusion. Then, after rejecting several girls who, using the power of the vessel, he had discovered were of different races to him in their past lives, Sinha·parákrama found one who, having been a lioness in her past life, was his equal, and he took her as his second wife, with the name

prāg|janma|bhinna|jātīyāḥ parihṛty' âiva kanyakāḥ.
tulyāṃ janm'|ântare siṃhīṃ pariṇinye vicintya saḥ
bhāryāṃ divtīyāṃ Siṃhaśrī|nāmnīṃ Siṃhaparākramaḥ.
4.3.50 kṛtvā Kalahakārīṃ ca tāṃ sa grām'|âika|bhāginīm†
nidhāna|prāpti|sukhitas tasthau nava|vadhū|sakhaḥ.
ittham dār"|ādayo 'p' îha bhavanti bhuvane nṛṇām
prāk|saṃskāra|vaś'|āyāta|vaira|snehā, mahī|pate.»
ity ākarṇya kathāṃ citrāṃ Vatsa|rājo Vasantakāt
bhṛśaṃ tutoṣa sahito devyā Vāsavadattayā.
evaṃ dineṣu gacchatsu rājñas tasya divā|niśam
a|tṛptasya lasad|garbha|devī|vaktr'|êndu|darśane.
mantriṇām udapadyanta sarveṣāṃ śubha|lakṣaṇāḥ
krameṇa tanayās tatra bhāvi|kalyāṇa|sūcakāḥ.
4.3.55 prathamaṃ mantri|mukhyasya jāyate sma kil' ātma|jaḥ
Yaugandharāyaṇasy' âiva Marubhūtir iti śrutaḥ.
tato Rumaṇvato jajñe suto Hariśikh'|âbhidhaḥ
Vasantakasy' âpy utpede tanayo 'tha Tapantakaḥ.
tato Nityodit'|ākhyasya pratīhār'|âdhikāriṇaḥ
Ityak'|âpara|saṃjñasya putro 'jāyata Gomukhaḥ.
«Vatsa|rāja|sutasy' êha bhāvinaś cakra|vartinaḥ
mantriṇo 'mī bhaviṣyanti vairi|vaṃś'|âvamardinaḥ.»
iti teṣu ca jāteṣu vartamāne mah"|ôtsave
tatr' â|śarīrā nabhaso niḥsasāra sarasvatī.
4.3.60 divaseṣv atha yāteṣu Vatsa|rājasya tasya sā
devī Vāsavadatt" âbhūd āsanna|prasav'|ôdayā.
adhyāsta sā ca tac citraṃ putriṇībhiḥ pariṣkṛtam
jāta|vāsa|gṛhaṃ s'|ârka|śamī|gupta|gavākṣakam.
ratna|dīpa|prabhā|saṅga|maṅgalair vividh'|āyudhaiḥ
garbha|rakṣā|kṣamaṃ tejo jvalayadbhir iv' āvṛtam.

Sinha·shri. He gave Kálaha·kari a village as her only posses- 4.3.50
sion and, happy now that he had acquired the treasure, he
lived with his new wife. Thus, great king, here in the world
of men, the affection and enmity of even people such as
wives are determined by prior conditioning."

On hearing this amazing story from Vasántaka, the king
of Vatsa, together with Queen Vásava·datta, was very pleased.

While days passed like this for the king, who could not
get enough of looking constantly at the resplendent moon-
face of his pregnant queen, one by one auspiciously marked
sons were born to all the ministers there, indicators of future
good fortune. First, it seems, there was born to the chief 4.3.55
minister, Yaugándharáyana, a son who was named Maru·
bhuti. Then a son called Hari·shikha was born to Rumánvat, after which Tapántaka was born to Vasántaka. Then to
the head chamberlain, who was called Nityódita (and had
another name, Ítyaka), was born his son Go·mukha. "These
boys shall be the ministers of the son of the king of Vatsa,
the future emperor here, and shall destroy the dynasties of
his enemies." When they had been born and a great celebration was being held, a disembodied divine voice said this
from the sky there.

The days passed and then the time drew near for Queen 4.3.60
Vásava·datta to bring good fortune to the king of Vatsa by
giving birth. She installed herself in a decorated birthing
chamber which had been prepared by ladies who had sons,
and its windows were concealed by *arka* and *shami* trees.
It was filled with various weapons made auspicious by the
touch of the light from jewel-fueled lamps, and it was as
if they were shining forth a light capable of protecting the

mantribhis tantrit'|ân|eka|mantra|tantr'|ādi|rakṣitam
jātaṃ mātṛ|gaṇasy' êva durgaṃ durita|dur|jayam.
tatr' âsūta ca sā kāle kumāraṃ kānta|darśanam
dyaur indum iva nirgacchad|acch'|âmṛta|maya|dyutim.
4.3.65 yena jātena na paraṃ mandiraṃ tat|prakāśitam
yāvadd hṛdayam apy asyā mātur niḥśoka|tāmasam.

tataḥ pramode prasaraty atr' āntaḥ|pura|vāsinām
Vats'|ēśaḥ suta|janm' aitac chuśrāv' âbhy'|ântarāj janāt.
tasmai sa rājyam api yat|prītaḥ priya|nivedine
na dadau tad|anaucitya|bhayena na tu tṛṣṇayā.
etya c' ântaḥ|puraṃ sadyo baddh'|âutsukyena cetasā
cirāt phalita|saṃkalpaḥ sa dadarśa sutaṃ nṛpaḥ.
rakt'|āyat'|ādhara|dalaṃ cal'|ôrṇā|cāru|*kesaram*
mukhaṃ dadhānaṃ sāmrājya|Lakṣmī|līl"|âmbuj'|ôpamam.
4.3.70 prāg ev' ânya|nṛpa|śrībhir bhity" êva nija|lāñchanaiḥ
ujjhitair aṅkitaṃ mṛdvoḥ padayoś chattra|cāmaraiḥ.

tato harṣa|bhar'|āpūra|pīḍan'|ôtphullayā dṛśā
s'|āsrayā sravat' îv' âsmin suta|snehaṃ mahī|patau.
nandatsv api ca Yaugandharāyaṇ'|ādiṣu mantriṣu
gaganād uccacār' âivaṃ kāle tasmin sarasvatī.
«Kāma|dev'|âvatāro 'yaṃ, rājan, jātas tav' ātma|jaḥ
Naravāhanadattaṃ ca jānīhy enam ih' ākhyayā.

unborn child. Guarded by sorcerers casting multiple spells, diagrams and so forth, it had become like the fortress of all the divine mothers, impossible for misfortune to conquer. At an auspicious moment she gave birth to a prince who was lovely to behold, and it was like the sky producing a moon which emits a pure light consisting of the nectar of immortality. By his birth not only was the palace illumi- 4.3.65
nated, but also the heart of his mother, which was freed from the darkness of sorrow.

Then, as the delight of the inhabitants of the harem at the news was spreading forth, the king of Vatsa heard about the birth of his son from the people within. And it was because he was worried that it would be inappropriate, not because of greed that he did not give his kingdom to the one who had delighted him by announcing the good news. With his mind full of longing, the king went straight to the women's apartments and, his wish at last fulfilled, beheld his son. With his lower lip a long red petal and his *hair : filaments* as lovely as wavy wool, he bore a face like the play-lotus of the goddess of the prosperity of empire. On his soft feet he 4.3.70
was marked with a parasol and a yak's tail fly whisk, as if in fear the fortune goddesses of other kings had already cast off their own insignia.

Then, while the king seemed to be pouring forth love for his son through his tearful eyes, which were bulging from the pressure of his great upwelling joy, and while Yaugándharáyana and the other ministers were rejoicing, at that moment a divine voice from the sky said the following. "O king, this son of yours that has been born is an incarnation

anena bhavitavyaṃ ca divyaṃ kalpam atandriṇā
sarva|vidyā|dhar'|êndrāṇām a|cirāc cakra|vartinā.»
4.3.75 ity uktvā virataṃ vācā tat|kṣaṇaṃ nabhasaḥ kramāt
puṣpa|varṣair nipatitaṃ prasṛtaṃ dundubhi|svanaiḥ.
tataḥ sura|kṛt'|ārambha|janit'|âbhyadhik'|ādaram
sa rājā sutarāṃ hṛṣṭaś cakāra param utsavam.
babhramus tūrya|ninadā nabhasto mandir'|ôdgatāḥ
vidyā|dharebhyaḥ sarvebhyo rāja|janm' êva śaṃsitum.
saudh'|âgreṣv anil'|ôddhūtāḥ śoṇa|rāgāḥ sva|kāntibhiḥ
patākā api sindūram anyonyam akirann iva.
bhuvi s'|âṅga|Smar'|ôtpatti|toṣād iva sur'|âṅganāḥ
samāgatāḥ pratipadaṃ nanṛtur vāra|yoṣitaḥ.
4.3.80 adṛśyata ca sarvā sā samāna|vibhavā purī
rājño baddh'|ôtsavāt prāptair nava|vastra|vibhūṣaṇaiḥ.
tadā hy arthān nṛpe tasmin varṣaty arthy|anujīviṣu
koṣād ṛte na tatratyo dadhau kaś|cana riktatām.
maṅgalya|pūrvāḥ sv'|ācāra|dakṣiṇā nartit'|âparāḥ
sat|prābhṛt'|ôttarās tais taiḥ su|rakṣibhir adhiṣṭhitāḥ
prasṛt'|ātodya|nirhrādāḥ sākṣād diśa iv' âkhilāḥ
samantād āyayuś c' âtra sāmant'|ântaḥ|pur'|âṅganāḥ.
ceṣṭā nṛtta|mayī tatra pūrṇa|pātra|mayaṃ vacaḥ
vyavahāro mahā|tyāga|mayas tūrya|mayo dhvaniḥ.
4.3.85 cīna|piṣṭa|mayo lokaś cāraṇ'|âika|mayī ca bhūḥ
ānanda|mayyāṃ sarvasyām api tasyām abhūt puri.

of the god of love. Know him now to be called Nara·váhana·datta. Before long he shall reign unwearied for an eon of the gods as the emperor of all the sorcerer kings."

After saying this the voice fell quiet and at that moment 4.3.75
a rain of flowers fell from the sky, followed by the sounds of drums coming forth. Then the king, who was utterly overjoyed, held a great celebration, which was made even more momentous by the gods having started it. As if announcing the birth of a king to all the sorcerers, the sound of musical instruments rang out from the palace and roamed about the sky. Even the blood-red banners fluttering in the wind on the tops of the mansions seemed, with their brilliant color, to be throwing vermilion over one another. As if the ladies of heaven had arrived on earth out of joy at the god of love being born with a body, courtesans were
dancing everywhere. And with new clothes and ornaments 4.3.80
received from the celebrating king, the whole city looked equally majestic.

Then, with the king raining down wealth on his needy subjects, nothing and no one there was empty, apart from the treasury. And from all sides women from the harems of the king's vassals arrived there, preceded by auspicious prayers, well-versed in etiquette, inciting other girls to dance, bearing fine gifts, attended by various excellent guards, and accompanied by the sound of musical instruments ringing forth, and it was as if all the directions had come in person.* All action there was dance, all words expressions of gratitude, all commerce was great generosity, all sound that of
musical instruments, all the people were covered in red and 4.3.85
the ground was strewn with bards everywhere in that city

evaṃ mah"|ôtsavas tatra bhūri|vāsara|vardhitaḥ
nivartate sma sa samaṃ pūrṇaiḥ paura|manorathaiḥ.

so 'pi vrajatsu divaseṣv atha rāja|putro
vṛddhiṃ śiśuḥ pratipad|indur iv' ājagāma
pitrā yathā|vidhi|nivedita|divya|vāṇī|
nirdiṣṭa|pūrva|Naravāhanadatta|nāmnā.
yāni sphuran|masṛṇa|mugdha|nakha|prabhāṇi
dvi|trāṇi yāni ca khacad|daśan'|âṅkurāṇi
tāni skhalanti dadato vadataś ca tasya
dṛṣṭvā niśamya ca padāni pitā tutoṣa.
atha tasmai mantri|varāḥ
sva|sutān ānīya rāja|putrāya
śiśave śiśūn mahī|pati|
hṛday'|ānandān samarpayām āsuḥ.

4.3.90 Yaugandharāyaṇaḥ prāṅ
Marubhūtiṃ Hariśikhaṃ Rumaṇvāṃś ca
Gomukham Ityaka|nāmā
Tapantak'|ākhyaṃ Vasantakaś ca sutam.
Śāntikaro 'pi purodhā
bhrātṛ|sutaṃ Śāntisomam aparaṃ ca
Vaiśvānaram arpitavān
Piṅgalikā|putrakau yama|jau.

tasmin kṣaṇe ca nabhaso nipapāta divyā
nāndī|nināda|subhagā sura|puṣpa|vṛṣṭiḥ
rājā nananda ca tadā mahiṣī|sametaḥ
sat|kṛtya tatra saciv'|ātmaja|maṇḍalaṃ tat.
bālye 'pi tair abhimatair atha mantri|putraiḥ
ṣaḍbhis tad|eka|nirataiś ca sa rāja|putraḥ
yuktaḥ sad" âiva Naravāhanadatta āsīd
yukto guṇair iva mah"|ôdaya|hetu|bhūtaiḥ.

where all was bliss. In this way the great celebrations increased for several days and they came to an end when the desires of the citizens were fulfilled.

And as the days progressed, the infant prince gradually grew up, like the new moon, and his father duly gave him the name Nara·váhana·datta, which the divine voice had earlier announced. When his father saw him take two or three faltering steps, showing his smooth, lovely toenails, and heard a few faltering words, in which two or three bud-like teeth were displayed, he was overjoyed. Then his excellent ministers brought their infant sons to the infant prince, and offered them as delights for the heart of the king. First 4.3.90
Yaugándharáyana offered Maru·bhuti, then Rumánvat offered Hari·shikha, then Ítyaka offered Go·mukha and then Vasántaka offered his son, who was called Tapántaka. And the priest Shanti·kara offered his brother's sons Shanti·soma and Vaishvánara, the twin sons of Píngalika.

And at that moment there fell from the sky a divine rain of heavenly flowers, made more lovely by sounds of celebration, and then the king celebrated together with his queens, having honored there all his ministers' sons. After that prince Nara·váhana·datta, even in childhood, was always accompanied by those six cherished ministers' sons, who were devoted to him alone, as if they were the qualities that are the cause of great prosperity.* While looking devotedly at his son, a smile on the boy's lotus face as he playfully cooed his sweet, indistinct and charming whims while moving from one to another of the laps of the kings,

taṃ ca krīḍā|kalita|lalit'|â|vyakta|narm'|âbhilāṣaṃ
yāntaṃ prīti|pravaṇa|manasām aṅkato 'ṅkaṃ nṛpāṇām
putraṃ smer'|ânana|sarasi|jaṃ s'|ādaraṃ paśyatas te
baddhv" ānandāḥ kim api divasā Vatsa|rājasya jagmuḥ.

iti mahā|kavi|śrī|Somadeva|bhaṭṭa|viracite Kathāsaritsāgare Naravāhanadatta|janana|lambake tṛtīyas taraṅgaḥ samāptaś c' âyaṃ Naravāhanadatta|janana|lambakaś caturthaḥ.

their minds brimful of affection, the king of Vatsa's days passed yet more blissfully.

Thus ends the third wave in the Attainment called Nara·váhana·datta's birth in the Ocean of the Rivers of Story composed by the glorious and learned great poet Soma·deva and this fourth Attainment, Nara·váhana·datta's birth, is complete.

ATTAINMENT V

FOUR GIRLS

MAHĀ|KAVI|ŚRĪ|SOMADEVA|bhaṭṭa|viracitaḥ Kathāsaritsāgaraḥ. caturdārikā nāma pañcamo lambakaḥ.

idaṃ guru|gir'|îndra|jā|
praṇaya|Mandar'|ândolanāt
purā kila kath"|âmṛtaṃ
Hara|mukh'|âmbudher udgatam
prasahya sarayanti ye
vigata|vighna|labdh'|arddhayo
dhuraṃ dadhati vaibudhīṃ
bhuvi Bhava|prasādena te.

The "Ocean of the Rivers of Story," composed by the glorious and learned great poet Soma·deva. The fifth Attainment, called Four Girls.

This nectar of story is said to have arisen long ago from the ocean of Hara's mouth as a result of its being churned by mount Mándara in the form of the insistent entreaties of the daughter of the lord of the mountains. Those who make it flow freely lose their troubles and gain riches, and through Bhava's grace it puts them on a divine pedestal on earth.

I

5.1.1 MADA|GHŪRṆITA|vaktr'|ôtthaiḥ
sindūraiś churayan mahīm
Herambaḥ pātu vo vighnān
sva|tejobhir dahann iva.

evaṃ sa devī|sahitas tasthau Vats'|ēśvaras tadā
Naravāhanadattaṃ tam eka|putraṃ vivardhayan.
tad|rakṣā|kātaraṃ taṃ ca dṛṣṭvā rājānam ekadā
Yaugandharāyaṇo mantrī vijana|sthitam abravīt.
«rājan, na rāja|putrasya kṛte cint" âdhunā tvayā
Naravāhanadattasya vidhātavyā kadā|cana.
5.1.5 asau bhagavatā bhāvī bhargeṇa hi bhavad|gṛhe
sarva|vidyā|dhar'|âdhīśa|cakra|vartī vinirmitaḥ.
vidyā|prabhāvād etac ca buddhvā vidyā|dhar'|âdhipāḥ
gatāḥ pāp'|êcchavaḥ kṣobhaṃ hṛdayair asahiṣṇavaḥ.
tad viditvā ca devena rakṣ"|ârthaṃ śaśi|maulinā
etasya Stambhako nāma gaṇ'|êśaḥ sthāpito nijaḥ.
sa ca tiṣṭhaty a|lakṣyaḥ san rakṣann etaṃ sutaṃ tava
etac ca kṣipram abhetya Nārado me nyavedayat.»
iti tasmin vadaty eva mantriṇi vyoma|madhyataḥ
kirīṭī kuṇḍalī divyaḥ khaḍgī c' âvātarat pumān.
5.1.10 praṇataṃ kalpit'|ātithyaṃ kṣaṇād Vats'|ēśvaro 'tha tam
«kas tvaṃ? kim iha te kāryam ity?» apṛcchat sa|kautukam.
so 'py avādīd «ahaṃ martyo bhūtvā vidyā|dhar'|âdhipaḥ
saṃpannaḥ Śaktiveg'|ākhyaḥ prabhūtāś ca mam' ârayaḥ.
so 'haṃ prabhāvād vijñāya bhāvy asmac|cakra|vartinam
bhavatas tanayaṃ draṣṭum āgato 'smy, avanī|pate.»

1

May Ganésha, sprinkling the earth with the vermilion 5.1.1
sent forth from his trunk as he whirls it around in
the exhilaration of rut, as if burning up obstacles with the
rays of his brilliance, protect you!

The king of Vatsa then lived like this with his queens,
bringing up their only son, Nara·váhana·datta. One day the
minister Yaugándharáyana having noticed that the king was
worried about protecting him, said to him when he was
alone, "Sire, now you need never worry about prince Nara·
váhana·datta, for he has been created in your house by the 5.1.5
blessed Shiva as the future emperor of all the sorcerer kings.
By means of their magical powers, the sorcerer kings are
aware of this. Unable to bear it in their hearts, they are troubled and want to make mischief. The god with the moon
as his crown has found out about this and has appointed
a *gana* chief called Stámbhaka to protect him. He is living
here unseen, protecting this son of yours. Nárada hurried
here and told me this."

At the very moment that the minister was saying this,
a divine man, wearing a crown and earrings and carrying
a sword came down to earth from the sky. After he had 5.1.10
bowed and been shown due hospitality, the king of Vatsa
straightaway eagerly asked him who he was and what he
had to do there.

He replied, "I used to be a man and have become a sorcerer king, with the name Shakti·vega. I have many enemies. I am here because through my powers I found out
that that your son is going to be our emperor, so I came to
see him, O king."

ity uktavantaṃ taṃ dṛṣṭa|bhaviṣyac|cakra|vartinam
prītaṃ Vats'|ēśvaro hṛṣṭaḥ punaḥ papraccha vismayāt.
«vidyā|dharatvaṃ prāpyeta kathaṃ kidṛg|vidhaṃ ca tat?
tvayā ca tat kathaṃ prāptam etat kathaya naḥ, sakhe.»
5.1.15 tac chrutvā vacanaṃ rājñaḥ sa tadā vinay'|ānataḥ
vidyā|dharaḥ Śaktivegas tam evaṃ pratyavocata.
«rājann, ih' âiva pūrve vā janmany ārādhya Śaṃkaram
vidyā|dhara|padaṃ dhīrā labhante tad|anugrahāt.
tac c' ân|eka|vidhaṃ vidyā|khaḍga|māl"|ādi|sādhanam
mayā ca tad yathā prāptaṃ kathayāmi tathā śṛṇu.»
evam uktvā sva|saṃbaddhāṃ Śaktivegaḥ sa saṃnidhau
devyā Vāsavadattāyāḥ kathām ākhyātavān imām.
«abhavad Vardhamān'|ākhye pure bhū|tala|bhūṣaṇe
nāmnā Paropakār" îti purā rājā paraṃ|tapaḥ.
5.1.20 tasy' ônnati|mataś c' âbhūn mahiṣī Kanakaprabhā
vidyud dhārā|dharasy' êva sā tu nirmukta|cāpalā.
tasyāṃ tasya ca kālena devyām ajani kanyakā
rūpa|darp'|ôpaśāntyai yā Lakṣmyā dhātr" êva nirmitā.
avardhata śanaiḥ sā ca loka|locana|candrikā
pitrā Kanakarekh" êti mātṛ|nāmnā kṛt" ātmajā.
ekadā yauvanasthāyāṃ tasyāṃ rājā sa tat|pitā
vijan'|ôpasthitāṃ devīṃ jagāda Kanakaprabhām.
‹vardhamānā sah' âiv' âitat|samān'|ôdvāha|cintayā
eṣā Kanakarekhā me hṛdayaṃ, devi, bādhate.
5.1.25 sthāna|prāpti|vihīnā hi gītivat kula|kanyakā

After he had said this and seen the future emperor, he was pleased and the delighted king of Vatsa, in his amazement, questioned him once again. "How does one become a sorcerer, and what is it like being one? And how did you become one? Tell us this, O friend."

When he heard these words from the king, the sorcerer 5.1.15
Shakti·vega then bowed humbly and answered him thus. "King, determined people become sorcerers through Shiva's grace, having propitiated him either in this life or an earlier one. And there are many types of sorcerer, signified by magical powers, swords, garlands and so forth. I shall tell you how I became one. Listen."

After saying this, in the presence of Queen Vásava·datta Shakti·vega told the following story about himself.

"Long ago there lived in a city called Vardhamána, which was an ornament to the world, a king called Paropakárin, who tormented his enemies. That lofty king had as his chief 5.1.20
wife Kánaka·prabha, Golden Hue, just as a rain cloud has lightning—but she was not fickle. And in time a daughter was born to him by her, and it was as if the creator had made her in order to put an end to Lakshmi's arrogance about her beauty. After her mother, the father gave his daughter, who was moonlight to the eyes of the world, the name Kánaka·rekha, and she gradually grew up.

One day when the girl had become a young woman, her father the king spoke to Queen Kánaka·prabha, who had come to him in a lonely place. 'As she grows up, this girl Kánaka·rekha is troubling my heart, O queen, with worry about marrying her to someone her equal. For a girl of good 5.1.25

udvejinī parasy' âpi śrūyamāṇ" âiva karṇayoḥ.
vidy" êva kanyakā mohād a|pātre pratipāditā
yaśase na na dharmāya jāyet' ânuśayāya tu.
tat kasmai dīyate hy eṣā mayā nṛpataye sutā
ko 'syāḥ samaḥ syād iti me, devi, cintā garīyasī.›

tac chrutvā sā vihasy' âivaṃ babhāṣe Kanakaprabhā
‹tvam evam āttha kanyā tu n' êcchaty udvāham eva sā.
ady' âiva narmaṇā sā hi kṛta|kṛtrima|putrakā
«vatse, kadā vivāhaṃ te drakṣyām' îty» uditā mayā.
5.1.30 sā tac chrutv" âiva s'|ākṣepam evaṃ māṃ pratyavocata
«mā m" âivam, amba! dātavyā n' âiva kasmai|cid apy aham.
mad|viyogo na c' ādiṣṭaḥ kany" âiv' âsmi su|śobhanā
anyathā māṃ mṛtāṃ viddhi. kiṃ|cid asty atra kāraṇam.»
evaṃ tay" ôktā tvat|pārśvaṃ, rājan, vign" âham āgatā
tan niṣiddha|vivāhāyāḥ kā varasya vicāraṇā?›

iti rājñī|mukhāc chrutvā samudbhrāntaḥ sa bhūpatiḥ
kanyak"|ântaḥ|puraṃ gatvā tām avādīt tadā sutām.
‹prārthayante 'pi tapasā yaṃ sur'|âsura|kanyakāḥ
bhartṛ|lābhaḥ kathaṃ, vatse, sa niṣiddhaḥ kila tvayā.›
5.1.35 etat pitur vacaḥ śrutvā bhū|tala|nyasta|locanā
tadā Kanakarekhā sā nijagāda nṛp'|ātmajā.
‹tāta, n' âiv' ēpsitas tāvad vivāho mama sāmpratam
tat tātasy' âpi kiṃ tena kāryaṃ kaś c' âtra vo grahaḥ.›

family who has not obtained a good position is like a discordant song—when heard of by the ears of even a stranger, she causes pain. Like learning, a daughter foolishly given to someone unsuitable leads to neither glory nor righteousness, but to regret. So, queen, to which king am I to betroth this daughter? Who could be equal to her? This is causing me great worry.'

When she heard this, Kánaka·prabha laughed and said the following: 'You are speaking thus, but the girl does not want to get married. Only today in fun she made a doll of a boy and I asked her, "My dear, when shall I see your wedding," to which she immediately replied reproachfully, 5.1.30
"Don't, don't speak thus, mother! I am not to be given to anyone. It is not ordained for me to be separated from you. I am only beautiful as a girl, but if I am married you must realize that I will be dead. There is a reason for this." After she said this, O king, I came to you in distress. So there is no point in discussing the bridegroom of a girl who refuses to get married.'

When the king heard this from the queen he hurried to the princess's apartment and then said to his daughter, 'When the maidens of the gods and *ásura*s seek to win a husband through austerities, how is it that you, my dear, have refused to take one?'

On hearing these words from her father, princess Kánaka· 5.1.35
rekha turned her eyes to the ground and then said, 'Father, for the moment I do not want to get married, so there is nothing for you to gain by it. Why are you insisting on it?'

ity uktaḥ sa tayā rājā duhitrā dhīmatāṃ varaḥ
Paropakārī sa punar evam etām abhāṣata.
‹kanyā|dānād ṛte, putri, kiṃ syāt kilbiṣa|śāntaye?
na ca bandhu|parādhīnā kanyā svātantryam arhati.
jāt" âiva hi parasy' ârthe kanyakā nāma rakṣyate
bālyād ṛte vinā bhartuḥ kīdṛk tasyāḥ pitur gṛham.
5.1.40 ṛtumatyāṃ hi kanyāyāṃ bāndhavā yānty adhogatim
vṛṣalī sā varaś c' âsyā vṛṣalīpatir ucyate.›

iti ten' ôditā pitrā rāja|putrī mano|gatām
vācaṃ Kanakarekhā sā tat|kṣaṇaṃ samudairayat.
‹yady evaṃ, tāta, tad yena vipreṇa kṣatriyeṇa vā
dṛṣṭā Kanakapury|ākhyā nagarī kṛtinā kila.
tasmai tvay" âhaṃ dātavyā sa me bhartā bhaviṣyati
n' ânyathā, tāta, mithy" âiva kartavyā me kadarthanā.›

evaṃ tay" ôkte sutayā sa rājā samacintayat
‹diṣṭy" ôdvāhasya tat tāvat prasaṅgo 'ṅgīkṛto 'nayā.
5.1.45 nūnaṃ ca kāraṇ'|ôtpannā dev" îyaṃ k" âpi mad|gṛhe
iyat kathaṃ vijānāti bālā bhūtv" ânyathā hy asau.›
iti saṃcintya tat|kālaṃ ‹tath" êty› uktvā ca tāṃ sutām
utthāya dina|kartavyaṃ sa cakāra mahī|patiḥ.
anyedyur āsthāna|gato jagāda sa ca pārśva|gān
‹dṛṣṭā Kanakapury|ākhyā purī yuṣmāsu kena|cit.
yena dṛṣṭā ca sā tasmai viprāya kṣatriyāya vā
mayā Kanakarekhā ca yauva|rājyaṃ ca dīyate.›

When his daughter said this to him, King Paropakárin, wisest of the wise, again spoke to her, saying the following. 'Without giving one's daughter's hand in marriage, how, my girl, is one to atone for one's sins? And a girl is dependent on her relatives and does not deserve independence. For indeed as soon as she is born, a daughter is looked after for the sake of someone else. Except in childhood, her father's house
is no place for her unless she has a husband. For when an 5.1.40
unmarried girl reaches puberty, her relatives are degraded, she is low caste and her groom is called the husband of a low caste girl.'

When her father said this, princess Kánaka·rekha immediately said the words she had in her mind. 'If that is the case, father, then you must betroth me to the capable man, brahmin or kshatriya, who is said to have seen the city called Kánaka·puri, City of Gold, and he shall become my husband. If that cannot be done, father, you must not needlessly harass me.'

After his daughter had said this, the king thought, 'It is good news at least that she has agreed on a condition
for her marriage. She must be some goddess, born in my 5.1.45
house for a reason. Otherwise how could she know so much when she is a child?' Having thought this through, the king then quickly said to his daughter, 'So be it,' stood up and attended to the day's duties. And on the next day, when he was in the assembly he said to those at his side, 'Has anyone among you seen a city called Kánaka·puri? To the man who has seen it, whether brahmin or kshatriya, I shall betroth Kánaka·rekha and make him crown prince.'

‹śrut" âpi n' âiva s" āsmābhir darśane, deva, kā kathā›
iti te c' âvadan sarve anyony'|ānana|darśinaḥ.
5.1.50 tato rājā pratīhāram ānīy' ādiśati sma saḥ
‹gaccha. bhramaya kṛtsne 'tra pure paṭaha|ghoṣaṇām.
jānīhi yadi ken' âpi dṛṣṭā sā nagarī na vā›
ity ādiṣṭaḥ pratīhāraḥ sa ‹tath" êti› viniryayau.
nirgatya ca samādiśya tat|kṣaṇaṃ rāja|pūruṣān
bhrāmayām āsa paṭahaṃ kṛta|śravaṇa|kautukam.
‹vipraḥ kṣatra|yuvā vā
Kanakapurīṃ yo 'tra dṛṣṭavān nagarīm
vadatu sa tasmai rājā
dadāti tanayāṃ ca yauva|rājyaṃ ca.›
iti c' êtas tatas tatra nagare datta|vismayam
tad aghoṣyata sarvatra paṭah'|ân|antaraṃ vacaḥ.
5.1.55 ‹k" êyaṃ pure 'smin Kanakapurī|nām" âdya ghoṣyate
yā vṛddhair api n' âsmābhir dṛṣṭā jātu na ca śrutā?›
ity evaṃ c' âvadan paurāḥ śrutvā tāṃ tatra ghoṣaṇām
na punaḥ kaś|cid eko 'pi ‹mayā dṛṣṭ" êty› abhāṣata.
tāvac ca tan|nivāsy ekaḥ Śaktideva iti dvijaḥ
Baladeva|tanūjas tām aśṛṇot tatra ghoṣaṇām.
sa yuvā vyasanī sadyo dyūtena vidhanī|kṛtaḥ
acintayad rāja|sutā|pradān'|ākarṇan'|ônmanāḥ.
‹dyūta|hārita|niḥśeṣa|vittasya mama n' âdhunā
praveśo 'sti pitur gehe n' âpi paṇy'|âṅganā|gṛhe.
5.1.60 tasmād a|gatikas tāvad varaṃ mithyā bravīmy aham
«mayā sā nagarī dṛṣṭ" êty» evaṃ paṭaha|ghoṣakān.
ko māṃ pratyety a|vijñānaṃ kena dṛṣṭā kadā hi sā?
syād evaṃ ca kadā|cin me rāja|putryā samāgamaḥ.›

And they all replied, looking at each other's faces, 'Sire, we have not even heard of it, let alone seen it.'

At this the king summoned the chamberlain and in- 5.1.50
structed him, 'Go and circulate a proclamation around the whole city to the beat of the drum and find out whether or not anyone has seen this city.' Instructed thus, the chamberlain agreed to it and left. After going out he immediately gave orders to some servants of the king and had the drum circulated, arousing the people's curiosity in hearing the proclamation: 'If any brahmin or kshatriya young man here has seen the city of Kánaka·puri, let him speak! The king shall give him his daughter and make him crown prince.' These were the astonishing words that were proclaimed all around that city immediately after the beating of the drum.

'What is this Kánaka·puri whose name is today being 5.1.55
proclaimed in this city, which we, even the elders, have neither seen nor heard of?' When the citizens said this after hearing that proclamation there, still not even one person said that they had seen it. Meanwhile one of the citizens, a brahmin called Shakti·deva, the son of Bala·deva, heard that proclamation there. That dissolute youth had quickly lost all his money at gambling and, excited at hearing that the princess was being offered, said to himself, 'Now that I have lost my entire fortune at gambling, I cannot enter my
father's house, nor even that of a prostitute. So while I have 5.1.60
no resource it would be best if I pretend to those making the proclamation by drum that I have seen that city. Who will realize that I do not know it, for who has ever seen it? And in this way I might get to marry the princess.'

iti saṃcintya gatvā tān sa rāja|puruṣāṃs tadā
Śaktidevo ‹mayā dṛṣṭā sā pur" îty› avadan mṛṣā.
‹diṣṭyā! tarhi pratīhāra|pārśvam eh' îti›† tat|kṣaṇam
uktavadbhiś ca taiḥ sākaṃ sa pratīhāram abhyagāt.
tasmai tath" âiva c' âśaṃsat tat|purī|darśanaṃ mṛṣā
ten' âpi sat|kṛtya tato rāj'|ântikam anīyata.
5.1.65 rāj'|âgre 'py avikalpaḥ saṃs tath" âiva ca tad abravīt
dyūtat"|ântasya kiṃ nāma kitavasya hi duṣkaram.
rāj" âpi niścayaṃ jñātuṃ brāhmaṇaṃ taṃ visṛṣṭavān
tasyāḥ Kanakarekhāyā duhitur nikaṭaṃ tadā.
tayā ca sa pratīhāra|mukhāj jñātv" ântik'|āgataḥ
‹kaccit tvayā sā Kanakapurī dṛṣṭ" êty› apṛcchyata.
‹bāḍhaṃ mayā sā nagarī dṛṣṭā vidy"|ârthinā satā
bhramatā bhuvam ity› evaṃ so 'pi tāṃ pratyabhāṣata.
‹kena mārgeṇa tatra tvaṃ gatavān kīdṛśī ca sā?›
iti bhūyas tayā pṛṣṭaḥ sa vipro 'py evam abravīt.
5.1.70 ‹ito Harapuraṃ nāma nagaraṃ gatavān aham
tato 'pi prāptavān asmi purīṃ Vārāṇasīṃ kramāt.
Vārāṇasyāś ca divasair nagaraṃ Pauṇḍravardhanam
tasmāt Kanakapury|ākhyāṃ nagarīṃ tāṃ gato 'bhavam.
dṛṣṭā mayā ca sā bhoga|bhūmiḥ su|kṛta|karmaṇām
a|nimeṣ'|ēkṣaṇ'|āsvādya|śobhā Śakra|purī yathā.
tatr' âdhigata|vidyaś ca kālen' âham ih' āgamam
iti ten' âsmi gatavān pathā s" âpi pur" īdṛśī.›
evaṃ viracit'|ôktau ca dhūrte tasmin dvi|janmani
Śaktideve sa|hāsaṃ sā vyājahāra nṛp'|ātmajā.
5.1.75 ‹aho satyaṃ, mahābrahman, dṛṣṭā sā nagarī tvayā
brūhi brūhi punas tāvat ken' âsi gatavān pathā.›

After thinking this through, Shakti·deva then went and lied to the king's officers that he had seen that city. They immediately said, 'Congratulations! In that case come to the chamberlain,' and he went with them to the chamberlain. In the same way he lied to him that he had seen that city. After being welcomed by him he was taken from there to
the king and in front of the king too he did not hesitate to 5.1.65
say the very same thing. Indeed, nothing is difficult for a rogue who has been ruined by gambling.

And the king, in order to be certain, then sent that brahmin to his daughter Kánaka·rekha. When she had been informed by the chamberlain and Shakti·deva had come in, she asked him whether he had seen Kánaka·puri and he replied to her, 'Yes, I saw that city when I was wandering about the world as a student.' When she then further asked him which road he had taken to get there and what it was
like, the brahmin replied, 'I went from here to the city called 5.1.70
Hara·pura and from there I eventually arrived at the city of Varánasi. And from Varánasi in a few days I reached the city of Paundra·várdhana. From there I went to that city called Kánaka·puri. I beheld a land of pleasure for those who do good deeds, like Indra's city, its beauty worthy of being savored by the unblinking eyes of the gods. After acquiring the sciences there, in time I came here. That was the route I took and that is what that city is like.'

After that rogue of a brahmin Shakti·deva had fabricated
this speech, the princess said with a laugh, 'Oh, great brah- 5.1.75
min, you have indeed seen that city. Tell me, just tell me again which route you took.'

tac chrutvā sa yadā dhārṣṭyaṃ Śaktidevo 'karot punaḥ
tadā taṃ rāja|putrī sā ceṭībhir niravāsayat.
nirvāsite yayau c' âsmin pituḥ pārśvaṃ tad" âiva sā
‹kiṃ satyam āha vipro 'sāv iti?› pitr" âpy apṛcchyata.
tataś ca sā rāja|sutā janakaṃ nijagāda tam
‹tāta, rāj" âpi bhūtvā tvam a|vicāry' âiva ceṣṭase.
kiṃ na jānāsi dhūrtā yad vañcayante janān ṛjūn?
sa hi mithy" âiva vipro māṃ pratārayitum īhate.
5.1.80 na punar nagarī tena dṛṣṭā s'|ālīka|vādinā
dhūrtair anek'|ākārāś ca kriyante bhuvi vañcanāḥ.
Śiva|Mādhava|vṛttāntaṃ tathā hi śṛṇu vacmi te›
ity uktvā rāja|kanyā sā vyājahāra kathām imām.
‹asti Ratnapuraṃ nāma yath"|ârthaṃ nagar'|ôttamam
Śiva|Mādhava|saṃjñau ca dhūrtau tatra babhūvatuḥ.
parivārī|kṛt'|ân|eka|dhūrtau tau cakratuś ciram
māyā|prayoga|niḥśeṣa|muṣit'|āḍhya|janaṃ puram.
ekadā dvau ca tāv evaṃ mantraṃ vidadhatur mithaḥ
«idaṃ nagaram āvābhyāṃ kṛtsnaṃ tāvad viluṇṭhitam.
5.1.85 ataḥ saṃprati gacchāmo vastum Ujjayinīṃ purīm
tatra tu śrūyate rājñaḥ purodhāḥ su|mahā|dhanaḥ
Śaṃkarasvāmi|nāmā ca tasmād yuktyā hṛtair dhanaiḥ
Mālava|strī|vilāsānāṃ yāsyāmo 'tra rasa|jñatām.
āskandī dakṣin'|ārdhasya sa tatra bhru|kuṭī|mukhaḥ
sapta|kumbhī|nidhāno hi *kīnāśo* gīyate dvijaiḥ.
kanyā|ratnaṃ ca tasy' âsti viprasy' âikam iti śrutam
tad apy etat|prasaṅgena dhruvaṃ tasmād avāpsyate.
iti niścitya kṛtvā ca mithaḥ kartavya|saṃvidam

When, on hearing this, Shakti·deva again displayed his audacity, the princess had her servants throw him out. And when he had been expelled, she immediately went to her father, and he asked her whether the brahmin had told the truth. At this the princess said to her father, 'Father, even though you are a king, you are behaving thoughtlessly. Do you not realize that there are rogues who cheat honest people? For that brahmin wants to lead me astray by speaking falsely. Besides, the liar has not seen the city. Rogues de- 5.1.80
ceive people in many different ways in this world. Just listen to the story of Shiva and Mádhava that I shall tell you.' After saying this, the princess told the following story.

'There is a fine city which is fittingly called Ratna·pura, City of Jewels. Two rogues called Shiva and Mádhava lived there. They had a gang of several rogues and for a long time they used deception to rob all the rich people in the city. One day they counseled one another thus: "We have plundered this entire city, so let's now go and live in the city 5.1.85
of Ujjain. It is said that the king's priest there is extremely rich and goes by the name of Shánkara·svamin. After cheating him of his fortune, we shall use it to become connoisseurs of the delights of the ladies of Málava there. Because he *gives them half their sacrificial fee : attacks the southern half of the world* with a frown while having a *fortune that fills : collection of* seven pots, the brahmins there call him *a miser : the god of death*. And it is said that that brahmin has a single jewel of a daughter, whom we are sure to get from him as a result of taking his money." After making this decision and arranging between them what had to be

Śiva|Mādhava|dhūrtau tu purāt prayayatus tataḥ.
5.1.90 śanaiś c' Ôjjayinīṃ prāpya Mādhavaḥ sa|paricchadaḥ
rāja|putrasya veṣeṇa tasthau grāme kva|cid bahiḥ.
Śivas tv a|vikalaṃ kṛtvā varṇi|veṣaṃ viveśa tām
nagarīm eka ev' âgre bahu|māyā|vicakṣaṇaḥ.
tatr' âdhyuvāsa Siprāyā maṭhikāṃ tīra|sīmani
dṛśya|sthāpita|mṛd|darbha|bhikṣā|bhāṇḍa|mṛg'|âjinām.
sa ca prabhāta|kāleṣu ghanay" âṅgaṃ mṛd" ālipat
Avīci|kardam'|ālepa|sūtra|pātam iv' ācaran.
sarit|toye ca sa ciraṃ nimajjy' āsīd avāṅ|mukhaḥ
ku|karma|jām iv' âbhyasyan bhaviṣyantīm adho|gatim.
5.1.95 snān'|ôtthito 'rk'|âbhimukhas tasthāv ūrdhvaṃ ciraṃ ca saḥ
śūl'|âdhiropaṇ'|āucityam ātmano darśayann iva.
tato dev'|âgrato gatvā kuśa|kūrca|karo japan
āsta padm'|āsan'|āsīnaḥ sa *dambha/caturānanaḥ.*
antarā hṛdayān" îva sādhūnāṃ kaitavena saḥ
svacchāny āhṛtya puṣpāṇi pur'|āriṃ paryapūjayat.
kṛta|pūjaś ca bhūyo 'pi mithyā japa|paro 'bhavat.
datt'|âvadhānaḥ ku|sṛtiṣv iva dhyānaṃ tatāna saḥ.

done, those two rogues Shiva and Mádhava set forth from the city.

They eventually reached Ujjain and Mádhava, together 5.1.90
with his entourage, stayed in some village outside the city disguised as a prince. Shiva, meanwhile, who was adept at several deceptions, disguised himself perfectly as a brahmin student and went into the city first, alone. He took up residence there at a small ashram on the banks of the Sipra, in which he placed clay, *darbha* grass, a begging bowl and a deer skin, in such a way that they were visible. In the mornings he would smear his body with thick clay, as if preparing to smear himself in the filth of the Avíchi hell. And he would immerse himself in the water of the river and remain for a long time looking downwards, as if practicing his forthcoming downward descent as a result of his evil deeds.
And after getting up from his bath he would stand upright 5.1.95
for an age facing the sun, as if demonstrating how fit he was for impalement. Then he would go before the Lord, and, repeating a mantra with a bundle of *kusha* grass in his hand, sitting in the lotus position, *his face fraudulent and cunning : the four-faced creator of deception,** he would offer *brightly colored* flowers in worship to Shiva, as if using deceit to offer up the *pure* hearts of virtuous men. And after carrying out the worship he would once more fraudulently devote himself to repeating a mantra and extend his meditation, as if concentrating on his deceptions.

apar'|âhṇe ca bhikṣ"|ârthī kṛṣṇa|sār'|âjin'|âmbaraḥ
puri tad|vañcanā|māyā|kaṭākṣa iva so 'bhramat.
5.1.100 ādāya dvija|gehebhyo maunī bhikṣā|trayaṃ tataḥ
sa|daṇḍ'|âjinakaś cakre triḥ satyam iva khaṇḍaśaḥ.
bhāgaṃ dadau ca kākebhyo bhāgam abhyāgatāya ca
bhāgena dambha|bījena kukṣi|bhastrām apūrayat.
punaḥ sa sarva|pāpāni nijāni gaṇayann iva
japann āvartayām āsa ciraṃ mithy" âkṣa|mālikām.
rajanyām a|dvitīyaś ca sa tasthau maṭhik'|ântare
api sūkṣmāṇi lokasya marma|sthānāni† cintayan.
evaṃ pratidinaṃ kurvan kaṣṭaṃ vyāja|mayaṃ tapaḥ
sa tatr' āvarjayām āsa nagarī|vāsināṃ manaḥ.
5.1.105 «aho tapasvī śānto 'yam iti» khyātiś ca sarvataḥ
udapadyata tatr' âsya bhakti|namre 'khile jane.

tāvac ca sa dvitīyo 'sya sakhā cāra|mukhena tam
vijñāya Mādhavo 'py etan|nagarīṃ praviveśa tām.
gṛhītvā vasatiṃ c' âtra dūre deva|kul'|ântare
sa rāja|putra|cchadmā san snātuṃ Siprā|taṭaṃ yayau.
snātvā s'|ânucaro dṛṣṭvā dev'|âgre japa|tatparam
taṃ Śivaṃ parama|prahvo nipapāt' âsya pādayoḥ.
jagāda ca janasy' âgre «n' âst' īdṛk tāpaso 'paraḥ
a|sakṛdd hi mayā dṛṣṭas tīrthāny eṣa bhramann iti.»
5.1.110 Śivas tu taṃ viloky' âpi dambha|stambhita|kaṃdharaḥ
tath" âiv' āsīt tataḥ so 'pi Mādhavo vasatiṃ yayau.
rātrau militvā c' âikatra bhuktvā pītvā ca tāv ubhau
mantrayām āsatuḥ śeṣaṃ kartavyaṃ yad ataḥ param.

In the afternoon he would wear the skin of a spotted antelope and wander about the city in search of alms as if he were a duplicitous side-glance ready to hoodwink it.
Observing a vow of silence and carrying his staff and deer 5.1.100
skin, he would then get three portions of alms from the brahmins' houses and divide it into three parts, as if it were the truth. And he would give a part to the crows, a part to an uninvited guest, and with one part, acquired through deception, he would fill his stomach. Then, as if counting his own sins, for an age he would deceitfully tell his beads while repeating a mantra. And at night he would stay alone in the little ashram, thinking about the people's subtle points of vulnerability. Thus performing every day fraudulent severe austerities, he attracted the minds of the citizens there.
And his fame for being a very composed ascetic became 5.1.105
widespread among all the devout people there.

Meanwhile, that companion of his, his friend Mádhava, having heard about him from a spy, went into the city. He set up residence inside a far off temple there and went in his disguise as a prince to the banks of the Sipra to bathe. After taking his bath, he and his retinue saw Shiva busy chanting before the Lord, and, with the utmost reverence, he fell at his feet. He said before the people, "There is no other ascetic like this one, for I have seen him many times as he
wanders about the places of pilgrimage." Shiva, meanwhile, 5.1.110
even though he had seen him, deceitfully kept his neck straight and remained as he was, at which Mádhava went to where he was staying. That night the two of them met somewhere and ate and drank together. Then they discussed what remained for them to do next. In the last watch of the

yāme ca paścime svairam āgāt sva|maṭhikāṃ Śivaḥ
Mādhavo 'pi prabhāte svaṃ dhūrtam ekaṃ samādiśat.
«etad gṛhītvā gaccha tvaṃ vastra|yugmam upāyanam
Śaṃkarasvāminaḥ pārśvam iha rāja|purodhasaḥ.
‹rāja|putraḥ parābhūto Mādhavo nāma gotra|jaiḥ
«pitryaṃ bahu gṛhītv" ârtham āgato dakṣiṇā|pathāt.
5.1.115 samaiḥ katipayair anyai rāja|putrair anudrutaḥ
sa c' êha yuṣmadīyasya rājñaḥ sevāṃ kariṣyati.
tena tvad|darśanāy' âhaṃ preṣito, yaśasāṃ nidhe›
iti tvayā sa|vinayaṃ sa ca vācyaḥ purohitaḥ.»
evaṃ sa Mādhaven' ôktvā dhūrtaḥ saṃpreṣitas tadā
jagām' ôpāyana|karo gṛhaṃ tasya purodhasaḥ.
upety' âvasare dattvā prābhṛtaṃ vijane ca tat
tasmai Mādhava|saṃdeśaṃ śaṃsati sma yath"|ôcitam.
so 'py upāyana|lobhāt tac chraddadhe kalpit'|āyatiḥ
upapradānaṃ lipsūnām ekaṃ hy ākarṣaṇ'|âuṣadham.
5.1.120 tataḥ pratyāgate tasmin dhūrte 'nyedyuḥ sa Mādhavaḥ
labdh'|âvakāśas tam agāt svayaṃ draṣṭuṃ purohitam.
dhṛta|kārpaṭik'|ākārai rāja|putr'|âpadeśibhiḥ
vṛtaḥ pārśva|carair ātta|kāṣṭha|khaṇḍaka|lāñchanaiḥ.
purog'|āveditaś c' âinam abhyagāt sa purohitam
ten' âpy abhyudgam'|ānanda|svāgatair abhyanandyata.
tatas tena saha sthitvā kath"|ālāpaiḥ kṣaṇaṃ ca saḥ
āyayau tad|anujñāto Mādhavo vasatiṃ nijām.
dvitīye 'hni punaḥ preṣya prābhṛtaṃ vastrayor yugam
bhūyo 'pi tam upāgacchat purohitam uvāca ca.
5.1.125 «parivār'|ânurodhena kila sev"|ârthino vayam
tena tvam āśrito 'smābhir artha|mātr" âsti naḥ punaḥ.

night Shiva sneaked off to his little hermitage, while Mádhava, in the morning, gave an order to one of his rogues: "Take these two pieces of clothing as a present and go to Shánkara·svamin, the king's priest here, humbly saying to him, 'A prince called Mádhava has been overthrown by his relatives and, taking his large ancestral fortune, has come
here from the south. He was accompanied by some other 5.1.115
princes like him, and he will serve your king here. He sent me to see you, O store of glory.'"

Mádhava said this and then sent the rogue on his way. Present in hand, he went to the house of the priest. When he got the chance, he went up and gave him the present in a quiet spot, and then told him Mádhava's message in an appropriate manner. The priest, out of greed for the present and in expectation of more, believed it, for a present is a
singular magic potion for attracting the greedy. The rogue 5.1.120
then went back and on the next day Mádhava got his chance and went in person to see the priest. Surrounded by attendants who were dressed as mercenary guards and were pretending to be princes, characterized by the wooden staffs they carried, and announced by a man who went ahead, he went up to the priest, who greeted him by getting up from his seat and gladly welcoming him. Then Mádhava stayed for a short while in conversation with him before taking his leave and returning to his own residence.

On the next day he again sent two pieces of clothing as a gift and then once more he went to see the priest. He said
to him, "In accordance with the wishes of my entourage, I 5.1.125
wish to serve the king, so I come to you for help, but I have no shortage of money."

tac chrutvā prāptim āśaṅkya tasmāt so 'tha purohitaḥ
pratiśuśrāva tat tasmai Mādhavāya samīhitam.
kṣaṇāc ca gatvā rājānam etad|arthaṃ vyajijñapat
tad|gauraveṇa rāj" âpi tat tathā pratyapadyata.

apare 'hni ca nītvā taṃ Mādhavaṃ sa|paricchadam
nṛpāy' âdarśayat tasmai sa purodhāḥ sa|gauravam.
nṛpo 'pi Mādhavaṃ dṛṣṭvā rāja|putr'|ôpam"|ākṛtim
ādareṇ' ânujagrāha vṛttiṃ c' âsya pradiṣṭavān.
5.1.130 tato 'tra sevamānas taṃ nṛpaṃ tasthau sa Mādhavaḥ
rātrau rātrau ca mantrāya Śivena samagacchata.
«ih' âiva vasa mad|gehe iti» tena purodhasā
so 'rthitaś c' âbhaval lobhād upacār'|ôpajīvinā.
tataḥ sahacaraiḥ sākaṃ tasy' âiv' āśiśriyad gṛham
vināśa|hetur vāsāya madguḥ skandhaṃ taror iva.
kṛtvā kṛtrima|māṇikya|mayair ābharaṇair bhṛtam
bhāṇḍaṃ ca sthāpayām āsa tadīye koṣa|veśmani.
antarā ca tad udghāṭya tais tair vyāj'|ârdha|darśitaiḥ
jahār' ābharaṇais tasya śaṣpair iva paśor manaḥ.
5.1.135 viśvaste ca tatas tasmin purodhasi cakāra saḥ
māndyam alpatar'|āhāra|kṛśī|kṛta|tanur mṛṣā.
yāte katipay'|âhne† ca taṃ śayy"|ôpānta|vartinam
purohitaṃ sa vakti sma dhūrta|rājo 'lpayā girā.
«mama tāvac charīre 'smin vartate viṣamā daśā
tad, vipra|vara, kaṃ|cit tvaṃ brāhmaṇ'|ôttamam ānaya.
yasmai dāsyāmi sarvasvam ihāmutra ca śarmaṇe
a|sthire jīvite hy āsthā kā dhaneṣu manasvinaḥ?»

When he heard this from him, thinking that it would be to his profit, he promised Mádhava that he would get what he wanted. Soon afterwards he went to the king and told him of Mádhava's request. Out of respect for the priest, the king agreed to it.

On the next day the priest brought Mádhava and his entourage, and solemnly presented them to the king. The king, on seeing that Mádhava looked like a prince, welcomed him respectfully and arranged some work for him.
After that Mádhava stayed there serving the king, and ev- 5.1.130
ery night he would meet Shiva for a discussion. The priest, who lived off charity, greedily asked him to stay there in his house. At this he and his companions took up residence in the priest's house and he was the cause of the dwelling's downfall, like a beaver in the trunk of a tree. He deposited a box filled with jewelry made of fake rubies in the priest's storeroom. By occasionally opening it and craftily letting some of the jewels be half seen, he captivated the mind of
the priest just as grass captivates that of a cow. Then, once 5.1.135
he had won the priest's trust, he feigned illness by eating very little and making his body grow thin. After a few days had passed, that king among rogues said in a soft voice to the priest, who was at his bedside, "While this body of mine is in a perilous state, O best of priests, please bring some noble brahmin to me, to whom I shall give my property to ensure my prosperity in this life and the next, for when life is impermanent, what do the wise care for riches?"

ity uktaḥ sa purodhāś ca tena dān'|ôpajīvakaḥ
«evaṃ karom' îty» āha sma so 'patac c' âsya pādayoḥ.
5.1.140 tataḥ sa brāhmaṇaṃ yaṃ yam ānināya purohitaḥ
viśeṣ'|êcchā|nibhāt taṃ taṃ śraddadhe na sa Mādhavaḥ.
tad dṛṣṭvā tasya pārśva|stho dhūrta eko 'bravīd idam
«na tāvad asmai sāmānyo vipraḥ prāyeṇa rocate.
tad ya eṣa Śivo nāma Siprā|tīre mahā|tapāḥ
sthitaḥ saṃprati bhāty asya na v" êty etan nirūpyatām.»
tac chrutvā Mādhavo 'vādīt kṛt'|ârtis taṃ purohitam
«hanta prasīd' ānaya taṃ vipro n' ânyo hi tādṛśaḥ.»
ity uktas tena ca yayau sa Śivasy' ântikaṃ tataḥ
purodhās tam apaśyac ca racita|dhyāna|niścalam.
5.1.145 upāviśac ca tasy' âgre tataḥ kṛtvā pradakṣiṇam
tat|kṣaṇaṃ so 'pi dhūrto 'bhūc chanair unmīlit'|ēkṣaṇaḥ.
tataḥ praṇamya taṃ prahvaḥ sa uvāca purohitaḥ
«na cet kupyasi tat kiṃ|cit, prabho, vijñāpayāmy aham.
tan niśamya ca ten' ôṣṭha|puṭ'|ônnamana|saṃjñayā
anujñātaḥ Śiven' âivaṃ tam avādīt purohitaḥ.
«iha sthito dākṣiṇātyo rāja|putro mahā|dhanaḥ
Mādhav'|ākhyaḥ sa c' â|svasthaḥ sarvasvaṃ dātum udyataḥ.
manyase yadi tat tubhyaṃ sa sarvaṃ tat prayacchati
nān"|ân|argha|mahā|ratna|may'|âlaṃkaraṇ'|ôjjvalam.
5.1.150 tac chrutvā sa śanair mukta|
maunaḥ kila Śivo 'bravīt
«brahman, bhikṣ"|âśanasy' ârthaiḥ
ko 'rtho me brahmacāriṇaḥ?»

On being addressed thus by him, the priest, who lived off donations, replied that he would do so and Mádhava fell at his feet. Then Mádhava wouldn't approve of whichever 5.1.140
brahmin the priest brought, saying that he wanted someone special. When he saw this, one of the rogues at his side said the following. "As a rule, he just doesn't like ordinary brahmins, so let us find out whether or not he likes the great ascetic called Shiva who is now living on the banks of the Sipra."

When he heard this, Mádhava, pretending to be suffering, said to the priest, "Oh, please fetch him, for there is no other brahmin like him."

After he said this to the priest, the latter then went to Shiva and found him pretending to be fixed in meditation. He circumambulated him and then sat down before him, 5.1.145
and at that moment the rogue slowly opened his eyes. Then the priest prostrated himself before him and said, while bowing, "If it doesn't anger you, my lord, I have something to ask you."

When he heard this, Shiva signaled his approval by pursing his lips, and the priest said the following to him, "There is a very rich prince from the south called Mádhava living here. He is unwell and wants to give away his property. If you approve, then he will give it all to you. It glitters with pieces of jewelry made from various huge priceless gems."

When he heard this, Shiva abandoned his vow of si- 5.1.150
lence and said slowly, "Brahmin, I am celibate and live off alms—what need do I have of wealth?" But the priest replied thus: "Don't speak like that, great brahmin. Do you not know the progression of life stages? By taking a wife and

tataḥ purohito 'py evaṃ
sa taṃ punar abhāṣata
«m" âivaṃ vādīr, mahā|brahman,
kiṃ na vetsy āśrama|kramam.
kṛta|dāro gṛhe kurvan deva|pitṛ|atithi|kriyāḥ
dhanais tri|vargaṃ prāpnoti gṛhī hy āśramiṇāṃ varaḥ.»
tataḥ so 'pi Śivo 'vādīt «kuto me dāra|saṃgrahaḥ
na hy ahaṃ pariṇeṣyāmi kulād yādṛśa|tādṛśāt?»
tac chrutvā sukha|bhogyaṃ ca matvā tasya tathā dhanam
sa prāpt'|âvasaro lubdhaḥ purodhās tam abhāṣata.
5.1.155 «asti tarhi sutā kanyā Vinayasvāmin" îti me
ati|rūpavatī sā ca tāṃ ca tubhyaṃ dadāmy aham.
yac ca pratigraha|dhanaṃ tasmāt prāpnoṣi Mādhavāt
tad ahaṃ tava rakṣāmi tad bhajasva gṛh'|āśramam.»
ity ākarṇya sa saṃpanna|yath"|êṣṭ'|ârthaḥ Śivo 'bravīt
«brahman, grahas tav' âyaṃ cet tat karomi vacas tava.
hema|ratna|sva|rūpe tu mugdha ev' âsmi tāpasaḥ
tvad|vāc' âiva pravarte 'haṃ yathā vetsi tathā kuru.»
etac Chiva|vacaḥ śrutvā parituṣṭas «tath" êti» tam
mūḍho nināya gehaṃ svaṃ tath" âiva sa purohitaḥ.
5.1.160 saṃniveśya ca tatr' âinaṃ Śiv'|ākhyam a|śivaṃ tataḥ
yathā|kṛtaṃ śaśaṃs' âitan Mādhavāy' âbhinandate.
tad" âiva ca dadau tasmai sutāṃ kleśa|vivardhitām
nijāṃ Śivāya saṃpattim iva mūḍhatva|hāritām.
kṛt'|ôdvāhaṃ tṛtīye 'hni pratigraha|kṛte ca tam
nināya vyāja|mandasya Mādhavasya tato 'ntikam.
«a|tarkya|tapasaṃ vande tvām ity» a|vitathaṃ vadan
Mādhavo 'py apatat tasya Śivasy' ôtthāya pādayoḥ.
dadau ca tasmai vidhivat koṣ'|āgārāt tad|āhṛtam

worshipping the gods, ancestors and guests in his house, a man uses wealth to attain the three goals, for the householder is the best of the followers of the stages of life.*

Shiva replied, "How can I take a wife, for I will not marry a girl from any old family?"

When the greedy priest heard this, thinking that he would thus be able to enjoy the ascetic's fortune with ease, he seized his chance and said, "In that case, I have a young 5.1.155
daughter called Vínaya·svámini. She is extremely beautiful and I shall give her to you. I shall look after for you the wealth you will receive as a donation from Mádhava, so adopt the householder's stage of life."

On hearing this, Shiva, having achieved just the thing he wanted, said, "Brahmin, if you are so insistent, then I shall do what you say. But I am an ascetic and completely ignorant of the nature of gold and jewels. I shall act exactly as you advise. Do what you think is right."

When he heard these words from Shiva, the foolish priest was overjoyed. Saying, "So be it," he took him to his home just as he was. Then he had that inauspicious man called 5.1.160
Shiva* go in there, and told the rejoicing Mádhava what had happened. There and then he gave to Shiva his daughter, who had been brought up carefully, and it was as if he were giving him his fortune, lost through his stupidity. Three days after he had got married, he took him to Mádhava, who was pretending to be ill, to get the donation. Saying—without being deceitful—"I welcome you whose asceticism is unfathomable," Mádhava stood up and then fell at Shiva's feet. With due ceremony he gave him the box full of jewelry made of fake rubies which he had fetched

bhūri|kṛtrima|māṇikya|may'|ābharaṇa|bhāṇḍakam.
5.1.165 Śivo 'pi pratigṛhy' âitat tasya haste purodhasaḥ
«n' âhaṃ vedmi tvam ev' âitad vets' îty» uktvā samarpayat.
«aṅgī|kṛtam idaṃ pūrvaṃ mayā cintā tav' âtra kā?»
ity uktvā tac ca jagrāha tat|kṣaṇaṃ sa purohitaḥ.
kṛt'|āśiṣi tato yāte sva|vadhū|vāsakaṃ Śive
nītvā sa sthāpayām āsa tan nije koṣaveśmani.
Mādhavo 'pi tad anyedyur māndya|vyājaṃ śanais tyajan
rog'|ôpaśāntiṃ vakti sma mahā|dāna|prabhāvataḥ.
«tvayā dharma|sahāyena samuttirṇo 'ham āpadaḥ»
iti c' ântikam āyāntaṃ praśaśaṃsa purohitam.
5.1.170 «etat|prabhāvād etan me śarīram iti» kīrtayan
prakāśam eva cakre ca Śivena saha mitratām.
Śivo 'pi yāteṣu dineṣv avādīt taṃ purohitam
«evam eva bhavad|gehe bhokṣyate ca kiyan mayā.
tat kiṃ tvam eva mūlyena gṛhṇāsy ābharaṇaṃ na tat
mah"|ârgham iti cen mūlyaṃ yathā|saṃbhavi dehi me.
tac chrutvā tad an|arghaṃ ca matvā tan|niṣkrayaṃ dadau
«tath" êti» tasmai sarvasvaṃ Śivāya sa purohitaḥ.
tad|arthaṃ ca sva|hastena
Śivaṃ lekhyam akārayat
svayaṃ c' âpy akarod buddhvā
tad dhanaṃ sva|dhan'|âdhikam.
5.1.175 anyonya|likhitaṃ haste gṛhītvā sa purohitaḥ
pṛthag āsīt pṛthak so 'pi Śivo bheje gṛha|sthitim.
tataś ca sa Śivaḥ so 'pi Mādhavaḥ saṃgatāv ubhau
purohit'|ârthān bhuñjānau yath"|êcchaṃ tatra tasthatuḥ.

from the storeroom. Shiva took it and said, "I don't know 5.1.165
about this, but you do," and put it into the priest's hand. Saying, "I have already agreed to this—there is no need for you to worry about it," the priest took it straight away. Then, when Shiva had given his blessings and gone to his wife's bedroom, the priest took the box and put it in his own storeroom.

Mádhava, meanwhile, slowly shaking off his fake illness, said on the next day that the disease had been cured as a result of his great generosity. When the priest came to him, he praised him, saying, "You, together with righteousness, have saved me from disaster." Singing his praises by an- 5.1.170
nouncing, "I have my body thanks to this man's powers," he very publicly struck up a friendship with Shiva. And Shiva, after a few days had passed, said to the priest, "How much hospitality am I to enjoy in your house like this? So why don't you take the jewelry for some money? If it is so valuable then give me an appropriate sum."

On hearing this, the priest, believing the jewelry to be priceless, agreed and gave Shiva his entire fortune as payment for it. He had him write an informal receipt for it with his own hand, and he himself also wrote one, believing that treasure to be more valuable than his fortune. Each 5.1.175
having taken in his hand the receipt written by the other, they went their separate ways and Shiva took up residence in a house. Shiva and Mádhava lived there both together, enjoying the priest's wealth as they so desired.

gate kāle ca mūly'|ârthī sa purodhāḥ kil' āpaṇe
tato 'laṃkāraṇād ekaṃ vikretuṃ kaṭakaṃ yayau.
tatr' âitad ratna|tattva|jñāḥ parīkṣya vaṇijo 'bruvan
«aho kasy' âsti vijñānaṃ yen' âitat kṛtrimaṃ kṛtam.
kāca|sphaṭika|khaṇḍā hi nānā|rāg'|ôparañjitāḥ
rīti|baddhā ime n' âite maṇayo na ca kāñcanam.»

5.1.180 tac chrutvā vihvalo gatvā sa purodhās tad" âiva tat
ānīy' ābharaṇaṃ gehāt kṛtsnaṃ teṣām adarśayat.
te dṛṣṭvā tad|vad ev' âsya sarvaṃ kṛtrimam eva tat
ūcire ca sa tac chrutvā vajr'|āhata iv' âbhavat.
tataś ca gatvā tat|kālaṃ sa mūḍhaḥ Śivam abhyadhāt
«gṛhṇīṣva svān alaṃkārāṃs tan me dehi nijaṃ dhanam.»
«kuto mam' âdy' âpi dhanaṃ tad dhy a|śeṣaṃ gṛhe mayā
kālena bhuktam iti?» taṃ Śivo 'pi pratyabhāṣata.
tato vivadamānau tau pārśv'|âvasthita|Mādhavam
purodhāś ca Śivaś c' ôbhau rājānam upajagmatuḥ.
5.1.185 «kāca|sphaṭikayoḥ khaṇḍai rīti|baddhaiḥ su|rañjitaiḥ
racitaṃ, deva, dattv" âiva† vyāj'|âlaṃkaraṇaṃ mahat.
Śivena mama sarvasvam a|jānānasya bhakṣitam»
iti vijñāpayām āsa nṛpatiṃ sa purohitaḥ.

tataḥ Śivo 'bravīd «rājann, ā bālyāt tāpaso 'bhavam
anen' âiva tad abhyarthya grāhito 'haṃ pratigraham.
tad" âiva bhāṣitaṃ c' âsya mugdhen' âpi satā mayā
‹ratn'|ādiṣv an|abhijñasya pramāṇaṃ me bhavān iti.›
‹ahaṃ sthitas tav' âtr' êti› pratyapadyata c' âiṣa tat
pratigṛhya ca tat† sarvaṃ haste 'sy' âiva may" ârpitam.

Time went by and then it seems that the priest, needing money, went to the royal camp to sell one of the ornaments in the market. After inspecting it, some merchants there who were connoisseurs of gemstones said, "Oh, who is the skillful man who made this fake? For these are pieces of glass and crystal, tinted with various dyes and fastened with brass. They are not gems and gold."

When he heard this, the priest was worried and imme- 5.1.180
diately went and fetched all the jewelry from his house and showed it to them. After looking at the jewelry, they said that, like the first piece, everything he had was fake. On hearing this it was as if he had been struck by a thunderbolt. The idiot went straight from there and said to Shiva, "Take your jewels and give me my money," to which Shiva replied, "But I don't have your money any more, for over time I have used it all up on my house." At this the priest and Shiva both took their argument to the king, at whose side was Mádhava. The priest said to the king, "Your high- 5.1.185
ness, after selling me a lot of fake jewelry which I did not realize was fashioned from pieces of glass and crystal fastened with brass and tinted, Shiva has consumed my entire fortune."

In response to this Shiva said, "Sire, I have been an ascetic since childhood and at this man's request I accepted the donation. At the time I said to him, even though I was being naive, "I am ignorant about jewels and so forth, so you are to appraise them." He agreed to this, saying, "I am on your side in this matter." I took the jewelry and entrusted it all to him. He then willingly bought it from me, my lord. 5.1.190

5.1.190 tato ʼnena gṛhītaṃ tat svecchaṃ mūlyena me, prabho
vidyate cʼ āvayor atra sva|hasta|likhitaṃ mithaḥ.
idānīṃ cʼ âiva sāhāyyaṃ paraṃ jānāty ataḥ prabhuḥ.»
evaṃ Śive samāptʼ|ôktāv uvāca sa ca Mādhavaḥ.
«mʼʼ âivam ādiśa. mānyas tvam. aparādho mamʼ âtra kaḥ?
na gṛhītaṃ mayā kiṃ|cid bhavato vā Śivasya vā.
paitṛkaṃ dhanam anyatra ciraṃ nyāsī|kṛtaṃ sthitam
tadā tad eva cʼ ānītaṃ mayā dattaṃ dvi|janmane.
satyaṃ yadi na tat svarṇaṃ na ca ratnāni tāni tat
rīti|sphaṭika|kācānāṃ pradānād astu me phalam.
5.1.195 nirvyāja|hṛdayatvena dāne ca pratyayo mama
dṛṣṭa evʼ âvatīrṇo ʼsmi yad rogam ati|dustaram.
ity a|bhinna|mukha|cchāyam uktavaty atra Mādhave
jahāsa mantri|sahito rājā tasmai tutoṣa ca.
«nʼ âivam a|nyāyataḥ kiṃ|cin Mādhavasya Śivasya vā»
iti tatra sabhā|sadbhiḥ sʼ|ântar|hāsam udīrite.
purohitaḥ so ʼtha yayau hāritʼ|ârtho vilajjitaḥ
kāsāṃ hi nʼ āpadāṃ hetur ati|lobhʼ|ândha|buddhitā.
tau ca dhūrtau tatas tatra tasthatuḥ Śiva|Mādhavau
parituṣṭa|nṛpʼ|âvāpta|prasāda|sukhitau ciram.
5.1.200 evaṃ sūtra|śatais tais tair jihvā|jālāni tanvate
jālʼ/ôpajīvino dhūrtā dhārāyāṃ dhīvarā iva.
tat, tāta, mithyā Kanakapurīṃ dṛṣṭām iva bruvan
eṣo ʼpi vañcayitvā tvāṃ vipro mat|prāptim icchati.
ataḥ saṃprati mā bhūt te mad|vivāha|kṛte tvarā
sthitʼʼ âsmi tāvat kanyʼʼ âiva paśyāmo bhavitʼʼ âtra kim.›

We have here the receipts that we each wrote with our own hands. And so now your highness knows how best to help."

When Shiva had thus finished speaking, Mádhava said, "Don't speak like this. You are a worthy man. How am I at fault here? I did not take anything of either yours or Shiva's. My ancestral fortune was for a long time stored elsewhere, then I fetched it and gave it to a brahmin. If in fact it isn't gold and jewels, then my reward must be from giving away brass, crystal and glass. The proof that I made the donation 5.1.195
with pure heart is seen from my having recovered from that very severe illness."

When Mádhava said this about the matter with a straight face, the king and his ministers laughed and were pleased with him. "Thus neither Mádhava nor Shiva has done anything unlawful." After the members of the assembly there had said this, stifling their laughter, the embarrassed priest left, his fortune lost. All disasters are caused by one's mind being blinded by excessive greed. After that those two rogues Shiva and Mádhava lived there for a long time in comfort, having obtained the favor of the delighted king.

In this way rogues, *living off deception*, weave the nets 5.1.200
from their tongues with hundreds of different threads and cast them into the stream, like fishermen *living off their nets*. Thus, father, this brahmin too, falsely claiming to have seen Kánaka·puri, has deceived you and wants to win me. So you must not be in a hurry to have me married right away. For the time being I shall remain an unmarried girl. Let's see what happens in this matter.'

ity uktaḥ sutayā rājā tayā Kanakarekhayā
Paropakārī sa tadā tām evaṃ pratyabhāṣata.
‹yauvane kanyakā|bhavaś ciraṃ, putri, na yujyate
mithyā vadanti doṣaṃ hi durjanā guṇa|matsarāḥ.
5.1.205 uttamasya viśeṣeṇa kalaṅk'|ôtpādako janaḥ
Harasvāmi|kathām atra śṛṇv etāṃ kathayāmi te

Gaṅg"|opakaṇṭhe Kusumapuraṃ nām" âsti yat puram
Harasvām" îti ko 'py āsīt tīrth'|ârthī tatra tāpasaḥ.
sa bhaikṣa|vṛttir vipro 'tra Gaṅgā|tīra|kṛt'|ôṭajaḥ
tapaḥ|prakarṣāl lokasya gaurav'|āspadatāṃ yayau.

kadā|cic c' âtra taṃ dṛṣṭvā dūrād bhikṣā|vinirgatam
jana|madhye jagād' âikas tad|guṇ'|âsahanaḥ khalaḥ.
«api jānītha jāto 'yaṃ kīdṛk kapaṭa|tāpasaḥ?
anen' âiv' ârbhakāḥ sarve nagare 'mutra bhakṣitāḥ.»
5.1.210 tac chrutvā ca dvitīyo 'tra tatr' âvocata tādṛśaḥ
«satyaṃ śrutaṃ may" âpy etad ucyamānaṃ janair iti.»
«evam etad iti» sm' āha tṛtīyo 'pi samarthayan
badhnāty ārya|parīvādaṃ khala|saṃvāda|śṛṅkhalā.

ten' âiva ca kramen' âiva gataḥ karṇa|paramparām
pravādo bahulī|bhāvaṃ sarvatr' âtra pure yayau.

When his daughter Kánaka·rekha said this to King Paropakárin, he replied as follows: 'My girl, it is not right for a maiden who has come of age to remain unmarried for long because bad people, jealous of virtue, will slander her. People are particularly inclined to malign those of noble 5.1.205
character. On this subject, listen to the story of Hara·svamin which I shall tell you.

Near the Ganga there is a city called Kúsuma·pura.* A certain ascetic pilgrim called Hara·svamin was staying there. That brahmin lived off alms and had made a hut of leaves on the banks of the Ganga. His intense asceticism earned him the respect of the people.

One day an evil man among them saw him from afar when he had gone out to beg there, and, unable to bear his virtue, he announced, "Do you realize how fraudulent this ascetic has become? It is he who has eaten all the children
here in this town." When he heard this, another man like 5.1.210
him there said about him, "It's true—I've also heard people saying this." A third man, voicing his opinion, also said that this was the case. The chain of the chatter of evil men tightens around reproach of the noble.

In this way the rumor passed through a series of ears and spread throughout the city. To a man the citizens forced

paurāś ca sarve gehebhyo balād bālān na tatyajuḥ
«Harasvāmī śiśūn nītvā bhakṣayaty akhilān» iti.
tataś ca brāhmaṇās tatra saṃtati|kṣaya|bhīravaḥ
saṃbhūya mantrayām āsuḥ purāt tasya pravāsanam.
5.1.215 «graseta kupitaḥ so 'smān iti» sākṣād bhayān na te
yadā tasy' âśakan vaktuṃ dūtān visasṛjus tadā.
te ca gatvā tadā dūtā dūrād eva tam abruvan
«nagarād gamyatām asmād ity» āhus tvāṃ dvi|jātayaḥ.»
«kiṃ nimittam? iti» proktā vismiten' âtha tena te
punar ūcus «tvam aśnāsi bāla|darśam ih' êti» tam.

tac chrutvā sa Harasvāmī svayaṃ pratyāyan'|êcchayā
viprāṇāṃ nikaṭaṃ teṣāṃ bhīti|naśyaj|jano yayau.
viprāś c' āruruhus trāsāt taṃ dṛṣṭv" âiva maṭh'|ôpari
pravāda|mohitaḥ prāyo na vicāra|kṣamo janaḥ.
5.1.220 atha dvijān Harasvāmī tān ekaikam adhaḥ sthitaḥ
nāma|grāhaṃ samāhūya sa jagād' ôpari sthitān.
«ko 'yaṃ moho 'dya vo, viprā, n' âvekṣadhvaṃ parasparam
kiyanto bālakāḥ kasya mayā kutra ca bhakṣitāḥ?»
tac chrutvā yāvad anyonyaṃ viprāḥ parimṛśanti te
tāvat sarve 'pi sarveṣāṃ jīvanto bālakāḥ sthitāḥ.
kramān niyuktāś c' ânye 'pi paurās tatra tath" âiva tat
pratyapadyanta sarve 'pi sa|vipra|vaṇijo 'bruvan.
«aho vimūḍhair asmābhiḥ sādhur mithy" âiva dūṣitaḥ
jīvanti bālāḥ sarveṣāṃ tat kasy' ânena bhakṣitāḥ?»

their children to stay in their houses, saying, "Hara·svamin takes all the young and eats them." At this the brahmins there, frightened that their lineage would be destroyed, got together and decided to make him leave the city. They could 5.1.215
not tell him in person because they were scared that in his anger he might eat them, so they sent messengers. Then the messengers went and told him from a distance that the brahmins were ordering him to leave the city. Surprised, he asked them why and they replied, "You eat the children here as soon as you see them."

When he heard this, Hara·svamin, out of a desire to win their confidence, went to the brahmins, causing the people to vanish in fear. The brahmins were so terrified that the moment they saw him they climbed on top of a monastery. People deluded by rumors tend to be incapable of reason.
Then Hara·svamin, standing below, one by one called by 5.1.220
name the brahmins who were up there and said, "What is this folly of yours today, O brahmins? Work out among yourselves how many children I have eaten, whose they were and where I ate them." After hearing this, in the course of inquiring from one another they established that all their children were there, alive. The other citizens there too, having been told to find out, eventually acknowledged that this was the case, and they all, together with the brahmins and merchants, said, "Oh we fools have falsely maligned a good man. Everyone's children are alive, so whose could he have eaten?"

5.1.225 ity uktavatsu sarveṣu Harasvāmī tad" âiva saḥ
saṃpanna|śuddhir nagarād gantuṃ pravavṛte tataḥ.
durjan'|ôtpādit'|â|vadya|viraktī|kṛta|cetasā
a|vivekini dur|deśe ratiḥ kā hi manasvinaḥ?
tato vaṇigbhir vipraiś ca prārthitaś caraṇ'|ānataiḥ
katham|cit sa Harasvāmī tatra vastum amanyata.

ittham sac|carit'|âvalokana|lasad|
vidveṣa|vācālitā
mithyā|dūṣaṇam evam eva dadati
prāyaḥ satāṃ durjanāḥ
kiṃ|cit kiṃ punar āpnuvanti yadi te
tatr' âvakāśaṃ manāg
draṣṭuṃ taj|jvalite 'nale nipatitaḥ
prājy'|ājya|dhār'|ôtkaraḥ.
tasmād viśalyayitum icchasi māṃ yadi tvaṃ,
vatse, tad unmiṣati nūtana|yauvane 'smin
na svecham arhasi ciraṃ khalu kanyakātvam
āsevituṃ sulabha|durjana|duṣpravādam.›

5.1.230 ity uktā nara|patinā
pitrā prāyeṇa Kanakarekhā sā
nijagāda rāja|tanayā
tam avasthita|niścayā bhūyaḥ.
‹dṛṣṭā Kanakapurī sā
vipreṇa kṣatriyeṇa vā yena
tarhi tam āśu gaveṣaya
tasmai māṃ dehi bhāṣitaṃ hi mayā.›

tac chrutvā dṛḍha|niścayāṃ vigaṇayañ
jāti|smarāṃ tāṃ sutāṃ
n' âsyāś c' ânyam abhīṣṭa|bhartṛ|ghaṭane
paśyann upāya|kramam

When everyone had said this, Hara·svamin, his name cleared, immediately started to leave that city, for what pleasure can a clever man take in a bad country, where the people cannot think straight because their hearts are turned against others as a result of accusations leveled by the wicked? Then, entreated by the merchants and brahmins prostrating at his feet, Hara·svamin reluctantly agreed to stay there. 5.1.225

In this way wicked men tend to slander the good, their tongues loosened by the hatred which springs forth when they witness good deeds. Furthermore, if they catch a glimpse of the slightest opportunity to do so, they pour torrents of ghee onto the fire that they have lit. So, if you want to free me from my torment, my dear, then while this fresh youthfulness is shining forth, you must not willingly remain unmarried for long, for such a condition is open to slander from bad people.'

Her father the king kept saying this to Kánaka·rekha, and 5.1.230
the princess would say to him, fixed in her resolve, 'I have told you: if that is how you feel then quickly find a brahmin or kshatriya who has seen Kánaka·puri and betroth me to him.'

After hearing this, the king realized that his daughter, who knew her past lives, was firm in her decision, and, unable to see another way of finding the husband she wanted, the king gave a new command that, in order to inquire of those who had newly arrived, every day from then on a

deśe tatra tataḥ prabhṛty anudinaṃ
prasṭuṃ nav'|āgantukān
bhūyo bhūmi|patiḥ sa nitya|paṭaha|
prodghoṣaṇām ādiśat.
‹yo vipraḥ kṣatriyo vā
nanu Kanakapurīṃ dṛṣṭavān so 'bhidhattām
tasmai rājā kila svāṃ
vitarati tanayāṃ yauva|rājyena sākam›
sarvatr' âghoṣyat' âivaṃ
punar api paṭah'|ân|antaraṃ c' âtra śaśvan
na tv ekaḥ ko 'pi tāvat
kṛta|Kanakapurī|darśano labhyate sma.

iti mahā|kavi|śrī|Somadeva|bhaṭṭa|viracite Kathāsaritsāgare caturdārikā|lambake prathamas taraṅgaḥ.

2

5.2.1 ATR' ÂNTARE dvija|yuvā Śaktidevaḥ sa durmanāḥ
acintayad abhipreta|rāja|kany"|âvamānitaḥ.
‹may" êha mithyā|Kanakapurī|darśana|vādinā
vimānanā paraṃ prāptā na tv asau rāja|kanyakā.
tad etat|prāptaye tāvad bhramaṇīyā mahī mayā
yāvat sā nagarī dṛṣṭā prāṇair v' âpi gataṃ mama.
tāṃ hi dṛṣṭvā purīm etya tat|paṇ'|ôpārjitaṃ na cet
labheya rāja|tanayām enāṃ kiṃ jīvitena tat?›
5.2.5 evaṃ kṛta|pratijñaḥ san Vardhamāna|purāt tataḥ
dakṣiṇāṃ diśam ālambya sa pratasthe tadā dvijaḥ.
krameṇa gacchaṃś ca prāpa so 'tha Vindhya|mah"|âṭavīm
viveśa ca nijāṃ vāñchām iva tāṃ gahan'|āyatām.
tasyāṃ ca mārut'|ādhūta|mṛdu|pādapa|pallavaiḥ
vījayantyām iv' ātmānaṃ taptam arka|kar'|ôtkaraiḥ
bhūri|caura|parābhūti|duḥkhād iva divā|niśam

proclamation announced by drum was to be made in that land. And again all around the city the following proclamation was made every day after the drum had been beaten: 'May the brahmin or kshatriya who has seen Kánaka·puri speak! To him shall the king give his daughter and the position of crown prince!' But no one who had seen Kánaka·puri was found.

Thus ends the first wave in the Four Girls Attainment in the "Ocean of the Rivers of Story" composed by the glorious and learned great poet Soma·deva.

2

MEANWHILE THE young brahmin Shakti·deva was down- 5.2.1
cast having been spurned by the princess he desired, and said to himself, 'By lying just now that I had seen Kánaka·puri, I didn't get the princess, but I was greatly humiliated. So to get her I must wander the earth until either I find that city or I die. For if I don't see that city and come back, and get the princess as the reward for doing so, what is the point of living?'

Having made this promise to himself, that brahmin then 5.2.5
left the city of Vardhamána and set out in a southerly direction. In the course of his journey he eventually arrived at the great forest of the Vindhyas and entered within. It was as impenetrable and extensive as his longing. With the soft leaves on its trees shaking in the wind it seemed to fan him, heated as he was by the sun's many rays; it seemed to cry out day and night with the horrible screams of animals being killed by lions and other beasts, as if in sadness at being

krośantyāṃ tīvra|siṃh'|ādi|hanyamāna|mṛg'|āravaiḥ.
svacchandī|cchalad|uddāma|mahā|maru|marīcibhiḥ
jigīṣantyām iv' âtyugrāṇy api tejāṃsi bhāsvataḥ.
5.2.10 jala|saṃhati|hīnāyām† apy aho sulabh'|āpadi
satat'|ôllaṅghyamānāyām api dūrī|bhavad|bhuvi.

divasair dūram adhvānam atikramya dadarśa saḥ
ekānte śītala|svaccha|salilaṃ su|mahat saraḥ.
puṇḍarīk'|ôcchrita|cchattraṃ prollasadd|haṃsa|cāmaram
kurvāṇam iva sarveṣāṃ sarasām adhirājatām.
tasmin snān'|ādi kṛtvā ca tat|pārśve punar uttare
apaśyad āśrama|padaṃ sa|phala|snigdha|pādapam.
tatr' âśvattha|taror mūle niṣaṇṇaṃ tāpasair vṛtam
sa Sūryatapasaṃ nāma sthaviraṃ munim aikṣata.
5.2.15 sva|vayo|'bda|śata|granthi|saṃkhyay" êv' âkṣa|mālayā
jarā|dhavala|karṇ'|âgra|saṃśrayiṇyā virājitam.
praṇāma|pūrvakaṃ taṃ ca munim abhyājagāma saḥ
ten' âpy atithi|sat|kārair muninā so 'bhyanandyata.
apṛcchyata ca ten' âiva saṃvibhajya phal'|ādibhiḥ
‹kutaḥ prāpto 'si gant" âsi kva ca, bhadr,' ôcyatām iti.›

‹Vardhamāna|purāt tāvad, bhagavann, aham āgataḥ
gantuṃ pravṛttaḥ Kanakapurīm asmi pratijñayā.
na jāne kva bhavet sā tu bhagavān vaktu vetti cet›
iti taṃ Śaktidevo 'pi sa prahvo munim abhyadhāt.
5.2.20 ‹vatsa, varṣa|śatāny aṣṭau mam' āśrama|pade tv iha
atikrāntāni na ca sā śrut" âpi nagarī mayā.›

overrun by so many thieves; with the shafts of light spontaneously springing from its great untamed wildernesses, it seemed to want to overcome even the extremely intense rays of the sun; even though it had no water-holes, calamities 5.2.10
were freely available;* and even on being continuously traversed, it extended far into the distance.

Some days later after he had gone a long way, he saw in a lonely spot a huge lake, its waters cool and pure. With lotuses as its lofty parasols and gleaming swans its yak's tail fly whisks, it seemed to be ruling over all lakes.* After performing his ablutions in it, he saw on its northern bank an ashram where there were lovely trees laden with fruit. In it, at the foot of an *ashváttha* tree, sitting surrounded
by ascetics, he saw an old sage called Surya·tapas. With his 5.2.15
rosary of beads, the number of its knots seeming to be the centuries of his life, touching the top of his ear, where old age had whitened his hair, he looked magnificent. Shakti·deva bowed and approached the sage, who welcomed him hospitably. After sharing some fruits and so forth, the sage asked him, 'From where have you come, and where are you going, good sir? Please tell me.'

With a bow, Shakti·deva said to the sage, 'I have just come from the city of Vardhamána, your reverence, and I am on my way to Kánaka·puri to honor a promise, but I do not know where it is. If your reverence knows, please tell me.'

'My boy, I have spent eight hundred years here in this 5.2.20
ashram but I haven't even heard of that city.'

iti ten' âpi muninā gaditaḥ sa viṣādavān
punar ev' âbravīt ‹tarhi mṛto 'smi kṣmāṃ bhramann iha.›
tataḥ krameṇa jñāt'|ârthaḥ sa munis tam abhāṣata
‹yadi te niścayas tarhi yad ahaṃ vacmi tat kuru.
asti Kāmpilya|viṣayo yojanānāṃ śateṣv itaḥ
triṣu tatr' Ôttar'|ākhyaś ca giris tatr' âpi c' āśramaḥ.
tatr' āryo 'sti mama bhrātā jyeṣṭho Dīrghatapā iti
tat|pārśvaṃ vraja jānīyāt sa vṛddho jātu tāṃ purīm.›
5.2.25 etac chrutvā ‹tath" êty› uktvā jāt'|āsthas tatra tāṃ niśām
nītvā pratasthe sa prātaḥ Śaktidevo drutaṃ tataḥ.
kleś'|âtikrānta|kāntāra|śataś c' āsādya taṃ cirāt
Kāmpilya|viṣayaṃ tasminn āruroh' Ôttare girau.
tatra taṃ Dīrghatapasaṃ munim āśrama|vartinam
dṛṣṭvā praṇamya ca prītaḥ kṛt'|ātithyam upāyayau.
vyajijñapac ca ‹Kanakapurīṃ rāja|sut'|ôditām
prasthito 'haṃ na jānāmi, bhagavan, kv' âsti sā purī.
sā ca me '|vaśya|gantavyā tatas tad|upalabdhaye
ṛṣiṇā Sūryatapasā preṣito 'smi tav' ântikam.›
5.2.30 ity uktavantaṃ taṃ Śaktidevaṃ so 'py abravīn muniḥ
‹iyatā vayasā, putra, purī s" âdya śrutā mayā.
deś'|ântar'|āgataiḥ kaiḥ kair jātaḥ paricayaś ca† me
na ca tāṃ śrutavān asmi dūre tad|darśanaṃ punaḥ.
jānāmy ahaṃ ca niyataṃ davīyasi tayā kva|cit
bhāvyaṃ dvīp'|ântare, vatsa, tatr' ôpāyaṃ ca vacmi te.
asti vāri|nidher madhye dvīpam Utsthala|saṃjñakam
tatra Satyavrat'|ākhyo 'sti Niṣād'|âdhipatir dhanī.

When the sage said this to him he was depressed and spoke again: 'In that case I shall die here in the course of my wanderings about the earth.'

When in the course of time the sage found out the truth of the matter, he said to him, 'If your mind is made up, then do what I shall tell you. There is a country called Kampílya three hundred *yójana*s from here. In it is a mountain called Úttara, and on that is an ashram. My noble elder brother Dirgha·tapas lives there. Go to him. He is old and may perhaps know of that city.'

When he heard this, Shakti·deva was heartened and 5.2.25
agreed to it. He spent the night there and hurried off in the morning. Having fought his way through hundreds of forests, he reached the land of Kampílya after an age and there climbed mount Úttara. On it he found the sage Dirgha·tapas in his ashram. After bowing and gladly accepting his hospitality, he said, 'I have set out for Kánaka·puri, which a princess has told me about, but, your reverence, I do not know where that city is. I must go there, so the sage Surya·tapas sent me to you to find out about it.'

When Shakti·deva said this, the sage replied, 'Even though 5.2.30
I am so old, my son, today is the first time I have heard of that city. I have met all sorts of people from foreign countries, and I have not heard of it, let alone seen it. I am certain it must be on some far off foreign island, my child, and I shall tell you a way to find it. There is in the middle of the ocean an island called Útsthala. The king of the Nishádas lives there. He is called Satya·vrata and is a rich man. He goes to and fro between all the other islands and he might
perhaps have seen or heard of that city. So you should first 5.2.35

tasya dvīp'|ântareṣv asti sarveṣv api gat'|āgatam
tena sā nagarī jātu bhaved dṛṣṭā śrut" âpi vā.
5.2.35 tasmāt prayāhi jaladher upakaṇṭha|pratiṣṭhitam
nagaraṃ prathamaṃ tāvad Viṭaṅkapura|saṃjñakam.
tataḥ ken' âpi vaṇijā samaṃ pravahaṇena tat
Niṣādasy' āspadaṃ gaccha dvīpaṃ tasy' êṣṭa|siddhaye.›

ity uktas tena muninā Śaktidevaḥ sa tat|kṣaṇam
‹tath" êty› uktvā tam āmantrya prayāti sma tad|āśramāt.

kālena prāpya c' ôllaṅghya deśān krośān vahaṃś ca saḥ
vāridhes tīra|tilakaṃ tad Vikaṭaṅkapuraṃ param.
tasmin Samudradatt'|ākhyam Utsthala|dvīpa|yāyinam
anviṣya vaṇijaṃ tena saha sakhyaṃ cakāra saḥ.
5.2.40 tadīyaṃ yāna|pātraṃ ca samaṃ ten' âdhiruhya saḥ
tat|prīti|pūrṇa|pātheyaḥ pratasthe 'mbudhi|vartmanā.
tato 'lpa|deśe gantavye samuttasthāv a|śaṅkitam
kālo vidyul|latā|jihvo garjan parjanya|rākṣasaḥ.
laghūn unnamayan bhāvān *gurūn apy avapātayan*
vavau vidher iv' ārambhaḥ pracaṇḍaś ca prabhañjanaḥ.
vāt'|āhatāś ca jaladher udatiṣṭhan mah"|ôrmayaḥ
āśray'|âbhibhava|krodhād iva śailāḥ sa|pakṣakāḥ.
yayau ca tat pravahaṇaṃ kṣaṇam ūrdhvam adhaḥ kṣaṇam
ucchrāya|pāta|paryāyaṃ darśayad dhaninām iva.
5.2.45 kṣaṇ'|ântare ca vaṇijām ākrandais tīvra|pūritam
bharād iva tad utpatya vahanaṃ samabhajyata.
bhagne ca tasmiṃs tat|svāmī sa vaṇik patito 'mbudhau
tīrṇaś ca phalak'|ārūḍhaḥ prāpy' ânyad vahanaṃ cirāt.
Śaktidevaṃ patantaṃ tu taṃ vyātta|mukha|kandaraḥ
a|parikṣata|sarv'|âṅgaṃ mahā|matsyo nigīrṇavān.

go to the city called Vitánka·pura on the shore of the ocean and from there go by boat with some merchant or other to the island home of that Nisháda in order to get what you want.'

When the sage told him this, Shakti·deva immediately said, 'So be it,' took his leave and set forth from the ashram.

In time, after reaching and crossing countries and traveling many *kroshas*, he arrived at Vitánka·pura, the tilak on the ocean's shore. There he found a merchant called Samúdra·datta who was going to the island of Útsthala and
he made friends with him. He boarded his boat with him 5.2.40
and set forth across the sea, fully equipped with provisions for the journey thanks to the kindness of the merchant. Then, with not far left to go, a black, roaring demon of a storm cloud, streaks of lightning for its tongue, appeared from nowhere and a terrifying hurricane raged, *lifting up light objects : exalting the insignificant* and *hurling down heavy : doing down the important* as if it were the efforts of fate. Whipped up by the wind, great waves rose up from the ocean as if they were winged mountains enraged at the assault on their home.* One moment the boat went up, the next down, as if demonstrating the alternating rise and fall
of rich men, and the next moment, as if overloaded by the 5.2.45
screams of the merchants, the boat keeled over and disintegrated. When it broke up, its owner the merchant fell into the sea and was rescued when after an age on top of a plank he reached another boat. But as he sank, Shakti·deva was swallowed, completely unhurt, by a huge fish with a cavernous gaping mouth.*

sa ca matsyo 'bdhi|madhyena tat|kālaṃ sv'|êcchayā caran
Utsthala|dvīpa|nikaṭaṃ jagāma vidhi|yogataḥ.
tatra tasy' âiva kaivarta|pateḥ Satyavratasya saḥ
śaphara|grāhibhir bhṛtyaiḥ prāpya daivād agṛhyata.
5.2.50 te ca taṃ su|mahā|kāyaṃ ninyur ākṛṣya kautukāt
tad" âiva dhīvarās tasya nijasya svāmino 'ntikam.
so 'pi taṃ tādṛśaṃ dṛṣṭvā tair eva sa|kutūhalaḥ
pāṭhīnaṃ pāṭayām āsa bhṛtyaiḥ Satyavrato nijaiḥ.
pāṭitasy' ôdarāj jīvañ Śaktidevo 'tha tasya saḥ
anubhūt'|âpar'|āścarya|garbha|vāso viniryayau.
niryātaṃ ca kṛta|svasti|kāraṃ taṃ ca sa|vismayaḥ
yuvānaṃ vīkṣya papraccha dāśaḥ Satyavratas tataḥ.
‹kas tvaṃ kathaṃ kutaś c' âiṣā
    śaphar'|ôdara|śāyitā
brahmaṃs, tvay" āptā? ko 'yaṃ te
    vṛttānto 'tyantam adbhutaḥ?›
5.2.55 tac chrutvā Śaktidevas taṃ dāś'|êndraṃ pratyabhāṣata
‹brāhmaṇaḥ Śaktidev'|ākhyo Vardhamāna|purād aham
avaśya|gamyā Kanakapurī ca nagarī mayā
a|jānānaś ca tāṃ dūrād bhrānto 'smi su|ciraṃ bhuvam.
tato Dīrghatapo|vākyāt saṃbhāvya dvīpa|gāṃ ca tām
taj|jñaptaye dāśa|pater Utsthala|dvīpa|vāsinaḥ.
pārśvaṃ Satyavratasy' âhaṃ gacchan vahana|bhaṅgataḥ
magno 'mbudhau nigīrṇo 'haṃ matsyena prāpito 'dhunā.›
ity uktavantaṃ taṃ Śaktidevaṃ Satyavrato 'bravīt
‹Satyavrato 'ham ev' âitad dvīpaṃ tac c' êdam eva te.
5.2.60 kiṃ tu dṛṣṭā bahu|dvīpa|dṛśvan" âpi na sā mayā
nagarī tvad|abhipretā dvīp'|ânteṣu śrutā punaḥ.›

By a stroke of fate, that fish, which at that time was wandering at will through the ocean, arrived near the island of Útsthala. Some servants of that same fisherman King Satya·vrata, out to catch *shápha ra* fish, happened to arrive there and catch it. The fishermen excitedly hauled in the huge fish 5.2.50
and took it straight to their lord. And Satya·vrata, seeing the *pathína* fish like that, was curious and had those same servants of his tear it open. Then Shakti·deva emerged alive from its belly once it had been ripped open, having experienced a second, amazing, stay in a womb. The fisherman Satya·vrata, on seeing a young man come out and hail him was astonished and asked him, 'Who are you and how and why did you come to be residing in the belly of a *shápha ra* fish, O brahmin? What is this exceedingly strange story of yours?'

Shakti·deva replied to the king of the fishermen, 'I am 5.2.55
a brahmin called Shakti·deva from the city of Vardhamána and I have to go to the city of Kánaka·puri. I do not know where it is and have been wandering far across the world for a very long time. Then Dirgha·tapas told me that it might be on an island. I was on my way to the king of the fishermen, Satya·vrata, who lives on the island of Útsthala, in order to find out, when the boat was destroyed and I sank into the sea where a fish swallowed me and brought me to where I am now.'

After Shakti·deva said this, Satya·vrata told him, 'I am Satya·vrata and this is the island you are after. However, 5.2.60
even though I have seen a lot of islands, I have not seen the city that you seek, but I have heard that it is on the far-off islands.'

ity uktvā Śaktidevaṃ ca viṣaṇṇaṃ vīkṣya tat|kṣaṇam
punar abhyāgata|prītyā taṃ sa Satyavrato 'bhyadhāt.
‹brahman, mā gā viṣādaṃ tvam ih' âiv' âdya niśāṃ vasa
prātaḥ kaṃ|cid upāyaṃ te vidhāsyam' îṣṭa|siddhaye.›
ity āśvāsya sa ten' âiva dāśena prahitas tataḥ
su|labh'|âtithi|satkāraṃ dvijo vipra|maṭhaṃ yayau.
tatra tad|vāsin" âikena kṛt'|āhāro dvi|janmanā
Viṣṇudatt'|âbhidhānena saha cakre kathā|kramam.
5.2.65 tat|prasaṅgāc ca ten' âiva pṛṣṭas tasmai samāsataḥ
nijaṃ deśaṃ kulaṃ kṛtsnaṃ vṛttāntaṃ ca śaśaṃsa saḥ.
tad buddhvā parirabhy' âinaṃ Viṣṇudattaḥ sa tat|kṣaṇam
babhāṣe harṣa|bāṣp'|âmbu|gharghar'|âkṣara|jarjaram.
‹diṣṭyā mātula|putras tvam eka|deśa|bhavaś ca me
ahaṃ ca bālya eva prāk tasmād deśād ih' āgataḥ.
tad ih' âiv' āssva nacirāt sādhayiṣyati c' âtra te
iṣṭaṃ dvīp'|ântar'|āgacchad|vaṇik|karṇa|paramparā.›
ity uktv" ânvayam āvedya Viṣṇudatto yath"|ôcitaiḥ
taṃ Śaktidevaṃ tat|kālam upacārair upācarat.
5.2.70 Śaktidevo 'pi saṃprāpa vismṛt'|âdhva|klamo mudam
videśe bandhu|lābho hi marāv amṛta|nirjharaḥ.
amaṃsta ca nij'|âbhīṣṭa|siddhim abhyarṇa|vartinīm
antar"|āpāti hi śreyaḥ kārya|saṃpatti|sūcakam.
tato rātrāv a|nidrasya śayanīye niṣeduṣaḥ
abhivāñchita|saṃprāpti|gata|cittasya tasya saḥ.
Śaktidevasya pārśva|stho Viṣṇudattaḥ samarthanam

After Satya·vrata had said this he saw that Shakti·deva was downcast and, in his fondness for unexpected guests, immediately spoke to him again: 'Brahmin, don't be sad. You must spend tonight right here. In the morning I shall arrange some way for you to get what you want.'

Thus heartened, the brahmin was sent off from there by
that same fisherman and went to a brahmin monastery,
where hospitality was freely available. There he was fed by
one of the brahmin inhabitants, who was called Vishnu·
datta, and he made conversation with him. When he was 5.2.65
questioned by Vishnu·datta in the course of their talking,
he told him in brief about his country, his family and everything that had happened to him. On hearing this, Vishnu·
datta immediately embraced him and, tears of joy obscur-
ing his words, stuttered 'What great luck! You are the son
of my maternal uncle and come from the same place as
me. Long ago in my childhood I came here from there. So
you must stay right here and before long the grapevine of
the merchants coming from other islands will enable you
to get what you want.' Straight after saying this and telling
him about his family, Vishnu·datta attended to Shakti·deva
with appropriate hospitality. Shakti·deva forgot the fatigue 5.2.70
of the journey and was happy, for finding a relative in a foreign land is like finding a stream of the nectar of immortality in a desert. He considered the accomplishment of his
aim to be near at hand, for good fortune happening in the
middle of an undertaking indicates that it will be successful. That night when Shakti·deva was lying sleepless on his
bed, thinking about getting what he wanted, Vishnu·datta

vinoda|pūrvakaṃ kurvan kathāṃ kathitavān imām.

‹pur" âbhūt su|mahā|vipro Govindasvāmi|saṃjñakaḥ
mah"|âgrahāre Kālindyā upakaṇṭha|niveśini.
5.2.75 jāyete sma ca tasya dvau sadṛśau guṇa|śālinaḥ
Aśokadatto Vijayadattaś c' êti sutau kramāt.
kālena tatra vasatāṃ teṣām ajani dāruṇam
durbhikṣaṃ tena Govindasvāmī bhāryām uvāca saḥ.
«ayaṃ durbhikṣa|doṣeṇa deśas tāvad vināśitaḥ
tan na śaknomy ahaṃ draṣṭuṃ suhṛd|bāndhava|durgatim.
dīyate ca kiyat kasya? tasmād annaṃ yad asti naḥ
tad dattvā mittra|bandhubhyo vrajāmo viṣayād itaḥ.
Vārāṇasīṃ ca vāsāya sa|kuṭumbāḥ śrayāmahe»
ity uktayā so 'numato bhāryay" ânnam adān nijam.
5.2.80 sa|dāra|suta|bhṛtyaś ca sa deśāt prayayau tataḥ
utsahante na hi draṣṭum uttamāḥ sva|jan'|āpadam.

gacchaṃś ca mārge jaṭilaṃ bhasma|pāṇḍuṃ kapālinam
s'|ârdha|candram iv' Īśānaṃ mahā|vratinam aikṣata.
upetya jñāninaṃ taṃ ca natvā snehena putrayoḥ
śubh'|â|śubhaṃ sa papraccha so 'tha yogī jagāda tam.
«putrau te bhāvi|kalyāṇau kiṃ tv etena kanīyasā
brahman, Vijayadattena viyogas te bhaviṣyati.
tato 'sy' Âśokadattasya dvitīyasya prabhāvataḥ
etena saha yuṣmākaṃ bhūyo bhāvī samāgamaḥ.»

was at his side and told this story, causing him to reflect and entertaining him.

"Long ago there lived a very great brahmin called Govínda·svamin in a large settlement of brahmins on the banks of the Yámuna granted to them by their king. In time two sons 5.2.75
called Ashóka·datta and Víjaya·datta were born to him, and they were as virtuous as he. When they had been living there for a while, a terrible famine occurred, as a result of which Govínda·svamin said to his wife, "Because of the famine, this country is now ruined. I cannot watch the distress of my friends and relations Nobody is giving anybody anything, so let us give what food we have to our friends and relations and leave the country. Let's flee to Varánasi with our family and stay there." On his saying this to her his wife agreed and he gave away his food and left that land with 5.2.80
her, his sons and his servants, for the lofty cannot bear to see disaster befall their own people.

As he was journeying along the road, he saw an ascetic who had taken the great vow.* With his matted locks, body white with ash and skull that he carried, he looked like Shiva with the half moon. He went up to the sage, bowed and out of love for his two sons asked what lay in store them, good or bad. Then the yogi said to him, "Your sons' futures are good, but, brahmin, you shall be separated from this younger one, Víjaya·datta. Then through the power of this other one, Ashóka·datta, you will be reunited with him."

5.2.85 ity uktas tena Govindasvāmī sa jñāninā tadā
sukha|duḥkh'|âdbhut'|ākrāntas tam āmantrya tato yayau.
prāpya Vārāṇasīṃ tāṃ ca tad|bāhye Caṇḍikā|gṛhe
dinaṃ tatr' âticakrāma devī|pūj"|ādi|karmaṇā.
sāyaṃ ca tatr' âiva bahiḥ sa|kuṭumbas taros tale
samāvasat kārpaṭikaiḥ so 'nya|deś'|āgataiḥ saha.
rātrau ca tatra supteṣu sarveṣv adhigat'|âdhvasu
śrānteṣv āstīrṇa|parṇ'|ādi|pāntha|śayyā|niṣādiṣu.
tadīyasya vibuddhasya tasy' â|kasmāt kanīyasaḥ
sūnor Vijayadattasya mahāñ śīta|jvaro 'jani.
5.2.90 sa tena sahasā bhāvi|bandhu|viśleṣa|hetunā
bhayen' êva jvareṇ' âbhūd ūrdhva|romā sa|vepathuḥ.
śīt'|ārtaś ca prabodhy' âiva pitaraṃ svam uvāca tam
«bādhate, tāta, tīvro mām iha śīta|jvaro 'dhunā.
tan me samidham ānīya śīta|ghnaṃ jvalay' ānalam
n' ânyathā mama śāntiḥ syān nayeyaṃ na ca yāminīm.»
tac chrutvā taṃ sa Govindasvāmī tad|vedan'|ākulaḥ
«tāvat kuto 'dhunā vahnir, vats,' êti?» ca samabhyadhāt.
«nanv ayaṃ nikaṭe, tāta, dṛśyate 'gnir jvalann itaḥ
bhūyiṣṭhe 'tr' âiva tad gatvā kiṃ n' âṅgaṃ tāpayāmy aham.
5.2.95 tasmāt sa|kampaṃ haste māṃ gṛhītvā prāpaya drutam»
ity uktas tena putreṇa punar vipro 'pi so 'bravīt.
«śmaśānam etad eṣā ca citā jvalati tat katham
gamyate 'tra piśāc'|ādi|bhīṣaṇe tvaṃ hi bālakaḥ.»

After the sage had said this to him, Govínda·svamin, overcome with happiness, sorrow and wonder, took his leave of him and went on his way. 5.2.85

On reaching Varánasi he spent the day outside the city in a temple to Chándika, worshipping the goddess and so forth. In the evening he stayed there with his family, outside under a tree, in the company of some mercenary guards who had come from other countries. That night when they were all asleep there tired after their journey, lying on wayfarers' beds made of strewn leaves and such like, that younger son of his, Víjaya·datta, suddenly woke
up with cold sweats and high fever. As if it were fear brought 5.2.90
on by his future separation from his relatives, the fever immediately made him shiver and shudder. Stricken with cold, he woke up his father and straightaway said to him, "Father, I'm right now suffering from a severe fever and cold sweats here, so bring me some fuel and light a fire to get rid of the cold. Otherwise I shall get no relief and won't get through the night."

When he heard this, Govínda·svamin, worried by his suffering, said to him, "But where am I to find fire now, my child?"

"Father, is that not a fire which I can see burning near here? It is very big: why don't I go to it and warm my body?
I'm trembling. Quickly, hold my hand and take me there." 5.2.95

When his son said this to him, the brahmin replied, "This is a cremation ground and it is a funeral pyre which is burning, so how can we go there—goblins and the like make it terrifying and you are a child."

etac chrutvā pitur vākyaṃ vatsalasya vihasya saḥ
vīro Vijayadattas taṃ s'|âvaṣṭambham abhāṣata.
«kiṃ piśāc'|ādibhis, tāta, varākaiḥ kriyate mama?
kim alpa|sattvaḥ ko 'py asmi? tad a|śaṅkaṃ nay' âtra mām.»
ity āgrahād vadantaṃ taṃ sa pitā tatra nītavān
so 'py aṅgaṃ tāpayan bālaś citām upasasarpa tām.
5.2.100 jvalantīm anala|jvālā|dhūma|vyākula|mūrdha|jām
nṛ|māṃsa|grāhiṇīṃ sākṣād iva rakṣo|'dhidevatām.
kṣaṇāt tatra samāśvasya so 'rbhakaḥ pitaraṃ ca tam
«cit"|ântar dṛśyate vṛttaṃ kim etad iti?» pṛṣṭavān.
«kapālaṃ mānuṣasy' aitac citāyāṃ, putra, dahyate»
iti taṃ pratyavādīc ca so 'pi pārśva|sthitaḥ pitā.
tataḥ sva|sāhasen' êva dīpt'|âgreṇa nihatya tam
kapālaṃ sphoṭayām āsa kāṣṭhen' âikena so 'rbhakaḥ.
ten' ôccaiḥ prasṛtā tasmān mukhe tasy' âpatad vasā
śmaśāna|vahninā naktaṃ|carī|siddhir iv' ârpitā.
5.2.105 tad|āsvādena bālaś ca saṃpanno 'bhūt sa rākṣasaḥ
ūrdhva|keśaḥ śikh'|ôtkhāta|khaḍgo daṃṣṭrā|viśaṅkaṭaḥ.
ākṛṣya ca kapālaṃ tad vasāṃ pītvā lileha saḥ
asthi|lagn'|ânala|jvālā|lolayā nija|jihvayā.
tatas tyakta|kapālaḥ san pitaraṃ nijam eva tam
Govindasvāminaṃ hantum udyat'|âsir iyeṣa saḥ.
«Kapālasphoṭa bho, deva, na hantavyaḥ pitā tava
ita eh' îti» tat|kālaṃ śmaśānād udabhūd vacaḥ.

When he heard these words from his devoted father, the brave Víjaya·datta laughed and resolutely said to him, "What are goblins and other vile creatures going to do to me, father? Am I some sort of coward? Take me there without fear."

With him insisting like this, his father took him there and, warming his body, the boy approached the funeral pyre, which, blazing and devouring the flesh of men, was 5.2.100
like the tutelary goddess of the demons in visible form, the smoke and flames of the fire her wild hair. After a moment, the boy, feeling better, asked his father, "What's that round thing I can see inside the pyre?" and his father, standing at his side, replied, "That is a man's skull, my boy, being burned in the pyre."

At this the boy, using, as if it were his own impetuousness, a piece of wood whose tip was alight, struck the skull and made it burst. The brains spurted up out of it and fell into the boy's mouth, as if the cremation ground fire were bestowing upon him the magical ability to become a nocturnal demon. By tasting it the boy became a *rákshasa*: his 5.2.105
hair stood on end, he carried a sword extracted from the flames and had hideous fangs. He took the skull, drank the brains and licked it with his tongue flickering like the flames of the fire clinging to the bones. Then he let go of the skull and went to kill his own father Govínda·svamin, sword at the ready. At that moment a voice came from the cremation ground: "Oh, your highness Kapála·sphota, your father is not to be killed, so come here!"

tac chrutvā nāma labdhvā ca Kapālasphoṭa ity adaḥ
sa baṭuḥ pitaraṃ muktvā rakṣo|bhūtas tiro|dadhe.
5.2.110 tat|pitā so 'pi Govindasvāmī «hā putra! hā guṇin!
hā hā Vijayadatt' êti» mukt'|ākrandas tato yayau.
etya Caṇḍī|gṛhaṃ tac ca prātaḥ patnyai sutāya ca
jyāyase 'śokadattāya yathā|vṛttaṃ śaśaṃsa saḥ.
tatas tābhyāṃ sah' ân|abhra|vidyud|āpāta|dāruṇam
yathā śok'|ânal'|āveśam ājagāma sa tāpataḥ.†
tathā† Vārāṇasī|saṃstho devī|saṃdarśan'|āgataḥ
tatr' ôpetya jano 'py anyo yayau tat|sama|duḥkhatām.
tāvac ca devī|pūj"|ârtham āgaty' âiko mahā|vaṇik
apaśyad atra Govindasvāminaṃ taṃ tathā|vidham.
5.2.115 Samudradatta|nām" âsāv upety' āśvāsya taṃ dvijam
tad" âiva sva|gṛhaṃ sādhur nināya sa|paricchadam.
snān'|ādin" ôpacāreṇa tatra c' âinam upācarat
nisargo hy eṣa mahatāṃ yad|āpann'|ânukampanam.
so 'pi jagrāha Govindasvāmī patnyā samaṃ dhṛtim
mahā|vrati|vacaḥ śrutvā jāt'|āsthaḥ suta|saṃgame.
tataḥ prabhṛti c' âitasyāṃ Vārāṇasyām uvāsa saḥ
abhyarthito mah"|āḍhyasya tasy' âiva vaṇijo gṛhe.
tatr' âiv' âdhīta|vidyo 'sya sa sutaḥ prāpta|yauvanaḥ
dvitīyo 'śokadatt'|ākhyo bāhu|yuddham aśikṣata.
5.2.120 krameṇa ca yayau tatra prakarṣaṃ sa tathā yathā
ajīyata na ken' âpi pratimallena bhū|tale.
ekadā deva|yātrāyāṃ tatra malla|samāgame

On hearing this and receiving the name Kapála·sphota, the brahmin boy let go of his father and, now a *rákshasa*, disappeared.

His father Govínda·svamin went from there, wailing, 5.2.110
"Oh my son! Oh virtuous one! Oh! Oh! Víjaya·datta!" He returned to the temple of Chándika and in the morning told his wife and elder son Ashóka·datta what had happened. Then, together with those two, as a result of his distress, he was possessed by the fire of grief which was as formidable as a bolt of lightning from a cloudless sky. As a result when the other people staying in Varánasi came to have darshan of the goddess, on reaching that place they became as upset as he. Meanwhile an important merchant arrived to worship the goddess and found Govínda·svamin
there in that state. The man, who was called Samúdra·datta, 5.2.115
went up to that brahmin and comforted him. Then the good fellow took him and his entourage straight to his home. There he attended to him hospitably, having him take a bath and so forth, for sympathy towards those in difficulty is a characteristic of the great. Govínda·svamin and his wife, who had heard the words of the *kapálika* and were hopeful of being reunited with their son, pulled themselves together. After that he stayed in Varánasi in the very rich merchant's house at his request.

There his other son, who was called Ashóka·datta, was taught the sciences, and when he had come of age he learned
to wrestle. In time he became so good at it that no wrestler 5.2.120
in the world could beat him. One day during a religious festival a great and famous wrestler from the south came

āgād eko mahā|mallaḥ khyātimān dakṣiṇā|pathāt.
ten' âtra nikhilā mallā rājño Vārāṇasī|pateḥ
Pratāpamukuṭ'|ākhyasya purato 'nye parājitāḥ.
tataḥ sa rājā mallasya yuddhe tasya samādiśat
ānāyy' Âśokadattaṃ taṃ śrutaṃ tasmād vaṇig|varāt.
so 'pi mallo bhujaṃ hatvā hasten' ārabhat' āhavam
mallaṃ c' Âśokadattas tu bhujaṃ hatvā nyapātayat.
5.2.125 tatas tatra mahā|malla|nipāt'|ôtthita|śabdayā
yuddha|bhūmy" âpi saṃtuṣya sādhu|vāda iv' ôdite.
sa rāj" Âśokadattaṃ taṃ tuṣṭo ratnair apūrayat
cakāra c' ātmanaḥ pārśva|vartinaṃ dṛṣṭa|vikramam.

so 'pi rājñaḥ priyo bhūtvā dinaiḥ prāpa parāṃ śriyam
śeva|dhiḥ śūra|vidyasya viśeṣa|jño viśāṃ|patiḥ.
so 'tha jātu yayau rājā caturdaśyāṃ bahiḥ pure
supratiṣṭhāpitaṃ dūre devam arcayituṃ Śivam.
kṛt'|ârcanas tato naktaṃ śmaśānasy' ântikena saḥ
āgacchann aśṛṇod etāṃ tan|madhyād udgatāṃ giram.
5.2.130 «ahaṃ daṇḍ'|âdhipen' êha mithyā vadhy'|ânukīrtanāt
dveṣeṇa viddhaḥ śūlāyāṃ tṛtīyaṃ divasaṃ, prabho.
ady' âpi na ca niryānti prāṇā me '|pāpa|karmaṇaḥ†
tad, deva, tṛṣito 'tyartham ahaṃ dāpaya me jalam.»

tac chrutvā kṛpayā rājā sa pārśva|stham uvāca tam
Aśokadattam «asy' âmbhaḥ prahiṇotu bhavān iti.»

there to a wrestlers' meet. There, before the king of Varánasi, who was called Pratápa·múkuta, he defeated all the king's other wrestlers. Then the king, having heard about Ashóka·datta from the eminent merchant, ordered him to be brought to fight that wrestler, who started the contest by striking him on the arm with his hand, but Ashóka·datta struck the wrestler on the arm and made him fall over. At 5.2.125
this even the wrestling arena seemed to call out "Bravo!" in delight with the sound made in it by the fall of the great wrestler. The pleased king gave Ashóka·datta lots of jewels and having witnessed his prowess made him his attendant.

Ashóka·datta, having become the king's favorite, acquired a great fortune within a few days. A king who appreciates special qualities is a store of treasure for one who has learned to be a hero. Then on the fourteenth day of the dark fortnight the king went out of the city to worship Shiva at a well endowed temple far away. After he had performed his worship and was near the cremation ground on his way back that night, he heard a voice come from inside it, saying the following: "After wrongly receiving a death sentence from a 5.2.130
hateful chief judge, I have been impaled on a stake for three days, your majesty. I have done nothing wrong and even now my life breaths will not leave me, so, your highness, I am extremely thirsty. Have some water given to me."

When he heard this, out of pity the king told Ashóka·datta, who was at his side, to send the man some water.

«ko 'tra rātrau vrajed, deva, tad gacchāmy aham ātmanā»
ity uktv" Âśokadattaḥ sa gṛhītv" âmbhas tato yayau.
yāte ca sva|purīṃ rājñi sa vīro gahan'|ântaram
mahattareṇa tamasā sarvato 'ntar|adhiṣṭhitam.
5.2.135 śiv"|âvakīrṇa|piśita|pratta|saṃdhyā|mahā|bali
kva|cit|kva|cic|citā|jyotir|dīpra|dīpa|prakāśitam.
lasad|uttāla|vetāla|tāla|vādyaṃ viveśa tat
śmaśānaṃ kṛṣṇa|rajanī|nivāsa|bhavan'|ôpamam.
«ken' âmbho yācitaṃ bhūpād ity?» uccais tatra sa bruvan
«mayā yācitam ity» evam aśṛṇod vācam ekataḥ.
gatvā tad|anusāreṇa nikaṭa|sthaṃ cit"|ânalam
dadarśa tatra śūl'|âgre viddhaṃ kaṃ|cit sa pūruṣam.
adhaś ca tasya rudatīṃ sad|alaṃkāra|bhūṣitām
a|dṛṣṭa|pūrvāṃ sarv'|âṅga|sundarīṃ striyam aikṣata.
5.2.140 kṛṣṇa|pakṣa|parikṣīṇe gate 'staṃ rajanī|patau
cit"|ārohāya tad|raśmi|ramyāṃ rātrim iv' āgatām.

«kā tvam, amba? kathaṃ c' êha rudaty evam avasthitā?»
iti pṛṣṭā ca sā tena yoṣid evaṃ tam abravīt.
«asy' âhaṃ śūla|viddhasya bhāryā vigata|lakṣaṇā
niścit'|āśā sthit" âsm' îha cit"|ārohe sah' âmunā.
kaṃ|cit kālaṃ pratīkṣe ca prāṇānām asya niṣkramam
tṛtīye 'hni gate 'py adya yānty etasya hi n' āsavaḥ.
yācate ca muhus toyam ānītaṃ ca may" êha tat
kiṃ tv ahaṃ n' ônnate śūle prāpnomy asya mukhaṃ, sakhe.»

"No one will go there at night, your highness, so I shall go there myself." With this Ashóka·datta took some water and set forth. When the king had left for his city, our 5.2.135
hero entered the cremation ground. It was pitch dark all around and its interior was impenetrable, jackals had scattered morsels of human flesh from the evening offerings, it was lit up here and there by shining torches that were the lights of the funeral pyres and the awful sound of *vetálas* clapping rang out: it was like the abode of black night. As he was calling out there, "Who asked the king for water?," he heard a voice say from one side, "I asked for it." Following it he went to a nearby funeral pyre and saw some man impaled there on top of a spike. Below him he saw crying a woman whom he had not seen before. She was adorned with fine jewelry and beautiful from head to toe. With the 5.2.140
moon, night's husband, having wasted away over the dark fortnight and disappeared, it was as if night herself, made lovely by his rays, had come to ascend the funeral pyre.*

"Who are you, mother? And why are you crying here like this?" When he asked her this, the woman replied, "I am the ill-starred wife of this man who has been impaled. I am waiting here in the firm hope that I might ascend the funeral pyre with him. I expect his life-breaths to depart at some time, but even though the third day has passed they still do not leave him. He keeps asking for water and I have brought some here, but he is on a tall stake and I cannot reach his mouth, my friend."

5.2.145 iti tasyā vacaḥ śrutvā sa pravīro 'py uvāca tām
«idaṃ tv asya nṛpeṇ' âpi haste me preṣitaṃ jalam.
tan me pṛṣṭhe padaṃ dattvā dehy etasy' âitad ānane
na para|sparśa|mātraṃ hi strīṇām āpadi dūṣaṇam.»

etac chrutvā «tath" êty» ātta|jalā dattvā pada|dvayam
śūla|mūl'|âvanamrasya pṛṣṭhaṃ tasy' āruroha sā.
kṣaṇād bhuvi sva|pṛṣṭhe ca rakta|binduṣv a|śaṅkitam
patatsu mukham unnamya sa vīro yāvad īkṣate
tāvat striyam apaśyat tāṃ chittvā churikayā muhuḥ
khādantīṃ tasya māṃsāni puṃsaḥ śūl'|âgra|vartinaḥ.
5.2.150 tatas tāṃ vikṛtiṃ matvā krodhād ākṛṣya sa kṣitau
āsphoṭayiṣyañ jagrāha pāde raṇita|nūpure.
s" âpi taṃ tarasā pādam ākṣipy' âiva sva|māyayā
kṣipraṃ gaganam utpatya jagāma kv' âpy a|darśanam.

tasya c' Âśokadattasya tat|pādān maṇi|nūpuram
tasmād ākarṣaṇa|srastam avatasthe kar'|ântare.
tatas tāṃ peśalām ādāv adhaḥ|kartrīṃ ca madhyataḥ
ante vikāra|ghorāṃ ca durjanair iva saṃgatim
naṣṭāṃ vicintayan paśyan haste divyaṃ ca nūpuram
sa|vismayaḥ s'|âbhitāpaḥ sa|harṣaś ca babhūva saḥ.
5.2.155 tataḥ śmaśānatas tasmāt sa jagām' ātta|nūpuraḥ
nija|gehaṃ prabhāte ca snāto rāja|kulaṃ yayau.
«kiṃ tasya śūla|viddhasya dattaṃ vār' îti» pṛcchate
rājñe sa ca «tath" êty» uktvā taṃ nūpuram upānayat.
«etat kuta iti?» svairaṃ pṛṣṭas tena sa bhūbhṛtā

When he heard these words from her, our hero replied, 5.2.145
"But this water in my hand has been sent for him by the king, so place your foot on my back and put the water his mouth, for in times of trouble there is no harm in a woman just touching another man."

When she heard this, she agreed and, taking the water, put both her feet on his back as he bent over at the foot of the stake, and climbed up. When after a moment drops of blood were unexpectedly falling on the ground and onto his back, our hero lifted his head and had a look. He saw the woman repeatedly using a knife to cut pieces of flesh from the man who was on top of the stake and eating them.
Then, believing her to be a ghoul, he angrily pulled her to 5.2.150
the ground and, wanting to smash her to pieces, seized her by the foot, its anklets tinkling. She quickly pulled back her foot and used her magical powers to shoot up into the sky and disappear.

Having slipped from her foot while it was being pulled, her jeweled anklet remained in Ashóka·datta's hand. Thinking how, like the company of evil men, she had been tender at first, wicked in the middle and had finally transformed into something terrifying before disappearing, and seeing in his hand the heavenly anklet, he was astonished, sorry and
delighted. Then, taking the anklet, he went from the crema- 5.2.155
tion ground to his house and in the morning, after bathing, he went to the palace. When the king asked him whether he had given water to the man impaled on the stake, he said he had and presented the king with the anklet. The king quietly asked him where it had come from and he told him the amazing and terrifying story of what had happened to

tasmai sva|rātri|vṛttāntaṃ śaśaṃs' âdbhuta|bhīṣaṇam.
tataś c' ân|anya|sāmānyaṃ sattvaṃ tasy' âvadhārya saḥ
tuṣṭo 'py anya|guṇ'|ôtkarṣāt tutoṣa sutarāṃ nṛpaḥ.
gṛhītvā nūpuraṃ taṃ ca gatvā devyai dadau svayam
hṛṣṭas tat|prāpti|vṛttāntaṃ tasyai ca samavarṇayat.
5.2.160 sā tad buddhvā ca dṛṣṭvā ca taṃ divyaṃ maṇi|nūpuram
Aśokadatta|ślāgh'|âika|tat|parā mumude rahaḥ.
tato jagāda tāṃ rājā «devi, jāty" êva vidyayā
satyen' êva ca rūpeṇa mahatām apy ayaṃ mahān.
Aśokadatto bhavyāyā bhartā ca duhitur yadi
bhaven Madanalekhāyās tad bhadram iti me matiḥ.
varasy' âmī guṇāḥ prekṣyā na lakṣmīḥ kṣaṇa|bhaṅginī
tad etasmai pravīrāya dadāmy etāṃ sutām aham.»
iti bhartur vacaḥ śrutvā devī sā s'|ādar" âvadat
«yuktam etad asau hy asyā yuvā bhart" ânurūpakaḥ.
5.2.165 sā ca tena madh'|ûdyāna|dṛṣṭena hṛta|mānasā
śūny'|āśayā dineṣv eṣu na śṛṇoti na paśyati.
tat|sakhītaś ca tad buddhvā sa|cint" âhaṃ niśā|kṣaye
suptā jāne striyā svapne kay" âpy ukt" âsmi divyayā.
‹vatse, Madanalekh" êyaṃ dey" ânyasmai na kanyakā
eṣa hy Aśokadattasya bhāryā janm'|ântar'|ârjitā.›
tac ca śrutvā prabuddhy' âiva gatvā pratyūṣa eva ca
svayaṃ tat|pratyayād vatsāṃ samāśvāsitavaty aham.
idānīṃ c' ārya|putreṇa svayam eva mam' ôditam
tasmāt sametu ten' âsau vṛkṣeṇ' êv' ārtavī latā.»

him during the night. At this the king, realizing that his valor was unlike that of anyone else, and even though he was already pleased with his other excellent qualities, was even more delighted. He took the anklet and went and gave it to the queen in person. In his delight he told her how it
had been obtained and when she heard the story and be- 5.2.160
held the divine jeweled anklet, she rejoiced inwardly and devoted herself solely to the praise of Ashóka·datta.

Then the king said to her, "Queen, in learning as in birth and in looks as in honesty, this man Ashóka·datta is great even among the great and I think it would be good if he became the husband of our lovely daughter Mádana·lekha. These are the qualities that are to be looked for in a groom, not wealth, which can disappear in an instant, so I shall betroth this daughter of ours to that hero."

When she heard these words from her husband, the queen respectfully said, "This is appropriate, because the boy is a
suitable husband for her. She saw him in the spring garden 5.2.165
and he stole her heart. In the days since her mind has been vacant and she doesn't hear or see anything. When I found out about this from her friends I was worried and on falling asleep at the end of the night I remember some heavenly lady saying to me in a dream, 'My child, this girl Mádana·lekha is not to be given to anyone other than Ashóka·datta, for he won her as his wife in an earlier life.' After hearing this, as soon as I woke up that morning I went straight to my child myself, and, convinced by the dream, comforted her. Now you, my respected husband, have yourself said this to me, so let that boy and girl be united, like a tree and a creeper in season."

5.2.170 ity uktaḥ priyayā prītaḥ sa rājā racit'|ôtsavaḥ
āhūy' Âśokadattāya tasmai tāṃ tanayāṃ dadau
tayoś ca so 'bhūd rāj'|êndra|putrī|vipr'|êndra|putrayoḥ
saṃgamo 'nyonya|śobhāyai lakṣmī|vinayayor iva.
tataḥ kadā|cid rājānaṃ taṃ devī vadati sma sā
Aśokadatt'|ānītaṃ tad uddiśya maṇi|nūpuram.
«ārya|putr,' âyam ekākī nūpuro na virājate
anurūpas tad etasya dvitīyaḥ parikalpyatām.»
tac chrutvā hema|kār'|ādīn ādideśa sa bhū|patiḥ
«nūpurasy' âsya sadṛśo dvitīyaḥ kriyatām iti.»
5.2.175 te tan nirūpya jagadur «n' edṛśo, deva, śakyate
aparaḥ kartum etad dhi divyaṃ śilpaṃ na mānuṣam.
ratnān' īdṛṃśi bhūyāṃsi na bhavanty eva bhū|tale
tasmād eṣa yataḥ prāptas tatr' âiv' ânyo gaveṣyatām.
etac chrutvā sa|devīke viṣaṇṇe rājñi tat|kṣaṇam
Aśokadattas tatra|sthas tad dṛṣṭvā sahas" âbravīt.
«aham ev' ānayāmy asya dvitīyaṃ nūpurasya te»
evaṃ kṛta|pratijñaś ca rājñā sāhasa|śaṅkinā.
snehān nivāryamāṇo 'pi niścayān na cacāla saḥ
gṛhītvā nūpuraṃ tac ca śmaśānaṃ sa punar yayau.
5.2.180 niśi kṛṣṇa|caturdaśyāṃ yatr' âiva tam avāptavān
praviśya tatra ca prājya|citā|dhūma|malī|masaiḥ.
pāś'|ôpaveṣṭita|gala|*skandh*'|ôllambita|mānuṣaiḥ
pādapair iva rakṣobhir ākīrṇe pitṛ|kānane.
a|paśyan pūrva|dṛṣṭāṃ tāṃ striyaṃ tan|nūpur'|āptaye

When his sweetheart said this to him, the king was de- 5.2.170
lighted and held a celebration. He summoned Ashóka·datta and gave his daughter to him, and the union of the daughter of the greatest of kings and the son of the greatest of brahmins, like that of fortune and modesty, led to their mutual splendor.

Then one day the queen said to the king, concerning the jeweled anklet that had been brought by Ashóka·datta, "My noble lord, on its own this anklet is not of note, so have another one like it made."

When the king heard this he instructed his goldsmiths and other craftsmen to make another anklet the same as that
one. After inspecting it, they said, "Your highness, another 5.2.175
one like this cannot be made, for this is divine craftsmanship, not that of men. There are no more gems like these on the earth, so another anklet must be found in the same place from which this one was obtained."

On hearing this, the king and queen were immediately upset. Ashóka·datta was there and on seeing this he rashly announced, "I shall personally bring you a match for this anklet." Having thus made this promise he would not sway from his decision and even though the king, worried that he was being rash, was out of love dissuading him, he took the anklet and went once more to the cremation ground.

He entered the place from where he had obtained the 5.2.180
anklet on the fourteenth night of the dark fortnight, the grove of the ancestors, and it was filled with *rákshasas*, who, dirty with the smoke from all the funeral pyres, and with men with nooses around their necks hanging from their *shoulders : boughs*, were like trees. Not finding the woman

upāyam ekaṃ bubudhe sa mahā|māṃsa|vikrayam.
taru|pāśād gṛhītv" âtha śavaṃ babhrāma tatra saḥ
«vikrīṇāno mahā|māṃsaṃ gṛhyatām iti» ghoṣayan.
«mahā|sattva, gṛhītv" âitad ehi tāvan mayā saha»
iti kṣaṇāc ca jagade sa dūrād ekayā striyā.
5.2.185 tac chrutvā sa tath" âiv' âitām upety' ânusaran striyam
ārāt taru|tale divya|rūpāṃ yoṣitam aikṣata.
strībhir vṛtām āsana|sthāṃ ratn'|ābharaṇa|bhāsurām
a|saṃbhāvya|sthitiṃ tatra marāv ambhojinīm iva.
striyā tay" ôpanītaś ca tām upetya tathā|sthitām
«nṛ|māṃsam asmi vikrīṇe gṛhyatām ity» uvāca saḥ.
«bho mahāsattva, mūlyena ken' âitad dīyate tvayā»
iti s" âpi tad" āha sma divya|rūpā kil' âṅganā.
tataḥ sa vīro hasta|sthaṃ tam ekaṃ maṇi|nūpuram
saṃdarśya skandha|pṛṣṭha|stha|preta|kāyo jagāda tām.
5.2.190 «yo dadāty asya sadṛśaṃ dvitīyaṃ nūpurasya me
māṃsaṃ tasya dadāmy etad asty asau yadi gṛhyatām.»
tac chrutvā s" âpy avādīt tam «asty anyo nūpuro mama
asau madīya ev' âiko nūpuro hi hṛtas tvayā.
s" âiv' âhaṃ yā tvayā dṛṣṭā śūla|viddhasya pārśvataḥ
kṛt'|ânya|rūpā bhavatā parijñāt" âsmi n' âdhunā.
tat kiṃ māṃsena yad ahaṃ vacmi te tat karoṣi cet
tad dvitīyaṃ dadāmy asya tulyaṃ tubhyaṃ sva|nūpuram.»
ity uktaḥ sa tadā vīraḥ pratipadya tad abravīt
«yat tvaṃ vadasi tat sarvaṃ karomy eva kṣaṇād iti.»
5.2.195 tatas tasmai jagād' âivam ā|mūlāt sā manīṣitam
«asti, bhadra, Trighaṇṭ'|ākhyaṃ himavac|chikhare puram.
tatr' āsīl Lambajihv'|ākhyaḥ pravīro rākṣas'|âdhipaḥ

whom he had seen before, he thought of a way to get the anklet—selling human flesh. Then he took a corpse from a noose on a tree and wandered about there, calling out, "Human flesh for sale!"

A moment later a woman called to him from far off, "O
hero, bring it with you and come with me." When he heard 5.2.185
this, he duly went up to her and followed her. From afar he saw a woman of divine appearance at the foot of a tree. She was on a throne, surrounded by women, and sparkled with jeweled ornaments. Her being in that place was unthinkable—she was like a lotus in a desert. Brought forward by the woman, he went up to her as she was and said, "I'm selling human flesh. Take it!" The woman of divine appearance then said, "O hero, for what price are you selling it?" at which our hero, a corpse on his shoulders and back, showed
her the single jeweled anklet in his hand and said to her, "I 5.2.190
shall give this flesh to the person who gives me an anklet which matches this one. If you have one, then take it."

On hearing this, she replied, "I have the other anklet, for the one that you took was mine. I am the same woman whom you saw by the man impaled on the stake. I have assumed a different form and you don't now recognize me. Forget about the flesh. If you do what I say then I shall give you my anklet, which is the match for that one."

When he was told this, our hero agreed and said, "I shall
do straightaway everything that you say." She then told him 5.2.195
all that she wanted: "There is, good sir, a city called Tri·ghanta on a peak of the Himálaya. A courageous *rákshasa* king called Lamba·jihva lived there. I am his wife, Vidyuc·chikha by name, and I can change my appearance as I wish.

tasya Vidyucchikhā nāma bhāry" âhaṃ kāma|rūpiṇī.
sa c' âikasyāṃ sutāyāṃ me jātāyāṃ daivataḥ patiḥ
prabhoḥ Kapālasphoṭasya purato nihato raṇe.
tato nija|puraṃ tan me prabhuṇā tena tuṣyatā
pradattaṃ tena ca sukhaṃ sthit" âsmi sa|sut" âdhunā.
sā ca mad|duhit" ēdānīm ārūḍhā nava|yauvanam
tat|pravīra|vara|prāpti|cintā ca mama mānasam.
5.2.200 atas tadā samaṃ rājñā yāntaṃ tvām amunā pathā
dṛṣṭvā naktaṃ caturdaśyām iha|sth" âham acintayam.
‹ayaṃ bhavyo yuvā vīro yogyo me duhituḥ patiḥ
tad etat|prāptaye kaṃ|cid upāyaṃ kiṃ na kalpaye.›
iti saṃkalpya yācitvā śūla|viddha|vaco|miṣāt
jalaṃ madhye|śmaśānaṃ tvam ānīto 'bhūr mayā mṛṣā.
māyā|darśita|rūp'|ādi|prapañc'|âlīka|vādinī
vipralabdhavatī c' âsmi tatra tvāṃ kṣaṇa|mātrakam.
ākarṣaṇāya bhūyas te yuktyā c' âikaṃ sva|nūpuram
saṃtyajya śṛṅkhalā|pāśam iva yātā tato 'py aham.
5.2.205 adya c' êtthaṃ mayā prāpto bhavāṃs tad gṛham etya naḥ
bhajasva me sutāṃ kiṃ ca gṛhāṇ' âpara|nūpuram.

ity uktaḥ sa niśācaryā «tath" êty» uktvā tayā saha
vīro gagana|mārgeṇa tat|siddhyā tat|puraṃ yayau.
sauvarṇaṃ tad apaśyac ca śṛṅge himavataḥ puram
nabho|'dhva|kheda|viśrāntam arka|bimbam iv' â|calam.

As fate would have it, after one daughter had been born to me, my husband was killed in battle in front of our lord, Kapála·sphota. That thankful king then gave me my own city and through his charity I now live in comfort with my daughter. That daughter of mine has now reached the fresh bloom of youth, and anxiety about finding a courageous groom for her has reached my mind. So at the time 5.2.200
when you were traveling along the road with the king that night on the fourteenth of the fortnight I was here and I saw you. I said to myself, 'This fine and courageous young man is a suitable husband for my daughter, so why don't I devise some way of winning him?' Having made this plan I imitated the voice of a man impaled on a stake and asked for water, thereby getting you into the cremation ground on false pretenses. There, tricking you by showing you my false appearance and so forth, which had been produced by magic, I took you in, just for a moment. And, again using a trick to attract you, I left one of my anklets as if it were a chain, before going on my way. I have thus now found 5.2.205
you, so come to our house, have my daughter and, what's more, take the other anklet."

After being addressed thus by that nocturnal demoness, our hero said yes and by means of her magic went through the sky with her to her city. He beheld that golden city on a peak of the Himálaya and it looked like the orb of the sun, unmoving because it was exhausted from the hard work of traveling through the sky.

rakṣo|'dhipa|sutāṃ tatra nāmnā Vidyutprabhāṃ sa tām
sva|sāhasa|mahā|siddhim iva mūrtām avāptavān.
tayā ca saha tatr' âiva kaṃ|cit kālam uvāsa saḥ
Aśokadattaḥ priyayā śvaśrū|vibhava|nirvṛtaḥ.
5.2.210 tato jagāda tāṃ śvaśrūṃ «mahyaṃ tad dehi nūpuram
yataḥ saṃprati gantavyā purī Vārāṇasī mayā.
tatra hy etat pratijñātaṃ svayaṃ nara|pateḥ puraḥ
eka|tvan|nūpura|spardhi|dvitīy'|ānayanaṃ mayā.»
ity uktā tena sā śvaśrūr dvitīyaṃ taṃ sva|nūpuram
tasmai dattvā punaś c' âikaṃ suvarṇa|kamalaṃ dadau.
prāpt'|âbja|nūpuras tasmāt sa purān niryayau tataḥ
Aśokadatto vacasā niyamy' āgamanaṃ punaḥ.
tayā śvaśrv" âiva c' ākāśa|pathena punar eva tam
śmaśānaṃ prāpitaḥ so 'bhūn nija|siddhi|prabhāvataḥ.
5.2.215 taru|mūle ca tatr' âiva sthitvā sā taṃ tato 'bravīt
«sadā kṛṣṇa|caturdaśyām iha rātrāv upaimy aham
tasyāṃ† niśi ca bhūyo 'pi tvam eṣyasi yadā yadā
tadā tadā vaṭa|taror mūlāt prāpsyasi mām itaḥ.»
etac chrutvā «tath" êty» uktvā tām āmantrya niśācarīm
Aśokadattaḥ sa tato yayau tāvat pitur gṛham.
kanīyaḥ|suta|viśleṣa|duḥkha|dvaiguṇya|dāyinā
tādṛśā tat|pravāsena pitarau tatra duḥkhitau.
a|tarkit'|āgato yāvad ānandayati tat|kṣaṇāt
tāvat sa buddhvā śvaśuras tatr' âiv' âsy' āyayau nṛpaḥ.
5.2.220 sa taṃ sāhasika|sparśa|bhītair iva sa|kaṇṭakaiḥ
aṅgaiḥ praṇatam āliṅgya mumude bhū|patiś ciram.
tatas tena samaṃ rājñā viveśa nṛpa|mandiram

Once there Ashóka·datta obtained that daughter of the king of the *rákshasa*s, who was called Vidyut·prabha, as if she were the incarnation of his boldness's great success. and he lived there with his sweetheart for some time, in comfort
thanks to his mother-in-law's riches. Then he said to his 5.2.210
mother-in-law, "Give me the anklet, because now I have to go to the city of Varánasi for I have promised in person before the king there that I would bring a second anklet to match that one of yours."

When he said this to her, his mother-in-law gave him that second anklet of hers and then also gave him a golden lotus. Taking the lotus and anklet, Ashóka·datta then left that city, having promised to return.

His mother-in-law used her magical powers to take him
through the sky again to the cremation ground. Stopping 5.2.215
at the foot of a tree there, she then said to him, "I always come here at night on the dark of the moon, and whenever you come here again at that time, you shall find me here at the foot of the banyan tree."

On hearing this, Ashóka·datta agreed to do so, took leave of the night-roving demoness and went straight from there to his father's house. Just at that moment when by his unexpected arrival he was bringing bliss to his parents there, who had been tormented by his disappearing like that—which had doubled their sorrow at their separation from their younger son—his father-in-law the king, having heard the
news, arrived there. The king, the hair on his body stand- 5.2.220
ing on end as if in fear of the touch of a brave hero, embraced him as he bowed, and he rejoiced for a long time. Then Ashóka·datta entered the palace with the king and he

Aśokadattaḥ sa tadā pramodo mūrtimān iva.
dadau rājñe sa saṃyuktaṃ tad divyaṃ nūpura|dvayam
kurvāṇam iva tad|vīrya|stutiṃ jhaṇa|jhaṇ'|āravaiḥ.
arpayām āsa tac c' âsmai kāntaṃ kanaka|paṅkajam
rakṣaḥ|koṣa|śriyo hastāl līl"|âmbujam iv' āhṛtam.
pṛṣṭo 'tha kautukāt tena rājñā devī|yutena saḥ
avarṇayad yathā|vṛttaṃ svaṃ karṇ'|ānanda|dāyi tat.
5.2.225 «vicitra|carit'|ôllekha|camatkārita|cetanam
prāpyate kiṃ yaśaḥ śubhram an|aṅgī|kṛtya sāhasam?»
evaṃ vadaṃs tatas tena jāmātrā kṛta|kṛtyatām
mene sa rājā devī ca prāpta|nūpura|yugmakā.
utsav'|ātodya|nirhrādi tadā rāja|gṛhaṃ ca tat
Aśokadattasya guṇān udgāyad iva nirbabhau.
anyedyuś ca sa rājā tat sva|kṛte sura|sadmani
hem'|âbjaṃ sthāpayām āsa sad|raupya|kalaś'|ôpari.
ubhau kalaśa|padmau ca śuśubhate sit'|āruṇau
yaśaḥ|pratāpāv iva tau bhū|pāl'|Âśokadattayoḥ.
5.2.230 tādṛśau ca viloky' âitau sa harṣ'|ôtphulla|locanaḥ
rājā māhêśvaro bhakti|ras'|āveśād abhāṣata.
«aho vibhāti padmena tuṅgo' yaṃ kalaśo 'munā
bhūti|śubhraḥ kapard" îva jaṭā|jūṭena babhruṇā
a|bhaviṣyad dvitīyaṃ ced īdṛśaṃ kanak'|âmbujam
asthāpayiṣyat" âmuṣmin dvitīye kalaśe 'pi tat.»
iti rāja|vacaḥ śrutv" Âśokadattas tato 'bravīt
«āneṣyāmy aham ambho|jaṃ dvitīyam api, deva, te.»

was like delight incarnate at that moment. He gave the king the matching pair of heavenly anklets, which seemed to be singing the praises of his heroism with their tinkling. He gave him that lovely golden lotus and it was as if he had taken the play lotus from the hand of the fortune goddess of the *rákshasas*' treasure trove. At this the curious king and queen questioned him and he described what had happened to him, which brought bliss to their ears.

"Shining glory, stories of whose amazing deeds aston- 5.2.225
ish the mind, is never won without embracing heroism!" As the king said this, he and the queen, having obtained the pair of anklets, realized that through their son-in-law they had achieved what they wanted to do. Then the palace resounded with the music of celebratory instruments and seemed to be hymning the virtues of Ashóka·datta. On the next day the king installed the golden lotus on top of a fine silver pot in a temple that he had built himself. The pot and the lotus, white and red, looked resplendent, as if they were
the glory and heroism of the king and Ashóka·datta. When 5.2.230
the king, who was a devotee of Shiva, saw them like that, his eyes widened with joy and, filled with the nectar of devotion, he said, "Oh, this lofty pot and lotus looks like Shiva white with ash with his ruddy topknot of matted locks. If there were a second golden lotus like this one, it could be installed on this second pot."

When he heard these words from the king, Ashóka·datta then said, "I shall bring you a second lotus too, O king."

tac chrutvā «na mam' ânyena paṅkajena prayojanam
alaṃ te sāhasen' êti!» rāj" âpi pratyuvāca tam.
5.2.235 divaseṣv atha yāteṣu hem'|âbja|haraṇ'|âiṣiṇi
Aśokadatte sā bhūyo 'py agāt kṛṣṇa|caturdaśī.
tasyāṃ c' âsya suvarṇ'|âbja|vāñchāṃ buddhvā bhayād iva
dyu|saraḥ|svarṇa|kamale yāte 'sta|śikharaṃ ravau
saṃdhy"|âruṇ'|ābhra|piśita|grāsa|garvād iva kṣaṇāt
tamo|rakṣaḥsu dhāvatsu dhūma|dhūmreṣu sarvataḥ
sphurad|dīp'|āvalī|danta|mālā|bhāsvara|bhīṣaṇe
jṛmbhamāṇe mahā|raudre niśā|naktaṃ|carī|mukhe
prasupta|rāja|putrīkāt svairaṃ nirgatya mandirāt
Aśokadattaḥ sa yayau śmaśānaṃ punar eva tat.
5.2.240 tatra tasmin vaṭa|taror mūle tāṃ punar āgatām
dadarśa rākṣasīṃ śvaśrūṃ vihita|sv'|āgat'|ādarām.
tayā ca saha bhūyas tad agamat tan|niketanam
sa yuvā himavac|chṛṅgaṃ mārg'|ônmukha|vadhū|janam.

kaṃ|cit kālaṃ samaṃ vadhvā tatra sthitv" âbravīc ca tām
śvaśrūṃ «dehi dvitīyaṃ me kutaś|cit kanak'|âmbujam.»
tac chrutvā s" âpy avādīt taṃ «kuto 'nyat paṅkajaṃ mama?
etat Kapālasphoṭasya vidyate 'smat|prabhoḥ saraḥ.
atr' ēdṛśāni jāyante hem'|âbjāni samantataḥ
tasmāt tad ekaṃ mad|bhartre prītyā padmaṃ sa dattavān.»
5.2.245 evaṃ tay" ôkte so 'vādīt «tarhi tan māṃ sarovaram
naya yāvat svayaṃ tasmād ādāsye kanak'|âmbujam.»

The king replied, "I have no need for another lotus. Enough of your impetuousness!"

The days went by with Ashóka·datta wanting to capture a golden lotus until the dark of the moon arrived once more. When on that day, as if terrified after finding out about Ashóka·datta's desire for a golden lotus, the sun, the golden lotus in the lake of the sky, had gone to the peak where it sets, and instantly the demons that are night, dark as smoke, were running everywhere as if proud at having eaten the chunks of flesh that were the red clouds in the twilight, and the awesome mouth of the demoness night was yawning open, frightening and brilliant with its garland of teeth, the rows of glittering lamps, Ashóka·datta crept out of his house, where the princess was asleep, and went once more to that cremation ground. There he saw at the foot of the banyan tree his mother-in-law the *rákshasi*, who had returned. She welcomed him respectfully and the young man went with her once more to her home, the peak of the Himálaya, where the young women were keenly watching their approach.

5.2.235

5.2.240

After he had spent some time there with his wife, he said to his mother-in-law, "Give me a second golden lotus from somewhere," to which she replied, "I don't have another lotus. Our lord Kapála·sphota has a lake in which golden lotuses like that one grow all around. He kindly gave my husband a lotus from there."

When she said this, he replied, "In that case take me to that lake, so that I can get a golden lotus from there myself." 5.2.245

«na śakyam etad rakṣobhir dāruṇais tad dhi rakṣyate.»
evaṃ niṣiddho 'pi tayā nirbandhaṃ na sa taṃ jahau.
tataḥ kathaṃ|cin nītaś ca tayā śvaśrvā dadarśa tat
dūrāt sarovaraṃ divyaṃ tuṅg'|âdri|kaṭak'|āśritam.
channaṃ nirantar'|ôddaṇḍa|dīpta|hema|saroruhaiḥ
satat'|ônmukhatā|pīta|saṃkrānt'|ârka|prabhair iva.
gatv" âiva tatra yāvac ca padmāny avacinoti saḥ
tāvat tad|rakṣiṇo ghorā rurudhus taṃ niśā|carāḥ.
5.2.250 sa|śastraḥ so 'vadhīc c' âinān anyān anye palāyya ca
gatvā Kapālasphoṭāya svāmine tan nyavedayan.
sa tad buddhv" âiva kupitas tatra rakṣaḥ|patiḥ svayam
āgaty' Âśokadattaṃ tam apaśyal luṇṭhit'|âmbujam.
«kathaṃ bhrātā mam' Âśokadattaḥ so 'yam ih' āgataḥ?»
iti pratyabhyajānāc ca tat|kṣaṇaṃ taṃ sa|vismayaḥ.
tataḥ śastraṃ samutsṛjya harṣa|bāṣp'|āplut'|ēkṣaṇaḥ
dhāvitvā pādayoḥ sadyaḥ patitvā ca jagāda tam.
«ahaṃ Vijayadatt'|ākhyaḥ sodaryaḥ sa tav' ânujaḥ
āvāṃ dvija|varasy' ôbhau Govindasvāminaḥ sutau.
5.2.255 iyac ciraṃ ca jāto 'haṃ daivād īdṛṅ niśācaraḥ
citā|kapāla|dalanāt Kapālasphoṭa|nāmakaḥ.
tvad|darśanād idānīṃ ca brāhmaṇyaṃ tat smṛtaṃ mayā
gataṃ ca rākṣasatvaṃ me moh'|ācchādita|cetanam.»

"That is impossible, because it is guarded by terrifying *rákshasas*." Even though she forbade him like this, he did not stop insisting. Then he managed to get his mother-in-law to take him and he saw from afar that heavenly lake on the side of a tall mountain, completely covered with upstanding lotuses of gleaming gold, as if, from facing it continually, they had drunk in and been imbued by the brightness of the sun. He went there and immediately started gathering the lotuses, but while he was doing so he was stopped by the terrifying *rákshasas* who guarded the
place. He killed some of them with his sword and the oth- 5.2.250
ers ran away to their master Kapála·sphota and told him the news. As soon as he heard it, the furious *rákshasa* king came there himself and saw Ashóka·datta, who had plundered the lotuses. In amazement he recognized him straight away, thinking, "It's my brother Ashóka·datta! How can he have come here?" Then he cast aside his sword and, tears of joy flooding his eyes, ran to him and fell straight at his feet before saying, "My name is Víjaya·datta and I am your younger brother, by the same mother. We are both sons of
that finest of brahmins, Govínda·svamin. Fate has willed 5.2.255
that for all this time I have been a *rákshasa* by the name of Kapála·sphota, because I split a skull in a funeral pyre. By seeing you now I have remembered that I am a brahmin, and I am no longer a *rákshasa* with a mind enshrouded in delusion."

evaṃ Vijayadattasya vadataḥ parirabhya saḥ
yāvat kṣālayat' îv' âṅgaṃ rākṣasī|bhāva|dūṣitam.
Aśokadatto bāṣp'|âmbu|pūrais tāvad avātarat
Prajñaptikauśiko nāma vidyā|dhara|gurur divaḥ.
sa tau dvāv apy upety' âiva bhrātarau gurur abravīt
«yūyaṃ vidyā|dharāḥ sarve śāpād etāṃ daśāṃ gatāḥ
5.2.260 adhunā ca sa śāpo vaḥ sarveṣāṃ śāntim āgataḥ
tad gṛhṇīta nijā vidyā bandhu|sādhāraṇīr imāḥ
vrajataṃ ca nijaṃ dhāma svī|kṛta|sva|janau yuvām.»
ity uktvā datta|vidyo 'sau tayor dyām udyayau guruḥ.
tau ca vidyā|dharī|bhūtau prabuddhau jagmatus tataḥ
vyomnā tad dhimavac|chṛṅgaṃ gṛhīta|kanak'|âmbujau.
tatra c' Âśokadattas tāṃ rakṣaḥ|pati|sutāṃ priyām
upāgāt s" âpy abhūt kṣīṇa|śāpā vidyā|dharī tadā.
tayā ca sākaṃ su|dṛśā bhrātarau tāv ubhāv api
Vārāṇasīṃ prayayatuḥ kṣaṇād gagana|gāminau.
5.2.265 tatra c' ôpetya pitarau viprayog'|âgni|tāpitau
niravāpayatāṃ sadyo darśan'|âmṛta|varṣiṇau.
a|deha|bhede 'py ākrānta|citra|janm'|ântarau ca tau
na pitror eva lokasy' âpy utsavāya babhūvatuḥ

While Víjaya·datta was saying this, Ashóka·datta embraced him, and it was as if he were washing his body, which had been defiled by his being a *rákshasa*, with the flood of his tears. Meanwhile the guru of the sorcerers, who was called Prajñápti·káushika, descended from the heavens. That guru went up to the two brothers and said, "You and your family are all sorcerers. You are like this because of
a curse and now the curse that befell you all has come to 5.2.260
an end, so take these your magical sciences, which are the common property of your family, and, taking your relations with you, go to your own home." After saying this and giving them the magical sciences, the guru flew up into the sky.

Having become sorcerers, those two then came to their senses and flew from there to the peak of the Himálaya, taking some golden lotuses with them. Once there, Ashóka·datta went up to his sweetheart, the daughter of the *rákshasa* king, and at that moment, her curse over, she too became a sorceress. In the company of that beautiful lady the two brothers reached Varánasi in an instant, going by way of the
sky. There they went to their parents, who were burning up 5.2.265
with the fire of separation, and, raining down the nectar of their appearance, extinguished the blaze. The two of them, who, even though their bodies had not changed, had experienced amazing different births, made not just their parents celebrate but the people too.

cirād Vijayadattaś ca gāḍham āśliṣyataḥ pituḥ
bhuja|madhyam iv' âtyarthaṃ manoratham apūrayat.
tatas tatr' âiva tad buddhvā Pratāpamukuṭo 'pi saḥ
Aśokadatta|śvaśuro rājā harṣād upāyayau.
tat|sat|kṛtaś ca tad|rāja|dhānīṃ s'|ôtka|sthita|priyām
Aśokadattaḥ sva|janaiḥ sārdhaṃ baddh'|ôtsavām agāt.
5.2.270 dadau ca kanak'|âbjāni rājñe tasmai bahūni saḥ
abhyarthit'|âdhika|prāpti|hṛṣṭaḥ so 'py abhavan nṛpaḥ.
tato Vijayadattaṃ taṃ sarveṣv atra sthiteṣu saḥ
pitā papraccha Govindasvāmī s'|āścarya|kautukaḥ.
«tadā śmaśāne yāminyāṃ rākṣasa|tvaṃ gatasya te
abhavat kīdṛśo, vatsa, vṛttānto? varṇyatām iti!»
tato Vijayadattas taṃ babhāṣe «tāta, cāpalāt
prasphoṭita|citā|dīpta|kapālo 'haṃ vidher vaśāt
mukha|praviṣṭayā sadyas tad|vasā|chaṭayā tadā
rakṣo|bhūtas tvayā tāvad dṛṣṭo māyā|vimohitaḥ.
5.2.275 Kapālasphoṭa ity evaṃ nāma kṛtvā hi rākṣasaiḥ
tato 'nyair aham āhūtas tan|madhye milito 'bhavam.
taiś ca nīto nijasy' âsmi pārśvaṃ rakṣaḥ|pateḥ kramāt
so 'pi dṛṣṭv" âiva māṃ prītaḥ senā|patye nyayojayat.
tataḥ kadā|cid gandharvān abhiyoktuṃ madena saḥ
gato rakṣaḥ|patis tatra saṅgrāme nihato 'ribhiḥ.
tad" âiva pratipannaṃ ca tad|bhṛtyair† mama śāsanam
tato 'haṃ rakṣasāṃ rājyam akārṣaṃ tat|pure sthitaḥ.
tatr' âkasmāc ca hem'|âbjahetoḥ prāptasya darśanāt
āryasy' Âśokadattasya praśāntā sā daśā mama.
5.2.280 an|antaraṃ yath" âsmābhiḥ śāpa|mokṣa|vaśān nijāḥ
vidyāḥ prāptās tath" āryo vaḥ kṛtsnam āvedayiṣyati.»

As his father embraced him tightly, Víjaya·datta fulfilled his great wish, just as he was filling his arms. Then when he heard the news, in his joy King Pratápa·múkuta, Ashóka·datta's father-in-law, came straight there too. After being welcomed by him, Ashóka·datta went with his family to his palace, where his sweetheart was waiting expectantly and celebrations were being held. He gave lots of golden lo- 5.2.270
tuses to the king, who was delighted at getting more than he had asked for. Then when everyone was there, his father Govínda·svamin, with wonder and curiosity, asked Víjaya·datta, "That night in the cremation ground when you became a *rákshasa*, what happened to you, my child? Tell us!"

Víjaya·datta replied, "Father, after I had thoughtlessly burst open the skull burning on the pyre, fate decreed it that at that moment a globule of its brains went straight into my mouth as a result of which, as seen at the time by you, deluded by magic I became a *rákshasa*. Some other *rákshasa*s 5.2.275
gave me the name Kapála·sphota because of this. At their invitation I joined their midst. In time they took me to the *rákshasa* king. On seeing me he was delighted and made me the commander of his army. Then one day in his arrogance the *rákshasa* king went to fight the *gandhárva*s and was killed in the battle there by his enemies. Straight away his subjects accepted my command and I then ruled over the *rákshasa*s, living in that city. When I suddenly saw the noble Ashóka·datta there, come to get a golden lotus, my existence as a *rákshasa* came to an end. The rest—how we 5.2.280
got back our magical sciences as a result of being freed from the curse—the noble Ashóka·datta shall tell you in full."

evaṃ Vijayadattena tena tatra nivedite
Aśokadattaḥ sa tadā tad ā|mūlād avarṇayat.
«purā vidyā|dharau santau gaganād Gālav'|āśrame
āvāṃ snāntīr apaśyāva Gaṅgāyāṃ muni|kanyakāḥ.
tuly'|âbhilāṣās tāś c' âtra
vāñchantau sahasā rahaḥ
buddhvā tad|bandhubhiḥ krodhāc
chaptau svo divya|dṛṣṭibhiḥ.
‹pāp'|ācārau prajāyethāṃ martya|yonau yuvām ubhau
tatr' âpi viprayogaś ca vicitro vāṃ bhaviṣyati.
5.2.285 mānuṣ'|â|gocare deśe viprakṛṣṭe 'py upāgatam
ekaṃ dṛṣṭvā dvitīyo vāṃ yadā prajñānam āpsyati.
tadā vidyā|dhara|guror vidyāṃ prāpya bhaviṣyathaḥ
punar vidyā|dharau yuktau śāpa|muktau sva|bandhubhiḥ.›
evaṃ tair munibhiḥ śaptau jātāv āvām ubhāv iha
viyogo 'tra yathā bhūtas tat sarvaṃ viditaṃ ca vaḥ.
idānīṃ padma|hetoś ca śvaśrū|siddhi|prabhāvataḥ
rakṣaḥ|pateḥ puraṃ gatvā prāpto 'yaṃ c' ânujo mayā.
tatr' âiva ca guroḥ prāpya vidyāḥ Prajñaptikauśikāt
sadyo vidyā|dharī|bhūya vayaṃ kṣipram ih' āgatāḥ.»

After Víjaya·datta had said this there, Ashóka·datta then told the story from the beginning. "Long ago when we two were sorcerers, we saw from the sky some sages' daughters bathing in the Ganga at Gálava's ashram. We immediately developed a secret longing for them and they felt the same. Their relatives had divine sight and when they found out they were so angry that they cursed us. 'You two wrongdoers shall both be born in the womb of a mortal, and once you are born you shall also undergo a miraculous separation. When one of you sees the other arrive in a distant land 5.2.285
beyond the range of men and recognizes him, then you shall receive your magical sciences from the guru of the sorcerers and, sorcerers once more, you shall be freed from the curse and united with your relatives.'

After thus being cursed by the sages, we were both born in this place. You know all about how we were separated here. Just now when through my mother-in-law's magical power I went to the city of the *rákshasa* king to get a lotus, I came across my younger brother there. After getting the magical sciences from guru Prajñápti·káushika in that same place, we immediately became sorcerers and came straight here."

5.2.290 ity uktvā pitarau ca tau priyatamāṃ
tāṃ c' ātmajāṃ bhū|pateḥ
sadyaḥ śāpa|tamo|vimokṣa|mudito
vidyā|viśeṣair nijaiḥ
tais taiḥ saṃvyabhajad vicitra|caritaḥ
so 'śokadattas tadā
yen' âite sapadi prabuddha|manaso
'jāyanta vidyā|dharāḥ.
tatas tam āmantrya nṛpaṃ sa sākaṃ
mātā|pitṛbhyāṃ dayitā|dvayena
utpatya dhanyo nija|cakra|varti|
dhāma dyu|mārgeṇa javī jagāma.
tatr' ālokya tam ājñām
prāpya ca tasmād Aśokavega iti
nāma sa bibhrat so 'pi ca
tad|bhrātā Vijayavega iti.
vidyā|dhara|vara|taruṇau
sva|jan'|ânugatāv ubhau nija|nivāsam
Govindakūṭa|saṃjñakam
acala|varaṃ bhrātarau yayatuḥ.
so 'py āścarya|vaśaḥ Pratāpamukuṭo
Vārāṇasī|bhū|patiḥ
svasmin deva|kule dvitīya|kalaśa|
nyast'|âika|hem'|âmbujaḥ
tad|dattair aparaiḥ suvarṇa|kamalair
abhyarcita|Tryambakas
tat|sambandha|mahattayā pramudito
mene kṛt'|ârthaṃ kulam.
5.2.295 evaṃ divyāḥ kāraṇen' âvatīrṇā
jāyante 'smiñ jantavo jīva|loke

After saying this, Ashóka·datta, who had had amazing 5.2.290
adventures and was delighted at being freed from the darkness of the curse, then immediately distributed his various special magical sciences among his parents and his sweetheart the king's daughter, as a result of which their minds were instantly awakened and they became sorcerers.

Then our lucky hero took his leave of the king and, together with his parents and his two sweethearts, took off and quickly flew to the abode of his emperor. He saw him there and at his command he took from him the name Ashóka·vega and his brother took the name Víjaya·vega. As fine young sorcerers and accompanied by their family, the two brothers went to their own home, that finest of mountains called Govínda·kuta. Pratápa·múkuta, the king of Varánasi, overcome with amazement, put a single golden lotus on the other pot, worshipped Shiva with the other golden lotuses given to him by Ashóka·datta, and, delighted by the honor of being related to him, considered his family to have achieved its purpose.

In this way divine beings come down and are born in 5.2.295
this world of men for a reason, and being suitably brave and energetic, accomplish impossible ends. So, O ocean of

sattv'|ôtsāhau sv'|ôcitau te dadhānā
duṣprāpām apy artha|siddhiṃ labhante.
tat, sattva|sāgara, bhavān api ko 'pi jāne
dev'|âṃśa eva bhavitā ca yath"|êṣṭa|siddhiḥ
prāyaḥ kriyāsu mahatām api duṣkarāsu
s'|ôtsāhatā kathayati prakṛter viśeṣam.
s" âpi tvad|īpsitā nanu
divyā rāj'|ātmajā Kanakarekhā
bāl" ânyathā hi vāñchati
Kanakapurī|darśinaṃ kathaṃ hi patim.›
iti rahasi niśamya Viṣṇudattāt
sa|rasa|kathā|prakaraṃ sa Śaktidevaḥ
hṛdi Kanakapurī|vilokan'|âiṣī
dhṛtim avalambya nināya ca tri|yāmām.

iti mahā|kavi|śrī|Somadeva|bhaṭṭa|viracite Kathāsaritsāgare
caturdārikā|lambake dvitīyas taraṅgaḥ.

3

5.3.1 TATAS TATR' Ôtsthala|dvīpe prabhāte taṃ maṭha|sthitam
Śaktidevaṃ sa dāś'|êndraḥ Satyavrata upāyayau.
sa ca prāk|pratipannaḥ sann upety' âinam abhāṣata
‹brahmaṃs tvad|iṣṭa|siddhy|artham upāyaś cintito mayā.
asti dvīpa|varaṃ madhye Ratnakūṭ'|ākhyam ambudheḥ
kṛta|pratiṣṭhas tatr' āste bhagavān Harir abdhinā.
Āṣāḍha|śukla|dvādaśyāṃ tatra yātr"|ôtsave sadā
āyānti sarva|dvīpebhyaḥ pūjāyai yatnato janāḥ.
5.3.5 tatra jñāyeta Kanakapurī sā jātu|cit purī
tad ehi tatra gacchāvaḥ pratyāsannā hi sā tithiḥ.›
iti Satyavraten' ôktaḥ Śaktidevas ‹tath" êti› saḥ
jagrāha hṛṣṭaḥ pātheyaṃ Viṣṇudatt'|ôpakalpitam.
tato vahanam āruhya sa Satyavrata|ḍhaukitam

courage, I think that you too must be some partial incarnation of a god and that you will accomplish what you desire. In deeds difficult for even the great, it is usually zeal which betrays a special nature. Surely the princess Kánaka·rekha whom you desire is divine, for otherwise how could a child want a husband who has seen Kánaka·puri?' Having thus heard in private from Vishnu·datta this delightful long tale, Shakti·deva, having a heartfelt desire to see Kánaka·puri, got through the night shored up by his resolve.

Thus ends the second wave in the Four Girls Attainment in the "Ocean of the Rivers of Story" composed by the glorious and learned great poet Soma·deva.

3

THE FOLLOWING morning there on the island of Útsthala, 5.3.1
Satya·vrata, the king of the fishermen, went to Shakti·deva in the monastery and, as he had promised earlier, went up to him and said, 'Brahmin, I have thought of a way for you to get what you want. There is an excellent island called Ratna·kuta in the middle of the sea. The ocean has established a temple to Lord Vishnu there. On the twelfth day of the bright fortnight of Ashádha a festival is always held there, and people from all the islands take pains to come to
worship. Perhaps the city of Kánaka·puri might be known 5.3.5
of there, so come, let's go there, for that day is at hand.'

Addressed thus by Satya·vrata, Shakti·deva agreed and, delighted, took provisions for the journey which Vishnu·datta gave him. Then he boarded the vessel brought by Satya·vrata and quickly journeyed with him across the sea.

ten' âiva sākaṃ tvaritaḥ prāyād vāridhi|vartmanā.
gacchaṃś ca tatra sa dvīpa|nibha|nakre 'dbhut'|ālaye
Satyavratam tam papraccha karṇa|dhāratayā sthitam.
‹ito dūraṃ mahā|bhogaṃ kim etad dṛśyate 'mbudhau
yadṛcchā|prodgat'|ôdagra|sa|pakṣa|giri|vibhramam.›
5.3.10 tataḥ Satyavrato 'vādīd ‹asau devo vaṭa|drumaḥ
asy' āhuḥ su|mah"|āvartam adhastād vaḍavā|mukham.
etaṃ ca parihṛty' âiva pradeśam iha gamyate
atr' āvarte gatānāṃ hi na bhavaty āgamaḥ punaḥ.›
iti Satyavrate tasmin vadaty ev' âmbu|vegataḥ
tasyām eva pravavṛte gantuṃ tad|vahanaṃ diśi.
tad dṛṣṭvā Śaktidevaṃ sa punaḥ Satyavrato 'bravīt
‹brahman, vināśa|kālo 'yaṃ dhruvam asmākam āgataḥ
yad a|kasmāt pravahaṇaṃ paśy' âtr' âiva prayāty adaḥ
śakyate n' âiva roddhuṃ ca katham apy adhunā mayā.
5.3.15 tad āvarte gabhīre 'tra vayaṃ mṛtyor iv' ānane
kṣiptā ev' âmbun" ākṛṣya karmaṇ" êva balīyasā.
etac ca n' âiva me duḥkhaṃ śarīraṃ kasya hi sthiram
duḥkhaṃ tu yan na siddhas te kṛcchreṇ' âpi manorathaḥ.
tad yāvad vārayāmy etad ahaṃ pravahaṇaṃ manāk
tāvad asy' âvalambethāḥ śākhāṃ vaṭa|taror drutam.
kadā|cij jīvit'|ôpāyo bhaved bhavy'|ākṛtes tava
vidher vilāsān abdheś ca taraṅgān ko hi tarkayet?›
iti Satyavratasy' âsya dhīra|sattvasya jalpataḥ
babhūva nikaṭe tasya taroḥ pravahaṇaṃ tataḥ.
5.3.20 tat|kṣaṇaṃ sa kṛt'|ôtphālaḥ Śaktidevo visādhvasaḥ
pṛthulām agrahīc chākhāṃ tasy' âbdhi|vaṭa|śākhinaḥ.

As he was going along on that abode of miracles, the sea, whose monsters look like islands, he asked Satya·vrata, who was at the helm, 'What is that huge object I can see far away from here in the sea, which looks like a tall winged mountain unexpectedly sprung forth?'

Satya·vrata replied, 'That is a sacred banyan tree. They 5.3.10
say that below it is a huge whirlpool, the opening to the undersea inferno. We must avoid that spot while we are traveling here, for those who enter that whirlpool do not return.'

Just as Satya·vrata was saying this, the boat started to go in that very direction driven by the current. When Satya·vrata noticed this he again spoke to Shakti·deva: 'Brahmin, the time of our demise has surely come, for see how the boat is suddenly going straight there and I am now unable
to stop it in any way. So the current, as if it were mighty 5.3.15
karma itself, has dragged us and flung us into that unfathomable whirlpool here as if into the mouth of death. This does not trouble me, for no one's body lasts forever, but what is a shame is that despite your pains, your wish has not been fulfilled. So while I hold back the boat a little, you should quickly hang on to a branch of this banyan tree. For someone who looks as handsome as you, there might perhaps be a way to stay alive, for who can fathom the vagaries of fate or the waves of the sea?'

As the courageous Satya·vrata was saying this, the boat
then drew near the tree. At that moment the terrified Shakti· 5.3.20
deva jumped and grabbed a broad branch of that banyan tree in the ocean. Satya·vrata, meanwhile, as his body and

Satyavratas tu vahatā dehena vahanena ca
par'|ârtha|kalpiten' âtra viveśa vaḍavā|mukham.
Śaktidevaś ca śākhābhiḥ *pūrit'|āśasya* tasya saḥ
āśrity' âpi taroḥ śākhāṃ nirāśaḥ samacintayat.
‹na tāvat sā ca Kanakapurī dṛṣṭā mayā purī
apade naśyatā tāvad dāś'|êndro 'py eṣa nāśitaḥ.
yadi vā satata|nyasta|padā sarvasya mūrdhani
kāmaṃ bhagavatī kena bhajyate bhavitavyatā?›
5.3.25 ity avasth"|ôcitaṃ tasya tataś cintayas tadā
vipra|yūnas taru|skandhe dinaṃ tat paryahīyata.
sāyaṃ ca sarvatas tasmin sa mahā|vihagān bahūn
vaṭa|vṛkṣe praviśataḥ śabd'|āpūrita|dik|taṭān.
apaśyat pṛthu|tat|pakṣa|vāta|dhūt'|ârṇav'|ōrmibhiḥ
gṛdhrān paricaya|prītyā kṛta|pratyudgamān iva.
tataḥ śākhā|vilīnānāṃ sa teṣāṃ pakṣiṇāṃ mithaḥ
manuṣya|vācā saṃlāpaṃ pattr'|âughaiś chādito 'śṛṇot.
kaś|cid dvīp'|ântaraṃ kaś|cid giriṃ kaś|cid dig|antaram
tad ahaś|caraṇa|sthānam ekaikaḥ samavarṇayat.
5.3.30 ekaś ca vṛddha|vihagas teṣāṃ madhyād abhāṣata
‹ahaṃ vihartuṃ Kanakapurīm adya gato 'bhavam
prātaḥ punaś ca tatr' âiva gant" âsmi carituṃ sukham
śram'|âvahena ko 'rtho me vidūra|gamanena hi?›
ity a|kāṇḍa|sudhā|sāra|sadṛśen' âsya pakṣiṇaḥ
vacasā śānta|tāpaḥ sañ Śaktidevo vyacintayat
‹diṣṭyā s" âsty eva nagarī! tat|prāptyai c' âyam eva me
upāyaḥ su|mahā|kāyo vihago vāhanī|kṛtaḥ!›
ity ālocya śanair etya tasya suptasya pakṣiṇaḥ

the boat journeyed on, made over to help another man, entered the mouth of the undersea inferno. Shakti·deva, even though he had found refuge on a branch of that tree, which *filled the sky: fulfilled hopes* with its branches, was desperate and said to himself, 'I still haven't seen the city of Kánaka·puri, and in perishing in an unsuitable place, I have brought about the death of the king of the fishermen too. But no one can willingly frustrate the blessed goddess fate, who always has her foot placed on the heads of all men.'

Then, while the young brahmin on the branch of the 5.3.25
tree was thinking these thoughts appropriate to the situation, the day drew to a close. In the evening he saw lots of large birds enter that banyan tree from all sides, filling the horizon with their cries, and when the ocean waves were whipped up by the wind from their broad wings, it was as if they had come forth to meet the vultures out of affection for old friends. Then, hidden by the abundant leaves, he listened to the birds perched on the branches talk to one another in a human voice. One talked of a foreign island, one a mountain and one a foreign land as the place of their
day's journey. And one old bird among them said, 'Today I 5.3.30
went to have some fun in Kánaka·puri and I shall go to that same place to feed in the morning, for there is no point in my going on a long and exhausting journey.'

His burning torment thus soothed by these words from the bird, which were like an unexpected rain of nectar, Shakti·deva said to himself, 'Thank goodness! The city does exist and by making this bird with its huge body my vehicle, I have a means of getting there!' After thinking this, Shakti·deva crept up to the sleeping bird and hid himself in the

pṛṣṭha|pakṣ'|ântare so 'tha Śaktidevo vyalīyata.
5.3.35 prātaś c' êtas tatas teṣu gateṣv anyeṣu pakṣiṣu
sa pakṣī darśit'|āścarya|*pakṣa/pāto* vidhir yathā
datt'|āskando vahan pṛṣṭhe Śaktidevam a|lakṣitam
kṣaṇād agacchat Kanakapurīṃ tāṃ carituṃ punaḥ.
tatr' ôdyān'|ântare tasmin upaviṣṭe vihaṃgame
sa Śaktidevo nibhṛtaṃ tasya pṛṣṭhād avātarat.
apasṛtya sa tat|pārśvād yāvad bhrāmyati tatra saḥ
dve puṣp'|âvacaya|vyagre tāvad aikṣata yoṣitau.
upagamya śanais te ca tad|vilokana|vismite
so 'pṛcchat ‹kaḥ pradeśo 'yaṃ ke ca, bhadre, yuvām iti?›
5.3.40 ‹iyaṃ Kanakapury|ākhyā purī vidyā|dhar'|āspadam
Candraprabh" êti c' âitasyām āste vidyā|dharī, sakhe.
tasyāś c' āvām ih' ôdyāne jānīhy udyāna|pālike
puṣp'|ôccayas tad|artho 'yam iti› te ca tam ūcatuḥ.
tataḥ so 'py avadad vipro ‹yuvāṃ me kurutaṃ tathā
yath" âham api paśyāmi tāṃ yuṣmat|svāminīm iha.›
etac chrutvā ‹tath" êty› uktvā nītavatyāv ubhe ca te
striyāv antar nagaryās taṃ yuvānaṃ rāja|mandiram.
so 'pi prāptas tad adrākṣīn māṇikya|stambha|bhāsvaram
sauvarṇa|bhitti saṃketa|ketanaṃ saṃpadām iva.
5.3.45 tatr' āgataṃ ca dṛṣṭvā taṃ sarvaḥ parijano 'bravīt
gatvā Candraprabhāyās tan mānuṣ'|āgaman'|âdbhutam.
s" âpy ādiśya pratīhāram a|vilambitam eva tam
abhyantaraṃ sva|nikaṭaṃ vipraṃ prāveśayat tataḥ.

feathers on its back. In the morning, when the other birds 5.3.35
had gone in their various directions, that bird, showing an amazing *beat of its wings : partiality*, as if it were fate, and carrying Shakti·deva on his back unnoticed, took off and in an instant reached Kánaka·puri to feed once more. When the bird had landed in a garden there, Shakti·deva quietly got down from its back. He moved away from its side and while he was wandering about there, he saw two women busy gathering flowers. He slowly went up to them and they were astonished at the sight of him. He asked, 'What is this place and who, good ladies, are you?'

They said to him, 'This city is called Kánaka·puri, home 5.3.40
to sorcerers, and in it, friend, there lives a sorceress called Chandra·prabha. Know us to be gardeners in her garden here. We have collected these flowers for her.'

The brahmin replied, 'Please arrange for me to meet this mistress of yours in this city.'

When they heard this, they agreed to it and the two women took the young man to the palace in the city. When he got there, he saw that it glittered with its columns of ruby and its walls were gold, as if it were a place of assignation for riches. On seeing him arrive there all the attendants 5.3.45
went and told Chandra·prabha of the miraculous arrival of a mortal. She then gave a chamberlain an order and without delay had the brahmin brought into her presence.

praviṣṭaḥ so 'py apaśyat tāṃ tatra netr'|ôtsava|pradām
dhātur adbhuta|nirmāṇa|paryāptim iva rūpiṇīm.
sā ca sad|ratna|paryaṅkād dūrād utthāya taṃ svayam
sv'|āgaten' ādṛtavatī tad|darśana|vaśī|kṛtā.
upaviṣṭam apṛcchac ca
‹kalyāṇin, kas tvam īdṛśaḥ?
kathaṃ ca mānuṣ'|â|gamyām
imāṃ prāpto bhavān bhuvam?›
5.3.50 ity uktaḥ sa tayā Candraprabhayā sa|kutūhalam
Śaktidevo nijaṃ deśaṃ jātiṃ c' āvedya nāma ca.
tat|purī|darśana|paṇāt prāptuṃ taṃ rāja|kanyakām
yathā Kanakarekh"|ākhyām āgatas tad avarṇayat.
tad buddhvā kim api dhyātvā dīrghaṃ niḥśvasya sā tataḥ
Candraprabhā taṃ vijane Śaktidevam abhāṣata.
‹śrūyatāṃ vacmi te kiṃ|cid idaṃ, subhaga, saṃprati
asty asyāṃ Śaśikhaṇḍ'|ākhyo vidyā|dhara|patir bhuvi.
vayaṃ tasya catasraś ca jātā duhitaraḥ kramāt
jyeṣṭhā Candraprabh" êty asmi Candrarekh" êti c' âparā.
5.3.55 Śaśirekhā tṛtīyā ca caturthī ca Śaśiprabhā
tā vayaṃ kramaśaḥ prāptā vṛddhim atra pitur gṛhe.
ekadā ca bhaginyo me snātuṃ tisro 'pi tāḥ samam
mayi kanyā|vrata|sthāyāṃ jagmur Mandākinī|taṭam.
tatr' Āgryatapasaṃ nāma muniṃ yauvana|darpataḥ
toyair jalastham asicann ārabdha|jala|kelayaḥ.
atinirbandhinīs tāś ca muniḥ kruddhaḥ śaśāpa saḥ
«ku|kanyakāḥ prajāyadhvaṃ martya|loke 'khilā iti!»

When he entered he saw her there, bringing delight to the eyes as if she were the creator's skill in creating miracles in bodily form. She got up from her finely jeweled bed and from afar welcomed him respectfully in person, beguiled by his appearance. When he had sat down, she asked him, 'Lucky fellow, who are you, to look like this? And how, sir, did you arrive at this land, which is inaccessible to mortals?'

When Chandra·prabha asked him this with interest, 5.3.50
Shakti·deva told her his country, his lineage and his name.
He described how he had come in order to win the hand of
a princess called Kánaka·rekha as the prize for seeing that
city.

On finding this out, Chandra·prabha thought a little,
gave a long sigh and then said to Shakti·deva in private, 'Listen, handsome man, I am now going to tell you something.
There lives in this land a sorcerer king called Shashi·khanda
and we four daughters were born to him in succession: I am
the eldest and am called Chandra·prabha, the next is called
Chandra·rekha, the third is Shashi·rekha and the fourth is 5.3.55
Shashi·prabha. In the course of time we grew up here in
our father's house. One day those three sisters of mine went
to bathe together on the banks of the Mandákini, while I
stayed at home because I was of marriageable age. There
they started playing about in the water and in the arrogance
of youth they splashed a sage called Agrya·tapas who was
in the river. The furious sage then cursed those boisterous
girls, saying, "You wicked girls! You shall all be born in the
world of men!"

tad buddhvā so 'smadīyena pitrā gatvā prasāditaḥ
pṛthak pṛthak sa śāp'|ântam uktvā tāsāṃ yathā|yatham.
5.3.60 jāti|smaratvaṃ divyena vijñānen' ôpabṛṃhitam
martya|bhāvena sarvāsām ādideśa mahā|muniḥ.
tatas tāsu tanūs tyaktvā martya|lokaṃ gatāsu saḥ
dattvā me nagarīm etāṃ pitā khedād gato vanam.
ath' êha nivasantīṃ māṃ devī svapne kil' Âmbikā
«mānuṣaḥ, putri, bhartā te bhavit" êti» samādiśat.
tena vidyā|dharāṃs tāṃs tān varān uddiśato bahūn
pitur vidhāraṇaṃ kṛtvā kany" âiv' âdy' âpy ahaṃ sthitā.

idānīṃ c' âmun" āścarya|mayen' āgamanena te
vapuṣā ca vaśī|kṛtya tubhyam ev' âham arpitā.
5.3.65 tad vrajāmi caturdaśyām āgāminyāṃ bhavat|kṛte
kartuṃ tātasya vijñaptim Ṛṣabh'|ākhyaṃ mahā|girim.
tatra tasyāṃ tithau sarve milanti prati|vatsaram
devaṃ Haraṃ pūjayituṃ digbhyo vidyā|dhar'|ôttamāḥ.
tātas tatr' âiva c' āyāti tad|anujñām avāpya ca
ih' āgacchāmy ahaṃ tūrṇaṃ tataḥ pariṇayasva mām.
tat tiṣṭha tāvad ity› uktvā sā taṃ vidyā|dhar'|ôcitaiḥ
Candraprabhā Śaktidevaṃ tais tair bhogair upācarat.
tasya c' âbhūt «tath" êty» atra tiṣṭhatas tat tadā sukham
yad|dāv|ānala|taptasya sudhā|hrada|nimajjane.
5.3.70 prāptāyāṃ ca caturdaśyāṃ sā taṃ Candraprabh" âbravīt
‹adya gacchāmi vijñaptyai tātasy' âhaṃ bhavat|kṛte.

When he found out about it, our father went and appeased that great sage, who then announced the different ways in which the curse would end for each of them and 5.3.60
ordained that when they were mortals all of them would remember their previous life, augmenting this power with divine sight. Then, when they had abandoned their bodies and gone to the world of mortals, my father was so upset that he gave me this city and went to the forest. After that, while I was living here, the goddess Párvati told me in a dream that my husband would be a mortal. As a result, my father showed me lots of different prospective sorcerer grooms but I stopped him and have remained unmarried until today.

Now I have been overcome by this miraculous arrival of yours here and your looks, and I offer myself to you. So on 5.3.65
the next fourteenth day of the fortnight, I shall go to the great mountain called Ríshabha to make a request to my father on your behalf. On that day each year all the sorcerers from every direction meet there to worship the god Shiva and my father goes there too. I shall get his permission and hurry back here. You must then marry me. In the meantime, wait.' So saying Chandra·prabha attended to Shakti·deva with various delights suitable for sorcerers. He agreed to what she said and then, while standing there, felt the pleasure of someone heated by a forest fire on plunging into a pool of nectar. When the fourteenth arrived Chandra· 5.3.70
prabha said to him, 'I am now going to my father to ask him if I can marry you, and my entire retinue will come with me. Nothing will happen to upset you by your being alone for a couple of days. But also, while you are staying here

sarvaḥ parijanaś c' âyaṃ may" âiva saha yāsyati
tvayā c' âikākinā duḥkhaṃ na bhāvyaṃ divasa|dvayam.
ekena punar etasmin mandire 'py avatiṣṭhatā
madhyamā bhavatā bhūmir n' āroḍhavyā katham|cana.›
ity uktvā sā yuvānaṃ taṃ nyasta|cittā tad|antike
tadīya|citt'|ânugatā yayau Candraprabhā tataḥ.
so 'py ekākī tatas tatra sthitaś ceto vinodayan
sthāna|sthāneṣu babhrāma Śaktidevo maha'|rddhiṣu.
5.3.75 kiṃ|svid atra niṣiddhaṃ me tayā pṛṣṭhe 'dhirohaṇam
vidyā|dhara|duhitr" êti jāta|kautūhalo 'tha saḥ.
tasy' âiva madhyamāṃ bhūmiṃ mandirasy' āruroha tām
prāyo vārita|vāmā hi pravṛttir manaso nṛṇām.
ārūḍhas tatra c' âpaśyad guptāṃs trīn ratna|maṇḍapān
ekaṃ c' ôdghāṭita|dvāraṃ tan|madhyāt praviveśa saḥ.
praviśya c' ântaḥ sad|ratna|paryaṅke nyasta|tūlike
paṭ'|āvaguṇṭhita|tanuṃ śayānaṃ kaṃ|cid aikṣata.
vīkṣate yāvad utkṣipya paṭaṃ tāvan mṛtāṃ tathā
Paropakāri|nṛpates tanayāṃ vara|kanyakām.
5.3.80 dṛṣṭvā c' âcintayat so 'tha ‹kim idaṃ mahad adbhutam?
kim a|prabodha|supt" êyaṃ kiṃ vā bhrāntir a|bādhakā?
yasyāḥ kṛte pravāso 'yaṃ mama s" âiv' êha tiṣṭhati
asāv apagata|prāṇā tatra deśe ca jīvati.
a|mlāna|kāntir asyāś ca tad vidhātrā mama dhruvam
ken' âpi kāraṇen' êdam Indra|jālaṃ vitanyate.›
iti saṃcintya nirgatya tāv anyau maṇḍapau kramāt
praviśy' ântaḥ sa dadṛśe tadvad anye ca kanyake.
tato 'pi nirgatas tasya s'|āścaryo mandirasya saḥ
upaviṣṭaḥ sthito 'paśyad vāpīm atyuttamām adhaḥ.
5.3.85 tat|tīre ratna|paryāṇaṃ dadarś' âikaṃ ca vājinam
ten' âvatīry' âiva tatas tat|pārśvaṃ kautukād yayau.

alone in the palace, in no way should you go up onto the middle floor.' After saying this to the young man, Chandra·prabha entrusted her heart to him and left, accompanied by his heart.

After this, Shakti·deva, staying alone there, wandered about in various magnificent spots amusing himself. Then 5.3.75
because the sorcerer's daughter had forbidden him from going up onto the terrace he became curious. He went up to the middle floor of the palace, for men's minds generally like that which has been forbidden. On going up there, he saw three secret jeweled pavilions. One had its door open and he went inside. Having gone inside he saw someone lying on a bed made of fine jewels on which had been placed a cotton sheet which concealed their body. When he lifted up the sheet he saw the beautiful young daughter of King Paropakárin, dead. On seeing her he said to himself, 'What 5.3.80
is this great miracle? Is she asleep never to wake up or is this a wild hallucination? The same girl for whose sake I left my country is here. Her life breaths have left her here, while in that land she is alive. Her beauty has not faded, so I am certain that this is a magic trick played by the creator for some reason.'

After thinking this he went out and one by one went into the other two pavilions where he saw two other girls like her. Then he left the palace in amazement, sat down and stayed there looking down at an exquisite pool. On 5.3.85
its banks he saw a horse with a jeweled saddle, so, curious, he went straight down from there to its side. Seeing that it had no rider, he tried to mount it and the horse kicked him, throwing him in the pool. Soon after plunging into

iyeṣa ca tam āroḍhuṃ śūnyaṃ dṛṣṭvā sa tena ca
aśven' āhatya pādena tasyāṃ vāpyāṃ nicikṣape.
tan|nimagnaḥ sa ca kṣipraṃ Vardhamāna|purān nijāt
udyāna|dīrghikā|madhyād unmamajja sa|saṃbhramaḥ.
dadarśa janma|bhūmau ca sadyo vāpī|jale sthitam
ātmānaṃ kumudais tulyaṃ dīnaṃ *Candraprabhāṃ vinā.*
‹Vardhamāna|puraṃ kv' êdaṃ kva sā vaidyādharī purī!
aho kim etad āścarya|māyā|ḍambara|jṛmbhitam?
5.3.90 kaṣṭaṃ kim api ken' âpi manda|bhāgyo 'smi vañcitaḥ
yadi vā ko 'tra jānāti kīdṛśī bhavitavyatā?›
ity|ādi cintayan so 'tha vāpī|madhyāt samutthitaḥ
sa|vismayaḥ Śaktidevo yayau pitṛ|gṛhaṃ nijam.
tatr' âpadiṣṭa|paṭaha|bhramaṇaḥ kṛta|kaitavaḥ
pitr" ābhinanditas tasthau s'|ôtsavaiḥ sva|janaiḥ saha.
dvitīye 'hni bahir gehān nirgataś c' âśṛṇot punaḥ
ghoṣyamāṇaṃ sa|paṭahaṃ pure tasminn idaṃ vacaḥ.
‹vipra|kṣatriya|madhyāt Kanakapurī yena tattvato dṛṣṭā
vaktu sa! tasmai tanayāṃ sa|yauva|rājyāṃ dadāti nṛpaḥ.›
5.3.95 tac chrutv" âiva sa gatvā tān paṭah'|ôdghoṣakān kṛtī
‹mayā dṛṣṭā purī s" êti› Śaktidevo 'bravīt punaḥ.
tais tūrṇaṃ nṛpater agraṃ sa nīto 'bhūn nṛpo 'pi tam
prāgvan mene parijñāya punar vitatha|vādinam.
‹mithyā ced vacmi na mayā dṛṣṭa sā nagarī yadi
tad idānīṃ śarīrasya nigraheṇa paṇo mama.
adya sā rāja|putrī māṃ pṛcchatv ity› udite tataḥ
gatvā c' ânucarai rājā tatr' âiv' ānāyayat sutām.
sā dṛṣṭvā dṛṣṭa|pūrvaṃ taṃ vipraṃ rājānam abhyadhāt
‹tāta, mithy" âiva bhūyo 'pi kiṃ|cid vakṣyaty asāv iti.›

it, to his amazement he surfaced in a tank in the park in his own city, Vardhamána. Suddenly finding himself in the water of a pool in the land of his birth, he realized that *without Chandra·prabha* he was as miserable as lotus flowers *separated from the light of the moon.* 'But this city of Vardhamána is worlds apart from that sorcerer stronghold! What is this amazing display of magic? Oh alas! Unlucky 5.3.90
me! Somehow someone has deceived me. But no one on earth knows how destiny will turn out.'

Thinking these and other thoughts, the astonished Shakti·deva then rose up from the middle of the pool and went to his father's house. Once there he pretended that he had been wandering about with the crier's drum and after being welcomed by his father he stayed there with his joyful family. On the next day he went out of the house and heard once more this proclamation being made in that city to the beat of a drum: 'If any brahmin or kshatriya has truly seen the city of Kánaka·puri, let him speak! The king shall give him his daughter and make him crown prince.'

When he heard this, Shakti·deva, who had done so, went 5.3.95
to the criers and said once again, 'I have seen that city.' They quickly took him before the king and when he recognized him, the king thought that like before he was once again telling lies. 'If I am lying and I have not seen that city, then this time execute me as a punishment. Now let the princess question me.' When he said this the king had his servants go and bring his daughter there. When she saw the brahmin whom she had seen before, she said to the king, 'Father, he is just going to tell lies again.'

5.3.100 Śaktidevas tato ’vādīd ‹ahaṃ satyaṃ mṛṣ” âiva vā
vacmi, rāja|sute, tvaṃ tu vad’ âivaṃ mama kautukam.
mayā Kanakapuryāṃ tvaṃ paryaṅke gata|jīvitā
dṛṣṭā c’ êha ca paśyāmi jīvantīṃ bhavatīṃ katham?›
ity uktā Śaktidevena s’|âbhijñānaṃ nṛp’|ātmajā
sadyaḥ Kanakarekhā sā jagād’ âivaṃ pituḥ puraḥ.
‹tāta, dṛṣṭ” âmunā satyaṃ nagarī sā mah”|ātmanā
a|cirāc c’ âiṣa bhartā me tatra|sthāyā bhaviṣyati.
tatra mad|bhaginīś c’ ânyās tisro ’yaṃ pariṇeṣyati
vidyā|dhar’|âdhirājyaṃ ca tasyāṃ puri kariṣyati.
5.3.105 mayā tv adya praveṣṭavyā svā tanuś ca purī ca sā
muneḥ śāpād ahaṃ hy atra jāt” âbhūvaṃ bhavad|gṛhe.
«yadā Kanakapuryāṃ te deham ālokya mānuṣaḥ
martya|bhāva|bhṛtas tattva|pratibhedaṃ kariṣyati.
tadā te śāpa|muktiś ca sa ca syān mānuṣaḥ patiḥ.»
iti me ca sa śāp’|ântaṃ punar ev’ ādiśan muniḥ.
jāti|smarā ca mānuṣye ’py ahaṃ jñānavatī tathā
tad vrajāmy adhunā siddhyai nijaṃ vaidyādharaṃ padam.›

ity uktvā rāja|putrī sā tanuṃ tyaktvā tiro|dadhe
tumulaś c’ ôdabhūt tasminn ākrando rāja|mandire.
5.3.110 Śaktidevo ’py ubhayato bhraṣṭas tais tair duruttaraiḥ
kleśaiḥ prāpy’ âpi na prāpte dhyāyaṃs te dve api priye.
nindan khinno ’pi c’ ātmānam a|saṃpūrṇa|manorathaḥ
nirgatya rāja|bhavanāt kṣaṇād evam acintayat.
‹abhīṣṭaṃ bhāvi me tāvad uktaṃ Kanakarekhayā
tat kim|arthaṃ viṣīdāmi sattv’|ādhīnā hi siddhayaḥ.
pathā ten’ âiva Kanakapurīṃ gacchāmi tāṃ punaḥ

Shakti·deva then said, 'I may speak the truth or lies, but, 5.3.100
O princess, please explain the following, about which I am curious. How is it that I have seen you dead on a bed in Kánaka·puri, and I am looking at you here, alive?'

When Shakti·deva said this to princess Kánaka·rekha by way of authentication, she immediately said the following in front of her father. 'Father, this great soul has indeed seen that city, and before long he will become my husband when I am there. And there he will marry my three other sisters
and become in that city the king of the sorcerers. But I must 5.3.105
now enter both my own body and that city, for I was born here in your house as the result of a curse from a sage and furthermore the sage decreed that my curse would end thus: "When a man sees your body in Kánaka·puri while you are a mortal, he will discover the truth. At that moment your curse shall end and that man shall be your husband." Even as a mortal I remember my past lives and possess the higher knowledge, so I shall now go to the happiness of my own sorcerers' abode.'

After saying this the princess abandoned her body and
disappeared. Noisy wailing arose in the palace. Shakti·deva, 5.3.110
deprived of both of his sweethearts and thinking about how they were not his despite his having won them with various insuperable hardships, and blaming himself even though he was upset, went out of the palace, his desires unfulfilled, and after a moment said to himself, 'Kánaka·rekha said that I would get what I wanted, so why am I being despondent, for success depends upon resolve. I shall go again by the same route to Kánaka·puri. Fate is sure once more to provide me with a means of getting there.' As soon as he had

bhūyo 'py avaśyaṃ daivaṃ me tatr' ôpāyaṃ kariṣyati.›
ity ālocy' âiva sa prāyāc Chaktidevaḥ purāt tataḥ
a|siddh'|ârthā nivartante na hi dhīrāḥ kṛt'|ôdyamāḥ.
5.3.115 gacchaṃś cirāc ca saṃprāpa jaladheḥ pulina|sthitam
tad Viṭaṅkapuraṃ nāma nagaraṃ punar eva saḥ.
tatr' âpaśyac ca vaṇijaṃ taṃ saṃmukham upāgatam
yena sākaṃ gatasy' âbdhiṃ potam ādāv abhajyata.
‹so 'yaṃ Samudradattaḥ syāt kathaṃ ca patito 'mbudhau
uttīrṇo 'yaṃ? na vā citram aham eva nidarśanam.›
ity ālocya sa yāvat tam abhyeti vaṇijaṃ dvijaḥ
tāvat sa taṃ parijñāya hṛṣṭaḥ kaṇṭhe 'grahīd vaṇik.
anaiṣīc ca nijaṃ gehaṃ kṛt'|ātithyaś ca pṛṣṭavān
‹pota|bhaṅge tvam ambhodheḥ katham uttirṇavān iti?›
5.3.120 Śaktidevo 'pi vṛttāntaṃ tathā taṃ kṛtsnam abravīt
yathā matsya|nigīrṇaḥ prāg Utsthala|dvīpam āpa saḥ.
an|antaraṃ ca tam api pratyapṛcchad vaṇig|varam
‹kathaṃ tadā tvam apy abdhim uttirṇo? varṇyatām iti.›
ath' âbravīt so 'pi vaṇik ‹tad" âhaṃ patito 'mbudhau
dina|trayaṃ bhramann āsam ekaṃ phalahakaṃ śritaḥ.
tatas tena path" â|kasmād ekaṃ vahanam āgatam
tatrasthaiś c' âham ākrandan dṛṣṭvā c' âtr' âdhiropitaḥ.
ārūḍhaś c' âtra pitaraṃ svam apaśyam ahaṃ tadā
gatvā dvīp'|ântaraṃ pūrvaṃ cirāt tat|kālam āgatam.
5.3.125 sa māṃ dṛṣṭvā parijñāya kṛta|kaṇṭha|grahaḥ pitā
rudann apṛcchad vṛttāntam ahaṃ c' âivaṃ tam abruvam.
«cira|kāla|prayāte 'pi, tāta, tvayy an|upāgate
sva|dharma iti vāṇijye svayam asmi pravṛttavān.

thought this through, Shakti·deva set forth from the city. When they have started something, resolute men do not stop without achieving their aim.

After traveling for a long time, he again arrived at the city 5.3.115
called Vitánka·pura on the ocean shore. There he saw come to meet him that merchant with whom he had first gone to sea and whose boat had been wrecked. 'It's Samúdra·datta! How can he have escaped after falling into the sea? But it's not that amazing—look at me.' Having reflected thus, the brahmin went up to the merchant, who was overjoyed on recognizing him and embraced him. He took him to his house where he welcomed him hospitably and asked him how he had escaped from the ocean after being shipwrecked
and Shakti·deva told him the whole story of how after being 5.3.120
swallowed by the fish he first reached the island of Útsthala. Immediately afterwards he in turn asked that fine merchant to tell him how he too had escaped from the ocean that time.

The merchant then said, 'When I fell into the sea I floated about for three days hanging on to a single plank. Then a boat suddenly came that way and as I cried out the men on it saw me and lifted me aboard. Once aboard the boat I saw my own father, who had earlier gone to a foreign island
and was now returning after a long time. When my father 5.3.125
saw me and recognized me, he embraced me and, crying, asked my story, and I told him the following: "When you had been gone a long time, father, and had not returned, I started to trade as a merchant myself, thinking it to be my duty. Then I was shipwrecked on my way to a foreign

tato dvīp'|ântaraṃ gacchann ahaṃ vahana|bhaṅgataḥ
ady' âmbudhau nimagnaḥ san prāpya yuṣmābhir uddhṛtaḥ.»

evaṃ may" ôktas tāto māṃ s'|ôpālambham abhāṣata
«ārohasi kim arthaṃ tvam īdṛśān prāṇa|saṃśayān?
dhanam asti hi me, putra, sthitaś c' âhaṃ tad|arjane
paśy' ānītaṃ may" êdaṃ te vahanaṃ hema|pūritam.»
5.3.130 ity uktv" āśvāsya ten' âiva vahanena nijaṃ gṛham
Viṭaṅkapuram ānītas ten' âiv' êdam ahaṃ tataḥ.›

ity etad vaṇijas tasmāc Chaktidevo niśamya saḥ
viśramya sa tri|yāmāṃ tām anyedyus tam abhāṣata.
‹gantavyam Utsthala|dvīpaṃ, sārthavāha, punar mayā
tat kathaṃ tatra gacchāmi sāmpratam kathyatām iti.›

‹gantuṃ pravṛttās tatr' âdya madīyā vyavahāriṇaḥ
tad|yāna|pātram āruhya prayātu saha tair bhavān.›
ity uktas tena vaṇijā sa tais tad|vyavahāribhiḥ
sākaṃ tad Utsthala|dvīpaṃ Śaktidevo yayau tataḥ.
5.3.135 ‹yaḥ sa bandhur mah"|ātmā me Viṣṇudatto 'tra tiṣṭhati
prāgvat tasy' âiva nikaṭaṃ vastum icchāmi tan maṭham.›
iti saṃprāpya ca dvīpaṃ tat|kālaṃ ca vicintya saḥ
vipaṇī|madhya|mārgeṇa gantuṃ prāvartata dvijaḥ.
tāvac ca tatra daivāt taṃ dṛṣṭvā dāśa|pateḥ sutāḥ
Satyavratasya tasy' ārāt parijñāy' âivam abruvan.
‹tātena sākaṃ Kanakapurīṃ cinvann itas tadā
brahmann, agās tvam ekaś ca katham ady' āgato bhavān.›

Śaktidevas tato 'vādīd ‹ambu|rāśau sa vaḥ pitā
patito 'mbubhir ākṛṣṭa|vahano vaḍavā|mukhe.›

island and today you found me floating in the sea and rescued me."

After I had told my father this, he said to me reproachfully, "Why do you take such risks with your life? For I have riches, my son, and I keep earning more. Look—I have brought you this boat filled with gold." After saying 5.3.130
this my father reassured me and then took me home here in Vitánka·pura in the boat.'

When Shakti·deva heard this from the merchant, he rested for the night and on the next day said to him, 'Eminent merchant, I have to go to the island of Útsthala again, so tell me now how I can reach there.'

'Some traders of mine are setting out for there today. Board their boat and go with them.' After the merchant said this to him, Shakti·deva then went to the island of Útsthala with the merchant's traders. 'Just as before I want to stay 5.3.135
at the monastery with my noble relative Vishnu·datta who lives here.' Thinking this as soon as he reached the island, the brahmin started to follow the road to the market. As fate would have it, the sons of Satya·vrata, the king of the fishermen, saw him there and when they recognized him immediately said the following. 'Brahmin, you left here that day with our father in search of Kánaka·puri, so why have you returned today alone?'

At this Shakti·deva said, 'While at sea your father fell into the mouth of the undersea inferno after his boat was drawn to it by the current.'

5.3.140 tac chrutvā dāśa|putrās te kruddhā bhṛtyān babhāṣire
‹badhnīt' âinaṃ durātmānaṃ hato 'nena sa naḥ pitā.
anyathā katham ekasmin sati pravahaṇe dvayoḥ
vaḍav"|âgnau pated eko dvitīyaś c' ôttaret tataḥ.
tad eṣa Caṇḍikā|devyāḥ purastāt pitṛ|ghātakaḥ
asmābhir upahantavyaḥ śvaḥ prabhāte paśū|kṛtaḥ.›

ity uktvā dāśa|putrās te bhṛtyān baddhv" âiva taṃ tadā
Śaktidevaṃ tato ninyur bhaya|kṛc|Caṇḍikā|gṛham
śaśvat|kavalit'|ân|eka|jīvaṃ *pravitat'|ôdaram*
khacad|ghaṇṭ'|āvalī|danta|mālaṃ mṛtyor iv' ānanam.
5.3.145 tatra baddhaḥ sthito rātrau saṃśayānaḥ sva|jīvite
sa Śaktidevo devīṃ tāṃ Caṇḍīm evaṃ vyajijñapat.
‹bāl'|ârka|bimba|nibhayā,
bhagavati, mūrtyā tvayā paritrātam
nirbhara|pīta|pravisṛta|
Ruru|dānava|kaṇṭha|rudhiray" êva jagat.
tan māṃ satata|praṇataṃ
niṣkāraṇa|vidhura|varga|hasta|gatam
rakṣasva su|dūr'|āgatam
iṣṭa|jana|prāpti|tṛṣṇayā, varade!›

iti devīṃ sa vijñapya prāpya nidrāṃ kathaṃ|cana
apaśyad yoṣitaṃ svapne tad|garbha|gṛha|nirgatām.
sā divy'|ākṛtir abhyetya sa|day" êva jagāda tam
‹bhoḥ Śaktideva mā bhaiṣīr na te 'niṣṭaṃ bhaviṣyati.
5.3.150 asty eṣāṃ dāśa|putrāṇāṃ nāmnā Bindumatī svasā
sā prātar vīkṣya kanyā tvāṃ bhartṛtve 'bhyarthayiṣyati.
tac ca tvaṃ pratipadyethāḥ s" âiva tvāṃ mocayiṣyati

When they heard this, the fisher boys were angry and said to some servants, 'Arrest this villain! He has killed our father. Otherwise how, when the two of them were in one boat, could one fall in the undersea fire and the other escape from it? So tomorrow morning we must make him, the killer of our father, a sacrificial offering to the goddess Chándika and slay him.' 5.3.140

After the fisher boys said this to the servants, they arrested Shakti·deva and took him from there to the terrifying temple of Chándika, which, constantly devouring hordes of creatures, its *stomach distended : interior wide*, its rows of teeth the lines of bells coming forth, was like the mouth of
death. Tied up there that night, Shakti·deva, fearing for his 5.3.145
life, made the following request to the goddess Chándika. 'Your holiness, looking like the orb of the morning sun after drinking your fill of the blood which spouted forth from the neck of the *dánava* Ruru, it is as if you saved the world. I am constantly devoted to you and after coming a very long way in my desire to win my beloved have for no reason fallen into the hands of a group of enemies, so rescue me, O giver of boons!'

After making this request to the goddess and somehow falling asleep, in a dream he saw a woman emerge from the temple's inner sanctum. She was of divine appearance and went up to him and said, as if in pity, 'O Shakti·deva, do
not be scared. Nothing undesirable shall befall you. These 5.3.150
fisher boys have a sister called Bíndumati. That girl will see you in the morning and want you as her husband. So you should agree and she will have you set free. She is not a fisherwoman, she is a divine woman who has fallen because

na ca sā dhīvarī sā hi divyā strī śāpataś cyutā.›
etac chrutvā prabuddhasya tasya netr'|âmṛta|cchaṭā
prabhāte dāśa|kanyā sā tad|devī|gṛham āyayau.
babhāṣe c' âinam abhyetya nivedy' ātmānam utsukā
‹ito 'haṃ mocayāmi tvāṃ tat kuruṣv' ēpsitaṃ mama.
bhrātṝṇāṃ saṃmatā hy ete pratyākhyātā varā mayā
tvayi dṛṣṭe tu me prītiḥ saṃjātā tad bhajasva mām.›
5.3.155 ity uktaḥ sa tayā Bindumatyā dāś'|êndra|kanyayā
Śaktidevaḥ smaran svapnaṃ hṛṣṭas tat pratyapadyata.
tay" âiva mocitas tāṃ ca su|mukhīṃ pariṇītavān
svapna|labdh'|âmbik"|ādeśair bhrātṛbhir vihit'|ēpsitām.
tasthau ca sukha|siddhy" êva tatra puṇy'|âika|labdhayā
rūp'|ântar'|ôpāgatayā sa tayā saha divyayā.
ekadā harmya|pṛṣṭha|stho dhṛta|go|māṃsa|bhārakam
mārg'|āgataṃ sa caṇḍālaṃ dṛṣṭvā tām abravīt priyām.
‹vandyās tri|jagato 'py etā yāḥ, kṛś'|ôdari, dhenavaḥ
tāsāṃ piśitam aśnāti paśy' âyaṃ pāpa|kṛt katham!›
5.3.160 tac chrutvā s" āpy avādīt taṃ patiṃ Bindumatī tadā
‹a|cintyam, ārya|putr,' aitat pāpam atra kim ucyate?
ahaṃ gavāṃ prabhāveṇa svalpād apy aparādhataḥ
jātā dāśa|kule 'muṣmin kā tv etasy' âtra niṣkṛtiḥ?›
evam uktavatīm eva Śaktidevo jagāda tām
‹citraṃ! brūhi, priye, kā tvaṃ dāśa|janma kathaṃ ca te›

of a curse.' After he had heard this and woken up, in the morning the fisher maiden arrived at the temple, a flood of the nectar of immortality to his eyes. Full of longing, she came up to him, introduced herself and said, 'I shall have you freed from here, so do what I want. The grooms approved of by my brothers have been turned down by me, but when I saw you I fell in love, so marry me.'

When Bíndumati, the daughter of the king of the fisher- 5.3.155
men, said this to him, Shakti·deva, remembering the dream, was delighted and said yes. She had him set free and he married the beautiful girl, her wishes carried out by her brothers, who had received instructions from the goddess in a dream. He stayed there with that heavenly girl who had assumed a different form, and it was as if she were the attainment of happiness, obtained only through good deeds.

One day he was on the terrace of his house and he saw a low caste man coming along the road carrying a load of cow flesh. He said to his sweetheart, 'Cows are worshipped by the three worlds, slender lady, and look how this sinner eats their flesh!'

When she heard this, Bíndumati said to her husband, 5.3.160
'My noble lord, this sin is unbelievable. What can be said of it? Due to the majesty of cows, I have been born in this family of fishermen as the result of a trifling misdemeanor, but how can this man atone for this?'

After she said this, Shakti·deva said to her, 'Amazing! Tell me, my dear, who you are and how you came to be born as a fisher girl.'

atinirbandhataś c' âivaṃ pṛcchantaṃ tam uvāca sā
‹vadāmi gopyam apy etad|vacanaṃ me karoṣi cet.›
‹bāḍhaṃ, priye, karom' îti› ten' ôkte śapath'|ôttaram
sā tad" âinaṃ jagād' âivam ādau tāvat samīhitam.
5.3.165 ‹asmin dvīpe dvitīy" âpi bhāryā te bhavit" âdhunā
sā c,' ārya|putra, nacirād dhṛta|garbhā bhaviṣyati.
aṣṭame garbha|māse ca pāṭayitv" ôdaraṃ tvayā
tasyāḥ sa garbhaḥ kraṣṭavyo n' âiva kāryā ghṛṇ" âtra ca.›
evam uktavatī tasmin ‹kim etad iti?› vismite
lasad|ghṛṇe ca bhūyaḥ sā dāś'|êndra|tanay" âbravīt.
‹ity etat tava kartavyaṃ hetoḥ kasy' âpi mad|vacaḥ
ath' êdaṃ śṛṇu yā c' âhaṃ dāśa|janma yathā ca me.
ahaṃ janm'|ântare 'bhūvaṃ k" âpi vidyā|dharī purā
martya|loke ca śāpena paribhraṣṭ" âsmi sāmpratam.
5.3.170 vidyā|dharatve ca yadā chittvā dantair ayojayam
vīṇāsu tantrīs ten' êha jāt" âhaṃ dāśa|veśmani.
tad evaṃ vadane spṛṣṭe śuṣkeṇa snāyunā gavām
īdṛśy adho|gatiḥ kā tu vārtā tan|māṃsa|bhakṣaṇe?›
ity evaṃ kathayantyāṃ ca tatra tasyāṃ sa|saṃbhramam
eko 'bhyupetya tad|bhrātā Śaktidevam abhāṣata.
‹uttiṣṭha sumahān eṣa kuto 'py utthāya sūkaraḥ
hat'|ân|eka|jano darpād ito 'bhimukham āgataḥ.›

When he was asking this so insistently, she said to him, 'I shall tell you, even though it is secret, if you do for me what I am about to tell you.'

When he replied with an oath, 'Of course I shall do it, my dear,' she then told him first what she wanted: 'On 5.3.165
this island you shall soon take a second wife, and she, noble lord, will before long become pregnant. In the eighth month of the pregnancy, you must split open her stomach and pull out the child from the womb. Don't feel squeamish about this.'

After she had said this, he was astonished and, looking disgusted, asked what it meant. The daughter of the fisher king spoke again. 'This is what you must do. There is a definite reason for what I am saying. Now hear who I am and how I was born among the fishermen. Long ago in a different life I was some sorceress or other and as a curse I have now fallen into the world of men. When I was a sorceress, 5.3.170
I cut some lute-strings with my teeth before fixing them on some lutes, as a result of which I was born here in the house of a fisherman. So if that is the debasement that happens when one's mouth is touched by a dried sinew from a cow, what can one say about eating their flesh?'

As she was saying this one of her brothers rushed in there in a panic and said to Shakti·deva, 'Get up! An enormous boar has appeared from somewhere. In its arrogance it has killed several people and is now on its way here.'

tac chrutvā so 'vatīry' âiva Śaktidevaḥ sva|harmyataḥ
āruhya śakti|hasto 'śvam adhāvat sūkaraṃ prati.
5.3.175 prajahāra ca dṛṣṭv" âiva tasmin vīre 'bhidhāvati
palāyya vraṇitaḥ so 'pi varāhaḥ prāviśad bilam.
Śaktidevo 'pi tatr' âiva tad|anveṣī praviśya ca
kṣaṇād apaśyat s'|āvāsam udyāna|gahanaṃ mahat.
tatra|sthaś ca dadarś' âikāṃ kanyām atyadbhut'|ākṛtim
sa|saṃbhramam upāyātāṃ prīty" êva vana|devatām.
tām apṛcchac ca ‹kalyāṇi, kā tvaṃ kiṃ saṃbhramaś ca te?›
tac chrutvā s" âpi sumukhī tam evaṃ pratyabhāṣata.
‹asti dakṣiṇa|diṅ|nātho nṛpatiś Caṇḍavikramaḥ
tasy' âhaṃ Bindurekh"|ākhyā sutā, subhaga, kanyakā.
5.3.180 ih' â|kasmāc ca pāpo māṃ daityo jvalita|locanaḥ
apahṛtya cchalen' âdya pitur ānītavān gṛhāt.
sa c' āmiṣ'|ârthī vārāhaṃ rūpaṃ kṛtvā bahir gataḥ
viddho 'dy' âiva kṣudh"|ārtaḥ sañ śaktyā vīreṇa kena|cit.
viddha|mātraḥ praviśy' êha pañcatām āgataś ca saḥ
tad|a|dūṣita|kaumārā palāyy' âhaṃ ca nirgatā.›
tac chrutvā Śaktidevas tām ūce ‹kas tarhi saṃbhramaḥ?
may" âiva sa varāho hi hataḥ śaktyā, nṛp'|ātmaje.›
tataḥ s" âpy avadat ‹tarhi brūhi me ko bhavān iti?›
«vipro 'haṃ Śaktidev'|ākhya iti» pratyabravīc ca saḥ.
5.3.185 ‹tarhi tvam eva me bhart" êty› uditaḥ sa tayā tataḥ

When he heard this, Shakti·deva came down from his terrace, mounted a horse with his spear in his hand and rushed after the boar. As soon as he saw it he threw the 5.3.175
spear. When that hero bore down on it, the boar fled, injured, and went into a hole. Shakti·deva went straight in there, chasing after it, and a moment later he saw a huge impenetrable garden and a house. While there, he saw a girl of quite amazing beauty rush up and approach him, as if she were the goddess of the forest approaching him out of affection. He asked her, 'Blessed lady, who are you and why are you flustered so?'

When she heard this, the lovely girl replied, 'There is a king, the lord of the South, called Chanda·víkrama. I, handsome sir, am his daughter, a maiden by the name of Bindu·rekha. An evil *daitya* with blazing eyes today sud- 5.3.180
denly abducted me by means of a trick and brought me here from my father's house. Desirous of flesh, he assumed the form of a boar and went out. Just now he was speared by some hero while stricken with hunger. As soon as he was speared he came in here and died. He had not violated my maidenhood and I ran away.'

When Shakti·deva heard this, he said to her, 'Then what's the panic, for it was I who killed the boar with a spear, O princess.'

She replied, 'In which case tell me who you are, sir.'

"I am a brahmin called Shakti·deva," he answered.

At this she said to him, 'Then you are my husband.' 5.3.185

‹tath" êty› ādāya tāṃ vīro bila|dvāreṇa niryayau.
gṛhaṃ gatvā ca bhāryāyai Bindumatyai nivedya tat
tac|chraddhitaḥ kumārīṃ tāṃ Bindurekhām udūḍhavān.
tatas tasya dvi|bhāryasya Śaktidevasya tiṣṭhataḥ
tatr' âikā Bindurekhā sā bhāryā garbham adhārayat.
aṣṭame garbha|māse ca tasyāḥ svairam upetya tam
ādyā Bindumatī bhāryā Śaktidevam uvāca sā.
‹vīra, tat smara yan mahyaṃ pratiśrutam abhūt tvayā
so 'yaṃ dvitīya|bhāryāyā garbha|māso 'ṣṭamas tava.
5.3.190 tad gatvā garbham etasyā vipāṭy' ôdaram āhara
an|atikramaṇīyaṃ hi nijaṃ satya|vacas tava.›
evam uktas tayā Śaktidevaḥ sneha|kṛp"|ākulaḥ
pratijñā|para|tantraś ca kṣaṇam āsīd an|uttaraḥ.
jāt'|ôdvegaś ca nirgatya Bindurekh"|ântikaṃ yayau
s" âpi khinnam upāyāntaṃ taṃ viloky' âivam abravīt.
‹ārya|putra, viṣaṇṇo 'si kim adya? nanu vedmy aham
Bindumatyā niyuktas tvaṃ garbhasy' ôtpāṭane mama.
tac ca te 'vaśya|kartavyaṃ kāryaṃ kiṃ|cid dhi vidyate
nṛśaṃsatā ca n' âsty atra kā|cit tan mā ghṛṇāṃ kṛthāḥ.
5.3.195 tathā hi śṛṇu, nāth,' âtra Devadatta|kathām imām
pur" âbhūd Haridatt'|ākhyaḥ Kambuk'|ākhye pure dvijaḥ.
tasya ca śrīmataḥ putraḥ kṛta|vidyo 'pi śaiśave
Devadatt'|âbhidhāno 'bhūd dyūt'|âika|vyasanī yuvā.
dyūta|hārita|vastr'|ādir gantuṃ n' âlaṃ pitur gṛham
ekadā ca viveś' âikaṃ sa śūnyaṃ devatā|gṛham.
tatra c' âpaśyad ekākī sādhit'|ân|eka|kārmaṇam
japantaṃ Jālapād'|ākhyaṃ mahā|vratinam ekakam.

Saying, 'So be it,' our hero took her and went out through the door of the hole. He went home and told his wife Bíndumati what had happened. With her approval he married the princess Bindu·rekha. Then when Shakti·deva was living there with his two wives, one of them, his wife Bindu·rekha, became pregnant. In the eighth month of the pregnancy, his first wife Bíndumati quietly went up to Shakti·deva and said to him, 'Brave warrior, remember what you promised me. It is the eighth month of your second wife's pregnancy so go and split open her stomach and take out 5.3.190
the unborn child, for you cannot go back on your word.'

When she said this to him, Shakti·deva was confused by his love and compassion. Committed to what he had promised, he stayed there for a moment without replying. Anxious, he left and went to Bindu·rekha. Seeing him arrive in a state of despair, she said, 'My noble lord, why are you sad today? But surely I know—Bíndumati has told you to tear out my unborn child. You must do it, because there is a reason for it, and there is no evil in it, so don't be squeamish. In the context of this, listen, my lord, to this story about 5.3.195
Deva·datta.

Long ago there was a brahmin called Hari·datta in a city called Kámbuka. That splendid fellow had a son called Deva·datta who even though he had been educated in his childhood, grew into a young man addicted to gambling. Having lost his clothes and so forth at the table, he couldn't go to his father's house. One day he went into a deserted temple and while alone there he saw repeating a mantra a solitary ascetic called Jala·pada who had undertaken the great vow and perfected several magical rites. He slowly

cakāra ca śanais tasya praṇāmam upagamya saḥ
ten' âpy apāsta|maunena svāgaten' âbhyanandyata.
5.3.200 sthitaḥ kṣaṇāc ca ten' âiva pṛṣṭo vaidhurya|kāraṇam
śaśaṃs' âsmai sva|vipadaṃ vyasana|kṣīṇa|vitta|jām.
tatas taṃ sa jagād' âivaṃ Devadattaṃ mahā|vratī
«n' âsti vyasaninām, vatsa, bhuvi paryāptaye dhanam.
icchā ca vipadaṃ hātuṃ yadi te kuru mad|vacaḥ
vidyā|dharatvaṃ prāptuṃ† yat|kṛtaḥ parikaro mayā.
tat sādhaya tvam apy etan mayā saha, su|lakṣaṇa,
mac|chāsanaṃ tu pālyaṃ te naśyantu vipadas tava.»
ity ukto vratinā tena pratiśrutya «tath" êti» tat
sa Devadattas tat|pārśve tad" âiva sthitim agrahīt.
5.3.205 anyedyuś ca śmaśān'|ânte gatvā vaṭa|taror adhaḥ
vidhāya rajanau pūjāṃ param'|ânnaṃ nivedya ca.
balīn dikṣu ca vikṣipya saṃpādita|tad|arcanaḥ
taṃ pārśva|vartinaṃ vipram uvāca sa mahā|vratī.
«evam eva tvayā kāryam iha pratyaham arcanam
‹Vidyutprabhe gṛhāṇ' êmāṃ pūjām› ity abhidhāyinā.
ataḥ paraṃ ca jāne 'haṃ siddhiś c' âivaṃ dhruv" âvayoḥ»
ity uktvā sa yayau tena samaṃ sva|nilayaṃ vratī.
so 'pi nityaṃ taros tasya mūle gatvā tath" âiva tat
Devadatto 'rcanaṃ cakre tath" âiva vidhinā tataḥ.
5.3.210 ekadā ca sapary"|ânte dvidhā|bhūtāt taros tataḥ
a|kasmāt paśyatas tasya divyā nārī viniryayau.
«ehy asmat|svāminī, bhadra, vakti tvām iti» vādinī
sā taṃ praveśayām āsa tasy' âiv' âbhyantaraṃ taroḥ.
sa praviśya dadarś' âtra divyaṃ maṇi|mayaṃ gṛham

went up and bowed before him. The sage abandoned his silence and greeted him with a welcome. After waiting for 5.3.200
a moment, the ascetic asked him why he was upset and he told him the disaster that had befallen him as a result of losing his money because of his addiction. At this the *kapálika* said to Deva·datta, "My child, there is not enough money in the world to satisfy those addicted to vice. If you want to get rid of your troubles, then do what I say. I have been making preparations to become a sorcerer, so, lucky man, finish them with me and obey my instructions and your troubles will disappear."

When the ascetic said this to him, Deva·datta agreed to it, saying, "So be it," and took residence at his side from then on. On the next night the *kapálika* went to the far end 5.3.205
of the cremation ground, performed his worship at the foot of a banyan tree, made an offering of rice pudding and cast the oblations into the directions. When his worship was over, he said to the brahmin, who was at his side, "You must perform worship exactly like this here every day, and say, 'Vidyut·prabha, accept this worship,' and I know that in this way we are both sure to achieve success as a result." After saying this the ascetic went with him to his home. After that Deva·datta would go regularly to the foot of the tree as he had been told and carry out worship in that fashion.

One day at the end of the worship, as he looked on, the 5.3.210
tree suddenly split in two and a divine woman emerged from it. "Come, good fellow, our mistress shall address you." Saying this she led him inside that very same tree. After going in he saw there a heavenly house made of jewels and inside it a beautiful girl on a bed. He immediately said

paryaṅka|vartinīm ekāṃ tatra c' ântar vara|striyam.
«rūpiṇī siddhir asmākam iyaṃ syād iti» sa kṣaṇāt
yāvad dhyāyati tāvat sā kṛt'|ātithyā var'|âṅganā
raṇit'|ābharaṇair aṅgair vihita|svāgatair iva
utthāya nija|paryaṅke tam upāveśayat svayam.
5.3.215 jagāda ca «mahā|bhāga, sutā yakṣa|pater aham
kanyā hi Ratnavarṣasya khyātā Vidyutprabh"|ākhyayā.
ārādhayac ca mām eṣa Jālapādo mahā|vratī
tasy' ârtha|siddhi|d" âiv' âsmi tvaṃ prāṇeṣv api me prabhuḥ.
tasmād dṛṣṭ'|ânurāgiṇyāḥ kuru pāṇi|grahaṃ mama!»
ity uktaḥ sa tayā cakre Devadattas «tath" êti» tat.
sthitvā ca kaṃ|cit kālaṃ sa garbha|bhāre tayā dhṛte
jagāma punar āgantuṃ taṃ mahā|vratinaṃ prati.
śaśaṃsa ca yathā|vṛttaṃ taṃ tasmai sa|bhayaṃ tataḥ
so 'py evam ātma|siddhy|arthī jagād' âinaṃ mahā|vratī.
5.3.220 «bhadra, sādhu kṛtaṃ kiṃ tu gatv" âsyā yakṣa|yoṣitaḥ
vipāṭy' ôdaram ākṛṣya śīghraṃ garbhaṃ tam ānaya.»
ity uktvā smārayitvā ca vratinā pūrva|saṃgaram
preṣitas tena bhūyas tāṃ Devadatto 'py agāt priyām.
tatra tiṣṭhati yāvac ca tad|vibhāvana|durmanāḥ
tāvad Vidyutprabhā sā taṃ yakṣī svayam abhāṣata.
«ārya|putra, viṣaṇṇo 'si kim|arthaṃ viditaṃ mayā
ādiṣṭaṃ Jālapādena tava mad|garbha|pāṭanam.
tad garbham etam ākarṣa pāṭayitvā mam' ôdaram
na cet svayaṃ karomy etat kāryaṃ hy asty atra kiṃ|cana.»
5.3.225 evaṃ tay" ôktaḥ sa yadā kartuṃ tan n' âśakad dvijaḥ
tad ākṛṣṭavatī garbhaṃ sā svayaṃ pāṭit'|ôdarā.
taṃ ca kṛṣṭaṃ puras tyaktvā Devadattaṃ tam abhyadhāt

to himself, "She could be the incarnation of our success," and just as he was thinking this, the beautiful lady greeted him hospitably, stood up, the ornaments on her body tinkling as if in welcome, and herself had him sit on her bed.
She said, "O most fortunate one, I am the maiden daughter 5.3.215
of Ratna·varsha, the king of the *yakshas*, and I am known as Vidyut·prabha. This *kapálika* ascetic Jala·pada has propitiated me. I shall grant him success in what he wants, but you rule my life. So having seen that I love you, marry me!" When she said this to Deva·datta, he agreed.

After he had stayed there for a while and she was pregnant, he went to visit the *kapálika* ascetic again. He then fearfully told him what had happened, and the *kapálika* ascetic, wanting to achieve his own aims, said to him, "Good 5.3.220
sir, you have done well, but now go and split open the stomach of this *yaksha* lady, take out the unborn child and bring it here." After saying this and reminding Deva·datta of their earlier agreement, the ascetic sent him off once more and he went to his sweetheart.

While he stood there, downcast as he thought about his task, the *yakshi* Vidyut·prabha said to him herself, "My noble lord, why are you sad? I know that Jala·pada has ordered you to split open my pregnant stomach. So split it open and take out the unborn child. If you don't, I shall do it
myself, for there is a purpose to this." When she said this 5.3.225
to him and the brahmin was then unable to do it, she split her stomach herself and took out the unborn child. She put down the extracted fetus in front of Deva·datta and said to him, "Take this. It will make the person who eats it a sorcerer. I am a sorceress but was born as a *yakshi* because of a

«bhoktur vidyā|dharatvasya kāraṇaṃ gṛhyatām ayam.
ahaṃ ca śāpād yakṣītve jātā vidyā|dharī satī
ayam īdṛk ca śāp'|ânto mama jāti|smarā hy aham.
idānīṃ yāmi dhāma svaṃ saṃgamaś c' āvayoḥ punaḥ
tatr' âiv' êty» abhidhāy' âiṣā kv' âpi Vidyutprabhā yayau.
Devadatto 'pi taṃ garbhaṃ gṛhītvā khinna|mānasaḥ
jagāma Jālapādasya tasya sa vratino 'ntikam.
5.3.230 upānayac ca taṃ garbhaṃ tasmai siddhi|pradāyinam
bhajanty ātmaṃbharitvaṃ hi durlabhe 'pi na sādhavaḥ.
so 'pi tat pācayitv" âiva garbha|māṃsaṃ mahā|vratī
vyasṛjad Devadattaṃ taṃ Bhairav'|ârcā|kṛte 'ṭavīm.
tato datta|balir yāvad etya paśyati sa dvijaḥ
tāvan māṃsam a|śeṣaṃ tad vratinā tena bhakṣitam.
«kathaṃ sarvaṃ tvayā bhuktam iti?» c' âtr' âsya jalpataḥ
jihmo vidyā|dharo bhūtvā Jālapādaḥ kham udyayau.
vyoma|śyāmala|nistriṃśe hāra|keyūra|rājite
tasminn utpatite so 'tha Devadatto vyacintayat.
5.3.235 «kaṣṭaṃ kīdṛg anen' âhaṃ vañcitaḥ pāpa|buddhinā
yadi v" âtyantam ṛjutā na kasya paribhūtaye.
tad etasy' âpakārasya katham adya pratikriyām
kuryāṃ? vidyā|dharī|bhūtam apy enaṃ prāpnuyāṃ katham?
tan n' âsty upāyo vetāla|sādhanād aparo 'tra me.»
iti niścitya sa yayau rātrau pitṛ|vanaṃ tataḥ.
tatr' āhūya taror mūle vetālaṃ nṛ|kalevare
pūjayitv" âkarot tasya nṛ|māṃsa|bali|tarpaṇam.
a|tṛpyantaṃ ca vetālaṃ tam any'|ānayan'|â|saham
tarpayiṣyan sva|māṃsāni cchettum ārabhate sma saḥ.
5.3.240 tat|kṣaṇaṃ taṃ sa vetālo mahā|sattvam abhāṣata

curse. My curse is to end like this, for I can remember my former lives. I shall now go home and we shall meet again there." After she had said this, Vidyut·prabha disappeared.

Deva·datta, meanwhile, down at heart, took the unborn child and went to the ascetic Jala·pada. He gave him that 5.3.230
unborn child, which could grant success, for good people do not behave selfishly, even in the case of things that are hard to obtain. As soon as the *kapálika* ascetic had cooked the unborn child's flesh he sent Deva·datta off to the forest to worship Bháirava. When he returned after making the offering, the brahmin saw that in the meantime the ascetic had eaten all the flesh. While he was asking him there why he had eaten it all, the crooked Jala·pada turned into a sorcerer and flew up into the sky.

Then, when he had flown off, resplendent with his garlands and armlets, his sword as blue as the sky, Deva·datta said to himself, "Oh dear. How this ill-intentioned fellow 5.3.235
has tricked me! But excessive honesty brings humiliation to everyone. So how now am I to take my revenge for this offense? And how am I to find him now that he has become a sorcerer? In this case there can be no means at my disposal other than winning the favor of a *vetála*."

Having decided thus, that night he left that place for the grove of the ancestors. At the foot of a tree there he invited a *vetála* to enter a corpse and having worshipped it he gratified it with a sacrificial offering of human flesh. The *vetála* was not satisfied and would not wait for him to fetch more, so, wanting to gratify it with an offering, he started to cut his own flesh. At that moment the *vetála* said to that very 5.3.240
brave man, "This courage of yours has pleased me. Do not

«sattven' ânena tuṣṭo 'smi tava mā sāhasaṃ kṛthāḥ.
tad, bhadra, kim abhipretaṃ tava yat sādhayāmi te?»
ity uktavantaṃ vetālaṃ sa vīraḥ pratyuvāca tam.
«viśvasta|vañcako yatra Jālapādo vratī sthitaḥ
vidyā|dhara|nivāsaṃ taṃ naya tan|nigrahāya mām.»
«tath" êty» uktavatā tena vetālena sa tat|kṣaṇāt
skandhe 'dhiropya nabhasā ninye vaidyādharaṃ padam.
tatr' âpaśyac ca taṃ Jālapādaṃ prāsāda|vartinam
sa vidyā|dhara|rājatva|dṛptaṃ ratn'|āsana|sthitam,
5.3.245 pratārayantaṃ tām eva labdha|vidyā|dharī|padām
Vidyutprabhām an|icchantīṃ bhāryātve tat|tad|uktibhiḥ.
dṛṣṭv" âiva ca sa|vetālo 'py abhyadhāvat sa taṃ yuvā
hṛṣyad|Vidyutprabhā|netra|cakor'|âmṛta|candramāḥ.
Jālapādo 'pi so 'kasmāt taṃ dṛṣṭv" âiv' āgataṃ tathā
vitrāsād bhraṣṭa|nistriṃśo nipapāt' āsanād bhuvi.
Devadatto 'pi tat khaḍgaṃ sa labdhv" âpy avadhīn na tam
ripuṣv api hi bhīteṣu s'|ânukampā mah"|āśayāḥ.
jighāṃsantaṃ ca vetālaṃ taṃ jagāda sa vārayan
«pākhaṇḍinā kim etena kṛpaṇena hatena naḥ?
5.3.250 sthāpyatāṃ bhuvi nītv" âyaṃ tasmāt sva|nilaye tvayā
āstāṃ tatr' âiva bhūyo 'pi pāpaḥ kāpāliko† varam.»
ity evaṃ vadatas tasya Devadattasya tat|kṣaṇam
divo 'vatīrya śarvāṇī devī pratyakṣatāṃ yayau.
sā jagāda ca taṃ prahvaṃ «putra, tuṣṭ" âsmi te 'dhunā
an|anya|sadṛśen' êha sattv'|ôtkarṣeṇa saṃprati.
tad vidyā|dhara|rājatvaṃ mayā dattam ih' âiva te.»
ity uktv" ârpita|vidyā sā devī sadyas tiro 'bhavat.

carry out this rash deed. So, good sir, what desire do you have that I may fulfill?"

When the *vetála* had said this, our hero replied, "Take me to the abode of sorcerers where stays the ascetic Jala·pada, who cheats those who trust him, so that he can be punished." The *vetála* said yes and immediately lifted him onto his shoulders and led him by way of the sky to the home of the sorcerers. There he found Jala·pada in a palace, on a jeweled throne, puffed up with pride at being a sorcerer king, using various utterances to persuade the reluc- 5.3.245
tant Vidyut·prabha, who had attained the rank of sorceress, to become his wife. As soon that young man, who was to the eyes of the overjoyed Vidyut·prabha like the full of the nectar of immortality to the *chakóra* bird, saw him, he and the *vetála* attacked him. Jala·pada, on suddenly seeing him come like that, immediately dropped his sword in terror and fell off his throne onto the ground. Deva·datta took the sword but did not kill him, for the noble take pity even on enemies when they are terrified. When the *vetála* wanted to kill him, he stopped him, saying, "Why should we kill this wretched heretic? You must take him from this place and 5.3.250
put him in his own house on earth. It would be better if the wicked *kapálika* lives there once more."

At the very moment that Deva·datta was saying this, Párvati came down from the sky and revealed herself. She said to him as he bowed humbly, "My son, I am now pleased because of this excellent and incomparable heroism you have just shown. So I give you right here the position of king of the sorcerers." Having said this and given him the magical sciences, the goddess suddenly vanished. The *vetála* took

Jālapādaś ca nītv" âiva vetālena sa bhū|tale
vibhraṣṭa|siddhir nidadhe n' â|dharmaś ciram ṛddhaye.
5.3.255 Devadatto 'pi sahitaḥ sa Vidyutprabhayā tayā
vidyā|dhar'|âdhirājyaṃ tat prāpya tatra vyajṛmbhata.›

ity ākhyāya kathāṃ patye Śaktidevāya sa|tvarā
sā Bindurekhā bhūyas taṃ babhāṣe mṛdu|bhāṣiṇī.
‹it' īdṛṃśi bhavanty eva kāryāṇi tad idaṃ mama
Bindumaty|uditaṃ garbhaṃ mukta|śokaṃ vipāṭaya.›
ity evaṃ Bindurekhāyāṃ vadantyāṃ pāpa|śaṅkite
Śaktideve ca gaganād udabhūt tatra bhāratī.
‹bhoḥ Śaktideva, niḥśaṅkaṃ garbho 'syāḥ kṛṣyatāṃ tvayā
kaṇṭhe muṣṭyā gṛhīto hi khaḍgo 'sau te bhaviṣyati.›
5.3.260 iti divyāṃ giraṃ śrutvā pāṭit'|ôdaram āśu saḥ
garbhaṃ tasyāḥ samākṛṣya pāṇinā kaṇṭhato 'grahīt.
gṛhīta|mātro jajñe ca sa khaḍgas tasya hasta|gaḥ
ākṛṣṭaḥ sattvataḥ siddheḥ keśa|pāśa iv' āyataḥ.
tato vidyā|dharaḥ kṣiprāt sa vipraḥ samajāyata
Bindurekhā ca tat|kālam a|darśanam iyāya sā.

tad dṛṣṭvā ca sa gatv" âiva dāśa|putryai nyavedayat
Bindumatyai dvitīyasyai patnyai sarvaṃ tathā|vidhaḥ.
sā tam āha ‹vayaṃ, nātha, vidyā|dhara|pateḥ sutāḥ
tisro bhaginyaḥ Kanakapurītaḥ śāpataś cyutāḥ.
5.3.265 ekā Kanakarekhā sā Vardhamāna|pure tvayā
yasyā dṛṣṭaḥ sa śāp'|ântaḥ sā ca tāṃ svāṃ purīṃ gatā.
śāp'|ânto h' īdṛśas tasyā vicitro vidhi|yogataḥ
aham eva tṛtīyā ca śāp'|ântaś c' âdhun" âiva me.
mayā c' âdy' âiva gantavyā nagarī sā nijā, priya
vidyā|dhara|śarīrāṇi tatr' âiv' âsmākam āsate.
Candraprabhā ca bhaginī jyāyasī hi sthit" âtra naḥ

Jala·pada, who had lost his powers, and immediately put him on the earth. Evil does not bring good fortune for long. Deva·datta, meanwhile, having become the king of the sor- 5.3.255
cerers, lived there in comfort with Vidyut·prabha.'

After telling this story to her husband Shakti·deva, Bindu·rekha hurriedly added in a gentle voice, 'Thus tasks such as this do arise, so, as Bíndumati said, split open my stomach without feeling sorrow.' While Bindu·rekha was saying this and Shakti·deva was worrying about committing a sin, a voice from the sky was heard there. 'O Shakti·deva, you must remove her unborn child without fear, for when you grip it by the neck, it will turn into your sword.' After hear- 5.3.260
ing this divine voice, he quickly split her stomach, pulled out the unborn child and held it by the throat in his hand. As soon as he took hold of it, it turned into a sword in his hand, as if through his courage he had drawn out the bound lock of hair on the head of success. The brahmin then immediately turned into a sorcerer and Bindu·rekha disappeared that very moment.

On seeing this, he straightaway went as he was and told the fisher girl Bíndumati, his second wife, everything. She said to him, 'We, my lord, are three sisters, the daughters of a sorcerer king, who have been cast out of Kánaka·puri as the result of a curse. Kánaka·rekha, the end of whose curse 5.3.265
you witnessed in the city of Vardhamána, is one of us and she has gone to her own city, for through the workings of

tad āyāhi tvam apy āśu khaḍga|siddhi|prabhāvataḥ.
tatra hy asmāṃś catasro 'pi bhāryāḥ saṃprāpya c' âdhikāḥ
vana|sthen' ârpitāḥ pitrā puri rājyaṃ kariṣyasi.›

5.3.270 iti nija|param'|ârtham uktavatyā
samam anayā punar eva Bindumatyā
atha Kanakapurīṃ sa Śaktidevo
gagana|pathena ‹tath" êti› tāṃ jagāma.
tasyāṃ ca yāni yoṣid|vapūṃṣi paryaṅka|talpa|vartīni
nirjīvitāny apaśyat pūrvaṃ triṣu maṇḍapeṣu divyāni.
tāni yathāvat sv'|ātmabhir
anupraviṣṭāḥ sa Kanakarekh"|ādyāḥ
prāpto bhūyaḥ praṇatā
adrākṣīt tā nija|priyās tisraḥ.
tāṃ ca caturthīm aikṣata taj|jyeṣṭhāṃ racita|maṅgalāṃ tatra
Candraprabhāṃ pibantīṃ cira|darśana|s'|ôtkayā dṛṣṭyā.
sva|sva|niyoga|vyāpṛta|
parijana|vanit"|âbhinandit'|āgamanaḥ
vāsa|gṛh'|ântaḥ
prāptaś Candraprabhayā tayā jagade.

5.3.275 ‹yā tatra Kanakarekhā
rāja|sutā, su|bhaga, Vardhamāna|pure
dṛṣṭā bhavatā s" êyaṃ
bhaginī me Candrarekh"|ākhyā.
yā dāś'|âdhipa|putrī Bindumatī prathamam Utsthala|dvīpe
pariṇīt" âbhūd bhavatā Śaśirekhā mat|svasā s" êyam.
yā tad|anu Bindurekhā rāja|sutā tatra dānav'|ānītā

fate her curse came to an end in that strange fashion. I am the third, and my curse has just ended.* I must go to that city of mine this very day, my dear: our sorcerer bodies await us there. And our elder sister Chandra·prabha is living in that place, so you too should hurry there by means of the sword's magical power. Having obtained all four of us as wives there, offered by our father while in the forest, you shall rule in the city.'

After Bíndumati had thus revealed the truth about her- 5.3.270
self, Shakti·deva agreed and flew once more to Kánaka·puri with her. On returning there he saw bowing humbly, having been duly entered by their souls, Kánaka·rekha and his other two sweethearts, whom he had seen before as lifeless heavenly ladies' bodies on the beds in the three pavilions. And he saw there Chandra·prabha, the fourth and eldest of them. She had performed rituals for good luck and was drinking him in with a gaze full of a long-held desire to see him.

His arrival was welcomed by the servant women, who were busy with their various tasks, and then Chandra·prabha said to him when he reached the inner apartment, 'Handsome sir, the princess Kánaka·rekha whom you saw 5.3.275
in the city of Vardhamána is my sister here. She is called Chandra·rekha. Bíndumati, the daughter of the fisher king, whom you first married on the island of Útsthala, is this sister of mine, Shashi·rekha. The princess Bindu·rekha who after that was brought there by the *dánava* and then became your wife, is my younger sister Shashi·prabha here. So now, O you who have achieved your aim, come with us to our

bhāryā ca te tad" âbhūc Chaśiprabhā s" êyam anujā me.
tad idānīm ehi, kṛtinn, asmat|pitur antikaṃ sah' âsmābhiḥ
tena prattāś c' âitā drutam akhilāḥ pariṇayasv' âsmān.›

iti kusuma|śar'|ājñā|sa|pragalbhaṃ ca tasyāṃ
tvaritam uditavatyām atra Candraprabhāyām
api catasṛbhir ābhiḥ sākam etat|pitus tan|
nikaṭam anuvan'|ântaṃ Śaktidevo jagāma.

5.3.280 sa ca caraṇa|natābhis tābhir āvedit'|ârtho
duhitṛbhir akhilābhir divya|vāk|preritaś ca
yugapad atha dadau tāḥ Śaktidevāya tasmai
mudita|matir a|śeṣās tatra vidyā|dhar'|êndraḥ.
tad|anu Kanakapuryām ṛddham asyāṃ sva|rājyaṃ
sapadi sa vitatāra svāś ca vidyāḥ samastāḥ
api ca kṛtinam enaṃ Śaktivegaṃ sva|nāmnā
vyadhita samucitena sveṣu vidyā|dhareṣu.

‹anyo na jeṣyati bhavantam ati|prabhāvād
Vats'|ēśvarāt punar udeṣyati cakra|vartī
yuṣmāsu yo 'tra Naravāhanadatta|nāmā
bhāvī vibhuḥ sa tava tasya natiṃ vidadhyāḥ.›
ity ūcivāṃś ca visasarja mahā|prabhāvo
vidyā|dhar'|âdhipatir ātma|tapo|vanāt tam
sat|kṛtya sa|priyatamaṃ nija|rāja|dhānīṃ
jāmātaraṃ sa Śaśikhaṇḍa|pad'|âbhidhānaḥ.

atha so 'pi Śaktivego rājā bhūtvā viveśa Kanakapurīm
sva|vadhūbhiḥ saha gatvā vidyā|dhara|loka|vaijayantīṃ tām.

5.3.285 tasyāṃ tiṣṭhan kanaka|racanā|visphuran|mandirāyām
aty|aunnatyād iva paṭu|patat|piṇḍit'|ârka|prabhāyām
vām'|âkṣībhiś catasṛbhir asau ratna|sopāna|vāpī|
hṛdy'|ôdyāneṣv alabhatatarāṃ nirvṛtiṃ preyasībhiḥ.»

father, and after he has given us away, quickly marry all of us here.'

After Chandra·prabha had hurriedly announced there this brazen command from the god of love, Shakti·deva went with the four girls to their father in the forest. Told 5.3.280
what had happened by all his daughters, who were bowing at his feet, and urged on by a divine voice, the delighted sorcerer king then and there simultaneously betrothed all the girls to him. Immediately after that he gave to Shakti·deva, who had achieved his aim, his prosperous throne in Kánaka·puri and all his magical sciences, and he bestowed upon him his name, Shakti·vega, which was dear to his sorcerers.

'No one else shall conquer you, but from the extremely powerful king of Vatsa shall arise among you an emperor, who shall have here the name Nara·váhana·datta. He shall be your ruler and you shall bow to him.' After saying this, the mighty sorcerer king, who was called Shashi·khanda, looked after his son-in-law hospitably and then sent him and his wives away from his penance grove to his capital.

Then Shakti·vega, now king, went with his wives to Kánaka·puri and entered the city which was the victory banner of the sorcerer world. Living there, its shining palaces 5.3.285
made from gold, its great height making it seem as if the bright light of the setting sun had solidified, he attained great bliss with his four beautiful sweethearts in lovely gardens whose tanks had steps made of jewels."

iti kathayitvā caritaṃ nijam eva vicitram eṣa tat|kālam
nijagāda Śaktivego vāgmī Vats'|ēśvaraṃ bhūyaḥ.
«taṃ māṃ, śaś'|âṅka|kula|bhūṣaṇa, Śaktivegaṃ
jānīhy upāgatam imaṃ khalu, Vatsa|rāja
utpanna|bhāvi|nija|nūtana|cakra|varti|
yuṣmat|sut'|âṅghri|yuga|darśana|s'|âbhilāṣam.
itthaṃ may" êha manujena sat" âpi labdhā
vidyā|dhar'|âdhipatitā pura|jit|prasādāt
gacchāmi c' âham adhunā, nṛ|pate, sva|dhāma
dṛṣṭa|prabhur.† bhavatu bhadram a|bhaṅguraṃ vaḥ.»
ity uktvā racit'|āñjalau ca vadati
prāpt'|âbhyanujñe tatas
tasminn utpatite mṛg'|âṅka|mahasi
dyāṃ Śaktivege kṣaṇāt
devībhyāṃ sahitaḥ sa|bāla|tanayo
Vats'|ēśvaro mantribhiḥ
sākaṃ kām api tatra saṃmada|mayīṃ
bheje tadānīṃ daśām.

iti mahā|kavi|śrī|Somadeva|bhaṭṭa|viracite Kathāsaritsāgare
caturdārikā|lambake tṛtīyas taraṅgaḥ.
samāpto 'yaṃ caturdārikā|lambakaḥ pañcamaḥ.

After thus telling his own amazing story, the loquacious Shakti·vega immediately carried on talking to the king of Vatsa. "Know me, O king of Vatsa, ornament to the lunar dynasty, to be that same Shakti·vega, come here with the desire to see the two feet of your son, who has been born to be our new emperor. Thus, although I was a man, through the grace of Shiva I became on earth a king of the sorcerers. Now that I have seen my lord, O king, I shall go home. May you always be fortunate."

Immediately after saying this with his hands joined together, Shakti·vega took permission to leave and flew up into the sky, as brilliant as the moon. The king of Vatsa, together with his queens, his young son and his ministers, then enjoyed there a state of indescribable happiness.

Thus ends the third wave in the Four Girls Attainment in the "Ocean of the Rivers of Story" composed by the glorious and learned great poet Soma·deva.

The fifth Attainment, Four Girls, is complete.

After thus telling his own amazing story, the fortunate Shakti·deva immediately went on talking to the king of Vatsa: "Know me, O king of Vatsa, ornament to the lunar dynasty, to be that same Shakti·deva, come here with the desire to see the two feet of your son who has been born to be our new emperor. Thus, although I was a man, through the grace of Shiva I became on earth a king of the sorcerers. Now that I have seen my lord, O king, I shall go home. May you always be fortunate."

Immediately after saying this with his hands joined together, Shakti·deva took permission to leave and flew up into the sky [illegible] king of Vatsa, together with [illegible] of his ministers, then enjoyed the [illegible] of [illegible] the happiness.

Thus ends the fifth wave in the Book Called [illegible] in the
Ocean of the Rivers of Story composed by the glorious
and excellent poet Soma·deva.
The Book [illegible] is complete.

ATTAINMENT VI

MÁDANA·MÁNCHUKA

MAHĀ|KAVI|ŚRĪ|SOMADEVA|bhaṭṭa|viracitaḥ Kathāsaritsāgaraḥ. Madanamañcukā nāma ṣaṣṭho lambakaḥ.

idaṃ guru|gir'|îndra|jā|
pranaya|Mandar'|āndolanāt
purā kila kath"|āmṛtaṃ
Hara|mukh'|âmbudher udgatam
prasahya sarayanti ye
vigata|vighna|labdh'|arddhayo
dhuraṃ dadhati vaibudhīṃ
bhuvi Bhava|prasādena te.

The "Ocean of the Rivers of Story," composed by the glorious and learned great poet Soma·deva. The sixth Attainment, called Mádana·mánchuka.

This nectar of story is said to have arisen long ago from the ocean of Hara's mouth as a result of its being churned by mount Mándara in the form of the insistent entreaties of the daughter of the lord of the mountains. Those who make it flow freely lose their troubles and gain riches, and through Bhava's grace it puts them on a divine pedestal on earth.

I

6.1.1 TARJAYANN IVA vighn'|âughān namit'|ônnamitena yaḥ
muhur vibhāti śirasā sa pāyād vo gaj'|ānanaḥ.
namaḥ Kāmāya yad|bāṇa|pātair iva nirantaram
bhāti kaṇṭakitaṃ Śaṃbhor apy Um"|āliṅgitaṃ vapuḥ.
ity|ādi|divya|caritaṃ kṛtv" ātmānaṃ kil' ânyavat
prāpta|vidyā|dhar'|āiśvaryo yad ā|mūlāt svayaṃ jagau
Naravāhanadatto 'tra sa|patnīkair maha'|rṣibhiḥ
pṛṣṭaḥ prasaṅge kutr' âpi tad idaṃ śṛṇut' âdhunā.
6.1.5 «atha saṃvardhyamāno 'tra pitrā Vats'|ēśvareṇa saḥ
Naravāhanadatto 'bhūd vyutkrānt'|âṣṭama|vatsaraḥ.
vinīyamāno vidyāsu krīḍann upavaneṣu ca
saha mantri|sutair āsīd rāja|putras tadā ca saḥ.
devī Vāsavadattā ca rājñī Padmāvatī tathā
āstām ekatama|snehāt tad|ekāgre divā|niśam.
ārohad|guṇa|namreṇa reje *sad|vaṃśa|janmanā*
śanair *āpūryamāṇena* vapuṣā dhanuṣā ca saḥ.
pitā Vats'|ēśvaraś c' âsya vivāh'|ādi|manorathaiḥ
āsanna|phala|saṃpatti|kāntaiḥ kālaṃ nināya tam.
6.1.10 atr' ântare kathā|saṃdhau yad abhūt tan niśamyatām
āsīt Takṣaśilā nāma Vitastā|puline purī.
tad|ambhasi babhau yasyāḥ pratimā saudha|saṃtateḥ
Pātāla|nagar" îv' âdhas|tac|chobh"|ālokan'|āgatā.
tasyāṃ Kaliṅgadatt'|ākhyo rājā parama|saugataḥ

I

WHILE SEEMING TO scold all the obstacles by repeatedly lowering and raising his head, may the elephant-faced one protect you. Homage to the god of love! When embraced by Párvati, the body of even Shiva, as if continually pricked by his arrows, is seen to horripilate. Now hear all the amazing adventures of Nara·váhana·datta, which he himself told from the beginning, in the third person, after he had become the ruler of the sorcerers and was questioned about them at some time or other by the great sages and their wives. 6.1.1

"In the course of being brought up there by his father the king of Vatsa, Nara·váhana·datta passed his eighth birthday. The prince then spent his time being instructed in the sciences and playing in the woods with the ministers' sons. The queens Vásava·datta and Padmávati had such a singular affection for him that day and night they thought only of him. His body *receptive to his increasing virtues* and *produced from a noble lineage* gradually *filling out*, and his bow *bending with the stretching string* and *made from good bamboo* gradually *increasing in size*, he was majestic. His father the king of Vatsa passed his time longing for his wedding and so forth, desires made lovely by their fruition being close at hand. Now listen to what happened at this juncture in the story. 6.1.5 6.1.10

There was a city called Taksha·shila on the banks of the Vitásta, in whose water the reflection of its row of palaces made it seem as if the city of Patála had come from below to behold its beauty. A great Buddhist king called Kalínga·datta lived there, and all his subjects were devoted to the

abhūt Tārā|vara|sphīta|jina|bhakt'|âkhila|prajaḥ.
rarāja sā purī yasya caitya|ratnair nirantaraiḥ
‹mat|tulyā nāma n' âst' îti› mada|śṛṅgair iv' ôditaiḥ.
prajānāṃ na paraṃ cakre yaḥ pit" êv' ânupālanam
yāvad gurur iva jñānam api svayam upādiśat.
6.1.15 tathā ca tasyāṃ ko 'py āsin nagaryāṃ saugato vaṇik
dhanī Vitastādatt'|ākhyo bhikṣu|pūj"|âika|tat|paraḥ.
Ratnadatt'|âbhidhānaś ca tasy' âbhūt tanayo yuvā
sa ca taṃ pitaraṃ śaśvat pāpa ity ājugupsata.
‹putra, nindasi kasmān mām iti?› pitrā ca tena saḥ
pṛcchyamāno vaṇik|putraḥ s'|âbhyasūyam abhāṣata.
‹tāta, tyakta|trayī|dharmas tvam a|dharmaṃ niṣevase
yad brāhmaṇān parityajya śramaṇāñ śaśvad arcasi.
snān'|ādi|yantraṇā|hīnāḥ sva|kāl'|âśana|lolupāḥ
apāsta|sa|śikh"|â|śeṣa|keśa|kaupīna|susthitāḥ.
6.1.20 vihār'|āspada|lābhāya† sarve 'py adhama|jātayaḥ
yam āśrayanti kiṃ tena saugatena nayena te?›

tac chrutvā sa vaṇik prāha ‹na dharmasy' âika|rūpatā
anyo lok'|ôttaraḥ, putra, dharmo 'nyaḥ sārva|laukikaḥ.
brāhmaṇyam api tat prāhur yad rāg'|ādi|vivarjanam
satyaṃ dayā ca bhūteṣu na mṛṣā jāti|vigrahaḥ.
kiṃ ca darśanam etat tvaṃ sarva|sattv'|â|bhaya|pradam
prāyaḥ puruṣa|doṣeṇa na dūṣayitum arhasi.
upakārasya dharmatve vivādo n' âsti kasya|cit
bhūteṣv a|bhaya|dānena n' ânyā c' ôpakṛtir mama.

prosperous conqueror, the groom of Tara.* The abundant jewels on the stupas made his city illustrious, as if they were the horns of pride, raised up because it thought that it had no equal. Not only did he look after the subjects like a father, but like a guru he himself also taught them knowledge.

Thus in that city there was a rich Buddhist merchant 6.1.15
called Vitásta·datta, who was particularly devoted to worshipping Buddhist monks. He had a son, a young man called Ratna·datta, who despised his father, thinking him to be a sinner. 'My son, why do you reproach me?' When his father would ask him this, the merchant boy said indignantly, 'Father, by abandoning the brahmins and always worshipping Buddhist monks, you have abandoned the religion of the three Vedas and follow a heretical teaching. With no obligations to bathe and so forth, they greedily eat whenever they want and are happy in loincloths having given up wearing topknots and all the other proper hairstyles: to a man they are of the lowest castes and it is 6.1.20
in order to get a place in a monastery that they follow the doctrine of the Buddha, so why do you bother with it?'

When the merchant heard this, he said, 'Religion does not take just one form. One religion can be transcendent, my son, another universal. They say that even the religion of the brahmins involves shunning passion and other vices, as well as truthfulness and compassion for living beings, not pointlessly dividing people according to their birth. Moreover, this philosophy gives shelter to all beings—you should not give it a blanket condemnation because of the faults of men. Nobody disputes the righteousness of helping others, and I give no assistance other than the granting of safe

6.1.25 tad a|hiṃsā|pradhāne 'smin, vatsa, mokṣa|pradāyini
darśane 'tiratiś cen me tad a|dharmo mam' âtra kaḥ?›
iti ten' ôditaḥ pitrā vaṇik|putraḥ prasahya saḥ
na tathā pratipede tan|ninind"|âbhyadhikaṃ punaḥ.
tataḥ sa tat|pitā khedād gatvā dharm'|ânuśāsituḥ
rājñaḥ Kaliṅgadattasya purataḥ sarvam abravīt.
so 'pi rājā tam āsthāne yukty" ānāyya vaṇik|sutam
mṛṣā|racita|kopaḥ sann evaṃ kṣattāram ādiśat.
‹śrutaṃ mayā vaṇik|putraḥ pāpo 'yam atiduṣkṛtī
nirvicāraṃ tad eṣo 'dya hanyatāṃ deśa|dūṣakaḥ.›
6.1.30 ity ūcivāṃs tataḥ pitrā kṛta|vijñāpanaḥ kila
nṛ|patir dharma|cary"|ârthaṃ dvau māsau vadha|nigraham.
saṃvidhārya tad|ante ca punar ānayanāya saḥ
tasy' âiva tat|pitur haste nyastavāṃs taṃ vaṇik|sutam.
so 'pi pitrā gṛhaṃ nīto vaṇik|putro bhay'|ākulaḥ
‹kiṃ may" âpakṛtaṃ rājño bhaved iti?› vicintayan.
a|kāraṇaṃ dvi|mās'|ânte maraṇaṃ bhāvi bhāvayan
a|nidro '|pacit'|āhāra|klāntas tasthau divā|niśam.
tato māsa|dvaye yāte rāj'|âgre kṛśa|pāṇḍuraḥ
punaḥ sva|pitrā ten' âsau vaṇik|sūnur anīyata.
6.1.35 rājā taṃ ca tathā|bhūtaṃ vīkṣy' āpannam abhāṣata
‹kim īdṛk tvaṃ kṛśī|bhūtaḥ? kiṃ ruddhaṃ te may" âśanam?›

haven to living creatures. So, my child, if I am very fond 6.1.25
of this philosophy, whose main tenet is non-violence and
which grants liberation, what is heretical about that?'

After his father said this to him, the merchant boy would
in no way agree with it, but reproached him still more. His
father was so troubled that he went before King Kalínga·
datta, the teacher of religion, and told him everything. The
king contrived to have the merchant's son brought into the
assembly, and, pretending to be angry, said to the chamberlain, 'I have heard that this merchant boy is a particularly
evil sinner, so he is to be killed today without deliberation
for bringing disgrace to the country.'

After the king had said this, it seems the boy's father then 6.1.30
made a request to him, for he stayed the execution for two
months so that the boy might conduct himself with righteousness and ordered that at the end of it the merchant
boy should be brought in again. He then entrusted him to
his father.

The merchant boy was taken home by his father, beside
himself with terror, wondering how he could have offended
the king. Thinking that at the end of the two months he was
going to be killed for no reason, he was unable to sleep and
ate less food, making him exhausted. When the two months
were over, his father took the emaciated and pale merchant
boy before the king once again. Seeing him in such a sorry 6.1.35
state, the king said to him, 'Why have you become so thin?
Did I stop you from eating?'

tac chrutvā sa vaṇik|putro rājānaṃ tam abhāṣata
‹ātm" âpi vismṛto bhītyā mama kā tv aśane kathā?
yuṣmad|ādiṣṭa|nidhana|śravaṇāt prabhṛti, prabho,
mṛtyum āyāntam āyāntam anvahaṃ cintayāmy aham.›
ity uktavantaṃ taṃ rājā sa vaṇik|putram abravīt
‹bodhito 'si mayā, vatsa, yuktyā prāṇa|bhayaṃ svataḥ.
īdṛg eva hi sarvasya jantor mṛtyu|bhayaṃ bhavet
tad|rakṣaṇ'|ôpakārāc ca dharmaḥ ko 'bhyadhiko vada.
6.1.40 tad etat tava dharmāya mumukṣāyai ca darśitam
mṛtyu|bhīto hi yatate naro mokṣāya buddhimān.
ato na garhaṇīyo 'yam etad|dharmā pitā tvayā.›
iti rāja|vacaḥ śrutvā prahvo 'vādīd vaṇik|sutaḥ.
‹dharm'|ôpadeśād devena kṛtī tāvad ahaṃ kṛtaḥ
mokṣāy' êcchā prajātā me tam apy upadiśa, prabho.›
tac chrutvā taṃ vaṇik|putraṃ prāpte tatra pur'|ôtsave
taila|pūrṇaṃ kare pātraṃ dattvā rājā jagāda saḥ.
‹idaṃ pātraṃ gṛhītvā tvam ehi bhrāntvā purīm imām
taila|bindu|nipātaś ca rakṣaṇīyas tvayā, suta.
6.1.45 nipatiṣyati yady ekas taila|bindur itas tava
sadyo nipātayiṣyanti tvām ete puruṣās tataḥ.›
evaṃ kil' ôktvā vyasṛjat taṃ bhrāmāya vaṇik|sutam
utkhāta|khaḍgān puruṣān dattvā paścāt sa bhūpatiḥ.
vaṇik|putro 'pi sa bhayād rakṣaṃs taila|lava|cyutim
purīṃ tām abhito bhrāntvā kṛcchrād āgān nṛp'|ântikam.
nṛpo 'py a|galit'|ānīta|tailaṃ dṛṣṭvā tam abhyadhāt

The merchant boy replied to the king, 'In my terror I forgot myself, let alone eating. Since hearing you order my execution, my lord, I have been constantly thinking of my ever approaching death.'

When the merchant boy said this, the king replied, 'I have tricked you, my child, into learning from yourself about the fear of death, for this same fear of death is present in all living beings and, tell me, what religious duty is better than helping them by protecting them from it? This was 6.1.40
therefore demonstrated in order for you to learn righteousness and the desire for liberation, for the wise man who is afraid of death strives for liberation. So you must not reproach your father here for following that religion.'

When he heard these words from the king, the merchant boy bowed and said, 'By instructing me in righteousness your highness has made me an accomplished man and now the desire for liberation has arisen in me. Teach me about that too, my lord.'

When the king heard this it was the time of the city festival and he put a pot full of oil in the merchant boy's hand and said to him, 'You must take this pot and make a round of the city before coming back here, and you must not let a drop of oil spill. If a single drop of oil should fall from it, 6.1.45
these men will immediately kill you.'

After saying this the king sent the boy out to make his round and had him followed by men with drawn swords. The merchant boy was so terrified that he somehow managed to make a round of the city without letting a drop of oil spill before returning to the king. The king, seeing that he had brought back the oil without having spilt it, said to

‹kaś|cit pura|bhrame 'py adya dṛṣṭo 'tra bhramatā tvayā.›
tac chrutvā sa vaṇik|putraḥ provāca racit'|âñjaliḥ
‹yat satyaṃ na mayā, deva, dṛṣṭaṃ kiṃ|cin na ca śrutam.
6.1.50 ahaṃ hy ek'|âvadhānena taila|leśa|paricyutam
khaḍga|pāta|bhayād rakṣaṃs tadānīm abhramaṃ purīm.›
evaṃ vaṇik|suten' ôkte sa rājā nijagāda tam
‹dṛśya|tail'|âika|cittena na tvayā kiṃ|cid īkṣitam.
tat ten' âiv' âvadhānena par'|ânudhyānam ācara
ek'|âgro hi bahir|vṛtti|nivṛttas tattvam īkṣate.
dṛṣṭa|tattvaś ca na punaḥ karma|jālena badhyate
eṣa mokṣ'|ôpadeśas te saṃkṣepāt kathito mayā.›
ity uktvā prahito rājñā patitvā tasya pādayoḥ
kṛt'|ârthaḥ sa vaṇik|putro hṛṣṭaḥ pitṛ|gṛhaṃ yayau.
6.1.55 evaṃ Kaliṅgadattasya prajās tasy' ânuśāsataḥ
Tārādatt'|âbhidhān" âbhūd rājñī rājñaḥ kul'|ôcitā.
yayā sa rājā śuśubhe *rītimatyā su/vṛttayā*
nānā/dṛṣṭ'/ânta/rasiko bhāratyā su|kavir yathā.
yā *prakāśa*|guṇa|ślāghyā jyotsn" êva śaśa|lakṣmaṇaḥ
tasy' âmṛta|mayasy' âbhūd a|vibhinn" âiva bhū|pateḥ.
tayā devyā samaṃ tatra sukhinas tasya tiṣṭhataḥ
nṛpasya jagmur divasāḥ Śacy" êva divi vajriṇaḥ.

him, 'During your tour of the city today, did you see anyone as you wandered about?'

When he heard this, the merchant boy put his palms together and said, 'In truth, your highness, I neither saw anything nor heard anything, for while I wandered about the 6.1.50
city I was so scared of being struck by the sword that my attention was focussed solely on preventing a drop of oil from spilling.'

When the merchant boy said this, the king replied, 'Your mind had the oil as its only object, which is why you did not notice anything. So practice meditating on the ultimate with that same concentration, for he who is focussed on one object and turns away from external events sees the ultimate reality and having seen the ultimate reality he is no longer bound by all his actions. I have thus given you a concise teaching about liberation.'

After the king had said this and dismissed him, the merchant boy fell at his feet and, satisfied and happy, went to his father's house.

That is how Kalínga·datta governed his subjects. He had 6.1.55
a queen called Tara·datta who was as high-born as him. *Cultured and virtuous*, she embellished the king, *a connoisseur of various philosophical analogies*, just as a good poet, *a connoisseur of various similes*, is embellished by speech *in good style and fine meter*. Praised like moonlight for her *celebrated : bright* qualities, she was inseparable from the king, as if from the moon, which consists of the nectar of immortality. Living there happily with that queen, the days went by for the king just as they do in heaven for Indra with Shachi.

atr' ântare kil' âitasmin kathā|saṃdhau śata|kratoḥ
kuto 'pi hetos tri|dive vartate sma mah"|ôtsavaḥ.
6.1.60 tatr' âpsaraḥsu sarvāsu nartituṃ militāsv api
ekā Surabhidatt'|ākhyā n' âdṛśyata var'|âpsarāḥ.
praṇidhānāt tataḥ Śakras tāṃ dadarśa rahaḥ|sthitām
vidyā|dhareṇa ken' âpi sahitāṃ Nandan'|ântare.
tad dṛṣṭvā jāta|kopo 'ntaḥ sa Vṛtr'|ârir acintayat
‹aho etau durācārau madan'|ândhāv ubhāv api
ekā yad ācaraty eva vismṛty' âsmān sva|tantravat
karoty a|vinayaṃ c' ânyo deva|bhūmau praviśya yat.
athav" âsya varākasya doṣo vidyā|dharasya kaḥ?
ākṛṣṭo hi vaśī|kṛtya rūpeṇ' âyam ih' ânayā.
6.1.65 kāntay" ântaḥ kil' āpūrṇa|tuṅga|stana|taṭ'|ântayā
lāvaṇy'|âmbu|taraṅgiṇyā hṛtaḥ syād ātmanaḥ prabhuḥ.
cakṣubhe kiṃ na Śarvo 'pi purā dṛṣṭvā Tilottamām
dhātrā gṛhītvā racitām uttamebhyas tilaṃ tilam.
tapaś ca Menakāṃ dṛṣṭvā Viśvāmitro na kiṃ jahau.
Śarmiṣṭhā|rūpa|lobhāc ca Yayātir n' āptavāñ jarām.
ato vidyā|dhara|yuvā n' âiv' âyam aparādhyati
tri|jagat|kṣobha|śaktena rūpeṇ' âpsarasā hṛtaḥ.
iyaṃ tu svar|vadhūḥ pāpā hīn'|āsakt" âparādhinī
praveśitaḥ surān hitvā yay" âyam iha Nandane.›

At this juncture in the middle of the story, Indra for some
reason held a great celebration in heaven. And when all the 6.1.60
*ápsaras*es came together there to dance, a beautiful *ápsaras*
called Súrabhi·datta was not to be seen. At this Indra went
into a trance and discovered her secreted away in Nándana
with some sorcerer or other. When he saw this Indra felt
anger in his heart and said to himself, 'Oh! These two, both
blinded by love, are misbehaving, one because she has forgotten us and is behaving as if she were her own master,
and the other because he is acting indecently having entered the land of the gods. But this poor sorcerer is not to
blame, for she has used her beauty to subjugate him and
entice him here. A man who is master of himself can have 6.1.65
his heart stolen by a sweetheart, the river of her loveliness
lapping at the banks of her full, high breasts. Was not even
Shiva shaken long ago after seeing Tilóttama, who was fashioned by the creator by taking tiny pieces from the finest beings. Did not Vishva·mitra abandon his austerities after seeing Ménaka? Did not Yayáti grow old because of his greed
for the beauty of Sharmíshtha? So this sorcerer lad has not
sinned in being enticed by an *ápsaras* with her beauty which
could disturb the three worlds. But this heavenly lady is a
wicked sinner, devoted to an inferior man. She has abandoned the gods and brought this sorcerer here to Nándana.'

6.1.70 ity ālocya vimucy' âinaṃ vidyā|dhara|kumārakam
Ahalyā|kāmukaḥ so 'syai śāpam apsarase dadau.
‹pāpe, prayāhi mānuṣyaṃ prāpya c' â|yoni|jāṃ sutām
divyaṃ kṛtvā ca kartavyam eṣyasi dyām imām iti.›
atr' ântare ca sā tasya rājñas Takṣaśilā|puri
rājñī Kaliṅgadattasya Tārādattā yayāv ṛtum.
tasyāḥ Surabhidattā sā Śakra|śāpa|cyut" âpsarāḥ
saṃbabhūv' ôdare devyā deha|saundarya|dāyinī.
tadā ca nabhaso bhraṣṭāṃ jvālāṃ devī dadarśa sā
Tārādattā kila svapne praviśantīṃ nij'|ôdare.
6.1.75 prātaś c' âvarṇayat svapnaṃ bhartre taṃ sā sa|vismayā
rājñe Kaliṅgadattāya so 'pi prīto jagāda tām.
‹devi, divyāḥ patanty eva śāpān mānuṣya|yoniṣu
taj jāne deva|jātīyaḥ ko 'pi garbhe tav' ârpitaḥ.
vicitra|sad|a|sat|karma|nibaddhāḥ saṃcaranti hi
jantavas tri|jagaty asmiñ śubh'|â|śubha|phal'|āptaye.›
ity uktā bhū|bhṛtā rājñī sā prasaṅgād uvāca tam
‹satyaṃ karm' âiva balavad bhoga|dāyi śubh'|â|śubham.
tathā c' êdam upodghātaṃ śrutaṃ vacmy atra te śṛṇu
abhavad Dharmadatt'|ākhyaḥ Kośal'|âdhipatir nṛpaḥ.
6.1.80 Nāgaśrīr iti tasy' āsīd rājñī yā pati|devatā
bhūmāv Arundhatī khyātā rundhanty api satī|dhuram.
kāle gacchati tasyāṃ ca devyāṃ tasya ca bhū|pateḥ
aham eṣā samutpannā duhit," āhita|sūdana.

After having these thoughts, Indra, the lover of Ahályа, let the sorcerer prince go and bestowed a curse on the *áp-saras*: 'Become a mortal, sinner. You shall have a daughter who has not been born from a womb and after then do-ing an important task for the gods, you shall return here to heaven.' 6.1.70

Meanwhile in the city of Taksha·shila, it was the time when Tara·datta, the queen of King Kalínga·datta, could conceive a child. Súrabhi·datta, the *ápsaras* who had fallen to earth as the result of Indra's curse, appeared in her womb and brought beauty to her body. It is said that at that time Queen Tara·datta saw in a dream a flame that had fallen from the sky entering into her own stomach. In the 6.1.75
morning she told the dream to her husband King Kalínga·datta in amazement. He was delighted and said to her, 'Queen, heavenly beings do fall into earthly wombs because of curses, so I think someone originally born divine has been offered into your womb. Beings journey through these three worlds bound by their various good and bad deeds in order to obtain pleasant and unpleasant rewards.'

After the king had said this to her, the queen said in con-nection with it, 'Karma is indeed powerful: it bestows re-wards and is good or bad. In illustration of this I shall tell you a story I have heard on this subject. Listen.

There was a king called Dharma·datta who ruled over Kóshala. He had a queen called Naga·shri who treated her 6.1.80
husband like a god. She was known as an earthly Arúndhati, for she was at the forefront of virtuous women.* As time went by I was born as that king and queen's daughter, O

tato mayy atibālāyāṃ, deva, sā jananī mama
a|kasmāt pūrva|jātiṃ svāṃ smṛtvā sva|patim abravīt.
«rājann, a|kāṇḍa ev' âdya pūrva|janma smṛtaṃ mayā
a|prītyai tad an|ākhyātam ākhyātaṃ mṛtaye ca me.
‹a|śaṅkitaṃ smṛtā jātiḥ syād ākhyāt" âiva mṛtyave›
iti hy āhur ato, deva, mayy atīva viṣāditā.»
6.1.85 ity uktaḥ sa tayā patnyā rājā tāṃ pratyabhāṣata
«priye, may" âpi prāg janma tvay" êva sahasā smṛtam.
tan mam' ācakṣva tāvat tvaṃ kathayiṣyāmy ahaṃ ca te
yad astu ko 'nyathā kartuṃ śakto hi bhavitavyatām?»
iti sā preritā tena bhartrā rājñī jagāda tam
«nirbandho yadi te, rājañ, śṛṇu tarhi vadāmy aham.
ih' âiva deśe viprasya Mādhav'|ākhyasya kasya|cit
gṛhe 'ham abhavaṃ dāsī suvṛttā pūrva|janmani.
Devadās'|âbhidhānaś ca patir atra mam' âbhavat
kasy' âpy ekasya vaṇijaḥ sādhuḥ karma|karo gṛhe.
6.1.90 tāv āvām avasāv' âtra kṛtvā gehaṃ nij'|ôcitam
sva|sva|svāmi|gṛh'|ānīta|pakv'|ânna|kṛta|vartanau.
vāri|dhānī ca kumbhaś ca mārjanī mañcakas tathā
ahaṃ ca mat|patiś c' êti yugma|tritayam eva nau.
a|kali|prasare gehe saṃtoṣaḥ sukhinor abhūt
deva|pitṛ|atithi|pratta|śeṣaṃ pramitam aśnatoḥ.
ekaikato 'dhikaṃ kiṃ|cid yad ācchādanam apy abhūt
sudurgatāya kasmai|cit tad āvābhyām adīyata.
ath' âtr' ôdabhavat tīvro durbhikṣas tena c' âvayoḥ

slayer of enemies. Then when I was very young, your highness, that mother of mine suddenly remembered her former life and said to her husband, "O king, without warning I have today remembered my former birth. If I don't tell it, I shall be unhappy, but if I do tell it, I shall die, because it is said that as soon as someone tells a birth that they have remembered, they are sure to die. So, your highness, I am extremely distressed."

When his wife said this to him, the king replied, "My 6.1.85
dear, I too, like you, have suddenly remembered my former birth, so tell me yours and I shall tell you mine and let it be, for no one can change the course of fate."

Urged on thus by her husband, the queen said to him, "If you insist, O king, then listen, I shall tell you. In my former life I was a well-behaved servant girl in the house of a certain brahmin called Mádhava in this very land. My husband at that time, who was called Deva·dasa, was a virtuous man who worked in the house of some merchant or
other. The two of us settled there, having built a house be- 6.1.90
fitting us, living off cooked food brought from the houses of our respective masters. We were three couples: a water tank and a pot, a broom and a bed, my husband and I. We were content in our house, where strife never arose, eating the small amount of food that was left after we had made offerings to the gods, the ancestors and guests. If either of us had any extra clothes we would give them to someone very poor. Then a severe famine happened there as a result of which each day we received a smaller and smaller amount
of food as our pay. Then, as we gradually wasted away, our 6.1.95
bodies emaciated with hunger, one day a weary brahmin

bhṛty|annam anvahaṃ prāpyam alpam alpam upānamat.
6.1.95 tataḥ kṣut|kṣāma|vapuṣoḥ śanair nāv avasīdatoḥ
kadā|cid āgād āhāra|kāle klānto 'tithir dvijaḥ.
tasmai niḥśeṣam āvābhyāṃ dvābhyām api nij'|âśanam
prāṇa|saṃśaya|kāle 'pi dattaṃ yāvac ca yac ca tat.
bhuktvā tasmin gate prāṇā bhartāraṃ me tam atyajan
‹arthiny asy' ādaro n' âsmāsv iti› manyu|vaśād iva.
tataś c' âhaṃ samādhāya patye samucitāṃ citām
ārūḍhā c' âvarūḍhaś ca vipad|bhāro mam' ātmanaḥ.
atha rāja|gṛhe jātā jāt" âhaṃ mahiṣī tava
a|cintyaṃ hi phalaṃ sūte sadyaḥ sukṛta|pādapaḥ.»

6.1.100 ity uktaḥ sa tayā rājñyā Dharmadatto nṛpo 'bravīt
«ehi, priye, sa ev' âhaṃ pūrva|janma|patis tava.
vaṇik|karma|karo 'bhūvaṃ Devadāso 'ham eva saḥ
etad eva may" âpy adya prāktanaṃ janma hi smṛtam.»

ity uktvā svāny abhijñānāny udīrya sa tayā saha
devyā viṣaṇṇo hṛṣṭaś ca rājā sadyo divaṃ gataḥ.
evaṃ tayoś ca mat|pitror lok'|ântaram upeyuṣoḥ
mātuḥ svasā vardhayituṃ mām anaiṣīn nijaṃ gṛham.
kanyāyāṃ mayi c' âbhyāgād ekas tatr' âtithir muniḥ
mātṛ|svasā ca māṃ tasya śuśrūṣāyai samādiśat.
6.1.105 sa ca Kunty" êva Durvāsā yatnen' ārādhito mayā
tad|varāc ca mayā prāpto dhārmikas tvaṃ patiḥ, prabho.
evaṃ bhavanti bhadrāṇi dharmād eva yad|ādarāt
pitṛbhyāṃ saha saṃprāpya rājyaṃ jātir api smṛtā.›

etat sa Tārādattāyā devyāḥ śrutvā vaco nṛpaḥ
Kaliṅgadatto dharm'|âika|sādaro nijagada tām.
‹satyaṃ samyak|kṛto 'lpo 'pi dharmo bhūri|phalo bhavet
tathā ca prāktanīṃ, devi, sapta|dvija|kathāṃ śṛṇu.

guest arrived at mealtime. We both gave him all of our food, even though at the time our lives were in danger. When he had eaten and gone, my husband's life-breaths left him as if they were angry that he had respected the man who had entreated him and not them. Then I kindled a suitable funeral pyre for my husband and mounted it, shedding the burden of my predicament. After that I was born in a palace and became your chief queen, for the tree of good deeds quickly bears unimaginable fruit."

After the queen had told him this, King Dharma·datta 6.1.100
said, "Come, my dear, I was that husband of yours in my former life. I was the merchant's servant Deva·dasa, for today I also remembered that very same former birth."

After saying this and making known his memories, the king, both sad and happy, suddenly went to heaven with his queen. With both my parents having thus gone to the next world, my mother's sister took me to her house to bring me up. While I was an unmarried girl, a sage arrived there as an unheralded guest and my aunt instructed me to wait
on him. Like Kunti with Durvásas, I strove hard to please 6.1.105
him, and because of a boon from him I obtained you as my dutiful husband, my lord. Thus good things come from piety alone, in respect of which my parents both became sovereigns and remembered their former lives.'

After hearing these words from Queen Tara·datta, King Kalínga·datta, who held only righteousness in regard, said to her, 'It's true—even a small amount of piety correctly performed can bear abundant fruit. Just listen to the old story of the seven brahmins.

Kuṇḍin"|ākhye pure pūrvam upādhyāyasya kasya|cit
brāhmaṇasy' âbhavañ śiṣyāḥ sapta brāhmaṇa|putrakāḥ.
6.1.110 sa tāñ śiṣyān upādhyāyo dhenuṃ durbhikṣa|doṣataḥ
gomataḥ śvaśurād ekāṃ yācituṃ prāhiṇot tataḥ.
te ca gatv" ânya|deśa|sthaṃ durbhikṣa|kṣāma|kukṣayaḥ
taṃ tad|girā tac|chvaśuraṃ tac|chiṣyā gāṃ yayācire.
so 'pi vṛtti|karīm ekāṃ dhenuṃ tebhyaḥ samarpayat
kṛpaṇaḥ kṣudhitebhyo 'pi na tu tebhyo 'śanaṃ dadau.
tatas te tāṃ gṛhītvā gām āyānto 'rdha|pathe kṣudhā
udgāḍha|pīḍitāḥ klāntā nipetur dharaṇī|tale.
«upādhyāya|gṛhaṃ dūraṃ dūre c' āpad|gatā vayam
durlabhaṃ sarvataś c' ânnaṃ tat prāṇair gatam eva naḥ.
6.1.115 evaṃ ca dhenur apy eṣā nistoya|vana|mānuṣe
araṇye 'smin vipann' âiva gurv|artho 'lpo 'pi kas tataḥ.
tad asyāḥ piśitaiḥ prāṇān saṃdhāry' āśu gurūn api
saṃbhāvayāmas tac|cheṣair āpat|kālo hi vartate.»

iti saṃmantrya sapt' âpi jaghnuḥ sa|brahma|cāriṇaḥ
śāstr'|ôkta|vidhinā dhenuṃ tāṃ paśū|kṛtya tatra te.
iṣṭvā devān pitṝn bhuktvā tan|māṃsaṃ vidhivac ca tat
jagmur ādāya tac|cheṣam upādhyāyasya c' ântikam.
tasmai praṇamya sarvaṃ te śaśaṃsus tad yathā kṛtam
sa tebhyaḥ s'|âparādhebhyo 'py atuṣyat satya|bhāṣaṇāt.
6.1.120 dinaiḥ sapt' âpi durbhikṣa|doṣāt te ca vipedire
jāti|smarāś ca bhūyo 'pi tena satyena jajñire.
itthaṃ phalati śuddhena siktaṃ saṃkalpa|vāriṇā

Long ago in a city called Kúndina, a certain brahmin
teacher had seven brahmin boys as his pupils. Then, because 6.1.110
of a famine, the teacher sent the pupils to ask his father-in-law, who was rich in cattle, for a cow. His pupils, their stomachs shrunken from the famine, went to his father-in-law, who lived in another land, and passed on his request for a cow. He gave them one cow to live off, but the niggardly fellow, even though they were famished, did not give them anything to eat. Then they took the cow and when they were half way back they were so severely afflicted with hunger that they collapsed, exhausted, onto the ground. "Our teacher's house is far away, we are in a disastrous situation in a remote place and food is impossible to find anywhere, so our lives are all but over. This cow too is similarly 6.1.115
stricken in this wilderness without water, vegetation or humans, and is not of the slightest use to our teacher. So we should keep ourselves alive by eating its flesh and hurry to feed the rest to our teacher and the other elders, for this is a time of emergency."

Having come to this decision together, the seven students made the cow a sacrificial victim and killed it there with due observance of the rules prescribed in the sacred texts. After worshipping the gods and ancestors and duly eating the cow's flesh, they took the rest to their teacher. They bowed and told him everything that they had done. Even though they had committed a sin, he was pleased with
them for telling the truth. After seven days they died be- 6.1.120
cause of the famine and because they had been truthful were reborn with the ability to remember their former births. Thus even a tiny seed of a good deed, sprinkled by the pure

puṇya|bījam api svalpaṃ puṃsāṃ kṛṣi|kṛtām iva.
tad eva dūṣitaṃ, devi, duṣṭa|saṃkalpa|pāthasā
phalaty an|iṣṭam atr' êdaṃ vacmy anyad api tac chṛṇu.

Gaṅgāyāṃ tulya|kālau dvau tapasy an|aśane janau
eko vipro dvitīyaś ca caṇḍālas tasthatuḥ purā.
tayor vipraḥ kṣudh"|ākrānto niṣādān vīkṣya tatra|gān
matsyān ādāya bhuñjānān evaṃ mūḍho vyacintayat.
6.1.125 «aho dāsyāḥ sutā ete dhanyā jagati dhīvarāḥ
ye yathā|kāmam aśnanti pratyahaṃ śaphar'|āmiṣam.
dvitīyas tu sa cāṇḍālo dṛṣṭvā tān eva dhīvarān
acintayad «dhig astv etān kravyādān prāṇi|ghātinaḥ.
tat kim evaṃ sthitasy' êha dṛṣṭair eṣāṃ mukhair mama?»
iti saṃmīlya netre sa tatr' āsīt sv'|ātmani sthitaḥ.

kramāc c' ân|aśanen' ôbhau vipannau tau dvij'|ântyajau
dvijas tatra śvabhir bhuktaḥ śīrṇo Gaṅgā|jale 'ntyajaḥ.
tato '|kṛt'|ātmā kaivarta|kula ev' âtra sa dvijaḥ
abhyajāyata tīrthasya guṇāj jāti|smaras tv abhūt.
6.1.130 caṇḍālo 'pi sa tatr' âiva Gaṅgā|tīre mahī|bhujaḥ
gṛhe jāti|smaro jajñe dhīro 'nupahat'|ātmakaḥ.
jātayoś ca tayor evaṃ prāg|janma|smarator dvayoḥ
eko 'nutepe dāsaḥ san rājā san mumude 'paraḥ.
iti dharma|taror mūlam a|śuddhaṃ yasya mānasam
śuddhaṃ yasya ca tad|rūpaṃ phalaṃ tasya na saṃśayaḥ.›

water of good intent, bears fruit for men as if to farmers, but, O queen, the same seed, contaminated by the water of evil intent, bears unwanted fruit. I shall tell you something else on this subject—listen.

Long ago two men spent an equal amount of time on the banks of the Ganga abstaining from food as a religious austerity. One was a brahmin, the other an outcaste. The brahmin among the two, overcome with hunger, saw some Nishádas arrive there with some fish, and while they ate
them, the idiot said to himself, "Oh how lucky are the 6.1.125
fishermen on earth! The sons of slave girls, they eat their fill of fish every day!" But the other one, the outcaste, when he saw those same fishermen, said to himself, "Shame on these murderous flesh eaters! I've had enough of sitting here like this looking at their faces." He then closed his eyes and remained there in inner contemplation.

In time, both the brahmin and the outcaste died because of their fasting. The brahmin was eaten there by dogs, the outcaste rotted in the waters of the Ganga. Then the brahmin, who had not mastered his self, was born into a family of fishermen there, but he could remember his former life
because of the power of the place of pilgrimage. The out- 6.1.130
caste, meanwhile, who was steadfast and had not let himself be led astray, was born in that same place on the banks of the Ganga in the house of a king, and could remember his former life. When those two were born like that remembering their past lives, one, being a servant, was regretful, the other, being a king, was happy. Thus the fruits reaped by he whose mind—the root of the tree of righteousness—is

ity etad uktvā devīṃ tāṃ Tārādattāṃ sa bhū|patiḥ
Kaliṅgadattaḥ punar apy uvāc' âināṃ prasaṅgataḥ.
‹kiṃ ca sattv'|âdhikaṃ karma, devi,† yan nāma yādṛśam
phalāya tad yataḥ sattvam anudhāvanti saṃpadaḥ.
6.1.135 tathā ca kathayāmy atra śṛṇu citrām imāṃ kathām
ast' îha bhuvana|khyāt" Âvantīṣ' Ûjjayinī purī.
rājate sita|harmyair yā Mahākāla|nivāsa|bhūḥ
tat|sevā|rasa|saṃprāpta|Kailāsa|śikharair iva.
sac|cakra|varti|pānīyaḥ praviśad|*vāhinī*|śataḥ
yad|ābhogo 'bdhi|gambhīraḥ *sa|pakṣa|kṣmā|bhṛd*|āśritaḥ.
tasyāṃ Vikramasiṃh'|ākhyo babhūv' ânvarthay" ākhyayā
rājā vairi|mṛgā yasya n' âiv' âsan saṃmukhāḥ kva|cit.
sa ca niṣpratipakṣatvād a|labdha|samar'|ôtsavaḥ
astreṣu bāhu|vīrye ca s'|âvajño 'ntar atapyata.
6.1.140 atha so 'maraguptena tad|abhiprāya|vedinā
kath'|ântare prasaṅgena mantriṇā jagade nṛpaḥ.
«deva, dor|daṇḍa|darpeṇa śastra|vidyā|madena ca
āśaṃsatām api ripūn rājñāṃ doṣo na durlabhaḥ.
tathā ca pūrvaṃ Bāṇena yuddha|yogyam ariṃ Haraḥ
darpād bhuja|sahasrasya tāvad ārādhya yācitaḥ.
yāvat prāpta|tathā|bhūta|tad|varaḥ sa Mur'|âriṇā
devena vairiṇā saṃkhye lūna|bāhu|vanaḥ kṛtaḥ.

impure and he whose mind is pure are sure to match their dispositions.'

After saying this to Queen Tara·datta, King Kalínga·datta spoke to her again in this connection. 'What's more, O queen, actions which are truly of the very courageous kind bear fruit, because prosperity follows after courage. Just 6.1.135
listen to this amazing story I'm going to tell you on the subject.

There is a world-famous city in the land of the Avántis called Ujjain. It is the place where Shiva resides as Maha·kala and its white palaces make it shine as if they were the peaks of Kailása come to have the pleasure of serving him. It is as vast as the ocean, the virtuous emperor is its swirling waters, hundreds of *rivers : armies* go into it, and it is resorted to by *allied kings : winged mountains.* In it there lived a king called Víkrama·sinha, "Lion of Courage," and it was an apt name, for the deer that were his enemies never stayed to face him. Because he had no enemies he could not enjoy himself in battle. He felt contempt for weapons and his mighty arms, and was consumed with inner torment.

Then, in the course of a conversation, the king's minis- 6.1.140
ter Ámara·gupta, who knew how he felt, said to him, "Your highness, trouble is not difficult to come by for kings who, out of pride in their strength and arrogance about their knowledge of weapons, merely express a desire for enemies. Thus in the past Bana was so proud of his thousand arms that he propitiated Shiva and kept asking him for an enemy worthy of a fight, until he got just what he had asked for and his forest of arms was lopped off in battle by his enemy Lord Vishnu. So you must not be dissatisfied by not

tasmāt tvay" âpi kartavyo n' â|saṃtoṣo yudhaṃ vinā
kāṅkṣaṇīyo na c' ân|iṣṭo vipakṣo 'pi kadā|cana.
6.1.145 śastra|śikṣā sva|vīryaṃ ca darśanīyaṃ tav' êha cet
yogya|bhūmāv aṭavyāṃ tan mṛgayāyāṃ ca darśaya.
rājñāṃ c' ākheṭakam api vyāyām'|ādi|kṛte matam
yuddh'|âdhvani na śasyante rājāno hy a|kṛta|śramāḥ.
āraṇyāś ca mṛgā duṣṭāḥ śūnyām icchanti medinīm
tena te nṛpater vadhyā ity apy ākheṭam iṣyate.
na c' âti te niṣevyante tat|sevā|vyasanena hi
gatā nṛpatayaḥ pūrvam api Pāṇḍv|ādayaḥ kṣayam.»
ity ukto 'maraguptena mantriṇā sa su|medhasā
rājā Vikramasiṃho 'tra «tath" êti» tad amanyata.
6.1.150 anyedyuś c' âśva|pādāta|sārameya|mayīṃ bhuvam
vicitra|vāgur"|ôcchrāya|mayīś ca sakalā diśaḥ.
sa|harṣa|mṛgayu|grāma|nināda|mayam ambaram
kurvan sa mṛgayā|hetor nagaryā niryayau nṛpaḥ.
nirgacchan gaja|pṛṣṭha|stho bāhye śūnye sur'|ālaye
puruṣau dvāv apaśyac ca vijane sahita|sthitau.
svairaṃ mantrayamāṇau ca mithaḥ kim api tāv ubhau
dūrāt sa tarkayan rājā jagāma mṛgayā|vanam.
tatra protkhāta|khaḍgeṣu vṛddha|vyāghreṣu ca vyadhāt
toṣaṃ sa|siṃha|nādeṣu bhū|bhāgeṣu nageṣu ca.
6.1.155 tāṃ sa vikrama|bīj'|ābhair mahīṃ tastāra mauktikaiḥ
siṃhānāṃ hasti|hantṝṇāṃ nihatānāṃ nakha|cyutaiḥ.
tiryañcas tiryag ev' âsya petur vakra|plutā mṛgāḥ
laghu nirbhidya tān pūrvaṃ harṣaṃ prāpad a|vakra|gaḥ.

having a war to fight, and never wish for an evil enemy. If 6.1.145
you must show off your knowledge of weapons and your heroism here, show them in the wilderness, a suitable arena, and in the chase. Hunting is also approved of for kings for purposes of exercise and so forth (but going to war is not recommended) for kings do not exert themselves. Wild animals are depraved and want the world to be empty, so they should be killed by the king, which is why hunting is desirable. But they are not to be pursued too much, for in the past Pandu and other kings have met their ends because of being addicted to hunting them."

After the very wise minister Ámara·gupta had said this to him on the subject, King Víkrama·sinha agreed, saying, "So
be it." On the next day, covering the ground in horses, men 6.1.150
and dogs, and filling all the directions by casting various different nets, and spreading the joyful cries of all the huntsmen across the sky, the king went out of the city to hunt. As he rode out on the back of an elephant, at a deserted temple outside the city he saw two men together in a quiet spot. Thinking from afar that the two of them were quietly talking among themselves about something, the king went to the hunting grounds. There he took pleasure in the landscape and the mountains, where there were drawn swords,
big tigers and the roars of lions. He scattered the earth with 6.1.155
pearls that had fallen from the claws of elephant-killing lions and they looked like the seeds of his valor. Deer, leaping this way and that, flew across his path. He, going straight, first deftly speared them and then attained delight.

kṛt'|ākheṭaś ca su|ciraṃ rāj" âsau śrānta|sevakaḥ
āgāc chithilita|jyena cāpen' Ôjjayinīṃ punaḥ.
tasyāṃ deva|kule tasmiṃs tāvat kālaṃ tath" âiva tau
sthitau dadarśa puruṣau nirgacchan yau sa dṛṣṭavān.
«kāv etau mantrayete ca kiṃ svid evam iyac ciram
nūnaṃ cārāv imau dīrgha|rahasy'|ālāpa|sevinau.»
6.1.160 ity ālocya pratīhāraṃ visṛjy' ānāyayat sa tau
puruṣau dvāv avaṣṭabhya rājā baddhau cakāra ca.
dvitīye 'hani c' âsthānaṃ tāv ānāyya sa pṛṣṭavān
«kau yuvāṃ su|ciraṃ kaś ca mantras tāvān sa vām iti?»
tatas tayoḥ svayaṃ rājñā tatra paryanuyuktayoḥ
yācit'|â|bhayayor eko yuvā vaktuṃ pracakrame.
«śrūyatāṃ varṇayāmy etad yathāvad adhunā, prabho.
abhūt Karabhako nāma vipro 'syām eva vaḥ puri.
tasya pravīra|putr'|êcchā|kṛt'|âgny|ārādhan'|ôdbhavaḥ
aham eṣa, mahā|rāja, veda|vidyā|vidaḥ sutaḥ.
6.1.165 tasmiṃś ca bhāry"|ânugate pitari svar|gate śiśuḥ
adhīta|vidyo 'py ānāthyāt sva|mārgaṃ tyaktavān aham.
pravṛttaś c' âbhavaṃ dyūtaṃ śastra|vidyāś ca sevitum
kasya n' ôcchṛṅkhalaṃ bālyaṃ guru|śāsana|varjitam.
tena krameṇa c' ôttīrṇe śaiśave jāta|dor|madaḥ
aṭavīm ekadā bāṇān ahaṃ kṣeptuṃ gato 'bhavam.
tāvat tena pathā c' âikā nagaryā nirgatā vadhūḥ
āgāt karṇī|rath'|ārūḍhā janyair bahubhir anvitā.

After spending a very long time hunting, the king, his servants tired, loosened his bowstring and returned to Ujjain. There in that temple he saw those two men whom he had seen on the way out in exactly the same position as they had been then. "Who are these two men and what can they have been discussing like this all this time? Surely they are spies, busy deliberating at length some secrets." After think- 6.1.160
ing this, he dispatched a chamberlain and had them both brought in. The king arrested the two men and imprisoned them. On the next day he had them brought to the assembly and asked them, "Who are you two and what have you been talking about for so very long?" At this, having been questioned there by the king himself, they asked for their safety to be assured and then one of them, a young man, started to speak. "Listen, I shall now tell you exactly what this is all about, my lord.

In this very city of yours, there lived a brahmin called Kárabhaka. I, great king, am the son of that knower of the Vedas and the sciences, and I was born as the result of his propitiating the god of fire in his desire for a distinguished son. I was a child when that father of mine went to heaven 6.1.165
followed by his wife and even though I had learned the sciences, because I had nobody to look after me I deviated from my path. I started to practice gambling and the study of weapons. Whose childhood would not become undisciplined if it were devoid of a teacher's instruction? In this way, by the time I came of age I had become proud of my strength. One day I went to the forest to shoot some arrows. In the meantime, a bride came out of the city along

a|kasmāc ca tad" âiv' âtra karī troṭita|śṛṅkhalaḥ
kuto 'py āgatya tām eva vadhūm abhyāpatan madāt.
6.1.170 tad|bhayena ca sarve 'pi tyaktvā tām anuyāyinaḥ
tad|bhartrā 'pi saha klībāḥ palāyy' êtas tato gatāḥ.
tad dṛṣṭvā sahas" âiv' âhaṃ sa|saṃbhramam acintayam
‹hā kathaṃ kātarair ebhis tyakt" âik" êyaṃ tapasvinī?
tad ahaṃ vāraṇād asmād rakṣyāmy a|śaraṇām imām
āpanna|trāṇa|vikalaiḥ kiṃ prāṇaiḥ pauruṣeṇa vā?›
ity ahaṃ mukta|nādas taṃ gaj'|êndraṃ prati dhāvitaḥ
gajo 'pi tāṃ striyaṃ hitvā sa māṃ ev' âbhyadudruvat.
tato 'haṃ bhītayā nāryā vīkṣyamāṇas tayā nadan
palāyamānaś ca gajaṃ taṃ dūram apakṛṣṭavān.
6.1.175 kramāt patra|ghanāṃ bhagnāṃ prāpya śākhāṃ mahā|taroḥ
ātmānaṃ ca tay" ācchādya taru|madhyam agām aham.
tatr' âgre sthāpayitvā tāṃ śākhāṃ tiryak su|lāghavāt
palāyito 'haṃ hastī ca sa tāṃ śākhām acūrṇayat.
tato 'haṃ yoṣitas tasyāḥ samīpam agamaṃ drutam
śarīra|kuśalaṃ c' âitām apṛccham iha bhīṣitām.
s" âpi māṃ vīkṣya duḥkh'|ârtā sa|harṣā c' âvadat tadā
‹kiṃ me kuśalam etasmai dattā kāpuruṣāya yā.
īdṛśe saṃkaṭe yo māṃ tyaktvā kv' âpi gataḥ, prabho.
etat tu kuśalaṃ yat tvam a|kṣataḥ punar īkṣitaḥ.
6.1.180 tan me sa katamo bhartā? tvam idānīṃ patir mama

the road in a covered palanquin, accompanied by several of the groom's party.

Suddenly there and then a rutting elephant that had broken its fetters appeared from somewhere and attacked the bride. In fear of it all her companions abandoned her, her 6.1.170
husband included, and the cowards fled in every direction. Seeing this I immediately said to myself in my excitement, 'Oh how could these faint-hearted men leave this poor lady on her own? I must protect the helpless woman from this elephant. There's no point in life or valor if they can't save those in distress.' While thinking this I shouted and ran at that great elephant and he put down the lady and attacked me. Then, watched by the terrified woman as I shouted and ran away, I drew the elephant a long way off. Eventually 6.1.175
I found a leaf-covered branch broken off from a huge tree and, using it to conceal myself, I made my way into the middle of the tree. I placed the branch in front of me there and by very quickly moving sideways I escaped and the elephant destroyed the branch. I then quickly went to the terrified woman, and asked her there if she was all right. She looked at me and then, both grief-stricken and joyful, said, 'How, my lord, could I be all right when I have been given away to that coward, who in an emergency like this has abandoned me and run away? But what is all right is that you have appeared again, uninjured. And what sort of 6.1.180
a protector is that husband of mine? You are now my husband, you who snatched me from the mouth of death with no regard for yourself. I can see my husband coming along here with his servants, so for the time being follow us discreetly, for when we get the chance we shall meet and run

yen' ātma|nirapekṣeṇa hṛtā mṛtyu|mukhād aham.
sa c' âiṣa dṛśyate bhṛtyaiḥ sah' âgacchan patir mama
ataḥ svairaṃ tvam asmākaṃ paścād āgaccha sāṃpratam.
labdhe 'ntare hi militā yāsyāmo yatra|kutra|cit.›
evaṃ tay" ôktas tad ahaṃ ‹tath" êti› pratipannavān.
su|rūp" âpy arpit'|ātm" âpi para|str" îyaṃ kim etayā
iti dhairyasya mārgo 'yaṃ na tāruṇyasya saṅginaḥ.
kṣaṇād etya ca sā bhartrā bālā saṃbhāvitā satī
tena sākaṃ sa|bhṛtyena gantuṃ prāvartata kramāt.
6.1.185 ahaṃ ca gupta|tad|datta|pātheyaḥ para|vartmanā
paścād a|lakṣitas tasya dūram adhvānam abhyagām.
sā ca hasti|bhaya|bhraṣṭa|bhaṅg'|âṅgaja|nitāṃ rujam
pathi mithyā vadantī taṃ patiṃ sparśe 'py avarjayat.
kasya rakt'|ônmukhī gāḍha|rūḍh'|ântar|viṣa|duḥsahā
tiṣṭhed an|apakṛtya strī bhujag" îva vikāritā.
kramāc ca Lohanagaraṃ prāptāḥ smas te puraṃ vayam
vaṇijy'|ājīvino yatra bhartus tasya gṛhaṃ striyāḥ.
sthitāḥ smas tad ahaś c' âtra sarve bāhye sur'|ālaye
tatra saṃmilitaś c' âiṣa dvitīyo brāhmaṇaḥ sakhā.
6.1.190 nave 'pi darśane 'nyonyam āśvāsaḥ samabhūc ca nau
cittaṃ jānāti jantūnāṃ prema janm'|ântar'|ârjitam.
tato rahasyam ātmīyaṃ sarvam asmai may" ôditam
tad buddhv" âiva tadā svairaṃ mām evam ayam abravīt.
‹tuṣṇīṃ bhav' âsty upāyo 'tra yat|kṛte tvam ih' āgataḥ
etasyā bhartṛ|bhaginī vidyate 'tra vaṇik|striyāḥ.
gṛhīt'|ârthā mayā sākam itaḥ sā gantum udyatā
tat kariṣye tadīyena sāhāyyena tav' ēpsitam.›

off wherever we can.' On her saying this to me, I agreed, saying, 'So be it.'

The way of self-restraint would have been to think that even though she was beautiful, even though she had offered herself, she was another man's wife and I should have nothing to do with her, but that is not the way of passionate youth. A moment later, her husband came and joined the virtuous girl and in time she set off with him and his servants. Eating provisions for the journey which she had se- 6.1.185
cretly given me, I went by a different path and followed them unseen by him for a long way. She, lying that she had pains in her body from hurting herself when falling over in fear of the elephant, avoided even being touched by her husband while on the way. Like a snake, a passionate woman who has been turned against a man, unbearable because of the mass of poison produced within her, will not remain without doing him harm.

In time we arrived at the city of Loha·nágara, where the lady's husband had a house and supported himself by doing business. That day we all stayed in a temple outside the city there, and there I met this other brahmin, my companion here. Even though we had just met, there arose a 6.1.190
mutual trust between us. The mind recognizes the affection of other beings earned in a different life. Then I told him all about my secret and as soon as he heard it he quietly said to me the following. 'Keep quiet about this. There is a way to accomplish what you have come here for. This merchant lady's husband has a sister here. She is ready to take her money and leave this place with me. So with her help I shall bring about what you desire.'

ity uktvā mām ayaṃ vipro gatvā tasyās tadā rahaḥ
vaṇig|vadhū|nanāndus tad yathā|vastu nyavedayat.
6.1.195 anyedyuḥ kṛta|saṃvic ca sā nanāndā sametya tām
prāveśayad bhrātṛ|jāyāṃ tatra deva|gṛh'|ântare.
tatr' ântaḥ sthitayor nau ca madhyād etaṃ tad" âiva sā
mittraṃ me bhrātṛ|jāyāyās tasyā veṣam akārayat.
kṛta|tad|veṣam enaṃ ca gṛhītvā nagar'|ântaram
bhrātrā sah' āviśad gehaṃ kṛtvā naḥ kārya|saṃvidam.
ahaṃ ca nirgatya tatas tayā puruṣa|veṣayā
vaṇig|vadhvā samaṃ prāptaḥ kramen' Ôjjayinīm imām.
tan|nanāndā ca sā rātrau tad ahaḥ s'|ôtsavāt tataḥ
matta|supta|janād gehād anena saha nirgatā.
6.1.200 tataś c' âyaṃ gṛhītvā tāṃ vipra|cchannaiḥ prayāṇakaiḥ
āgato nagarīm etām ath' āvāṃ militāv iha.

ity āvābhyām ubhe bhārye prāpte pratyagra|yauvane
nanāndṛ|bhrātṛ|jāye te sv'|ânurāga|samarpite.
ato nivāse sarvatra, deva, śaṅkāmahe vayam
kasy' āśvasiti ceto hi vihita|svaira|sāhasam.
tad avasthāna|hetoś ca vitt'|ârthaṃ ca rahaś ciram
āvāṃ mantrayamāṇau hyo dṛṣṭau devena dūrataḥ.
dṛṣṭv" ānāyya ca saṃyamya sthāpitau cāra|śaṅkayā
adya pṛṣṭau ca vṛttāntaṃ sa c' âiṣa kathito mayā.
6.1.205 devaḥ prabhavat' īdānīm ity» anen' ôdite tadā
rājā Vikramasiṃhas tau viprau dvāv apy abhāṣata.
«tuṣṭo 'smi vāṃ bhayaṃ mā bhūd ih' âiva puri tiṣṭhatam
aham eva ca dāsyāmi paryāptaṃ yuvayor dhanam.»

After saying this to me, this brahmin then went and secretly informed the merchant woman's sister-in-law of everything. Having arranged a meeting, on the next day the 6.1.195
sister-in-law met her brother's wife and brought her into the temple. Of the two of us waiting inside there, she then chose my friend here to put on her sister-in-law's clothes. After dressing him up in them, she took him into the city and went into her house with her brother, having made arrangements with us for what was to be done. I then left with the merchant's wife, who was dressed as a man, and eventually arrived here in Ujjain. That night her sister-in-law and this man left her house, where there had been a party and everyone was in a drunken sleep. He then took 6.1.200
her and came to this city with some travelers disguised as brahmins, at which point we met here.

Thus we two obtained two wives in the bloom of youth, the sister-in-law and her brother's wife, who had offered themselves out of love. So, your highness, wherever we stay we are worried, for no one's mind is at ease when it has done something willful and rash. Thus yesterday when your highness saw us from afar, we were discussing at length and in private where we should stay and how we could get money. After seeing us you had us brought in and imprisoned on the suspicion that we were spies, and today we were asked our story, which is what I have just told. The matter is 6.1.205
now in your majesty's hands." On being told this by him, King Víkrama·sinha then said to the two brahmins, "I am pleased. Have no fear while you are staying in this city. I shall give you all the wealth you need." After saying this the

ity uktvā sa dadau rājā yath"|êṣṭaṃ jīvanaṃ tayoḥ
tau ca bhāry"|ânvitau tasya nikaṭe tasthatuḥ sukham.
itthaṃ kriyāsu nivasanty api yāsu tāsu
puṃsāṃ śriyaḥ prabala|sattva|bahiṣ|kṛtāsu
evaṃ ca sāhasa|dhaneṣv atha buddhimatsu
saṃtuṣya dāna|niratāḥ kṣiti|pā bhavanti.
ity aihikena ca purā|vihitena c' âpi
sven' âiva karma|vibhavena śubh'|â|śubhena
śaśvad bhavet tad|anurūpa|vicitra|bhogaḥ
sarvo hi nāma sasurāsura eṣa sargaḥ.
6.1.210 tat svapna|vṛtta|nibhato nabhasaś cyutā yā
jvālā tvay" ântar udaraṃ viśat' îha dṛṣṭā
sā k' âpi, devi, sura|jātir a|saṃśayaṃ te
garbhaṃ kuto 'pi khalu karma|vaśāt prapannā.›

iti nija|bhartur vadanāc chrutvā nṛ|pateḥ Kaliṅgadattasya devī Tārādattā prāpa sa|garbhā paraṃ pramadam.

iti mahā|kavi|śrī|Somadeva|bhaṭṭa|viracite Kathāsaritsāgare
Madanamañcukā|lambake prathamas taraṅgaḥ.

2

6.2.1 TATAḤ KALIṄGADATTASYA rājño garbha|bhar'|â|lasā
rājñī Takṣaśilāyāṃ sā Tārādattā śanair abhūt.
udeṣyac|candra|lekhāṃ ca prācīm anucakāra sā
āsanna|prasavā pāṇḍu|mukhī tarala|*tārakā*.
jajñe ca tasyā nacirād an|anya|sadṛśī sutā
vedhasaḥ sarva|saundarya|sarga|varṇaka|saṃnibhā.
‹īdṛk putro na kiṃ jāta it'› ? îva *sneha*|śālinaḥ
rakṣā|pradīpās tat|kānti|jitā vicchāyatāṃ yayuḥ.

king gave them as much as they wanted to live on and the two of them and their wives lived in comfort near him.

Thus success also inhabits men's actions when they are the result of great heroism, and so in this way kings, when pleased, delight in generosity to clever men rich in daring. So it is always by the power of its actions, good or bad and performed in this life or the past, that this entire creation, including the gods and *ásuras*, reaps the various rewards appropriate to those actions. Thus the flame that appeared 6.1.210
in your dream and which you saw fall from the sky and enter your belly here must, O queen, be some type of deity which because of its karma has arrived in your womb from somewhere.'

After hearing this from the mouth of her own husband, King Kalínga·datta, the pregnant Queen Tara·datta was overjoyed.

Thus ends the first wave in the Mádana·mánchuka Attainment in the "Ocean of the Rivers of Story" composed by the glorious and learned great poet Soma·deva.

2

IN TAKSHA·SHILA TARA·DATTA, King Kalínga·datta's queen, 6.2.1
slowly became tired from the burden of her pregnancy. When the birth was close at hand, with her pale face and flickering *pupils : stars* she looked like the East with a sliver of a moon about to rise. Before long a daughter of unrivaled appearance was born to her, and she looked like a specimen of the creator's creation of absolute beauty. The lights,

6.2.5 pitā Kaliṅgadattaś ca jātāṃ tāṃ tādṛśīm api
dṛṣṭvā tad|rūpa|putr'|āśā|vaiphalya|vimanā abhūt.
divyāṃ tām api saṃbhāvya sa putr'|êcchur adūyata
śoka|kandaḥ kva kanyā hi kv' ānandaḥ kāyavān sutaḥ?
tataś ceto|vinodāya khinno nirgatya mandirāt
yayau nānā|jin'|ākāraṃ vihāraṃ sa mahī|patiḥ.
tatr' âika|deśe śuśrāva dharma|pāṭhaka|bhikṣuṇā
jana|madhy'|ôpaviṣṭena kathyamānam idaṃ vacaḥ.
«artha|pradānam ev' āhuḥ saṃsāre su|mahat|tapaḥ
artha|daḥ prāṇa|daḥ proktaḥ prāṇā hy artheṣu kīlitāḥ.
6.2.10 Buddhena ca parasy' ârthe karuṇ"|ākula|cetasā
ātm" âpi tṛṇavad dattaḥ kā varāke dhane kathā?
tādṛśena ca dhīreṇa tapasā sa gata|spṛhaḥ
saṃprāpta|divya|vijñāno Buddho Buddhatvam āgataḥ.
ā śarīram ataḥ sarveṣv iṣṭeṣv āśā|nivartanāt
prājñaḥ sattva|hitaṃ kuryāt samyak|saṃbodha|labdhaye.
tathā ca pūrvaṃ kasy' âpi Kṛta|nāmno mahī|pateḥ
ajāyant' âti|subhagāḥ kramāt sapta kumārikāḥ.
bālā eva ca tās tyaktvā vairāgyeṇa pitur gṛham
śmaśānaṃ śiśriyuḥ pṛṣṭā jagaduś ca paricchadam.
6.2.15 «a|sāraṃ viśvam ev' âitat tatr' âp' îdaṃ śarīrakam

full of *oil: love* kept burning for her protection were overwhelmed by her brilliant beauty and grew dim, as if thinking, 'Why hasn't a son like her been born?' When her fa- 6.2.5
ther Kalínga·datta saw her after her birth, even though she was so beautiful he was sad that his hopes for an equally beautiful son had not come to fruition. Despite supposing her to be divine, he was upset because he wanted a son, for how can one compare a daughter, a lump of sorrow, with a son, bliss incarnate? Then the depressed king, to take his mind off it, left the palace and went to a monastery with lots of images of the Buddha. In some place there he heard the following story being told by a monk who gave religious discourses and was sitting among some people.

'It is said that in the mundane world the very greatest asceticism is giving away one's wealth. The giver of wealth is called the giver of life because life is bound up in wealth. For the sake of someone else, the Buddha, his mind over- 6.2.10
come with compassion, gave away, as if it were a piece of straw, even his life—forget vile wealth! It was through such resolute asceticism that the Buddha cast off desire, attained divine knowledge and became a Buddha. So in order to attain right knowledge the wise man should work for the benefit of living beings, by renouncing desires for all things, including the body.

In illustration of this, seven very beautiful daughters were once born in succession to a certain king called Krita. While still young they abandoned their father's house out of distaste for the world and took to living in the cremation ground. On being questioned they said to their servants,

tatr' âpy abhīṣṭa|saṃyoga|sukh'|ādi svapna|vibhramaḥ.
ekaṃ para|hitaṃ tv atra saṃsāre sāram ucyate
tad anen' âpi dehena kurmaḥ sattva|hitaṃ vayam.
kṣipāmo jīvad ev' âitac charīraṃ pitṛ|kānane
kravyād|gaṇ'|ôpayogāya kānten' âpi hy anena kim.

tathā ca rāja|putro 'tra viraktaḥ ko 'py abhūt purā
sa yuv" âpi su|kānto 'pi parivrajyām aśiśriyat.
sa jātu bhikṣuḥ kasy' âpi praviṣṭo vaṇijo gṛham
dṛṣṭas taruṇyā tat|patnyā padma|patr'|āyat'|ēkṣaṇaḥ.
6.2.20 sā tal|locana|lāvaṇya|hṛta|cittā tam abravīt
‹katham āttam idaṃ kaṣṭam īdṛśena tvayā vratam?
sā dhanyā strī tav' ânena cakṣuṣā yā nirīkṣyate!›

pratyuktaḥ sa tayā bhikṣuś cakṣur ekam apāṭayat.
ūce ca haste kṛtvā tan ‹mātaḥ, paśy' êdam īdṛśam
jugupsitam asṛṅ|māṃsaṃ gṛhyatāṃ yadi rocate.
īdṛg eva dvitīyaṃ ca vada ramyaṃ kim etayoḥ?›

ity uktā tena tad dṛṣṭvā vyaṣīdat sā vaṇig|vadhūḥ.
uvāca ca ‹hahā! pāpaṃ mayā kṛtam a|bhavyayā
yad ahaṃ hetutāṃ prāptā locan'|ôtpāṭane tava.›

"This entire world is without substance and in it this body 6.2.15
and pleasures such as making love to one's sweetheart are as illusory as dreams. Doing good for others is said to be the one substantial thing in this mundane world, so we shall use even our bodies for the good of other living beings. We shall cast off these bodies, while they are still alive, into the grove of the ancestors for the use of the packs of carnivorous animals. They may be lovely, but we have no need of them.

In the same way, there lived long ago a certain prince, who, disgusted with this world, became a wandering ascetic, despite being young and very handsome. One day that monk with eyes as wide as a lotus leaf went into the house of some merchant or other and was seen by his young
wife. The beauty of his eyes captivated her mind and she 6.2.20
said to him, 'Why has someone like you undertaken this difficult observance? Lucky is the woman on whom this eye of yours falls!'

After she had spoken to him, the monk ripped out one of his eyes and, holding it in his hand, said, 'Mother, see this for what it is: disgusting blood and flesh. If you like it then take it. The other one is the same. Tell me what's lovely about them.'

When he said this to her and she saw the eye, the merchant's wife was distressed and said, 'Oh no! I am wicked and have committed a sin by causing you to rip out your eye.'

6.2.25 tac chrutvā bhikṣur avadan ‹mā bhūd, amba, tava vyathā
mama tvayā hy upakṛtaṃ yataḥ śṛṇu nidarśanam.
āsīt ko 'pi purā kānte kutr' âpy upavane yatiḥ
anujāhnavi vairāgya|niḥśeṣa|nikaṣ'|êcchayā.
tapasyataś ca ko 'py asya rājā tatr' âiva daivataḥ
vihartum āgataḥ sākam avarodha|vadhū|janaiḥ.
vihṛtya pāna|suptasya pārśvād utthāya tasya ca
nṛpasya cāpalād rājñyas tad|udyāne kil' âbhraman.
dṛṣṭvā tatr' âika|deśe ca taṃ samādhi|sthitaṃ munim
atiṣṭhan parivāry' âinaṃ «kim etad iti?» kautukāt.
6.2.30 cira|sthitāsu tāsv atra prabuddhaḥ so 'tha bhū|patiḥ
a|paśyan dayitāḥ pārśve tatra babhrāma sarvataḥ.
dadarśa c' âtra rājñīs tāḥ parivārya muniṃ sthitāḥ
kupitaś c' ērṣyayā tasmin khaḍgena prāharan munau.
aiśvaryam īrṣyā nairghṛṇyaṃ kṣībatvaṃ nirvivekitā
ekaikaṃ kiṃ na yat kuryāt pañc'|âṅgitve tu kā kathā?
tato gate nṛpe tasmin kṛtt'|âṅgam api taṃ munim
a|kruddhaṃ prakaṭī|bhūya k" âpy uvāc' âtra devatā.
«mah"|ātman, yena pāpena krodhen' âitat kṛtaṃ tvayi
sva|śaktyā tam ahaṃ hanmi manyate yadi tad bhavān.»
6.2.35 tac chrutvā sa jagāda 'rṣir «devi, mā sm' âivam ādiśaḥ
sa hi dharma|sahāyo me na vipriya|karaḥ punaḥ.
tat|prasādāt kṣamā|dharmaṃ, bhagavaty, āptavān aham
kasya kṣameya kiṃ, devi, n' âivaṃ cet sa samācaret?

When he heard this, the monk said, 'Mother, do not be alarmed. You have done me a favor. Listen, I shall explain it to you with a story. 6.2.25

Long ago there lived in some beautiful grove on the banks of the Ganga a certain ascetic who wanted to be the touchstone of absolute detachment. It so happened that while he was practicing austerities there, some king or other came to that very spot to have fun with some wives from his harem. After enjoying themselves and getting up from the side of the king, who was in a drunken sleep, it seems that the queens, being flighty, wandered about that grove. When in some spot there they saw the sage deep in meditation, they were so curious that they stood around him, wondering what was going on. Then, after they had been stand- 6.2.30
ing there for a long time, the king awoke. Seeing that the queens were not at his side, he wandered all about that place and he found the queens there, standing around the sage. Enraged by jealousy, he attacked the sage with his sword. Power, jealousy, cruelty, drunkenness and lack of discernment: there is nothing that each of these cannot do on its own, let alone all five together. When the king had gone, some goddess or other appeared there and said to the sage, whose body had been cut but who was not angry, "O great soul, I shall use my power to kill the sinner who in his anger has done this to you, if you so approve."

The sage replied, "O goddess, do not talk like this, for 6.2.35
he has not been disagreeable to me, but has helped me in my religious duty. Thanks to him, O blessed one, I have acquired the virtue of forgiveness. If he did not behave thus, O goddess, then whom am I to forgive for what? A wise man

kaḥ kopo naśvarasy' âsya dehasy' ârthe manasvinaḥ
priy'|â|priyeṣu sāmyena kṣamā hi brahmaṇaḥ padam.»

ity uktā muninā s" âtha tapasā tasya toṣitā
aṅgāni devatā kṛtvā nirvraṇāni tiro|dadhe.

tad yathā so 'pi tasya' rṣer upakārī mato nṛpaḥ
netr'|ôtkhanana|hetos tvaṃ tapo|vṛddhyā tath," âmba, me.›

6.2.40 ity uktvā sa vaśī bhikṣur vinamrāṃ tāṃ vaṇig|vadhūm
kānte 'pi vapuṣi svasminn an|āsthaḥ siddhaye yayau.
tasmād bāle 'pi ramye 'pi kaḥ kāye gatvare grahaḥ
sattv'|ôpakāras tv etasmād ekaḥ prājñasya śasyate.
tad imā vayam etasmin nisarga|sukha|sadmani
śmaśāne prāṇinām arthe vinyasyāma śarīrakam.»

ity uktvā parivāraṃ tāḥ sapta rāja|kumārikāḥ
tath" âiva cakruḥ prāpuś ca saṃsiddhiṃ paramāṃ tataḥ.
evaṃ nije śarīre 'pi mamatvaṃ n' âsti dhīmatām
kiṃ punaḥ suta|dār"|ādi|parigraha|tṛṇ'|ôtkare.›

6.2.45 ity|ādi sa nṛpaḥ śrutvā vihāre dharma|pāṭhakāt
Kaliṅgadatto nītvā ca dinaṃ prāyāt sva|mandiram.
tatr' ânubādhyamānaś ca kanyā|janma|śucā punaḥ
sa rājā gṛha|vṛddhena ken' âpy ūce dvi|janmanā.
‹rājan, kiṃ kanyakā|ratna|janmanā paritapyase?
putrebhyo 'py uttamāḥ kanyāḥ śivāś c' êha paratra ca.

does not get angry over this body, which is impermanent. For forgiveness by means of viewing all things, pleasant and unpleasant, as the same, is the mark of having attained the status of Brahma."

After the sage had said this, the goddess, pleased by his asceticism, healed his body and disappeared.

So just as that king was considered to have helped the sage, so, mother, have you helped me by increasing my asceticism through causing me to rip out my eye.'

After saying this to the merchant's bowing wife, that self- 6.2.40
controlled monk, who had no concern for his own body even though it was beautiful, attained perfection. Therefore, even though our bodies are young and lovely, they are transient and there is no point in hanging on to them. However, for the wise one use is prescribed for the body: helping living beings. So we girls here shall lay down our bodies in this abode of natural happiness, the cremation ground, for the sake of living creatures."

After saying this to their attendants, those seven princesses did just that and as a result attained the ultimate perfection. Thus for the wise there is no sense of "I" even in the case of one's own body, much less for all the worthless things like sons, wives and families.'

After hearing this and more like it from the preacher in 6.2.45
the monastery, at the day's end King Kalínga·datta went to his palace. There the king was still afflicted by sorrow over the birth to him of a daughter. A certain brahmin who had grown old in the palace said to him, 'Sire, why are you sad about the birth of this jewel of a daughter? Daughters are better even than sons, and are auspicious both in this world

rājya|lubdheṣu kā teṣu putreṣv āsthā mahī|bhujām
ye bhakṣayanti janakaṃ bata markaṭakā iva?
nṛpās tu Kuntibhoj'|ādyaḥ Kunty|ādi|tanayā|guṇaiḥ
tīrṇā duḥsaha|Durvāsaḥ|prabhṛtibhyaḥ parābhavam.
6.2.50 phalaṃ yac ca sutā|dānāt kutaḥ putrāt paratra tat?
Sulocanā|kathām atra kiṃ ca vacmi niśamyatām.
āsīd rājā Suṣeṇ'|ākhyaś Citrakūṭ'|âcale yuvā
Kāmo 'nya iva yo dhātrā nirmitas Tryambak'|ērṣyayā.
sa cakre divyam ārāmaṃ mūle tasya mahā|gireḥ
surāṇāṃ Nandan'|ôdyāna|vāsa|vairasya|dāyinam.
tan|madhye ca cakār' âikāṃ vāpīm utphulla|paṅkajām
Lakṣmī|līl"|âravindānāṃ nav'|ākara|mahīm iva.
tasyās tasthau ca sad|ratna|sopānāyās taṭe sadā
patnīnaṃ sv'|ânurūpāṇām a|bhāvād a|vadhū|sakhaḥ.
6.2.55 ekadā tena mārgeṇa nabhasā sura|sundarī
Rambhā Jambh'|âri|bhavanād ājagāma yadṛcchayā.
sā taṃ dadarśa rājānaṃ tatr' ôdyāne vihāriṇam
sākṣān Madhum iv' ôtphulla|puṣpa|kānana|madhya|gam.
«vāpikā|padma|patitāṃ divo 'nu patitaḥ Śriyam
candraḥ kim eṣa n' âitad vā śrīr asya hy an|apāyinī.
nūnaṃ puṣp'|êṣur udyānaṃ puṣp'|êcchuḥ so 'yam āgataḥ
kiṃ tu sā Ratir etasya kva gatā saha|cāriṇī?»
ity autsukya|kṛt'|ôllekhā s" âvatīrya nabho|'ntarāt
Rambhā mānuṣa|rūpeṇa rājānaṃ tam upāgamat.

and the next. What regard can one have for those sons of kings who, alas, in their greed for the throne devour their fathers like spiders? But through the virtues of daughters such as Kunti, kings like Kunti·bhoja have avoided being destroyed by irresistible sages like Durvásas. And how can 6.2.50
one get from a son the reward that one reaps in the next world by giving away a daughter? Moreover, on this subject I shall tell the story of Sulóchana. Listen.

A young king called Sushéna lived on mount Chitra·kuta. It was as if the creator, irked with Shiva, had made another god of love. At the foot of that great mountain the king created a heavenly garden which made the gods find living in the garden of Nándana insipid. In its middle he built a tank with blooming lotuses, and it was like a new source of play lotuses for Lakshmi. It had steps of fine jewels and the king would frequent its edge, without a wife as company because there were no brides suitable for him.
One day the heavenly beauty Rambha spontaneously came 6.2.55
that way through the sky from the home of Indra. She saw the king enjoying himself in the garden there like the embodiment of Spring in the midst of a garden of blooming flowers.

"Is this the moon fallen from the sky in pursuit of Lakshmi, who has fallen among the lotuses of the tank? But it can't be—she never leaves him. Surely this is the god who has flowers for arrows, come here in search of flowers. But where has his companion Rati gone?" Her curiosity having made her speak of him thus, Rambha came down from the sky in the form of a woman and went up to the

6.2.60 upetāṃ tāṃ ca sahasā dṛṣṭvā rājā sa|vismayaḥ
acintayad «aho k" êyam a|saṃbhavya|vapur bhavet?
na tāvan mānuṣī yena pādau n' âsyā† rajaḥ|spṛśau
na cakṣuḥ sa|nimeṣaṃ vā tasmād divy" âiva k" âpy asau.
praṣṭavyā tu mayā n' êyaṃ palāyeta hi jātu|cit
pratibhed'|â|sahāḥ† prāyo divyāḥ kāraṇa|saṃgatāḥ.»
iti dhyāyan sa nṛ|patiḥ kṛta|saṃbhāṣaṇas tayā
tat|kramen' âiva tat|kālaṃ tat|kaṇṭh'|āśleṣam āptavān.
cikrīḍa ca ciraṃ so 'tra sākam apsarasā tayā
divaṃ s" âpi na sasmāra ramyaṃ prema na janma|bhūḥ.
6.2.65 tat|sakhī|yakṣiṇī|vṛṣṭair apūri svarṇa|rāśibhiḥ
s" âsya bhūmir nar'|êndrasya dyaur Meru|śikharair iva.
kālena c' âsya rājñaḥ sā Suṣeṇasya var'|âpsarāḥ
asūt' ân|anya|sadṛśīṃ dhṛta|garbhā satī sutām.
prasūta|mātr" âiva ca sā jagād' âinaṃ mahī|patim
«rājan, śāpo 'yam īdṛn me kṣīṇo jātaḥ sa c' âdhunā.
ahaṃ hi Rambhā nāka|strī tvayi dṛṣṭe 'nurāgiṇī
jāte ca garbhe muktvā taṃ gacchāmas tat|kṣaṇaṃ vayam.
samayo h' īdṛśo 'smākaṃ tad rakṣeḥ kanyakām imām
etad|vivāhān nāke nau bhūyo bhāvī samāgamaḥ.»
6.2.70 evam uktv" âpsarā Rambhā vivaśā sā tirodadhe
tad|duḥkhāc ca sa rāj" âbhūt tadā prāṇa|vyay'|ôdyataḥ.
«nirāsthen' âpi kiṃ tyaktaṃ Viśvāmitreṇa jīvitam
Menakāyāṃ prayātāyāṃ prasūy' âiva Śakuntalām.»
ity|ādi sacivair ukto jñāt'|ârthaḥ sa nṛpo dhṛtim
śanair ādatta kanyāṃ ca punaḥ|saṃgama|kāraṇam.

king. When he suddenly saw her approach, the astonished 6.2.60
king said to himself, "Who might this lady of unimaginable beauty be? She isn't human, because the dust does not stick to her feet, nor do her eyes blink, so she is some divine lady. But I must not question her, for she might run away. When divine beings meet one for a reason, they tend to be intolerant of revealing things about themselves." While the king was thinking this, she struck up a conversation with him, in the course of which he suddenly embraced her. He sported there with that *ápsaras* for a long time. She did not
think of heaven. Love is lovely, not one's birthplace. Like 6.2.65
heaven being filled with the peaks of Meru, the king's land was filled with heaps of gold, rained down by the *yakshi*s who accompanied her. In time the beautiful and virtuous *ápsaras* became pregnant and bore King Sushéna a daughter of incomparable looks. As soon as she had given birth, she said to the king, "O King, I was cursed and the curse is now spent. I am Rambha, a divine woman, who fell in love with you at first sight. When we give birth to a child, we leave it and immediately go away, because that is how our rules work. So you must look after our daughter. We shall be reunited after she is married in heaven."

After saying this, the *ápsaras* Rambha had no choice but 6.2.70
to vanish. The king was then so upset by this that he was ready to end his life.

"Did Vishva·mitra, even though he cared for nothing, give up his life when Ménaka went away immediately after giving birth to Shakúntala?" When his ministers said things like this to him, the king realized their truth and slowly

tāṃ ca bālāṃ tad|ek'|âgraḥ pitā sarv'|âṅga|sundarīm
so 'tilocana|saundaryān nāmnā cakre Sulocanām.
kālena yauvana|prāptām udyāna|sthāṃ dadarśa tām
yuvā yadṛcchayā bhrāmyan Vats'|ākhyaḥ Kāśyapo muniḥ.
6.2.75 sa tapo|rāśi|rūpo 'pi dṛṣṭv" âiv' âitāṃ nṛp'|ātmajām
anurāga|rasa|jño 'bhūd iti c' âtra vyacintayat.
«aho rūpaṃ kim apy asyāḥ
kanyāyāḥ param'|âdbhutam!
n' êmāṃ prāpnomi ced bhāryāṃ
kim anyat tapasaḥ phalam?»
iti dhyāyan muni|yuvā sa Sulocanayā tayā
adarśi prajvalat|tejā vidhūma iva pāvakaḥ.
taṃ vīkṣya s" âpi sa|premā s'|âkṣa|sūtra|kamaṇḍalum
«śāntaś ca kamanīyaś ca ko 'yaṃ syād ity?» acintayat.
varaṇāy' êva c' ôpetya nayan'|ôtpala|mālikām
kṣipantī tasya vapuṣi praṇāmam akaron muneḥ.
6.2.80 «patiṃ samāpnuh' īty» āśīs tasyās ten' âbhyadhīyata
sur'|âsura|durullaṅghya|Manmath'|ājñā|vaś'|ātmanā.
tato 'sāmānya|tad|rūpa|lobha|luṇṭhita|lajjayā
tay" âpy ūce sa vinamad|vaktrayā muni|puṃgavaḥ.
«eṣā yad' îcchā bhavato narm'|ālāpo na ced ayam
tad, deva, dātā nṛ|patiḥ pitā me yācyatām iti.»

pulled himself together and devoted himself to his daughter, the means to their reunion. Her father could think of nothing but her, and because her eyes were so particularly beautiful, he called the beautiful girl Sulóchana.

When in time she came of age, a young sage called Vatsa of Káshyapa's lineage who was wandering about at will saw her in a park. Even though he was a vision of accumulated 6.2.75
ascetic power, as soon as he saw the princess he understood the pleasures of love and consequently said to himself there, "Oh how supremely amazing is the beauty of this girl! What could be the reward of asceticism other than winning her as one's wife?"

As the young sage, who with his blazing splendor was like fire without smoke, was thinking this, he was seen by Sulóchana. She, on seeing him with his rosary and pot, fell in love and said to herself, "Who might this serene and lovely man be?" As if to choose him as her husband, she went up to the sage, throwing the garland of the lotuses of her eyes on his body, and bowed before him. Under the 6.2.80
orders of the god of love, which are hard for the gods and *ásuras* to disobey, he gave her a blessing: "Take a husband."

Then, her modesty removed by her lust for his unusual beauty, she said to that fine sage, her face looking down, "If that is your desire, sir, and you are not joking, then, your holiness, it is my father the king who will betroth me—ask him."

ath' ânvayaṃ parijanān munis tasyā niśamya saḥ
gatvā nṛpaṃ tat|pitaraṃ Suṣeṇaṃ tām ayācata.
so 'pi taṃ vīkṣya tapasā vapuṣā c' âtibhūmi|gam
uvāca racit'|ātithyo rājā muni|kumārakam.
6.2.85 «jāt" âpsarasi Rambhāyāṃ kany" âiṣā, bhagavan, mama
asyā vivāhān nāke me tayā bhāvī samāgamaḥ.
evaṃ tayā vrajantyā dyāṃ Rambhay" âiva mam' ôditam
etat kathaṃ, mahābhāga, bhaved iti? nirūpyatām.»
tac chrutvā muni|putro 'sau kṣaṇam evam acintayat
«kiṃ purā Menak"|ôdbhūtā sarpa|daṣṭā Pramadvarā.
dattv" āyuṣo 'rdhaṃ muninā na bhāryā Ruruṇā kṛtā
Triśaṅkuḥ kiṃ na nīto dyāṃ Viśvāmitreṇa lubdhakaḥ.
tad idaṃ sva|tapo|bhāga|vyayāt kiṃ na karomy aham?»
ity alocya «na bhāro 'yam ity» uktvā so 'bravīn muniḥ.
6.2.90 «he devatās! tapo|'ṃśena madīyen' âiṣa bhū|patiḥ
sa|śarīro divaṃ yātu Rambhā|saṃbhoga|siddhaye.»
ity ukte tena muninā śṛṇvantyāṃ rāja|saṃsadi
«evam astv iti» su|vyaktā divyā vāg udabhūt tataḥ.
tataḥ Sulocanāṃ tasmai munaye Kāśyapāya tām
Vatsāya dattvā tanayāṃ sa rājā divam udyayau.
tatra divyatvam āsādya tayā Śakra|niyuktayā
sa reme Rambhayā sākaṃ bhūyo divy'|ânubhāvayā.
itthaṃ kṛt'|ârthatāṃ, deva, Suṣeṇaḥ prāpa kanyayā
kanyā yuṣmādṛśāṃ geheṣv īdṛśyo 'vataranti hi.
6.2.95 tad eṣā k" âpi divyā te jāta śāpa|cyutā gṛhe
kanyā nūnam ato mā gāḥ śucaṃ taj|janmanā, vibho.›

Then the sage, after hearing about her lineage from her servants, went to her father, King Sushéna, and asked for her hand. The king, on seeing the young sage and his extraordinary asceticism and beauty, showed him due hospitality and said, "This daughter of mine, O blessed one, was 6.2.85
born to the *ápsaras* Rambha, with whom I shall be reunited in heaven after my daughter is married. Thus Rambha herself told me as she went up into the sky. So tell me, O illustrious one, how is that to come about?"

When the young sage heard this he reflected thus for a moment: "Long ago, was not Pramádvara, Ménaka's daughter, when bitten by a snake, given half his life by the sage Ruru and made his wife? Was not the hunter Tri·shanku taken to heaven by Vishva·mitra? So why don't I expend a part of my ascetic power in order to do the same?" After thinking this, the sage declared that it would be no trouble
and said, "Oh Gods! Using some of my ascetic power, have 6.2.90
this king go to heaven in his body so that he can make love to Rambha." After the sage had said this while the king's assembly listened on, a divine voice was clearly heard to say, "So be it." Then the king betrothed his daughter Sulóchana to the sage Vatsa, who was of Káshyapa's lineage, and went up to heaven. There he became divine and enjoyed himself with Rambha, who had been commissioned by Indra and once again had divine authority.

In this way, your highness, Sushéna achieved what he wanted through his daughter, for daughters like her descend to earth in the houses of people like you. So this 6.2.95
daughter of yours must be some divine lady born in your house having fallen to earth because of a curse, therefore

iti śrutvā kathāṃ rājā gṛha|vṛddhād dvi|janmanaḥ
Kaliṅgadatto nṛpatir jahau cintāṃ tutoṣa ca.
tāṃ ca cakre nija|sutāṃ nayan'|ānanda|dāyinīm
nāmnā Kaliṅgasen" êti bālām indu|kal"|ôpamām.

s" âpi tasya pitur gehe rāja|putrī tataḥ kramāt
Kaliṅgasenā vavṛdhe vayasyā|madhya|vartinī.
vijahāra ca harmyeṣu sā gṛheṣu vaneṣu ca
krīḍā|rasa|mayasy' êva laharī śaiśav'|âmbudheḥ.

6.2.100 kadā|cid atha harmya|sthāṃ keli|saktāṃ dadarśa tām
Māy"|âsura|sutā yāntī vyomnā Somaprabh"|âbhidhā.
sā tām ālokya rūpeṇa muni|mānasa|mohinīm
Somaprabhā nabhaḥ|sth" âiva jāta|prītir acintayat.
‹k" êyaṃ? kim aindavī mūrtiḥ? kāntis tasyā divā kutaḥ?
Ratir vā yadi Kāmaḥ kva? kanyakā tad avaimy aham.
atra rāja|gṛhe k" âpi divyā śāpa|cyutā bhavet
jāne janm'|ântare c' âbhūn nūnaṃ sakhyaṃ mam' âitayā.
etad dhi me vadaty asyām atisneh'|ākulaṃ manaḥ
tad yuktaṃ kartum etāṃ me svayaṃvara|sakhīṃ punaḥ.›

6.2.105 iti saṃcintya bālāyās tasyāḥ saṃtrāsa|śaṅkayā
Somaprabhā sā gaganād a|lakṣitam avātarat.
manuṣya|kanyakā|bhāvam āśrity' āśvāsa|kāraṇam
s" âsyāḥ Kaliṅgasenāyāḥ śanair upasasarpa ca.

you must not be sad about her birth, my lord.' After hearing this story from the brahmin who had grown old in his house, King Kalínga·datta stopped worrying and was happy. He named his daughter, who brought bliss to the eyes, Kalínga·sena, and the girl was like a digit of the moon.

In time princess Kalínga·sena grew up among her friends in her father's house. She played about in palaces, in houses and in forests, and was like a wave of the ocean of childhood, full of the nectar of fun.

Then one day, as the daughter of the *ásura* Maya, who 6.2.100
was called Soma·prabha, was flying through the sky, she came across Kalínga·sena busy having fun on the palace terrace. On seeing that she was so beautiful that she could bewitch the minds of sages, Soma·prabha was drawn to her, even in the sky, and said to herself, 'Who is this girl? Is she an incarnation of the moon? But how could she be so brilliantly lovely by day? If she were Rati then where is the god of love? So I presume she is a girl. I think she might be some divine lady who has fallen to earth in the king's house here because of a curse and I must have been friendly with her in her former life, for my mind is beside itself with its excessive affection for her and is telling me this. Therefore it is all right for me to choose her to be my friend once again.'

After thinking this, Soma·prabha, worried about fright- 6.2.105
ening the girl, descended from the sky unseen. Turning herself into a human girl to inspire trust, she slowly approached Kalínga·sena.

‹diṣṭyā rāja|sutā k" âpi svayam atyadbhut'|ākṛtiḥ
asau samāgatā pārśvam ucit" êyaṃ sakhī mama.›
iti tad|darśanād eva vicinty' otthāya c' ādarāt
Kaliṅgasen" âpy āliṅgat sā tāṃ Somaprabhāṃ tadā.
upaveśya ca papraccha kṣaṇād anvaya|nāmanī
‹vaksyāmi sarvaṃ tiṣṭh' êti› tāṃ ca Somaprabh" âbravīt.
6.2.110 tataḥ kathā|krameṇ' âiva vācā sakhyam abadhyata
tābhyām ubhābhyām anyonya|hasta|graha|puraḥ|saram.
atha Somaprabh" âvādīt ‹sakhi, tvaṃ rāja|kanyakā
rāja|putraiḥ samaṃ sakhyaṃ kṛcchrād apy ativāhyate.
alpen' âpy aparādhena te hi kupyanty a|mātrayā
rāja|putra|vaṇik|putra|kathāṃ śṛṇv atra vacmi te.
nagaryāṃ Puṣkarāvatyāṃ Gūḍhasen'|âbhidho nṛpaḥ
āsīt tasya ca jāto 'bhūd eka eva kil' ātmajaḥ.
sa rāja|putro dṛptaḥ sann eka|putratayā śubham
a|śubhaṃ v" âpi yac cakre pitā tasy' âsahiṣṭa tat.
6.2.115 bhrāmyat" ôpavane jātu dṛṣṭas ten' âika|putrakaḥ
vaṇijo Brahmadattasya sva|tulya|vibhav'|ākṛtiḥ.
dṛṣṭvā ca sadyaḥ so 'nena svayaṃvara|suhṛt|kṛtaḥ
tad" âiva c' âika|rūpau tau jātau rāja|vaṇik|sutau.
sthātuṃ na śekatuḥ kṣipraṃ tāv anyonyam a|darśanam
āśu badhnāti hi prema prāg|janm'|ântara|saṃstavaḥ.
n' ôpabhuṅkte sma taṃ bhogaṃ rāja|putraḥ kadā|cana
vaṇik|putrasya yas tasya n' ādāv ev' ôpakalpitaḥ.

'Excellent! Here is some princess of quite wonderful appearance who has come in person to my side and is an appropriate companion for me.' Kalínga·sena said this to herself as soon as she saw Soma·prabha, then got up and embraced her before having her sit down and immediately asking her her name and family.

Soma·prabha replied, 'I shall tell you everything. Wait.' Then in the course of that very conversation each of them 6.2.110
sealed their friendship with a promise, while holding each other's hands. Then Soma·prabha said, 'My friend, you are the daughter of a king and it is difficult to maintain friendships with the children of kings, for they get angry beyond measure because of even a trifling wrongdoing. On this subject, listen to the story of the prince and the merchant's son that I am going to tell you.

"In the city of Pushkarávati there lived a king called Gudha·sena and he had just one son. The prince was spoiled —his father, because he had only one son, put up with whatever he did, whether good or bad. One day when he 6.2.115
was wandering about in a park, the prince saw the merchant Brahma·datta's only son, who was his equal in wealth and looks. As soon as he saw him he chose him to be his friend and at that moment the son of the king and the son of the merchant became indistinguishable. Soon they could not bear to be out of each other's sight, for acquaintance in former births quickly produces affection. The prince would never partake of any pleasure without it first being made ready for the merchant's son.

ekadā suhṛdas tasya niścity' odvāham āditaḥ
Ahicchatraṃ vivāhāya sa pratasthe nṛp'|ātmajaḥ.
6.2.120 mittreṇa tena sākaṃ ca gaj'|ārūḍhaḥ sa|sainikaḥ
gacchann Ikṣumatī|tīraṃ prāpya sāyaṃ samāvasat.
tatra candr'|ôdaye pānam āsevya śayanaṃ śritaḥ
arthito nijayā dhātryā kathāṃ vaktuṃ pracakrame.
upakrānta|katho jahre śrānto mattaś ca nidrayā
dhātrī ca tadvat so 'py āsīt snehāj jāgrad vaṇik|sutaḥ.
tataḥ supteṣu c' ânyeṣu strīṇām iva mithaḥ kathā
gagane śuśruve tena vaṇik|putreṇa jāgratā.
«an|ākhyāya kathāṃ suptaḥ pāpo 'yaṃ tac chapāmy aham
paridrakṣyaty asau hāraṃ prātas taṃ ced grahīṣyati.
6.2.125 kaṇṭha|lagnena ten' âiṣa tat|kṣaṇaṃ mṛtyum āpsyati.»
ity uktvā virarām' âikā dvitīyā ca tato 'bravīt.
«ato yady ayam uttīrṇas tad drakṣyaty āmra|pādapam
viyokṣyate phalāny asya tataḥ prāṇair vimokṣyate.»
ity uktvā vyaramat s" âpi tṛtīy" âbhidadhe tataḥ
«yady etad api tīrṇo 'yaṃ tad vivāha|kṛte gṛham
praviṣṭaś cet tad ev' âsya hantuṃ pṛṣṭhe patiṣyati.»
uktv" êti nyavṛtat s" âpi caturthī vyāharat tataḥ.
«ato 'pi yadi nistīrṇas tan naktaṃ vāsa|veśmani
praviṣṭaḥ śata|kṛtvo 'yaṃ kṣutaṃ sadyaḥ kariṣyati.
6.2.130 śata|kṛtvo 'pi yady asya ‹jīv' êti› na vadiṣyati
kaś|cid atra tataś c' âiṣa mṛtyor vaśam upaiṣyati.
yena c' êdaṃ śrutaṃ so 'sya rakṣ"|ârthaṃ yadi vakṣyati
tasy' âpi bhavitā mṛtyur ity» uktvā sā nyavartata.

One day, having first arranged his friend's wedding, the
prince set out for Ahi·cchatra in order to get married. Riding 6.2.120
along on an elephant with his friend and accompanied by an army, in the evening he reached the banks of the Íkshumati and made camp. When the moon rose he had a drink and lay down on his bed. At the request of his nurse he started to tell a story. After beginning it, tired and drunk, sleep took him, and the nurse too, but out of affection for the prince the merchant's son stayed awake. Then, when the others were asleep, the vigilant merchant's son heard in the sky a conversation which seemed to be between some women. "This sinner has gone to sleep without finishing his story so I shall bestow a curse. In the morning he shall see
a necklace. If he takes it and puts it on his neck, he will in- 6.2.125
stantly die," said the first woman before falling quiet. A second then said, "If he escapes this, then he will see a mango tree. If he picks its fruit, his life will leave him." That voice said this and stopped. Then a third said, "If he escapes this too, then if he enters a house in order to get married, it will collapse on top of him and kill him." Having said this, that voice ceased. Then a fourth said, "If he avoids that as well, then when he goes into his bedroom at night, he shall suddenly sneeze one hundred times. If someone there does not 6.2.130
say, 'Stay alive,' to him one hundred times too, then death will take him. If he who has heard this relates it in order to save him, he too shall die." After saying this, that voice fell quiet.

vaṇik|sutaś ca tat sarvaṃ śrutvā nirghāta|dāruṇam
sa tasya rāja|putrasya sneh'|ôdvigno vyacintayat.
«upakrāntām an|ākhyātāṃ dhik kathāṃ yad† a|lakṣitāḥ
devatāḥ śrotum āyātāḥ śapantyas tu kutūhalāt.
tad etasmin mṛte rāja|sute ko 'rtho mam' āsubhiḥ?
ato 'yaṃ rakṣaṇīyo ‹m" êty› uktyā prāṇa|samaḥ suhṛt.
6.2.135 vṛttānto 'pi na vācyo 'sya mā bhūd doṣo mam' âpy ataḥ.»
ity ālocya niśāṃ ninye sa kṛcchreṇa vaṇik|sutaḥ.

rāja|putro 'pi sa prātaḥ prasthitas tat|sakhaḥ pathi
dadarśa purato hāraṃ tam ādātum iyeṣa ca.
tato 'bravīd vaṇik|putro «hāraṃ mā sma grahīḥ, sakhe.
māy" êyam anyathā n' âite paśyeyuḥ sainikāḥ katham?»

tac chrutvā taṃ parityajya gacchann agre dadarśa saḥ
āmra|vṛkṣaṃ phalāny asya bhoktuṃ c' āicchan nṛp'|ātmajaḥ.
vaṇik|putreṇa ca prāgvat tato 'pi sa nivāritaḥ
s'|ântaḥ|khedaḥ śanair gacchan prāpa śvaśura|veśma tat.
6.2.140 tatr' ôdvāha|kṛte veśma viśan dvārān nivartitaḥ
ten' âiva sakhyā yāvac ca tāvat tat patitaṃ gṛham.
tataḥ kathaṃ|cid uttīrṇaḥ kiṃ|cit|sa|pratyayo niśi
nivāsakaṃ viveś' ânyaṃ rāja|putro vadhū|sakhaḥ.
tatra tasmin vaṇik|putre praviśy' â|lakṣita|sthite
śata|kṛtvaḥ kṣutaṃ cakre śayanīy'|āśrito 'tha saḥ.
śata|kṛtvo 'pi tasy' âtra nīcair «jīv' êty» udīrya saḥ
kṛta|kāryo vaṇik|putro hṛṣṭaḥ svairaṃ bahir yayau.

After hearing all this, which was as frightening as an earthquake, he was anxious because of his love for the prince and said to himself, "Curse this story that was started but not told! Unseen gods have come to hear it but are issuing curses in their curiosity. If the prince dies then my life will have no purpose, so my friend, who is as dear to me as life, must be protected by being told, 'Don't do it!' He must not 6.2.135
be told what has happened lest I too should come to harm as a result." After thinking this, the merchant's son struggled to get through the night.

The prince, after setting out along the road in the morning accompanied by the merchant's son, saw in front of him a necklace and wanted to take it. At this the merchant's son said, "Don't take the necklace, my friend. It's a trick—otherwise why wouldn't these soldiers be able to see it?"

When he heard this, he left it. Journeying further on, the prince saw a mango tree and wanted to eat its fruit. As before he was prevented from doing so by the merchant's son. Traveling slowly and feeling inwardly aggrieved, he arrived at his father-in-law's house. As he was entering the house 6.2.140
there in order to get married, he was turned back at the door by that same friend and in the meantime the house collapsed. After having this narrow escape the prince began to trust his friend's advice and that night he went to another house with his wife. The merchant's son entered it and waited unseen. Then the prince went to bed and sneezed a hundred times. At this the merchant's son quietly said, "Stay alive," for him a hundred times too and then, happy to have done his job, he slipped out. As he was leaving the

niryāntaṃ tam apaśyac ca rāja|putro vadhū|sakhaḥ
īrṣyā|vismṛta|tat|snehaḥ kruddho dvāḥ|sthān uvāca ca.
6.2.145 «pāp'|ātm" âyaṃ rahaḥ|sthasya praviṣṭo 'ntaḥ|puraṃ mama
tad baddhvā sthāpyatāṃ yāvat prabhāte 'sau nigṛhyate.»
tad buddhvā rakṣibhir baddho niśāṃ ninye vaṇik|sutaḥ
prātar vadhya|bhuvaṃ taiś ca nīyamāno 'bravīt sa tān.
«ādau nayata māṃ tāvad rāja|putr'|ântikaṃ yataḥ
vakṣyāmi kāraṇaṃ kiṃ|cit tataḥ kuruta me vadham.»
ity uktais tena tair gatvā vijñaptaḥ sa nṛp'|ātmajaḥ
sacivair bodhitaś c' ânyais tasy' ānayanam ādiśat.
ānītaḥ so 'bravīt tasmai vṛttāntaṃ rāja|sūnave
pratyayād gṛha|pāt'|ôtthān mene satyaṃ ca so 'pi tat.
6.2.150 tatas tuṣṭaḥ samaṃ sakhyā vadha|muktena tena saḥ
āyayau rāja|tanayaḥ kṛta|dāro nijāṃ purīm.
tatra so 'pi suhṛt tasya kṛta|dāro vaṇik|sutaḥ
stūyamāna|guṇaḥ sarvair janair āsīd yathā|sukham.
evam *ucchṛṅkhalā* bhūtvā *sva|niyantṛ|pramāthinaḥ*
rāja|putrā na manyante hitaṃ mattā gajā iva.
vetālais taiś ca kā maittrī ye vihasya haranty asūn?
tad, rāja|putri, sakhyaṃ me mā sma vyabhicaraḥ sadā.›
iti śrutvā kathām etāṃ harmye Somaprabhā|mukhāt
Kaliṅgasenā sa|snehaṃ tāṃ sakhīṃ pratyabhāṣata.
6.2.155 ‹ete piśācā na tv ete rāja|putrā matāḥ, sakhi
piśāca|durgraha|kathām aham ākhyāmi te śṛṇu.

prince and his wife saw him. Forgetting, in his indignation, his love for him, the enraged prince said to the guards at the door, "This wretch entered my inner apartments when 6.2.145
I was to be left alone, so arrest him and keep him until the morning when he will be punished." When they heard this, the guards arrested the merchant's son and took him away for the night. In the morning, as they were taking him to the place of execution, he said to them, "First take me to the prince's inner apartments so that I can just tell him why I did it, then execute me."

On his saying this to them, they went and told the prince, who, on the advice of his other counselors, ordered him to be brought in. On being fetched he told the prince what had happened and the prince, convinced by the collapse of the house, believed it to be true. Pleased with his friend, 6.2.150
the prince stayed his execution and returned to his city as a married man. His friend the merchant's son got married there and lived in comfort, his virtues being praised by all the people.

Thus, like rutting elephants, the children of kings become *uncontrolled : free from their fetters, torment their governors : crush their restrainers* and don't take heed of what is good for them. One can't be friends with *vetálas* like them—they take lives with a smile! So, princess, please never violate your friendship with me.'

After hearing this story from Soma·prabha on the terrace, Kalínga·sena fondly replied to her friend, 'But you are talk- 6.2.155
ing about *pisháchas*, my friend, not the children of kings. I shall tell you a story about the obstinacy of *pisháchas*. Listen.

Yajñasthal'|ākhye ko 'py āsīd agra|hāre purā dvijaḥ
sa jātu durgataḥ kāṣṭhāny āhartum aṭavīṃ yayau.
tatra kāṣṭhaṃ kuṭhāreṇa pātyamānaṃ vidher vaśāt
āpatya tasya jaṅghāyāṃ bhittv" ântaḥ praviveśa tat.
tataḥ sa prasravad|rakto dṛṣṭvā ken' âpi mūrcchitaḥ
utkṣipy' ānīyata gṛhaṃ puṃsā pratyabhijānatā.
tatra vihvalayā patnyā tasya prakṣālya śoṇitam
āśvāsya tasya jaṅghāyāṃ nibaddho vraṇa|paṭṭakaḥ.
6.2.160 tataś cikitsyamānaḥ san vraṇas tasya dine dine
na paraṃ na ruroh' âiva yāvan nāḍītvam āyayau.
tato nāḍī|vraṇāt khinno daridro maraṇ'|ôdyataḥ
abhyetya sakhyā vipreṇa ken' âpi jagade rahaḥ.
«sakhā me Yajñadatt'|ākhyaś ciraṃ bhūtv" âtidurgataḥ
piśāca|sādhanaṃ kṛtvā dhanaṃ prāpya sukhī sthitaḥ.
tac ca tat|sādhanaṃ tena mam' âpy uktaṃ tvam apy ataḥ
piśācaṃ sādhaya, sakhe, sa te ropayitā vraṇam.»

ity uktv" ākhyāta|mantro 'sāv uvāc' âsya kriyām imām
«utthāya paścime yāme mukta|keśo dig|ambaraḥ.
6.2.165 an|ācāntaś ca muṣṭī dvau taṇḍulānāṃ yathā|kṣamam
dvābhyām ādāya hastābhyāṃ japan gaccheś catuṣ|patham.
tatra taṇḍula|muṣṭī dvau sthāpayitvā tataḥ, sakhe
maunen' âiva tvam āgaccher mā vīkṣiṣṭhāś ca pṛṣṭhataḥ.
evaṃ kuru sadā yāvat piśāco vyaktatāṃ gataḥ
‹ahaṃ hi hanmi te vyādhim iti› tvāṃ vakṣyati svayam.
tato 'bhinandes taṃ so 'tha tava rogaṃ hariṣyati.»

Long ago, in a brahmin settlement called Yajña·sthala which had been granted by the king, there lived a certain brahmin. He was a poor man and one day he went to the forest to fetch wood. There, by a stroke of fate, a piece of wood fell onto his thigh as it was being split by the axe, cut it and entered within. Then as the blood flowed forth and he fainted, some man, recognizing him, picked him up and took him to his home. There his distraught wife cleaned away the blood, brought him round and tied a bandage on his thigh. Then his wound was treated every day but did 6.2.160
not heal and eventually became infected. As a result the poor man became debilitated by the infected wound and was about to die. Some brahmin friend of his went to him and said to him in private, "A friend of mine called Yajña·datta was for a long time extremely poor. After propitiating *pishácha*s he obtained wealth and was happy. He told me how to propitiate them, so you too should propitiate a *pishácha*, my friend, and he will heal your wound."

After saying this he told him a spell and taught him the following practice. "Get up in the last watch of the night. Without tying up your hair, wearing any clothes, or ritually 6.2.165
rinsing out your mouth, take two handfuls of rice, as much as you can take in your fists, and go to a crossroads while repeating the spell. Place the two handfuls of rice there, after which, my friend, you should return in silence. And don't look back. Keep doing this until a *pishácha* appears. He will say to you in person, 'It is I who shall destroy your disease.' At this you should welcome him. He will then remove your disease."

ity uktas tena mittreṇa sa dvijas tat tath" âkarot.
tataḥ siddhaḥ piśācaḥ sa tasy' ārtasya mah"|âuṣadhīḥ
him'|âcal'|êndrād ānīya ropayām āsa taṃ vraṇam.
6.2.170 jagāda ca prahṛṣṭaṃ taṃ so 'tha lagna|graho dvijam
«dehi vraṇaṃ dvitīyaṃ me yāvat taṃ ropayāmy aham!
na cet sṛjāmy an|arthaṃ te śarīraṃ saṃharāmi vā.»
tac chrutvā sa dvijo bhītaḥ
sadyo muktyai tam abhyadhāt.
«vraṇaṃ dvitīyaṃ dāsyāmi saptabhis te dinair iti»
tatas ten' ôjjhitaḥ so 'bhūn nirāśo jīvite dvijaḥ.›
ity uktvā viratā madhyād a|ślīl'|ākhyāna|lajjayā
Kaliṅgasenā bhūyaḥ s" âvādīt Somaprabhām idam.
‹tato vraṇ'|ântar'|â|lābhād ārtaṃ vipram uvāca tam
dṛṣṭvā pṛṣṭvā ca duhitā vidagdhā mṛta|bhartṛkā.
6.2.175 «vañcaye 'haṃ piśācaṃ taṃ gaccha tvaṃ brūhi taṃ punaḥ
‹nāḍī|vraṇo mad|duhitur bhavatā ropyatām iti.› »
tac chrutvā mudito gatvā tath" âiv' ôktvā ca sa dvijaḥ
anaiṣīd duhitus tasyāḥ piśācaṃ taṃ tato 'ntikam.
sā ca tasya piśācasya varāṅgaṃ svam adarśayat
«ropay' êmaṃ vraṇaṃ, bhadra, mam' êti» bruvatī rahaḥ.
sa ca mūḍhaḥ piśāco 'syā varāṅge satataṃ dadau
piṇḍī|lep'|ādi na tv āsīt sa taṃ ropayituṃ kṣamaḥ.
dinaiś ca khinnas tasyāḥ sa kṛtvā jaṅghe nij'|âṃsayoḥ
«kiṃ|svin na rohat" îty?» evaṃ tad|varāṅgaṃ vyalokayat.
6.2.180 yāvad dvitīyaṃ tasy' âdhaḥ sa pāyu|vraṇam aikṣata
taṃ dṛṣṭv" âiva ca saṃbhrāntaḥ sa piśāco vyacintayat.

After being told this by his friend, the brahmin did what he had been told. Then a *pishácha* propitiated by that sick man fetched some magical herbs from the Himálaya and healed his wound. Afterwards the *pishácha* became insis- 6.2.170
tent, saying to the delighted brahmin, "Give me a second wound to heal! If you don't I shall make something bad happen for you or steal your body."

When he heard this, so that he might be freed of him the terrified brahmin quickly said, "I shall provide you with a second wound within seven days." At this the *pishácha* left and the brahmin felt that there was no hope for his life.'

After saying this Kalínga·sena fell quiet in the middle of the story, embarrassed that the story was vulgar. She then continued, saying to Soma·prabha, 'Next, his clever daughter, a widow, seeing the brahmin troubled at not having a second wound, questioned him and said, "I shall play a 6.2.175
trick on the *pishácha*. You should go and speak to him again, saying, 'My daughter has an infected wound. Please heal it, sir.'" When the brahmin heard this he was delighted and went and said just that. Then he brought the *pishácha* to his daughter. In private she showed the *pishácha* her vagina, saying, "Heal this wound of mine, good sir." The stupid *pishácha* kept smearing her vagina with lotions and so forth, but he was unable to heal it. After some days he had had enough and put her lower legs on his shoulders to inspect her vagina, wondering why it wouldn't heal. Then he no- 6.2.180
ticed below it a second wound—her anus—and as soon as he saw that the *pishácha* was confused and said to himself, "One wound hasn't healed and now this other one has appeared. True is the saying that calamities multiply in *weak*

«eko na ropito yāvad utpanno 'yaṃ vraṇo 'paraḥ
satyaḥ pravādo yac *chidreṣv* an|arthā yānti bhūritām.
prabhavanti yato *lokāḥ* pralayaṃ yānti yena ca
saṃsāra/vartma vivṛtaṃ kaḥ pidhātuṃ tad īśvaraḥ?»
ity ālocya viruddh'|ârtha|siddhyā bandhana|śaṅkayā
sa piśācas tato mūrkhaḥ palāyy' â|darśanaṃ yayau.
evaṃ ca vañcayitvā taṃ piśācaṃ mocitas tayā
duhitrā sa dvijas tasthau rog'|ôttīrṇo yathā|sukham.

6.2.185 itthaṃ piśācās tat|tulyā bālā rāja|sutāś ca ye
te siddhā apy an|arthāya, sakhi, rakṣyās tu buddhibhiḥ.
rāja|putryaḥ kulīnās tu n' âitādṛśyaḥ śrutāḥ kva|cit
ato 'nyathā na bhāvyaṃ te, sakhi, mat|saṃgataṃ prati.›

evaṃ Kaliṅgasenāyā mukhāc chrutvā yathā|kramam
sa|hāsa|citra|madhuraṃ toṣaṃ Somaprabhā yayau.
‹ito me ṣaṣṭi|yojanyāṃ gṛhaṃ yāti ca vāsaraḥ
ciraṃ sthit" âsmi tat, tanvi, yām' îty› etām uvāca ca.

tato 'sta|giri|śekharaṃ vrajati vāsar'|êśe śanaiḥ
sakhīṃ punar upāgamat praṇayinīṃ samāpṛcchya tām
kṣaṇaṃ janita|vismayā gagana|mārgam utpatya sā
jagāma vasatiṃ nijāṃ prasabham eva Somaprabhā.

spots : orifices. Once it has been flung open, no one can shut the *gateway to worldly existence : vagina,* from which *people : worlds* appear and into which they dissolve." After thinking this, in fear of being captured now that the successful accomplishment of his aims had been thwarted, the stupid *pishácha* ran off and disappeared. Once his daughter had delighted him by tricking the *pishácha* like this, the brahmin lived happily, freed from his disease.

That's how *pishácha*s are, and the young children of kings, 6.2.185
who, even when befriended, can bring about misfortune, are like them, but, my friend, one can use one's wits to keep them on side. But princesses from good families are never said to be like this, so you should not imagine otherwise about your relationship with me, my friend.'

When she heard this from Kalínga·sena's mouth, Soma·prabha attained a happiness that was colored in turn by laughter, wonder and delight, and she said to her, 'My house is sixty *yójana*s from here and the day is passing. I have been here for a long time, so, slender lady, I shall go.'

Then, as the sun slowly journeyed to the peak of the western mountain, Soma·prabha approached her friend once more and said goodbye to her. She caused astonishment by instantly flying up into the sky and then she went at great speed to her home.

6.2.190 vilokya ca tad adbhutaṃ bahu|vitarkam atyadbhutaṃ
pravišya samacintayat kila Kaliṅgasenā ca sā
‹na vedmi kim asāv aho mama sakhī hi siddh'|âṅganā
bhavet kim athav" âpsarāḥ kim athav" âpi vidyā|dharī.
divyā tāvad iyaṃ bhavaty a|vitathaṃ
vyom'|âgra|saṃcāriṇī
divyā yānti ca mānuṣībhir a|sama|
sneh'|āhṛtāḥ saṃgatim.
bheje kiṃ nṛpateḥ Pṛthos tanayayā
sakhyaṃ na s" Ârundhatī?
tat|prītyā Pṛthur ānināya Surabhiṃ
svargān na kiṃ bhū|tale?
tat|kṣīr'|âśanato na kiṃ punar asau
bhraṣṭo 'pi yāto divaṃ?
saṃbhūtāś ca tataḥ prabhṛty a|vikalā
gāvo na kiṃ bhū|tale?
tad dhany" âsmi śubh'|ôdayād upanatā
divyā sakh" îyaṃ mama
prātaś c' ânvaya|nāmanī su|nipuṇaṃ
prakṣyāmi tām āgatām.›
ity|ādi rāja|tanayā hṛdi cintayantī
tāṃ yāminīm anayad atra Kaliṅgasenā
Somaprabhā ca nija|veśmani bhūya eva
tad|darśan'|ôtsuka|manā rajanīṃ nināya.

iti mahā|kavi|śrī|Somadeva|bhaṭṭa|viracite Kathāsaritsāgare
Madanamañcukā|lambake dvitīyas taraṅgaḥ.

3

6.3.1 TATAḤ SOMAPRABHĀ prātas tad|vinod'|ôpapādinīm
nyasta|dāru|may'|ân|eka|māyā|sad|yantra|putrikām.

Kalínga·sena, when she saw this miracle, went inside thinking about it at length, and she said to herself in great amazement, 'Oh, I don't know whether that friend of mine is a *siddha* lady or an *ápsaras* or even a sorceress. But she travels through the upper atmosphere so she must be divine. Drawn by an unequal affection divine ladies can become friends with mortal women. Did not Arúndhati enjoy friendship with the daughter of King Prithu? As a result of her friendship, did not Prithu bring the cow Súrabhi from heaven to the earth? And from consuming her milk, did he not return to heaven despite having fallen from it? And were not healthy cows born on earth from then on? So I am blessed that through good luck this divine lady has become my friend. When she comes in the morning, I shall very delicately ask her her family and name.' 6.2.190

While princess Kalínga·sena was passing that night with these and other thoughts in her heart, Soma·prabha spent the night in her own house, eager to see her again.

Thus ends the second wave in the Mádana·mánchuka Attainment
in the "Ocean of the Rivers of Story" composed by the
glorious and learned great poet Soma·deva.

3

THE NEXT MORNING Soma·prabha, traveling through the sky, arrived once again at Kalínga·sena's house, bringing with her a basket in which she had put several fine mechan- 6.3.1

karaṇḍikāṃ samādāya sā nabhas|tala|cāriṇī
tasyāḥ Kaliṅgasenāyā nikaṭaṃ punar āyayau.
Kaliṅgasen" âpy ālokya tām ānand'|âśru|nirbharā
utthāya kaṇṭhe jagrāha pārśv'|āsīnām uvāca ca.
‹tvadīya|mukha|pūrṇ'|êndu|darśanena vinā, sakhi
tamo|mayī tri|yām" âdya śata|yām" êva me gatā.
6.3.5 taj janm'|ântara|saṃbandhaḥ kīdṛśaḥ syāt tvayā mama
yasy' âyaṃ pariṇāmo 'dya tvaṃ, devi, vetsi ced vada.›

tac chrutvā rāja|putrīṃ tām evaṃ Somaprabh" âbravīt
‹īdṛṅ me n' âsti vijñānaṃ na hi jātiṃ smarāmy aham.
na c' âtra munayo 'bhijñāḥ ke cit tu yadi jānate
taiḥ kṛtaṃ tādṛśaṃ pūrvaṃ para|tattva|vidaś ca te.›
evam uktavatīṃ bhūyaḥ prema|viśrambha|peśalam
Kaliṅgasenā papraccha vijane tāṃ sa|kautukā.
‹brūhi me, sakhi, kasy' êha deva|jāteḥ pitus tvayā
janman" âlaṃkṛto *vaṃśo* muktay" êva *su/vṛttayā*?
6.3.10 jagat|karṇ'|âmṛtaṃ kiṃ ca tava nāma, su|lakṣaṇe?
karaṇḍikā kim|arth" êyam asyām asti ca vastu kim?›

evaṃ Kaliṅgasenāyāḥ śrutvā sa|praṇayaṃ vacaḥ
Somaprabha sā sarvaṃ tat kramād vaktuṃ pracakrame.

ical magic dolls made of wood with which to amuse her. When Kalínga·sena saw her she got up, overflowing with tears of joy, embraced her, and, when Soma·prabha had sat next to her, said, 'Without a view of the full moon of your face, my friend, the dark night with its three watches that just passed seemed to me to take a hundred watches. What 6.3.5
must my relationship with you in a past life have been like to have resulted in this now? If you know, O goddess, then speak.'

When she heard this, Soma·prabha replied to the princess as follows: 'I do not have that sort of knowledge, for I cannot remember my past lives. Nor do the sages here have knowledge of it, but if anyone does know, they will have to have done something similar in the past and be acquainted with the ultimate reality.' After she had said this, Kalínga·sena, her voice tender with love and trust, eagerly questioned her some more in a private place. 'Tell me, my friend, who is the divine father here on earth whose *lineage : bamboo* you, being *well-behaved*, have adorned with your birth like a *perfectly round* pearl?* And, auspicious 6.3.10
lady, what is the nectar of immortality to the ears of the world, your name? What purpose has this basket and what is inside it?'

After hearing these affectionate words from Kalínga·sena, Soma·prabha started to tell her everything in the order in which it happened.

‹asti tri|jagati khyāto Mayo nāma mah"|âsuraḥ
āsuraṃ bhāvam utsṛjya Śauriṃ sa śaraṇaṃ śritaḥ.
tena datt'|â|bhayaś cakre sa ca vajra|bhṛtaḥ sabhām
daityāś ca deva|pakṣo 'yam iti taṃ prati cukrudhuḥ.
tad|bhayāt tena Vindhy'|âdrau māyā|vivara|mandiram
a|gamyam asur'|êndrāṇāṃ bahv|āścarya|mayaṃ kṛtam.
6.3.15 tasy' āvāṃ dve duhitarau Mayasya brahma|cāriṇī
jyeṣṭhā Svayaṃprabhā nāma kumārī tad|gṛha|sthitā.
ahaṃ Somaprabhā nāma kaniṣṭhā sā tv ahaṃ, sakhi
Nalakūbara|saṃjñāya dattā dhana|da|sūnave.
pitrā ca śikṣit" âsm' îha māyā|yantrāṇy an|ekadhā
tvat|prītyā c' êyam ānītā pūrṇā tava karaṇḍikā.›
ity uktv" âdarśayat tasyāḥ prodghāṭya bahu|kautukāḥ
Somaprabhā kāṣṭha|mayīḥ sva|māyā|yantra|putrikāḥ.
kīlik'|āhati|mātreṇa kā|cid gatvā vihāyasā
tad|ājñayā puṣpa|mālām ādāya drutam āyayau.
6.3.20 kā|cit tath" âiva pānīyam ānināya yadṛcchayā
kā|cin nanarta kā|cic ca kath"|ālāpam ath' âkarot.
ity|ādibhir mah"|āścaryaiḥ kaṃ|cit kālaṃ vinodya tām
su|rakṣitāṃ sthāpayitvā tāṃ ca yantra|karaṇḍikām
Kaliṅgasenām āmantrya s'|ôtkāṃ Somaprabhā tataḥ
yayau bhartṛ|parāyattā nabhasā nija|mandiram.
Kaliṅgasen" âpy āścarya|darśana|dhvastayā kṣudhā
prahṛṣṭā tad|ahas tasthau sarv'|āhāra|parāṅ|mukhī.
tad dṛṣṭvā ca tatas tasyā jananī roga|śaṅkinī

'There is a great *ásura* called Maya who is famous in the three worlds. He went against his *ásura* nature and approached Vishnu for protection. After Vishnu had granted him safety, he built a hall for Indra. The *ásuras*, thinking that he had sided the gods, were angry with him. In fear of them he built a most marvelous magical underground palace in the Vindhya hills, inaccessible to the *ásura* kings.
Maya has two daughters, myself and my elder sister, a celi- 6.3.15
bate maiden called Svayam·prabha who lives in his house. But I, my friend, the younger sister, called Soma·prabha, was given in marriage to a son of the lord of wealth called Nala·kúbara. My father has taught me how to make all sorts of magical machines and out of affection for you I have brought you this basket full of them.'

After saying this, Soma·prabha opened the basket and showed her the fascinating wooden mechanical dolls created by her magic. One of them, just at the push of a button, flew off and at her command quickly fetched a garland
of flowers. In the very same way one spontaneously fetched 6.3.20
some water. One danced and then one held a conversation. After amusing her for a while with these and other great marvels, she put down the basket of mechanical toys in a safe place, said goodbye to the wistful Kalínga·sena and then Soma·prabha, obedient to her husband, flew to her own house. After seeing this miracle, Kalínga·sena was so overjoyed that she lost her appetite and would not look at any food that day. On noticing this, her mother, worried that she was ill, had a doctor called Anánda look at her
and he pronounced her healthy. 'Something has made her 6.3.25

Ānand'|ākhyena bhiṣajā nirūpy' â|vikal'|ôditā.
6.3.25 ‹kuto 'pi hetor harṣeṇa naṣṭ" âsyāḥ kṣun na rogataḥ
utphulla|netraṃ vakty etad asyā hasad iv' ānanam.›
ity uktā bhiṣajā harṣa|hetuṃ taj|jananī ca sā
papraccha tāṃ yathā|vṛttaṃ s" âpi tasyai tad abravīt.
tataḥ ślāghya|sakhī|saṅga|hṛṣṭāṃ matv" âbhinandya ca
āhāraṃ kārayām āsa jananī tāṃ yath"|ôcitam.
ath' ânyedyur upāgatya vidit'|ârthā krameṇa sā
Kaliṅgasenāṃ tām eva rahaḥ Somaprabh" âbhyadhāt.
‹mayā tvat|sakhyam āvedya tvat|pārśv'|āgamane 'nvaham
anujñā jñānino bhartur gṛhītā vidit'|ârthataḥ.
6.3.30 tasmāt tvam apy anujñātā pitṛbhyāṃ bhava sāṃpratam
yena svairaṃ mayā sākaṃ niḥśaṅkā vihariṣyasi.›
evam uktavatīṃ haste tāṃ gṛhītv" âiva tat|kṣaṇam
Kaliṅgasenā sva|pitur mātuś ca nikaṭaṃ yayau.
tatra nām'|ânvay'|ākhyāna|pūrvaṃ c' âitām adarśayat
pitre Kaliṅgadattāya rājñe Somaprabhāṃ sakhīm.
mātre ca Tārādattāyai tath" âiv' âitām adarśayat
tau ca dṛṣṭvā yath"|ākhyānam enām abhinanandatuḥ.
ūcatuś c' ākṛti|prītau daṃpatī tāv ubhau tataḥ
sat|kṛtya duhitṛ|snehāt tāṃ mah'|âsura|sundarīm.
6.3.35 ‹vatse, Kaliṅgasen" êyaṃ haste tava samarpitā
tad idānīṃ yatha|kāmam ubhe viharatāṃ yuvām.›
etat tayor vaco dve c' âpy abhinandya nirīyatuḥ
samaṃ Kaliṅgasenā ca sā ca Somaprabhā tataḥ.

happy which is why she has lost her appetite—it's not because of an illness. Her face, which with its wide eyes looks to be laughing, gives it away.'

After the doctor said this to her, Kalínga·sena's mother asked her the reason for her joy and she told her what had happened. At this, thinking that she was happy because of her friendship with a praiseworthy friend, her mother was happy with her and had her eat some proper food.

Then on the next day Soma·prabha arrived and, having been told in turn what had happened, she said to Kalínga·sena in private, 'I have informed my wise husband that I am friends with you and have taken permission from him, having told him the truth, to come to you every day. So hence- 6.3.30
forth you too should get permission from your parents, so that you can play with me freely and without worry.'

After she had said this, Kalínga·sena immediately took her by the hand and went straight to her father and mother. There, after announcing her name and family, she introduced her friend Soma·prabha to her father, King Kalínga·datta. In the same way she then introduced her to her mother Tara·datta. On seeing that she was just as they had been told, her parents were delighted. Pleased by her appearance, the two of them then both said to the beautiful daughter of the great *ásura*, after welcoming her hospitably out of affection for their daughter, 'My child, we put this 6.3.35
girl Kalínga·sena in your care, so now you can both have as much fun together as you want.' Kalínga·sena and Soma·prabha rejoiced at these words from that couple and then left together. They went to play at a temple that the king

jagmatuś ca vihārāya vihāraṃ rāja|nirmitam
āninyatuś ca tāṃ tatra māyā|yantra|karaṇḍikām.
tato yantra|mayaṃ yakṣaṃ gṛhītvā prāhiṇot tadā
Somaprabhā sva|prayogād Buddh'|ârc'|ānayanāya sā.
sa yakṣo nabhasā gatvā dūram adhvānam āyayau
ādāya muktā|sad|ratna|hem'|âmbu|ruha|saṃcayam.
6.3.40 ten' âbhipūjya su|gatān bhāsayām āsa tatra sā
Somaprabhā sa|nilayān sarv'|āścarya|pradāyinaḥ.†
tad buddhv" āgatya dṛṣṭvā ca vismito mahiṣī|sakhaḥ
rājā Kaliṅgadattas tām apṛcchad yantra|ceṣṭitam.
tataḥ Somaprabh" âvadīd ‹rājann, etāny an|ekadhā
māyā|yantr'|ādi|śilpāni pitrā sṛṣṭāni me purā.
yathā c' êdaṃ jagad|yantraṃ pañca|bhūt'|ātmakaṃ tathā
yantrāṇy etāni sarvāṇi śṛṇu tāni pṛthak pṛthak.
pṛthvī|pradhānaṃ yantraṃ yad dvār'|ādi pidadhāti tat
pihitaṃ tena śaknoti na c' ôdghāṭayituṃ paraḥ.
6.3.45 ākāras toya|yantr'|ôtthaḥ sa|jīva iva dṛśyate
tejo|mayaṃ tu yad yantraṃ taj jvālāḥ parimuñcati.
vāta|yantraṃ ca kurute ceṣṭā gaty|āgam'|ādikāḥ
vyaktī|karoti c' ālāpaṃ yantram ākāśa|saṃbhavam.
mayā c' âitāny avāptāni tātāt kiṃ tv amṛtasya yat
rakṣakaṃ cakra|yantraṃ tat tāto jānāti n' âparaḥ.›
iti tasyā vadantyās tad|vacaḥ śraddadhatām iva
madhy'|âhne pūryamāṇānāṃ śaṅkhānām udabhūd dhvaniḥ.
tataḥ sv'|ôcitam āhāraṃ dātuṃ vijñāpya taṃ nṛpam
prāpy' ânujñāṃ vimāne tāṃ s'|ânugāṃ yantra|nirmite.
6.3.50 Kaliṅgasenām ādāya pratasthe gaganena sā
Somaprabhā pitṛ|gṛhaṃ jyeṣṭhāyāḥ svasur antikam.

had built, taking there with them the basket of magical machines. Then Soma·prabha took hold of a mechanical *yaksha* and using her magic sent it off to fetch materials for worshipping the Buddhas. The *yaksha* quickly flew a long way and returned with a collection of pearls, fine jewels,
gold and lotuses. After using it to worship them, she made 6.3.40
the Buddhas, those producers of all marvels, appear there together with their residences. When he heard about this, and came and saw it with his queen, the astonished King Kalínga·datta asked her how the machines worked. Soma·prabha answered, 'King, these various magical machines and other artifacts were made by my father long ago. Just as this machine the world is made of five elements, so are all these machines. Listen to them described individually.

The machine whose main constituent is earth closes doors
and so forth. Nothing else can open what it has closed. The 6.3.45
figures produced by the water machine appear to be alive, while the machine which consists of fire gives off flames. The wind machine produces motion, such as going or coming, and the machine which is made from ether talks. I obtained these machines from my father, but he and no one else understands the wheel machine which protects the nectar of immortality.'

As she was saying this, the sound of conches being blown was heard in the middle of the day, as if lending credence
to her words. Then Soma·prabha asked the king to give 6.3.50
her some food that she liked, after which, with permission, she took Kalínga·sena and her companions and set forth for her father's house through the sky in a flying machine to see her elder sister. In an instant she reached

kṣaṇāc ca prāpya Vindhy'|âdri|varti tat|pitṛ|mandiram
tasyāḥ Svayaṃprabhāyāś ca pārśvaṃ tām anayat svasuḥ.
tatr' âpaśyaj jaṭā|jūṭa|mālinīṃ tāṃ Svayaṃprabhām
Kaliṅgasenā lamb'|âkṣa|mālāṃ sā brahma|cāriṇīm.
su|sit'|âmbara|saṃvītāṃ hasantīm iva Pārvatīm
kāma|bhoga|mahā|bhoga|gṛhīt'|ôgra|tapaḥ|kriyām.
s" âpi Somaprabh"|ākhyātāṃ praṇatāṃ tāṃ nṛp'|ātma|jām
Svayaṃprabhā kṛt'|ātithyā saṃvibheje phal'|âśanaiḥ.
6.3.55 ‹sakhi, bhuktaiḥ phalair etair jarā te na bhaviṣyati
vināśiny asya rūpasya padmasy' êva him'|āhatiḥ.
etad|artham iha snehād ānītā bhavatī mayā.›
iti Somaprabhā c' âitāṃ rāja|putrīm abhāṣata.
tataḥ Kaliṅgasen' âtra tāny abhuṅkta phalāni sā
sadyo 'mṛta|ras'|āsāra|sikt'|âṅg" îva babhūva ca.

dadarśa ca pur'|ôdyānaṃ bhramantī tatra kautukāt
sa|suvarṇ'|âbja|vāpīkaṃ sudhā|svādu|phala|drumam.
haima|citra|khag'|ākīṛṇaṃ san|maṇi|stambha|vibhramam
bhitti|buddhi|karaṃ śūnye bhittau śūnya|pratīti|dam.
6.3.60 jale sthala|dhiyaṃ kurvat sthale ca jala|buddhi|kṛt
lok'|ântaram iv' â|pūrvaṃ Maya|māyā|vinirmitam.
praviṣṭa|pūrvaṃ plava|gaiḥ purā Sītā|gaveṣibhiḥ
Svayaṃprabhā|prasādena cirāt saṃprāpta|nirgamaiḥ.

her father's house in the Vindhya hills and took Kalínga·sena to her sister Svayam·prabha. Kalínga·sena saw Svayam·prabha there garlanded with a mass of matted locks and a long rosary, a chaste nun wearing a bright white robe, who seemed to be mocking Párvati, her fearsome ascetic practices having taken away the great pleasure, the pleasure of love. When Soma·prabha introduced the bowing princess to her, Svayam·prabha welcomed her hospitably and gave
her some fruit to eat. 'My friend, by eating these fruits, old 6.3.55
age, which would destroy your beauty as snowfall does that of the lotus, will not affect you. I love you so much that this is why I brought you here,' said Soma·prabha to the princess. At this Kalínga·sena ate the fruits there and it was as if her body had suddenly been showered with the nectar of immortality.

Wandering about that place out of curiosity, she came across the city park, which had tanks containing golden lotus flowers and trees with fruits as delicious as nectar. It was full of golden and brightly colored birds and looked as if it contained columns of fine jewels. In the open spaces it gave the impression of walls and in the walls it made one think
of open spaces. In the water it suggested land and on land it 6.3.60
gave the impression of water. It was like some strange other world, created by Maya's magic. It had already been entered long ago by monkeys searching for Sita, who after an age found a way out thanks to Svayam·prabha.

tatas tad|adbhuta|pura|prakām'|āloka|vismitām
a|jarā|bhājanī|bhūtāṃ tām āpṛcchya Svayaṃprabhā.†
Kaliṅgasenām āropya yantre bhūyo vihāyasā
Somaprabhā Takṣaśilām ānināya sva|mandiram.
tatra sā tad yathā|vastu pitroḥ sarvam avarṇayat
Kaliṅgasenā tau c' âpi paraṃ saṃtoṣam īyatuḥ.
6.3.65 itthaṃ tayor dvayoḥ sakhyor gacchatsu divaseṣv atha
ūce Kaliṅgasenāṃ tām evaṃ Somaprabh" âikadā.
‹yāvan na pariṇītā tvaṃ tāvat sakhyaṃ mama tvayā
tvad|bhartṛ|bhavane paścān mama syād āgamaḥ kutaḥ.
na dṛśyo hi sakhī|bhartā n' âṅgī|kāryaḥ kathaṃ|cana
aver vṛk" îva snuṣāyāḥ śvaśrūr māṃsāni khādati.
tathā ca śṛṇu vacmy etāṃ Kīrtisenā|kathāṃ tava
[- - - - - - - - - - - - - - - -]*

pure Pāṭaliputr'|ākhye dhuryo dhanavatāṃ vaṇik
nāmnā yath"|ârthena purā Dhanapālita ity abhūt.
6.3.70 Kīrtisen"|âbhidhānā ca tasy' âjāyata kanyakā
rūpeṇ' ân|anya|sadṛśī prāṇebhyo 'py adhika|priyā.
sā ca tena samānāya Magadheṣu maha'|rddhaye
Devasen'|âbhidhānāya datt" âbhūd vaṇije sutā.
tasya c' âti|su|vṛttasya Devasenasya durjanī
vipanna|janakasy' āsīj jananī svāminī gṛhe.
sā snuṣāṃ Kīrtisenāṃ tāṃ paśyantī pati|saṃmatām
krudhā jvalantī putrasya parokṣam akadarthayat.
Kīrtisenā ca sā patyur vaktuṃ n' âiva śaśāka tat
kaṣṭā hi kuṭila|śvaśrū|para|tantra|vadhū|sthitiḥ.

Then Soma·prabha said goodbye to Svayam·prabha, who was astonished at seeing the delights of that amazing city and had received the gift of not growing old, and put her on the flying machine before taking her back through the sky to her palace in Taksha·shila. There Kalínga·sena told her parents everything just as it had happened, and they were delighted.

While the days were passing in this way for the two 6.3.65
friends, one day Soma·prabha said to Kalínga·sena, "I shall be your friend until you are married. After that I will not be able to come to your husband's house. For the husband of a friend is not to be seen and never to be made a friend. A mother-in-law eats the flesh of a daughter-in-law like a she-wolf eats that of a sheep. Just listen to the story of Kirti·sena which I am going to tell you.

Long ago there lived in the city of Pátali·putra a merchant who, since he was the richest of rich men, was appropriately called Dhana·pálita, "Protected by wealth." A 6.3.70
daughter called Kirti·sena was born to him. She was unrivaled in beauty and dearer to him than life. She was given in marriage by him to a very rich merchant called Deva·sena, who was of equal standing in Mágadha. He was extremely virtuous but his father was dead and his mother, the mistress of the house, was an evil woman. She, seeing that her daughter-in-law Kirti·sena was held in high esteem by her husband, was on fire with anger and mistreated her behind her son's back. Kirti·sena, however, was unable to tell her husband about it, for difficult is the lot of a bride subject to a deceitful mother-in-law.

6.3.75 ekadā sa patis tasyā Devaseno vaṇijyayā
gantuṃ pravavṛte bandhu|prerito Valabhīṃ purīm.
tataḥ sā Kīrtisenā taṃ patim evam abhāṣata
«iyac ciraṃ mayā n' âitad, ārya|putra, tav' ôditam.
kadarthayati mām eṣā tav' âmbā tvayy api sthite
tvayi tu proṣite kiṃ me kuryād iti na vedmy aham.»
tac chrutvā sa samudbhrāntas tat|snehāt sa|bhayaḥ śanaiḥ
Devasenas tadā gatvā mātaraṃ praṇato 'bravīt.
«Kīrtisen" âdhunā haste tav,' âmba, prasthitasya me
n' âsyā niḥsnehatā kāryā kulīna|tanayā hy asau.»
6.3.80 tac chrutvā Kīrtisenāṃ tām āhūy' ôdvartit'|ēkṣaṇā
taṃ Devasenaṃ mātā sā tat|kālaṃ samabhāṣata.
«kṛtaṃ mayā kiṃ pṛcch' âitām evaṃ tvāṃ prerayaty asau.
gṛha|bheda|karī, putra, mama tu dvau yuvāṃ samau.»
śrutv" âitac chānta|citto 'bhūt tat|kṛte sa vaṇig|varaḥ
vyāja|sa|praṇayair vākyair jananyā ko† na vañcyate?
Kīrtisenā tu sā tūṣṇīm āsīd udvega|sa|smitā
Devasenas tu so 'nyedyuḥ pratasthe Valabhīṃ vaṇik.
tatas tad|viraha|kleśa|juṣas tasyāḥ krameṇa sā
tan|mātā Kīrtisenāyā dāsīḥ pārśvān nyavārayat.
6.3.85 kṛtvā ca gṛha|cāriṇyā sva|ceṭyā saha saṃvidam
ānāyy' âbhyantaraṃ guptaṃ tāṃ vivastrāṃ cakāra sā.
«pāpe! harasi me putram ity!» uktvā sa|kaca|graham
pādair dantair nakhaiś c' âitāṃ ceṭyā samam apāṭayat.
cikṣepa c' âināṃ bhū|gehe sa|pidhāne dṛḍh'|ârgale
tatratye 'bhyuddhṛt'|â|śeṣa|pūrva|jāt'|ârtha|saṃcaye.

One day her husband, on the instructions of his relatives, was about to go to the city of Válabhi on business, so Kirti·sena said to him, "For a long time, my noble lord, I have not told you this. Your mother mistreats me even when you are present. What she will do to me while you are away, I do not know." When he heard this, Deva·sena was upset. Out of affection for his wife, he then slowly and fearfully went to his mother and humbly said, "Mother, Kirti·sena is in your hands now that I am going away. She is not to be treated unlovingly, for she is a girl of good family." 6.3.75

On hearing this, his mother rolled her eyes, summoned Kirti·sena and straightaway said to Deva·sena, "Ask her what I have done. The girl is going to split up this house and this is how she eggs you on, my son, but in my eyes the two of you are the same." 6.3.80

When he heard this, that fine merchant stopped worrying on his wife's behalf. Who would not be deceived by falsely affectionate words from his mother? Kirti·sena, however, stayed quiet, wearing a puzzled smile, and the merchant Deva·sena set out for Válabhi the next day. Then his mother one by one stopped the servant girls from attending to Kirti·sena, who was feeling sorrow at being separated
from him. After hatching a plan with her own maidservant, 6.3.85
she secretly had her brought inside and stripped her. "You wicked girl! You are stealing my son from me!" Saying this, she and the servant girl pulled her hair and tore at her with kicks, bites and scratches. Then she threw her into a cellar with a door that had a strong bolt, having removed all the things that had been in it before. At the end of each day, that evil woman would put half a plate of food in there for

nyadhāc ca tasyās tatr' ântaḥ pratyahaṃ sā din'|âtyaye
pāpā tādṛg|avasthāyā bhaktasy' ârdha|śarāvakam.
acintayac ca «‹dūra|sthe patyāv evaṃ mṛtā svayam
imāṃ vyutthāpya yāt' êti› vakṣyāmi divasair iti.»

6.3.90 itthaṃ bhūmi|gṛhe kṣiptā śvaśrvā pāpa|kṛtā tayā
sukh'|ārhā rudatī tatra Kīrtisenā vyacintayat.
«āḍhyaḥ patiḥ kule janma saubhāgyaṃ sādhu|vṛttatā
tad apy aho mama śvaśrū|prasādād īdṛśī vipat.
etad|arthaṃ ca nindanti kanyānāṃ janma bāndhavāḥ
śvaśrū|nanāndṛ|saṃtrāsam a|saubhāgy'|ādi|dūṣitam.»
iti śocanty a|kasmāt sā Kīrtisenā khanitrakam
lebhe 'smād bhū|gṛhād dhātrā manaḥ śalyam iv' ôddhṛtam.
ayo|mayena ten' âtra suruṅgāṃ nicakhāna sā
tāvad yāvat tay" ôttasthe daivāt svād vāsa|veśmanaḥ.

6.3.95 dadarśa ca pradīpena prāktanen' âtha tad|gṛham
a|kṣīṇena kṛt'|ālokā dharmeṇ' êva nijena sā.
ādāy' âtaś ca vastrāṇi svaṃ svarṇaṃ ca niśā|kṣaye
nirgaty' âiva tato guptaṃ jagāma nagarād bahiḥ.
«evaṃ|vidhāyā gantuṃ me na yuktaṃ pitṛ|veśmani
kiṃ vakṣye tatra lokaś ca pratyeṣyati kathaṃ mama?
ataḥ sva|yuktyā gantavyaṃ patyur ev' ântikaṃ mayā
ihāmutra ca sādhvīnāṃ patir ekā gatir yataḥ.»

her while she was in that state and she said to herself, "I shall announce in a few days that with her husband far away she died spontaneously, and then ask for her body to be taken away."

Having been thrown into the cellar in this fashion by 6.3.90
her wicked mother-in-law, Kirti·sena, who deserved happiness, sobbed as she said to herself, "My husband is rich, I was born into a good family, and I am attractive and well-behaved, nevertheless look at the disaster that has befallen me thanks to my mother-in-law. This is why relatives hate the birth of a daughter: with the attendant fear of mothers- and sisters-in-law it is stained with unhappiness and other difficulties."

While lamenting thus, Kirti·sena suddenly found a small spade in the cellar and it was as if the creator had extracted a needle from her heart. The spade was made of iron and she used it to dig a tunnel there until, as fate would have it, she
appeared in her own bedroom. Then, using an old lamp to 6.3.95
cast light as if it were her intact virtue, she looked about the house. She took from there her clothes and her gold, and at the end of the night she emerged from the house and went straight out of the city in secret.

"It would not be right for me to go to my father's house like this. What would I say there and how could the people trust me? So I must use my wits to find my husband, because in this world and the next for virtuous women their husband is their only refuge."

ity ālocya cakār' âtra taḍāg'|âmbu|kṛt'|āplavā
rāja|putrasya veṣaṃ sā Kīrtisenā su|bṛṃhitam.
6.3.100 tato gatv" āpaṇe dattvā kiṃ|cin mūlyena kāñcanam
kasy' âpi vaṇijo gehe dine tasminn uvāsa sā.

anyedyus tatra cakre ca Valabhīṃ gantum icchatā
Samudrasena|nāmnā sā vaṇijā saha saṃstavam.
tena sākaṃ sa|bhṛtyena prāptuṃ prāk|prasthitaṃ patim
sad|rāja|putra|veṣā sā pratasthe Valabhīṃ prati.
jagāda taṃ ca vaṇijaṃ «gotra|jair asmi bādhitaḥ
tat tvayā saha gacchāmi Valabhīṃ sva|jan'|ântikam.»

tac chrutvā sa vaṇik|putro mārge paryacarac ca tām
«rāja|putro dhruvaṃ bhavyaḥ ko 'py asāv iti» gauravāt.
6.3.105 yayau ca sa vaṇik|sārthaḥ puraskṛty' âṭavī|patham
bahu|śulka|bhaya|tyakta|mārg'|ântara|jan'|āśritam.
dinaiḥ prāpy' âṭavī|dvāraṃ sāyaṃ sārthe kṛta|sthitau
cakre kṛt'|ânta|dūt" îva śabdaṃ bhaya|karaṃ śivā.
tad|abhijñe vaṇig|loke caur'|âdy|āpāta|śaṅkini
haste gṛhīta|śastreṣu sarvato ripu|rakṣiṣu.
dhvānte dhāvati dasyūnām agra|yāyi|bal'|ôpame
Kīrtisenā tad ālokya puṃ|veṣā sā vyacintayat.
«aho duṣkṛtināṃ karma saṃtānen' âiva vardhate
paśya śvaśrū|kṛtā vyāpad ih' âpi phalitā mama.
6.3.110 prathamaṃ mṛtyun" êv' âhaṃ śvaśrū|kopena bhakṣitā
praviṣṭā bhū|gṛhaṃ paścād garbha|vāsam iv' âparam.
daivāt tato 'pi niṣkrāntā jāt" êva punar apy aham

After thinking this, Kirti·sena bathed in the water of a tank there and dressed herself in the sumptuous clothes of a prince. Then she went and exchanged some gold for money 6.3.100
in the market and stayed that day in the house of some merchant or other.

On the next day she made the acquaintance of a merchant called Samúdra·sena who wanted to go to Válabhi. In order to find her husband, who had set forth previously, she set out for Válabhi with that man and his servants in her splendid guise as a prince. She said to the merchant, "I have been harassed by my relatives, so I shall go with you to my family in Válabhi."

When he heard this the merchant's son, thinking that she must be some noble prince, respectfully attended to her on the way. The trading caravan followed a forest track to 6.3.105
which people resorted after leaving the other road in fear of the heavy duties. After a few days they reached the gateway to the forest and in the evening when the caravan had halted, a jackal, as if it were a harbinger of death, gave a terrifying howl. Recognizing it for what it was, the merchants feared an attack by bandits or such like, and the guards on all sides drew their weapons. With darkness coming on as fast as the vanguard of the robbers, Kirti·sena, in her guise as a man, saw this and said to herself, "Oh the actions of those who do bad increase with their descendants! See how the calamity imposed on me by my mother-in-law has borne fruit here too! First I was eaten up by my mother-in-law's 6.3.110
anger as if by death, then I entered the cellar as if it were another womb. Then by chance I escaped from there as if being reborn and now having come here my life is once more

ih' âdy' āgatya saṃprāptā bhūyo jīvita|saṃśayam.
caurair yadi hat" âsm' îha tac chvaśrūr mama vairiṇī
any'|āsaktā gatā kv'|âp' îty abhidhāsyati me patim.
str" îti jñāt" âsmi ken' âpi hṛta|vastr" ântarā yadi
tato mṛtyur mama śreyān na punaḥ śīla|viplavaḥ.
tena c' ātm" âiva me rakṣyo n' âpekṣyo 'yaṃ suhṛd vaṇik
satī|dharmo hi su|strīṇāṃ cintyo na suhṛd|ādayaḥ.»

6.3.115 iti niścitya sā prāpa cinvatī taru|madhya|gam
gartaṃ gṛh'|ākṛtiṃ dattaṃ kṛpay" êv' ântaraṃ bhuvā.
tatra praviśya c' ācchādya tṛṇa|parṇ'|ādibhis tanum
tasthau saṃdhāryamāṇā sā pati|saṃgama|vāñchayā.
tato niśīthe sahasā nipaty' âiv' ôdyat'|āyudhā
caura|senā su|mahatī sārthaṃ veṣṭayati† sma tam.
ninadad|dasyu|kāl'|âbhraṃ śastra|jvāl'|â|cira|prabham
tataḥ sa|rudhirā|sāraṃ tatr' âbhūd yuddha|durdinam.
hatvā Samudrasenaṃ ca s'|ânugaṃ taṃ vaṇik|patim
balino 'tha yayuś caurā gṛhīta|dhana|saṃcayāḥ.

6.3.120 tadā ca Kīrtisenā sā śruta|kolāhalā balāt
yan na mukt'|āsubhis tatra kāraṇaṃ kevalo vidhiḥ.

tato niśāyāṃ yātāyām udite tigma|tejasi
nirjagāma ca sā tasmād gartād viṭapa|madhyataḥ.
kāmaṃ bhartṛ|eka|bhaktānām a|viskhalita|tejasām
devatā eva sādhvīnāṃ trāṇam āpadi kurvate.
yat tatra nirjane 'raṇye siṃho dṛṣṭv" âpi tāṃ jahau
na paraṃ yāvad abhyetya kutaś|cit ko 'pi tāpasaḥ.

in peril. If the bandits kill me here, my hateful mother-in-law will tell my husband that I ran off with someone else. Meanwhile, if someone takes my clothes and I am discovered to be a woman, then it would be better for me to die than to have my virtue violated. So I must save myself and not look out for my friend the merchant here, for good women should observe the duties of the virtuous wife, not worry about their people like their friends."

After deciding this, she looked about and found in a tree 6.3.115
a hollow the shape of a house, as if the earth had taken pity and presented her with a chance. She went in there, concealed her body with grass, leaves and other foliage, and waited, sustained by the hope of being reunited with her husband. Then in the middle of the night a huge bandit army suddenly fell upon the caravan, weapons at the ready, and surrounded it. There followed a tempestuous battle, the roaring robbers its black thunder clouds, swords its flashes of lightning and blood its downpours. Then the mighty bandits killed Samúdra·sena, the head merchant, and his
followers, took all the valuables and went away. During the 6.3.120
fight Kirti·sena was forced to hear the clamor and only destiny can be responsible for her not breathing her last.

When the night was over and the sun had risen, she came out from the hole in the middle of the tree. It must surely be the gods who rescue virtuous women who are solely devoted to their husbands and do not let their dignity falter when they are in distress, because in that lonely wilderness not only did a lion see her and leave her alone, but some ascetic appeared from somewhere, asked her what had happened, comforted her, gave her a drink of water from his

pṛṣṭ'|ôdantāṃ samāśvāsya jala|pānaṃ kamaṇḍaloḥ
dattv" ôpadiśya panthānaṃ tasyāḥ kv' âpi tiro|dadhe.
6.3.125 tatas tṛpt" âmṛten' êva kṣut|pipāsā|vinā|kṛtā
tāpas'|ôktena mārgeṇa pratasthe sā pati|vratā.
ath' âsta|śikhar'|ārūḍhaṃ prasārita|karaṃ ravim
«rātrim ekāṃ kṣamasv' êti» vadantam iva vīkṣya sā.
mahato 'raṇya|vṛkṣasya gṛh'|ābhaṃ mūla|koṭaram
viveśa pidadhe c' âsya dvāram anyena dāruṇā.

pradoṣe ca dadarś' âtra dvāra|cchidr'|ântareṇa sā
rākṣasīm āgatāṃ ghorāṃ bālakair anvitāṃ sutaiḥ.
tīrṇ" ânya|vipad ady' âham anayā bhakṣit" êti sā
trastā yāvat tarau tāvad ārūḍhā tatra rākṣasī.
6.3.130 anvārūḍhāś ca tat|putrās tatra tāṃ kila rākṣasīm
abruvann «amba, naḥ kiṃ|cid bhakṣyaṃ deh' îti» tat|kṣaṇam.

tataḥ sā rākṣasī bālāṃs tān uvāc' «âdya, putrakāḥ,
mahā|śmaśānaṃ gatv" âpi bhakṣyaṃ n' āsāditaṃ mayā.
yācito ḍākinī|saṃgho 'py atra bhāgam adān na me
tat|khedād atha vijñapya yācito Bhairavo mayā.
sa ca nām'|ânvayau pṛṣṭvā devo mām evam ādiśat
‹bhayaṃkari, kulīn" âsi Khara|Dūṣaṇa|vaṃśa|jā.
tad ito n' âti|dūra|sthaṃ Vasudatta|puraṃ vraja
tatr' āste Vasudatt'|ākhyo rājā dharma|paro mahān.
6.3.135 yaḥ kṛtsnām aṭavīm etāṃ paryanta|stho 'bhirakṣati
svayaṃ gṛhṇāti śulkaṃ ca nigṛhṇāti ca taskarān.
tasy' âṭavyāṃ ca mṛgayā|śrama|suptasya bhū|pateḥ
a|jñāt" âiva praviṣṭ" ântaḥ karṇe śata|padī laghu.

pot, showed her the way and then vanished. After that, freed 6.3.125
from hunger and thirst as if she had drunk her fill of the nectar of immortality, that virtuous wife set forth along the road that the ascetic had told her about. Then after seeing the sun spreading its rays on top of the western mountain as if telling her to wait for a night, she went into a hollow that was like a house in the roots of a large tree in the forest and concealed its opening with another piece of wood.

In the morning she saw through a hole in the door that a terrifying *rákshasi* had come there with her young children. While she was worrying that having escaped from a different disaster she was now going to be eaten by the *rákshasi*,
the *rákshasi* climbed the tree there. Her children climbed 6.3.130
up after her and once there it seems they immediately said to the *rákshasi*, "Mother, give us something to eat."

The *rákshasi* replied, "Children, today I went to the great burning ground but I did not find anything to eat. Even when I asked a group of witches there, they wouldn't give me a share. Upset by this, I then addressed Bháirava and asked him. That god asked me my name and family and then instructed me thus: 'O terrifying one, born of the lineage of Khara and Dúshana, you are from a good family. So go from here to the city of Vasu·datta, which is not far from
here. A great and pious king called Vasu·datta lives there, on 6.3.135
the edge of this forest, and he protects it all. He personally collects duties and punishes robbers. When the king was in the forest, sleeping off the fatigue of the chase, a centipede slipped into his ear unnoticed. In time it produced lots of offspring inside the ear, and from the resulting illness the king's muscles have now withered. His doctors do not know

sā ca kālena bahuśaḥ prasūt" âsya śiro|'ntare
tena rogeṇa rāj" âsau snāyu|śeṣo 'dya vartate.
vaidyāś c' âsya na taṃ vyādhiṃ vidanty anyo 'pi ko 'pi cet
na jñāsyati tataś c' âiṣa dinair alpair vipatsyate.
tasya māṃsāni bhuñjīthā vipannasya sva|māyayā
bhakṣitais tarhi ṣaṇ|māsān paritṛptā bhaviṣyasi.›
6.3.140 itthaṃ me Bhairaveṇ' âpi saṃvibhāgaḥ sa|saṃśayaḥ
kālavāṃś c' âdya vihitas. tat, putrāḥ, kiṃ karomy aham?»
evaṃ tay" ôktā rākṣasyā putrās te tām ath' âbruvan
«jñāt'|âpanīte roge 'smin kiṃ sa rāj," âmba, jīvati?
kathaṃ ca tādṛśo rogo vada tasy' âpanīyate.»
evam uktavatas tān sā tanayān rākṣasī jagau.
«jñāt'|âpanīte roge 'smiñ jīvaty eva sa bhū|patiḥ
śrūyatāṃ ca yathā so 'sya mahā|rogo 'panīyate.
śiraḥ pūrvaṃ ghṛt'|âbhyaktaṃ tasya nyast'|ôṣṇa|sarpiṣā
kṛtvā madhy'|âhna|kaṭhine sthāpitasy' ātape ciram.
6.3.145 niveśya karṇa|kuhare suṣirāṃ vaṃśa|nāḍikām
śīt'|âmbu|ghaṭa|pṛṣṭha|stha|śarāva|cchidra|saṅginīm.
tena sved'|ātapa|klāntā nirgaty' âsya śiro|'ntarāt
karṇa|randhreṇa ten' âiva vaṃśa|nāḍīṃ praviśya tām.
ghaṭe śīt'|âbhilāṣiṇyaḥ śata|padyaḥ patanti tāḥ
evaṃ sa nṛ|patis tasmān mahā|rogād vimucyate.»
ity uktvā rākṣasī putrān vṛkṣa|sthān virarāma sā
Kīrtisenā ca tat sarvam aśṛṇot koṭara|sthitā.
śrutvā ca cintayām āsa «nistariṣyāmi ced itaḥ
tad gatv" âiv' âitayā yuktyā jīvayiṣyāmi taṃ nṛpam.
6.3.150 etām ev' âṭavīṃ so 'lpa|śulkaḥ prānta|sthito 'vati
tat saukaryāc ca vaṇijaḥ sarve yānty amunā pathā.

what the illness is and if no one else recognizes it he will die within a few days. When he is dead you should use your magic to eat his flesh. By eating it you shall be satisfied for six months.'

Bháirava has thus today apportioned food for me that 6.3.140
may not be available and, if it is, will take time to get. So, children, what am I to do?"

After the *rákshasi* had said this to them, her children replied, "Mother, if the illness is diagnosed and cured, will the king survive? And tell us, how can such a disease as his be cured?"

Questioned thus, the *rákshasi* said to her children, "If this disease is diagnosed and cured, the king is sure to survive. Hear how this serious illness of his is cured. After his head has been anointed by having warm ghee put on it, he is to
be put in the harsh midday heat for a long time. Then a 6.3.145
bamboo tube is to be inserted into the opening in his ear. The tube goes to a hole in a plate on the top of a pot of cold water. Distressed by the heat and the sweat, the centipedes will come out from inside his head through that opening in his ear and go into the bamboo tube. In their desire to cool down, they will jump into the pot. In this way the king will be freed from that serious illness."

The *rákshasi* told this to her children in the tree and then fell quiet. Kirti·sena heard it all while in the hollow and having heard it, she said to herself, "If I escape from here, then I shall go straightaway and use this stratagem to revive the
king. He lives on the edge of this forest and guards it, taking 6.3.150
small taxes, so all the merchants go this way because it is convenient. The merchant Samúdra·sena, who has gone to

etat Samudraseno 'pi svar|gāmī so 'bravīd vaṇik
tad eten' âiva mārgeṇa sa me bhart" āgamiṣyati.
ato gatv" âṭavī|prānte Vasudatta|pure nṛpam
rogād uttārya tatra|sthā pratīkṣe bhartur āgamam.»
evaṃ vicintayantī sā kṛcchrāt tām anayan niśām
prātar naṣṭeṣu rakṣaḥsu niragāt koṭarāt tataḥ.
kramāt tato 'ṭavī|madhye yāntī puruṣa|veṣa|bhṛt
prāpte 'par'|âhṇe gopālam ekaṃ sādhuṃ dadarśa sā.
6.3.155 tat|saukumārya|dūr'|âdhva|darśan'|ârdrī|kṛtaṃ ca tam
papracch' ôpetya sā «ko 'yaṃ pradeśaḥ? kathyatām iti.»
so 'pi gopālako 'vādīd «Vasudattasya bhū|pateḥ
Vasudattapuraṃ nāma puram etat puraḥ sthitam.
rāj" âpi sa mah"|ātm" âtra mumūrṣur vyādhitaḥ sthitaḥ»
tac chrutvā Kīrtisenā taṃ gopālakam abhāṣata.
«yadi māṃ nayate kaś|cid rājñas tasy' ântikaṃ tataḥ
ahaṃ taṃ tasya jānāmi nivārayitum āmayam.»
tac chrutv" âiv' âvadad gopaḥ
«pure 'tr' âiva vrajāmy aham
tad āyāhi mayā sākaṃ
yāvad yatnaṃ karomi te.»
6.3.160 «tath" êty» uktavatīṃ tāṃ ca Kīrtisenāṃ tad" âiva saḥ
Vasudatta|puraṃ gopaḥ puṃ|veṣāṃ nayati sma tām.
tac ca tatra tathā vastu nivedy' ārtāya tat|kṣaṇāt
pratīhārāya kalyāṇa|lakṣaṇāṃ tāṃ samarpayat.
pratīhāro 'pi rājānaṃ vijñapy' âiva tad|ājñayā
praveśayām āsa sa tāṃ tasy' ântikam a|ninditām.
rājā ca so 'tra rog'|ārtas tāṃ dṛṣṭv" âiv' âdbhut'|ākṛtim

heaven, told me this, and it means my husband will return by this very road, so I shall go to the city of Vasu·datta on the edge of the forest, cure the king of the disease and await my husband's arrival there."

Deep in these thoughts, she struggled to get through that night. In the morning, when all the *rákshasas* had disappeared, she came out from the hole. In the afternoon, as she was traveling along through the forest in her disguise as a
man, she came across a lone kind cowherd. Seeing how del- 6.3.155
icate she was and that she had come a long way, he felt pity for her, and when she approached him and asked him to tell her what country they were in, the cowherd said, "The city of King Vasu·datta, which is called Vasu·datta lies here ahead and the noble king there is on the point of death from an illness."

When she heard this, Kirti·sena said to the cowherd, "If someone takes me to the king, then I can cure his disease."

The cowherd immediately replied, "I am going to that
very city, so come with me and I shall help you." Kirti· 6.3.160
sena agreed and the cowherd led her, disguised as a man, straight to the city of Vasu·datta. As soon as they arrived he told a distressed chamberlain what she had said and presented that auspiciously marked lady to him. No sooner had the chamberlain informed the king than the virtuous lady was brought in to him at his command. The moment the disease-stricken King Vasu·datta saw her there with her amazing appearance, he cheered up. The soul knows what is good for it and what isn't. He said to her in her guise as a man, "If you cure this disease, I shall give you half this

āśvasto Vasudatto 'bhūd vetty ātm" âiva hit'|āhitam.
uvāca c' âitāṃ puṃ|veṣāṃ «yad' îmām apaneṣyasi
rujam etat pradāsyāmi rājy'|ârdhaṃ te, su|lakṣaṇa.
6.3.165 jāne jahāra pṛṣṭhān me svapne strī kṛṣṇa|kambalam
tan niścitam imaṃ rogaṃ hariṣyati bhavān mama.»
tac chrutvā Kīrtisenā taṃ jagād' «âdya dinaṃ gatam
deva, śvas te 'paneṣyāmi rogaṃ mā sm' â|dhṛtiṃ kṛthāḥ.»
ity uktvā mūrdhni rājño 'sya gavyaṃ ghṛtam adāpayat
tena tasy' āyayau nidrā yayau sā c' âti|vedanā.
«bhiṣag|rūpeṇa devo 'yaṃ puṇyair naḥ ko 'py upāgataḥ»
iti tatra ca tāṃ sarve Kīrtisenāṃ tato 'stuvan.
mahādevī ca tais tais tām upacārair upācarat
naktaṃ veśma pṛthak c' âsyāḥ sa|dāsīkam akalpayat.
6.3.170 ath' âparedyur madhy'|âhne mantriṣv antaḥ|pureṣu ca
paśyatsu tasya bhūpasya Kīrtisenā cakarṣa sā.
śirasaḥ karṇa|mārgeṇa s'|ârdhaṃ śata|padī|śatam
rākṣasy|uditayā pūrvaṃ yukty" âty|adbhutayā tayā.
sthāpayitvā ca ghaṭake sā tāḥ śata|padīs tataḥ
ghṛta|kṣīr'|ādi|sekena taṃ nṛpaṃ samatarpayat.
kramāt tasmin samāśvaste roga|mukte mahī|patau
ghaṭe tān prāṇino dṛṣṭvā ko na tatra visismiye?
rājā ca sa viloky' âitān ku|kīṭān mūrdha|nirgatān
tatrāsa dadhyau mumude mene janma nijaṃ punaḥ.
6.3.175 kṛt'|ôtsavaś ca sa snātaḥ Kīrtisenām apūjayat
tām an|ādṛta|rājy'|ârdhāṃ grāma|hasty|aśva|kāñcanaiḥ.
devī ca mantriṇaś c' âitāṃ hemnā vastrair apūrayan
«prabhu|prāṇa|prado 'smākaṃ pūjyo bhiṣag asāv iti.»
sā ca tasy' âiva rājñas tān haste 'rthān saṃprati nyadhāt

kingdom, auspicious sir. I think that since in a dream a lady 6.3.165
removed a black blanket from my back, you, sir, are sure to remove this disease of mine."

Kirti·sena replied, "Today is at an end, your highness. I shall cure your disease tomorrow. Do not be impatient."

After saying this she put cow's ghee on the king's head, as a result of which sleep came to him and his severe pain left. At this everyone there praised Kirti·sena, saying, "He is some god come in the form of a doctor as a result of our good deeds." The queen attended to her with various favors and at night arranged a separate chamber for her with servant girls.

Then at noon on the following day, as the ministers and 6.3.170
ladies of the harem looked on, Kirti·sena extracted one hundred and fifty centipedes from the head of the king via the opening of his ear using that extremely amazing method taught previously by the *rákshasi*. After having the centipedes go into a pot, she refreshed the king by anointing him with things like ghee and milk. When the king had eventually recovered and was free of the disease, everyone looked at the creatures in the pot there and was astonished. When the king saw the unpleasant insects that had come out of his head, he was frightened, he was thoughtful, he was delighted and he considered himself to have been born
again. He celebrated and bathed and then honored Kirti· 6.3.175
sena, who was not interested in having half of the kingdom, with villages, elephants, horses and gold. The queen and the ministers gave her a mass of gold and clothes, saying that the doctor who had saved the life of their king should be honored. She was waiting for her husband and entrusted

«kaṃ|cit kālaṃ vrata|stho 'ham ity» uktvā bhartṛ|apekṣiṇī.
tataḥ saṃmānyamān' âtra sarvaiḥ kāny apy ahāni sā
yāvat puruṣa|veṣeṇa Kīrtisen" âvatiṣṭhate.

tavāc chuśrāva lokāt taṃ Valabhītaḥ samāgatam
sārthavāhaṃ pathā tena Devasenaṃ nijaṃ patim.
6.3.180 puri tatr' âtha taṃ sārthaṃ
prāptaṃ buddhv" âiva s" âbhyagāt
bhartāraṃ tam apaśyac ca
mayūr" îva nav'|âmbu|dam.
citten' êva cir'|âutsukya|saṃtāpa|pravilāyinā
datt'|ârgh'|ānanda|bāṣpeṇa pādayos tasya c' âpatat.
so 'pi pratyabhyajānāc ca veṣa|cchannāṃ nirūpya tām
bhartā bhāsvat|kar'|â|lakṣyāṃ divā mūrtim iv' āindavīm.
tasya tad|vadan'|ênduṃ ca *candra|kāntasya* paśyataḥ
Devasenasya hṛdayaṃ citraṃ na galati sma yat.

ath' âsyāṃ Kīrtisenāyām evaṃ prakaṭit'|ātmani
«kim etad iti?» s'|āścaryaṃ sthite tasmiṃś ca tat|patau.
6.3.185 vismite ca vaṇig|grāme tad buddhv" âiva sa|vismayaḥ
sa rājā Vasudatto 'tra svayam eva kil' āyayau.
tena pṛṣṭā ca sā Kīrtisenā patyuḥ puro 'khilam
śvaśrū|duścarit'|ôtpannaṃ sva|vṛttāntam avarṇayat.
Devasenaś ca tac chrutvā tad|bhartā sa sva|mātari
parāṅ|mukho 'bhavat kopa|kṣamā|vismaya|harṣavān.
«bhartṛ|bhakti|rath'|ārūḍhāḥ śīla|saṃnāha|rakṣitāḥ
dharma|sārathayaḥ sādhvyo jayanti mati|hetayaḥ!»
iti tatra sthito 'vādīd ākarṇy' âiva tad adbhutam

the wealth to the king for the time being, saying that she was observing a vow for a certain period. After that Kirti·sena remained there in her guise as a man for a few days, being feted by all.

Meanwhile, she heard from people that her husband the caravan leader Deva·sena had come along the road from Válabhi. As soon as she discovered that the caravan had ar- 6.3.180
rived in the city, she went and met her husband and beheld him like a peacock looking at a newly arrived cloud. As if to soothe the burning pain of their long separation, her heart gave him a welcome offering of tears of joy as she fell at his feet. After examining her in her disguise, in which she was like the embodiment of the moon made invisible in the day by the rays of the sun, her husband recognized her. The amazing thing was that as he looked at the moon of her face, the heart of Deva·sena, who was *as handsome as the moon : a moonstone* did not dissolve.*

Then, after Kirti·sena had revealed herself like this and her husband stood in amazement wondering what it could mean, and all the merchants were astonished, it seems that 6.3.185
as soon as he found out about it the astonished King Vasu·datta came there in person. When he questioned Kirti·sena in front of her husband, she related everything that had happened to her as a result of the bad behavior of her mother-in-law. When her husband Deva·sena heard this, he turned against his own mother, feeling anger, forgiveness, amazement and joy. "Mounted on the chariot of devotion to their husbands, protected by the armor of virtue, righteousness as their charioteer, intelligence their weapons, good women win out!" All the people there joyfully said

caritaṃ Kīrtisenāyāḥ s'|ānandaḥ sakalo janaḥ.
6.3.190 rāj" âpy uvāca «paty|artham āśrita|kleśay" ânayā
Sītā devy api Rāmasya parikleśa|vahā jitā.
tad eṣā dharma|bhaginī mama prāṇa|pradāyinī»
ity uktavantaṃ taṃ bhūpaṃ Kīrtisen" âtha s" âbravīt.
«deva, tvat|prīti|dāyo yas tava haste mama sthitaḥ
grāma|hasty|aśva|ratn'|ādiḥ sa me bhartre samarpyatām.»
evam uktas tayā rājā dattvā grām'|ādi tasya tat
tad|bhartur Devasenasya prītaḥ paṭṭaṃ babandha saḥ.
atha nara|pati|dattais tair vaṇijy'|ârjitaiś ca
prasabha|bharita|koṣo Devaseno dhan'|ôghaiḥ
parihṛta|jananīkaḥ saṃstuvan Kīrtisenāṃ
kṛta|vasatir amuṣminn eva tasthau pure saḥ.
6.3.195 sukham apagata|pāpa|śvaśrukaṃ Kīrtisen" âpy
a|sama|carita|labdha|khyātir āsādya tatra
nyavasad akhila|bhog'|āiśvarya|bhāg'|ântika|sthā
su|kṛta|phala|samṛddhir deha|baddh" êva bhartuḥ.
evaṃ viṣahya vidhurasya vidher niyogam
āpatsu rakṣita|caritra|dhanā hi sādhvyaḥ
guptāḥ sva|sattva|vibhavena mahattamena
kalyāṇam ādadhati patyur ath' ātmanaś ca.
itthaṃ ca, pārthiva|kumāri, bhavanti doṣāḥ
śvaśrū|nanāndṛ|vihitā bahavo vadhūnām
tad bhartṛ|veśma tava tādṛśam arthaye 'haṃ
śvaśrūr na yatra na ca yatra śaṭhā nanāndā.›

this as soon as they heard about Kirti·sena's amazing adventures. The king declared, "With the hardships she suffered 6.3.190
for the sake of her husband, this woman has surpassed even Queen Sita, who bore the afflictions of Rama. So she, who gave me life, is my sister in righteousness."

When the king said this, Kirti·sena replied, "Your highness, please give to my husband your kind gift of villages, elephants, horses, jewels and so forth which I entrusted to you."

When she said this to him, the king gave her husband Deva·sena the villages and so forth, and, delighted, he tied a ceremonial turban on him.

Deva·sena, his coffers overflowing with the gifts from the king and the proceeds from his trading, turned his back on his mother and, singing the praises of Kirti·sena, took
up residence in that city. Kirti·sena, famous for her unique 6.3.195
adventures, found happiness in separation from her evil mother-in-law and lived there enjoying absolute pleasure and power as if she were the incarnation of the fruits of her husband's good deeds. For in this way virtuous women who overcome the vicissitudes of fate and in times of peril guard the wealth that is their virtue are then protected by the mighty power of their courage and bring good fortune on their husbands and themselves. Thus, O princess, the misfortunes that befall wives at the hands of their mothers-in-law and sisters-in-law are many, so I want the house of your husband to be such that there is no wicked mother- or sister-in-law.'

it' îdam ānandi|kath"|âdbhutaṃ sā
mukhān niśamy' âsura|rāja|putryāḥ
Somaprabhāyā manuj'|êndra|putrī
Kaliṅgasenā paritusyati sma.
tato vicitr'|ârtha|kath"|âvasānaṃ
dṛṣṭv" êva gantuṃ mihire pravṛtte
s'|ôtkāṃ samāliṅgya Kaliṅgasenāṃ
Somaprabhā svaṃ bhavanaṃ jagāma.

iti mahā|kavi|śrī|Somadeva|bhaṭṭa|viracite Kathāsaritsāgare
Madanamañcukā|lambake tṛtīyas taraṅgaḥ.

4

6.4.1 TATAḤ SVA|SADMA yātāyāḥ paścān mārgam avekṣitum
Somaprabhāyāḥ snehena mārga|harmy'|āgram āsthitām.
Kaliṅgasenām ārāt tāṃ dadarśa gagan'|āgataḥ
daivān Madanaveg'|ākhyo yuvā vidyā|dhar'|âdhipaḥ.
sa tāṃ dṛṣṭv" âiva rūpeṇa jagat|tritaya|mohinīm
kṣobhaṃ jagāma Kām'|āindra|jālikasy' êva picchikām.
‹alaṃ vidyā|dhara|strībhiḥ kā kath" âpsarasām api
yatr' ēdṛg etad etasyā mānuṣyā rūpam adbhutam!
6.4.5 tad eṣā yadi me na syād bhāryā kiṃ jīvitena tat
kathaṃ ca mānuṣī|saṅgaṃ kuryāṃ vidyā|dharo 'pi san.›
ity ālocya sa dadhyau ca vidyāṃ Prajñapti|saṃjñikām
sā c' āvir|bhūya s'|ākārā tam evam avadat tadā.
‹tattvato mānuṣī n' êyam eṣā śāpa|cyut'|âpsarāḥ
jātā Kaliṅgadattasya gṛhe, su|bhaga, bhū|pateḥ.›
ity ukte vidyayā so 'tha hṛṣṭo gatvā sva|dhāmani

After hearing this happy and amazing story from the mouth of Soma·prabha the *ásura* princess, the mortal princess Kalínga·sena was overjoyed. Then, with the sun having started on its way after seeing that these stories with their wonderful different subjects had come to an end, Soma·prabha embraced Kalínga·sena, who longed to see her again, and went to her own palace.

Thus ends the third wave in the Mádana·mánchuka Attainment in the "Ocean of the Rivers of Story" composed by the glorious and learned great poet Soma·deva.

4

WHEN SOMA·PRABHA had left for her home, out of affec- 6.4.1
tion for her Kalínga·sena then went to the top of a palace on the road to watch her route. By chance a young sorcerer king called Mádana·vega who was coming through the sky saw her from afar. She could bewitch the three worlds with her beauty and as soon as he saw her he was as disturbed as if she had been the peacock feather of that magician the god of love. 'Enough of sorcerer women—to say nothing of *ápsaras*es—when a mortal woman is as amazingly beautiful
as this! So if she won't be my wife then there's no point in 6.4.5
living. But how can I associate with a mortal woman when I am a sorcerer?'

After thinking this, he called to mind the magical science called Prajñápti and when it appeared in physical form it said to him, 'This lady is not really human, O lucky one, she is an *ápsaras* who has fallen to earth because of a curse and been born in the house of King Kalínga·datta.' When the magical science said this, the sorcerer was happy and went

vidyā|dharo 'nya|vimukhaḥ kām'|ārtaḥ samacintayat.
‹haṭhād yadi harāmy etāṃ tad etan me na yujyate
strīṇāṃ haṭh'|ôpabhoge hi mama śāpo 'sti mṛtyu|daḥ.
6.4.10 tad etat|prāptaye Śaṃbhur ārādhyas tapasā mayā
tapo|'dhīnāni hi śreyāṃsy upāyo 'nyo na vidyate.›
iti niścitya c' ânyedyur gatvā Ṛṣabha|parvatam
eka|pāda|sthitas tepe nirāhāras tapāṃsi saḥ.
atha tuṣṭo 'cirāt tīvrais tapobhir datta|darśanaḥ
evaṃ Madanavegaṃ tam ādideś' Âmbikā|patiḥ.
‹eṣā Kaliṅgasen"|ākhyā khyātā rūpeṇa bhū|tale
kanyā n' âsyāś ca bhart" âpi sadṛśo rūpa|saṃpadā.
ekas tu Vatsa|rājo 'sti sa c' âitām abhivāñchati
kiṃ tu Vāsavadattāyā bhītyā n' ârthayate sphuṭam.
6.4.15 eṣ" âpi rūpa|lubdhā taṃ śrutvā Somaprabhā|mukhāt
svayaṃvarāya Vats'|ēśaṃ rāja|putry abhivāñchati.
tatra yāvad vivāho 'syā na bhavet tāvad antarā
kṛtvā kāl'|â|sahasy' êva rūpaṃ Vats'|ēśvarasya tat.
gatvā gāndharva|vidhinā bhāryāṃ kuryād bhavān imām.
evaṃ Kaliṅgasen" âsau tava setsyati sundarī.›
ity|ādiṣṭaḥ sa Śarveṇa praṇipaty' âtha taṃ yayau
gṛhaṃ Madanavegaḥ svaṃ Kālakūṭa|gires taṭam.
atr' ântare pratiniśaṃ gacchantyā nija|mandiram
pratiprabhātam āyāntyā yantreṇa vyoma|gāminā
6.4.20 tayā Takṣaśilā|puryāṃ sā Somaprabhayā saha
Kaliṅgasenā krīḍantī tāṃ jagād' âikadā rahaḥ.
‹sakhi, vācyaṃ na kasy' âpi tvayā yat te bravīmy aham

home. Stricken by love, he turned away from other things and said to himself, 'It would not be right for me to take her by force, for I have been cursed that if I enjoy a woman by force I shall die. So in order to get her I shall propitiate 6.4.10
Shiva with asceticism, for the best things can be won with asceticism and there is no other way for me to get what I want.'

Having decided this, on the next day he went to mount Ríshabha and practiced austerities, standing on one leg and going without food. Before long Shiva was pleased with Mádana·vega's severe austerities and, showing himself to him, instructed him thus: 'This girl called Kalínga·sena is world-famous for her beauty, but she has no husband to match her wealth of looks. But there is one man, the king of Vatsa, and he does desire her. However, in fear of Vásava·
datta, he will not openly ask for her hand. She is greedy for 6.4.15
beauty and when she hears about him from Soma·prabha the princess will want to choose the king of Vatsa as her husband. So before she gets married, make yourself look like the impatient king of Vatsa and go and marry her according to the *gandhárva* rite. In this way the beautiful Kalínga·sena will become yours.'

After being instructed thus by Shiva, Mádana·vega bowed and went to his house on the flanks of mount Kala·kuta.

Meanwhile, there in the city of Taksha·shila Kalínga·sena 6.4.20
was having fun with Soma·prabha, who every night would go to her own palace on her flying machine and return in the morning. One day Kalínga·sena said to Soma·prabha in private, 'My friend, you mustn't tell anyone what I am going to tell you. The time for my wedding has arrived.

vivāho mama saṃprāpta iti jāne yataḥ śṛṇu.
iha māṃ yācituṃ dūtāḥ preṣitā bahubhir nṛpaiḥ
te ca tātena saṃvṛtya tath" âiva preṣitā itaḥ.
yas tu Prasenajin|nāma Śrāvastyām asti bhū|patiḥ
tadīyaḥ kevalaṃ dūtaḥ sādaraṃ tena sat|kṛtaḥ.
mantritaṃ c' âmbay" âpy etat tan manye mad|varo nṛpaḥ
sa tātasya tath" âmbāyāḥ kulīna iti saṃmataḥ.
6.4.25 sa hi tatra kule jāto yatr' Âmb"|Âmbālik'|Âmbikāḥ†
pitāmahyaḥ Kurūṇāṃ ca Pāṇḍavānāṃ ca jajñire.
tat Prasenajite tasmai, sakhi, datt" âsmi sāṃpratam
tātena rājñe Śrāvastyāṃ nagaryām iti niścayaḥ.›

etat Kaliṅgasenātaḥ śrutvā Somaprabhā śucā
sṛjant" îv' âparaṃ hāraṃ sadyo dhār"|âśruṇ" ârudat.
jagāda c' âitāṃ pṛcchantīṃ vayasyām aśru|kāraṇam
dṛṣṭa|niḥśeṣa|bhū|lokā sā May'|âsura|putrikā.

‹vayo rūpaṃ kulaṃ śīlaṃ vittaṃ c' êti varasya yat
mṛgyate, sakhi, tatr' ādyaṃ vayo vaṃś'|ādikaṃ tataḥ.
6.4.30 Prasenajic ca pravayāḥ sa dṛṣṭo nṛpatir mayā
jātī|puṣpasya jāty" êva jīrṇasy' âsya kulena kim.
hima|śubhreṇa tena tvaṃ hemanten' êva padminī
parimlān'|âmbuja|mukhī yuktā śocyā bhaviṣyasi.
ato jāto viṣādo me praharṣas tu bhaven mama
yadi syād Vatsa|rājas te, kalyāṇy, Udayanaḥ patiḥ.
tasya n' âsti hi rūpeṇa lāvaṇyena kulena ca
śauryeṇa ca vibhūtyā ca tulyo 'nyo nṛpatir bhuvi.
tena ced yujyase bhartrā sadṛśena, kṛś'|ôdari

Listen to how I know. Many kings have sent envoys here to ask for my hand. After meeting them my father sends them off the same way that they came. But there is a king called Prasénajit in Shravásti whose envoy is the only one that he has treated with respect. My mother has approved of it too, so I think that king has been chosen as my groom having been deemed to be of good family by my father and mother,
for he was born into the family into which Amba, Ambálika 6.4.25
and Ámbika, the paternal grandmothers of the Kurus and the Pándavas, were born. So, my friend, I am convinced that my father has now betrothed me to that King Prasénajit in the city of Shravásti.'

When Soma·prabha heard this from Kalínga·sena, she was so upset that she suddenly cried a stream of tears, seeming to fashion another necklace for herself. With her friend asking her the reason for her tears, the daughter of the *ásura* Maya, who had seen the entire world, said to her:

'Youth, looks, family, conduct and riches are looked for in a groom, my friend, and of them the most important
is youth, and then family and the rest. I have seen King 6.4.30
Prasénajit and he is advanced in years. He is an old man so his noble family is of no consequence, like the lineage of a jasmine flower. He is as white as snow and married to him you will be as miserable as a lily pond in the company of winter, your face a faded lotus. That is why I am sad, but I would be overjoyed if Údayana, the king of Vatsa, were to be your husband, O auspicious one, for there is no other king on earth his equal in looks, charm, family, courage, or wealth. So if, O slender-waisted one, you were to marry a

dhātuḥ phalati lāvaṇya|nirmāṇaṃ tad idaṃ tvayi.›
6.4.35 iti Somaprabhā|kḷptair vākyair yantrair iv' ēritam
yayau Kaliṅgasenāyā mano Vats'|ēśvaraṃ prati.
tataś ca sā tāṃ papraccha rāja|kanyā May'|ātma|jām
‹kathaṃ sa Vatsa|rāj'|ākhyaḥ, sakhi, kiṃ|vaṃśa|saṃbhavaḥ?
kathaṃ c' Ôdayano nāmnā tvayā me kathyatām iti.›
s" âtha Somaprabh" âvādīc ‹chṛṇu tat, sakhi, vacmi te.
Vatsa ity asti vikhyāto deśo bhūmer vibhūṣaṇam
purī tatr' âsti Kauśāmbī dvitīy" êv' Âmarāvatī.
tasyāṃ sa kurute rājyaṃ yato Vats'|ēśvaras tataḥ
vaṃśaṃ ca tasya, kalyāṇi, kīrtyamānaṃ mayā śṛṇu.
6.4.40 Pāṇḍavasy' Ârjunasy' âbhūd Abhimanyuḥ kil' ātmajaḥ
cakra|vyūha|bhidā yena nītā Kuru|camūḥ kṣayam.
tasmāt Parīkṣid abhavad rājā Bharata|vaṃśa|bhṛt
sarpa|sattra|praṇet" âbhūt tato 'pi Janamejayaḥ.
tato 'bhavac Chatānīkaḥ Kauśāmbīm adhyuvāsa yaḥ
yaś ca dev'|âsura|raṇe daityān hatvā vyapadyata.
tasmād rājā jagac|chlāghyaḥ Sahasrānīka ity abhūt
yaḥ Śakra|preṣita|ratho divi cakre gat'|āgatam.
tasya devyāṃ Mṛgāvatyām asāv Udayano 'jani
bhūṣaṇaṃ śaśino vaṃśe jagan|netr'|ôtsavo nṛpaḥ.
6.4.45 nāmno nimittam apy asya śṛṇu. sā hi Mṛgāvatī
antarvatnī sati rājño janany asya su|janmanaḥ.
utpanna|rudhira|snāna|dohadā pāpa|bhīruṇā
bhartrā racita|lākṣ'|ādi|rasa|vāpī|kṛt'|āplavā.

husband like him, this fashioning of loveliness in you by the creator will have borne fruit.'

By these words concocted by Soma·prabha, Kalínga·sena's 6.4.35
mind was driven towards the king of Vatsa as if by engines. Then the princess asked Maya's daughter, 'Why is he called the king of Vatsa, my friend and into what lineage was he born? And why does he have the name Údayana? Please tell me.'

Soma·prabha replied, 'Listen, I shall explain it to you. There is a land known as Vatsa which is an ornament to the world. In it is the city of Kaushámbi which is like a second Amarávati. He rules from there, which is why he is called the king of Vatsa. Now hear me describe his lineage, O lucky lady. Abhimányu was the son of the Pán- 6.4.40
dava Árjuna and by smashing their circular troop formation he destroyed the army of the Káuravas. His son was King Paríkshit, the bearer of the lineage of Bhárata, and from him arose Janaméjaya, the performer of the snake sacrifice. From him was born Shataníka, who lived in Kaushámbi and who died in a battle between the gods and the *ásura*s after killing some *daitya*s. From him was born the world-renowned King Sahasraníka, who went to heaven and back in a chariot sent to him by Indra. To him was born by Queen Mrigávati this king Údayana, an ornament to the lunar dynasty who brings joy to the eyes of the world.

And listen to why he has this name. While pregnant, that 6.4.45
same Mrigávati, the mother of that noble king, developed a craving to bathe in blood. Her husband, worried about committing a sin, had her bathe in a pool filled with lac and other liquids. By a stroke of fate, a bird of Gáruda's

pakṣiṇā Tārkṣya|vaṃśyena nipaty' āmiṣa|śaṅkayā
nītvā vidhi|vaśāt tyaktā jīvanty" êv' Ôday'|ācale.
tatra c' āśvāsitā bhūyo bhartṛ|saṃgama|vādinā
Jamadagnya'|ṛṣiṇā dṛṣṭā sthit" âsau tatra c' āśrame.
avajñā|janit'|ērṣyāyāḥ kaṃ|cit kālaṃ hi tādṛśaḥ
śāpas Tilottamāto 'bhūt tad|bhartus tad|viyoga|daḥ.
6.4.50 divasaiḥ sā ca tatr' âiva Jamadagny|āśrame sutam
Uday'|âdrau prasūte sma dyaur indum iva nūtanam.
«asāv Udayano jātaḥ sārvabhaumo mahī|patiḥ
janiṣyate ca putro 'sya sarva|vidyā|dhar'|âdhipaḥ.»
ity uccāry' âmbarād vāṇīm a|śarīrāṃ tadā kṛtam
nām' Ôdayana ity asya devair udaya|janmataḥ.
so 'pi śāp'|ânta|baddh'|āśaḥ kālaṃ Mātali|bodhitaḥ
kṛcchrāt Sahasrānīkas tāṃ vin" ānaiṣīn Mṛgāvatīm.
so 'pi śāp'|ânta|baddh'|āśaḥ kālaṃ Mātali|bodhitaḥ
kṛcchrāt Sahasrānīkas tāṃ vin" ānaiṣīn Mṛgāvatīm.
prāpte śāp'|âvasāne tu śabarād vidhi|yogataḥ
Uday'|âdrer upāyātāt prāpy' âbhijñānam ātmanaḥ.
6.4.55 āvedit'|ârthas tat|kālaṃ gagan'|ôdgatayā girā
śabaraṃ taṃ puras|kṛtya jagām' âiv' Ôday'|ācalam.
tatra vāñchita|saṃsiddhim iva prāpya Mṛgāvatīm
bhāryām Udayanaṃ taṃ ca mano|rājyam iv' ātmajam.
tau gṛhītv" âtha Kauśāmbīm āgaty' âiv' âbhiṣiktavān
yauva|rājye tanūjaṃ taṃ tad|guṇ'|ôtkarṣa|toṣitaḥ.
Yaugandharāyaṇ'|ādīṃś ca tasmai mantri|sutān dadau
ten' ātta|bhāro bubhuje bhogān bhāryā|sakhaś ciram.

race, thinking she was a piece of meat, flew down, took her off and then abandoned her, alive, on mount Údaya. She was seen there by the sage Jamad·agni, who consoled her by saying that she would be reunited with her husband, and she stayed there in his ashram. For Tilóttama, who had been made jealous by his treating her disrespectfully, had put a curse on her husband which was such that it kept them apart for a certain amount of time.

After some days in Jamad·agni's ashram there on mount 6.4.50
Údaya, she gave birth to a son, and it was like heaven giving birth to the new moon. "Údayana, the ruler of the whole earth has been born here, and he shall have a son who shall be the emperor of all the sorcerers." Thus the gods then proclaimed in a disembodied voice from the sky, giving him the name Údayana because he was born on mount Údaya.

Sahasraníka, longing for the end of the curse, having been informed of it by Mátali, struggled to pass the time without Mrigávati. But as fate would have it, when the time came for the curse to end he obtained from a tribal who had come from mount Údaya something that he recognized as
his own. At that instant he was appraised of the facts by a 6.4.55
voice that came from the sky, and he followed the tribal to mount Údaya. There, like a wish come true, he found his wife Mrigávati and, like the kingdom of his dreams, his son Údayana. He then returned to Kaushámbi with them and, delighted with his excellent qualities, immediately anointed his son as crown prince and appointed to him Yaugándharáyana and the other sons of his ministers. The burden of the duties of state taken from him by his son, for a long time he enjoyed pleasures in the company of his wife. In time

kālen' āropya rājye ca tam ev' Ôdayanaṃ sutam
vṛddhaḥ sa|bhāryā|sacivo yayau rājā mahā|patham.
6.4.60 evaṃ sa pitryaṃ rājyaṃ tat prāpya jitvā tato 'khilām
Yaugandharāyaṇa|sakhaḥ praśāsty Udayano mahīm.›
ity āśu kathayitvā sā kathām Somaprabhā rahaḥ
sakhīṃ Kaliṅgasenāṃ tāṃ punar evam abhāṣata.
‹evaṃ Vatseṣu rājatvād Vatsa|rājaḥ, sugātri, saḥ
Pāṇḍav'|ânvaya|saṃbhūtyā soma|vaṃś'|ôdbhavas tathā.
nāmn" âpy Udayanaḥ prokto devair udaya|janmanā
rūpeṇa c' âtra saṃsāre Kaṃdarpo 'pi na tādṛśaḥ.
sa ekas tava tulyo 'sti patis, trailokya|sundari
sa ca vāñchati lāvaṇya|lubdhas tvāṃ prārthitāṃ dhruvam.
6.4.65 kiṃ tu Caṇḍamahāsena|mahī|pati|tan'|ûdbhavā
asti Vāsavadatt'|ākhyā tasy' āgrya|mahiṣī, sakhi.
tathā sa ca vṛtas tyaktvā bāndhavān atiraktayā
Uṣā|Śakuntal"|ādīnāṃ kanyānāṃ hṛta|lajjayā.
Naravāhanadatt'|ākhyas tasyāṃ jāto 'sya c' ātmajaḥ
ādiṣṭaḥ kila devair yo bhāvī vidyā|dhar'|âdhipaḥ.
atas tasyāḥ sa Vats'|ēśo bibhyat tvāṃ n' êha yācate
sā ca dṛṣṭā mayā na tvāṃ spardhate rūpa|saṃpadā.›
evam uktavatīṃ tāṃ ca sakhīṃ Somaprabhāṃ tadā
Kaliṅgasenā Vats'|ēśa|s'|ôtsukā nijagāda sā.
6.4.70 ‹jāne 'ham etad vaśyāyāḥ pitroḥ śakyaṃ tu kiṃ mama?
sarva|jñā sa|prabhāvā ca tat tvam ev' âtra me gatiḥ.›
‹daiv'|āyattam idaṃ kāryaṃ tathā c' âtra kathāṃ śṛṇu.›
Somaprabhā tām ity uktvā śaśaṃs' âsyai kathām imām.

the king grew old and had that same son of his, Údayana, take the throne, and with his wife and ministers he went on the great journey. Having thus inherited his father's king- 6.4.60
dom, Údayana then conquered the whole world and rules accompanied by Yaugándharáyana.'

After quickly telling her this tale in private, Soma·prabha went on to say to her friend Kalínga·sena, 'Thus, O beautiful one, he is the king of Vatsa because he rules in Vatsa, and, by being descended from the Pándavas, he was born into the lunar dynasty. The gods called him by the name Údayana because he was born on mount Údaya, and in this universe even the god of love is no match for him in looks. He is the only husband equal to you, O beauty of the three worlds, and, being one who lusts after loveliness, he is sure to want you, who are an object of desire. However, 6.4.65
my friend, he has a chief queen called Vásava·datta, who is the daughter of King Chanda·maha·sena and she, madly in love, took him after abandoning her relations, sparing the blushes of girls like Usha and Shakúntala.* She has borne him a son called Nara·váhana·datta, who the gods have apparently said is going to be the king of the sorcerers. So in fear of her, the king of Vatsa does not ask for your hand here. I have seen her and she does not rival you in looks.'

After her friend Soma·prabha had said this, Kalínga·sena, longing for the king of Vatsa, said to her, 'I'm sure that's 6.4.70
true, but I am in the sway of my parents. What can I do? You are omniscient and have great powers, so my destiny in this matter lies with you.' Soma·prabha then said to her, 'This matter depends on fate. Just listen to this story on the subject,' and told her the following tale.

‹rājā Vikramasen'|ākhya Ujjayinyām abhūt purā
tasya Tejasvat" îty āsīd rūpeṇ' â|pratimā sutā.
tasyāś c' âbhimataḥ kaś|cit prāyo n' âbhūd varo nṛpaḥ
ekadā ca dadarś' âikaṃ puruṣaṃ sā sva|harmya|gā.
tena sv|ākṛtinā daivāt saṃgatiṃ vāñchati sma sā
sv'|âbhiprāyaṃ ca saṃdiśya tasmai svāṃ vyasṛjat sakhīm.
6.4.75 sā gatvā tat|sakhī tasya puṃsaḥ sāhasa|śaṅkinaḥ
an|icchato 'pi prārthy' âivaṃ yatnāt saṃketakaṃ vyadhāt.
«etad deva|kulaṃ, bhadra, viviktaṃ paśyas' îha yam
atra rātrau pratīkṣethā rāja|putryās tvam āgamam.»
ity uktvā sā tam āmantrya gatvā tasyai tad abhyadhāt
Tejasvatyai tataḥ s" âpi tasthau sūry'|âvalokinī.
pumāṃś ca so 'numāny" âpi bhayāt kv' âpy anyato yayau
na bhekaḥ koka|nadinī|kiṃjalk'|āsvāda|kovidaḥ.

atr' ântare ca ko 'py atra rāja|putraḥ kul'|ôdgataḥ
mṛte pitari tan|mittraṃ rājānaṃ draṣṭum āyayau.
6.4.80 sa c' âtra sāyaṃ saṃprāptaḥ Somadatt'|âbhidho yuvā
dāyāda|hṛta|rājy'|ādir ekākī kānta|darśanaḥ.
viveśa daivāt tatr' âiva netuṃ deva|kule niśām
rāja|putryāḥ sakhī yatra puṃsaḥ saṃketam ādiśat.
taṃ tatra sthitam abhyetya rāja|putry a|vibhāvya sā
niśāyām anurāg'|ândhā svayaṃvara|patiṃ vyadhāt.
so 'py abhyanandat tūṣṇīṃ tāṃ prājño vidhi|samarpitām
saṃsūcayantīṃ bhāvinyā rāja|lakṣmyā samāgamam.
tataḥ kṣaṇād rāja|sutā sā viloky' âivam eva tam
kamanīyatamaṃ mene dhātr" ātmānam a|vañcitam.

'Long ago there lived in Ujjain a king called Víkrama·sena. He had a daughter of unrivaled beauty called Tejásvati who would turn down any king who sought to marry her. One day when she was on the terrace of her palace, she saw a man who was very handsome. It so happened that she wanted to meet him and she communicated her intention to him by sending out her handmaiden. That friend of hers 6.4.75
went and made the request to him and with difficulty arranged a meeting with the reluctant man, who was worried that it would be rash. "Good sir, tonight you should await the arrival of the princess in this deserted temple which you can see here." After saying this she took her leave of him and went and told Tejásvati, who then waited, watching the sun. The man, despite having said yes, was so worried that he fled somewhere else. A frog does not know how to savor the filaments of the red water-lily.

Meanwhile some aristocratic prince whose father had died came there to see his father's friend the king and, as 6.4.80
fate would have it, that handsome young man, who was called Soma·datta and whose kingdom and so forth had been seized by his kinsmen, having arrived there in the evening on his own, went into that very same temple in which the princess's handmaiden had arranged for her to meet the man, in order to spend the night. While he was there the princess went up to him and, both blinded by love and unable to see him clearly in the night, chose him for her husband. That wise man welcomed her in silence as an offering from fate, indicating union with his future royal fortune. After a moment the princess saw who he was, but she considered him to be particularly lovely and did not think

6.4.85 an|antaraṃ kathāṃ kṛtvā yathā|svaṃ saṃvidā tayoḥ
ekā sva|mandiram agād anyas tatr' ānayan niśām.
prātar gatvā pratīhāra|mukhen' āvedya nāma saḥ
rāja|putraḥ parijñāto rājñaḥ prāviśad antikam.
tatr' ôkta|rājya|hār'|ādi|duḥkhasya sa kṛt'|ādaraḥ
aṅgī|cakre sahāyatvaṃ rājā tasy' āri|mardane.
matiṃ cakre ca tāṃ tasmai dātuṃ prāg|ditsitāṃ sutām
mantribhyaś ca tad" âiv' âitam abhiprāyaṃ śaśaṃsa saḥ.
ath' âitasmai ca rājñe taṃ sutā|vṛttāntam abhyadhāt
devī svā bodhitā pūrvaṃ tay" âiv' āpta|sakhī|mukhaiḥ.
6.4.90 a|siddh'|ân|iṣṭa|siddh'|êṣṭa|kākatālīya|vismitam
tatas taṃ tatra rājānam eko mantrī tad" âbravīt.
«vidhir eva hi jāgarti bhavyānām artha|siddhiṣu
a|saṃcetayamānānāṃ sad|bhṛtyaḥ svāminām iva.
tathā ca kathayāmy etāṃ, rājann, atra kathāṃ śṛṇu

babhūva Hariśarm'|ākhyaḥ ko 'pi grāme kva|cid dvijaḥ.
sa daridraś ca mūrkhaś ca vṛtty|a|bhāvena duḥsthitaḥ
pūrva|duṣkṛta|bhogāya jāto 'ti|bahu|bālakaḥ.
sa|kuṭumbo bhraman bhikṣāṃ prāpy' âikaṃ nagaraṃ kramāt
śiśriye Sthūladatt'|ākhyaṃ gṛha|sthaṃ sa mahā|dhanam.
6.4.95 gav|ādi|rakṣakān putrān bhāryāṃ karma|karīṃ nijām
tasya kṛtvā gṛh'|âbhyarṇe praiṣyaṃ kurvann uvāsa saḥ.

that she had been cheated by the creator. They immediately 6.4.85
started to talk and by mutual agreement one of them, the girl, went to her palace and the other, the prince, spent the night there. In the morning the prince went and announced himself via the chamberlain, and on being recognized went in to see the king. The king treated him respectfully and, when he told him about his kingdom being seized and so forth, he agreed to help him defeat his enemies and he made up his mind to betroth to him his daughter, whom he had tried to betroth before. He immediately told his ministers of his intention. Then the king's queen told him what had happened to their daughter, having earlier been informed of it by the girl herself through the mouths of her trusted
girlfriends. The king was then amazed at how what wasn't 6.4.90
wanted had by chance not happened and what was had. Then a minister said to him there, "Fate alone makes sure that good men get what they want, just as good servants do for inattentive masters. Just listen to this story on the matter that I am going to tell, sire.

A certain brahmin called Hari·sharman lived in some village or other. He was poor and stupid and in dire straits because he had no way to support himself and so that he should reap the rewards of his past misdeeds far too many children were born to him. Wandering about with his family in search of alms, he eventually arrived at a city and took refuge with a very rich householder called Sthula·
datta. Making his sons look after the cows and other ani- 6.4.95
mals and his wife do chores, he took up residence there near the house, working as a servant.

ekadā Sthūladattasya sutā|pariṇay'|ôtsavaḥ
tasy' âbhūd āgat'|ân|eka|janya|yātrā|jan'|ākulaḥ.
tadā ca Hariśarm" âtra tad|gṛhe sa|kuṭumbakaḥ
ākaṇṭha|ghṛta|māṃs'|ādi|bhojan'|āsthāṃ babandha saḥ.
tad|velāṃ vīkṣamāṇo 'tha smṛtaḥ ken' âpi n' âtra saḥ
tato 'n|āhāra|nirviṇṇo bhāryām ity abravīn niśi.
‹dāridryād iha maurkhyāc ca mam' ēdṛśam a|gauravam
tad atra kṛtrimaṃ yuktyā vijñānaṃ prayunajmy aham.
6.4.100 yen' âsya Sthūladattasya bhaveyaṃ gaurav'|āspadam
tvaṃ prāpte 'vasare c' âsmai jñāninaṃ māṃ nivedaya.›
ity uktvā tāṃ vicinty' âtra dhiyā supte jane hayaḥ
Sthūladatta|gṛhāt tena jahre jāmātṛ|vāhanaḥ.
dūre pracchannam etena sthāpitaṃ prātar atra tam
itas tato vicinvanto 'py aśvaṃ janyā na lebhire.
ath' â|maṅgala|vitrastaṃ haya|caura|gaveṣiṇam
Hariśarma|vadhūr etya Sthūladattam uvāca sā.
‹bhartā madīyo vijñānī jyotir|vidy"|ādi|kovidaḥ
aśvaṃ vo lambhayaty enaṃ kim|arthaṃ sa na pṛcchyate?›
6.4.105 tac chrutvā Sthūladattas taṃ Hariśarmāṇam āhvayat
‹hyo vismṛto hṛte 'śve tu smṛto 'smy ady' êti› vādinam.
‹vismṛtaṃ naḥ kṣamasv' êti› prārthitaṃ brāhmaṇaṃ ca saḥ
papraccha ‹ken' âpahṛto hayo naḥ kathyatām iti.›
Hariśarmā tato mithyā rekhāḥ kurvann uvāca saḥ
‹ito dakṣiṇa|sīm'|ânte cauraiḥ saṃsthāpito hayaḥ.

One day Sthula·datta held a celebration for the wedding of his daughter and it was crowded with the many people who had come in the bridegroom's procession. Then Hari·sharman and his family thought that they would be able to eat their fill of ghee and meat and so forth in his house there. But nobody remembered him there while he was awaiting his turn to eat, as a result of which, depressed at not getting any food, he said to his wife that night, 'It is because I am poor and stupid that I am treated without respect like this, so on this occasion I shall use a trick to pretend that I have special knowledge and then Sthula·datta will hold me in 6.4.100
respect. When you get an opportunity, tell him that I am a sage.'

After saying this to his wife and thinking it over in his head, when everyone was asleep he stole from Sthula·datta's house the horse which was his son-in-law's steed. He hid it far away and in the morning, despite looking all over the place, the groom's party could not find the horse. Then, with Sthula·datta aghast at this inauspicious event and searching for the thief of the horse, Hari·sharman's wife went to him and said, 'My husband is a sage and knows sciences such as that of astrology. He can find the horse for you. Why don't you ask him?'

When he heard this, Sthula·datta summoned Hari· 6.4.105
sharman, who said, 'Yesterday I was forgotten, but today, now that the horse has been stolen, I have been remembered.' Sthula·datta requested the brahmin to forgive them for having forgotten him and then asked him to tell them who had stolen the horse. Then Hari·sharman, while drawing fake diagrams, said, 'The thieves have put the horse

pracchanna|stho din'|ânte ca dūraṃ yāvan na nīyate
tāvad ānīyatāṃ gatvā tvaritaṃ sa turaṃgamaḥ.›
tac chrutvā dhāvitaiḥ prāpya kṣaṇāt sa bahubhir naraiḥ
āninye 'śvaḥ praśaṃsadbhir vijñānaṃ Hariśarmaṇaḥ.
6.4.110 tato jñān" îti sarveṇa pūjyamāno janena saḥ
uvāsa Hariśarm" âtra Sthūladatt'|ârcitaḥ sukham.
atha gacchatsu divaseṣv atra rāja|gṛh'|ântarāt
hema|ratn'|ādi caureṇa bhūri ken' âpy anīyata.
n' âjñāyata yadā cauras tadā jñāni|prasiddhitaḥ
ānāyayām āsa nṛpo Hariśarmāṇam āśu tam.
sa c' ānītaḥ kṣipan kālaṃ ‹vakṣye prātar iti› bruvan
vāsake sthāpito '|jñāna|vigno† rājñ" â|surakṣitaḥ.
tatra rāja|kule c' āsīn nāmnā Jihv" êti ceṭikā
yayā bhrātrā samaṃ tac ca nītam abhyantarād dhanam.
6.4.115 sā gatvā niśi tatr' âsya vāsake Hariśarmaṇah
jijñāsayā dadau dvāri karṇaṃ taj|jñāna|śaṅkitā.
Hariśarmā ca tat|kālam ekako 'bhyantare sthitaḥ
nijāṃ jihvāṃ ninind' âivaṃ mṛṣā|vijñāna|vādinīm.
‹bhoga|lampaṭayā, jihve, kim idaṃ vihitaṃ tvayā?
durācāre, sahasva tvam idānīm iha nigraham.›
tac chrutvā ‹jñānin" ânena jñāt" âsm' îti› bhayena sā
Jihv"|ākhyā ceṭikā yuktyā praviveśa tad|antikam.
patitvā pādayos tasya jnāni|vyañjanam abravīt
‹brahmann, iyaṃ sā Jihv" âhaṃ tvayā jñāt" ârtha|hāriṇī.

on the boundary south from here. The horse is hidden. Quickly go and fetch it before it is taken far away at the end of the day.'

On hearing this, several men immediately ran off, found the horse and brought it back, praising Hari·sharman's special knowledge. After this Hari·sharman lived there in com- 6.4.110
fort, held in respect by Sthula·datta and with everyone worshipping him as a sage.

Then as the days passed there, a large amount of gold and jewels and so forth was taken from inside the king's palace there by some thief or other. When the thief could not be discovered, the king quickly had Hari·sharman brought in on account of his renown as a sage. When he was summoned, he was terrified because he had no special knowledge and played for time by saying that he would speak in the morning. The king had him put in an unguarded bedroom. In that palace there lived a servant girl called Jihva, 'Tongue,' who together with her brother had taken the riches from there. That night she went to Hari·sharman's 6.4.115
bedroom and, in her desire to know more and worried about his special knowledge, she put her ear to the door. At that moment Hari·sharman was inside alone, reproaching his tongue for pretending he had special knowledge: 'O tongue, what have you done in your greed for pleasure? Now, you sinner, you must suffer punishment here.' When she heard this, terrified that the sage had found her out, the servant girl called Jihva used a trick to go in and see him. Falling at his feet, she said to the pretend sage, 'Brahmin, I am that Jihva whom you have found out, the thief of the

6.4.120 nītvā tac ca may" âsy' âiva mandirasy' êha pṛṣṭhataḥ
udyāne dāḍimasy' âdho nikhātaṃ bhū|tale dhanam.
tad rakṣa māṃ gṛhāṇ' êmaṃ kiṃ|cin me hema hasta|gam.›

etac chrutvā sa|garvaṃ sa Hariśarmā jagāda tām.
‹gaccha jānāmy ahaṃ sarvaṃ bhūtaṃ bhavyaṃ bhavat tathā
tvāṃ tu n' ôdghāṭayiṣyāmi kṛpaṇāṃ śaraṇ'|āgatām.
yac ca hasta|gataṃ te' sti tad dāsyasi punar mama.›

ity uktā tena sā ceṭī ‹tath" êty› āśu tato yayau.
Hariśarmā ca sa tato vismayād ity acintayat
‹a|sādhyaṃ sādhayaty arthaṃ helay" âbhimukho vidhiḥ.
6.4.125 yad ih' ôpasthite 'n|arthe siddho 'rtho '|śaṅkitaṃ mama
sva|jihvāṃ nindato Jihvā caurī me patitā puraḥ.
śaṅkay" âiva prakāśante bata pracchanna|pātakāḥ›
ity|ādy ākalayan so 'tra hṛṣṭo rātriṃ nināya tām.
prāyaś c' ālīka|vijñāna|yuktyā nītvā sa taṃ nṛpam
tatr' ôdyāne nikhāta|sthaṃ prāpayām āsa tad dhanam.
cauraṃ c' âpy apanīt'|âṃśaṃ śaśaṃsa prapalāyitam
tatas tuṣṭo nṛpas tasmai grāmān dātuṃ pracakrame.
‹kathaṃ syān mānuṣ'|â|gamyaṃ jñānaṃ śāstraṃ vin" ēdṛśam
tan nūnaṃ caura|saṃketa|kṛt" êyaṃ dhūrta|jīvikā.
6.4.130 tasmād eṣo 'nyayā yuktyā vāram ekaṃ parīkṣyatām
deva, jñān" îti› karṇe taṃ mantrī rājānam abhyadhāt.

tato 'ntaḥ kṣipta|maṇḍūkaṃ sa|pidhānaṃ navaṃ ghaṭam
svairam ānāyya rājā taṃ Hariśarmāṇam abravīt.
‹brahman, yad asmin ghaṭake sthitaṃ jānāsi tad yadi
tad adya te kariṣyāmi pūjāṃ su|mahatīm aham.›

valuables, and I took them and buried them in the ground 6.4.120
under a pomegranate tree in the garden here behind this very palace. So save me and take this small amount of gold which I have in my hand.'

When he heard this, Hari·sharman said to her with pride, 'Go. I know everything in the past, present and future, but you are pitiful and have come for refuge, so I shall not expose you. But you will give me what you have in your hand.'

When he said this to her, the servant girl agreed and quickly left. In his astonishment, Hari·sharman then said to himself, 'Fate is friendly and playfully achieves ends which
are unachievable! For, disaster having been close at hand, I 6.4.125
have surely achieved what I wanted in this matter. As I was rebuking my tongue, the thief Jihva fell before me. It is, alas, through misapprehension that hidden crimes are revealed.' Thinking these and other thoughts, he spent the night there in happiness. In the morning, using the trick of pretending to have special knowledge, he took the king to that garden, found for him the buried valuables and said that the thief had fled having taken part of it. Pleased, the king was then about to give him some villages, when a minister whispered to him, 'It is impossible for someone to have supernatural knowledge such as this without studying the scriptures, so this rogue must support himself by collaborating with
thieves. Therefore, your highness, let's use another trick to 6.4.130
test this sage one more time.'

At this the king quietly had a new pot with a lid brought in, inside which had been put a frog, and said to Hari·sharman, 'Brahmin, if you know what is inside this pot, then today I shall honor you very greatly.'

tac chrutvā nāśa|kālaṃ taṃ matvā smṛtvā tato nijam
pitrā krīḍā|kṛtaṃ bālye Maṇḍūka iti nāma saḥ.

vidhātṛ|preritaḥ kurvaṃs ten' âtra paridevanam
brāhmaṇo Hariśarm" âtra sahas" âiv' âivam abravīt.

6.4.135 ‹sādhor eva tu, maṇḍūka, tav' â|kāṇḍe ghaṭo 'dhunā
a|vaśasya vināśāya saṃjāto 'yaṃ haṭhād iha!›

tac chrutv" ‹âho mahā|jñānī! bheko 'pi vidito 'munā!›
iti jalpan nanand' âtra prastut'|ârth'|ânvayāj janaḥ.

tatas tat prātibha|jñānaṃ manvāno Hariśarmaṇe
tuṣṭo rājā dadau grāmān sa|hema|cchatra|vāhanān.

kṣaṇāc ca Hariśarmā sa jajñe sāmanta|saṃnibhaḥ
itthaṃ daivena sādhyante sad|arthāḥ śubha|karmaṇām.

tat Somadattaṃ sadṛśaṃ daiven' âiv' âbhisāritā
nivāry' â|sadṛśaṃ, rājaṃs, tava Tejasvatī sutā.»

6.4.140 iti mantri|mukhāc chrutvā tasmai rāja|sutāya tām
rājā Vikramaseno 'tha dadau Lakṣmīm iv' ātmajām.

tataḥ śvaśura|sainyena gatvā jitvā ripūṃś ca saḥ
Somadattaḥ sva|rājya|sthas tasthau bhāryā|sakhaḥ sukham.

When he heard this he thought that his end had come. Then, thinking of the name 'Frog' which in his childhood his father had given him as a joke and urged on by fate, the brahmin Hari·sharman, using it as a lament, burst out,
'You are a fine fellow, O frog, but this pot has now suddenly 6.4.135
appeared here to destroy helpless you by force!'

When they heard this, because it made sense in connection with the object in question, the people there were delighted, saying, 'Oh what a great sage! He even knew it was a frog!' Then, considering this to have been divine insight, the king was pleased and gave Hari·sharman some villages, together with gold, parasols and vehicles and he instantly became the equal of a feudal chief.

Thus fate brings about good things for those who do good deeds and it was fate, O king, that made your daughter Tejásvati have a rendezvous with a suitable man like Soma·datta, having warded off someone unsuitable."

After hearing these words from his minister, King 6.4.140
Víkrama·sena then gave his daughter to the prince and it was as if she were Lakshmi, the goddess of fortune. Soma·datta then went and conquered his enemies with his father-in-law's army and lived happily in his own kingdom with his wife.

evaṃ vidher bhavati sarvam idaṃ viśeṣāt
tvām īdṛśīṃ ghaṭayituṃ ka iha kṣameta
Vats'|ēśvareṇa sadṛśena vin' âiva daivaṃ?
kuryām ahaṃ, sakhi, kim atra, Kaliṅgasene?›
itthaṃ kathāṃ rahasi rāja|sutā niśamya
Somaprabhā|vadanato 'tra Kaliṅgasenā
tat|prārthinī śithila|bandhu|bhaya|trapā sā
Vats'|ēśa|saṃgama|samutka|manā babhūva.
ath' âstam upayāsyati
tri|bhuvan'|âika|dīpe ravau
prabhāta|samay'|āgam'|â-
vadhi kathaṃ|cid āmantrya tām
sakhīm abhimat'|ôdyama|
sthita|matiṃ kha|mārgeṇa sā
May'|âsura|sutā yayau
nija|gṛhāya Somaprabhā.

iti mahā|kavi|śrī|Somadeva|bhaṭṭa|viracite Kathāsaritsāgare
Madanamañcukā|lambake caturthas taraṅgaḥ.

5

6.5.1 TATO 'NYEDYUR upetāṃ tāṃ prātaḥ Somaprabhāṃ sakhīm
Kaliṅgasenā viśrambhāt kathāṃ kurvaty uvāca sā.
‹māṃ Prasenajite rājñe tāto dāsyati niścitam
etac chrutaṃ may" âmbāto dṛṣṭo vṛddhaḥ sa ca tvayā.
Vats'|ēśas tu yathā rūpe tvay" âiva kathitas tathā
śruti|mārga|praviṣṭena hṛtaṃ tena yathā manaḥ.
tat Prasenajitaṃ pūrvaṃ pradarśya naya tatra mām
āste Vats'|ēśvaro yatra kiṃ tātena kim ambayā?›

Thus this all happens through the peculiarity of fate. What in this world other than fate could unite a girl like you with a man like the king of Vatsa and what, my friend Kalínga·sena, can I do in this matter?'

After hearing this story from Soma·prabha there in private, princess Kalínga·sena began to long to be united with the king of Vatsa and in her desire for him she shook off her fear of her relatives and her modesty.

Then, as the one light of the three worlds, the sun, was setting, Soma·prabha, the daughter of the *ásura* Maya, somehow took leave, until her return in the morning, of her friend, whose mind was fixed on striving after what she wanted, and flew home.

Thus ends the fourth wave in the Mádana·mánchuka Attainment in the "Ocean of the Rivers of Story" composed by the glorious and learned great poet Soma·deva.

5

WHEN HER FRIEND Soma·prabha arrived the next morn- 6.5.1
ing, Kalínga·sena said to her in the course of a private conversation, 'My father is definitely going to betroth me to King Prasénajit. I heard it from my mother. You have seen him to be an old man, but you have said the king of Vatsa to be so beautiful that, entering by way of my ear, he has stolen my heart. So first show me Prasénajit and then take me to where the king of Vatsa lives—forget my father and mother!'

6.5.5 evam uktavatīṃ tāṃ ca s'|ôtkāṃ Somaprabh" âbravīt
‹gantavyaṃ yadi tad yāmo yantreṇa vyoma|gāminā.
kiṃ tu sarvaṃ gṛhāṇa tvaṃ nijaṃ parikaraṃ yataḥ
dṛṣṭvā Vats'|ēśvaraṃ bhūyo n' āgantum iha śakṣyasi.
na ca tvaṃ drakṣyasi punaḥ pitarau na smariṣyasi
dūra|sthāṃ prāpta|dayitā vismariṣyasi māṃ api.
na hy evam aham eṣyāmi bhartṛ|veśmani te, sakhi.›
tac chrutvā rāja|kanyā sā rudatī tām abhāṣata.
‹tarhi Vats'|ēśvaraṃ taṃ tvam ih' âiv' ānaya me, sakhi
n' ôtsahe tatra hi sthātuṃ kṣaṇam ekaṃ tvayā vinā.
6.5.10 n' āninye c' Âniruddhaḥ kim upāyāc Citralekhayā
jānaty api tathā c' âitāṃ mattas tvaṃ tat kathāṃ śṛṇu.
Bāṇ'|âsurasya tanayā babhūv' Ôṣ" êti viśrutā
tasyāś c' ārādhitā Gaurī pati|prāptyai varaṃ dadau.
«svapne prāpsyasi yat|saṅgaṃ sa te bhartā bhaved iti»
tato deva|kumār'|ābhaṃ kaṃ|cit svapne dadarśa sā.
gāndharva|vidhinā tena pariṇītā tath" âiva ca
prāpta|tat|satya|saṃbhogā prābudhyata niśā|kṣaye.
a|dṛṣṭvā taṃ patiṃ dṛṣṭaṃ dṛṣṭvā saṃbhoga|lakṣaṇam
smṛtvā Gaurī|varaṃ s" âbhūt s'|ātaṅka|bhaya|vismayā.
6.5.15 tāmyantī ca tataḥ sā taṃ svapne dṛṣṭaṃ priyaṃ vinā
pṛcchantyai Citralekhāyai sakhyai sarvaṃ śaśaṃsa tat.
s" âpi nām'|ādy|abhijñānaṃ na kiṃ|cit tasya jānatī
yog'|ēśvarī Citralekhā tām Uṣām evam abravīt.
«sakhi, devī|varasy' âyaṃ prabhāvo 'tra kim ucyate?

After Kalínga·sena had eagerly said this, Soma·prabha 6.5.5
replied, 'If we must go then let's go in the flying machine. But bring all of your retinue, for after you have seen the king of Vatsa you will not be able to return here and you will neither see nor think of your parents again. When you have won your sweetheart and I am far away you shall forget me too, for I shall never enter your husband's house, my friend.'

When she heard this, the sobbing princess replied, 'In that case you must bring the king of Vatsa here, my friend, for I couldn't bear to spend one moment there without you.
Did not Chitra·lekha fetch Anirúddha by means of a ruse? 6.5.10
Even though you know the story, listen to me tell it.

The *ásura* Bana had a daughter who was known as Usha. Gauri, on being propitiated, gave her a boon so that she would get a husband, saying, "The man with whom you make love in a dream shall become your husband." Then she saw in a dream some man who looked like a divine prince. He married her there and then according to the *gandhárva* rite and she enjoyed the now legitimate pleasure of making love to him. At the end of the night she woke up. When she couldn't see the husband that she had met, but could see the traces of lovemaking, she remembered Gauri's boon and was upset, scared and astonished.

Afterwards, as she suffered in separation from that sweet- 6.5.15
heart whom she had met in the dream, her friend Chitra·lekha questioned her and she told her everything. Chitra·lekha had mastered magic, but, not knowing his name nor any other means of recognizing him, she said to Usha, "My friend, this is the result of a boon from the goddess: what

kiṃ tv abhijñāna|śūnyas te so 'nveṣṭavyaḥ priyaḥ katham?
parijānāsi cet taṃ te sa|sur'|âsura|mānuṣam
jagal likhāmi tan|madhye taṃ me darśaya yena saḥ
ānīyate may" êty» uktā sā «tath" êty» udite tayā
Citralekhā kramād viśvam alikhad varṇa|vartibhiḥ.
6.5.20 tatr' Ôṣā «so 'yam ity» asyā hṛṣṭ" âṅgulyā sa|kampayā
Dvārāvatyāṃ Yadu|kulād Aniruddham adarśayat.

Citralekhā tato 'vādīt «sakhi, dhany" âsi yat tvayā
bhart" Âniruddhaḥ prāpto 'yaṃ pautro bhagavato Hareḥ.
yojanānāṃ sahasreṣu ṣaṣṭau vasati sa tv itaḥ.»

tac chrutvā s'|âdhik'|āutsukya|vaśāt tām abravīd Uṣā.
«n' âdya cet, sakhi, tasy' âṅkaṃ śraye śrī|khaṇḍa|śītalam
tad aty|uddāma|kām'|âgni|nirdagdhāṃ viddhi māṃ mṛtām.»

śrutv" âitac Citralekhā sā tām āśvāsya priyāṃ sakhīm
tad" âiv' ôtpatya nabhasā yayau Dvāravatīṃ purīm.
6.5.25 dadarśa ca pṛth'|ûttuṃgair mandirair abdhi|madhya|gām
kurvatī taṃ punaḥ kṣipta|manth'|âdri|śikhara|bhramam.
tasyāṃ suptaṃ niśi prāpya s" Âniruddhaṃ vibodhya ca
Uṣ"|ânurāgaṃ taṃ tasmai śaśaṃsa svapna|darśanāt.
ādāya c' ātta|tad|rūpa|svapna|vṛttāntam eva tam
s'|ôtkaṃ siddhi|prabhāveṇa kṣaṇen' âiv' āyayau tataḥ.
etya c' âvekṣamāṇāyās tasyāḥ sakhyāḥ kha|vartmanā
prāveśayad Uṣāyās taṃ guptam antaḥ|puraṃ priyam.

can one say about it? However, there is nothing by which your sweetheart can be identified, so he cannot be searched for. I shall draw a picture of the world, with gods, *ásuras* and men. If you recognize him, point him out to me in it, so that I can bring him here." When she said this Usha agreed to it, and, using colored pens, Chitra·lekha then gradually drew
the whole world. Usha, delighted, used a trembling finger 6.5.20
to point out Anirúddha among the family of the Yadus in Dvarávati, saying, "There he is."

At this Chitra·lekha said, "My friend you are blessed to have won Anirúddha as your husband. He is the grandson of Lord Vishnu. However, he lives sixty thousand *yójanas* from here."

When she heard this Usha was so overcome by her excessive desire that she said to her, "If, my friend, I cannot be in his arms, which are as cool as sandal, on this very day, then know that I shall die, consumed by the overbearing fire of love."

On hearing this, Chitra·lekha consoled her dear friend before immediately afterwards rising up and flying through
the sky to the city of Dvarávati. She saw it in the middle 6.5.25
of the ocean. With its broad, towering palaces it made it look as if the peaks of the mountain that churned the ocean had once more been thrown into it.* That night she found Anirúddha asleep, woke him up, and told him of Usha's love for him after seeing him in a dream. He told her that he had had the same dream. He was full of longing and she used her magical powers to bring him back from there in an instant. After returning through the sky to where her friend Usha was expecting her sweetheart, she secretly brought

sā dṛṣṭv" âiv' Âniruddhaṃ tam Uṣā sākṣād upāgatam
amṛt'|âṃśum iv' âmbhodhi|velā n' âṅgeṣv avartata.
6.5.30 tatas tena samaṃ tasthau sakhī|dattena tatra sā
jīviten' êva mūrtena vallabhena yathā|sukham.
taj|jñānāt pitaraṃ c' âsyāḥ kruddhaṃ Bāṇaṃ jigāya saḥ
Aniruddhaḥ sva|vīryeṇa pitāmaha|balena ca.
tato Dvāravatīṃ gatvā tāv a|bhinna|tanū ubhau
Uṣ"|Âniruddhau jajñāte giri|jā|Śaṃkarāv iva.
ity Uṣāyāḥ priyo 'hn' âiva melitaś Citralekhayā
tvaṃ sa|prabhāv" âpy adhikā tato 'pi, sakhi, me matā.
tan mam' ānaya Vats'|ēśam iha mā sma ciraṃ kṛthāḥ!›
evaṃ Kaliṅgasenātaḥ śrutvā Somaprabh" âbravīt.
6.5.35 ‹Citralekhā sura|strī sā samutkṣipy' ānayat param
mādṛśī kiṃ vidadhyāt tu para|sparś'|ādy a|kurvatī?
tat tvāṃ nayāmi tatr' âiva yatra Vats'|ēśvaraḥ, sakhi
prāk Prasenajitaṃ taṃ te darśayitvā tvad|arthinam.›
iti Somaprabh"|ôktā sā ‹tath" êty› uktvā tayā saha
Kaliṅgasenā tat|kḷptaṃ māyā|yantra|vimānakam.
tad" âiv' āruhya nabhasā sa|koṣā sa|paricchadā
kṛta|prāsthānikā prāyāt pitror a|viditā tataḥ.
na hi paśyati tuṅgaṃ vā śvabhraṃ vā strī|jano 'grataḥ
Smareṇa nītaḥ paramāṃ dhārāṃ vāj" îva sādinā.
6.5.40 Śrāvastīṃ prāpya pūrvaṃ ca taṃ Prasenajitaṃ nṛpam
mṛgayā|nirgataṃ dūrāj jarā|pāṇḍuṃ dadarśa sā.

him into Usha's inner apartment. When Anirúddha arrived in person, as soon as she saw him, who was like the moon, Usha, like the ocean tides, could not be contained in her
body. Then she lived there in happiness together with her 6.5.30
beloved, who had been given by her friend as if he were the gift of life incarnate. When her father Bana found out about it and was angry, Anirúddha defeated him using his own might and the forces of his grandfather. Afterwards Usha and Anirúddha both went to Dvarávati and, their bodies inseparable, became like the daughter of the mountains and Shiva. Thus in one day Chitra·lekha brought Usha and her sweetheart together. I consider you to be even more powerful than her, my friend, so bring the king of Vatsa to me here and don't be long!'

When she heard this from Kalínga·sena, Soma·prabha
replied, 'Chitra·lekha is a divine woman and fetched a strange 6.5.35
man by picking him up, but what is a girl like me, who won't do things such as touch another man, to do? So, my friend, I shall take you to where the king of Vatsa is, having first shown you your suitor Prasénajit.'

On being told this by Soma·prabha, Kalínga·sena agreed and, together with her, immediately climbed aboard the magical flying machine that she had made, and, after making preparations for their departure, took her fortune and her entourage and flew away from there without her parents knowing, for, like a horse led on at a gallop by its rider, when led on by the god of love women do not see great
heights or gaping defiles in front of them. She first went 6.5.40
to Shravásti and saw from afar King Prasénajit, who had gone out hunting. He was white with old age and could be

‹vṛddhād vraj' âsmād iti!› tāṃ dūrād iva niṣedhatā
uddhūyamānena muhuś cāmareṇ' ôpalakṣitam.
‹so 'yaṃ Prasenajid rājā pitr" âsmai tvaṃ praditsitā
paśy' êti!› Somaprabhayā darśitaṃ s'|ôpahāsayā.

‹jaray" âyaṃ vṛto rājā kā vṛṇīte 'parā tv amum
tad itaḥ, sakhi, śīghraṃ māṃ naya Vats'|ēśvaraṃ prati.›

iti Somaprabhāṃ c' ôktvā tat|kṣaṇaṃ sā tayā saha
Kaliṅgasenā vyomn' âiva Kauśāmbīṃ nagarīṃ yayau.
6.5.45 tatr' ôdyāna|gataṃ sā taṃ Vats'|ēśaṃ sakhy|udīritam
dadarśa dūrāt s'|ôtkaṇṭhā cakor" îv' âmṛta|tviṣam.
sā tad utphullayā dṛṣṭyā hṛn|nyastena ca pāṇinā
‹praviṣṭo 'yaṃ path" ânena mām atr' êty› abravīd iva.
‹sakhi, saṃgamay' âdy' âiva Vatsa|rājena mām iha
enaṃ vilokya hi sthātuṃ na śaktā kṣaṇam apy aham.›
iti c' ôktavatīṃ tāṃ sā sakhī Somaprabh" âbravīt
‹ady' â|śubhaṃ mayā kiṃ|cin nimittam upalakṣitam.
tad idaṃ divasaṃ tūṣṇīm udyāne 'sminn a|lakṣitā
adhitiṣṭhasva mā kārṣīḥ, sakhi, dūraṃ gat'|āgatam.
6.5.50 prātar āgatya yuktiṃ vāṃ ghaṭayiṣyāmi saṃgame
adhunā gantum icchāmi, bhartuś citta|gṛhe, gṛham.›

ity uktvā tām avasthāpya yayau Somaprabhā tataḥ
Vatsa|rājo 'pi c' ôdyānāt sva|mandiram ath' āviśat.
tataḥ Kaliṅgasenā sā tatra|sthā sva|mahattaram
yathā|tattvaṃ sva|saṃdeśaṃ dattvā Vats'|ēśvaraṃ prati.
prāhiṇot prāṅ|niṣiddh" âpi sva|sakhyā śakuna|jñayā

picked out by the yak's tail fly whisk being continuously waved over him. It seemed to be warding her off from afar, saying, 'Move on from this old man!' With a laugh Soma·prabha pointed him out and said, 'Look, that is the King Prasénajit whom your father wants you to marry!'

'Old age has chosen this king for herself—no other woman will choose him! So, quickly, my friend, take me from here to the king of Vatsa!'

As soon as she had said this to Soma·prabha, Kalínga·sena went with her through the sky to the city of Kaushámbi. Once there, with longing she beheld from afar in a garden 6.5.45
the king of Vatsa, pointed out by her friend, and it was like a *chakóra* hen seeing the moon. With her wide eyes and her hand placed on her heart, it was as if she were saying, 'This is the route by which he has entered me here.' When she then said, 'My friend, have me meet the king of Vatsa here this very day, for having seen him I cannot wait for even a moment,' her friend Soma·prabha replied, 'I have noticed a certain bad omen today, so wait out this day in silence, unseen in this garden, and don't, my friend, travel far from here. In the morning I shall come and contrive to 6.5.50
bring about a meeting between the two of you. Now, O you who are the home of your husband's heart, I want to go to home.'

After saying this and having her wait there, Soma·prabha left. The king of Vatsa then went from the garden to his palace. At this Kalínga·sena stayed where she was but gave her chamberlain a message for the king of Vatsa from her explaining the situation and sent him off, despite having earlier been told not to do so by her friend, who knew how

sva|tantro 'bhinav'|ārudho yuvatīnāṃ mano|bhavaḥ.
sa ca gatvā pratīhāra|mukhen' āvedya tat|kṣaṇam
mahattaraḥ praviśy' âivaṃ Vatsa|rājaṃ vyajijñapat.
6.5.55 ‹rājan, Kaliṅgadattasya rājñas Takṣaśilā|pateḥ
sutā Kaliṅgasen"|ākhyā śrutvā tvāṃ rūpavattaram.
svayaṃvar'|ârtham iha te saṃprāptā tyakta|bāndhavā
māyā|yantra|vimānena s'|ânugā vyoma|gāminā.
ānītā guhya|cāriṇyā sakhyā Somaprabh"|ākhyayā
May'|âsurasy' ātma|jayā Nalakūbara|bhāryayā.
tayā vijñāpanāy' âhaṃ preṣitaḥ svī|kuruṣva tām
yuvayor astu yogo 'yaṃ kaumudī|candrayor iva.›

evaṃ mahattarāc chrutvā taṃ ‹tath" êty› abhinandya ca
prahṛṣṭo hema|vastr'|ādyair Vatsa|rājo 'bhyapūjayat.
6.5.60 āhūya c" âbravīn mantri|mukhyaṃ Yaugandharāyaṇam
‹rājñaḥ Kaliṅgadattasya khyāta|rūpā kṣitau sutā.
svayaṃ Kaliṅgasen'|ākhyā varaṇāya mam' āgatā
tad brūhi śīghram a|tyājyāṃ kadā pariṇayāmi tām.›

ity ukto Vatsa|rājena mantrī Yaugandharāyaṇaḥ
asy' āyati|hit'|âpekṣī kṣaṇam evam acintayat.
‹Kaliṅgasenā sā tāvat khyāta|rūpā jagat|traye
n' âsty anyā tādṛśī tasyai spṛhayanti surā api.
tāṃ labdhvā Vatsa|rājo 'yaṃ sarvam anyat parityajet
devī Vāsavadattā ca tataḥ prāṇair viyujyate.
6.5.65 Naravāhanadatto 'pi naśyed rāja|sutas tataḥ

to read omens. When love is newly arisen in the heart of a young woman, it has no master. So the chamberlain left and, after announcing himself via the door-keeper, went straight in and said to the king, 'O king, the daughter of 6.5.55
Kalínga·datta, king of Taksha·shila, Kalínga·sena by name, having heard that you are very handsome has abandoned her family and come here in order to ask you to be her husband. She and her entourage were brought here in a magical mechanical flying chariot by a friend of hers called Soma·prabha, the daughter of the *ásura* Maya, who is the wife of Nala·kúbara and moves in mysterious ways. She has sent me to make this request. Take her for your own and may the two of you be united like moonlight and the moon.'

When the king of Vatsa heard this from the chamberlain, he was delighted and said he would do just that before honoring him with gold, clothes and other gifts. He sum- 6.5.60
moned his chief minister Yaugándharáyana and said to him, 'King Kalínga·datta has a daughter whose beauty is famous throughout the world. She is called Kalínga·sena and has come in person to ask me to be her husband. So quickly, tell me: when shall I marry her? She is not to be rejected.'

After the king of Vatsa had said this to him, the minister Yaugándharáyana, thinking for a moment of the king's long-term good, said this to himself: 'Kalínga·sena is famed in the three worlds for her beauty and there is no other girl like her—even the gods desire her. Once he has won her, the king of Vatsa here will turn his back on everything else and Queen Vásava·datta's life-breaths will leave her. Then 6.5.65
the king's son Nara·váhana·datta will also perish and Padmávati loves him so much that she too will find it hard to

Padmāvaty api tat|snehād devī jīvati duṣkaram.
tataś Caṇḍamahāsena|Pradyotau pitarau dvayoḥ
devyor vimuñcataḥ prāṇān vikṛtiṃ v' âpi gacchataḥ.
evaṃ ca sarva|nāśaḥ syān na ca yuktaṃ niṣedhanam
rājño 'sya vyasanaṃ yasmād vāritasy' âdhikī|bhavet.
tasmād anupraveśasya siddhyai kālaṃ harāmy aham.›
ity ālocya sa Vats'|ēśaṃ prāha Yaugandharāyaṇaḥ.
‹deva, dhanyo 'si yasy' âiṣā svayaṃ te gṛham āgatā
Kaliṅgasenā bhṛtyatvaṃ prāptaś c' âitat|pitā nṛpaḥ.
6.5.70 tat tvayā gaṇakān pṛṣṭvā su|lagne 'syā yathā|vidhi
kāryaḥ pāṇi|graho rājño bṛhato duhitā hy asau.
ady' âsyā dīyatāṃ tāvad yogyaṃ vāsa|gṛhaṃ pṛthak
dāsī|dāsā visṛjyantāṃ vastrāṇy ābharaṇāni ca.›
ity ukto mantri|mukhyena Vatsa|rājas ‹tath" êti› tat
prahṛṣṭa|hṛdayaḥ sarvaṃ sa|viśeṣaṃ cakāra saḥ.
Kaliṅgasenā ca tataḥ praviṣṭā vāsa|veśma tat
sva|mano|ratham āsannaṃ matvā prāpa parāṃ mudam.
Yaugandharāyaṇaḥ so 'pi kṣaṇād rāja|kulāt tataḥ
nirgatya sva|gṛhaṃ gatvā dhīmān evam acintayat.
6.5.75 ‹prāyo '|śubhasya kāryasya kāla|hāraḥ pratikriyā
tathā ca Vṛtra|śatrau prāg brahma|hatyā|palāyite.
deva|rājyam avāptena Nahuṣeṇ' âbhivāñchitā
rakṣitā deva|guruṇā Śacī śaraṇam āśritā.
«adya prātar upaiti tvām ity» uktvā kāla|hārataḥ
yāvat sa naṣṭo Nahuṣo huṃkārād brahma|śāpataḥ.
prāptaś ca pūrvavac Chakraḥ sa punar deva|rājatām

live. At this Chanda·maha·sena and Pradyóta, the fathers of the two queens, will cast off their life-breaths or turn hostile. Thus utter ruin shall result. But it would not be right to forbid him, because if he is thwarted, the king's lust will intensify. Therefore I shall delay the wedding in order to ensure a successful outcome.'

'Your highness, you are lucky that this girl Kalínga·sena has come to your house in person and that her father, a king,
has become your servant. So you must ask the astrologers 6.5.70
when would be an auspicious time and marry her with due ceremony, for she is the daughter of a powerful king. In the meantime, she should be given a suitable and separate place to stay, and sent servant men and women, clothes and ornaments.'

When his chief minister said this to him, the king of Vatsa agreed and with delight in his heart took care of everything down to the finest detail.

Kalínga·sena then entered her quarters and, thinking that the fulfillment of her wish was close at hand, was overjoyed. As for Yaugándharáyana, well, a moment later he left the palace and went home, where the clever fellow said to
himself, 'A delay often prevents something bad happening. 6.5.75
Thus in the past, when Indra, the enemy of the brahmin Vritra, had fled after killing him, Náhusha, now king of the gods, lusted after his wife Shachi. She was protected by the guru of the gods after going to him for refuge. He played for time by saying, "She will come to you today or tomorrow," until Náhusha was destroyed with a roar as the result of a curse from a brahmin and Indra became the king of the gods again, just as before. Thus I must hold up the king

evaṃ Kaliṅgasen"|ârthe kālaḥ kṣepyo mayā prabhoḥ.›
iti saṃcintya sarveṣāṃ gaṇakānāṃ sa saṃvidam
dūra|lagna|pradānāya mantrī guptaṃ vyadhāt tadā.
6.5.80 atha vijñāya vṛttāntaṃ devyā Vāsavadattayā
āhūya sa mahā|mantrī sva|mandiram anīyata.
tatra praviṣṭaṃ praṇataṃ rudatī sā jagāda tam
‹ārya, pūrvaṃ tvay" ôktaṃ me yathā «devi, mayi sthite
Padmāvatyā ṛte n' ânyā sa|patnī te bhaviṣyati»
Kaliṅgasen" âpy ady' âiṣā paśy' êha pariṇeṣyate!
sā ca rūpavatī tasyām ārya|putraś ca rajyati
ato vitatha|vādī tvaṃ jāto 'haṃ ca mṛt" âdhunā!›
tac chrutvā tām avocat sa mantrī Yaugandharāyaṇaḥ
‹dhīrā bhava kathaṃ hy etad, devi, syān mama jīvataḥ?
6.5.85 tvayā tu n' âtra kartavyā rājño 'sya pratikūlatā
pratyutālambya dhīratvaṃ darśanīy" ânukūlatā.
n' āturaḥ pratikūl'|ôktair vaśe vaidyasya vartate
vartate tv anukūl'|ôktaiḥ sāmn" aiv' ācarataḥ kriyām.
pratīpaṃ kṛṣyamāṇo hi n' ôttared uttaren naraḥ
vāhyamāno 'nukūlaṃ tu n' ôdyogād vyasanāt tathā.
ataḥ samīpam āyāntaṃ rājānaṃ tvam a|vikriyā
upacārair upacareḥ saṃvṛty' ākāram ātmanaḥ.
Kaliṅgasenā|svī|kāraṃ śraddadhyās tasya sāmpratam
vṛddhiṃ bruvāṇā rājyasya sahāye tat|pitary api.
6.5.90 evaṃ kṛte ca mahātmya|guṇaṃ dṛṣṭvā paraṃ tava
pravṛddha|sneha|dākṣiṇyo rāj" âsau bhavati tvayi.
matvā Kaliṅgasenāṃ ca sv'|âdhīnāṃ n' ôtsuko bhavet

in his pursuit of Kalínga·sena.' After thinking this through, the minister secretly made an arrangement with all the astrologers for them to set the date for the wedding in the distant future.

Then Queen Vásava·datta found out what had happened 6.5.80
and summoned the chief minister to her palace. When he came in there and bowed, she sobbed as she said to him, 'Noble sir, some time ago you said to me, "Queen, while I hold my position, you shall have no rival as queen other than Padmávati," and now, look, this Kalínga·sena is also going to be made a wife here! She is beautiful and my husband delights in her, so you are a liar and now I shall die!'

When he heard this, the minister Yaugándharáyana replied: 'Be strong, your highness, for while I am alive it
won't happen. But you must not oppose the king in this 6.5.85
matter. For now remain composed and pretend to approve: the patient does not give himself up to the doctor through unpleasant words, but through agreeable utterances from a doctor who goes about his work in a conciliatory fashion, because a man is not rescued, from either a struggle or from a vice, by being pulled against the current, but by being carried with it. So when the king comes to you, you should not be hostile to him and attend to him with favors, disguising how you feel. You should approve for the time being of his engagement to Kalínga·sena, speaking of the benefit to the
kingdom of her father being an ally too. If you do this, when 6.5.90
the king sees how very magnanimous you are, his love and kindness towards you will increase. Thinking that Kalínga·sena is in his power, he will not be impatient, for it is when a man is being restrained that his desire for the objects of

vāryamāṇasya vāñchā hi viṣayeṣv abhivardhate.
devī Padmāvatī c' âitac chikṣaṇīyā tvay," ân|aghe
evaṃ sa rājā kārye 'smin kāla|kṣepaṃ saheta naḥ.
ataḥ paraṃ ca jāne 'haṃ paśyer yukti|balaṃ mama
saṃkaṭe hi parīkṣyante prājñāḥ śūrāś ca saṃgare.
tad, devi, mā viṣaṇṇā bhūr iti› devīṃ prabodhya tām
tay" ādṛt'|ôktiḥ sa yayau tato Yaugandharāyaṇaḥ.

6.5.95 Vats'|ēśvaraś ca tad ahar na divā na rātrau
devyor dvayor api sa vāsa|gṛhaṃ jagāma
tādṛk|svayaṃvara|ras'|ôpanamat|Kaliṅga-
senā|samāna|nava|saṃgama|s'|ôtka|cetāḥ.
rātriṃ ca durlabha|ras'|ôtsukat"|âtigāḍha|
cintā|mah"|ôtsava|mayīm iva tāṃ tatas te
ninyuḥ sva|sadmasu pṛthak pṛthag eva devī|
Vats'|ēśa|tat|saciva|mukhya|Kaliṅgasenāḥ.

iti mahā|kavi|śrī|Somadeva|bhaṭṭa|viracite Kathāsaritsāgare
Madanamañcukā|lambake pañcamas taraṅgaḥ.

6

6.6.1 TATAḤ PRATĪKṢAMĀṆAṂ taṃ Vatsa|rājam upetya saḥ
Yaugandharāyaṇo dhūrtaḥ prātar mantrī vyajijñapat.
‹lagnaḥ Kaliṅgasenāyā devasya ca śubh'|āvahaḥ
vivāha|maṅgalāy' êha kiṃ n' âdy' âiva vilokyate.»
tac chrutvā so 'bravīd rājā ‹mam' âpy evaṃ hṛdi sthitam
tāṃ vinā hi muhūrtaṃ me sthātuṃ na sahate manaḥ.›

the senses increases. You should also instruct Padmávati in this, O blameless one, and in this way the king will put up with our delaying this matter. I know that later you will witness the strength of my plan, for the wise are tested in a crisis and the brave in battle. So, your highness, do not be downcast.' After thus advising the queen and having his words received respectfully by her, Yaugándharáyana left.

That day the king of Vatsa did not go to the houses of 6.5.95
either of his two queens by day or by night, for his mind was eager for a similar, but new union with Kalínga·sena, who had come to ask him to be her groom with such passion. Then, with them all in their separate dwellings, that night passed with the two queens finding pleasure hard to come by, the king of Vatsa full of longing, his chief minister profoundly anxious and Kalínga·sena in great celebration.

Thus ends the fifth wave in the Mádana·mánchuka Attainment in the "Ocean of the Rivers of Story" composed by the glorious and learned great poet Soma·deva.

6

THE NEXT MORNING that cunning minister Yaugándhará- 6.6.1
yana went to the expectant king of Vatsa and said to him, 'Why don't you find out right away when will be an auspicious time for the marriage ceremony of Kalínga·sena and your highness?'

The king replied, 'I too was thinking this, for my heart cannot bear to be without her for a moment.'

ity uktv" âiva sa tat|kālaṃ pratīhāraṃ puraḥ|sthitam
ādiśy' ānāyayām āsa gaṇakān saral'|āśayaḥ.
6.6.5 tena pṛṣṭā mahā|mantri|pūrva|sthāpita|saṃvidaḥ
ūcur ‹lagno 'nukūlo 'sti rājño māseṣu ṣatsv itaḥ.›

tac chrutv" âiva mṛṣā kopaṃ kṛtvā Yaugandharāyaṇaḥ
‹a|jñā ime dhig ity!› uktvā rājānaṃ nipuṇo 'bravīt.
‹yo 'sau jñān" îti devena pūjito gaṇakaḥ purā
sa n' āgato 'dya taṃ pṛṣṭvā yathā|yuktaṃ vidhīyatām.›
etan mantri|vacaḥ śrutvā Vats'|ēśo gaṇakaṃ tadā
tam apy ānāyayām āsa dol"|ārūḍhena cetasā.
so 'py asya kāla|hārāya sthita|saṃvit tath" âiva tam
lagnaṃ pṛṣṭo 'bravīd dhyātvā ṣaṇ|mās'|ânte vyavasthitam.
6.6.10 tato rājānam udvigna iva Yaugandharāyaṇaḥ
jagāda ‹deva, kartavyaṃ kim atr' ādiśyatām iti.›
rāj" âpy utkaḥ su|lagn'|âiṣī sa vimṛśya tato 'bhyadhāt
‹Kaliṅgasenā praṣṭavyā sā kim āh' êty avekṣyatām.›

tac chrutvā sa ‹tath" êty› uktvā gṛhītvā gaṇaka|dvayam
pārśvaṃ Kaliṅgasenāyā yayau Yaugandharāyaṇaḥ.
tayā kṛt'|ādaro dṛṣṭvā tad|rūpaṃ sa vyacintayat
‹prāpy' êmāṃ vyasanād rājā sarvaṃ rājyaṃ tyajed iti.›
uvāca c' âinām ‹udvāha|lagnaṃ te gaṇakaiḥ saha
niścetum āgato 'smy etair janma'|rkṣaṃ tan nivedyatām.›
6.6.15 tac chrutvā janma|nakṣatraṃ tasyāḥ parijan'|ôditam

No sooner had he said this than the guileless king gave
an order to a chamberlain who was standing in front of him
and had the astrologers brought in. Having already made an 6.6.5
agreement with the chief minister, on being questioned by
the king they said, 'The favorable time for the king's wedding is six months from now.'

The moment he heard this, the clever Yaugándharáyana
pretended to be angry and, after exclaiming, 'Curse these
fools!,' said to the king, 'The astrologer whom your highness
honored for his wisdom some time ago has not come today. Ask him and then act accordingly.' After hearing these
words from the minister, the king of Vatsa, his mind sitting
on the swing of vacillation, had that astrologer
brought in as well. When asked about the right time for the
wedding, he too, having made that same agreement to play
for time, reflected and then said it was fixed at six months
thence. At this Yaugándharáyana, as if upset, said to the 6.6.10
king, 'Your highness, give an instruction as to what must
be done in this matter.' The eager king wanted the wedding
to be at an auspicious moment and after consideration he
said, 'Kalínga·sena must be asked. Let's see what she says.'

When he heard this, Yaugándharáyana agreed, took two
astrologers and went to Kalínga·sena. She greeted him respectfully and when he saw her beauty, he said to himself,
'After he gets this girl, the king will be so consumed with
desire that he will neglect the whole kingdom.' To her he
said, 'I have come with these astrologers to ascertain an appropriate time for your wedding so please say under which
star you were born.' When the astrologers heard from her 6.6.15

gaṇakās te mṛṣā kṛtvā vicāraṃ mantri|saṃvidā.
lagnaṃ tam eva tatr' âpi māsa|ṣaṭk'|ânta|vartinam
‹n' ârvāg ataḥ puro 'st' îti› vadantaḥ punar abhyadhuḥ.
śrutvā dūrataraṃ taṃ ca lagnam āvigna|cetasi
tataḥ Kaliṅgasenāyāṃ tan mahattarako 'bhyadhāt.
‹prekṣyo lagno 'nukūlaḥ prāg yena syād etayoḥ śubham
yāvat kālaṃ hi dampatyoḥ kiṃ cireṇ' â|cireṇa vā.›
etan|mahattara|vacaḥ śrutvā sarve 'pi tat|kṣaṇam
‹sad|uktam evam ev' âitad iti› tatra babhāṣire.
6.6.20 Yaugandharāyaṇo 'py āha ‹hā ku|lagne kṛte ca naḥ
Kaliṅgadattaḥ saṃbandhī rājā khedaṃ vrajed iti.›
tataḥ Kaliṅgasen' âpi sarvāṃs tān a|vaśā satī
‹yathā bhavanto jānant' îty› uktvā tūṣṇīṃ babhūva sā.
tad eva ca vacas tasyā gṛhītv" āmantrya tāṃ tataḥ
Yaugandharāyaṇo rājñaḥ pārśvaṃ sa|gaṇako yayau.
tatra tasmai tad āvedya Vats'|ēśāya tath" âiva saḥ
yuktyā ca tam avasthāpya sa jagāma nijaṃ gṛham.
siddha|kāl'|âtipātaś ca kārya|śeṣāya tatra saḥ
Yogeśvar'|ākhyaṃ suhṛdaṃ sasmāra brahma|rākṣasam.
6.6.25 sa pūrva|pratipannas taṃ svairaṃ dhyānād upasthitaḥ
rākṣaso mantriṇaṃ natvā ‹kiṃ smṛto 'sm' îty?› avocata.
tataḥ sa mantrī tasmai taṃ kṛtsnaṃ vyasana|daṃ prabhoḥ
Kaliṅgasenā|vṛttāntam uktvā bhūyo jagāda tam.

attendants under which star she had been born, in accordance with their agreement with the minister, after pretending to deliberate, there too they again gave the same time, six months thereafter, saying that no moment before then was presenting itself.

When she heard that the auspicious date for the wedding was so far off, Kalínga·sena was distressed. Then her chamberlain said, 'The most important thing is that a favorable date be found so that this couple will be happy—it does not matter whether it is a long time hence or soon.' The moment they heard these words from the chamberlain, everyone there announced that they were well said. Yaugándharáyana himself declared, 'Indeed. And if an in- 6.6.20
auspicious date were chosen then King Kalínga·datta, with whom we are to be allied, would be upset.'

At this Kalínga·sena too, having no choice, said to them all that it should be as they determined and fell silent. Accepting her words, Yaugándharáyana then said goodbye to her and went with the astrologers to the king. There he told the king of Vatsa exactly what had happened and, having contrived to stall him, he went home. Now that he had successfully delayed the marriage, in order to achieve the rest of what he wanted to do, he called to mind there his friend the brahmin *rákshasa* called Yogéshvara. Arriving directly 6.6.25
upon being thought of, as he had promised previously, the *rákshasa* bowed to the minister and asked why he had summoned him. At this the minister told him all about the episode with Kalínga·sena which was consuming his master with desire and then he said to him, 'I have bought some time, my friend, during which you should use your magic

‹kālo mayā hṛto, mitra, tan|madhye tvaṃ sva|yuktitaḥ
vṛttaṃ Kaliṅgasenāyāḥ pracchanno 'syā nirūpayeḥ.
vidyā|dhar'|ādayas tāṃ hi channaṃ vāñchanti niścitam
yato 'nyā tādṛśī n' âsti rūpeṇ' âsmiñ jagat|traye.
ataḥ ken' âpi siddhena saṅgaṃ vidyā|dhareṇa vā
gacchet sā yadi tac ca tvaṃ paśyes tad bhadrakaṃ bhavet.
6.6.30 anya|rūp'|āgataś c' âtra lakṣyas te divya|kāmukaḥ
svāpa|kāle yato divyāḥ suptāḥ sve rūpa āsate.
evaṃ tvad|dṛṣṭitas tasyā doṣo 'smābhir vilokyate
tasyāṃ rājā virajyec ca tat kāryaṃ nirvahec ca naḥ.›
ity ukto mantriṇā tena so 'bravīd brahma|rākṣasaḥ
‹yukty" âham eva kiṃ n' âitāṃ dhvaṃsayāmi nihanmi vā?›
tac chrutv" âiva mahā|mantrī taṃ sa Yaugandharāyaṇaḥ
uvāca ‹n' âitat kartavyam a|dharmo hi mahān bhavet.
yaś ca dharmam a|bādhitvā svena saṃsarate pathā
tasy' ôpayāti sāhāyyaṃ sa ev' âbhīṣṭa|siddhiṣu.
6.6.35 tat tasyāḥ sv'|ôtthito doṣaḥ prekṣaṇīyas tvayā, sakhe
yen' âsmābhir bhavan|maitryā rāja|kāryaṃ kṛtaṃ bhavet.›
iti mantri|var'|ādiṣṭaḥ sa gatvā brahma|rākṣasaḥ
gṛhaṃ Kaliṅgasenāyā yoga|cchannaḥ praviṣṭavān.
atr' ântare sakhī tasyāḥ sā May'|âsura|putrikā
āgāt Kaliṅgasenāyāḥ pārśvaṃ Somaprabhā punaḥ.
sā pṛṣṭvā rātri|vārtāṃ tāṃ yukta|bandhuṃ May'|ātma|jā
rāja|putrīm uvāc' âivaṃ tasmiñ śṛṇvati rākṣase.
‹adya pūrv'|āhṇa ev' âhaṃ vicitya tvām ih' āgatā
channā tv atiṣṭhaṃ tvat|pārśve dṛṣṭvā Yaugandharāyaṇam.
6.6.40 śrutaś ca yuṣmad|ālāpaḥ sarvaṃ c' âvagataṃ mayā

to watch in secret the behavior of Kalínga·sena. Sorcerers and other supernatural beings are sure to be lusting after her in secret, for there is no other girl as beautiful as she in these three worlds. So it would be good if she were to make love with some *siddha* or sorcerer and you were to witness it. Her divine lover will come in disguise, so you will need 6.6.30
to look at him when he is asleep because divine beings assume their own forms while they are sleeping. When she is thus found to be at fault by us as a result of your surveillance, the king will lose interest in her and we shall achieve our end.'

When the minister said this, the brahmin *rákshasa* replied, 'Why don't I just use magic to ravish or kill her?'

The chief minister Yaugándharáyana replied, 'That must not be done, for it would be a great sin and he who follows his path without sinning gets help in accomplishing his aims. So you must watch for a transgression that occurs 6.6.35
in her of its own accord, my friend, in order that through your friendship we can do what must be done for the king.'

After being instructed thus by the chief minister, the brahmin *rákshasa* went to Kalínga·sena's house and, using magic to make himself invisible, went inside. Meanwhile Kalínga·sena's friend Soma·prabha, the daughter of the *ásura* Maya, had come to her once more. Maya's daughter asked the princess, who was with her friends, what had happened in the night and then said to her, while the *rákshasa* listened on, "After searching for you this morning I came here. When I saw Yaugándharáyana at your side I stood out of sight and listened to your conversation. I found 6.6.40
out about everything. So why did you make the first move

tat kiṃ tvayā hya ev' aitad ārabdhaṃ man|niṣiddhayā.
a|vyapohy' â|nimittaṃ hi kāryaṃ yat kriyate, sakhi
tad an|iṣṭāya kalpeta tathā c' êmāṃ kathāṃ śṛṇu.

Antarvedyām abhūt pūrvaṃ Vasudatta iti dvijaḥ
Viṣṇudatt'|âbhidhānaś ca putras tasy' ôdapadyata.
sa Viṣṇudatto vayasā pūrṇa|ṣoḍaśa|vatsaraḥ
gantuṃ pravavṛte vidyā|prāptaye Valabhīṃ purīṃ.
milanti sma ca tasy' ânye sapta vipra|sutāḥ samāḥ
sapt' âpi te punar mūrkhāḥ sa vidvān sat|kul'|ôdgataḥ.
6.6.45 kṛtv" ânyonya|parityāga|śapathaṃ taiḥ samaṃ tataḥ
Viṣṇudattaḥ pratasthe sa pitror a|vidito niśi.

prasthitaś c' âgrato 'kasmād a|nimittam upasthitam
dṛṣṭvā so 'tra vayasyāṃs tān saha|prasthāyino 'bhyadhāt.
«a|nimittam idaṃ hanta yuktam adya nivartitum
punar eva prayāsyāmaḥ siddhaye śakun'|ânvitāḥ.»
tac chrutv" âiva sakhāyas taṃ mūrkhāḥ sapt' âpi te 'bruvan
«mṛṣā m" âjīgaṇaḥ śaṅkāṃ na hy ato bibhimo vayam.
tvaṃ ced bibheṣi tan mā gā vayaṃ yāmo 'dhun' âiva tu
prātar vidita|vṛttāntā n' âsmāṃs tyakṣyanti bāndhavāḥ.»
6.6.50 ity uktavadbhir a|jñais taiḥ sākaṃ śapatha|yantritaḥ
Viṣṇudatto yayāv eva sa smṛtv" âgha|haraṃ Harim.
rātry|ante ca viloky' ânyad a|nimittaṃ punar vadan
mūrkhais taiḥ sakhibhiḥ sarvaiḥ sa evaṃ nirabhartsyata.
«etad ev' â|nimittaṃ naḥ kim anyen,' âdhva|bhīluka
yat tvam asmābhir ānītaḥ kāka|śaṅkī pade pade.»

yesterday when I had told you not to? A task undertaken without first averting misfortune will lead to undesirable results, my friend. Just listen to this story.

Long ago there lived in the region between the Ganga and Yámuna rivers a brahmin called Vasu·datta. A son called Vishnu·datta was born to him, who, on reaching sixteen years of age, prepared to go to the city of Válabhi to acquire learning. Seven others joined him, brahmin boys like him, but those seven were fools while he was clever, having been
born into a good family. Then, after they had vowed never 6.6.45
to desert one another, Vishnu·datta set out with them at night without his parents knowing.

After setting forth, he saw a bad omen suddenly appear in front of them and spoke to his traveling companions about it, "Oh dear, this is a bad omen. We should turn back now and set out again when we have favorable signs for success." But as soon as they heard this, those seven stupid friends said, "It's pointless you deeming it dangerous. Don't bother, for we aren't scared of it. If you're frightened then don't journey on, but we shall continue forthwith. When our families find out in the morning what has happened, they will not let us go."

After those fools had said this, Vishnu·datta, bound by 6.6.50
his promise to them, meditated on Vishnu, the remover of sin, and continued on his way. At the end of the night he saw another bad omen, but while he was speaking of it, his foolish companions all scolded him thus: "With your worries about crows at every step, you stay-at-home, it's enough of a bad omen to have brought you with us. Let's not have

ity|ādi bhartsanāṃ kṛtvā gacchadbhis taiḥ samaṃ ca saḥ
vivaśaḥ prayayau Viṣṇudattas tūṣṇīṃ babhūva ca.
«n' ôpadeśo vidhātavyo mūrkhasya sv'|âbhicāriṇaḥ
saṃskāro 'vaskarasy' êva tiras|kāra|karo hi saḥ.
6.6.55 eko bahūnāṃ mūrkhāṇāṃ madhye nipatito budhaḥ
padmaḥ pāthas|taraṅgāṇām iva viplavate dhruvam.
tasmād eṣāṃ na vaktavyaṃ mayā bhūyo hit'|â|hitam
tūṣṇīm eva prayātavyaṃ vidhiḥ śreyo vidhāsyati.»
ity|ādy ākalayan mūrkhaiḥ prakramaṃs taiḥ samaṃ pathi
Viṣṇudatto dinasy' ânte śabara|grāmam āpa saḥ.

tatra bhrāntvā niśi prāpa taruṇy" âdhiṣṭhitaṃ striyā
gṛham ekaṃ yayāce ca nivāsaṃ so 'tha tāṃ striyam.
tayā datte 'pavarake sah' ânyais tair viveśa saḥ
sakhibhis te ca supt' âpi tatra nidrāṃ kṣaṇaṃ yayuḥ.
6.6.60 sa eko jāgrad ev' āsīd a|manuṣya|gṛh'|āśrayāt
svapanty a|jñā hi niśceṣṭāḥ kuto nidrā vivekinām?

tāvac ca tatra puruṣaḥ ko 'py eko nibhṛtaṃ yuvā
abhyantara|gṛhaṃ tasyāḥ praviveś' ântikaṃ striyāḥ.
tena sākaṃ ca sā reme ciraṃ gupt'|âbhibhāṣiṇī
rati|śrāntau ca tau daivān nidrāṃ dvāv api jagmatuḥ.
tac ca dīpa|prakāśena sarvaṃ dvār'|ântareṇa saḥ
Viṣṇudatto viloky' âivaṃ sa|nirvedam acintayat.
«kaṣṭaṃ kathaṃ praviṣṭāḥ smo duścāriṇyāḥ striyā gṛham?
dhruvaṃ jñāto 'yam etasyā na kaumāraḥ patiḥ punaḥ.
6.6.65 n' ânyathā hi bhavaty eṣā sa|śaṅka|nibhṛtā gatiḥ
mayā capala|citt" êyam ādāv eva ca lakṣitā.

any more!" After they had abused him like this, Vishnu·datta had no choice but to continue with them on their way and he kept quiet. "The self-deluded fool is not to be given instruction for, like polishing a turd, doing so incurs abuse.
A lone wise man fallen in the midst of a mass of fools is sure 6.6.55
to perish, like a lotus in waves. Therefore I shouldn't say anything more to these fellows about what is good or bad for them, but journey on in silence. Fate shall bring about what's best." Thinking these and other thoughts, Vishnu·datta continued along the road with those fools and at the end of the day they reached a tribal village.

After wandering around there that evening, he arrived at a house inhabited by a young woman and asked her for a place to stay. She gave them a room in which to sleep and he went in there with the others, his companions, and the
seven of them went straight to sleep. He alone remained 6.6.60
awake because he was staying in the house of a savage. The stupid sleep like logs but for the wise sleep is difficult.

Meanwhile some young man or other slipped into that woman's bedroom there and she, whispering sweet nothings, enjoyed herself with him for a long time until, as fate would have it, the two of them went to sleep, exhausted by their lovemaking. Vishnu·datta had seen everything through the door by the light of a lamp. Disillusioned, he said to himself, "Alas, how can we have entered the house of an immoral woman? She knows this man, but
he is surely not the man who married her, for otherwise 6.6.65
they would not be behaving fearfully and secretively, and

any'|â|lābhāt praviṣṭāḥ smaḥ kiṃ tv atr' ânyonya|sākṣiṇaḥ»

ity evaṃ cintayañ śabdaṃ janānāṃ so 'śṛṇod bahiḥ.
dadarśa praviśantaṃ ca sva|sva|sthāna|sthit'|ânugam
yuvānam abhipaśyantaṃ sa|khaḍgaṃ śabar'|âdhipam.
«ke yūyam iti?» pṛcchantaṃ matvā gṛha|patiṃ sa tam
bhītaḥ «pānthāḥ sma ity» āha Viṣṇudattaḥ pulinda|pam.
sa c' ântaḥ śabaro gatvā dṛṣṭvā bhāryāṃ tathā|sthitām
ciccheda tasya suptasya taj|jārasy' āsinā śiraḥ.
6.6.70 bhāryā tu nigṛhītā na tena sā n' âpi bodhitā
bhuvi nyast'|āsin" ânyatra paryaṅke suptam eva tu.
tad dṛṣṭvā sa|pradīpe 'tra Viṣṇudatto vyacintayat
«yuktaṃ str" îti na yad bhāryā hatā dāra|haro hataḥ.
kiṃ tu kṛtv" ēdṛśaṃ karma yad anen' âtra supyate
visrabdhaṃ tad aho citraṃ vīryam udrikta|cetasām!»

ity atra cintayaty eva Viṣṇudatte prabudhya sā
ku|strī dadarśa jāraṃ svaṃ hataṃ suptaṃ ca taṃ patim.
utthāya ca gṛhītvā tat|skandhe jāra|kabandhakam
hasten' âikena c' ādāya tac|chiraḥ sā viniryayau.
6.6.75 gatvā bahiś ca nikṣipya bhasma|kūṭ'|ântare drutam
kabandhaṃ sa|śiraskaṃ tam āyayau nibhṛtaṃ tataḥ.
Viṣṇudattaś ca nirgatya sarvaṃ dūrād vilokya tat
madhye sakhīnāṃ suptānāṃ praviśy' āsīt tath" âiva saḥ.
sā c' āgatya praviśy' ântaḥ patyuḥ suptasya durjanī

right from the start I noticed that she was wayward in nature. But we came in here because we didn't find anywhere else and we can vouch for each other."

While thinking this he heard voices outside. Then he saw a young tribal chieftain come in, carrying a sword and looking about, his attendants in their respective rightful places. He asked Vishnu·datta, "Who are you people," and thinking him to be the master of the house, the terrified Vishnu·datta replied to the tribal chief, "We are travelers." The tribal went in, saw his wife lying there like that and with his sword
cut off the head of her lover sleeping there. He did not, 6.6.70
however, punish his wife. He didn't even wake her up, but put his sword down on the ground and went straight to sleep on a different bed. When he saw this by the light of a lamp, Vishnu·datta said to himself there, "It is right that he killed the adulterer but did not kill his wife, because she is a woman. However, to sleep here soundly after doing such a deed—oh how amazing is the bravery of men of noble mind!"

While Vishnu·datta was there thinking this, that wicked woman woke up and saw her lover slain and her husband asleep. She got up, put her lover's headless corpse on her shoulders and, carrying his head in one hand, left the house.
On going outside she hurriedly threw the headless corpse 6.6.75
and head into a pile of ash and then sneaked back in. Vishnu·datta had gone out and seen all this from afar. He then returned to his sleeping companions and lay down as he was before. After coming back, that wicked woman went into the bedroom and, using that very same sword of his, cut off the head of her sleeping husband. Then she came

ten' âiva tat|kṛpāṇena tasya mūrdhānam acchinat.
nirgatya śrāvayantī ca bhṛtyāñ śabdaṃ cakāra sā
«hā hat" âsmi hato bhartā mam' âibhiḥ pathikair iti!»
tataḥ parijanāḥ śrutvā pradhāvy' ālokya taṃ prabhum
hataṃ tān Viṣṇudatt'|ādīn abhyadhāvann udāyudhāḥ.
6.6.80 etaiś c' ā|hanyamāneṣu teṣu trast'|ôtthiteṣv atha
anyeṣu tat|sahāyeṣu Viṣṇudatto 'bravīd drutam.
«alaṃ vo brahma|hatyābhir n' âiv' âsmābhir idaṃ kṛtam
etay" âiva kṛtaṃ hy etat ku|striy" ânya|prasaktayā.
mayā c' âpāvṛta|dvāra|mārgeṇ' ā|mūlam īkṣitam
nirgatya ca bahir dṛṣṭaṃ kṣamadhvaṃ yadi vacmi tat.»
ity uktvā tān sa śabarān Viṣṇudatto nivārya ca
tebhyo niḥśeṣam ā|mūlād vṛttāntaṃ tam avarṇayat.
nītvā c' âdarśayat teṣāṃ kabandhaṃ taṃ śiro|'nvitam
sadyo hataṃ tayā kṣiptaṃ striyā tasminn avaskare.
6.6.85 tataḥ svena *vivarṇena mukhen'* âṅgī|kṛte tayā
kulaṭāṃ tāṃ tiras|kṛtya sarve tatr' âivam abruvan.
«Smar'|ākṛṣṭā tanoty eva yā sāhasam a|śaṅkitā
sā para|svī|kṛtā ku|strī kṛpāṇ" îva na hanti kam?»
ity uktvā Viṣṇudatt'|ādīn sarvāṃs te mumucus tataḥ.
Viṣṇudattaṃ ca sapt' ânye sahāyās te 'tha tuṣṭuvuḥ.
«rakṣā|ratna|pradīpas tvaṃ jāto naḥ svapatāṃ niśi
tvat|prasādena tīrṇāḥ smo mṛtyum ady' â|nimitta|jam.»
stutv" âivaṃ Viṣṇudattaṃ taṃ śamayitvā ca durvacaḥ
praṇatās te yayuḥ prātaḥ sva|kāryāy' âiva tad|yutāḥ.›

out and shouted, so that her servants could hear, "Oh alas! My husband has been killed by these travelers!" On hearing this, her staff came running and when they saw their murdered master they fell upon Vishnu·datta and the others, weapons raised. While they were attacking the rest of 6.6.80
his companions, who had stood up in alarm, Vishnu·datta hurriedly said, "You must stop murdering brahmins! It was not we who did this! This woman did it herself, for the evil lady is in love with another man! I saw it from the start through the open door and then I went outside and saw what happened there. Bear with me and I shall tell you."

With these words Vishnu·datta held the tribals at bay and he then told them, from the beginning, everything that had happened. He took them and showed them the freshly slain headless corpse, and the head, which the woman had thrown into the rubbish heap. She then confirmed it with 6.6.85
her own *pale face : silent mouth* and everyone there abused her as a harlot and said, "The wicked wife who, taken by another man, behaves rashly under the influence of the god of love, will, like a dagger, kill anyone!"

After saying this they released Vishnu·datta and all the others. Vishnu·datta's seven companions now sang his praises. "While we were asleep at night you became our jewel-fueled lamp of protection. Thanks to you we have today been saved from a death born of bad omens." After praising Vishnu·datta thus, they stopped speaking ill of him and, bowing humbly, they set out in the morning to do what they had to do, accompanied by him.'

6.6.90 ittham Kaliṅgasenāyāḥ kathayitvā kathāṃ mithaḥ
Somaprabhā sā Kauśāmbyāṃ sakhīṃ punar uvāca tām.
‹evaṃ kārya|pravṛttānām a|nimittam upasthitam
vilamb'|ādy|a|pratihataṃ, sakhy, an|iṣṭaṃ prayacchati.
tataś c' âtr' ânutapyante prājña|vāky'|âvamāninaḥ
pravartamānā rabhasāt paryante manda|buddhayaḥ.
ato '|śubhe nimitte hyo Vats'|ēśaṃ prati yat tvayā
ātma|grahāya prahito dūto yuktaṃ na tat kṛtam.
tad a|vighnaṃ vivāhaṃ ca vidadhātu vidhis tava
ku|lagnen' āgatā gehād vivāhas tena dūrataḥ.
6.6.95 devā api ca lubhyanti tvayi rakṣyam idaṃ tataḥ
cintyaś ca nīti|nipuṇo mantrī Yaugandharāyaṇaḥ.
rāja|vyasana|śaṅkī san so 'tra vighnaṃ samācaret
vihite 'pi vivāhe vā doṣam utpādayet tava.
dhārmikaḥ san na kuryād vā doṣaṃ tad api te, sakhi
sa|patnī sarvathā cintyā kathāṃ vacmy atra te śṛṇu.

ast' îh' êkṣumatī nāma purī tasyāś ca pārśvataḥ
nadī tad|abhidhān' âiva Viśvāmitra|kṛte ubhe.
tat|samīpe mahac c' âsti vanaṃ tatra kṛt'|āśramaḥ
ūrdhva|pādas tapaś cakre munir Maṅkaṇak'|âbhidhaḥ.
6.6.100 tapasyatā ca ten' âtra gaganen' āgat" âpsaraḥ
adarśi Menakā nāma vātena calit'|âmbarā.
tato labdh'|âvakāśena Kāmena kṣobhit'|ātmanaḥ

After telling this story to Kalínga·sena in the course of 6.6.90
their conversation in Kaushámbi, Soma·prabha continued to speak to her friend. 'Thus a bad omen which presents itself to those who have undertaken a task, if not thwarted by delaying tactics or other methods, brings about undesirable results, my friend. And if those who are dimwitted ignore advice from the wise and behave rashly, they regret it in the end. So when yesterday, after there had been a bad omen, you sent an envoy to the king of Vatsa asking him to marry you, you did something wrong. So let fate arrange for you to be married without hindrance. You arrived from your home at an inauspicious moment. As a result your wedding
is a long way off. The gods are also lusting after you, so 6.6.95
watch out for that. And you must keep in mind the minister Yaugándharáyana who is skilled in statecraft. Worried about the king becoming consumed by passion he might move to obstruct the wedding, or even after the wedding is over he might raise complaints against you. Nevertheless, being pious, he will not do anything to harm you, my friend. However, you absolutely must bear your rival wife in mind. I shall tell you a story on this subject. Listen.

In this land there is a city called Íkshumati which is on the banks of a river of the same name. Both were created by Vishva·mitra. Near it there is a great forest in which a sage called Mánkanaka has made an ashram and performs
austerities standing on one leg. While performing austeri- 6.6.100
ties there, he saw an *ápsaras* called Ménaka arrive through the sky, her robe moving in the breeze. At this the god of love found his chance and disturbed the sage, so that his semen fell into a young banana tree. An utterly beautiful girl

nūtane kadalī|garbhe vīryaṃ tasy' âpatan muneḥ.
jajñe tataś ca kanyā sā sadyaḥ sarv'|âṅga|sundarī
a|moghaṃ hi maha"|rṣīṇāṃ vīryaṃ phalati tat|kṣaṇam.
saṃbhūtā kadalī|garbhe yasmāt tasmāc cakāra tām
nāmnā sa Kadalīgarbhāṃ pitā Maṅkaṇako muniḥ.
tasy' āśrame sā vavṛdhe Gautamasya Kṛpī yathā
Droṇa|bhāryā purā Rambhā|darśana|cyuta|vīrya|jā.
6.6.105 ekadā ca viveś' âitam āśramaṃ mṛgayā|rasāt
Dṛḍhavarmā hṛto 'śvena madhya|deśa|bhavo nṛpaḥ.
sa tāṃ dadarśa Kadalīgarbhāṃ prāvṛta|valkalām
muni|kany"|ôciten' âtra veṣeṇ' âtyanta|śobhitām.
sā ca dṛṣṭ" âsya nṛ|pateḥ svī|cakre hṛdayaṃ tathā
yath" âvakāśo 'pi hṛtas tatr' ântaḥ|pura|yoṣitām.
«ap' îmāṃ prāpnuyāṃ bhāryāṃ kasy' âp' îha sutām ṛṣeḥ
Duṣyanta iva Kaṇvasya muneḥ kanyāṃ Śakuntalām?»
iti saṃcintayann eva saṃgṛhīta|samit|kuśam
so 'tr' âpaśyat tam āyāntaṃ munim Maṅkaṇakaṃ nṛpaḥ.
6.6.110 vavande c' âinam abhyetya pādayor mukta|vāhanaḥ
pṛṣṭaś c' ātmānam etasmai munaye sa nyavedayat.
tataḥ sa Kadalīgarbhāṃ munir ādiśati sma tām
«vatse, rājño 'tither asya tvay" ârghyaṃ kalpyatām iti.»
«tath" êti» kalpit'|ātithyas tayā rājā sa namrayā
«īdṛk kutas te kany" êyam iti?» papraccha taṃ munim.
muniś ca sa tatas tasyās tām utpattiṃ ca nāma ca
anvarthaṃ Kadalīgarbh" êty asmai rājñe nyavedayat.
tatas tāṃ sa muneḥ kanyāṃ Menakā|bhāvan'|ôdbhavām

was instantly born from it, for the semen of great sages is potent and immediately bears fruit. Because she had been born inside a banana tree, her father the sage Mánkanaka called her Kádali·garbha. She grew up in his ashram just as Kripi, the wife of Drona, grew up long ago in Gáutama's ashram, having been born when his seed fell at the sight of Rambha.

One day Dridha·varman, a king from the middle re- 6.6.105
gions, was carried off by his horse in his love for the chase and entered that ashram. There he saw Kádali·garbha wearing bark and in the garb befitting the daughter of a sage she was particularly beautiful. On being seen she stole the heart of the king to such an extent that there was no room in it for the women of his harem. "Can I win as my wife this girl here, who is the daughter of some sage, in the same way that Dushyánta won Shakúntala, the daughter of the ascetic Kanva?"

Just as he was thinking this, the king saw the sage Mánkanaka arrive carrying fuel and *kusha* grass. He greeted him, 6.6.110
dismounted, and touched his feet, and on being questioned introduced himself to the sage. Then the sage gave Kádali·garbha an order: "Dear girl, prepare a welcome offering for our guest, the king here." She agreed and respectfully showed the king due hospitality. He asked the sage, "How did you get such a daughter?" and at this the sage told the king about her birth and how she bore the fitting name Kádali·garbha, "Born of a banana tree." Then, thinking the sage's daughter, having been born as a result of his thinking of Ménaka, to be an *ápsaras*, the king asked him for her

matv" âpsarasam aty|utko rājā tasmād ayācata.
6.6.115 so 'py etāṃ Kadalīgarbhāṃ dadau tasmai sutām ṛṣiḥ
divy'|ânubhāvaṃ pūrveṣām a|vicāryaṃ hi ceṣṭitam.
tac ca buddhvā prabhāveṇa tatr' âbhyetya sur'|âṅganāḥ
Menakā|prītitas tasyāś cakrur udvāha|maṇḍanam.
dattvā ca sarṣapān haste jagadus tāṃ tad" âiva tāḥ
«yāntī mārge vapasv' aitāṃs tvam abhijñāna|siddhaye.
yadi bhartrā kṛt'|âvajñā kadā|cit tvam ih' âiṣyasi
taj|jātair ebhir āyāntī panthānaṃ, putri, vetsyati.»
ity uktāṃ tābhir āropya kṛt'|ôdvāhāṃ sva|vājini
sa rājā Kadalīgarbhāṃ Dṛḍhavarmā yayau tataḥ.
6.6.120 prāpt'|ânvāgata|sainyo 'tha vapantyā sarṣapān pathi
vadhvā tayā saha prāpa rāja|dhānīṃ nijāṃ ca saḥ.
tatr' ânya|patnī|vimukhaḥ Kadalīgarbhayā tayā
samaṃ sa tasthāv ākhyāta|tad|vṛttāntaḥ sva|mantriṣu.
tatas tasya mahā|devī tadīyaṃ mantriṇaṃ rahaḥ
smārayitv" ôpakārān svāñ jagād' âtyanta|duḥkhitā.
«rājñā nūtana|bhāry"|âika|sakten' âdy' âham ujjhitā
tat tathā kuru yen' âiṣā sa|patnī me nivartate.»
tac chrutvā so 'bravīn mantrī «devi, kartuṃ na yujyate
mādṛśānāṃ prabhoḥ patnyā vināśo 'tha viyojanam.
6.6.125 eṣa pravrājaka|strīṇāṃ viṣayaḥ kuhak'|ādiṣu
prayogeṣv abhiyuktānāṃ saṃgatānāṃ tathā|vidhaiḥ.
tā hi kaitava|tāpasyaḥ praviśy' aiv' â|nivāritāḥ
gṛheṣu māyā|kuśalāḥ karma kiṃ kiṃ na kurvate?»

hand and the sage betrothed his daughter Kádali·garbha to 6.6.115
him, for our forefathers' actions had divine authority and were spontaneous. The ladies of heaven, having found out about it using their powers, came there and, because of their fondness for Ménaka, made up the girl for her wedding. Immediately afterwards they put some mustard seeds in her hand and said to her, "On your way, you should scatter these seeds along the path so that you will be able to recognize it. If your husband should ever treat you with disrespect and you come back here, my girl, you will recognize the path as you journey along it by the plants produced from them."

After they had said this to her, King Dridha·varman put
his new bride Kádali·garbha on his horse and left. He then 6.6.120
found the army that had accompanied him and together with his bride, who scattered the mustard seeds along the way, he arrived at his capital. After he had told his ministers her story, he lived there with Kádali·garbha, ignoring his other wives. At this his chief queen, extremely distressed, said in private to his minister, having reminded him of the favors she had done him, "The king is devoted to his new wife alone and has now abandoned me, so please arrange for the disposal of my rival." When he heard this, the minister said, "Queen, it is not right for men like me to bring about the demise or exile of their masters' wives.
That is for mendicants' wives devoted to cheating and so 6.6.125
forth who dally with men like themselves, for with their skills in magic such dishonest lady ascetics can go straight into houses unchecked and do whatever they want."

ity uktā tena sā devī vinat" êv' āha taṃ hriyā
«alaṃ tarhi mam' ânena garhitena satām iti.»

tad|vaco hṛdi kṛtvā tu taṃ visṛjya ca mantriṇam
kāṃ|cit pravrājikāṃ ceṭī|mukhen' ānayati sma sā.
tasyāḥ śaśaṃsa c' ā|mūlāt tat sarvaṃ sva|manīṣitam
aṅgī|cakāra dātuṃ ca siddhe kārye dhanaṃ mahat.
6.6.130 s" âpy artha|lobhād ārtāṃ tām ity uvāca ku|tāpasī
«devi, kiṃ nāma vastv etad ahaṃ te sadhayāmy adaḥ.
nānā|vidhān hi jānāmi prayogān subahūn aham.»

evam āśvāsya tāṃ devīṃ s" âtha pravrajikā yayau.
maṭhikāṃ prāpya ca nijāṃ bhīt" êv' êttham acintayat
«aho atīva bhog'|āśā kaṃ nāma na viḍambayet
yan mayā sahasā devyāḥ pratijñā purataḥ kṛtā?
vijñānaṃ c' âtra tādṛṅ me samyak kiṃ|cin na vidyate.
anyatr' êva ca na vyājaṃ kartuṃ rāja|gṛhe kṣamam
jñātvā jātu hi kurvīran nigrahaṃ prabhaviṣṇavaḥ.
6.6.135 ekas tatr' âbhyupāyaḥ syād yat suhṛn me 'sti nāpitaḥ
īdṛg|vijñāna|kuśalaḥ sa cet kuryād ih' ôdyamam.»

ity ālocy' âiva sā tasya nāpitasy' ântikaṃ yayau
tasmai manīṣitaṃ sarvaṃ tac chaśaṃs' ârtha|siddhidam.
tataḥ sa nāpito vṛddho dhūrtaś c' âivam acintayat
«upasthitam idaṃ diṣṭyā lābha|sthānaṃ mam' âdhunā.
tan na bādhyā navā rāja|vadhū rakṣyā tu sā yataḥ
divya|dṛṣṭiḥ pitā tasyāḥ† sarvaṃ prakhyāpayed idam.

When he said this to the queen, she, as if downcast, said to him embarrassedly, "In that case I won't have anything to do with this proposal of mine: it has been censured by the virtuous."

However she took his words to heart and after dismissing the minister she had a servant girl bring in some ascetic lady or other and she told her from the beginning everything she wanted, agreeing to give her a large fortune if her aims were achieved. That wicked ascetic lady, in her greed for wealth, 6.6.130
said to the stricken queen, "Your highness, this is a trifling matter and I shall accomplish it for you, for I know a great many magic tricks of various kinds."

Having thus reassured the queen, the ascetic lady went on her way. After reaching her cell, she said to herself, seemingly afraid, "Oh dear! The overblown desire for riches which made me rashly make the promise to the queen could make a fool of anyone. I do not have any special knowledge whatsoever of the kind required for this and I can't fake it in the palace like elsewhere, for those in power might find out and punish me. There might be one way out of this: I 6.6.135
have a friend, a barber who is skilled in trickery of this sort, and he might perhaps apply himself in this matter."

After thinking this, she went straight to the barber and told him everything she had in mind for bringing about what she wanted. At this the cunning old barber said to himself: "Lucky me! I've just been presented with a chance to make some profit. So the king's new wife is not to be harassed but protected, because her father has divine sight and might reveal everything. However, let's profit from that queen for the time being by separating her from the king,

viśliṣy' âitāṃ tu nṛ|pater devīṃ saṃprati bhuñjmahe
ku|rahasya|sahāye hi bhṛte bhṛtyāyate prabhuḥ.
6.6.140 saṃśleṣya kāle rājñe ca vācyam etat tathā mayā
yathā syād upajīvyo me rājā sā ca' ṛṣi|kanyakā.
evaṃ ca n' âtipāpaṃ syād bhaved dīrghā ca jīvikā»
ity ālocya sa tāṃ prāha nāpitaḥ kūṭa|tāpasīm.

«amba, sarvaṃ karomy etat kiṃ tu yoga|balena cet
eṣā rājño navā bhāryā hanyate tan na yujyate.
buddhvā kadā|cid rājā hi sarvān asmān vināśayet
strī|hatyā|pātakaṃ ca syāt tat|pitā ca muniḥ śapet.
tasmād buddhi|balen' âiṣā rājño viśleṣyate param
yena devī sukhaṃ tiṣṭhed artha|prāptir bhavec ca naḥ
6.6.145 etac ca me kiyat kiṃ hi na buddhyā sādhayāmy aham
prajñānaṃ māmakīnaṃ ca śrūyatāṃ varṇayāmi te.

abhūd asya pitā rājño duḥśīlo Dṛḍhavarmaṇaḥ
ahaṃ ca dāsas tasy' êha rājñaḥ sv'|ôcita|karma|kṛt.
sa kadā|cid iha bhrāmyan bhāryām aikṣata māmakīm
tasyāṃ tasya su|rūpāyāṃ taruṇyāṃ ca mano yayau.
nāpita|str" îti c' âbodhi pṛṣṭvā parijanaṃ sa tām
kiṃ nāpitaḥ karot' îti praviśy' âiva sa me gṛham.
upabhujy' âiva tāṃ svecchaṃ mad|bhāryāṃ ku|nṛpo yayau
ahaṃ ca tad|ahar daivād gṛhād āsaṃ bahiḥ kva|cit.
6.6.150 anyedyuś ca praviṣṭena dṛṣṭā s' ânyādṛśī mayā
pṛṣṭā bhāryā yathā|vṛttaṃ s'|âbhimān" êva me 'bhyadhāt.
tat|krameṇ' âiva tāṃ bhāryām a|śaktasya niṣedhane
nityam ev' ôpabhuñjānaḥ sa mam' ôttabdhavān nṛpaḥ.

for by taking help in a wicked intrigue a master becomes a servant. And after in time reuniting them, I must explain 6.6.140
this to the king, so that he and the sage's daughter might provide me with a living. And in this way I shall not commit too great a sin and be supported for a long time." After thinking this through, the barber said to the dishonest lady ascetic:

"Mother, I shall do all of this, but it would not be right if by the power of the magic the king's new wife should be killed, for if the king were one day to find out, he would destroy us all. We would have committed the sin of killing a woman and her father the sage would curse us. Therefore we should use our wits to separate her completely from the king, so that the queen is happy and we get our money. And this is nothing for me, because using my wits I can do 6.6.145
anything. I'll tell you how clever I am. Listen.

This King Dridha·varman had a badly behaved father. I was his servant here, and performed duties appropriate to my position. One day he was wandering about here and saw my wife. She was beautiful and young and she captivated his mind. When he asked his entourage about her and found out that she was a barber's wife, that wicked king went straight into my house, thinking that a barber wouldn't do anything about it. He had his fill of fun with my wife and left straight after. As fate would have it, I was away from the house that day. When I returned the next 6.6.150
day I noticed that my wife looked strange. On being questioned she told me what had happened, as if proud. That lecherous king kept on enjoying himself with my wife in that very same fashion and I was powerless to stop him.

kuto gamyam a|gamyaṃ vā ku|śīl'|ônmādinaḥ prabhoḥ?
vāt'|ôdbhūtasya dāv'|âgneḥ kiṃ tṛṇaṃ kiṃ ca kānanam?
tato yāvad gatir me 'sti na kā|cit tan|nivāraṇe
tāvat svalp'|âśana|kṣāmo māndya|vyājam aśiśriyam.
tādṛśaś ca gato 'bhūvaṃ rājñas tasy' âham antikam
sva|vyāpār'|ôpasev"|ârthaṃ niḥśvasan kṛśa|pāṇḍuraḥ.
6.6.155 tatra mandam iv' ālokya s'|âbhiprāyaḥ sa māṃ nṛpaḥ
papraccha ‹re, kim īdṛk tvaṃ saṃjātaḥ kathyatām iti.›
nirbandha|pṛṣṭas taṃ c' âhaṃ vijane yācit'|â|bhayaḥ
pratyavocaṃ nṛpaṃ ‹deva, bhāry" âsti mama ḍākinī.
sā ca suptasya me 'ntrāṇi guden' ākṛṣya cūṣati
tath" âiva c' ântaḥ kṣipati ten' âhaṃ kṣāmatāṃ gataḥ.
poṣaṇāya ca me nityaṃ bṛṃhaṇaṃ bhojanaṃ kutaḥ?›
ity uktaḥ sa mayā rājā jātā|śaṅko vyacintayat.
‹kiṃ satyaṃ ḍākinī sā syāt? ten' âhaṃ kiṃ hṛtas tayā?
kiṃ|svid āhāra|puṣṭasya cūṣed antraṃ mam' âpi sā.
6.6.160 tad adya tām ahaṃ yuktyā jijñāsiṣye svayaṃ niśi.›
iti saṃcintya rājā me so 'tr' āhāram adāpayat.
tato gatvā gṛhaṃ tasyā bhāryāyāḥ saṃnidhāv aham
aśrūṇy amuñca pṛṣṭaś ca tayā tām evam abravam.
‹priye, na vācyaṃ kasy' âpi tvayā śṛṇu vadāmi te
asya rājño gude jātā dantā vajr'|âśri|saṃnibhāḥ.
tac ca bhagno 'dya jātyo 'pi kṣuro me karma kurvataḥ
evaṃ c' âtra mam' êdānīṃ kṣuras truṭyet pade pade.
tan navaṃ navam āneṣye kuto nityam ahaṃ kṣuram?

How is a king crazed by decadence to know what is and what is not fair game? A wildfire fanned by the wind makes no distinction between grass and forest. So while there was no way for me to stop him, I feigned illness by making myself thin through eating very little and I went to the king in that state, wheezing, thin and pale, to carry out my duties.
Seeing me there looking ill, the king asked me, betraying 6.6.155
intent, 'Hey, tell me, why have you become like this?'

He questioned me insistently and after asking him to promise not to punish me I answered him in private. 'Your highness, my wife is a witch and when I am asleep she pulls my entrails out of my anus, sucks them and then puts them back in as they were. That is why I have become thin. The regular consumption of wholesome food cannot nourish me.'

When I said this to him, the king grew worried and said to himself, 'Could she really be a witch? If so, why has she seduced me? I am well-fed—perhaps she is going to suck
my entrails too. So tonight I shall use a trick to test her my- 6.6.160
self.' After thinking this, the king had me given some food there. Then I went home and in the presence of my wife I cried. When she questioned me I said to her, 'My dear, you must not tell anyone what I am about to tell you. Listen. In the king's bottom teeth have appeared which are like spikes of diamond and because of this when I was doing my job today my razor broke, even though it is of the finest quality. My razor is now going to break on it like that every time. How am I to keep on getting new razors? So I am crying
because my livelihood is finished.' When I said this to my 6.6.165

ato rodimi naṣṭā hi jīvik" êyaṃ gṛhe mama.›
6.6.165 ity uktā sā mayā bhāryā matim ādhād upaiṣyataḥ
rātrau rājño 'sya suptasya guda|dant'|âdbhut'|ēkṣaṇe.
ā|saṃsārād a|dṛṣṭaṃ tad a|satyaṃ na tv abodhi sā
vidagdhā api vañcyante viṭa|varṇanayā striyaḥ.
ath' âitya tāṃ niśi svairaṃ mad|bhāryām upabhujya saḥ
rājā śramād iv' âlīkaṃ suptavān mad|vacaḥ smaran.
mad|bhāry" âpy atha taṃ suptaṃ matvā tasya śanaiḥ śanaiḥ
hastaṃ prasārayām āsa gude dant'|ôpalabdhaye.
guda|prāpte ca tat|pāṇāv utthāya sahas" âiva saḥ
‹ḍākinī! ḍākin" îty!› uktvā trasto rājā tato yayau.
6.6.170 tataḥ prabhṛti sā tena bhītyā tyaktā nṛpeṇa me
bhāryā gṛhīta|saṃtoṣā mad|ek'|āyattatāṃ gatā.
evaṃ pūrvaṃ nṛpād buddhyā gṛhiṇī mocitā mayā.»
iti tāṃ tāpasīm uktvā nāpitaḥ so 'bravīt punaḥ.
«tad etat prajñayā kāryam, ārye, yuṣman|manīṣitam
yathā ca kriyate, mātas, tad idaṃ vacmi te śṛṇu.
ko 'py antaḥ|pura|vṛddho 'tra svī|kāryo yo bravīty amum
‹jāyā te Kadalīgarbhā ḍākin" îti› nṛpaṃ rahaḥ.
āraṇyakāyā na hy asyāḥ kaś|cit parijanaḥ svakaḥ
sarvaḥ paro bheda|saho lobhāt kurvīta kiṃ na yat.
6.6.175 tato 'smin rājñi sāśaṅke śravaṇān niśi yatnataḥ
hasta|pād'|ādi Kadalīgarbhā|dhāmni nidhīyate.
tat prabhāte vilokỳ' âiva rājā satyam avetya tat
vṛddh'|ôktaṃ Kadalīgarbhāṃ bhītas tāṃ tyakṣyati svayam.
evaṃ sa|patnī|virahād devī sukham avāpnuyāt
tvāṃ ca sā bahu manyeta lābhaḥ kaś|cid bhavec ca naḥ.»

wife, she decided to examine the strange tooth in the bottom of the king, who was due to visit that night, while he slept. Such a thing had never been seen anywhere in the world, but she did not think it a lie. Even clever women are deceived by the tales of rogues. That night the king came and enjoyed himself to his heart's content with my wife, after which, bearing in mind what I had said, he pretended to go to sleep as if he were exhausted. Then my wife, thinking him to be asleep, very slowly extended her hand in order to find the tooth in his bottom. When her hand reached his anus, the king jumped up and, saying, 'A witch! A witch!,' fled in terror. From then on the king left my wife alone out 6.6.170
of fear, and she, having found happiness, became devoted to me alone. I have thus already used my wits to free a wife from the king."

After saying this to the lady ascetic, the barber continued to speak. "So, noble lady, your wish can be achieved through wisdom. I shall tell you what is to be done, mother. Listen. Some old retainer in the harem here is to be won over so that in private he will tell the king that his wife Kádali·garbha is a witch. She is from the forest and has no entourage of her own, and all strangers can be won over and made to do anything out of greed. Then, with the king 6.6.175
alarmed at hearing this, we must make efforts to put body parts such as hands and feet in Kádali·garbha's house by night. As soon as he sees them in the morning, the king will think what the old man has said about Kádali·garbha to be true and he will abandon her in terror. With her rival wife thus deserted the queen will be happy and hold you in high esteem, and we should make some profit."

ity uktā tāpasī tena nāpitena «tath" êti» sā
gatvā rājño mahā|devyai yathā|vastu nyavedayat.
devī ca tat tathā cakre sā tad|yuktyā nṛpo 'pi tām
pratyakṣaṃ vīkṣya Kadalīgarbhāṃ «duṣṭ" êti» tāṃ jahau.
6.6.180 tuṣṭayā ca tato devyā tayā guptam adāyi yat
pravrājikā tad bubhuje sā yath"|êṣṭaṃ sa|nāpitā.
tyaktā ca Kadalīgarbhā sā tena Dṛḍhavarmaṇā
rājñ" âbhiśāpa|saṃtaptā niryayau rāja|mandirāt.

yen' ājagāma ten' âiva prayayau pitur āśramam
pūrv'|ôpta|jāta|siddh'|ârtha|s'|âbhijñānena sā pathā.
tatra tām āgatāṃ dṛṣṭvā so 'kasmāt tat|pitā muniḥ
tasyā duścarit'|āśaṅkī tasthau Maṅkaṇakaḥ kṣaṇam.
praṇidhānāc ca taṃ kṛtsnaṃ tad|vṛttāntam avetya saḥ
āśvāsya ca svayaṃ snehāt tām ādāya yayau tataḥ.
6.6.185 etya tasmai yad ācakhyau svayaṃ prahvāya bhū|bhṛte
devyā sa|patnī|doṣeṇa kṛtaṃ kapaṭa|nāṭakam.
tat|kālaṃ svayam abhyetya rājñe tasmai sa nāpitaḥ
yathā|vṛttaṃ tad ācaṣṭa punar evam uvāca ca.
«itthaṃ viśleṣya Kadalīgarbhā rājñī mayā, prabho
abhicāra|vaśād yuktyā devīṃ saṃtoṣya rakṣitā.»
tac chrutvā niścayaṃ dṛṣṭvā mun'|îndra|vacanasya saḥ
jagrāha Kadalīgarbhāṃ saṃjāta|pratyayo nṛpaḥ.
anuvrajya muniṃ taṃ ca saṃvibheje sa nāpitam
«bhakto mam' âyam ity» arthair dhūrtair bhojyā bat' ēśvarāḥ.
6.6.190 tatas tayā samaṃ tasthau Kadalīgarbhay" âiva saḥ
rājā sva|devī|vimukho Dṛḍhavarmā su|nirvṛtaḥ.

On being told this by the barber, the lady ascetic agreed and went and communicated it in detail to the king's chief queen. The queen did what the lady ascetic had said and as a result of her ploy, the king, when he saw Kádali·garbha in
front of him, thought she was evil and abandoned her. Then 6.6.180
the delighted queen secretly presented the lady ascetic with gifts which she and the barber enjoyed as they had wished. Kádali·garbha, abandoned by King Dridha·varman, left the royal palace aggrieved at the false accusation.

She went to her father's ashram by the same path that she had come, the seeds she had sown earlier in order to recognize it having grown up and achieved their purpose. When her father the sage Mánkanaka saw her arrive there unexpectedly he paused for a moment, worried that she had misbehaved herself. By entering a trance he found out everything that had happened. He lovingly comforted her
himself before taking her with him and leaving. He went in 6.6.185
person and told the bowing king about the deceitful drama cooked up by the queen to denounce her rival. At that moment the barber himself went up to the king, told him in detail what had happened and then said to him, "By thus distancing your Queen Kádali·garbha, I contrived to protect her from black magic and appeased the chief queen." On hearing this and realizing that what the great sage had said was true, the king was convinced and took back Kádali·garbha. After respectfully accompanying the sage on his way home he bestowed wealth on the barber, thinking that he was devoted to him—kings are to be profited from by

evaṃ|vidhān vidadhate su|bahūn sa|patnyo
doṣān mṛṣ" âpy, an|avam'|âṅgi Kaliṅgasene
tvaṃ kanyakā ca cira|bhāvi|vivāha|lagnā
vāñchanty a|cintya|gatayaś ca surā api tvām.
tat sarvataḥ sāṃpratam ātmanā tvam
ātmānam ekaṃ jagad|eka|ratnam
Vats'|ēśvar'|âik'|ârpitam atra rakṣer
vairaṃ tav' âyaṃ hi nijaḥ prakarṣaḥ.
ahaṃ hi n' êṣyāmi, sakhi, tvad|antikaṃ
sthit" âdhunā tvaṃ pati|mandire yataḥ
sakhī|pateḥ sadma na yānti sat|striyaḥ,
sugātri, bhartr" âdya nivārit" âsmi ca.
na ca guptam ih' āgamaḥ kṣamo me
tvad|atisneha|vaśāt sa divya|dṛṣṭiḥ
tad avaiti hi mat|patiḥ kathaṃ|cit
tam anujñāpya kil' āgat" âham adya.
6.6.195 iha n' âsty adhunā hi māmakīnaṃ,
sakhi, kāryaṃ tava yāmi tad gṛhāya
yadi mām anumaṃsyate ca bhartā
tad ih' âiṣyāmi punar vilaṅghya lajjām.›
itthaṃ sa|bāṣpam abhidhāya Kaliṅgasenāṃ
tām aśru|dhauta|vadanāṃ manuj'|êndra|putrīm
āśvāsya c' âhni vigalaty asur'|êndra|putrī
Somaprabhā sva|bhavanaṃ nabhasā jagāma.

iti mahā|kavi|śrī|Somadeva|bhaṭṭa|viracite Kathāsaritsāgare Madanamañcukā|lambake ṣaṣṭhas taraṅgaḥ.

rogues! Then, turning his back on his queen, King Dridha·varman lived in great happiness with no one but Kádali·garbha. 6.6.190

Rival wives impute many such wrongdoings, even falsely, O Kalínga·sena, you of the exalted body. You are a virgin girl, the time for whose marriage has been fixed far in the future, and even the gods, whose ways are unthinkable, desire you. So for the time being you yourself must guard your person here in every way, you who are unique, the one jewel of the world, who have been dedicated to the king of Vatsa alone, for this preeminence of yours gives rise to hostility. I, my friend, shall not visit you, now that you are living in your husband's house, because good women do not go to the houses of their friends' husbands, O lovely lady, and I have just been forbidden to do so by my husband. Nor can I come here in secret, driven by my excessive love for you, for my husband has divine sight and will find out; indeed, it was with difficulty that I got his permission to come here
today. Now there is nothing left here for me to do for you 6.6.195
so I shall go home. If my husband gives me leave, then I shall put aside shame and come here again.'

After saying these words through sobs and reassuring Kalínga·sena, the daughter of the mortal king, her face awash with tears, Soma·prabha, the daughter of the *ásura* king, flew home as the day ebbed away.

Thus ends the sixth wave in the Mádana·mánchuka Attainment in the "Ocean of the Rivers of Story" composed by the glorious and learned great poet Soma·deva.

7

6.7.1 TATAḤ SOMAPRABHĀṂ yātāṃ smarantī tāṃ priyāṃ sakhīm
Kaliṅgasenā saṃtyakta|nija|deśa|sva|bāndhavā
sā vilambita|Vats'|ēśa|pāṇi|graha|mah"|ôtsavā
nar'|êndra|kanyā Kauśāmbyāṃ mṛg" îv' āsīd vana|cyutā.
Kaliṅgasenā|vivāha|vilambana|vicakṣaṇān
gaṇakān prati s'|āsūya iva Vats'|ēśvaro 'pi ca
autsukya|vimanās tasmin dine ceto vinodayan
devyā Vāsavadattāyā nivāsa|bhavanaṃ yayau.
6.7.5 tatra sā taṃ patiṃ devī nirvikārā viśeṣataḥ
upācarat sv'|ôpacāraiḥ prāṅ|mantri|vara|śikṣitā.
‹Kaliṅgasenā|vṛttānte khyāte 'py a|vikṛtā katham
dev" îyam iti?› sa dhyātvā rājā jijñāsur āha tām.
‹kaccid, devi, tvayā jñātaṃ svayaṃvara|kṛte mama
Kaliṅgasenā nām' âiṣā rāja|putrī yad āgatā.›
tac chrutv" âiv' â|vibhinnena mukha|rāgeṇa s" âbravīt
‹jñātaṃ may" âti|harṣo me Lakṣmīḥ sā hy āgat" êha naḥ.
vaśa|ge hi mahā|rāje tat|prāptyā tat|pitary api
Kaliṅgadatte pṛthvī te sutarāṃ vartate vaśe.
6.7.10 ahaṃ ca tvad|vibhūty' âiva sukhitā tvat|sukhena ca
ārya|putra, tav' âitac ca viditaṃ prāg api sthitam.
tan na dhany" âsmi kiṃ yasyā mama bhartā tvam īdṛśaḥ
yaṃ rāja|kanyā vāñchanti vāñchyamānā nṛp'|ântaraiḥ?›

7

THEN, THINKING OF her dear absent friend Soma·prabha, 6.7.1
princess Kalínga·sena, who had left her own country and family, and the great celebrations of whose wedding to the king of Vatsa had been delayed, was like a doe that has quit the forest while she remained in Kaushámbi. The king of Vatsa, a little annoyed with the astrologers who were craftily delaying his wedding to Kalínga·sena, was beside himself with longing and in order to distract himself he went that
day to Queen Vásava·datta's quarters. There the queen be- 6.7.5
stowed her favors on her husband as attentively as normal, having previously been told what to do by the chief minister. The king, wondering how the queen could be her usual self despite the news about Kalínga·sena being well known, was curious and said to her, 'Might you be aware, O queen, that this princess called Kalínga·sena who has arrived has chosen me as her husband?'

As soon as she heard this she said, the color of her face unchanged, 'I am aware and I am extremely happy, for she is the goddess of fortune come here to us in person, for when her father Kalínga·datta, who is a great king, is subservient as a result of her being won, you will control even more of
the earth. It is your glory, as well as your happiness, that 6.7.10
has made me happy, my noble lord. Furthermore, I knew previously that you had decided on this. Am I not lucky to have a husband like you, who is desired by princesses who are desired by other kings?'

evaṃ Vats'|ēśvaraḥ prokto devyā Vāsavadattayā
Yaugandharāyaṇa|pratta|śikṣay" ântas tutoṣa saḥ.
tay" âiva ca sah' āsevya pānaṃ tad|vāsake niśi
tasyāṃ suṣvāpa madhye ca prabuddhaḥ samacintayat.
‹kiṃ|svin mah"|ânubhāv" êtthaṃ devī mām anuvartate
Kaliṅgasenām api yat sa|patnīm anumanyate?
6.7.15 kathaṃ vā śaknuyād etāṃ soḍhuṃ s" âiṣā tapasvinī
Padmāvatī|vivāhe 'pi yā daivān na jahāv asūn?
tad asyāś ced an|iṣṭaṃ syāt sarva|nāśas tato bhavet
etad|ālambanāḥ putra|śvaśurya|śvaśurāś ca me.
Padmāvatī ca rājyaṃ ca kim abhyadhikam ucyate?
ataḥ Kaliṅgasen" âiṣā pariṇeyā kathaṃ mayā?›
evam ālocya Vats'|ēśo niś"|ânte nirgatas tataḥ
apar'|âhṇe yayau devyāḥ Padmāvatyāḥ sa mandiram.
s" âpy enam āgataṃ datta|śikṣā Vāsavadattayā
tath" âiv' ôpācarat tadvat pṛṣṭ" âvocat tath" âiva ca.
6.7.20 tato 'nyedyus tayor devyor ekaṃ cittaṃ vacaś ca tat
Yaugandharāyaṇāy' âsau śaśaṃsa vimṛśan nṛpaḥ.
so 'pi taṃ vīkṣya rājānaṃ vicāra|patitaṃ śanaiḥ
kāla|vedī jagād' âivaṃ mantrī Yaugandharāyaṇaḥ.
‹jāne 'haṃ n' âitad etāvad abhiprāyo 'tra dāruṇaḥ
devībhyāṃ jīvita|tyāga|dārḍhyād uktaṃ hi tat tathā.
any'|āsakte gate ca dyāṃ striyo maraṇa|niścitāḥ
bhavanty a|dainya|gambhīrāḥ sādhvyaḥ sarvatra niḥspṛhāḥ.

When Queen Vásava·datta, at the instruction of Yaugándharáyana, said this to him, the king of Vatsa was inwardly delighted. That night he enjoyed a drink with her in her apartment and then went to sleep. In the middle of the night he woke up and said to himself, 'Is the high-minded queen so obedient to me that she even approves of having Kalínga·sena as her rival wife? But how can she be such a 6.7.15
stoic that she puts up with her when at my wedding to Padmávati it was only through a stroke of fate that she did not give up her life? If something bad were to happen to her, absolute disaster would follow. My son, my brothers-in-law and my father-in-law depend on her, as well as Padmávati and the kingdom. There is nothing more important than them so how can I marry this girl Kalínga·sena?'

These were the king of Vatsa's thoughts when at the end of the night he left there. That afternoon he went to the palace of Queen Padmávati. When he arrived she too, having been given instructions by Vásava·datta, attended to him in the same way and on being asked the same question gave an identical answer.

Then on the next day the king, thinking about how the 6.7.20
two queens had been of one mind and voice, told his minister Yaugándharáyana, who, knowing how to pick his moment and having noticed that the king had become unsure, said, 'I think that this is not the whole story. There is an awful intention behind it. The queens spoke thus because they have resolved to abandon their lives. When their men fall in love with someone else or have gone to heaven, virtuous women, their lack of sorrow making them inscrutable, have no desire for anything and become intent on dying. Wives

a|sahyaṃ hi puraṃdhrīṇāṃ premṇo gāḍhasya khaṇḍanam
tathā ca, rājaṃs, tatr' âitāṃ Śrutasena|kathāṃ śṛṇu.
6.7.25 abhūd dakṣiṇa|bhūmau prāg Gokarṇ'|ākhye pure nṛpaḥ
Śrutasena iti khyātaḥ kula|bhūṣā śrut'|ânvitaḥ.
tasya c' âik" âbhavac cintā rājñaḥ saṃpūrṇa|saṃpadaḥ
ātm"|ânurūpāṃ bhāryāṃ yat sa na tāvad avāptavān.
ekadā ca nṛpaḥ kurvaṃś cintāṃ tāṃ tat|kath'|ântare
Agniśarm'|âbhidhānena jagade so 'gra|janmanā.
«āścarye dve mayā dṛṣṭe te, rājan, varṇaye śṛṇu
tīrtha|yātrā|gataḥ Pañcatīrthīṃ tām aham āptavān.
yasyām apsarasaḥ pañca grāhatvaṃ ṛṣi|śāpataḥ
prāptāḥ satīr udaharat tīrtha|yātrā|gato 'rjunaḥ.
6.7.30 tatra tīrtha|vare snātvā pañca|rātr'|ôpavāsinām
Nārāyaṇ'|ânucaratā|dāyini snāyināṃ nṛṇām.
yāvad vrajāmi tāvac ca lāṅgal'|ôllikhit'|âvanim
gāyantaṃ kaṃ|cid adrākṣaṃ kārṣikaṃ kṣetra|madhya|gam.
sa pṛṣṭaḥ kārṣiko mārgaṃ mārg'|āyātena kena|cit
pravrājakena tad|vākyaṃ n' âśṛṇod gīta|tat|paraḥ.
tataḥ sa tasmai cukrodha parivrāḍ vidhuraṃ bruvan
so 'pi gītaṃ vimucy' âtha kārṣikas tam abhāṣata.
‹aho pravrājako 'si tvaṃ dharmasy' âṃśaṃ na vetsyasi
mūrkheṇ' âpi mayā jñātaṃ sāraṃ dharmasya yat punaḥ.›
6.7.35 tac chrutvā ‹kiṃ tvayā jñātam iti?› tena ca kautukāt
pravrājakena pṛṣṭaḥ san kārṣikaḥ sa jagāda tam.
‹ih' ôpaviśa pracchāye śṛṇu yāvad vadāmi te
asmin pradeśe vidyante brāhmaṇā bhrātaras trayaḥ.
Brahmadattaḥ Somadatto Viśvadattaś ca puṇya|kṛt

cannot bear it when a heartfelt love is broken off. On this subject, O king, just listen to this story about Shruta·sena.

In a city called Go·karna in the south, there lived a king 6.7.25
called Shruta·sena who was learned and an ornament to his family. The king was very rich and had but one worry: he had not yet found a suitable wife. One day when the king was worrying about this, in the course of a conversation about the matter a brahmin called Agni·sharman said to him, "Sire, I have seen two miracles and I shall tell you about them. Listen. On a pilgrimage I arrived at Pancha·tirthi, where five *ápsaras*es who had become crocodiles because of a sage's curse were saved by Árjuna when he went
there on a pilgrimage. I bathed in that finest of pilgrimage 6.7.30
places, which makes companions of Vishnu of men who bathe in it and fast for five nights, and then as I was leaving I saw some farmhand in the middle of a field who had finished furrowing the earth with his plow and was singing. A certain wandering ascetic who had come that way asked the farmhand for directions but he was engrossed in his singing and did not hear him. As a result the wandering ascetic became angry with him, hurling abuse. The farmhand then stopped singing and said to him, 'Oh! You are an ascetic but you will never know a fraction of righteousness, while I, even though I am a fool, have understood its essence.'

When the ascetic heard this he was intrigued and asked 6.7.35
the farmhand what he had found out, to which he replied, 'Sit here in the shade and listen while I tell you. In this land there are three brahmin brothers, Brahma·datta, Soma·datta and the virtuous Vishva·datta. The elder two have

teṣāṃ jyeṣṭhau dāravantau kaniṣṭhas tv a|parigrahaḥ.
sa tayor jyeṣṭhayor ājñāṃ kurvan karma|karo yathā
mayā sah' āsīd a|krudhyann ahaṃ teṣāṃ hi kārṣikaḥ.
tau ca jyeṣṭhāv abudhyetāṃ mṛduṃ taṃ buddhi|varjitam
sādhum a|tyakta|san|mārgam ṛjum āyāsa|varjitam.
6.7.40 ekadā bhrātṛ|jāyābhyāṃ sa|kāmābhyāṃ raho 'rthitaḥ
kaniṣṭho Viśvadatto 'tha mātṛvat te nirākarot.
tatas te nijayor bhartror ubhe gatvā mṛṣ" ôcatuḥ
«vāñchaty āvāṃ rahasy eṣa kanīyān yuvayor iti.»
tena taṃ prati tau jyeṣṭhau s'|ântaḥ|kopau babhūvatuḥ
sad a|sad vā na vidatuḥ ku|strī|vacana|mohitau.
ath' âitau bhrātarau jātu
Viśvadattaṃ tam ūcatuḥ
«gaccha tvaṃ kṣetra|madhya|sthaṃ
valmīkaṃ tam samī|kuru.»
«tath" êty» āgatya valmīkaṃ kuddālen' âkhanat sa tam
«mā m" âivaṃ! kṛṣṇa|sarpo 'tra vasat' îty» udito mayā.
6.7.45 tac chrutv" âpi sa valmīkam akhanad «yad bhavatv iti»
pāp'|âiṣiṇor apy ādeśaṃ jyeṣṭha|bhrātror a|laṅghayan.
khanyamānāt tataḥ prāpa kalaśaṃ hema|pūritam
na kṛṣṇa|sarpaṃ dharmo hi sāṃnidhyaṃ kurute satām.
taṃ ca nītvā sa kalaśaṃ bhrātṛbhyāṃ sarvam arpayat
nivāryamāṇo 'pi mayā jyeṣṭhābhyāṃ dṛḍha|bhaktitaḥ.
tau punas tata ev' âṃśaṃ dattvā prerya ca ghātakān
tasy' âcchedayatāṃ pāṇi|pādaṃ dhana|jihīrṣayā.
tath" âpi na sa cukrodha nirmanyur bhrātarau prati

wives but the youngest does not. He worked as their servant, doing what they told him to do without getting angry, and he lived with me, for I am their plowman. The two elder brothers considered him to be meek, slow-witted, decent, unswervingly honorable, honest and unambitious.

One day Vishva·datta, the youngest brother, was propo- 6.7.40
sitioned in private by his two sisters-in-law, who were in love with him, and he rejected them as if they were his mother. They then both went to their husbands and lied that that younger brother of theirs had been lusting after them in private. The two elder brothers became inwardly angry with him. Deceived by the wicked women's words they did not know what was true and what was false. Then one day the two brothers told Vishva·datta to go and flatten a termite mound in the middle of a field. He said he would and went and started to dig it out with a spade, when I said, "Don't! Don't do that! A black snake lives there."
Despite hearing this, he still dug at the termite mound, say- 6.7.45
ing, "What will be, will be," and refusing to disobey the order from his two elder brothers, even though they wished him ill.

Then while he was digging it out, he found not a black snake but a pot filled with gold, for justice accompanies the virtuous. He took the pot and was so firm in his loyalty that he gave everything to his two elder brothers, despite my telling him not to. In their greed for wealth, however, they used a part of that same gold to hire some thugs and had his hands and feet cut off. Even after this he was not aggrieved and failed to get angry with his brothers, and as

tena satyena tasy' âtra hasta|pādam ajāyata.
6.7.50 tadā|prabhṛti tad dṛṣṭvā tyaktaḥ krodho 'khilo mayā
tvayā tu tāpasen' âpi krodho 'dy' âpi na mucyate.
a|krodhena jitaḥ svargaḥ paśy' âitad adhun' âiva bhoḥ›
ity uktv" âiva tanuṃ tyaktvā kārṣikaḥ sa divaṃ gataḥ.
ity āścaryaṃ mayā dṛṣṭaṃ. dvitīyaṃ śṛṇu, bhū|pate.»
ity uktvā Śrutasenaṃ sa nṛpaṃ vipro 'bravīt punaḥ.
«tato 'pi tīrtha|yātr"|ârthaṃ paryaṭann ambudhes taṭe
ahaṃ Vasantasenasya rājño rāṣṭram avāptavān.
tatra bhoktuṃ praviṣṭaṃ māṃ rāja|sattre 'bruvan dvijāḥ
‹brahman, path" âmunā mā gāḥ sthitā hy atra nṛp'|ātmajā.
6.7.55 Vidyuddyot"|âbhidhānā tāṃ paśyed api munir yadi
sa kāma|śara|nirbhinnaḥ prāpy' ônmādaṃ na jīvati.›
tato 'haṃ pratyavocaṃ tān ‹n' âitac citraṃ sadā hy aham
paśyāmy apara|Kandarpaṃ Śrutasena|mahī|patim.
yātr"|ādau nirgate yasmin rakṣibhir dṛṣṭi|gocarāt
utsāryante satī|vṛtta|bhaṅga|bhītyā kul'|âṅganāḥ.›
ity uktavantaṃ vijñāya bhāvatkaṃ bhojanāya mām
nṛp'|ântikaṃ nītavantau sattr'|âdhipa|purohitau.
tatra sā rāja|tanayā Vidyuddyotā may" ēkṣitā
Kāmasy' êva jagan|moha|mantra|vidyā śarīriṇī.
6.7.60 cirāt tad|darśana|kṣobhaṃ
niyamy' âham acintayam
‹asmat|prabhoś ced bhāry" êyaṃ
bhaved rājyaṃ sa vismaret.
tath" âpi kathanīyo 'yam udantaḥ svāmine mayā
Unmādinī|Devasena|vṛttānto hy anyathā bhavet.›

a result of his goodness his hands and feet grew back. Ever 6.7.50
since I witnessed this I have renounced anger altogether, but you, despite being an ascetic, have not given it up even now. Heaven is conquered by he who is free from anger. Now watch this!' As soon as he said this the plowman cast off his body and went to heaven. Thus I beheld a miracle. Hear the second one, O king."

After saying this to King Shruta·sena, the brahmin continued. "And then, while wandering about on the ocean shore in order to visit sacred sites, I arrived at the dominion
of King Vasánta·sena. When I went into a royal almshouse 6.7.55
there to eat, the brahmins said, 'Brahmin, do not go that way, for a princess called Vidyud·dyota is there and if even a sage sees her he is pierced by the arrow of the god of love, goes mad and dies.'

At this I replied to them, 'That is not so strange, for I regularly see King Shruta·sena, who is a second god of love. When he goes out for festivals and the like, ladies of good family are ushered out of his sight by the guards in fear that they will stop behaving like virtuous women.' After I said this the man in charge of the almshouse and the chaplain realized that I was one of your subjects and took me to the king to eat. There I saw princess Vidyud·dyota and she was like the embodiment of the god of love's spell for bewitching the world. A long time later, when I had recovered from 6.7.60
the shock of having seen her, I said to myself, 'If this girl were to become the wife of our king he would forget the kingdom. Even so I must tell my master this news, for otherwise an Unmádini and Deva·sena episode might happen.'

Devasenasya nṛpateḥ purā rāṣṭre vaṇik|sutā
Unmādin" îty abhūt kanyā jagad|unmāda|kāriṇī.
āvedit" âpi sā pitrā na ten' āttā mahī|bhṛtā
vipraiḥ ‹ku|lakṣaṇ" êty› uktā tasya vyasana|rakṣibhiḥ.
pariṇītā tadīyena mantri|mukhyena sā tataḥ
vātāyan'|âgrād ātmānaṃ rājñe 'smai jātv adarśayat.
6.7.65 tayā bhujaṃgyā rāj'|êndro durād dṛṣṭi|viṣ'|āhataḥ
muhur mumūrccha na ratiṃ lebhe n' āhāram āharat.
prārthito 'pi ca tad|bhartṛ|pramukhaiḥ so 'tha mantribhiḥ
dhārmikas tāṃ na jagrāha tat|saktaś ca jahāv asūn.
tad īdṛśe pramāde 'tra vṛtte drohaḥ kṛto bhavet
ity ālocya may" ôktaṃ te citram etya tato 'dya tat.»

śrutv" âitat sa dvijāt tasmān Madan'|ājñā|nibhaṃ vacaḥ
Vidyuddyot"|āhṛta|manāḥ Śrutasena|nṛpo 'bhavat.
tat|kṣaṇaṃ ca visṛjy' âiva tatra vipraṃ tam eva saḥ
tath" âkarod yath" ānīya śīghraṃ tāṃ pariṇītavān.
6.7.70 tataḥ sā nṛpates tasya Vidyuddyotā nṛp'|ātmajā
śarīr'|â|vyatirikt" āsīd bhāskarasya prabhā yathā.
atha svayaṃvarāy' āgāt taṃ nṛpaṃ rūpa|garvitā
kanyakā Mātṛdatt'|ākhyā mahā|dhana|vaṇik|sutā.
a|dharma|bhītyā jagrāha sa rājā tāṃ vaṇik|sutām
Vidyuddyot" âtha tad buddhvā hṛt|sphoṭena vyapadyata.
rāj" âpy āgatya tāṃ kāntāṃ paśyann eva tathā|gatām
aṅke kṛtvā sa vilapan sadyaḥ prāṇair vyayujyata.

Long ago in the country of King Deva·sena there was a merchant's daughter, a maiden called Unmádini who drove the whole world crazy. Her father told the king about her, but he did not take her hand because the brahmins, who protected him from disaster, said that she had inauspicious markings. She was then married to his chief minister and one day she showed herself to the king from a window. That 6.7.65
great king, struck from afar by that lady serpent with the poison of her gaze, kept fainting and took no pleasure in anything nor ate any food. He was pious and despite being entreated by his ministers, the chief minister at their head, would not marry her and cast off his breaths while devoted to her. So I have come today and told you this amazing story after realizing that if such an infatuation were to happen in this instance I would have committed a crime."

After hearing from that brahmin these words, which were like a command from the god of love, King Shruta·sena's mind was captivated by Vidyud·dyota. He immediately dismissed the brahmin there, arranged for the girl to be fetched and quickly married her. After this princess 6.7.70
Vidyud·dyota was inseparable from the king, like light from the sun. Then the daughter of a very rich merchant, a maiden called Matri·datta who was proud of her beauty, came to choose the king as her husband. In fear of not observing his duty, the king married the merchant's daughter. Then Vidyud·dyota found out and died of a broken heart. When the king arrived and found his sweetheart dead, he held her in his arms and while he was sobbing his

tato vaṇik|sutā vahniṃ Mātṛdattā viveśa sā
itthaṃ praṇaṣṭaṃ sarvaṃ tad api rāṣṭraṃ sa|rājakam.
6.7.75 ato, rājan, prakṛṣṭasya bhaṅgaḥ premṇaḥ su|duḥsahaḥ
viśeṣeṇa manasvinyā devyā Vāsavadattayā.
tasmāt Kaliṅgasen" âiṣā pariṇītā yadi tvayā
devī Vāsavadattā tat|prāṇāñ jahyān na saṃśayaḥ.
devī Padmāvatī tadvat tayor ekaṃ hi jīvitam
Naravāhanadattaś ca putras te syāt kathaṃ tataḥ?
tañ ca devasya hṛdayaṃ soḍhuṃ jāne na śaknuyāt
evam eka|pade sarvam idaṃ naśyen, mahī|pate.
devyor yac c' ôkti|gāmbhīryaṃ tad eva kathayaty alam
hṛdayaṃ jīvita|tyāga|gāḍha|niścita|niḥspṛham.
6.7.80 tat sv'|ârtho rakṣaṇīyas te tiryañco 'pi hi jānate
sva|rakṣāṃ kiṃ punar, deva, buddhimanto bhavādṛśāḥ.›

iti mantri|varāc chrutvā svairaṃ Yaugandharāyaṇāt
samyag|viveka|padavīṃ prāpya Vats'|ēśvaro 'bravīt.
‹evam etan na saṃdeho. naśyet sarvam idaṃ mama.
tasmāt Kaliṅgasenāyāḥ ko 'rthaḥ pariṇayena me?
ukto lagnaś ca dūre yat tad yuktaṃ gaṇakaiḥ kṛtam
svayaṃvar'|āgatā|tyāgād a|dharmo vā kiyān bhavet?›

ity ukto Vatsa|rājena hṛṣṭo Yaugandharāyaṇaḥ
cintayām ‹āsa kāryaṃ naḥ siddha|prāyaṃ yath"|ēpsitam.
6.7.85 upāya|rasa|saṃsiktā deśa|kāl'|ôpabṛṃhitā
s" êyaṃ nīti|mahā|vallī kiṃ nāma na phalet phalam.›

life breaths suddenly left him. Then Matri·datta, the merchant's daughter, ascended the funeral pyre and so, as well as its king, that entire kingdom was destroyed.

Thus, O king, the breaking off of a particularly strong 6.7.75
love is very hard to bear, especially for a proud lady like Queen Vásava·datta. So if you marry this girl Kalínga·sena, Queen Vásava·datta is sure to give up her life and Queen Padmávati will do the same, for the two of them share one life. Your son Nara·váhana·datta could never survive their deaths and I don't think your highness's heart could bear that. Thus, O king, everything here would be lost in one fell swoop. The earnestness of the two queens' utterances is in itself enough to betray how their hearts have lost hope and
they are firmly decided on giving up their lives, so you must 6.7.80
protect your own interests, for even animals know how to look after themselves—how much more wise men like you, your highness.'

After willingly listening to these words from that finest of ministers Yaugándharáyana, the king of Vatsa saw sense and said, 'That is absolutely right. Everything I have would be lost. Therefore there is nothing to be gained by my marrying Kalínga·sena. It was right for the astrologers to fix a far off date, and it is not so great a sin to reject a girl who has come to ask one to be her husband.'

When the king of Vatsa said this to him, Yaugándharáyana was delighted and said to himself, 'What we need to do
has almost been accomplished just as we hoped. Witness the 6.7.85
great creeper of statecraft—sprinkled with the water of correct method and nourished with the right time and place, it is sure to bear fruit.'

iti saṃcintya sa dhyāyan deśa|kālau praṇamya tam
rājānaṃ prayayau mantrī gṛhaṃ Yaugandharāyaṇaḥ.
rāj" âpi racit'|ātithya|gūḍha|kārām upetya saḥ
devīṃ Vāsavadattāṃ tāṃ sāntvayann evam abravīt.
‹kim|arthaṃ vacmi jānāsi tvam eva, hariṇ"|âkṣi, yat
vāri vāri|ruhasy' êva tvat|prema mama jīvitam.
nām' âpi hi kim anyasyā grahītum aham utsahe
Kaliṅgasenā tu haṭhād upāyātā gṛhaṃ mama.
6.7.90 prasiddhaṃ c' âtra yad Rambhā tapaḥ|sthena nirākṛtā
Pārthena ṣaṇḍhatā|śāpaṃ dadau tasyai haṭh'|āgatā.
sa śāpas tiṣṭhatā tena varṣam Vairāṭa|veśmani
strī|veṣeṇa mah"|āścarya|rūpeṇ' âpy ativāhitaḥ.
ataḥ Kaliṅgasen" âiṣā niṣiddhā na tadā mayā
vinā tvad|icchay" âhaṃ tu na kiṃ|cid vaktum utsahe.›
ity āśvāsy' ôpalabhy' âtha hṛdayen' êva *rāginā*
mukh'|ârpitena madyena satyaṃ krūraṃ tad|āśayam.
tay" âiva saha rātriṃ tāṃ rājñyā Vāsavadattayā
mantri|mukhya|mati|prauḍhi|tuṣṭo Vats'|ēśvaro 'vasat.
6.7.95 atr' ântare ca yaṃ pūrvaṃ divā|rātrau prayuktavān
Kaliṅgasenā|vṛttānta|jñaptyai Yaugandharāyaṇaḥ.
sa brahma|rākṣaso 'bhyetya suhṛd Yogeśvar'|âbhidhaḥ
tasyām eva niśi svairaṃ taṃ mantri|varam abhyadhāt.
‹Kaliṅgasenā|sadane sthito 'smy antar bahiḥ sadā
divyānāṃ mānuṣāṇāṃ vā paśyāmi na tath" āgamam.

After thinking this, while reflecting on right time and place, the minister Yaugándharáyana bowed before the king and went home. The king went to Queen Vásava·datta, who dissembled by treating him hospitably, and, comforting her, he said, 'There's no need for me to say this for you yourself know, O doe-eyed lady, that your love is my life, like water to the water-lily. How could I bear to take even the name of another woman? But Kalínga·sena came to my
house and imposed herself and it is well known how when 6.7.90
Rambha imposed herself on Árjuna when he was practicing austerities and was spurned by him, she cursed him to become a eunuch. He got through that curse by staying for a year in the house of the king of Viráta in the clothes of a woman, even though he looked very strange. So at that time I did not turn down this girl Kalínga·sena, but I would not dare to say anything without your willing it.'

After thus reassuring her and then surmising from the *red wine offered by her mouth : blushing happiness shown by her face*, as if it were her *enamored* heart, that she really had had that awful intention, the king of Vatsa spent that night with Queen Vásava·datta alone, pleased with the assurance of his chief minister.

Meanwhile, Yaugándharáyana's friend the brahmin *rák-* 6.7.95
shasa called Yogéshvara whom he had previously commissioned to watch day and night what Kalínga·sena was doing, came to him out of the blue that same night and said to the chief minister, 'I have remained either inside or outside Kalínga·sena's house at all times, and I have not seen any divine beings or mortals come there. Today at dusk when I was hiding there near the roof terrace, I suddenly heard

ady' â|vyakto mayā śabdaḥ śruto '|kasmān nabhas|tale
pracchannen' âtra harmy'|âgra|saṃnikarṣe niśā|mukhe.
prabhāvaṃ tasya vijñātuṃ prayukt' âpi tato mama
vidyā na prābhavat tena vimṛśy' âham acintayam.
6.7.100 «ayaṃ divya|prabhāvasya śabdaḥ kasy' âpi niścitam
Kaliṅgasenā|lāvaṇya|lubdhasya bhramato 'mbare.
yena na kramate vidyā tad vīkṣe kiṃ|cid antaram
na duṣprāpaṃ para|cchidraṃ jāgradbhir nipuṇair yataḥ.
‹divyānāṃ vāñchit" âiṣ" êti› proktaṃ mantri|vareṇa ca
Somaprabhā sakhī c' âsyā vadanty etan mayā śrutā.»
iti niścitya tat tubhyam ih' âhaṃ vaktum āgataḥ
idaṃ prasaṅgāt pṛcchāmi tan me tāvat tvay" ôcyatām.
«tiryañco 'pi hi rakṣanti sv'|ātmānam iti» yat tvayā
ukto rajā tad aśrauṣaṃ yogād aham a|lakṣitaḥ.
6.7.105 nidarśanaṃ ced atr' âsti tan me kathaya, san|mate.›
iti Yogeśvareṇ' ôktaḥ sm' āha Yaugandharāyaṇaḥ.
‹asti, mittra, tathā c' âtra kathām ākhyāmi te śṛṇu
Vidiśā|nagarī|bāhye nyagrodho 'bhūt purā mahān.
catvāraḥ prāṇinas tatra vasanti sma mahā|tarau
nakul'|ôlūka|mārjāra|mūṣakāḥ pṛthag|ālayāḥ.
bhinne bhinne bile mūla āstāṃ nakula|mūṣakau
mārjāro madhya|bhāga|sthe taror mahati koṭare.
ulūkas tu śiro|bhāge 'n|anya|labhye lat"|ālaye
mūṣako 'tra tribhir vadhyo mārjāreṇa trayo 'pare.
6.7.110 annāya mārjāra|bhayān mūṣako nakulas tathā
sva|bhāven' âpy ulūkaś ca paribhremur niśi trayaḥ.
mārjāraś ca divā|rātrau nirbhayaḥ prabhramaty asau

an indistinct voice in the sky. I then used my powers to find out where it had come from, but they did not work, so after thinking about it I said to myself, "This must be the 6.7.100
voice of someone with divine powers who is lusting after Kalínga·sena's loveliness as he roams about the sky. I shall look for some opportunity when his magic is not working, because a chink in an opponent's armor is not hard to find for those who are alert and skillful. The chief minister has said that she is desired by divine beings, and I heard her friend Soma·prabha saying it too."

After working this out, I came here to speak to you. In passing, I ask you the following. Just tell me this. Using magic I secretly heard you tell the king that even animals protect themselves. If there is an example of this then tell 6.7.105
me, O wise one.'

When Yogéshvara said this to him, Yaugándharáyana replied, 'There is an example, my friend. Just listen to the story I shall tell you on the subject. Long ago outside the city of Vídisha there was a great banyan tree. Four animals lived in separate homes in that great tree: a mongoose, an owl, a cat and a mouse. The mongoose and the mouse lived in different holes at the foot of the tree and the cat in a large hollow in its middle, but the owl lived in a nest of creepers in its crown, out of reach of the others. The mouse was the prey of three of them; the cat preyed on the three other than itself. Out of fear of the cat, those three, the mouse, 6.7.110
the mongoose and the owl (whose nature it was to do so anyway) would wander about at night to find food. The cat would roam about fearlessly day and night in a field of barley near there, hoping to catch the mouse. The others,

tatr' āsanne yava|kṣetre sadā mūṣaka|lipsayā.
ye 'nye 'pi yuktyā jagmus tat sva|kāle 'nn'|âbhivāñchayā
ekadā lubdhakas tatra caṇḍālaḥ kaś|cid āyayau.
sa mārjāra|pada|śreṇiṃ dṛṣṭvā tat|kṣetra|gāminīm
tad|vadhāy' âbhitaḥ kṣetraṃ pāśān dattvā tato yayau.
tatra rātrau ca mārjāraḥ sa mūṣaka|jighāṃsayā
etya praviṣṭas tat|pāśaiḥ kṣetre tasminn abadhyata.
6.7.115 mūṣako 'pi tato 'nn'|ârthī sa tatra nibhṛt'|āgataḥ
baddhaṃ taṃ vīkṣya mārjāraṃ jaharṣa ca nanarta ca.
yāvad viśati tat kṣetraṃ dūrād ekena vartmanā
tatra tau tāvad āyātāv ulūka|nakulāv api.
dṛṣṭa|mārjāra|bandhau ca mūṣakaṃ labdhum aicchatām
mūṣako 'pi ca tad dṛṣṭvā dūrād vigno vyacintayat.
«nakul'|ôlūka|bhaya|daṃ mārjāraṃ saṃśraye yadi
baddho 'py eka|prahāreṇa śatrur mām eṣa mārayet.
mārjārād dūra|gaṃ hanyād ulūko nakulaś ca mām
tac chatru|saṃkaṭa|gataḥ. kva gacchāmi? karomi kim?
6.7.120 hanta! mārjāram ev' êha śrayāmy āpad|gato hy ayam
ātma|trāṇāya māṃ rakṣet pāśa|cched'|ôpayoginam.»
ity ālocya śanair gatvā mārjāraṃ mūṣako 'bravīt
«baddhe tvayy atiduḥkhaṃ me tat te pāśaṃ chinadmy aham.
ṛjūnāṃ jāyate snehaḥ saha|vāsād ripuṣv api
kiṃ tu me n' âsti viśvāsas tava cittam a|jānataḥ.»
tac chrutv" ôvāca mārjāro «bhadra, viśvasyatāṃ tvayā!
adya prabhṛti me mittraṃ bhavān prāṇa|pradāyakaḥ!»

meanwhile, used their wits to go there at their own particular times in the hope of finding food.

One day some outcaste hunter arrived there. When he saw the cat's tracks leading into the field, he laid traps around the field to kill it and then left. That night the cat went into the field hoping to kill the mouse and was caught
in one of the traps. Then the mouse, having arrived there 6.7.115
in secret in search of food, saw the captured cat and danced for joy. As the mouse was entering the field, the owl and the mongoose also arrived there, coming from afar on the same path. When they saw that the cat had been snared, they wanted to catch the mouse. The mouse, on seeing them from afar, was worried and said to itself, "If I go for refuge to the cat, who poses a threat to the mongoose and the owl, as an enemy of mine he might kill me in one blow, even though he is trapped. If I am far from the cat, the owl and the mongoose might kill me, so I am stuck between my
enemies. Where can I go? What can I do? Oh dear! I shall 6.7.120
go to the cat for refuge, for he is in a tight spot and might protect me to save himself, for I can be useful in cutting his snare."

After thinking this through, the mouse slowly approached the cat and said, "I am very upset that you have been trapped, so I shall cut through your snare. By living with them, the virtuous develop affection for even their enemies. However I am not sure for I don't know your intentions."

The cat replied, "Good sir, you must trust me! From today onwards, as the one who has given me life, you shall be my friend!"

iti śrutv” âiva mārjārāt tasy’ ôtsaṅgaṃ sa śiśriye
tad dṛṣṭvā nakul’|ôlūkau nirāśau yayatus tataḥ.
6.7.125 tato jagāda mārjāro mūṣakaṃ pāśa|pīḍitaḥ
«gata|prāyā niśā, mittra, tat pāśāṃś chindhi me drutam.
mūṣako ’pi śanaiś chindal̐ lubdhak’|āgaman’|ônmukhaḥ
mṛṣā kaṭakaṭāyadbhir daśanair akaroc ciram.
kṣaṇād rātrau prabhātāyāṃ lubdhake nikaṭ’|āgate
mārjāre ’rthayamāne drāk pāśāṃś ciccheda mūṣakaḥ.
chinna|pāśe ’tha mārjāre lubdhaka|trāsa|vidrute
mūṣako mṛtyu|muktaḥ san palāyya prāviśad bilam.
n’ âśvasat punar āhūto mārjāreṇa jagāda ca
«kāla|yuktyā hy arir mittraṃ jāyate na ca sarvadā.»
6.7.130 evaṃ bahubhyaḥ śatrubhyaḥ prajñay” ātm” âbhirakṣitaḥ
mūṣakena tiraśc” âpi kiṃ punar mānuṣeṣu yat?

etad uktas tadā rājā mayā yat tat tvayā śrutam
buddhyā kāryaṃ nijaṃ rakṣed devī|saṃrakṣaṇād iti.
buddhir nāma ca sarvatra mukhyaṃ mittraṃ na pauruṣam
Yogeśvara, tathā c’ âitām atr’ âpi tvaṃ kathāṃ śṛṇu.

Śrāvast” îty asti nagarī tasyāṃ pūrvaṃ Prasenajit
rāj” âbhūt tatra c’ âbhyāgāt ko ’py a|pūrvo dvijaḥ puri.
so ’śūdr’|ânna|bhug ekena vaṇijā guṇavān iti
brāhmaṇasya gṛhe tatra kasya|cit sthāpito dvijaḥ.
6.7.135 tatr’ âiva tena śuṣk’|ânna|dakṣiṇ”|ādibhir anvaham
āpūryata tato ’nyaiś ca śanair buddhvā vaṇig|varaiḥ.

As soon as he heard this from the cat, he took refuge in his lap. On seeing this, the mongoose and the owl lost hope and went away.

Then the cat, pained by the snare, said to the mouse, 6.7.125
"The night is almost over, my friend, so, quickly, cut the snares." The mouse, meanwhile, slowly gnawing away as it awaited the arrival of the hunter, played for time by making a fake chewing noise with its teeth. Before long dawn broke and the hunter drew near. With the cat entreating him, the mouse quickly cut the snares. Its snares cut, the cat then ran off in fear of the hunter, while the mouse, saved from death, ran off and went into its hole. When the cat called it, the mouse did not trust it any more, saying, "Circumstances can make an enemy a friend, but it does not last forever."

Thus the mouse, though an animal, used its wits to save 6.7.130
itself from a host of enemies—men do the same much more often!

This is what I said to the king when you overheard me tell him that he should use his wits to safeguard the queen and thereby protect his own interests. Indeed it is always one's wits that are one's best friend, not courage, Yogéshvara. On this subject, just listen to this story.

There is a city called Shravásti in which long ago there lived King Prasénajit. A certain brahmin stranger arrived in that city unannounced. The brahmin did not eat the food of low caste men, and a merchant, thinking him to be a virtuous man, had him lodged in the house of some brahmin
in the city. There each day the merchant would present him 6.7.135
with uncooked rice and other gifts suitable for a brahmin and then, on hearing about him, other eminent merchants

ten' âsau hema|dīnāra|sahasraṃ kṛpaṇaḥ kramāt
saṃcitya gatv" âraṇye tan nikhanya† kṣiptavān bhuvi.

ekākī pratyahaṃ gatvā tac ca sthānam avaikṣata
ekadā hema|śūnyaṃ tat|khātaṃ vyāttaṃ ca dṛṣṭavān.

śūnyaṃ tat khātakaṃ tasya paśyato hata|cetasaḥ
na paraṃ hṛdi saṃkrāntā citraṃ dikṣv api śūnyatā.

ath' ôpāgāc ca vilapaṃs taṃ vipraṃ yad|gṛhe sthitaḥ
pṛṣṭas taṃ ca sva|vṛttāntaṃ tasmai sarvaṃ nyavedayat.

6.7.140 gatvā tīrtham a|bhuñjānaḥ prāṇāṃs tyaktum iyeṣa ca
buddhvā ca so 'nna|dāt" âsya vaṇig anyaiḥ sah' āyayau.

sa taṃ jagāda «kiṃ, brahman, vitta|hetor mumūrṣasi?
a|kāla|meghavad vittam a|kasmād eti yāti ca.»

ity|ādy ukto 'pi ten' âsau na jahau maraṇa|graham
prāṇebhyo 'py artha|mātrā hi kṛpaṇasya garīyasī.

tataś ca mṛtaye tīrthaṃ gacchato 'sya dvi|janmanaḥ
svayaṃ Prasenajid rājā tad buddhv" ântikam āyayau.

papraccha c' âinaṃ «kiṃ kiṃ|cid asti tatr' ôpalakṣaṇam
yatra bhūmau nikhātās te dīnārā brāhmaṇa tvayā?»

6.7.145 tac chrutvā sa dvijo 'vādīd «asti kṣudro 'tra pādapaḥ
aṭavyāṃ, deva, tan|mūle nikhātaṃ tan mayā dhanam.»

gradually started to do the same. As a result that niggardly man eventually amassed a thousand gold dinars. He went to the forest, dug a hole and put it in the ground. Every day he would go alone and check on the spot and one day he saw that the hole which he had dug had been opened and was empty of gold. As he looked at that empty hole he was perplexed and the emptiness took over not only his heart but, strangely enough, his whole world. He then went sobbing to the brahmin in whose house he was staying and on being questioned he told him everything that had happened to him. He wanted to go to a place of pilgrimage 6.7.140
and fast to death. When the merchant who gave him food found out about this he arrived with some others and said to him, "Why, brahmin, are you willing to die over money? Money is like a cloud out of season—it comes and goes for no reason."

Even after the merchant had said this and more like it to the brahmin, he would not give up his determination to kill himself, for wealth is more important to a miser than his life breaths. Then as that brahmin was on his way to a place of pilgrimage to die, King Prasénajit himself came to him having heard what had happened and asked him if there was any way of recognizing the place where he had buried
the dinars in the ground. The brahmin replied, "There is a 6.7.145
small tree there in the forest, your highness, and I buried the money at its foot."

ity ākarṇy" âbravīd rājā «dāsyāmy anviṣya tat tava
dhanaṃ sva|koṣād athavā mā tyākṣīr jīvitaṃ, dvija.»
ity uktvā maraṇ'|ôdyogān nivārya vinidhāya ca
dvijaṃ taṃ vaṇijo haste sa rāj" âbhyantaraṃ gataḥ.
tatr' ādiśya pratīhāraṃ śiro|'rti|vyapadeśataḥ
vaidyān ānāyayat sarvān dattvā paṭaha|ghoṣaṇām.
«āturās te kiyanto 'tra kasy' âdāḥ kiṃ tvam auṣadham?»
ity upānīya papraccha tān ekaikaṃ vivikta|gaḥ.
6.7.150 te 'pi tasmai tad" âikaikaḥ sarvam ūcur mahī|pateḥ
eko 'tha vaidyas tan|madhyāt krama|pṛṣṭo 'bravīd idam.
«vaṇijo Mātṛdattasya, deva, nāgabalā mayā
a|svasthasy' ôpadiṣṭ" âdya dvitīyaṃ dinam oṣadhiḥ.»

tac chrutvā sa tam āhūya rājā vaṇijam abhyadhāt
«nanu nāgabalā kena tav' ānīt" ôcyatām iti.»
«deva, karma|kareṇ' êti» ten' ôkte vaṇijā tadā
kṣipram ānāyya taṃ rājā sa karma|karam abravīt.
«tvayā nāgabalā|hetoḥ khanatā śākhinas talam
dīnāra|jātaṃ yal labdhaṃ brahma|svaṃ tat samarpaya.»
6.7.155 ity ukto bhū|bhṛtā bhītaḥ pratipady' âiva tat|kṣaṇam
sa tān ānīya dīnārāṃs tatra karma|karo jahau.
rāj" âpy upoṣitāy' âsmai dvijāy' āhūya tān dadau
dīnārān hārita|prāptān prāṇān iva bahiś|carān.

On hearing this, the king said, "I shall find the money and give it to you; if not, I shall give it to you out of my own treasury. Do not kill yourself, brahmin." After saying this and deterring him from his plan of killing himself, the king entrusted the brahmin to the merchant and went home. There, on the pretext of having a headache, he instructed a chamberlain to make an announcement to the beat of a drum and summon all the doctors. He took each one of them aside and asked him how many patients he had in the city, what they were suffering and what medicine he
was giving them. One by one they then answered in full 6.7.150
the king's question. Then, when it was his turn to be asked, one doctor among them said, "Your highness, the merchant Matri·datta is unwell and for the second day in a row today I prescribed him the herb *naga·bala*."

On hearing this, the king summoned that merchant and asked him to say who had fetched the *naga·bala* for him. When the merchant said that a servant had fetched it, the king quickly had the servant brought in and said to him, "Hand over the dinars which you found while digging for *naga·bala* at the foot of the tree and which are the property of a brahmin."

When the king said this to him, the terrified servant im- 6.7.155
mediately confessed. He then fetched the dinars and left them there. The king summoned the fasting brahmin and gave him the dinars, which, lost and then found, were like an external manifestation of his life-breaths.

evaṃ sa labdhavān buddhyā nītaṃ mūla|talāt taroḥ
dvij'|ârthaṃ bhū|patir jānann oṣadhiṃ tāṃ tad|udbhavām.
tad evaṃ sarvadā buddheḥ prādhānyaṃ jita|pauruṣam
īdṛśeṣu ca kāryeṣu kiṃ vidadhyāt parākramaḥ?
tad, Yogeśvara, kurvīthās tvam api prajñayā tathā
yathā Kaliṅgasenāyā doṣo jñāyata kaś|cana.
6.7.160 asti c' âitad yathā tasyāṃ lubhyant' îha sur'|âsurāḥ
tathā ca divi kasy' âpi niśi śabdaḥ śrutas tvayā.
labdhe 'tha doṣe tasyāś ca bhaved a|kuśalaṃ na naḥ
n' ôpayaccheta tāṃ rājā na c' â|dharmaḥ kṛto bhavet.›
ity udāra|dhiyaḥ śrutvā sarvaṃ Yaugandharāyaṇāt
Yogeśvaras taṃ saṃtuṣya jagāda brahma|rākṣasaḥ.
‹kas tvayā sadṛśo nītāv anyo devād Bṛhaspateḥ
ayaṃ tv amṛta|seko 'sya tvan|mantro rājya|śākhinaḥ.
so 'haṃ Kaliṅgasenāyā jijñāsiṣye gatiṃ sadā
buddhyā śakty" âpi c' êty› uktvā tato Yogeśvaro yayau.
6.7.165 tat|kālaṃ sā ca harmy'|ādau paryaṭantaṃ sva|harmyagā
Kaliṅgasenā Vats'|ēśaṃ dṛṣṭvā dṛṣṭvā sma tāmyati.
tan|manāḥ Smara|saṃtaptā mṛṇāl'|âṅgada|hāriṇī
sā śrī|khaṇḍ'|âṅga|rāgā ca na lebhe nirvṛtiṃ kva|cit.
atr' ântare sa tāṃ pūrvaṃ dṛṣṭvā vidyā|dhar'|âdhipaḥ
tasthau Madanaveg'|ākhyo gāḍh'|Ân|aṅga|śar'|ârditaḥ.
tat|prāptaye tapaḥ kṛtvā vare labdhe 'pi Śaṃkarāt
s" âny'|āsakt" ânya|deśa|sthā sukha|prāpy" âsya n' âbhavat.
yatas ten' ântaraṃ labdhum asau vidyā|dhar'|ēśvaraḥ

Thus the king used his intelligence to find for the brahmin what had been taken away from the foot of the tree, knowing that that herb grew there. So in this way intelligence is always paramount, beating courage, and in undertakings like this, bravery can do nothing. Therefore, Yogéshvara, you should use your wisdom in such a way that
Kalínga·sena is found to be at fault in some way. It is true 6.7.160
that the gods and *ásura*s lust after her here, which is why you heard the sound of someone in the sky tonight. If she is found to be at fault, then misfortune will befall her, not us, the king will not marry her and no injustice will have been done.'

After hearing all this from the high-minded Yaugándharáyana, the brahmin *rákshasa* Yogéshvara was delighted and said to him, 'Who other than Brihas·pati is your equal in statecraft? This advice of yours waters the tree of this realm with the nectar of immortality. So I shall constantly scrutinize the conduct of Kalínga·sena, using both my intelligence and my powers.' After saying this, Yogéshvara left.

At that time Kalínga·sena was in her palace, gasping for 6.7.165
breath as she kept beholding the king of Vatsa in his wanderings on the palace terrace and elsewhere. Thinking of him and burned up by the god of love, she wore an armlet and necklace of lotus fiber and applied sandal on her body, but she couldn't in any way find relief.* In the meantime the sorcerer king called Mádana·vega who had seen her previously was still badly wounded by the arrow of the god of love. In order to win her he had performed austerities but, although he had obtained a boon from Shiva, she had not become easy to win because she loved another man and

rajanīṣu divi bhrāmyann āsīt tan|mandir'|ôpari.

6.7.170 saṃsmṛtya tu tam ādeśaṃ tapas|tuṣṭasya dhūr|jaṭeḥ
ekasyāṃ niśi Vats'|ēśa|rūpaṃ cakre sva|vidyayā.
tad|rūpaś ca viveś' âsyā† mandiraṃ dvāḥ|stha|vanditaḥ
kāla|kṣep'|â|kṣamo guptaṃ mantriṇāṃ sa iv' āgataḥ.
Kaliṅgasen" âpy uttasthau taṃ dṛṣṭv" ôtkampa|viklavā
‹na so 'yam iti› s'|ārāvair vāryamāṇ" êva bhūṣaṇaiḥ.
tato Vats'|ēśa|rūpeṇa kramād viśvāsya tena sā
bhāryā Madanavegena gāndharva|vidhinā kṛtā.

tat|kālaṃ ca praviṣṭas tad dṛṣṭvā yogād a|lakṣitaḥ
Yogeśvaro viṣaṇṇo 'bhūd Vats'|ēś'|ālokana|bhramāt.
6.7.175 Yaugandharāyaṇāy' âitad gatv" ôktvā tan|nideśataḥ
yuktyā Vāsavadattāyā Vats'|ēśaṃ vīkṣya pārśva|gam.
hṛṣṭo mantri|var'|ôkty" âiva rūpaṃ suptasya veditum
Kaliṅgasenā|pracchanna|kāminaḥ so 'gamat punaḥ.
gatvā Kaliṅgasenāyāḥ suptāyāḥ śayanīyake
suptaṃ Madanavegaṃ taṃ sva|rūpe sthitam aikṣata.
chatra|dhvaj'|âṅka|nirdhūli|pād'|âbjaṃ divya|mānuṣam
svāp'|ântar|hita|tad|vidyā|vīta|rūpa|vivartanam.
tatra gatvā yathā|dṛṣṭaṃ nivedya paritoṣavān
Yogeśvaro jagād' âsau hṛṣṭo Yaugandharāyaṇam.

was in someone else's country. In consequence of this the sorcerer king was spending his nights roaming about the sky above her palace in order to find a way to get what he wanted.

Then one night he remembered what Shiva, he of the 6.7.170
heavy matted locks, had taught him when pleased by his austerities, and used his magic to assume the appearance of the king of Vatsa. Disguised as him, he entered her palace as if he were in a hurry and had not told his ministers, and was saluted by the guards on the door. When Kalínga·sena saw him she got up trembling and perplexed, her tinkling ornaments seeming to her hold her back, saying 'This is not he.' Then Mádana·vega, in his guise as the king of Vatsa, gradually won her confidence and made her his wife according to the *gandhárva* rite.

Having entered at that very moment, using magic so that he was unnoticed, Yogéshvara saw this and was saddened, mistakenly thinking he was looking at the king of Vatsa. He 6.7.175
went and told Yaugándharáyana what had happened and then at his instruction he used his powers to find out that the king of Vatsa was at the side of Vásava·datta. Delighted, at the chief minister's bidding he then went back to examine the appearance of Kalínga·sena's sleeping secret lover. When he reached there, he found Mádana·vega asleep in the bed of the sleeping Kalínga·sena, having assumed his usual form, that of a divine man, his lotus feet free from dust and marked with a parasol and a flag, his disguise gone because his magical powers disappeared when he was asleep. After going there, Yogéshvara was overjoyed and gladly told

6.7.180 ‹na vetti mādṛśaḥ kiṃ|cid vetsi tvaṃ nīti|cakṣuṣā
tava mantreṇa duḥsādhyaṃ siddhaṃ kāryam idaṃ prabhoḥ.
kiṃ vā vyoma vin" ârkeṇa? kiṃ toyena vinā saraḥ?
kiṃ mantreṇa vinā rājyaṃ? kiṃ satyena vinā vacaḥ?›
ity uktavantam āmantrya prīto Yogeśvaraṃ tataḥ
prātar Vats'|ēśvaraṃ draṣṭum āgād Yaugandharāyaṇaḥ.
tam upetya yathāvac ca kathā|prastāvato 'bravīt
nṛpaṃ Kaliṅgasen"|ârthe pṛṣṭa|kārya|viniścayam.
‹svacchand" âsau na te, rājan, pāṇi|sparśam ih' ârhati
eṣā hi sv'|êcchayā draṣṭuṃ Prasenajitam āgatā.
6.7.185 viraktā vīkṣya taṃ vṛddhaṃ tvāṃ prāptā rūpa|lobhataḥ
tad|anya|puruṣ'|āsaṅgam api sv'|êcchaṃ karoty asau.›
tac chrutvā ‹kula|kany" êyaṃ katham evaṃ samācaret?
śaktiḥ kasya praveṣṭuṃ vā madīy" ântaḥ|pur'|ântare?›
iti rājñ" ôdite 'vādīd dhīmān Yaugandharāyaṇaḥ
‹ady' âiva darśayāmy etat pratyakṣaṃ niśi, deva, te.
divyās tām abhivāñchanti siddh'|ādyā mānuṣo 'tra kaḥ
divyānāṃ ca gatī roddhuṃ, rājan, ken' êha śakyate?
tad ehi sākṣāt paśy' êti› vādinā tena mantriṇā
saha gantuṃ matiṃ cakre tatra rātrau sa bhū|patiḥ.

Yaugándharáyana what he had seen. 'My sort know nothing; you, with the eye of statecraft, have knowledge. By your advice, this difficult business of the king's has been successfully accomplished. But what is the sky without the sun? What is a lake without water? What is a kingdom without counsel? What is speech without truth?' 6.7.180

When Yogéshvara had said this, the delighted Yaugándharáyana said goodbye to him and then in the morning went to see the king of Vatsa. After approaching him with due decorum, in the course of a conversation he said to the king, who had asked him for a decision about what was to be done with regard to Kalínga·sena, 'The girl is wanton, O king, and does not deserve to take your hand here, for she
went of her own free will to see Prasénajit. She lost interest 6.7.185
when she saw that he was old, came to you out of a desire for your good looks and now she is even enjoying the company of a man other than him!'

When he heard this, the king said, 'She is a girl from a good family: how could she behave so? And who has the power to enter my harem?' to which the wise Yaugándharáyana replied, 'I shall show you clearly this very night, your highness. *Siddha*s and other divine beings are lusting after her—no man could be involved. No one here, O king, is able to obstruct the movements of divine beings. So come and see with your own eyes.'

When the minister said this, the king made up his mind to go there with him that night.

6.7.190 ‹Padmāvatyā ṛte rājñyā na vivāhy' âpar' êti yat
proktaṃ, devi, pratijñātaṃ mayā nirvyūḍham adya tat.›
ity ath' âbhyetya tāṃ devīm uktvā Yaugandharāyaṇaḥ
Kaliṅgasenā|vṛttāntaṃ taṃ tasyai sarvam uktavān.
‹tvadīya|śikṣ"|ânuṣṭhāna|phalam etan mam' êti› sā
devī Vāsavadatt" âpi praṇat" âbhinananda tam.
tato niśīthe saṃsupte jane Vats'|ēśvaro yayau
gṛhaṃ Kaliṅgasenāyāḥ sa ca Yaugandharāyaṇaḥ.
a|dṛṣṭaś ca praviṣṭo 'tra tasyā nidrā|juṣo 'ntike
suptaṃ Madanavegaṃ taṃ sva|rūpa|sthaṃ dadarśa saḥ.
6.7.195 hantum icchati yāvac ca sa taṃ sāhasikaṃ nṛpaḥ
tāvat sa vidyayā vidyā|dharo 'bhūt pratibodhitaḥ.
prabuddhaś ca sa nirgatya jhagity udapatan nabhaḥ
kṣaṇāt Kaliṅgasen' âpi sā prabuddh" âbhavat tataḥ.
śūnyaṃ śayanam ālokya
    jagāda ca ‹kathaṃ hi mām
pūrvaṃ prabudhya Vats'|ēśaḥ
    suptāṃ muktv" âiva gacchati?›
tad ākarṇya sa Vats'|ēśam āha Yaugandharāyaṇaḥ
‹eṣā vidhvaṃsit" ânena śṛṇu tvad|rūpa|dhāriṇā.
eṣa† yoga|balāj jñātvā sākṣāt te darśito mayā
kiṃ tu divya|prabhāvatvād asau hantuṃ na śakyate.›
6.7.200 ity uktvā sa ca rājā ca saha tām upajagmatuḥ
Kaliṅgasenā s" âpy etau dṛṣṭvā tasthau kṛt'|ādarā.
‹adhun' âiva kva gatvā tvaṃ, rājan, prāptaḥ sa|mantrikaḥ?›
iti bruvāṇām avadat tāṃ sa Yaugandharāyaṇaḥ.
‹Kaliṅgasene, ken' âpi māyā|Vats'|ēśa|rūpiṇā
saṃmohya pariṇīt" âsi na tvaṃ mat|svāmin" âmunā.›

Yaugándharáyana then went to the queen and after saying to her, 'Today, O queen, I have carried out my promise to make sure that no woman other than Queen Padmávati is to be married to the king,' he told her everything that had happened with Kalínga·sena. 6.7.190

Queen Vásava·datta humbly applauded him, saying, 'This is my reward for carrying out your instructions.'

Then when everyone was asleep that night, the king of Vatsa, accompanied by Yaugándharáyana, went to Kalínga·sena's house. He went in there unseen and saw Mádana·vega at the side of the sleeping lady, asleep and in his usual form. When the king was about to kill him, that headstrong sorcerer was alerted by his magic powers. He woke up, went outside and immediately flew up into the sky. A moment later Kalínga·sena also woke up. When she saw the empty bed, she said, 'How can the king of Vatsa have woken up before me and left, leaving me asleep?' On hearing this Yaugándharáyana said to the king of Vatsa, 'Listen, by assuming your appearance, this fellow has violated the girl. I found him out using magic and showed him to you directly. However, because of his divine powers he cannot be killed.' 6.7.195

After saying this, he and the king approached the girl together and when Kalínga·sena saw them she stood there, greeted them respectfully and said, 'Where did you go just now, O king, before arriving with the minister?,' and as she was saying this, Yaugándharáyana said to her, 'O Kalínga·sena, someone magically disguised as the king of Vatsa has deceived you and married you, not my master here.' 6.7.200

tac chrutvā s" âtisaṃbhrāntā viddh" êva hṛdi pattriṇā
Kaliṅgasenā Vats'|ēśaṃ jagād' ôdaśru|locanā.
‹gāndharva|vidhin" âhaṃ te pariṇīt" âpi vismṛtā
kiṃ|svid, rājan, yathā pūrvaṃ Duṣyantasya Śakuntalā.›

6.7.205 ity uktaḥ sa tayā rājā tām uvāc' ānat'|ānanaḥ
‹satyaṃ na pariṇīt" âsi may" âdy' âiv' āgato hy aham.›
ity uktavantaṃ Vats'|ēśaṃ mantrī Yaugandharāyaṇaḥ
‹eh' îty› uktvā tataḥ svairam anaiṣīd rāja|mandiram.

tataḥ sa|mantrike rājñi gate s" âtra videśa|gā
mṛg" îva yūtha|vibhraṣṭā parityakta|sva|bāndhavā.
saṃbhoga|vidalat|pattra|mukh'|ābjā gaja|pīḍitā
padmin" îva parikṣipta|kabarī|bhramar'|āvaliḥ.
vinaṣṭa|kanyakā|bhāvā nir|upāya|kramā satī
Kaliṅgasenā gaganaṃ vīkṣamāṇ" êdam abravīt.

6.7.210 ‹Vats'|ēśa|rūpiṇā yena pariṇīt" âsmi kena|cit
prakāśaḥ so 'stu kaumāraḥ sa eva hi patir mama.›
evaṃ tay" ôkte gaganāt so 'tra vidyā|dhar'|âdhipaḥ
avātarad divya|rūpo hāra|keyūra|rājitaḥ.
‹ko bhavān iti?› pṛṣṭaś ca tay" âivaṃ sa jagāda tām
‹ahaṃ Madanaveg'|ākhyas, tanvi, vidyā|dhar'|âdhipaḥ.
mayā ca prāg vilokya tvāṃ purā pitṛ|gṛhe sthitām
tvat|prāpti|das tapaḥ kṛtvā varaḥ prāpto Maheśvarāt.

When she heard this Kalínga·sena was so upset it was as if she had been struck in the heart by an arrow, and with tears pouring from her eyes she said to the king of Vatsa, 'O king, even though you married me according to the *gandhárva* rite, have you forgotten me just as long ago Dushyánta forgot Shakúntala?'

After she said this to him, the king, bowing his head, 6.7.205
said, 'Truly I did not marry you, for I have only just arrived here.'

When the king of Vatsa had said this, the minister Yaugándharáyana said to him, 'Come,' and quietly took him to the palace.

Then, when the king and his minister had gone, Kalínga·sena, having abandoned her family, was there in a foreign country like a doe that has strayed from its herd. The petals of her lotus face blown open by her lovemaking as if she were a bed of water-lilies crushed by an elephant, her locks tossed about like its line of bees, her virginity lost, helpless and hopeless, Kalínga·sena said while looking at the sky,
'May whoever it was that married me while disguised as the 6.7.210
king of Vatsa reveal himself, for he took my virginity and is my husband!'

When she said this, the sorcerer king came down there from the sky in his divine form, resplendent with garland and armlet. On being asked by her who he was he replied, 'I am called Mádana·vega, slender lady, and I am a sorcerer king. I first saw you long ago when you were in your father's house. After performing austerities I received a boon from Shiva that would make you mine. You were in love with the king of Vatsa, so by assuming his appearance I quickly

Vats'|ēśvar'|ânuraktā ca tad|rūpeṇa mayā drutam
a|vṛtta|tad|vivāh" âiva pariṇīt" âsi yuktitaḥ.›
6.7.215 iti vāk|sudhayā tasya śruti|mārga|praviṣṭayā
kiṃ|cit Kaliṅgasen" âbhūd ucchvāsita|hṛd|ambujā.
atha sa Madanavegas tāṃ samāśvāsya kāntāṃ
vihita|dhṛti|vitīrṇa|svarṇa|rāśiḥ sa tasyai
ucita iti tay" ântar|baddha|sad|bhartṛ|bhaktiḥ
punar upagamanāya dyāṃ tad" âiv' ôtpapāta.
divy'|āspadaṃ sva|pati|sadma na martya|gamyaṃ
kāmāt pitur bhavanam ujjhitam ity avekṣya
tatr' âiva vastum atha s" âpi Kaliṅgasenā
cakre dhṛtiṃ Madanavega|kṛt'|âbhyanujñā.

iti mahā|kavi|śrī|Somadeva|bhaṭṭa|viracite Kathāsaritsāgare
Madanamañcukā|lambake saptamas taraṅgaḥ.

8

6.8.1 TATAḤ KALIṄGASENĀYĀḤ smarann an|upamaṃ vapuḥ
ekadā Manmath'|āviṣṭo niśi Vats'|ēśvaro 'bhavat.
utthāya khaḍga|hastaḥ san gatv" âiva praviveśa saḥ
ekākī mandiraṃ tasyāḥ kṛt'|ātithy'|ādaras tayā.
tatra prārthayāmānas tāṃ bhāry"|ârthe sa mahī|patiḥ
‹para|patny aham asm' îti› pratyākhyātas tay" âbravīt.
‹tṛtīyaṃ puruṣaṃ prāptā yatas tvam asi bandhakī
para|dāra|gato doṣo na me tvad|gamane tataḥ.›

tricked you into marrying me before your wedding to him was carried out.' When the nectar of these words entered 6.7.215
her ears, the lotus of Kalínga·sena's heart was revived a little. Then Mádana·vega comforted his sweetheart, helped her regain her composure and gave her a pile of gold. Thinking him to be suitable, she became inwardly firm in her devotion to her virtuous husband, and he then flew straight up into the sky to return again. Then after saying goodbye to Mádana·vega, Kalínga·sena, reflecting that her husband's house was an abode of divine beings and inaccessible to mortals, and that she had abandoned her father's house for love, made up her mind to stay right where she was.

Thus ends the seventh wave in the Mádana·mánchuka Attainment in the "Ocean of the Rivers of Story" composed by the glorious and learned great poet Soma·deva.

8

THEN ONE NIGHT, while recalling Kalínga·sena's unpar- 6.8.1
alleled beauty, the king of Vatsa was possessed by passion. Getting up, he went to her palace sword in hand and alone, and walked straight in. She greeted him with due respect. There, while the king was asking her to be his wife, she said that she was the wife of another man, to which he replied, 'Because you have now had three men, you are a harlot, so I shall not be committing the sin of adultery if I make love to you.'

6.8.5 evaṃ Kaliṅgasenā sā rājñ" ôktā pratyuvāca tam
‹tvad|artham āgatā, rājann, ahaṃ vidyā|dhareṇa hi
vyūḍhā Madanavegena svairaṃ tvad|rūpa|dhāriṇā
sa ev' âikaś ca bhartā me tat kasmād asmi bandhakī?
kiṃ v" âtikrānta|bandhūnāṃ sv'|êcch"|ācāra|hat'|ātmanām
imās tā vipadaḥ strīṇāṃ kumārīṇāṃ kath" âiva kā?
dṛṣṭ'|â|śakunayā sakhyā niṣiddh" âpi vyasarjayam
tvat|pārśvaṃ yad ahaṃ dūtaṃ tasya c' êdaṃ phalaṃ mama.
tat spṛśyasi balān māṃ cet prāṇāṃs tyakṣyāmy ahaṃ tataḥ
kā nāma kula|jā hi strī bhartṛ|drohaṃ kariṣyati.
6.8.10 tathā ca kathayāmy atra tava, rājan, kathāṃ śṛṇu
pur" âbhūd Indradatt'|ākhyaś Cedi|deśa|mahī|patiḥ.
sa Pāpaśodhane tīrthe kīrtyai deva|kulaṃ mahat
cakre yaśaḥ|śarīr'|ârthī śarīraṃ vīkṣya bhaṅguram.
tac ca bhakti|rasāc chaśvad īkṣituṃ sa yayau nṛpaḥ
sarvaś ca tīrtha|snānāya sadā tatr' āyayau janaḥ.
ekadā ca dadarś' âikāṃ tīrtha|snān'|ârtham āgatām
sa rāj" âtra vaṇig|bhāryāṃ pravāsa|sthita|bhartṛkām.
svaccha|kānti|sudhā|siktāṃcitra|rūpa|vibhūṣaṇām
jaṅgamām iva Kaṃdarpa|rāja|dhānīṃ mano|ramām.
6.8.15 «tvay" âhaṃ vijaye viśvam iti» prīty" êva pādayoḥ
āśliṣṭāṃ pañca|bāṇasya tūṇīra|dvaya|śobhayā.
sā dṛṣṭ" âiva manas tasya jahāra nṛpates tathā
yath" ânviṣya gṛhaṃ tasyāḥ sa yayau vivaśo niśi.
tāṃ ca prārthayamānaḥ sañ jagade sa tayā nṛpaḥ

When the king said this to Kalínga·sena, she replied, 'I 6.8.5
came to win you, O king, but I was willingly married to the sorcerer Mádana·vega because he had assumed your appearance. He is my one and only husband, so why am I a harlot? But such are the disasters that befall adult women—to say nothing of young maidens—who leave their families and ruin themselves by behaving according to their desires. Even though I had been told not to by a friend who had noticed a bad omen, I sent a messenger to you and I am now reaping the reward of that. So if you force yourself on me then I shall give up my life, for what woman of respectable
family could be unfaithful to her husband? To this end I 6.8.10
shall tell you a story on the subject. Listen, O king.

Long ago there was a king of the land of Chedi called Indra·datta. Having realized that the physical body is impermanent, he wanted to create a body of good works and built a great temple at the pilgrimage place of Papa·shódhana in order to glorify himself. Because of his fondness for worship, the king regularly went to visit it, and all his people kept coming there to bathe in the holy waters. One day the king saw there a merchant's wife who had come to bathe in the holy waters and whose husband was abroad. *Wet with the nectar of her pure radiance* : and *decorated by her amazing beauty* :, she was charming and looked like a moving palace of the god of love *washed white by the radiant moonlight* and *with various beautiful decorations*. Her 6.8.15
feet were embraced by the beauty of the two quivers of he who has five arrows, the god of love, as if he were fondly saying, "Through you I shall conquer the world." As soon as he saw her she stole the king's heart, such that he sought

«rakṣitā tvaṃ na yuktaṃ te para|dār'|âbhimarśanam.
haṭhāt spṛśasi vā māṃ ced a|dharmas te mahān bhavet
mariṣyāmi ca sadyo 'haṃ na sahiṣye ca dūṣaṇam.»
ity ukte 'pi tayā tasmin balaṃ rājñi cikīrṣati
śīla|bhraṃśa|bhayāt tasyāḥ sadyo hṛdayam asphuṭat.
6.8.20 tad dṛṣṭvā sapadi hrītaḥ sa gatv" âiva yath"|āgatam
dinais ten' ânutāpena rājā pañcatvam āyayau.›
ity ākhyāya kathām etāṃ sa|bhaya|praśray'|ānatā
bhūyaḥ Kaliṅgasenā sā Vats'|ēśvaram abhāṣata.
‹tasmād a|dharme mat|prāṇa|haraṇe mā matiṃ kṛthāḥ
ih' āśritāyā vastuṃ me dehi yāmy anyato 'nyathā.›
etat Kaliṅgasenātaḥ śrutvā Vats'|ēśvaro 'tha saḥ
vicārya virato bhūtvā dharma|jñas tām abhāṣata.
‹rāja|putri, vasa sv'|êcchaṃ bhartrā samam ih' âdhunā
n' âhaṃ vakṣyāmi te kiṃ|cid idānīṃ mā bhayaṃ kṛthāḥ.›
6.8.25 ity uktv" âiva gate tasmin svairaṃ rājñi sva|mandiram
śrutvā Madanavegas tan nabhaso 'vatatāra saḥ.
‹priye, sādhu kṛtaṃ! n' âivam akariṣyaḥ, śubhe, yadi
n' âbhaviṣyac chubhaṃ yasmān n' âsahiṣyata tan mayā.›

out her house and, out of control, went there that night. While he was entreating her, she said to the king, "You are a guardian and it is not right for you to touch the wife of another man. If you force yourself on me you will have committed a great sin and I shall die straight away, unable to bear the ignominy."

Despite her saying this to him, the king did try to force himself on her and as he was doing so, in fear of her virtue being violated, the woman's heart burst spontaneously. As 6.8.20
soon as the king saw this he left the way he had come in shame. A few days later he died out of remorse for what he had done.'

After telling this tale, Kalínga·sena, bowing with fear and humility, addressed the king of Vatsa once again. 'Therefore do not think to commit a sin that would take away my life. I came here for refuge. Let me stay or I shall go elsewhere.' On hearing this from Kalínga·sena, the king of Vatsa, who knew his duty, deliberated, desisted and said to her, 'Princess, from now on you must live here with your husband as you wish. I shall not say anything to you. You must no longer be scared.'

When the king had said this and gone of his own ac- 6.8.25
cord to his palace, Mádana·vega, having heard what was said, came down from the sky. 'Well done, my dear! If you had not behaved thus, good lady, then things would not have turned out well for I could not have put up with such behavior.'

ity uktvā sāntvayitvā tāṃ niśāṃ nītvā tayā saha
tatr' âiva gacchann āgacchann āsīd vidyā|dharo 'tha saḥ.
Kaliṅgasen' âpi ca sā patyau vidyā|dhar'|ēśvare
tatr' āsta martya|bhāve 'pi divya|bhoga|sukh'|ânvitā.
Vatsa|rājo 'pi tac|cintāṃ muktvā mantri|vacaḥ smaran
nananda labdhaṃ manvāno devīṃ rājyaṃ sutaṃ tathā.
6.8.30 devī Vāsavadattā ca mantrī Yaugandharāyaṇaḥ
abhūtāṃ nirvṛtau siddhe nīti|kalpa|latā|phale.

atha gacchatsu divasesv āpāṇḍu|mukha|paṅkajā
dadhre Kaliṅgasenā sā garbham utpanna|dohadā.
tuṅgau virejatus tasyāḥ stanāv āśyāma|cūcukau
nidhāna|kumbhau Kāmasya mada|mudr"|āṅkitāv iva.
tato Madanavegas tām upetya patir abhyadhāt
‹Kaliṅgasene, divyānām asmākaṃ samayo 'sty ayam.
jātaṃ mānuṣa|garbhaṃ yan muktvā yāmo vidūrataḥ
Kaṇv'|āśrame na tatyāja Menakā kiṃ Śakuntalām?
6.8.35 tvaṃ yady apy apsarāḥ pūrvaṃ tad apy a|vinayān nijāt
Śakra|śāpena saṃprāptā mānuṣyaṃ, devi, sāṃpratam.
ten' âiva bandhakī|śabdo jātaḥ sādhvyā ap' îha te
tasmād apatyaṃ rakṣes tvaṃ sthānaṃ yāsyāmy ahaṃ nijam.
smariṣyasi yadā māṃ ca saṃnidhāsye tadā tava.›

evaṃ Kaliṅgasenāṃ tām uktvā s'|âśru|vilocanām
samāśvāsy' âtha dattvā ca tasyai tad ratna|saṃcayam
tac|cittaḥ samay'|ākṛṣṭo yayau vidyā|dhar'|ēśvaraḥ.
Kaliṅgasen" âpy atr' āsīd apaty'|āśāṃ sakhīm iva

After saying this and reassuring her, the sorcerer spent the night with her and then kept coming and going from that same place. Kalínga·sena, her husband a sorcerer king, lived there enjoying divine luxury and happiness even though she was a mortal. The king of Vatsa, meanwhile, stopped worrying about her and, recalling the words of his minister, rejoiced, thinking that he had regained his queen, his kingdom and his son. Queen Vásava·datta and the minister 6.8.30
Yaugándharáyana were content, the wish-fulfilling tree of statecraft having successfully born fruit.

Then as the days went by, Kalínga·sena, her lotus face a little pale, fell pregnant and developed cravings. Her pert breasts, their nipples slightly dark, looked splendid, like pots of treasure belonging to the god of love marked with the seal of passion. Then her husband Mádana·vega went up to her and said, 'Kalínga·sena, we heavenly beings have this custom: when a mortal child is born, we leave it and go far away. Did not Ménaka abandon Shakúntala in Kanva's ashram? Even though you were once an *ápsaras*, O queen, 6.8.35
by Indra's curse you have for the time being become a mortal as a result of your own misconduct. It is because of this that even though you are virtuous, the word harlot has been used for you here. So you must look after your offspring. I am going to my own abode and I shall come to you when you think of me.'

After saying this to Kalínga·sena, who had tears in her eyes, he comforted her and gave her a mass of jewels. His mind set on her, the sorcerer king left, bound by custom. Kalínga·sena remained there, supported by her hopes for

ālambya Vatsa|rājasya bhuja|cchāyām apāśritā.
6.8.40 atr' ântare kṛtavatīṃ s'|âṅga|bhartr|āptaye tapaḥ
ādideśa Ratiṃ bhāryām Anaṅgasy' Âmbikā|patiḥ.
‹Vatsa|rāja|gṛhe jāto dagdha|pūrvaḥ sa te patiḥ
Naravāhanadatt'|ākhyo yoni|jo mad|vilaṅghanāt.
mad|ārādhanatas tvaṃ tu martya|loke 'py a|yoni|jā
janiṣyase tatas tena bhartrā s'|âṅgena yokṣyase.›
evam uktvā Ratiṃ Śaṃbhuḥ Prajāpatim ath' ādiśat
‹Kaliṅgasenā tanayaṃ soṣyate divya|saṃbhavam.
taṃ hṛtvā māyayā tasyās tat|sthāne tvam imāṃ Ratim
nirmāya mānuṣīṃ kanyāṃ tyakta|divya|tanuṃ kṣipeḥ.›
6.8.45 it' Îśvar'|ājñām ādāya mūrdhni vedhasy atho gate
Kaliṅgasenā prasavaṃ prāpte kāle cakāra sā.
jāta|mātraṃ sutaṃ tasyā hṛtv" âiv' âtra sva|māyayā
Ratiṃ tāṃ kanyakāṃ kṛtvā nyadhād vidhir a|lakṣitam.
sarvaś ca tatra tām eva kanyāṃ jātām alakṣata
div" âpy a|kāṇḍa|pratipac|candra|lekhām iv' ôditām.
kānti|dyotita|tad|vāsa|gṛhāṃ nirjitya kurvatīm
ratna|dīpa|śikhā|śreṇīr lajjitā iva niṣprabhāḥ.
Kaliṅgasenā tāṃ dṛṣṭvā jātām a|sadṛśīṃ sutām
putra|janm'|âdhikaṃ toṣād utsavaṃ vitatāna sā.

her offspring as if by a friend, having taken refuge in the shade of the mighty arm of the king of Vatsa.

In the meantime Ámbika's husband Shiva gave an order 6.8.40
to Rati, the wife of the god of love, who had performed austerities in order to get back her husband with his body restored. 'Your husband, who was earlier burned up, has been born in the home of the king of Vatsa. He has the name Nara·váhana·datta and was born in a mortal womb because he had offended me. You, on the other hand, because you have propitiated me, will be born in the world of mortals, but not in a womb. You will then be united with your now embodied husband.'

After saying this to Rati, Shiva gave a command to Praja·pati, the creator. 'Kalínga·sena shall give birth to a son of divine origin. Use magic to take him from her and, having fashioned Rati here in the form of a mortal maiden, her divine body cast aside, put her in his place.'

Honoring this order from Shiva, the creator then left. 6.8.45
When her time arrived Kalínga·sena gave birth. As soon as her son was born, the creator used his magic to take him and, immediately and without being noticed, put in his place Rati, whom he had turned into a girl. Everyone there saw only that a girl had been born, and she was like the sliver of the new moon unexpectedly appearing by day, lighting up the bedroom with her radiance and making the rows of flames from the jeweled lamps grow faint, as if ashamed. When Kalínga·sena saw that she had given birth to a daughter of unparalleled appearance, she was so happy that she celebrated more than she would have done if a son had

6.8.50 atha Vats'|éśvaro rājā sa|devīkaḥ sa|mantrikaḥ
kanyāṃ Kaliṅgasenāyā jātāṃ śuśrāva tādṛśīm.
śrutvā ca sa nṛpo 'kasmād uvāc' Eśvara|coditaḥ
devīṃ Vāsavadattāṃ tāṃ sthite Yaugandharāyaṇe.
‹jāne Kaliṅgasen" âiṣā divyā strī śāpataś cyutā
asyāṃ jātā ca kany" êyaṃ divy" âiv' āścarya|rūpa|dhṛk.
tad asau kanyakā tulyā rūpeṇa tanayasya me
Naravāhanadattasya mahā|devītvam arhati.›

tac chrutvā jagade rājā devyā Vāsavadattayā
‹mahā|rāja, kim evaṃ tvam a|kasmād adya bhāṣase?
6.8.55 kula|dvaya|viśuddho 'yaṃ kva putras te bata kva sā
Kaliṅgasenā|tanayā bandhakī|garbha|saṃbhavā.›

śrutv" âitad vimṛśan rājā so 'bravīn ‹na hy ahaṃ svataḥ
vadāmy etat praviśy' ântaḥ ko 'pi jalpayat' îva mām.
«Naravāhanadattasya kany" êyaṃ pūrva|nirmitā
bhāry" êty» evaṃ vadantīṃ ca śṛṇom' îva giraṃ divaḥ.
Kaliṅgasenā kiṃ c' âsāv eka|patnī kul'|ôdgatā
pūrva|karma|vaśāt tv asyā bandhakī|śabda|saṃbhavaḥ.›

iti rājñ" ôdite prāha mantrī Yaugandharāyaṇaḥ
‹śrūyate, deva, yac cakre Ratir dagdhe Smare tapaḥ.
6.8.60 «martya|lok'|âvatīrṇena sa|śarīreṇa saṃgamaḥ
martya|bhāva|gatāyās te svena bhartrā bhaviṣyati.»
iti c' ādād varaṃ Śarvo Ratyai sva|patim īpsave
Kām'|âvatāraś c' ôktaḥ prāg divya|vācā sutas tava.

been born. Then the king of Vatsa and his queens and min- 6.8.50
isters found out that a daughter of such beauty had been born to Kalínga·sena and hearing this, the king, urged on by Shiva, suddenly said to Queen Vásava·datta in the presence of Yaugándharáyana, 'I'm sure that this girl Kalínga·sena is a divine woman fallen to earth because of a curse, and the daughter born to her with this amazing beauty must be divine. So the girl is the equal in looks of my son Nara·váhana·datta and should become his chief queen.'

When she heard this, Queen Vásava·datta said to the king, 'Great king, why do you suddenly now speak like this?
How on earth can one compare your son here, who, being 6.8.55
born to two good families, is of pure origin, with this girl, the offspring of Kalínga·sena, conceived in the womb of a harlot?'

When the king heard this, on reflection he replied, 'But I am not saying this of my own accord. Someone seems to have entered me and be making me speak, and it is as if I am hearing a voice from the sky saying, "This girl was created to be the wife of Nara·váhana·datta." Furthermore, Kalínga·sena is a faithful wife and comes from a good family, but it is because of her actions in a former life that she is being called a harlot.'

After the king said this, the minister Yaugándharáyana spoke. 'It is said, your highness, that when the god of love was consumed by fire, Rati, wanting to find her husband,
performed austerities and Shiva bestowed on her the follow- 6.8.60
ing boon: "You shall be reunited with your husband when he descends, embodied, to the world of mortals and you have become a mortal." A divine voice has already said that

Raty" âvataraṇīyaṃ ca martya|bhāve Har'|ājñayā
garbha|grāhikayā c' âdya mam' âivaṃ varṇitaṃ rahaḥ.
«mayā Kaliṅgasenāyā garbhaḥ prāg garbha|śayyayā
yukto dṛṣṭas tad" âiv' ânyad apaśyam tad|vivarjitam.
tad āścaryaṃ viloky' âhaṃ tav' ākhyātum ih' āgatā»
iti striyā tay" ôktaṃ me jāt" âiṣā pratibh" âpi te.
6.8.65 taj jāne māyayā devaiḥ s" âiṣā Ratir a|yoni|jā
Kaliṅgasenā|tanayā garbha|cauryeṇa nirmitā.
bhāryā Kām'|âvatārasya putrasya tava, bhū|pate.
  tathā c' âtra kathām etāṃ yakṣa|saṃbandhinīṃ śṛṇu.
  bhṛtyo Vaiśravaṇasy' âbhūd Virūpākṣa iti śrutaḥ
yakṣo nidhāna|lakṣāṇāṃ pradhān'|âdhyakṣatāṃ gataḥ.
Mathurāyāṃ bahiḥ|saṃsthaṃ nidhānaṃ sa ca rakṣitum
yakṣaṃ niyuktavān ekaṃ śilā|stambham iv' âcalam.
tatra taṃ nagarī|vāsī kaś|cit pāśupato dvijaḥ
nidhān'|ânveṣaṇāy' āgāt khanya|vādī kadā|cana.
6.8.70 sa mānuṣa|vasā|dīpa|hasto yāvat parīkṣate
sthānaṃ tat tāvad asy' âtra karād dīpaḥ papāta saḥ.
lakṣaṇena ca ten' âtra sthitaṃ nidhim avetya saḥ
udghāṭayitum ārebhe sah' ânyaiḥ sakhibhir dvijaiḥ.
atha yo 'sau niyukto 'bhūd yakṣo rakṣā|vidhau sa tat
dṛṣṭvā gatvā yathā|vastu Virūpākṣaṃ vyajijñapat.
  «gaccha vyāpādaya kṣipraṃ kṣudrāṃs tān khanya|vādinaḥ»
ity ādideśa taṃ yakṣaṃ Virūpākṣaḥ sa kopanaḥ.
tataḥ sa yakṣo gatv" âiva sva|yuktyā nijaghāna tān
nidhāna|vādino viprān a|saṃprāpta|manorathān.

your son is an incarnation of the god of love and Rati is to descend to earth as a mortal by the order of Shiva. Today the midwife said to me in private, "I first saw Kalínga·sena's baby attached to the afterbirth and then that same instant I saw it as something else, detached from it. On seeing this miracle I came here to tell you." That is what the woman told me and now you have had this revelation. Thus I think 6.8.65
that this girl here is Rati, not born of a womb, but magically made by the gods to be Kalínga·sena's daughter, by stealing her newborn child, and she is to be the wife of your son, who is an incarnation of the god of love, O king.

On this subject listen to the following tale about a *yaksha*.

The god of wealth had as a servant a *yaksha* called Virupáksha who was the head guard of a hundred thousand treasures. Virupáksha appointed a *yaksha* to guard a treasure outside Máthura and he was as steadfast as a pillar of stone. One day a certain *páshupata* brahmin* who lived in the city and knew the magical science of locating underground treasure, came there looking for a buried hoard. While he was 6.8.70
searching about that spot carrying a lamp burning human fat, the lamp fell from his fingers. By this sign he knew that there was a treasure there and with some other brahmin friends of his, he started to uncover it. Then the *yaksha* who had been appointed to guard, having seen this, went and told Virupáksha everything that had happened.

Virupáksha was furious and gave the *yaksha* the following order: "Quickly go and kill those wretched treasure-hunting magicians!" The *yaksha* then went and immediately used his powers to kill the treasure-hunting brahmins,

6.8.75 tad buddhvā dhana|daḥ kruddho Virūpākṣam uvāca tam
«brahma|hatyā kathaṃ pāpa kāritā sahasā tvayā?
durgato vārtika|jano lobhāt kiṃ nāma n' ācaret?
nivāryate sa vitrāsya vighnais tais tair na hanyate.»
ity uktv" âtha śaśāp' âinaṃ Virūpākṣaṃ dhan'|âdhipaḥ
«martya|yonau prajāyasva duṣkṛt'|ācaraṇād iti.»
  prāpta|śāpo 'tha kasy' âpi bhū|tale brāhmaṇasya saḥ
Virūpākṣaḥ suto jāto brāhmaṇyasy' âgra|hāriṇaḥ.
tato 'sya yakṣiṇī patnī dhan'|âdhyakṣaṃ vyajijñapat
«deva, yatra sa bhartā me kṣiptas tatr' âiva māṃ kṣipa.
6.8.80 prasīda na hi śaknomi viyuktā tena jīvitum.»
  evaṃ tayā sa vijñaptaḥ sādhvyā Vaiśravaṇo 'bhyadhāt.
«yasya† viprasya sadane jāto bhartā sa te, 'naghe
tasy' âiva dāsyā gehe tvaṃ nipatiṣyasy a|yoni|jā.
tatra tena samaṃ bhartrā saṃgamas te bhaviṣyati
tvat|prasādāt sa śāpaṃ ca tīrtvā mat|pārśvam eṣyati.»
  iti Vaiśravaṇ'|ādeśāt sādhvī sā patitā tataḥ
dāsyās tasyā gṛha|dvāri kanyā bhūtv" âiva mānuṣī.
a|kasmāc ca tayā dāsyā kanyā dṛṣṭ" âdbhut'|ākṛtiḥ
gṛhītvā darśitā c' âsya svāmino 'tra dvi|janmanaḥ.
6.8.85 «‹divy" êyaṃ kanyakā k" âpi niḥsaṃdeham a|yoni|jā›
ity ātmā mama vakt' îh' ānaya tāṃ tvam a|śaṅkitam.

before they had got what they wanted. When the god of 6.8.75
wealth found out what had happened he was furious and said to Virupáksha, "Why did you rashly have the sin of brahmin murder committed, you wicked fellow? In their greed, poor people will do anything to support themselves. They are to be stopped by frightening them and putting various obstacles in their way, not killed." After saying this, the lord of wealth then cursed Virupáksha, saying, "Be born in the womb of a mortal for your wicked behavior."

After being cursed, Virupáksha was born on earth as the son of some brahmin who lived off land donated by the king. Then his *yakshi* wife made a request to the lord of wealth: "Your highness, please cast me down to the same
place where my husband was cast down, for I cannot live 6.8.80
apart from him."

When that virtuous *yakshi* made this request, the god of wealth said, "Your husband has been born in the house of a brahmin, O blameless lady, and you shall fall down into the house of a servant girl of that same brahmin, without being born in a womb. There you shall be united with your husband and thanks to you he will be freed from the curse and return to my side."

In accordance with this command from the god of wealth, the virtuous *yakshi* then instantly became a mortal maiden and appeared down on earth at the door of the house of that servant girl. When the servant girl suddenly saw a strange-looking maiden, she took her and showed her to her master there, the brahmin. "She is undoubtedly some divine 6.8.85
maiden and has not been born in a womb—that is what my soul is saying. You must move her in here immediately, for

iyaṃ hi mama putrasya manye bhāryātvam arhati»
iti so ’pi dvijo dāsīṃ tām uvāca nananda ca.
kramād atra vivṛddhā sā kanyā vipr’|ātmajaś ca saḥ
anyonya|darśan’|ābaddha|gāḍha|snehau babhūvatuḥ.
tataḥ kṛta|vivāhau tau tena vipreṇa daṃpatī
a|jāti|smaraṇe ’py āstām uttīrṇa|virahāv iva.
atha kālena deh’|ânte tayā so ’nugataḥ patiḥ
tat|tapaḥ|kṣata|pāpaḥ san yakṣaḥ svaṃ prāptavān padam.
6.8.90 it’ îh’ âvataranty eva nirāgastvād a|yoni|jāḥ
bhū|tale kāraṇa|vaśād divyā daivata|nirmitāḥ.
kulaṃ kiṃ, nṛpate, te ’syās tasmād bhāryā sutasya te
Kaliṅgasenā|putr” îyaṃ yath”|ôktaṃ daiva|nirmitā.›

Yaugandharāyaṇen’ âivam ukte Vats’|ēśvaraś ca tat
devī Vāsavadattā ca ‹tath” êti› hṛdi cakratuḥ.
tatas tasmin gṛhaṃ yāte mantri|mukhye sa bhū|patiḥ
pān’|ādi|krīḍayā ninye sa|bhāryas tad|dinaṃ sukhī.

tato dineṣu gacchatsu† moha|bhraṣṭa|svaka|smṛtiḥ
Kaliṅgasenā|tanayā sā samaṃ rūpa|saṃpadā.
6.8.95 krameṇa vavṛdhe nāmnā kṛtā Madanamañcukā
sutā Madanavegasy’ êty ato mātrā janena ca.
nūnaṃ sā śiśriye rūpaṃ sarv’|ânya|vara|yoṣitām
anyathā tāḥ puras tasyā virūpā jajñire katham?

I think this girl would make a worthy wife for my son." The brahmin said this to the servant girl and rejoiced. The girl gradually grew up there, and she and the brahmin's son fell deeply in love from looking at one another. Then the brahmin arranged their marriage and, although they did not remember their previous births, the couple felt as if they had been reunited after a separation. Then in time her husband the *yaksha* died and she followed him. He reached his home with his sins having been wiped out by her austerities.

Thus divine beings come down here to earth for a rea- 6.8.90
son, created by a deity and, because they are without sin, not born in wombs. The girl's family should be of no importance to you, O king: this daughter of Kalínga·sena, as I have said, has been fashioned by fate to be the wife of your son.'

When Yaugándharáyana said this, the king of Vatsa and Queen Vásava·datta both agreed with him in their hearts. Then when the chief minister had gone home, the happy king spent that day enjoying drinking and other pleasures with his wife.

Afterwards, as the days went by, delusion having deprived her of the memory of her true self, Kalínga·sena's daughter gradually grew up and her wealth of beauty increased accordingly. Her mother and the people called her 6.8.95
Mádana·mánchuka because she was the daughter of Mádana·vega, and she must surely have appropriated the beauty of all other beautiful women, otherwise why did they become ugly before her?

śrutvā rūpavatīṃ tāṃ ca kautukāt svayam ekadā
devi Vāsavadattā tām āninīy' ātmano 'ntikam.
tatra dhātryā mukh'|āsaktāṃ Vatsa|rājo dadarśa tām
Yaugandharāyaṇ'|ādyāś ca varter dīpa|śikhām iva.
dṛṣṭvā c' â|dṛṣṭa|pūrvaṃ tat tasyā netr'|âmṛtaṃ vapuḥ
‹Ratir ev' âvatīrṇ" êyam iti› mene na tatra kaḥ.
6.8.100 tataś c' ānāyayāṃ cakre devyā Vāsavadattayā
Naravāhanadatto 'tra jagan|netr'|ôtsavaḥ sutaḥ.
so 'tra phulla|mukh'|âmbhojo dīprāṃ Madanamañcukām
tām apaśyan navāṃ saurīm iva padm'|ākaraḥ prabhām.
s" âpi taṃ locan'|ānandaṃ paśyantī vikac'|ānanā
na tṛptim āyayau bālā cakor" îv' âmṛta|tviṣam.
tataḥ prabhṛti tau bālāv api sthātuṃ na śekatuḥ
dṛṣṭi|pāśair iv' ābaddhau pṛthag|bhūtāv api kṣaṇam.

dinair niścitya saṃbandhaṃ deva|nirmitam eva tu
vivāha|vidhaye buddhiṃ vyadhād Vats'|ēśvaras tayoḥ.
6.8.105 Kaliṅgasenā tad buddhvā nananda ca babandha ca
Naravāhanadatte 'smiñ jāmātṛ|prītito dhṛtim.
saṃmantrya mantribhiḥ sārdhaṃ tataś c' âkārayat pṛthak
Vatsa|rājaḥ sva|putrasya tasya svam iva mandiram.
tataḥ sambhṛtya saṃbhārān putraṃ rājā sa kāla|vit
yauva|rājye 'bhyaṣiñcat taṃ dṛṣṭa|ślāghya|guṇa|graham.
pūrvaṃ tasy' âpatan mūrdhni pitror ānanda|bāṣpa|jam
tataḥ śrauta|mahā|mantra|pūtaṃ sat|tīrtha|jaṃ payaḥ.
abhiṣek'|âmbubhis tasya dhaute vadana|paṅkaje
citraṃ nirmalatāṃ prāpur mukhāni kakubhām api!

One day, Queen Vásava·datta, curious herself after having heard how beautiful she was, had the girl brought to her. There the king of Vatsa and Yaugándharáyana and the others beheld her clinging to the face of her nurse like the flame of a lamp clinging to its wick. On seeing her unprecedented beauty, the nectar of immortality to the eyes, everyone there thought that she must indeed be an incarnation of Rati. Then Queen Vásava·datta had her son Nara·váhana· 6.8.100
datta, who brought cheer to the eyes of the world, brought in there. His lotus face blooming, he looked at the radiant Mádana·mánchuka there and it was like a bed of lotuses looking at the morning sunlight. Like a *chakóra* hen looking at the moon, the girl, her face beaming, could not get enough of looking at that delight for the eyes. From then on the two children, as if bound by the chain of their gazes, could not bear to be apart for a moment.

After a few days the king of Vatsa became certain that their relationship had been forged by the gods and he decided to arrange their wedding ceremony. When Kalínga· 6.8.105
sena found out about this, she was overjoyed and took delight in Nara·váhana·datta, out of affection for her daughter's future husband. Having deliberated with his ministers, the king of Vatsa then had a separate palace like his own made for his son. Then the king, knowing that the time was right, gathered the requisite materials and anointed his son as crown prince, his qualities having been shown to be commendable. The first water to fall on his head came from his parents' tears of joy; then it was water from sacred bathing places, purified by great mantras from learned brahmins. Amazingly, when the lotus of his face was washed in the

6.8.110 maṅgalyā|mālya|puṣpeṣu tasya kṣipteṣu mātṛbhiḥ
mumoca divya|māly'|âugha|varṣaṃ dyaur api tat|kṣaṇam.
deva|dundubhi|nirhrāda|spardhay" êva jajṛmbhire
ānanda|tūrya|nirghoṣa|pratiśabdā nabhas|tale.
praṇanām' âbhiṣiktaṃ taṃ yuva|rājaṃ na tatra kaḥ
sva|prabhāvād ṛte ten' âiv' ônnanāma tadā hi saḥ.

tato Vats'|ēśvaras tasya sūnor bāla|sakhīn sataḥ
sva|mantri|putrān āhūya sacivatve samādiśat.
Yaugandharāyaṇa|sutaṃ mantritve Marubhūtikam
senā|patye Hariśikhaṃ Rumaṇvat|tanayaṃ tataḥ.
6.8.115 Vasantaka|sutam krīḍā|sakhitve tu Tapantakam
Gomukhaṃ ca pratīhāra|dhurāyām Ityak'|ātmajam.
paurohitye ca pūrv'|ôktāv ubhau Piṅgalikā|sutau
Vaiśvānaraṃ Śāntisomaṃ bhrātuḥ putrau purodhasaḥ.
ity ājñapteṣu putrasya sācivye teṣu bhū|bhṛtā
gaganād udabhūd vāṇī puṣpa|vṛṣṭi|puraḥ|sarā.
‹sarv'|ârtha|sādhakā ete bhaviṣyanty asya mantriṇaḥ
śarīrād a|vibhinno 'sya Gomukhas tu bhaviṣyati.›

ity ukto divyayā vācā hṛṣṭo Vats'|ēśvaraś ca saḥ
sarvān saṃmānayām āsa vastrair ābharaṇaiś ca tān.
6.8.120 anujīviṣu tasmiṃś ca vasu varṣati rājani
daridra|śabdasy' âikasya n' āsīt tatr' *ârtha*|saṃgatiḥ.
pavan'|ôllāsit'|ākṣipta|patākā|paṭa|paṅktibhiḥ
āhūtair iva s" âpūri nartakī|cāraṇaiḥ purī.

waters of his consecration, even the quarters of the sky became clean! And when his mothers threw flowers from good 6.8.110
luck garlands on him, at that same moment the heavens released a downpour of heavenly garlands. As if to emulate the sound of the gods' drums, echoes of the sounds of celebratory musical instruments spread across the sky. Everyone there bowed before him once he was anointed as crown prince; not having power of his own, at that moment it was only thus that he was held in high esteem.

Then the king of Vatsa summoned the virtuous young friends of his son, the sons of his ministers, and appointed them as his attendants. Yaugándharáyana's son Maru·bhuti was made minister, Rumánvat's son Hari·shikha was put in charge of his army, Vasántaka's son Tapántaka was made his 6.8.115
playfellow, and Go·mukha, Ítyaka's son, was given the task of being his chamberlain. Píngalika's two sons, Vaishvánara and Shanti·soma, the king's priest's brother's boys mentioned earlier, were made his chaplains. After the king had thus appointed these men to assist his son, a voice was heard from the sky, accompanied by a rain of flowers: 'These ministers shall accomplish all his aims for him, and Go·mukha shall be inseparable from him.'

When the divine voice said this to him, the king of Vatsa was delighted and honored them all with clothes and ornaments. With the king showering wealth on his dependents, 6.8.120
nothing but the word poor was dissociated from *meaning: wealth* there. The city was filled with dancers and singers, as if the rows of painted flags unfurled and fluttering in the breeze had summoned them. Kalínga·sena, as if she were the incarnation of the sorcerer goddess of fortune who was

āgād vaidyādharī sākṣāl Lakṣmīs tasy' êva† bhāvinī
Kaliṅgasenā jāmātur utsave 'tra bhaviṣyataḥ.
tato Vāsavadattā ca sā ca Padmāvatī tathā
harṣeṇa nanṛtus tisro militā iva śaktayaḥ.
mārut'|ândolita|latāḥ pranṛtyann iva sarvataḥ
udyāna|taravo 'py atra cetaneṣu kath" âiva kā.
6.8.125 tataḥ kṛt'|âbhiṣekaḥ sann āruhya jaya|kuñjaram
Naravāhanadattaḥ sa yuva|rājo viniryayau.
avākīryata c' ôtkṣiptair netrair nīla|sit'|âruṇaiḥ
paura|strībhiḥ sa nīl'|âbja|lāja|padm'|âñjali|prabhaiḥ.

dṛṣṭvā ca tat|purī|pūjya|devatā bandi|māgadhaiḥ
stūyamānaḥ sa|sacivaḥ sa viveśa sva|mandiram.
tatra divyāni bhojyāni tathā pānāny upāharat
Kaliṅgasenā tasy' ādau sva|vibhūty|adhikāni sā
dadau tasmai su|vastrāṇi divyāny ābharaṇāni ca
sa|mantri|sakhi|bhṛtyāya jāmātṛ|sneha|kātarā.
6.8.130 evaṃ mah"|ôtsaven' âsāv amṛt'|āsvāda|sundaraḥ
eṣāṃ Vats'|ēśvar'|ādīnāṃ sarveṣāṃ vāsaro yayau.

tato niśāyāṃ prāptāyāṃ sut"|ôdvāha|vimarśinī
Kaliṅgasenā sasmāra tāṃ sā Somaprabhāṃ sakhīm.
etayā smṛta|mātrāṃ tāṃ May'|âsura|sutāṃ tadā
bhavyāṃ bhartā mahā|jñānī jagāda Nalakūbaraḥ.
‹Kaliṅgasenā tvām adya s'|ôtsukā smarati, priye
tad gaccha divyam udyānaṃ kuru c' âitat|sutā|kṛte.›
ity uktvā bhāvi bhūtaṃ ca kathayitvā ca tad|gatam
tad" âiva preṣayām āsa patnīṃ Somaprabhāṃ patiḥ.

going to accompany him, arrived there at the celebrations of her future son-in-law, and then she, Vásava·datta and Padmávati danced for joy as if they were the three royal powers united.* With their creepers swinging in the wind, even the trees in the gardens there seemed to dance, to say nothing of the sentient beings. Then after he had been anointed, Nara· 6.8.125
váhana·datta mounted a victory elephant and went out as crown prince. The dark pupils, the whites and the red edges of the upturned eyes of the ladies of the city which they cast over him looked like offerings of handfuls of blue lotuses, parched grain and lilies.

After visiting the gods worshipped in that city, he entered his own palace in the company of his advisers, while being hymned by bards and minstrels. There Kalínga·sena first of all treated him with divine delicacies and drinks even more splendid than usual and then, cowed by love for her son-in-law, she gave him and his ministers, friends and servants fine clothes and divine ornaments. Thus that day passed in great 6.8.130
celebration for the king of Vatsa and the rest of them, and it was as beautiful as the taste of the nectar of immortality.

When night had fallen and Kalínga·sena was thinking about her daughter's marriage, she recalled her friend Soma·prabha. Merely by Kalínga·sena calling her to mind, Nala·kúbara, the clairvoyant husband of that noble daughter of the *ásura* Maya, said to Soma·prabha, 'Kalínga·sena is now thinking of you with longing, my dear, so go and create a divine garden for her daughter.' Immediately after saying this and telling her Kalínga·sena's past and future, her husband dispatched his wife Soma·prabha. She, on reaching 6.8.135
her friend, who gave her an embrace born of having missed

6.8.135 sā c' āgatya cir'|ôtkaṇṭhā|kṛta|kaṇṭha|grahāṃ sakhīm
Kaliṅgasenāṃ kuśalaṃ pṛṣṭvā Somaprabh" âbravīt.
‹vidyā|dhareṇa tāvat tvaṃ pariṇītā maha"|rddhinā
avatīrṇā Ratis te ca sutā śārvād anugrahāt.
Kām'|âvatārasy' âiṣā ca Vats'|ēśāl labdha|janmanaḥ
Naravāhanadattasya pūrva|bhāryā vinirmitā.
vidyā|dhar'|âdhirājyaṃ sa divyaṃ kalpaṃ kariṣyati
tasy' âiṣ" âny'|âvarodhānāṃ mūrdhni mānyā bhaviṣyati.
tvaṃ c' âvatīrṇā bhū|loke Śakra|śāpa|cyut" âpsarāḥ
niṣpanna|kārya|śeṣā ca śāpa|muktim avāpsyasi.
6.8.140 etan me sarvam ākhyātaṃ bhartrā jñānavatā, sakhi
tasmāc cintā na te kāryā bhāvi sarvaṃ śubhaṃ tava.
ahaṃ c' êha karomy eṣā divyaṃ tvat|tanayā|kṛte
udyānaṃ n' âsti pātāle na bhūmau yan na vā divi.›
ity uktvā divyam udyānaṃ sā nirmāya sva|māyayā
Kaliṅgasenām āmantrya s'|ôtkāṃ Somaprabhā yayau.
tato niśi prabhātāyām a|kasmān Nandanaṃ divaḥ
bhūmāv iva cyutaṃ loko dadarś' ôdyānam atra tat.
buddhv" âtha rājā Vats'|ēśaḥ sa|bhāryaḥ sacivaiḥ saha
Naravāhanadattaś ca s'|ânugo 'tra samāyayau.
6.8.145 dadṛśus te tam udyānaṃ sadā|puṣpa|phala|drumam
nānā|maṇi|maya|stambha|bhitti|bhū|bhāga|vāpikam.
suvarṇa|varṇa|vihagaṃ divya|saurabha|mārutam
dev'|ādeś'|âvatīrṇaṃ tat|svarg'|ântaram iva kṣitau.

her for so long, asked Kalínga·sena if she was well and then said, 'You have been taken in marriage by a mighty sorcerer and, by the grace of Shiva, Rati has incarnated as your daughter. She has been created after being in her previous life the wife of Nara·váhana·datta, who is an incarnation of the god of love and was born to the king of Vatsa. He shall rule over the sorcerers for an eon of the gods and she shall be held in esteem at the head of his other wives. You are an *ápsaras* who has come down to earth after being condemned by a curse from Indra, and when everything you have left to do is complete you shall be freed from the curse. My husband, who is a sage, told me all this, my friend, so 6.8.140
you need not worry: your future is all good. I am here to create a divine garden for your daughter, the like of which is not to be found in the underworld, on earth or in heaven.'

After saying this Soma·prabha used her magic powers to fashion a divine garden, said goodbye to the wistful Kalínga·sena, and left. When dawn had broken, the people saw the garden there looking like Nándana suddenly fallen to earth from heaven. When he found out about it, the king of Vatsa, along with his wives and his ministers, and Nara·váhana·datta and his attendants, came there together. They 6.8.145
beheld that garden where the trees always had flowers and fruit, its pillars, walls, terraces and tanks made from various different jewels, its birds colored gold, its breezes divinely scented, like a heaven other than theirs brought down to earth at the command of the gods.

dṛṣṭvā tad adbhutaṃ rājā ‹kim etad iti?› pṛṣṭavān
Kaliṅgasenām ātithya|vyagrāṃ Vats'|ēśvaras tadā.
sā pratyuvāca sarveṣu śṛṇvatsu nṛpatiṃ ca tam
‹Viśvakarm'|âvatāro 'sti Mayo nāma mah"|âsuraḥ
Yudhiṣṭhirasya yaś cakre puraṃ ramyaṃ ca vajriṇaḥ
tasya Somaprabhā nāma tanay" âsti sakhī mama.
6.8.150 tayā rātrāv ih' āgatya mat|samīpaṃ sva|māyayā
prītyā kṛtam idaṃ divyam udyānaṃ mat|sutā|kṛte.›
ity uktvā yac ca sakhy" âsyā bhūtaṃ bhāvy uditaṃ tayā
tat tay" âiv' ôktam ity uktvā tadā sarvaṃ śaśaṃsa sā.
tataḥ Kaliṅgasen"|ôktiṃ sa|saṃvādām avekṣya tām
nirasta|saṃśayāḥ sarve toṣaṃ tatr' â|tulaṃ yayuḥ.
Kaliṅgasen"|ātithyena nināya divasaṃ ca tam
udyāne 'tr' âiva Vats'|ēśo bhāryā|putr'|ādibhiḥ saha.

anyedyur nirgato draṣṭuṃ devaṃ deva|kule ca saḥ
dadarśa nṛpatir bahvīḥ su|vastr'|ābharaṇāḥ striyaḥ.
6.8.155 ‹kā yūyam iti?› pṛṣṭāś ca tena tās taṃ babhāṣire
‹vayaṃ vidyāḥ kalāś c' âitās tvat|putr'|ârtham ih' āgatāḥ.
gatvā viśāmas tasy' ântar› ity uktvā tās tiro 'bhavan
sa|vismayaḥ sa rāj" âpi Vats'|ēśo 'bhyantaraṃ yayau.
tatra Vāsavadattāyai devyai mantri|gaṇāya ca
tac chaśaṃs' âbhyanandaṃs te devat"|ânugrahaṃ ca tam.
tato rāja|nideśena vīṇā Vāsavadattayā
Naravāhanadatte 'tra praviṣṭe jagṛhe kṣaṇāt.
vādayantīṃ tatas tāṃ ca mātaraṃ vinayena saḥ
rāja|putro 'bravīd ‹vīṇā cyutā sthānād asāv iti.›

When he saw that marvel, the king of Vatsa asked Kalínga·sena, who was busy being hospitable, how it had come about. As everyone listened on, she said in reply to the king, 'There is a great *ásura* called Maya who is an incarnation of Vishva·karman. He built for Yudhi·shthira, and created the lovely abode of Indra. He has a daughter called Soma·
prabha, who is my friend.* She came to me here last night 6.8.150
and out of affection used her magic to create this divine garden for my daughter.' After saying this, she told them that that same friend had told her her past and future, and then reported it all. At this everyone there, realizing that what Kalínga·sena had said tallied with what they knew, cast aside their doubts and attained an unparalleled happiness. The king of Vatsa spent the day in that very garden with his wives and son, being shown due hospitality by Kalínga·sena.

On the next day the king went out to visit a god in a temple and saw lots of women wearing fine clothes and ornaments. When he asked them who they were, they replied, 6.8.155
'We are the sciences and arts and we have come here for your son. We shall go and enter him.' After saying this they vanished and the astonished king of Vatsa went home. There he told Queen Vásava·datta and his ministers what had happened and they welcomed the favor from that god. Then immediately after Nara·váhana·datta came in there, at the king's instruction Vásava·datta picked up a lute. While his mother was playing it the prince humbly announced that
the lute was out of tune. His father then told him to pick 6.8.160
it up and play it, and his playing brought astonishment to even the *gandhárvas*. Once his father had examined him

6.8.160 ‹tvaṃ vādaya gṛhāṇ' âitām iti› pitr" ôdite 'tha saḥ
vīṇām avādayat kurvan gandharvān api vismitān.
evaṃ sarvāsu vidyāsu kalāsu ca parīkṣitaḥ
pitrā yāvad vṛtas tābhiḥ svayaṃ sarvaṃ viveda saḥ.
vīkṣya taṃ sa|guṇaṃ putraṃ Vats'|ēśas tām aśikṣayat
Kaliṅgasenā|tanayāṃ nṛttaṃ Madanamañcukām.
yathā yathā pūrṇa|*kalā* s" ābhūt tanur iv' āindavī
Naravāhanadatt'|âbdhiś cakṣubhe sa tathā tathā.
araṃsta tāṃ ca gāyantīṃ nṛtyantīṃ ca vilokayan
paṭhantīm iva Kām'|ājñām aṅg'|ādy'|abhinayair vṛtām.
6.8.165 s" âpi kṣaṇam a|paśyantī tam udaśruḥ *sudhā|mayam*
kāntam āsīd uṣaḥ|kāle jal'|ārdr" êva kumudvatī.
satataṃ c' â|sahaḥ sthātuṃ tan|mukh'|ālokanaṃ vinā
Naravāhanadatto 'sau tat tad|udyānam āyayau.
tatra pārśvaṃ tay" ānīya sutāṃ Madanamañcukām
Kaliṅgasenayā prītyā rajyamānaḥ sa tasthivān.

Gomukhaś c' âsya citta|jñaḥ svāmino 'tra cira|sthitim
icchan Kaliṅgasenāyai tāṃ tām akathayat kathām.
citta|graheṇa ten' âsya rāja|putras tutoṣa saḥ
hṛday'|ânupraveśo hi prabhoḥ saṃvananaṃ param.
6.8.170 nṛtt"|ādi|yogyāṃ kurute tasmin Madanamañcukām
tatra svayaṃ ca saṃgīta|veśmany udyāna|vartini.
Naravāhanadattaḥ sa hrepayan vara|cāraṇān
tasyāṃ priyāyāṃ nṛtyantyāṃ sarv'|ātodyāny avādayat.
jigāya c' āgatān digbhyo vividhān paṇḍitāṃs tathā
gaj'|âśva|ratha|śastr'|âstra|citra|pust'|ādi|kovidaḥ.
evaṃ viharato vidyā|svayaṃvara|vṛtasya te
Naravāhanadattasya śaiśave vāsarā yayuḥ.

like this in all the sciences and arts, he possessed them all and knew everything for himself.

When the king of Vatsa saw that his son was so talented, he had Kalínga·sena's daughter Mádana·mánchuka taught dance. As if her body were that of the moon, the more that she was filled with *arts : digits*, the more the ocean that was Nara·váhana·datta became disturbed. He took pleasure in watching her singing and dancing: she had the full complement of physical and other dramatic gestures and it was as if she were reciting a command from the god of love. She, 6.8.165
if she didn't see her *nectar-filled lover : beloved moon* for a moment, wept like a lotus bedewed at dawn. Unable to live without continuously gazing at her face, Nara·váhana·datta used to come to that garden of hers. Kalínga·sena would kindly bring her daughter Mádana·mánchuka to his side there, and he would stay there flushed with love.

Go·mukha, knowing what his master was feeling and wanting him to remain there for a long time, would keep telling Kalínga·sena stories. By grasping the prince's feelings for the girl, Go·mukha made him happy, for the best way to please one's master is by empathizing with him. Nara· 6.8.170
váhana·datta would himself make Mádana·mánchuka practice dancing and other arts in the music hall in that garden. Bringing shame to the finest bards, Nara·váhana·datta accompanied his dancing sweetheart on all the instruments. Skilled in riding elephants, horses and chariots, armed and unarmed combat, and painting and modeling, he surpassed all the various experts who had come there from all around. The childhood days of Nara·váhana·datta, who had been

ekadā c' âtra yātrāyām udyānaṃ sa priyā|sakhaḥ
yayau Nāgavanaṃ nāma rāja|putraḥ sa|mantrikaḥ.
6.8.175 tatr' âbhilāṣiṇī kā|cid vaṇig|bhāryā nirākṛtā
iyeṣa Gomukhaṃ hantuṃ sa|viṣ'|āhṛta|pānakā.
tad viveda ca tat|sakhyā mukhād atra sa Gomukhaḥ
n' ādade pānakaṃ tac ca striya evaṃ nininda ca.
‹aho dhātrā purā sṛṣṭaṃ sāhasaṃ tad|anu striyaḥ
n' âitāsāṃ duṣkaraṃ kiṃ|cin nisargād iha vidyate.
nūnaṃ strī nāma sṛṣṭ" êyam amṛtena viṣeṇa ca
anurakt" âmṛtaṃ sā hi viraktā viṣam eva ca.
jñāyate kānta|vadanā kena pracchanna|pātakā
ku|strī praphulla|kamalā gūḍha|nakr" êva padminī.
6.8.180 divaḥ patati kā|cit tu guṇa|cakra|pracodinī
bhartṛ|ślāghā|sahā su|strī prabhā bhānor iv' â|malā.
hanty ev' āśu gṛhīt" ânyā para|raktā gata|spṛhā
pāpā virāga|viṣa|bhṛd bhartāraṃ bhujag" îva sā.

tathā hi kutra|cid grāme Śatrughna iti ko 'py abhūt
puruṣas tasya bhāryā ca babhūva vyabhicāriṇī.
sa dadarś' âikadā sāyaṃ bhāryāṃ tāṃ jāra|saṃgatām
jaghāna taṃ ca taj|jāraṃ khaḍgen' ântar|gṛha|sthitam.
rātry|apekṣī ca tasthau sa dvāri bhāryāṃ nirudhya tām
tat|kālaṃ ca nivās'|ârthī tam atra pathiko 'bhyagāt.

chosen by the sciences to be their husband, went by with
him enjoying himself thus.

One day there the prince and his sweetheart, together
with his ministers, went to a garden called Naga·vana, Snake
Forest, for a festival. Some merchant's wife there who de- 6.8.175
sired Go·mukha and had been spurned, tried to kill him by
offering him a poisoned drink. Go·mukha found out about
it from a friend of hers there and did not accept the drink
but poured scorn on women thus: 'Oh! Long ago the creator brought forth rashness and he followed it with women.
Because of their innate disposition, there is nothing in this
world that they won't do. This creature called woman must
have been fashioned from nectar and poison, for when she
is in love she is nectar but when she isn't, she is nothing but
poison. Who can read a wicked woman, her lovely face hiding evil intent as if she were a bed of blossoming lotuses con-
cealing a crocodile? But a good woman can descend from 6.8.180
heaven, inspiring a host of virtues and causing her husband
to be praised, like spotless sunlight and her husband the
sun. Other women are as evil as she-snakes and, when taken
as wives, love other men, take no pleasure in their husbands
and, wielding the poison of indifference, kill them.

Thus there lived in some village or other a certain man
called Shatrúghna, and his wife was unfaithful to him. One
evening he found his wife with her lover and he killed her
lover with a sword when he was inside his house. Then he
stood at the door waiting for night, stopping his wife from
going out, and when night fell a traveler arrived there unannounced, looking for a place to stay. He gave him shelter 6.8.185

6.8.185 dattvā tasy' āśrayaṃ yuktyā ten' âiva saha taṃ hatam
pāradārikam ādāya rātrau tatr' âṭavīṃ yayau.
tatr' ândha|kūpe yāvat sa śavaṃ kṣipati taṃ tayā
tāvad āgatayā paścāt kṣiptaḥ so 'py atra bhāryayā.
evaṃ ku|yoṣit kurute kiṃ kiṃ nāma na sāhasam›
iti strī|caritaṃ bālo 'py anindat so 'tra Gomukhaḥ.
tato Nāgavane tatra nāgān abhyarcya sa svayam
Naravāhanadatto 'gāt sv'|āvāsaṃ sa|paricchadaḥ.

tatra jijñāsur anyedyuḥ sacivān Gomukh'|ādikān
jānann api sa papraccha rāja|nīteḥ samuccayam.
6.8.190 ‹sarvajñas tvaṃ tath" âpy etad brūmaḥ pṛṣṭā vayaṃ tvayā›
ity uktvā sāram anyonyaṃ te niścity' âivam abruvan.
‹āruhya nṛ|patiḥ pūrvam indriy'|âśvān vaśī|kṛtān
kāma|krodh'|ādikāñ jitvā ripūn ābhyantarāṃś ca tān
jayed ātmānam ev' ādau vijayāy' ânya|vidviṣām
a|jit'|ātmā hi vivaśī vaśī|kuryāt kathaṃ param.

tato jānapadatv'|ādi|guṇa|yuktāṃś ca mantriṇaḥ
purohitaṃ c' âtharva|jñaṃ kuryād dakṣaṃ tapo|'nvitam.
upādhibhir bhaye lobhe dharme kāme parīkṣitān
yogyeṣv amātyān kāryeṣu yuñjīt' ântara|vittamaḥ.
6.8.195 satyaṃ dveṣa|prayuktaṃ vā sneh'|ôktaṃ sv|ârtha|saṃhatam
vacas teṣāṃ parīkṣeta mithaḥ kāryeṣu jalpatām.
satye tuṣyed a|satye tu yath"|ârhaṃ daṇḍam ācaret
jijñāseta pṛthak c' âiṣāṃ cārair ācaritaṃ sadā.
ity an|āvṛta|dṛk paśyan kāryāṇy utkhāya kaṇṭakān

and then tricked him into helping him take the slain adulterer to the forest that night. While he was throwing the body into a hidden well there, his wife arrived and threw him in after it. Thus there is no rash act of any kind that a wicked woman will not do.' With these words, Go·mukha, though but a boy, denounced the conduct of women. Then Nara·váhana·datta himself worshipped the snakes there in Naga·vana before going home with his entourage.

The next day he wanted to test Go·mukha and his other ministers there and, even though he knew the answer, he asked them for a summary of statecraft. They told him that 6.8.190
he knew everything but even so they would give the answer because he had asked them. Then, having determined among themselves how to sum it up, they said, 'A king should first tame and mount the horses that are his senses, then conquer passion and anger and his other internal enemies, for in order to conquer one's other enemies, one should first conquer one's self, for he who has not mastered his self is uncontrolled and cannot control others.

Then he should appoint ministers who have qualities such as being inhabitants of his country, and a priest who knows the Athárva Veda, is competent and has accumulated ascetic power. After staging events whereby he can test his ministers' fear, greed, piety and passion, he will know them intimately and should give them suitable duties. When they are talking to one another in the course of their 6.8.195
duties, he should check whether their words are truthful, used maliciously, spoken with affection or attended with self-interest. If truthful he should be happy, but if not he

upārjya koṣa|daṇḍ'|ādi sādhayed baddha|mūlatām.
utsāha|prabhutā|mantra|śakti|traya|yutas tataḥ
para|deśa|jigīṣuḥ syād vicārya sva|par'|ântaram.
āptaiḥ śrut'|ânvitaiḥ prājñair mantraṃ kuryād an|āyatam
tair niścitaṃ sva|buddhyā tat sarv'|âṅgaṃ pariśodhayet.
6.8.200 sāma|dān'|ādy|upāya|jño yoga|kṣemaṃ prasādhayet
prayuñjīta tataḥ saṃdhi|vigrah'|ādīn guṇāṃś ca ṣaṭ.

evaṃ vitandro vidadhat sva|deśa|para|deśayoḥ
cintāṃ rājā jayaty eva na punar jātu jīyate.
a|jñas tu kāma|lobh'|ândho vṛthā|mārga|pradarśibhiḥ
nītvā śvabhreṣu nikṣipya muṣyate dhūrta|ceṭakaiḥ.
n' âiv' âvakāśaṃ labhate rājñas tasy' ântike 'paraḥ
dhūrtair nibaddha|vāṭasya śāler iva kṛṣīvalaiḥ.
antar|bhūya rahasyeṣu tair vaśī|kriyate hi saḥ
tataḥ Śrīr a|viśeṣa|jñāt khinnā tasmāt palāyate.
6.8.205 tasmāj jit'|ātmā rājā syād yukta|daṇḍo viśeṣa|vit
praj"|ânurāgād evaṃ hi sa bhaved bhājanaṃ śriyaḥ.

should mete out a suitable punishment. He should constantly use spies to check on the activities of each of them individually. Thus observing his affairs with an unblinkered eye and extracting the thorns, he should amass a fortune and an army and so forth, and strive to give his position a firm foundation. Then, endowed with the three royal powers—energy, majesty and good counsel—he should seek to conquer other countries, having weighed up the differences between him and his enemies. He should take regular advice from trusted and learned wise men, and use his own intelligence to refine in every detail what they decide upon.
Knowing conciliation, charity and the other ways of win- 6.8.200
ning over an enemy, he should protect what he has and then employ treaties, battles and the other four tactics to be used in foreign policy.*

A king thus tirelessly thinking about his and his enemy's lands can only be victorious and is never conquered, but an ignorant man blinded by passion and greed is robbed by roguish servants who show him the wrong path, lead him along and throw him into a pit. Like a paddyfield fenced in by farmers, the king is guarded by the rogues and no one else gets a chance to come near him, for they become intimate with his secrets and he falls under their control. He does not know how to discriminate and the goddess of
fortune runs away from him in distress. So a king should 6.8.205
have mastered his self, have the means to govern and know how to discriminate. For when the people thus love him, he becomes a worthy home for the goddess of fortune.

pūrvaṃ ca Śūrasen'|ākhyo bhṛty'|âika|pratyayo nṛpaḥ
sacivaiḥ peṭakaṃ kṛtvā bhujyate sma vaśī|kṛtaḥ.
yas tasya sevako rājñas tasmai tan|mantriṇo 'tra te
dātuṃ n' âicchaṃs tṛṇam api ditsaty api ca bhū|patau.
teṣāṃ tu sevako yo 'tra dadus tasmai svayaṃ ca te
te ca vijñapya rājānam an|arhāy' âpy adāpayan.
tad dṛṣṭvā sa nṛpo buddhvā śanais tad|dhūrta|peṭakam
anyonyaṃ prajñayā yuktyā sacivāṃs tān abhedayat.
6.8.210 bhinneṣu teṣu naṣṭeṣu mithaḥ paiśunya|kāriṣu
samyak chaśāsa rājyaṃ tat sa rāj" ânyair a|vañcitaḥ.

Harisiṃhaś ca rāj" âbhūt s'|âmātyo nīti|tattva|vit
kṛta|bhakta|budh'|âmātyaḥ sa|durgaḥ s'|ârtha|saṃcayaḥ.
anuraktāḥ prajāḥ kṛtvā ceṣṭate sma yathā tathā
cakra|varty|abhiyukto 'pi na jagāma parābhavam.
evaṃ vicāraś cintā ca sāraṃ rājye 'dhikaṃ nu kim.›

ity|ādy uktvā yathā|svaṃ te viremur Gomukh'|ādayaḥ.
Naravāhanadattaś ca teṣāṃ śraddhāya tad|vacaḥ
cintye puruṣa|kartavye 'py a|cintyaṃ daivam abhyadhāt.
6.8.215 tataś c' ôtthāya tair eva sākaṃ tāṃ prekṣituṃ yayau
sa vilamba|kṛt'|ôtkaṇṭhāṃ priyāṃ Madanamañcukām.
prāpte tan|mandiraṃ tasminn āsana|sthe kṛt'|ādarā
kṣaṇaṃ Kaliṅgasen" âtra Gomukhaṃ vismit" âbravīt.
‹Naravāhanadatte 'tra rāja|sūnāv an|āgate

Long ago there lived a king called Shura·sena who put absolute faith in his servants. His ministers formed a cabal, took control of him and enjoyed his fortune. His ministers there would not give even a piece of straw to anyone who was the king's servant, even if the king wanted to reward them, but they themselves would bestow gifts on any man who worked for them there and would tell the king to give to him, even if he was undeserving. When the king saw this and slowly found out about that cabal of rogues, he used his wisdom to trick the ministers into breaking apart from one another. When they had split up and were ruined 6.8.210
after informing on each other, the king duly ruled over the kingdom and was not cheated by anyone else.

And there was a king, Hari·sinha, who had ministers and knew the essence of statecraft. He made wise and devoted men his ministers, and had a citadel and a store of wealth. He made his subjects love him and behaved in such a way that even when attacked by an emperor he was not defeated.

Thus deliberation and consideration are the essence of ruling a kingdom. There is nothing more important.'

After they had each spoken like this, Go·mukha and the others fell quiet. Nara·váhana·datta approved of what they had said and then announced that even though one should think about human endeavor, fate was beyond the realm of thought. Then he got up and went with them to see 6.8.215
his sweetheart Mádana·mánchuka, whom their lateness had made anxious. Once he had reached her palace and was sitting down, Kalínga·sena quickly and respectfully welcomed him there and then said to Go·mukha in amazement, 'When prince Nara·váhana·datta didn't come here,

utsukā padavīm asya draṣṭuṃ Madanamañcukā.
harmy'|âgra|bhūmim ārūḍhā, Gomukh,' ânugatā mayā
yāvat tāvat pumān eko nabhaso 'tr' âvatīrṇavān.
sa kirīṭī ca khaḍgī ca māṃ divy'|ākṛtir abravīt
«ahaṃ Mānasaveg'|ākhyo rājā vidyādhar'|ēśvaraḥ.
6.8.220 svaḥ|strī Surabhidatt"|ākhyā tvaṃ ca śāpa|cyutā bhuvi
sutā ca tava divy" êyam etan me viditaṃ kila.
tad dehi me sutām etāṃ saṃbandhaḥ sadṛśo hy ayam.»
ity ukte tena sahasā vihasy' âhaṃ tam abravam.
«Naravāhanadatto 'syā bhartā devair vinirmitaḥ
sarveṣāṃ yo 'tra yuṣmākaṃ cakra|vartī bhaviṣyati.»
ity uktaḥ sa may" ôtpatya vyoma vidyā|dharo gataḥ
mat|putrī|nayan'|ôdveg'|â|kāṇḍa|vidyul|lat"|ôpamaḥ.›
tac chrutvā Gomukho 'vādīj
‹jāte 'smin svāmin' îha naḥ
rāja|putre 'ntarikṣ'|ôkter
buddhv" âmuṃ bhāvinaṃ prabhum
6.8.225 pāpaṃ vidhātum apy aicchan sadyo vidyā|dharā hi te
ucchṛṅkhalo niyantāraṃ ka icched balinaṃ prabhum.
tato 'yaṃ rakṣitaḥ sākṣād gaṇān ādiśya Śaṃbhunā
Nārad'|ôktir iyaṃ tāten' ôcyamānā śrutā mayā.
ato vidyā|dharāḥ saṃpraty ete 'smākaṃ virodhinaḥ.›
śrutvā Kaliṅgasen" âitat sva|vṛttānta|bhiy" âbravīt.
‹māyayā tarhi no yāvan madvan Madanamañcukā
vañcyate rāja|putreṇa kiṃ na tāvad vivāhyate?›
etat Kaliṅgasenātaḥ śrutvā tāṃ Gomukh'|ādayaḥ
ūcus ‹tvay" âiva kārye 'smin Vats'|ēśaḥ preryatām iti.›

O Go·mukha, Mádana·mánchuka was so filled with longing that she climbed up to the roof terrace with me to watch his approach, and in the meantime a man came down here from the sky. He wore a crown, carried a sword and was of divine appearance. He said to me, "I am a king called Mánasa·vega, a sorcerer lord and you are a divine lady called 6.8.220
Súrabhi·datta who has fallen to earth because of a curse. This girl of yours is divine—I am sure of it—so give me your daughter for it is a fitting union."

After he had said this with such temerity, I laughed and replied, "The gods have created Nara·váhana·datta to be her husband and he shall become the emperor of all you sorcerers here on earth."

After I had said this to him the sorcerer flew off into the sky, putting fear into the eyes of my daughter like an unheralded streak of lightning.'

On hearing this, Go·mukha said, 'When our master this 6.8.225
prince was born here, the sorcerers heard from that voice from the sky that he was their future lord and they immediately wanted to do him harm. No one who is free would want a mighty lord to rule over him. As a result Shiva has ordered the *gana*s themselves to guard him. Nárada said this and I heard my father repeating it. That is why for the time being these sorcerers are hostile to us.'

When she heard this, Kalínga·sena, worried about what had happened to her, said, 'In that case, before she is deceived by magic like I was, why doesn't the prince marry Mádana·mánchuka now?' On hearing this from Kalínga·sena, Go·mukha and the others said to her, 'It is you who must urge the king of Vatsa to proceed with this matter.'

6.8.230 tatas tad|gata|dhīs tasminn udyāne vyāharad dinam
Naravāhanadattas tāṃ paśyan Madanamañcukām.
utphulla|padma|vadanāṃ dalat|kuvalay'|ēkṣaṇām
bandhūka|kamanīy'|âuṣṭhīṃ mandāra|stabaka|stanīm.
śirīṣa|su|kumār'|âṅgīṃ pañca|puṣpa|mayīm iva
ekām eva jagaj|jetrīṃ Smareṇa vihitām iṣum.
Kaliṅgasen" âpy anyedyur gatvā Vats'|ēśvaraṃ svayam
sutā|vivāha|hetos tad yath"|âbhīṣṭaṃ vyajijñapat.
Vats'|ēśo 'pi visṛjy' âitām āhūya nija|mantriṇaḥ
devyāṃ Vāsavadattāyāṃ sthitāyāṃ nijagāda tān.
6.8.235 ‹Kaliṅgasenā tvarate sut'|ôdvāhāya tat katham
kurmo yad bandhak" îty etāṃ loko vakty uttamām iti?
lokaś ca sarvadā rakṣyas tat|pravādena kiṃ purā
Rāma|bhadreṇa śuddh" âpi tyaktā devī na Jānakī?
Ambā hṛt" âpi Bhīṣmeṇa yatnād bhrātuḥ kṛte tathā
pratīpaṃ kiṃ na vā tyaktā vṛta|pūrv'|ânya|bhartṛkā?
evaṃ Kaliṅgasen" âiṣā svayaṃvara|vṛte mayi
vyūḍhā Madanavegena ten' âitāṃ garhate janaḥ.
ato 'syās tanayām etāṃ gāndharva|vidhinā svayam
Naravāhanadatto 'sāv udvahatv anurūpikām.›
6.8.240 ity ukte Vatsa|rājena sm' āha Yaugandharāyaṇaḥ
‹icchet Kaliṅgasen" âitad an|aucityaṃ kathaṃ, prabho?
divy" âiṣā hi na sāmānyā sa|sut" êty a|sakṛd|gatam
mittreṇa c' âitad uktaṃ me jñāninā brahma|rakṣasā.›

Nara·váhana·datta then spent the day having fun in that 6.8.230
garden, his mind fixed on Mádana·mánchuka as he gazed on her. With her face a full-blown lotus, her eyes blossoming water-lilies, her lovely lips *bandhúka* flowers, her breasts clusters of *mandára* blooms and her body a tender *shirísha* flower, she seemed to consist of five flowers, a single arrow created by the god of love to conquer the world.* In order to have her daughter married, on the next day Kalínga·sena went in person to the king of Vatsa and told him her wishes. After dismissing her, the king of Vatsa summoned his ministers and, in the presence of Queen Vásava·datta,
said to them, 'Kalínga·sena is anxious for her daughter to 6.8.235
be married soon, so how are we to arrange it, since the people are calling that exalted woman a harlot? One must always be on guard against the people: did not Lord Rama long ago abandon Queen Sita because of what they were saying, even though she was innocent? And was not Amba, though Bhishma had taken pains to carry her off for his brother's sake, also unfortunately abandoned, because she had previously chosen a different husband? In the same way Kalínga·sena here, having chosen me as her husband, was married to Mádana·vega. That is why the people are censuring her. So let our Nara·váhana·datta marry this daughter of hers himself according to the *gandhárva* rite—she is suitable for him.'

When the king of Vatsa had said this, Yaugándharáyana 6.8.240
replied, 'How could Kalínga·sena wish for something so improper, my lord? She is a divine lady, not an ordinary one, and the same is true for her daughter. My clairvoyant friend the brahmin *rákshasa* has told me this many times.'

ity|ādi tatra te yāvad vimṛśanti parasparam
evaṃ māheśvarī tāvad vāṇī prādur abhūd divaḥ.
‹man|netr'|ānala|dagdhasya sṛṣṭasy' âtra mano|bhuvaḥ
Naravāhanadattasya may" âiv' âiṣā vinirmitā.
tapas|tuṣṭena bhāry" âsya Ratir Madanamañcukā
etayā sahitaś c' âyaṃ sarv'|ântaḥ|pura|mukhyayā.
6.8.245 vidyā|dhar'|âdhirājyaṃ sa divyaṃ kalpaṃ kariṣyati
mat|prasādād vijity' ârīn› ity uktvā virarāma vāk.
śrutv" âitāṃ bhagavad|vāṇīṃ Vats'|ēśaḥ sa|paricchadaḥ
taṃ praṇamya sut'|ôdvāhe sa|nando niścayaṃ vyadhāt.
atha sa saciva|mukhyaṃ pūrva|vijñāta|tattvaṃ
nara|patir abhinandy' āhūya mauhūrtikāṃś ca
śubha|phala|dam apṛcchal lagnam ūcus tu te taṃ
katipaya|dina|madhye bhāvinaṃ prāpta|pūjāḥ.
‹kālaṃ manāg anubhaviṣyati kaṃ|cid atra
putro viyogam anayā saha bhāryayā te
jānīmahe vayam idaṃ nija|śāstra|dṛṣṭyā,
Vats'|ēśvar' êti› jagadur gaṇakāḥ punas te.
tataḥ sa sūnor nija|vaibhav'|ôcitaṃ
vivāha|saṃbhāra|vidhiṃ vyadhān nṛpaḥ
tathā yath" âsya sva|purī na kevalaṃ
pṛthivy āpi kṣobham agāt tad|udyamāt.
6.8.250 prāpte vivāha|divase 'tha Kaliṅgasenā
pitrā nisṛṣṭa|nija|divya|vibhūṣaṇāyāḥ
tasyāḥ prasādhana|vidhiṃ duhituś cakāra
Somaprabhā pati|nideśa|vaś" āgatā ca.

As they talked it over like this among themselves, Shiva's voice was heard from the sky: 'After he was burned up by the fire from my eye, I brought forth the god of love here as Nara·váhana·datta and, pleased with her austerities, I created his wife Rati as Mádana·mánchuka. With her at the head of his entire harem, he shall rule over the sorcerers for 6.8.245
an eon of the gods after defeating his enemies through my grace.' After saying this, the voice fell quiet. When the king of Vatsa and his entourage heard this speech from the Lord, he bowed before Him and joyfully came to the conclusion that his son should be married.

Then the king congratulated his chief minister, who had already divined the truth, summoned the astrologers and asked them what would be an auspicious time for the wedding. After being honored with presents they replied that it would be in a few days. Then the astrologers spoke again: 'For a short while your son will experience here some sort of separation from this wife of his. We know this by looking at our treatises, O king of Vatsa.' Then the king made the many arrangements for his son's wedding, appropriate to his greatness, and they were such that not only his city but the whole world was disturbed by the undertaking. When 6.8.250
the day of the wedding arrived, Kalínga·sena made up her daughter, to whom her father had sent his own divine ornaments, and Soma·prabha arrived, obeying her husband's command.

kṛta|divya|kautukā sā
    sutarām atha Madanamañcukā vibabhau
nanv evam eva kāntā
    candra|tanuḥ Kārttik'|ânugatā.
divy'|âṅganāś ca tasyā
    Har'|ājñayā śrūyamāṇa|gīta|ravāḥ
tad|rūpa|jit'|ācchannā
    hrītā iva maṅgalaṃ vidadhuḥ.
‹bhakt'|ânukampini, jay,' âdri|sute! tvay" âdya
    Ratyās tapaḥ svayam upetya kṛtaṃ kṛt'|ârtham›
ity|ādi divya|vara|cāraṇa|vādya|miśra|
    vāky'|ânumeyam api saṃdadhate 'tra Gauryāḥ.
  atha Naravāhanadattaḥ
    praviveśa sa Madanamañcuk"|âdhyuṣitam
kṛta|vara|kautuka|śobhī
    vividha|mahā|todya|bhṛd|vivāha|gṛham.
6.8.255 nirvartya tatra bahal'|ôdyata|vipram aṣṭa|†
    vīvāha|maṅgala|vidhiṃ ca vadhū|varau tau
vedīṃ samāruruhatur jvalit'|âgnim uccai
    rājñāṃ śiro|bhuvam iv' â|mala|ratna|dīpām.
yadi yugapad ih' êndu|mūrti|bhānū
    kanaka|giriṃ bhramato 'bhitaḥ kadā|cit
bhavati tad upamā tayos tadānīṃ
    jagati vadhū|varayoḥ pradakṣiṇe 'gneḥ.
yathā vivāh'|ôtsava|tūrya|nādān
    apothayan dundubhayo 'ntarikṣe
tathā vadh"|ûtsārita|homa|lājāḥ
    sur'|ôjjhitāḥ kausuma|vṛṣṭayo 'tra.

In her divine marriage-thread Mádana·mánchuka looked even lovelier. Does not the body of the moon look similarly more lovely when attended by the month of Kárttika? Divine ladies bestowed blessings upon her at the order of Shiva; the sound of their songs was audible, but, cowed by her beauty, they were hidden, as if ashamed. 'Victory to you, who are compassionate to your devotees, O daughter of the mountain! You have come in person today and made Rati's austerities successful.' They composed this and other incomparable hymns to Gauri, and were accompanied by music from the finest divine minstrels.

Then Nara·váhana·datta, resplendent after being invested with an exquisite marriage string, went into the wedding house, which was occupied by Mádana·mánchuka and full of all sorts of huge musical instruments. After there com- 6.8.255
pleting the rite of the eight auspicious items* for good luck in marriage, which was diligently carried out by several brahmins, the bride and groom ascended the altar, where the fire had been lit, and it was as if they were taking their place, lit by flawless jewels, at the head of the kings. If the full moon and the sun were simultaneously to revolve around the golden mount Meru here on earth, then there would be something in the world comparable to that bride and groom's circumambulation of the fire at that time. Just as the drums in heaven drowned out the sounds of the instruments celebrating the wedding, so the showers of flowers sent down by the gods swamped the parched grain thrown by the bride in the fire offering. It is said that

tataḥ kanaka|rāśibhir maṇi|mayaiś ca jāmātaraṃ
samarcayad udāra|dhīḥ kila Kaliṅgasenā tathā
yath' âtra bubudhe janair api su|durgato 'syāḥ puraḥ
sa kāmam Alakā|patiḥ kṛpaṇa|bhū|bhṛto 'nye tu ke?

niṣpanna|tādṛśa|cir'|âbhimat'|ânurūpa|
pāṇi|grah'|ôtsava|vidhī ca vadhū|varau tau
abhyantaraṃ viviśatuḥ *pramad"|ôparuddham*
lokasya mānasam iv' *â|mala|citra|bhakti*.

6.8.260 sad|*vāhinī*|parigatair api *viśva|vandya|*
śaury'|āśritair api jit'|âvanatair nar'|êndraiḥ
sā vāri|rāśibhir iv' āśu purī pupūre
Vats'|ēśvarasya sad|upāyana|ratna|hastaiḥ.

anujīvi|janāya so 'pi rājā
vyakirad dhema tathā mah"|ôtsave 'smin
yadi param abhavan *na jāta|rūpā*
jananī|garbha|gatā yath" âsya rāṣṭre.

vara|cāraṇa|nartakī|samūhair
vividha|dig|anta|samāgatais tad" âtra
paritaḥ stava|nṛtta|gīta|vādyair
bubudhe tan|maya eva jīva|lokaḥ.

vāt'|ôddhūta|patākā|
bāhulatā c' ôtsave 'tra Kauśāmbī

the noble-minded Kalínga·sena then honored her son-in-law with piles of gold mixed with jewels to such an extent that before her the lord of wealth was happily considered poverty-stricken by the people there, and the wretched other kings were nothing.

The bride and groom, their celebratory marriage rite completed according to those long held desires of theirs, went inside, where it was *crammed with women* and *hung with perfect paintings*, and it was as if they had entered the hearts of the people, which were *purely and wondrously devoted to them* and *full of joy*. The king of Vatsa's city 6.8.260
was soon filled with kings, who, despite being *endowed with heroism worthy of praise throughout the world*, had their heads bowed in submission, accompanied by their fine *armies⁝ rivers inhabited by Vishnu who is worthy of praise throughout the world* and, with them carrying in their hands splendid presents of jewels, it was if the city were filled with the oceans.* The king, too, scattered so much gold among his dependents during that great celebration that it seemed as if the children still in their mother's wombs were the only ones in his kingdom *not made of gold⁝ who had not taken form.*

Then, with the groups of fine singers and dancing girls who had come from various corners of the world playing hymns, dancing and singing on all sides, mankind appeared to consist of nothing but them. During the celebrations the city of Kaushámbi also seemed to dance, her banners waving in the wind her creeper-like arms, the ornaments put on by the women of the city her jewelry. Growing like this day by day, that great festival there did not come to an end

s" âpi nanart' êva purī
 paura|strī|racita|maṇḍan'|ābharaṇā.
evaṃ ca sa pratidinaṃ parivardhamāno
 nirvartyate sma sucireṇa mah"|ôtsavo 'tra
sarvaḥ sad" âiva ca suhṛt|sva|jano janaś ca
 hṛṣṭas tataḥ kim api pūrṇa|manoratho 'bhūt.

6.8.265 sa ca Naravāhanadatto yuva|rājo Madanamañcukā|sahitaḥ bhajate sma su|cira|kāṅkṣitam uday'|âiṣī jīva|loka|sukham.»

iti mahā|kavi|śrī|Somadeva|bhaṭṭa|viracite Kathāsaritsāgare Madanamañcukā|lambake 'ṣṭamas taraṅgaḥ.
samāptaś c' âyaṃ Madanamañcukā|lambakaḥ ṣaṣṭhaḥ.

for a very long time and all the friends, family and people were constantly and indescribably happy, their wishes having come true. Together with Mádana·mánchuka, crown 6.8.265
prince Nara·váhana·datta, striving for glory, enjoyed the earthly pleasure he had desired for so long."

Thus ends the eighth wave in the Mádana·mánchuka Attainment
in the "Ocean of the Rivers of Story" composed by the
glorious and learned great poet Soma·deva.
And the sixth Attainment, that of Mádana·mánchuka,
is complete.

NOTES

Bold *references are to the English text;* ***bold italic*** *references are to the Sanskrit text. An asterisk (*) in the body of the text marks the word or passage being annotated.*

3.5.73 **Shesha** is the thousand-headed serpent said to support the world.

3.5.74 The **Kapálikas** were ascetics who carried skulls.

3.5.80 **Yoga·karándaka** means "Box of Tricks."

3.5.90 **Vanga** covered an area similar to that of modern Bengal.

3.5.97 The river **Godávari** splits into seven streams before reaching the sea.

3.5.105 **Mount Mándara** was used by the gods and demons to churn the ocean of milk.

3.5.107 **Álaka** is the city of Kubéra, the god of wealth, and is situated in the Himálaya. In their resemblance to teeth in an open mouth, mountains such as Kailása are often said to be laughing.

3.5.113 The **parasol** is an emblem of royalty.

3.6.64 **"Whom shall I drive mad?"** is a translation of ***kaṃ darpayāmi***, hence the name **Kandárpa.**

3.6.87 **Ganas** are demigods. They are Shiva's regular attendants.

3.6.134 The **six enemies** are passion (*kāma*), anger (*krodha*), greed (*lobha*), pleasure (*harṣa*), pride (*māna*) and rapture (*mada*).

3.6.172 **Prayága** is modern-day Allahabad, where the Ganga and Yámuna rivers meet.

3.6.228 ***bahudhānya***° is a pun and can be read as either *bahudh" ânya*° or *bahu|dhānya*°.

4.2.3 **Rati** and **Priti** are the wives of the god of love.

4.2.76 The protrusions on **elephants**' foreheads are said to contain **pearls.**

4.2.155 **Bhagírathi** is the name of the Ganga in the upper reaches of the Himálaya.

4.2.159 **Old age grabbed me by the chin**: i.e. his beard began to turn gray.

4.2.200 *Kuśa* grass is notoriously sharp.

4.3.7 This *pādayuga* is not found in all the manuscripts.

4.3.83 **From all sides women … all the directions had come in person**: multiple puns on the names of the directions are made here. Each of the first four epithets of the women is a compound whose final member is the name of one of the cardinal points, but which is not to be taken that way in translation. Furthermore, like the women, the cardinal points are **attended by guards**.

4.3.93 The six **qualities** or acts that bring about **prosperity** are those which are to be practiced by a warring king: appeasement (*sandhi*), war (*vigraha*), marching (*yāna*), staying in one place (*āsana*), dividing the enemy (*dvaidhībhāva*), and taking refuge with someone else (*saṃśraya*).

5.1.96 ***dambhacaturānanaḥ*** can be read in two ways: *dambha/catur'/ ānanaḥ* and *dambha/catur/ānanaḥ*. In the second, Shiva is the four-faced creator (Brahma has four faces) of deceit. His other attributes here, holding *kuśa* grass and sitting on a lotus, are also attributes of Brahma.

5.1.152 The four **stages of life** for the orthodox brahmin are student (*brahmacārin*), householder (*gṛhastha*), forest dweller (*vanaprastha*), and renunciate (*saṃnyāsin*). The three ends of man are righteousness (*dharma*), wealth (*artha*), and pleasure (*kāma*).

5.1.160 There is a pun here: *śiva* means auspicious.

5.1.206 **Kúsuma·pura**, Flower City, is a name for Pátali·putra.

5.2.10 As Tawney notes, this is "probably a poor pun" on the word *āpad* (calamity), which could also be understood to mean a store of water.

5.2.12 **Parasols** and **yak's tail fly whisks** are emblems of royalty.

5.2.43 When Indra started to cut off the mountains' wings, some of them fled to the sea.

5.2.47 **A huge fish with a cavernous gaping mouth**: I have been unable to identify the species of this fish. It is called both *śaphara* and *pāṭhīna* which are said by Monier-Williams to be carp and sheatfish respectively, but they are both freshwater fish.

5.2.81 The **great vow** is the vow taken by the skull-bearing *kāpālika* Shaiva ascetics.

5.2.140 Widowed, **night** wants to commit sati.

5.3.266 There appears to be a verse describing Bindu·rekha missing before 5.3.266.

6.1.12 The **groom of Tara** is the Buddha.

6.1.80 **Arúndhati**, the wife of Vasíshtha, is a paradigm of womanly virtue.

6.3.9 **Bamboo** is said to be a source of pearls.

6.3.68 A half-verse appears to be missing here.

6.3.183 **Moonstone** is said to dissolve when put in moonlight.

6.4.66 Soma·prabha is saying that compared to Vásava·datta who betrayed her family by running away, **Usha and Shakúntala** need feel no shame for being seduced in their parental homes.

6.5.25 This is a reference to mount Mándara, which was used by the gods and *asuras* to churn the ocean of milk.

6.7.166 **Lotus fiber** and **sandal** are cooling.

6.8.69 The **páshupatas** were members of a sect which worshipped Shiva.

6.8.123 The **three royal powers** are majesty (*prabhutva*), good counsel (*mantra*), and energy (*utsāha*).

6.8.149 Maya famously built Yudhi·shthira's assembly hall. The verse here is odd—there is no mention of what Maya built for Yudhi·shthira.

6.8.200 There are four ways to success against an enemy: sowing dissension, negotiation, bribery, and attack. There are six tactics to be used in **foreign policy**: treaty, war, marching, halting, fomenting dissent, and going to a more powerful king for protection.

6.8.232 The **five flowers** are those said to be the arrows of Kama, the god of love.

6.8.255 The **eight auspicious items** are variously said to be a lion, a bull, an elephant, a water-jar, a fan, a flag, a trumpet, and a lamp; or a brahmin, a cow, fire, gold, ghee, the sun, water, and a king.

6.8.260 The **oceans** are said to contain fabulous treasures.

EMENDATIONS TO THE SANSKRIT TEXT

3.6.159 *śikṣitaṃ śruta/vismṛtam* em. : *śikṣituṃ śruta/vismitam* Ed

3.6.200 *sūpa/kṛd* em. : *sūpa/kṛt* Ed

4.2.8 *vitāna°* em. Aklujkar : *vimāna°* Ed

4.2.38 *yukt'/āspadaṃ* em. : *mukt'/āspadaṃ* Ed

4.3.44 *devyā* em. : *devyāḥ* Ed

4.3.46 *ṛkṣīṃ* em. : *ukṣīṃ* Ed

4.3.50 *grām'/âika/* em. : *grās'/âika/* Ed

5.1.63 *eh' îti* em. : *ehīhi* Ed

5.1.103 *marma/sthānāni* em. : *tarka/sthānāni* Ed

5.1.136 *katipay'/âhne* em. : *katipayāhe* Ed

5.1.185 *dattv" âiva* em. T : *tatr' âiva* Ed

5.1.189 *tat* em. : *sat* Ed

5.2.10 */saṃhati/* em. : */saṃgati/* Ed

5.2.31 *ca* em. : *na* Ed

5.2.112 *tāpataḥ* conj. : *tāpasaḥ* Ed

5.2.113 *tathā* em. : *yathā* Ed

5.2.131 *'/pāpa/karmaṇaḥ* em. : *pāpa/karmaṇaḥ* Ed

5.2.216 *tasyāṃ* em. T : *tasmān* Ed

5.2.278 *tad/bhṛtyair* em. T's translation : *mad/bhṛtyair* Ed

5.3.202 *prāptuṃ* em. : *prāptaṃ* Ed

5.3.250 *kāpāliko* em. : *kāpālikā* Ed

5.3.288 *dṛṣṭa/prabhur* em. : *dṛṣṭaḥ prabhur* Ed

6.1.20 */lābhāya* em. : */lobhāya* Ed

6.1.134 *devi* em. : *devī* Ed

6.2.61 ***n' âsyā*** em. : *n' âsya* Ed

6.2.62 ***pratibhed'|â|sahāḥ*** em. : *ratibhed'|â|sahāḥ* Ed

6.2.133 ***yad*** em. : *yady* Ed

6.3.40 ***pradāyinaḥ*** em. : *pradāyinā* Ed

6.3.62 ***Svayaṃprabhā*** em. : *Svayaṃprabhām* Ed

6.3.82 ***ko*** em. : *yo* Ed

6.3.117 ***veṣṭayati*** em. : *vaiṣṭayati* Ed

6.4.25 ***Âmbikāḥ*** em. AKLUJKAR : *ādikāḥ* Ed

6.4.113 ***'|jñāna|vigno*** em. : *jñāna|vigno* Ed

6.6.138 ***tasyāḥ*** em. AKLUJKAR : *tasya* Ed

6.7.136 ***nikhanya*** em. : *nihatya* Ed

6.7.171 ***viveś' âsyā*** em. : *viveś' âsya* Ed

6.7.199 ***eṣa*** em. : *s' âiṣa* Ed

6.8.81 ***yasya*** em. AKLUJKAR : *tasya* Ed

6.8.94 ***gacchatsu*** em. : *gacchasu* Ed

6.8.122 ***tasy' êva*** em. AKLUJKAR : *tasy' âiva* Ed

6.8.255 ***aṣṭa|*** em. : *atta|* Ed

INDEX

Sanskrit words are given in the English alphabetical order, according to the accented CSL pronuncuation aid. They are followed by the conventional diacritics in brackets.

THE CLAY SANSKRIT LIBRARY

The volumes in the series are listed here in order of publication.
Titles marked with an asterisk* are also available in the
Digital Clay Sanskrit Library (eCSL).
For further information visit www.claysanskritlibrary.org

1. The Emperor of the Sorcerers (*Bṛhatkathāślokasamgraha*) (vol. 1 of 2) by *Budhasvāmin*. SIR JAMES MALLINSON
2. Heavenly Exploits (*Divyāvadāna*). JOEL TATELMAN
3. Maha·bhárata III: The Forest (*Vanaparvan*) (vol. 4 of 4)* WILLIAM J. JOHNSON
4. Much Ado about Religion (*Āgamaḍambara*) by *Bhaṭṭa Jayanta*. CSABA DEZSŐ
5. The Birth of Kumára (*Kumārasambhava*) by *Kālidāsa*. DAVID SMITH
6. Ramáyana I: Boyhood (*Bālakāṇḍa*) by *Vālmīki*. ROBERT P. GOLDMAN
7. The Epitome of Queen Lilávati (*Līlāvatīsāra*) (vol. 1 of 2) by *Jinaratna*. R.C.C. FYNES
8. Ramáyana II: Ayódhya (*Ayodhyākāṇḍa*) by *Vālmīki*. SHELDON I. POLLOCK
9. Love Lyrics (*Amaruśataka, Śatakatraya & Caurapañcāśikā*) by *Amaru, Bhartṛhari & Bilhaṇa*. GREG BAILEY & RICHARD GOMBRICH
10. What Ten Young Men Did (*Daśakumāracarita*) by *Daṇḍin*. ISABELLE ONIANS
11. Three Satires (*Kaliviḍambana, Kalāvilāsa & Bhallaṭaśataka*) by *Nīlakaṇṭha, Kṣemendra & Bhallaṭa*. SOMADEVA VASUDEVA
12. Ramáyana IV: Kishkíndha (*Kiṣkindhākāṇḍa*) by *Vālmīki*. ROSALIND LEFEBER
13. The Emperor of the Sorcerers (*Bṛhatkathāślokasamgraha*) (vol. 2 of 2) by *Budhasvāmin*. SIR JAMES MALLINSON
14. Maha·bhárata IX: Shalya (*Śalyaparvan*) (vol. 1 of 2)* JUSTIN MEILAND

32. "Friendly Advice" (*Hitopadeśa*) by *Nārāyaṇa* &
"King Víkrama's Adventures" (*Vikramacarita*). Judit Törzsök

33. Life of the Buddha (*Buddhacarita*)
by *Aśvaghoṣa*. Patrick Olivelle

34. Maha·bhárata V: Preparations for War (*Udyogaparvan*) (vol. 1 of 2)
Kathleen Garbutt. Foreword by Gurcharan Das

35. Maha·bhárata VIII: Karna (*Karṇaparvan*) (vol. 2 of 2)
Adam Bowles

36. Maha·bhárata V: Preparations for War (*Udyogaparvan*) (vol. 2 of 2)
Kathleen Garbutt

37. Maha·bhárata VI: Bhishma (*Bhīṣmaparvan*) (vol. 1 of 2)*
Including the "Bhagavad Gita" in Context
Alex Cherniak. Foreword by Ranajit Guha

38. The Ocean of the Rivers of Story (*Kathāsaritsāgara*) (vol. 2 of 7)
by *Somadeva*. Sir James Mallinson

39. "How the Nagas were Pleased" (*Nāgānanda*) by *Harṣa* &
"The Shattered Thighs" (*Ūrubhaṅga*) by *Bhāsa*.*
Andrew Skilton

40. Gita·govínda: Love Songs of Radha and Krishna (*Gītagovinda*)*
by *Jayadeva*. Lee Siegel. Foreword by Sudipta Kaviraj

41. "Bouquet of Rasa" & "River of Rasa" (*Rasamañjarī & Rasataraṅgiṇī*) by *Bhānudatta*. Sheldon Pollock

42. Garland of the Buddha's Past Lives (*Jātakamālā*) (vol. 1 of 2)*
by *Āryaśūra*. Justin Meiland

43. Maha·bhárata XII: Peace (*Śāntiparvan*) (vol. 3 of 5)*
"The Book of Liberation" (*Mokṣadharma*). Alexander Wynne

44. The Little Clay Cart (*Mṛcchakaṭikā*) by *Śūdraka*.
Diwakar Acharya. Foreword by Partha Chatterjee

45. Bhatti's Poem: The Death of Rávana (*Bhaṭṭikāvya*)*
by *Bhaṭṭi*. Oliver Fallon

46. “Self-Surrender,” “Peace,” “Compassion,” and “The Mission of the Goose”: Poems and Prayers from South India (*Ātmārpaṇastuti, Śāntivilāsa, Dayāśataka & Haṃsasaṃdeśa*) by *Appayya Dīkṣita, Nīlakaṇṭha Dīkṣita & Vedānta Deśika.* YIGAL BRONNER & DAVID SHULMAN
Foreword by GIEVE PATEL
47. Maha·bhárata VI: Bhishma (*Bhīṣmaparvan*) (vol. 2 of 2)* ALEX CHERNIAK
48. How Úrvashi Was Won (*Vikramorvaśīya*) by *Kālidāsa* VELCHERU NARAYANA RAO & DAVID SHULMAN
49. The Quartet of Causeries (*Caturbhāṇī*) by *Śūdraka, Śyāmilaka, Vararuci & Īśvaradatta.* CSABA DEZSŐ & SOMADEVA VASUDEVA
50. Garland of the Buddha's Past Lives (*Jātakamālā*) (vol. 2 of 2)* by *Āryaśūra.* JUSTIN MEILAND
51. Princess Kadámbari (*Kādambarī*) (vol. 1 of 3) by *Bāṇa.* DAVID SMITH
52. The Rise of Wisdom Moon (*Prabodhacandrodaya*)* by *Kṛṣṇamiśra.* MATTHEW T. KAPSTEIN
Foreword by J.N. MOHANTY
53. Maha·bhárata VII: Drona (*Droṇaparvan*) (vol. 2 of 4)* VAUGHAN PILIKIAN
54. Maha·bhárata X & XI: Dead of Night & The Women (*Sauptikaparvan & Strīparvan*).* KATE CROSBY
55. Seven Hundred Elegant Verses (*Āryāsaptaśatī*)* by *Govardhana.* FRIEDHELM HARDY
56. Málavika and Agni·mitra (*Mālavikāgnimitram*) by *Kālidāsa.* DÁNIEL BALOGH & ESZTER SOMOGYI